# LATIN: *An Intensive Course*

# LATIN
## *An Intensive Course*

by FLOYD L. MORELAND *and* RITA M. FLEISCHER

*Brooklyn College of the City University of New York*

UNIVERSITY OF CALIFORNIA PRESS

*Berkeley   Los Angeles   London*

University of California Press
Berkeley and Los Angeles, California
University of California Press, Ltd.
London, England
Copyright © 1977 by
The Regents of the University of California
ISBN 0–520–03183–0
Library of Congress Catalog Card Number: 75–36500
Printed in the United States of America

6  7  8  9

# CONTENTS

v

# PREFACE
## to the Preliminary Edition

These materials have been written to meet the needs of students who desire a comprehensive, intensive introduction to Latin forms and syntax in a relatively short period of time. They were originally structured to fit the specific format of the Latin Workshop of the University of California at Berkeley and the Summer Latin Institute of Brooklyn College of the City University of New York. Both of these programs aim to provide a rapid introduction to Latin forms and syntax in a period of approximately four weeks of concentrated study, leading to an additional six weeks in which selected classical and medieval texts are treated in depth. However, this book may also be used, at a slower pace, by instructors of less intensive or regular classes.

The introduction of the subjunctive early in the course will permit the supplementary reading of real or slightly altered texts at an early point in the student's career, given substantial vocabulary and syntactical glosses. Selections of connected reading (real, doctored, or manufactured, as need requires) will be found at the end of each Unit. Notes which will aid in the memorization of vocabulary as well as present some of the rules for word formation are provided after each new vocabulary list. In addition, the book contains a complete appendix, divided into two parts:

1. FORMS. All paradigms are included in full for reference and review. This will be particularly helpful in those cases where paradigms are not written out in full in the body of the text (e.g., **iste, ista, istud**, Unit 12G). The future imperative, which has been omitted from the actual text because of its infrequent use, appears in the appendix for the first time.

2. SYNTAX. An outline of syntax is presented for reference and review. Each construction is illustrated with several examples and so should supplement amply the explanations and illustrations in the main body of the text. In addition, several constructions which do not appear earlier in the book are included so as to make the text a more useful tool for those students who plan to continue with their study of Latin.

Each Unit was originally designed to be covered in a single day of the Berkeley and Brooklyn intensive summer programs, although regular-paced classes may wish to spend an entire week on each one. Drills which illustrate the new morphological and grammatical concepts are supplied in the text for each Unit. Wherever possible, the vocabulary used in these drills has been limited to words which have already been met, and so the drills may be done without knowledge of the new vocabulary in the Unit. The exercises, in whole or in part, should be prepared by the student at home, and the connected readings, with their ample glosses, provide an excellent opportunity for sight reading in class.

The review Units consist of sentences which illustrate the morphological and grammatical principles taught in the lessons being reviewed. In the first three review Units, these sentences are followed by two review tests which the student may work out on his own or with the aid of an instructor. The six sample review tests in the book are followed by answer keys so as to enable the student to use them as a means of self-review. Maximum benefits may be obtained in reviewing the last Units by reading and carefully parsing the selections from Caesar which form the last part of Unit 18. By this time, students should be able to handle, with the aid of vocabulary glosses, any piece of reasonably straightforward Latin prose.

It is the belief of the authors that the best way to understand the structure of Latin is first through literal English translations, then smoother ones. For this reason, literal translations of illustrative sentences are almost invariably given first, followed by smoother English variants. For example,

Fēmina ā mīlitibus vīsa domum cucurrit.
The woman having been seen by the soldiers ran home; after she had been seen by the soldiers, the woman ran home; since she had been seen by the soldiers, the woman ran home, etc.

Dīcit sē fēlīcem esse.
He says himself to be happy; he says that he is happy.

In preparing these materials, the following works have been consulted:

Allen and Greenough, *New Latin Grammar* (Boston, 1903)
Gildersleeve and Lodge, *Latin Grammar* (London, 1957)
Krebs and Schmalz, *Antibarbarus der Lateinischen Sprache* (Basel, 1905)
Lane, *A Latin Grammar* (New York, 1898)
Woodcock, *A New Latin Syntax* (London, 1959)

Lewis and Short, *A Latin Dictionary* (Oxford, 1962) is the authority for the meanings of words; long quantities are for the most part based on those found in Walde-Hofmann, *Lateinisches etymologisches Wörterbuch* (Heidelberg, 1938).

For help with the present volume, we are grateful to Ms. Judith Rosner for her contributions to the initial stages of the project, to Mr. Robert E. Kenney for his kind assistance with xeroxing and duplication, to Ms. Stephanie Russell for help with typing part of the manuscript, and especially to Professors William S. Anderson of the University of California at Berkeley and Charles William Dunmore of New York University for reading through segments of the manuscript and offering many constructive criticisms. In addition, Mr. August Frugé of the University of California Press has been most cooperative and helpful. To Brooklyn College and Professor Ethyle R. Wolfe, Dean of the School of Humanities, go our thanks for encouragement, the opportunity to bring the program to New York City, and for a grant in the summer of 1972 which enabled us to begin the project. Gratitude must also be expressed to those colleagues in the Departments of Classics and Comparative Literature who gave us support, in particular to Professor Anna Griffiths, who has helped us in many ways. Last but not least, it would be remiss of us to conclude without a very special vote of thanks to the department chairman when this was being written, Professor Dennis J. Spininger. If it were not for his eager support of the program, the chances of completing this project would have been diminished severely.

There is one additional group of people, many of whom must remain nameless, who deserve perhaps the most recognition of all — those who have played a role in building the intensive summer Latin programs which inspired this book and for which it was originally written. To Professors W. Ralph Johnson and Alain Renoir of the University of California at Berkeley, Mary-Kay Gamel Orlandi of the University of California at Santa Cruz, John Wyatt of Beloit College, Ms. Catherine R. Freis, current director of the Berkeley Latin Workshop, and Ms. Joan Plotnick and Professor Gail Smith of Brooklyn College go our thanks for their many explicit and implicit contributions to the program and all for which it stands. Most of all, however, we are indebted to the students who have participated in the Berkeley Latin Workshop and the Brooklyn Summer Latin Institute. Their patience and dedication, met only by that of superb teaching staffs, were vital to the success which both programs have enjoyed. It is to them, and to all those who follow them, that this book is dedicated.

Needless to say, the errors and infelicities of style which remain in the following pages are the result of our own short-sightedness and do not bear in the least on the people mentioned above. We hope to iron them out in the final version of the text.

FLOYD L. MORELAND
RITA M. FLEISCHER

*New York*
*February, 1974*

# PREFACE
## *to this Edition*

Two summers and an academic year of use in beyond-the-intensive, intensive, accelerated, and regular courses have caused this book to be revised in a number of ways. Many errors have been eliminated and some sentences have been rewritten to illustrate better the concepts under consideration as well as to bring them into line with correct Latin usage. Some of the Units have undergone revision, modification, or expansion in order to give a more complete picture of the various syntactical functions. Unit Seven has been reorganized in the interest of greater lucidity, and the treatment of clauses of result and characteristic has been considerably revamped. The Review Tests have been retitled "Self Review" and one of these has been added to the Review of Units 12–18.

So as to make the book adaptable to regular-paced classes which meet three or four times per week, a group of Preliminary Exercises has been added for the first seventeen Units. These will permit breaking down each Unit into two or more manageable parts. Several users have suggested the following arrangement for presentation: the first day is spent rendering (at sight) the reading selections from the previous Unit, while the vocabulary for the new Unit is assigned for homework. On the second day, the first segment of the new Unit is presented and the Preliminary Exercises are assigned. The third day is spent presenting the second segment of the new Unit and then assigning selected sentences from the Unit Exercises. Grammatical principles can be reinforced at any time by going through the Unit Drills. A fourth day can be used doing additional sentences from the Exercises, or the vocabulary for the next Unit might be assigned while the readings are done at sight in class. Of course, other arrangements may be preferred and some instructors will find it useful to spend more time on some Units than on others. The initial four Units, for example, are extremely compact and may well require more time.

A substantial number of the sentences beyond Unit Seven have been built around phrases or thought-patterns from the ancient authors (although references are consistently not given). They have been adapted (in some cases, very slightly) to fit the controlled vocabulary and to afford concentrated practice with new forms and syntax. The problem of including "real" Latin in a beginner's text is a massive one, particularly in the light of the authors' efforts to control the vocabulary and the constructions. Selections with glosses have, however, been included in most of the Units for the benefit of those who prefer that their students have contact with the original sources at an early stage. These selections have been coordinated as much as possible to the forms and syntax of the Unit.

The introduction of the subjunctive and some sophisticated constructions near the beginning of the course will permit reading of unaltered texts early in the term. Rather than include a greater variety of suggested readings in the book, we felt it more useful to leave it to the individual instructor to provide the students with sight material which he or she deems appropriate and interesting. We have found that several of the poems of Catullus are easy to handle from Unit Seven onwards, but others will have different preferences.

There continue to be more than ample exercises and opportunity for practice. The Unit Drills do not, where possible, use the new vocabulary for the Unit and so they permit the drilling of new syntactical functions before the student has mastered the vocabulary. The Preliminary Exercises and the Exercises do use the new vocabulary and provide more than enough practice on forms and syntax. The readings (after Unit Five) attempt to integrate the material of the Unit with actual (or slightly altered) selections from the authors and so a consistent progression from grammar and forms, to practice with synthetic or slightly altered Latin, to exposure to actual excerpts is maintained.

Throughout this book, every attempt has been made to present the grammar in as lucid and clear a way as possible while not oversimplifying it. The exercises and readings tend to be complex from the beginning so as not to give the student a false sense of confidence, but rather to minimize the traditionally difficult transition into the continuous reading of ancient texts. The book does not presume to be a definitive grammar and so many points have of necessity been omitted in order not to overburden the student with a plethora of exceptions and alternate ways of expressing ideas. A great deal about the function of independent subjunctives in hypotaxis, for example, has been omitted on the assumption that this kind of information and analysis can either be supplied by the instructor or might profitably be delayed until such time as the student begins to read continuously and so to expand his or her knowledge of syntax and style.

The book has a complete appendix of morphology and syntax which not only reviews in capsule form the material included in the main text, but also includes other constructions and terms to aid the student as he or she goes on to read. In the few instances where complete paradigms are not included in the body of the text, they will appear in full in the Appendix. The vocabularies at the end are geared to the exercises in the book and by no means are to be considered complete either in their inclusiveness or in the definitions of words.

Users have stated that the book has proved useful both as a beginner's text and as a review text for intermediate Latin classes. The Appendix will be especially valuable as a reference for the latter.

Detailed notes and suggestions submitted by Professors John R. Clark, J. B. Clinard, Elizabeth Constantinides, Gerald M. Quinn, Mr. Steven Lund, Ms. Stephanie Russell, and others have proved most valuable and have caused us to rethink and revise many things; but we have remained stubborn about others. The difficulties involved in editing a text of this kind and in attempting to achieve some degree of consistency in the presentation were greater than we could possibly have imagined. The patient, efficient services of Ms. Susan Peters of the University of California Press and the trained eye and skill of our copy editor, Ms. Ramona Michaelis, have been indispensable in this regard. To them and to other colleagues, students, and friends, we extend our gratitude, not only for whatever polish this edition has acquired over the preliminary one, but also for the opportunity afforded us to reassess our own notions and to learn a great deal more about this language.

F.L.M.
R.M.F.

*New York*
*January, 1976*

**An Additional Note:**

In using the book at the Latin Institute of the City University of New York, we have found that the following poems of Catullus integrate nicely with the Units of the book as indicated below. We provide this information for the reference of instructors who may be looking for appropriate original material to supplement the exercises in the Units.

Unit 8, Catullus 13
Unit 9, Catullus 51
Unit 10, Catullus 9
Unit 11, Catullus 12
Unit 13, Catullus 41 and 43
Unit 14, Catullus 42
Unit 15, Catullus 5 and 7
Unit 16, Catullus 101
Unit 17, Catullus 8
Unit 18, Catullus 11

# INTRODUCTION

## A. The Alphabet and Pronunciation

There are twenty-four letters in the Latin alphabet. These are the same as in the English alphabet, except that there is no *j* or *w*. The letters *i* and *u* were used as both vowels and consonants (*u*, when used as a consonant, is written *v* in this book). The sounds for the letters correspond roughly to the sounds in English, but the following observations should be noted.

VOWELS: All vowels are either long or short by nature.

ā  (as in f*a*ther)                    frāter, hās
a  (as in *a*like)                      multa, parentum
ē  (as in the *a* in s*a*ve)            valē, tētē
e  (as in b*e*t)                        vectus, mūnere
ī  (as in mach*i*ne)                    prīscō, dormīre
i  (as in *i*s, *i*t)                   mortis, miser
ō  (as in *o*h, *O*hio)                 frāternō, mōre, dōnārem
o  (as in *o*ften)                      locus, adloquerer
ū  (as in r*u*de)                       flētū, fortūna
u  (as in the *oo* in lo*o*k)           vectus, ut

DIPHTHONGS: (A diphthong occurs when two vowels are pronounced together as one sound.)

ae  (as *i* in al*i*ke)                 haec, aequora
au  (as *ou* in f*ou*l)                 laudō, aut
ei  (as in r*ei*n)                      deinde
eu  (a combination of *e* as           heu
    in b*e*t and an *oo* sound
    as in f*oo*d)
oe  (as *oi* in b*oi*l)                 coepit, proelium
ui  (as in r*ui*n)                      huic, cui

1

CONSONANTS:

| | | |
|---|---|---|
| b | (+ s, pronounced like *p*; otherwise like English *b*) | abstulit, barbarus, urbs |
| c | (always hard, like a *k*) | accipe, haec, cinerem |
| g | (always hard, as in *g*et) | gentēs |
| h | (always pronounced as an aspirate, as in *h*at) | huius, haec, huic |
| i | (consonantal; pronounced like *y* in *y*es) | Iūnō, iūdex (In some texts, consonantal *i* is written as *j*.) |
| q(u) | (pronounced like *kw* as in *qu*ick) | aequora, nēquīquam |
| s | (always a sibilant, as in *s*eek) | īnferiās, abstulit, trīstī |
| t | (always as in *t*ell) | abstulit, trīstī, trādita, mānantia |
| v | (pronounced like *w*) | avē atque valē; adveniō, vīvit (In some texts, *v* is written as *u*. This is called consonantal *u*.) |
| x | (pronounced like *ks*) | dīxit |
| ch | (pronounced like the *k h* in par*k h*ere) | character, charta |
| ph | (pronounced like the *p h* in to*p h*at) | philosophia |
| th | (pronounced like the *t h* in ho*t h*ead) | theātrum |
| gu | (pronounced like *gw*) | lingua |

Every letter in a Latin word is pronounced; there are no silent letters.

## B. Syllabification

Every Latin word has as many syllables as it has vowels or diphthongs. In dividing a word into syllables, a consonant after a vowel goes with the following syllable:

mū/tam;   ta/men

When a vowel or diphthong is followed by two or more consonants, the first consonant goes with the first syllable, the remainder with the next syllable:

for/tū/na; ad/lo/que/rer

Thus:

| | |
|---|---|
| fortūna | 3 syllables |
| mānantia | 4 syllables |
| atque | 2 syllables (que = qve) |
| nunc | 1 syllable |
| mūtam | 2 syllables |
| cinerem | 3 syllables |
| tamen | 2 syllables |
| postrēmō | 3 syllables |
| īnferiās | 4 syllables |

### C. Accentuation

Every Latin word has one syllable which is slightly stressed over the others. In order to illustrate the rule by which accentuation is determined, it will be necessary to present some terminology.

ulti*ma* (**syllaba ultima**, 'last syllable') = the last syllable
*pe*nult (**syllaba paene ultima**, 'almost
    last syllable') = the second syllable from the end
an*te*penult (**syllaba ante paene ultima**,
    'before the almost last syllable') = third syllable from the end

The only two syllables in a Latin word which may receive accent are the penult and the antepenult. Accent is determined by applying the *law of the penult*:
In words of two syllables, the *penult* receives the accent:

múltās géntēs véctus

In words of more than two syllables, the *penult* receives the accent *if it is long*; *if the penult is short*, the accent is placed on the *antepenult*.
A syllable can be long in one of two ways:

1. *Length by nature.* If the syllable contains a long vowel or a diphthong, it is said to be long *by nature*.
2. *Length by position.* If the syllable contains a vowel which is followed by two consonants, it is said to be long *by position*. $x$ ($= ks$) is said to be a double consonant.

| | | |
|---|---|---|
| postrḗmō | aéquora | áccipe |
| paréntum | frātérnō | múnere |

Read the following poem aloud, applying the rules for pronunciation, syllabification, and accentuation that have just been presented:

> Multās per gentēs et multa per aequora vectus
> 　adveniō hās miserās, frāter, ad īnferiās,
> ut tē postrēmō dōnārem mūnere mortis
> 　et mūtam nēquīquam adloquerer cinerem,
> quandoquidem fortūna mihī tētē abstulit ipsum,
> 　heu miser indīgnē frāter adempte mihi.
> Nunc tamen intereā haec, prīscō, quae mōre parentum
> 　trādita sunt trīstī mūnere ad īnferiās,
> accipe frāternō multum mānantia flētū,
> 　atque in perpetuum, frāter, avē atque valē.

(Catullus 101)

## D. Word Order

The meaning of an English sentence is often dependent on the order of its words. For example, in the sentence:

*Maria sees Anna*

the word order tells us clearly that "Maria" is the subject of the verb "sees", while "Anna" is its object. Switch the words around, and we have altered the sense:

Anna sees Maria.

And, given English idiom, other arrangements are not possible:

Sees Anna Maria　　Maria Anna sees　　Sees Maria Anna

Latin word order is far more flexible, for the order of words does not rigidly determine their grammatical relationship. Latin nouns, pronouns, adjectives, and verbs are *inflected*; that is, they change their form, usually at the end of the word, to show their grammatical relationship to other words around them. The word *bends* (**flectere**, 'to bend') away from its original form in order to assume different grammatical relationships. The inflection of verbs is called *conjugation*, and one is said to *conjugate* a verb. The inflection of nouns, pronouns, and adjectives is called *declension*, and one is said to *decline* these words.

Thus, if we translate the sentence "Maria sees Anna" into Latin, we have **Maria videt Annam**. The -m ending of **Annam** indicates that this word *must* function as the object of the verb **videt**. The words can appear in any order, but the basic meaning will still be clear:

Maria Annam videt.
Annam videt Maria.
Videt Annam Maria.
Videt Maria Annam.
. . .etc.

This does not mean that the order of words in a Latin sentence is strictly fortuitous. Word order shifts because of *emphasis*. The two really emphatic positions in a Latin sentence or clause are the *first* and the *last*. Since the subject and the verb are usually the most emphatic words in a sentence, the normal word order is subject first, verb last. But variations occur. The following will give some idea of what shifts of emphasis can do.

| Maria videt Annam. | Maria sees Anna. | (both"Maria"and"Anna" mildly emphasized) |
| Maria Annam videt. | Maria sees Anna. | (normal or neutral order: subject and verb in equal emphasis) |
| Annam Maria videt. | Anna is the one whom Maria sees. | ("Anna" emphasized) |
| Videt Annam Maria. | Maria *sees* Anna. | ("Maria" *actually sees* "Anna"; emphasis on the verbal action) |

Of course, the exact thrust or nuance of the emphasis achieved by word order must also be determined from the context in which a given arrangement appears.

What may emerge from this brief illustration is the observation that the more *unusual* a position is for any word, the more *emphatic* it is for that word.

In order to apply this observation, the following remarks about word order are offered:

1. The *subject* of the sentence stands at the beginning of or early in the sentence.
2. The *verb* (or some important part of the predicate) usually comes at the end. *But* forms of the verb **sum**, 'be', when used as a link verb, rarely come last.
3. The accusative and dative, expressing the direct and indirect objects of the verb, usually come *before* the verb. Latin in this respect differs decidedly from English:

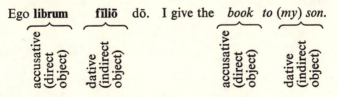

Ego **librum** **fīliō** dō. I give the *book* to *(my) son.*

accusative (direct object)    dative (indirect object)    accusative (direct object)    dative (indirect object)

4. A genitive usually follows the word on which it depends:

   librum *fēminae*   (a, the) book *of (a, the) woman*; (a, the) *woman's* book

5. Adjectives, when used to describe or give an attribute of the noun, regularly
   come *after* the noun; but demonstratives, interrogatives, numerals, and
   adjectives denoting size or quantity regularly come *before* their nouns:

   | vir **bonus** | (a, the) *good* man | (attributive adjective) |
   | puella **pulchra** | (a, the) *beautiful* girl | (attributive adjective) |
   | **haec** urbs | *this* city | (demonstrative adjective) |
   | **multī** hominēs | *many* men | (adjective denoting quantity) |
   | **ūnus** vir | *one* man | (numerical adjective) |
   | **quae** fēmina? | *which* woman? | (interrogative adjective) |

6. Adverbs and their equivalents regularly precede the word or words they
   qualify:

   | Ille mīles **diū** vīxit. | That soldier lived *for a long time*. |
   | Hominem **gladiō** interfēcit. | He killed the man *with a sword*. |
   | Tē **nōn** amō. | I do *not* love you. |

When writing sentences in Latin, we would suggest that, at the beginning, you
observe the guidelines for word order listed above. As the course progresses,
variations in word order will be called to your attention, and when your feel
for Latin idiom and emphasis begins to grow, you will discover the multiple
nuances you can create in a Latin sentence just by ordering its words skillfully
and artistically.

# ABBREVIATIONS
## Used in This Book

The following abbreviations appear throughout:

*Case*
nom. (nominative)
gen. (genitive)
dat. (dative)
acc. (accusative)
abl. (ablative)

*Parts of Speech*
pron. (pronoun)
adj. (adjective)
adv. (adverb)
prep. (preposition)
interj. (interjection)
conj. (conjunction)

*Mood*
indic. (indicative)
subj. (subjunctive)

*Tense*
pres. (present)
imperf. (imperfect)
perf. (perfect)
pluperf. (pluperfect)
fut. (future)
fut. perf. (future perfect)

*Number*
sing. (singular)
pl. (plural)

*Gender*
masc. *or* M. (masculine)
fem. *or* F. (feminine)
neut. *or* N. (neuter)

*Other abbreviations*:
inf. (infinitive)
lit. (literally)
rel. (relative)

Note: A star (★) before a word denotes that the form is a hypothetical one.

# GRAMMATICAL REVIEW

There are eight parts of speech: *noun, pronoun, adjective, verb, adverb, conjunction, interjection, preposition.*

A *noun* is a word used to express the name of a person, place, or thing.

> Examples: boy, dog, horses, Chicago, window, feet.

A *pronoun* is a word used in place of a noun.

> Examples: he, she, it, we, us, them, ours, mine.

An *adjective* is a word used to describe a noun.

> Examples: big, small, red, tall, new, old.

A *verb* is a word used to express action or a state of being.

> Examples: run, walk, eat, sleep, cough, chew, am, is, are, stand, was, were, appear, seem.

An *adverb* is a word used to describe a verb, adverb, or an adjective.

> Examples: quickly, very, beautifully, happily, too.

A *conjunction* is a word used to connect sentences, clauses, phrases, or words.

> Examples: and, if, or, but, since, although.

An *interjection* is a word or sound which expresses an emotion.

> Examples: oh, ouch, phew, damn!, ugh.

A *preposition* is a word placed before a noun or a pronoun which is used to indicate position, direction, time, or some other abstract relation.

> Examples: by, from, to, with, at, in, on, for.

Nouns and pronouns have the qualities of *gender*, *number*, and *case*.
There are three *genders*: masculine, feminine, and neuter. In English, nouns are feminine if they are the name of a female creature: "woman, girl, mare, ewe,

8

hen, doe, aviatrix, actress, sow, cow, bitch"; masculine if they are the name of a male creature: "man, boy, gander, stallion, actor, aviator, rooster, bull"; neuter if the noun is neither masculine nor feminine. Usually, we think of a neuter noun as an inanimate one: "window, blackboard, chalk, chair, table". However, in English, we sometimes personify a neuter noun and change its gender; for example, many people speak of their car (a neuter word) as a feminine creature. They will say of a new car: "She's a beauty. She gets 38 miles to the gallon," etc. Ships, too, are often referred to as females: "She was listing at a forty-five degree angle." In Latin, the gender of each noun must be memorized as each noun is learned, since its gender is not readily apparent in many instances.

In Latin, there are two *numbers*: singular and plural. Singular refers to one object, plural, to more than one. In English, for the most part, the plural is formed by adding -s to the singular form: "house, houses"; "dog, dogs"; "girl, girls". However, some words change their spelling altogether to indicate that they are plural: "mouse, mice"; "foot, feet"; "die, dice". These forms have to be learned; they cannot be guessed at.

English has three *cases*: subjective, possessive, and objective. The subjective case is used for the subject of a verb: "I, he, we". The objective case is used for the object (either of a verb or a preposition): "me, him, us". The possessive case is used to show possession: "Mary's, mine, his, ours". Latin has six cases and some words show a trace of a seventh case.

VERBS have the qualities of *person, number, tense, voice,* and *mood.*

By *person* is meant first, second, or third. The *first* person is "I" in the singular, "we" in the plural. The *second* person is "you". (Note that in Latin there is no special polite form for the pronoun "you"; the singular is used for one "you" and the plural is used for more than one "you".) The *third* person is "he, she, it" in the singular, "they" in the plural.

By *number* is meant singular and plural.

*Tense* indicates *time* and *aspect*; we speak of the present tense, past tense, and future tense. In addition, we speak of simple aspect, continuous (progressive) aspect, and completed aspect. In Latin there are six tenses.

Latin has two *voices*: active and passive. A verb in the *active* voice has a *subject* which is *doing* the action of the verb:

The pitcher *is throwing* the ball.
The dog *bit* the child.
*Will* the ball *break* the window?

A verb in the *passive* voice has a subject which is *not doing* the action of the verb, but which is *having the action* of the verb *done* to it:

> The ball *is being thrown* by the pitcher.
> The child *was bitten* by the dog.
> Will the window *be broken* by the ball?

The *mood* of the verb expresses *how* the action of the verb is conceived. If the action is conceived of as a *command*, then the *imperative* mood will be used:

> *Get* me a drink of water.

If the action is conceived of as a statement of *fact*, then the *indicative* mood will be used:

> She *got* me a drink of water.

If the action is conceived of as an *idea* or a *possibility* (rather than an actual fact), then the *subjunctive* mood will be used:

> If I *were* thirsty (but I'm not; therefore, it is not a fact), would you get me a drink of water?

In Latin there are three moods.

An ADJECTIVE may be used as a noun; when it is, it is called a *substantive*.

Examples:

> Only *the brave* deserve *the fair*.
> Blessed are *the meek*.
> Fortune favors *the brave*.

In Latin when the substantive is *masculine*, it refers to *men*; when it is *feminine*, it refers to *women*; and when it is *neuter*, it refers to *things*.

Latin does not have an article; there is no word for "a, an", or "the". Latin uses far fewer words than English does: it can omit such words as "his, her, its", and the verb "to be" may be omitted frequently. There need not be a separate word to express the subject of a verb; the subject may simply be indicated in the verb itself. Thus, it is conceivable that the following is a complete Latin sentence:

> Docent.    They are teaching.

Latin is an inflected language. *Inflection* is the change made in the form of a word to show its grammatical relations. The inflection of a *noun, pronoun,* or *adjective* is called *declension*. The inflection of a *verb* is called *conjugation*. Inflection can be seen in English in the following ways:

| boy | singular |
| boy's | singular possessive case |
| boys | plural |
| boys' | plural possessive case |
| I, he, she | subjective |
| me, him, her | objective |

Note that, for nouns, -'s or -s' indicates possession.

In the conjugation of the verb "to be"

am
are
is

"am" is obviously first person singular and "is" is third person singular.

Inflection was more common in older English, where -st was the ending for the second person singular of the verb and -th was the ending for the third person singular present.

| do | say |
| dost | sayest |
| doth | saith |

Nowadays, the only remnant of inflection in most verbs is the final -s of the third person singular in the present tense.

| say | want | see |
| says | wants | sees |

# A SELECTED GLOSSARY

## *of Important Terms*

This glossary is provided as a reference for some of the basic terminology which a student of Latin will encounter. Presented from the point of view of English, it will serve as a partial review of grammatical terms and as a foundation on which one's study of Latin may be built. It should be used in conjunction with the main text and the appendix.

A nominative *absolute* is a participial construction which is not in close grammatical connection with the main sentence. Example:

> *This being a legal holiday,* ("This" is in the nominative (subjective) case,
> I refuse to work. as is the participle "being", which agrees with it.)

An *abstract noun* is the name of a quality or a general idea. Examples:

> thoughtfulness, loyalty, freedom

*Agreement* is the correspondence in one or more categories between a noun and the adjective which describes it, a subject and its verb, or a pronoun and its antecedent. Examples:

> *much* noise (noun and adjective both singular)
> *many* noises (noun and adjective both plural)
> he knows (subject and verb both singular)
> The *book which* he lost is mine. (antecedent and pronoun both neuter)

*Antecedent.* The word for which the pronoun stands. Example:

> The *man* whom you know is good.

*Apodosis.* The conclusion in a conditional sentence (cf. *Protasis*). Example:

> If it should rain, *I'll take an umbrella.*

*Apposition.* A word placed next to another one which means or indicates the same thing. Example:

> John, *the farmer*, is a good man.

The appositive must be in the same case as the word to which it refers.

12

*Aspect.* The category of the verb which indicates whether the action is simple, continuous (progressive), or completed. Examples from the point of view of present time:

| | |
|---|---|
| he walks | (simple) |
| he is walking | (continuous or progressive) |
| he has walked | (completed) |

*Attributive.* An attributive adjective is one which describes or modifies a noun (as opposed to a substantive adjective). An adjective is said to be in attributive position if, in English, it precedes the noun it modifies ("the *brave* man"). This is in contrast with the predicate adjective which, in English, comes after the linking verb ("he seems *brave*").

*Clause.* A group of words which contains a subject and a verb but is in itself not a complete sentence, but a part of a complex or compound sentence.

A *causal* clause is introduced by "since" or "because".

A *circumstantial* clause is introduced by "when" or "after" and stresses the circumstances in which the action occurs.

A *concessive* clause is introduced by "although, though, granted that".

A *temporal* clause indicates the time at which the action occurs and is introduced by "when, after, before, as, while".

A *collective noun* is a word in the singular which names a group of people. Examples:

group, crowd, populace, senate

The *comparative* degree of the adjective indicates an increased amount of the quality of the positive form of the adjective. In English, the comparative degree is shown by adding *-er* to the simple form of the adjective or by adding "more", "rather", or "too" to the positive degree. Examples:

fatter, more beautiful, rather pretty, too big

A *complementary infinitive* is used to complete the meanings of certain verbs such as "be able, try, ought". Example:

He ought *to go.*

A *complex* sentence is a sentence which contains at least one dependent and one independent clause. Example:

While we were away, our house was robbed.

A *compound* sentence is a sentence which contains two or more independent clauses. Example:

My sister went to the beach and I stayed home.

A *conditional* sentence is a sentence which contains two clauses: a protasis and an apodosis. Example:

If it should rain, I'll take an umbrella.

A *contrafactual* (contrary-to-fact) condition is a condition which is not true. Example:

If I were an elephant, I would have a trunk (but I'm not an elephant; therefore, I don't have a trunk).

A *coordinating conjunction* is a conjunction used to join two elements of a sentence without subordinating one to the other. Examples:

and, but, or

*Correlatives* are words regularly used together which balance each other. Examples:

both...and; either...or; the more...the....

A *demonstrative* is a word which points out something. Examples:

this, that, these, those

A *denominative* verb is a verb made from a noun. Examples:

broadcast, flag (i.e., flag down a train).

A *dependent* clause is a clause which does not make a complete statement by itself. Example:

because we are busy

*Diminutives* are nouns which indicate a small size, endearment, or contempt. Examples:

duckling, pussykin, pup

The most common diminutive endings in English are: *-et (-ette), -y, -ie, -ey*. Examples:

piglet, statuette, Bobby, bookie, lovey

*Ellipsis* is the omission of a word or words which are necessary for grammatical completeness. Example:

The man we saw was drunk. *instead of* The man whom we saw was drunk.

An *enclitic* is a word which in pronunciation is so closely connected to the preceding word that it loses its own accent. Examples:

give me (often pronounced "gimme"), want to (often pronounced "wanna"), should have (often pronounced "shoulda").

An *epexegetical* infinitive is an infinitive which depends on and limits an adjective. Example:

difficult *to imagine*

An *expletive* is a word which serves no grammatical function, but which fills up a sentence or gives emphasis. Example:

*There* are five people here.

A *finite* verb is a verb which is limited by person, number, tense, voice, and mood. Examples:

was, am, eats

The *frequentative* (iterative) aspect of a verb expresses repeated action. Example:

He keeps walking.

A *gerund* is a verbal noun. Example:

*Swimming* is good exercise.

*Hypotaxis* (subordination) is the subordination of one clause to another

An *idiom* is an expression which is peculiar to a language. Example:

to be on the up and up

*Idiom* also refers to the characteristic modes of expression of a given language.

An *impersonal* verb is a verb which lacks a personal subject and is found only in the third person singular. Example:

It is raining.

The *inchoative* (inceptive) aspect of a verb expresses the beginning of an action. Example:

He is beginning to crawl.

An *indefinite* pronoun refers to a not specific person or thing. Examples:

someone, somebody, anyone, anybody

An *independent* clause is a main clause, one that is not subordinate.

An *indirect object* is found with verbs of giving, telling, and showing. Someone gives or tells or shows something *to somebody*; the "somebody" is the indirect object. Example:

John gave *Mary* the book.

*Indirect discourse* is of three types:

An *indirect statement*, regularly introduced by the subordinating conjunction *that*, expresses what someone says, thinks, feels, or believes without using a direct quotation. Example:

> "I do not feel good."        (direct statement)
> He says *that he does not feel good.*    (indirect statement)

An *indirect question*, introduced by an interrogative word, expresses what someone asks, considers, wonders, or states without using a direct quotation. Example:

> "Why did you do that?"     (direct question)
> I wonder *why you did that.*     (indirect question)

An *indirect command* expresses what someone commands, urges, warns, or begs without using a direct quotation. Example:

> "Don't go."          (direct command)
> I urge you *not to go.*    (indirect command)

The *infinitive* is the form of the verb which is not limited by person or number. Example:

> to see, to have done

*Inflection* is the change made in the form of a word to show its grammatical relationship to the other words around it.

The *intensive adjective* is used to emphasize the word it describes. Example:

> He is the *very* man I meant.

An *interrogative* asks a question. An interrogative sentence is a sentence which asks a question. The interrogative pronoun in English is "who" or "what"; the interrogative adjective is "what, which".

An *intransitive* verb is a verb which does not take a direct object. Examples:

> fall, go, die

A *macron* is a mark (ˉ) placed above a long vowel to mark its quantity.

*Morphology* is the study of the basic formations of words.

The *object* receives the action of the verb. Example:

> The child broke the *pitcher*.

A *paradigm* is a model or pattern which contains all the inflectional variations of a given word. Examples:

man, man's, men, men's; he, his, him, they, their (theirs), them

*Parataxis* (coordination) is the absence of subordination and the arrangement of several clauses side by side. Example:

We left; she stayed.

A *participle* is a verbal adjective. Example:

The *screaming* woman caught our attention.

*Periphrasis* (circumlocution) is a roundabout expression of a simple idea. Example:

Illumination is required to be extinguished *is a periphrasis for* Lights must be put out.

*Phonology* is the study of the sounds of a language.

A *phrase* is a group of words without a subject or verb. It may be used as an adjective or an adverb. Examples:

on time, without money, by whom

A *possessive* pronoun or adjective shows ownership. Example:

mine, yours, my, your, his

The *predicate*, in English, is the verb and the part of the sentence that comes after the verb. A *predicate nominative* is a noun or pronoun which follows a linking verb (such as the verbs "to be, seem, appear") and which is the same as the subject. Example:

Tom is a *farmer.*

The same case follows the linking verb as precedes it; the linking verb can *not* take an object. Thus, in the example given above, both "Tom" and "farmer" are in the nominative case. A *predicate adjective* is an adjective which follows a linking verb. Example:

Tom is *tall.*

Once again, "tall" is in the nominative case; the verb "to be" can *not* take an object.

*Protasis* is the clause containing the condition in a conditional sentence (cf. *Apodosis*). Example:

*If it should rain,* I'll take an umbrella.

*Proviso.* A clause of proviso expresses a conditional or a provisional idea. Example:

They will come, *provided that we invite them.*

A *reflexive* pronoun refers to the subject of the main verb. Example:

He cut *himself.*

A *relative* pronoun, "who, which, that", introduces an adjectival clause which modifies the antecedent of that pronoun. Example:

The man *whom* we saw was very tall.

The relative pronoun has the same gender as its antecedent, but it takes its case from its use in its own clause.

The *root* of a word is the basic element that gives the meaning of the word. Examples:

ex*port*, re*port*er, trans*port*ation

A *sentence* is a group of words with a subject and a verb; it expresses a complete thought, feeling, question, or command.

The *stem* is that part of a word to which endings are added. Example:

*annihilat*ed, *annihilat*ion

The *subject* performs the action of the verb. Example:

The *pitcher* threw the ball.

A *subordinate* clause is a dependent clause.

A *subordinating conjunction* is a conjunction used to join two elements of a sentence in a way in which one will be subordinate to or dependent upon the other. Examples:

since, when, although, that

A *substantive* is an adjective used as a noun. Example:

Blessed are *the meek.*

It is also any noun.

The *superlative* degree of an adjective indicates the greatest amount of the quality of the positive form of that adjective. In English, the superlative degree is shown by adding *-est* to the simple form of the adjective, or by adding "most, very" or "extremely" to the positive degree. Examples:

youngest, most expensive, very tall, extremely handsome

A *synopsis* is a summary outline of a given verb that shows at a glance the major inflectional variations of that verb.

*Syntax* is the portion of grammar which deals with the relationship of words to each other in the sentence.

A *transitive* verb is a verb which may take an object. Examples:

see, eat, hit

## A. The Verbal System

The inflection of verbs is called *conjugation*, and one is said to *conjugate* a verb. Finite verb forms have the qualities of person, number, tense, voice, and mood.

1. PERSON: The Latin verb form, without the aid of pronouns, indicates whether the subject is in the *first* ("I, we"), *second* ("you"), or *third* ("he, she, it, they") persons.
2. NUMBER: The inflection of a verb shows whether the subject is *singular* or *plural*.
3. TENSE: The tense of a verb tells us *when* the action occurs, has occurred, or will occur. The simplest categories of tense (time) are *present, past*, and *future,* but since there is the additional concern as to the completeness or the continuation of the stated act, some refinements of the present, past, and future divisions are required.
4. VOICE: There are two grammatical voices in Latin: the *active* indicates that the subject is the doer of the act; the *passive* shows the subject as the recipient of the verbal action.
5. MOOD: There are three moods or tones of verbal action. By mood we refer to the manner in which the speaker conceives of the action. The *indicative* mood is the mood of *fact* and is used for making direct statements and asking direct questions. The *subjunctive* is the mood used to express *idea, intent, desire, uncertainty, potentiality,* or *anticipation.* The *imperative* mood expresses the action as a *command.*

## B. The Tenses of the Indicative

There are six tenses in the indicative mood.

1. PRESENT: The present tense indicates an action which is going on now or is habitual.

    optat   he desires, he is desiring, he (always) desires, he does desire

NOTE: The Latin form makes no distinction between the simple present tense and the present progressive.

2. IMPERFECT: (**imperfectum** = 'not completed'): The imperfect describes an action which was going on or was habitual in the past. The imperfect is in some respects a motion picture of past action.

> optābat   he desired (continually, habitually), he was desiring, he used to desire, he kept on desiring

3. FUTURE: The future refers to an action which will occur at some later time.

> optābit   he will desire, he will be desiring

NOTE: Again, the Latin form makes no distinction between the simple future and the future progressive.

4. PERFECT (**perfectum** = 'completed'): The perfect tense describes one of two types of action:

a. one which was completed at some time before the present.

> optāvit   he desired

NOTE: This aspect of the perfect is most nearly equivalent to the English past tense. It is a snapshot of past action.

b. one which was started in the past but has some relevance to the present. The relevance may be either that the action is completed from the point of view of the present, or that it is operative in the present.

> optāvit   he has desired (the implications are that he no longer desires and/or that he still desires in the present)

NOTE: This aspect is most nearly equivalent to the English present perfect.

5. PLUPERFECT [PAST PERFECT] (**plūs quam perfectum** = 'more than completed'): This tense describes an action which was already completed at some time in the past.

> optāverat   he had desired

6. FUTURE PERFECT: The future perfect indicates an action which will be completed before some point of time in the future.

> optāverit   he will have desired (i.e., by next week)

The six Latin tenses in the indicative, then, express not only matters of *time* but also those of *aspect*. The following chart will illustrate the uses of the tenses in these terms.

TENSES

|  | Present | Past | Future |
|---|---|---|---|
| Simple | optat<br>he desires<br>(Present) | optāvit<br>he desired<br>(Perfect) | optābit<br>he will desire<br>(Future) |
| Continuous<br>(Progressive) | optat<br>he is desiring<br>(Present) | optābat<br>he was desiring<br>(Imperfect) | optābit<br>he will be desiring<br>(Future) |
| Completed | optāvit<br>he has desired<br>(Perfect) | optāverat<br>he had desired<br>(Pluperfect) | optāverit<br>he will have desired<br>(Future Perfect) |

ASPECTS

The tenses in the second vertical column, that is, all those which refer to past time, are called *secondary* tenses. Those in the first and third columns, which refer to present and future time, are called *primary* tenses.

PRIMARY TENSES OF INDICATIVE
Present
Future
Future Perfect
Perfect (when equivalent to
   English present perfect)

SECONDARY TENSES OF INDICATIVE
Imperfect
Perfect (when equivalent to English
   past tense)
Pluperfect

Both lists above will prove very valuable to you as you progress with your study of Latin. Refer to them frequently.

## C. The Infinitive

The verb forms discussed above are *finite* forms. The Latin word **fīnis** means 'boundary' or 'limit', and so finite forms are those which are bounded or limited by person, number, tense, voice, and mood. The infinitive is *not* limited as to person, number, and mood, but it does show tense and voice.

|  | ACTIVE | PASSIVE |
|---|---|---|
| Present | optāre<br>to desire | optārī<br>to be desired |
| Perfect | optāvisse<br>to have desired | optātus esse<br>to have been desired |
| Future | optātūrus esse<br>to be going to desire | optātum īrī<br>to be going to be desired (this form is rare<br>   in classical Latin) |

The infinitive is in fact an abstract verbal noun. **Optāre** can thus be translated not only as 'to desire' but as 'desiring' and so expresses a verbal activity.

## D. The Four Conjugations

With the exception of the verb "to be", every verb in Latin belongs to one of four classes or *conjugations*: the first, second, third, or fourth. These conjugations are distinguished from one another by the form of the present infinitive.

Verbs of the first conjugation have a present infinitive in -**āre**.

optāre   to desire

Verbs of the second conjugation have a present infinitive in -**ēre**.

implēre   to fill

Verbs of the third conjugation have a present infinitive in -**ere**.

incipere   to begin

Verbs of the fourth conjugation have a present infinitive in -**īre**.

sentīre   to feel, perceive

## E. The Principal Parts

Most verbs in Latin have four principal parts. For example, the vocabulary entry for the verb **optō**, 'to desire', appears thus:

optō, -āre, -āvī, -ātus

The forms, written in full, are

optō, optāre, optāvī, optātus

and are explained as follows.

| | | |
|---|---|---|
| optō | first person singular, present active indicative | I desire |
| optāre | present active infinitive | to desire |
| optāvī | first person singular, perfect active indicative | I desired, I have desired |
| optātus | perfect passive participle | having been desired, desired |

It is essential that the four principal parts for each verb be learned as part of the vocabulary, for without these parts it will not be possible to conjugate the verb fully. This fact will become obvious shortly.

## F. The Present Active Indicative System of the First Two Conjugations

1. A Latin verb usually consists of a stem, a tense sign, and an ending.
2. The stem for the present, imperfect, and future tenses is called the *present stem* and is derived from the second principal part of the verb, i.e., from the present infinitive: the -**re** ending is dropped. This is true for all four conjugations.

STEM
| | |
|---|---|
| optō, -āre | optā/re |
| impleō, -ēre | implē/re |
| incipiō, -ere | incipe/re |
| sentiō, -īre | sentī/re |

3. The present tense has no tense sign. However, the tense sign of the imperfect for all conjugations is **-bā-**, and that of the future for the first and second conjugations is **-bi-**. These tense signs are added to the stem.

> optō, optāre:
> optā- (present), optābā- (imperfect), optābi- (future)
> impleō, implēre:
> implē- (present), implēbā- (imperfect), implēbi- (future)

4. Finally, the personal endings are added, indicating the person (first, second, or third) and number (singular or plural) of the verb. The endings for the active voice are as follows:

FIRST CONJUGATION:

SINGULAR

| | | Present | Imperfect | Future |
|---|---|---|---|---|
| 1 | -ō or -m | optō | optābam* | optābō |
| 2 | -s | optās | optābās | optābis |
| 3 | -t | optat* | optābat | optābit |

PLURAL

| | | | | |
|---|---|---|---|---|
| 1 | -mus | optāmus | optābāmus | optābimus |
| 2 | -tis | optātis | optābātis | optābitis |
| 3 | -nt | optant* | optābant | optābunt |

* Note that a long vowel is shortened before final -m, -t, or -nt.

SECOND CONJUGATION:

SINGULAR

| | | Present | Imperfect | Future |
|---|---|---|---|---|
| 1 | -ō or -m | impleō | implēbam | implēbō |
| 2 | -s | implēs | implēbās | implēbis |
| 3 | -t | implet | implēbat | implēbit |

PLURAL

| | | | | |
|---|---|---|---|---|
| 1 | -mus | implēmus | implēbāmus | implēbimus |
| 2 | -tis | implētis | implēbātis | implēbitis |
| 3 | -nt | implent | implēbant | implēbunt |

The only irregularities which are obvious above are really not problematic. In the first person singular of the first conjugation, the -ā- of the stem is absorbed into the -ō personal ending. This is true of all verbs of the first conjugation, but there is no trouble with this since the first person singular form is learned as a vocabulary item. Note that the -ō and -m endings for the first person singular are *not* interchangeable. The paradigms will illustrate which ending is to be used for each tense. (The future of the first and second conjugations and the present indicative of all conjugations use the -ō endings in the first person singular. All other tenses in the present system use the -m ending.)

In the future of the first two conjugations, the -i- of the tense sign is absorbed into the -ō personal ending and changes to -u- in the third person plural.

Therefore, in order to interpret a Latin verb form in the present system, one reads backwards:

optābant **nt** = 'they'
**ba** = imperfect tense
**optā** = 'desire'

THEREFORE: 'they used to desire' (third person plural imperfect active indicative)

clāmābis **s** = 'you' (sing.)
**bi** = future tense
**clāmā** = 'shout'

THEREFORE: 'you will shout' (second person singular future active indicative)

terrēmus **mus** = 'we'
**--** = present tense (no tense sign)
**terrē** = 'frighten'

THEREFORE: 'we frighten' (first person plural present active indicative)

## G. The Irregular Verb *sum,* 'be'

As in all Indo-European languages, the verb "to be" is somewhat irregular and must be learned thoroughly. The present, imperfect, and future tenses of this verb are given below. Despite the irregularities, note that the personal endings are those which one would normally expect.

### sum, esse, fuī, futūrus, 'be'

| PRESENT | | IMPERFECT | | FUTURE | |
|---|---|---|---|---|---|
| SING. | PL. | SING. | PL. | SING. | PL. |
| sum | sumus | eram | erāmus | erō | erimus |
| es | estis | erās | erātis | eris | eritis |
| est | sunt | erat | erant | erit | erunt |

## H. The Noun System

The inflection of nouns, pronouns, and adjectives is called *declension*, and such words are said to be *declined*.

Every Latin noun belongs to one of three grammatical *genders*: *masculine*, *feminine*, or *neuter*. The gender of each noun must be learned as a vocabulary item, for it is important in the matter of noun and adjective agreement.

The inflection, or declension, of nouns shows the qualities of *number* and *case*. The case endings indicate the grammatical and syntactical relationship of the given noun to the other words in the sentence. Whereas English relies largely on word order to illustrate such relationships, Latin relies on its inflections. In addition, where the English uses a prepositional phrase, the Latin frequently needs only the one inflected word. See examples under GENITIVE and DATIVE below.

There is no definite or indefinite article in Latin. The articles "the, a, an" are frequently supplied in an English translation.

There are five cases which will be of concern to us at the present. These are: Nominative, Genitive, Dative, Accusative, Ablative. The basic uses of each case are described below.

1. NOMINATIVE: This is the case of the subject and the predicate nominative.

> **Fēmina** optat. *The woman desires.*
> **Fēmina** est **rēgīna**. *The woman is a queen.*

2. GENITIVE: In general, the genitive case is used for a noun which is dependent upon another noun and is often introduced by the preposition "of" in English (except where "of" means 'concerning').

> patria **fēminae** the native land *of the woman, the woman's* native land
> timor **aquae** fear *of water*
> urna **pecūniae** a jar *of money*

3. DATIVE: This case generally expresses the person (or thing), with the exception of the subject and object, *with reference to* whom (or what) the action or idea of the main verb is relevant. It is usually rendered in English by the prepositions "to" or "for", and one of its uses includes the indirect object.

> Taedam **fēminae** dat. He gives the torch *to the woman*. (*Fēminae* is the *referent* of the action; that is, the action of the verb occurs *with reference to* her.)
> Taedam **fēminae** optat. He chooses a torch *for the woman*.

4. ACCUSATIVE: Essentially, the accusative case is used as the direct object of a verb or as the object of certain prepositions.

**Fēminam** videt.               He sees *the woman.*
Fēmina in **aquam** ambulābit.   The woman will walk into *the water.*

5. ABLATIVE: The ablative generally expresses notions connected with the English prepositions "from, with, in", and "by". Sometimes prepositions are required to express these notions; other times the case ending alone serves this purpose. Distinctions will be pointed out in later Units.

Cum **fēminā** ambulat.          He walks with *the woman.*
Fēmina est in **aquā**.          The woman is in *the water.*
Nauta fēminam **taedā** terret.  The sailor frightens the woman *with a torch.*

## I. The First Declension

There are five basic groups of nouns in Latin. Each of these is called a *declension*. These declensions are distinguished from one another by the ending of the genitive singular: for the first declension, this is -ae, for the second, -ī, for the third, -is, for the fourth, -ūs, and for the fifth, -eī. At present we shall be concerned only with the first of these groups, the first declension.

Noun entries in the vocabulary lists are given in three parts:

fēmina, -ae, F.

The first of these parts is the nominative singular form; the second indicates the ending of the genitive singular; the third reveals the gender of the noun (*M.* for masculine, *F.* for feminine, *N.* for neuter). Most nouns of the first declension are feminine, but there are a few which are masculine.

A noun form consists of a stem and a case ending. In order to arrive at the stem of any noun in Latin, take the full genitive singular form and drop the ending.

fēmin / ae
(stem)   (ending)

For the first declension, it may seem pointless to go to the genitive form to arrive at the stem when the same results might be obtained by using the nominative form. But for many nouns the genitive form is significantly different from the nominative, so that the stem for all nouns can only be found by this procedure.

To this stem the endings of the particular declension are added. The endings for the first declension are:

**SINGULAR**

| Nominative | -a | fēmina | (the, a) woman (subject) |
|---|---|---|---|
| Genitive | -ae | fēminae | of (the, a) woman, (the, a) woman's |
| Dative | -ae | fēminae | to/for (the, a) woman |
| Accusative | -am | fēminam | (the, a) woman (object) |
| Ablative | -ā | fēminā | from/with/in/by (the, a) woman |

**PLURAL**

| Nominative | -ae | fēminae | (the) women (subject) |
|---|---|---|---|
| Genitive | -ārum | fēminārum | of (the) women, (the) women's |
| Dative | -īs | fēminīs | to/for (the) women |
| Accusative | -ās | fēminās | (the) women (object) |
| Ablative | -īs | fēminīs | from/with/in/by (the) women |

# UNIT ONE — VOCABULARY

| | |
|---|---|
| **ambulō** (1)* | walk |
| **aqua, -ae,** F. | water |
| **clāmō** (1) | shout |
| **corōna, -ae,** F. | crown, wreath |
| **corōnō** (1) | crown |
| **cum** (prep. + abl.) | with |
| **cūra, -ae,** F. | care, concern, anxiety |
| **dē** (prep. + abl.) | concerning, about; (down) from |
| **dō, dare, dedī, datus** | give, grant |
| **dōnō** (1) | give, present, reward |
| **ē, ex** (prep. + abl.) | out of, from[1] |
| **enim** (postpositive conj.) | indeed, of course |
| **et** (conj.) | and |
| **et...et** | both...and |
| (adv.) | even |
| **fāma, -ae,** F. | talk, report, rumor, fame, reputation |
| **fēmina, -ae,** F. | woman |
| **fōrma, -ae,** F. | form, shape, figure, beauty |
| **habeō, -ēre, habuī, habitus** | have, hold, possess, consider |
| **impleō, -ēre, implēvī, implētus** | fill, fill up |
| **in** (prep. + acc.) | into, onto (motion toward) |
| (prep. + abl.) | in, on (place where) |
| **īnsula, -ae,** F. | island |
| **nauta, -ae,** M. | sailor |

| -ne (enclitic) | (added to the first word of an interrogative sentence or clause; it indicates a question)² |
| **nōn** (adv.) | not |
| **optō** (1) | desire, wish (for); choose |
| **patria, -ae,** F. | native land, country |
| **pecūnia, -ae,** F. | money |
| **poena, -ae,** F. | penalty, punishment |
|   **poenās dare** | to pay a penalty |
| **poēta, -ae,** M. | poet |
| **porta, -ae,** F. | gate |
| -que (enclitic) | and³ |
| **rēgīna, -ae,** F. | queen |
| sed (conj.) | but |
| **sum, esse, fuī, futūrus** | be, exist |
| **taeda, -ae,** F. | torch |
| **terreō, -ēre, terruī, territus** | frighten, alarm, terrify |
| **timeō, -ēre, timuī, --** | fear, be afraid (of) |
| **turba, -ae,** F. | crowd, uproar |
| **via, -ae,** F. | way, road, path, street |
| **videō, -ēre, vīdī, vīsus** | see |

\* The entry (1) after a verb indicates that the verb belongs to the first conjugation and has the regular principal parts in -āre, -āvī, -ātus.

1 ē before a word beginning with a consonant; ex before a vowel or h and sometimes before a consonant.

2 e.g., Timetne?          Is he afraid?
    Fēmināsne vidēs?   Do you see the women?

3 e.g., poēta rēgīnaque = poēta et rēgīna

## UNIT ONE — NOTES ON VOCABULARY

Many verbs in Latin derive from nouns. For example, **corōnō, corōnāre, corō-nāvī, corōnātus**, 'crown', comes from **corōna, corōnae,** F., 'crown'. Such verbs are called denominatives.

The preposition **cum**, 'with', always takes the ablative case: **cum cūrā**, 'with care', **cum fēminā**, 'with a woman'.

Note that **dē** has both the meaning 'concerning' and 'down from'. It always takes the ablative case.

Although most first conjugation verbs follow the pattern -āre, -āvī, -ātus, the verb **dō, dare**, 'give', does not. The -a- in the infinitive is short and the other principal parts are **dedī, datus**. When an infinitive is used with this verb, it is best to use the meaning 'grant, allow' for **dō**. For example:

Rēgīna fēminās vidēre corōnam dat.    The queen grants (allows) the women
to see (her) crown.

The first conjugation verb **dōnō**, 'give, present, award', may govern an accusative and a dative *or* an accusative and ablative. In other words, with **dōnō**, one
may present something to someone or present someone with something:

Aquam nautīs dōnābimus.   We shall give water to the sailors.
Nautās aquā dōnābimus.   We shall present the sailors with water.

**Enim**, 'indeed, of course', is a postpositive conjunction. This means that it
cannot be the first word of a clause. Usually, a word that is postpositive is placed
as the second word of a clause. **Enim** generally introduces a statement which
corroborates what precedes.

**Et** means 'and'. In a series, the first **et** means 'both'. For example:

Et fēminae et nautae in viā ambulant.   Both the women and the sailors
are walking in the street.

As an adverb, **et** means 'even':

Et rēgīna poenās dabat.   Even the queen was paying the penalty.

One cannot know for sure exactly what the principal parts of a verb in the
second conjugation will be:

habeō, habērę, habuī, habitus       have
impleō, implēre, implēvī, implētus  fill
videō, vidēre, vīdī, vīsus          see

Thus, each verb must be learned thoroughly; one cannot simply guess at the
principal parts.

The preposition **in** may take either the accusative or the ablative case, with a
difference in meaning. The accusative case is used to express movement toward;
thus **in** with the accusative means 'into' or 'onto': **in turbam**, 'into the crowd'.
Sometimes this movement can be in a hostile sense, as 'The man led his troops
against the sailors' (**in nautās**). The ablative case, on the other hand, is not
associated with movement, but with location. Thus **in** with the ablative means
'in' or 'on': **in turbā**, 'in the crowd'.

A vowel before -**ns**- is long; thus, **īnsula, īnsulae**, F., 'island'.

Literally, the idiom **poenās dare** means 'to give punishments', but the actual
meaning is the opposite, 'to pay a penalty'. Of course, the verb is conjugated:

Poenās dabit.   He will pay the penalty.

Although most nouns of the first declension are feminine, **poēta, poētae**,
'poet', and **nauta, nautae**, 'sailor', are masculine. These words are declined in
the same way as the feminine nouns of the first declension.

An enclitic is attached to the end of a word and is pronounced with it. In English we translate -que, 'and' *before* the word to which it is attached:

poētae nautaeque                                the poets and sailors
Fēminās vidēbunt rēgīnamque corōnābunt.   They will see the women and
                                                crown the queen.

The verb "to be" is irregular in most languages; Latin is no exception. Note that **est** may be translated 'there is' as well as 'he, she, it is'. Thus, **erat**, 'there was'; **erit**, 'there will be'. Since the verb "to be" cannot logically have a passive voice, it does not have a perfect passive participle (which, for most verbs, is given as the fourth principal part). In its place, the future active participle has been provided. Translate **futūrus** as 'going to be'. Of course the verb "to be" cannot take an object. When this verb is used as a "linking" verb, one finds the same case preceding and following it.

Nauta est poēta.   The sailor is a poet.

**Timeō, timēre, timuī, ––**, 'fear', lacks a fourth principal part. In order not to confuse the meanings of **terreō, terrēre, terruī, territus**, 'frighten', and **timeō**, remember that **terreō** means 'terrify' and that a timid person is one who is afraid.

Caesar's famous expression, **Vēnī, vīdī, vīcī**, 'I came, I saw, I conquered', is a very handy way of remembering the third principal parts of these verbs (**veniō**, 'come', Unit Two; **videō, vidēre, vīdī, vīsus**, 'see'; and **vincō**, 'conquer', Unit Fourteen).

Note that the -ī- in the perfect tenses of **video** is long (**vīdī**). Very often in Latin the short vowel in the present stem lengthens in the perfect.

# UNIT ONE — DRILL

## I.

Translate:

1. Fēminae in viā ambulant.
2. Fēminaene in viā ambulābunt?
3. Fēminae in viā nōn ambulābant.
4. Estne rēgīna in īnsulā?
5. Rēgīna in īnsulā nōn erat sed erit.
6. Pecūniam habētis? Nōn habēmus.
7. Pecūniam habēs? Nōn habeō.
8. Et pecūniam et fāmam habēbis.
9. Pecūniam habēbāmus sed fāmam habēbātis.

10. Pecūniam nōn habēbō sed fāmam habēbimus.
11. Turbamne terrēbās? Nōn terrēbam.
12. Aquam nautīs dabitis?

**II.**

A. Decline **porta, turba,** and **rēgīna** fully.
B. Change each of the following from the singular to the plural (in some instances there may be two possible answers):

|   |   |   |
|---|---|---|
| 1. rēgīnam | 3. fēminā | 5. nauta |
| 2. fāmae | 4. corōna | |

**III.**

Translate into Latin:

|   |   |
|---|---|
| 1. with the queens | 6. I am |
| 2. to the poet | 7. we shall shout |
| 3. of women | 8. they used to be afraid |
| 4. on the gates | 9. you (pl.) are desiring |
| 5. crown (object) | 10. to give |

# UNIT ONE — PRELIMINARY EXERCISES
## (SECTIONS A, B, C, D, E, F, G)

**I.**

A. What are the stems of **impleō, implēre; corōnō, corōnāre; dō, dare; videō, vidēre?**
B. Conjugate **dōnō** in the imperfect active indicative.
C. Conjugate **timeō** in the future active indicative.
D. Conjugate **habeō** in the present active indicative.
E. Give the second person singular of **clāmō** in the present, imperfect, and future tenses, active indicative.

**II.**

A. Identify each of the following forms:

|   |   |
|---|---|
| 1. vidētis | 6. es |
| 2. vidēbās | 7. erat |
| 3. vidēbis | 8. erit |
| 4. clāmātis | 9. est |
| 5. ambulābātis | 10. habēre |

B. Change from singular to plural:

1. ambulat     6. implēs
2. corōnō     7. optās
3. habēs      8. sum
4. erit       9. videt
5. est      10. erō

# UNIT ONE — EXERCISES

**I.**
1. Nauta in patriā poenās rēgīnae timet.
2. Poēta pecūniam fāmamque nōn optat.
3. Pecūniam poētārum habēmus.
4. Poētīsne rēgīna pecūniam dabit?
5. Rēgīnam īnsulae cum turbā nautārum vidēre optābāmus.
6. Fēminae enim poētās corōnīs corōnābunt.
7. Fēminās in viīs vidēbātis, sed dē fōrmā nōn clāmābātis. Poenās dabitis.
8. Poētae rēgīnam patriae ē turbā fēminārum optant.
9. Est cūra dē poenā poētae.
10. Taedās in viā vidēre timēbō.
11. Taedamne in īnsulā vidētis?
12. Turbamne fēminārum in īnsulā vidēs (vidēbās)?
13. Cum poētā ē portīs in viam ambulō (ambulābam).
14. Poētae et poenam et fāmam timent.
15. Viās turbā implēbunt.
16. Nautae fēminās taedīs terrēbant.
17. a) Et pecūniam et corōnās poētīs dōnābis.
     b) Et pecūniā et corōnīs poētās dōnābis.
18. Erisne (eruntne, erantne, suntne) in īnsulā cum rēgīnā?
19. Fēminae est fōrma, fāma nautae; fēminīs est fōrma, fāma nautīs.
20. Poena nautārum erat cūra rēgīnae.
21. Rēgīnaene corōnam vidēre optābās?
22. Rēgīnae dē patriā cūram habent.
23. Nauta enim poenās dare nōn optat.
24. Ex aquā ambulāmus.
25. Patria poētae est īnsula.
26. Īnsulam esse patriam habēbat.
27. Vidēre taedās patriae est nautīs cūra.

## II.

1. The poets will crown a queen from the women of the island.
2. Shall we be with the poet on the island?
3. The sailors kept on shouting about the punishment of the women.
4. We fear the reputation of the poet.
5. You [pl.] kept on giving money to the crowds of sailors.
6. We desire to see women in (our) native land.
7. The sailor was a poet, but he kept on fearing both money and fame.

## III. Reading

Poēta fābulam[1] nārrat[2] dē rēgīnā et nautā. Rēgīna cum turbā incolārum[3] ē patriā exit[4] et ad[5] Africam[6] appropinquat.[7] Ibi[8] novam[9] patriam aedificābat[10] sed nōn timēbat. Subitō[11] nauta cum turbā et incolārum[3] et fēminārum ē patriā Trōiā[12] ad rēgīnae patriam appropinquat.[7] In Africā[6] diū[13] manent.[14] Rēgīna nautam amat[15] et nauta rēgīnam. Fāma enim rēgīnae nōn erat cūra. Postrēmō[16] nauta rēgīnam relinquit[17] et rēgīna vītam.[18]

[1] fābula, -ae, F., 'story'   [2] nārrō (1), 'tell'   [3] incola, -ae, M., 'inhabitant'   [4] exit, 'goes out' (3rd person sing.)   [5] ad (prep. + acc.), 'to, toward'   [6] Africa, -ae, F., 'Africa'   [7] appropinquō (1) (+ ad + acc.), 'approach'   [8] ibi (adv.), 'there'   [9] nova (adj.) 'new'   [10] aedificō (1), 'build'   [11] subitō (adv.), 'suddenly'   [12] Trōia, -ae, F., 'Troy'   [13] diū (adv.), 'for a long time'   [14] maneō, -ēre, mānsī, mānsus, 'remain'   [15] amō (1), 'love'   [16] postrēmō (adv.), 'finally'   [17] relinquit ,'abandons' (3rd person sing.)   [18] vīta, -ae, F., 'life'

# UNIT TWO

## A. The Perfect Active Indicative System of All Verbs

1. All verbs in Latin, regardless of the conjugation to which they belong, are formed identically in the perfect, pluperfect, and future perfect tenses respectively. As in the present system, the verb form in these tenses usually consists of a stem, a tense sign, and an ending.

2. The perfect stem is derived by dropping the -ī from the third principal part of the verb.

|  |  | STEM |
|---|---|---|
| optō, -āre, -āvī, -ātus | desire |  |
| optāvī |  | optāv/ī |
| impleō, -ēre, -ēvī, -ētus | fill |  |
| implēvī |  | implēv/ī |
| incipiō, -ere, -cēpī, -ceptus | begin |  |
| incēpī |  | incēp/ī |
| sentiō, -īre, sēnsī, sēnsus | feel, perceive |  |
| sēnsī |  | sēns/ī |

This process also applies to the few irregular verbs in Latin; irregularities do not appear in the perfect system.

3. There is a special set of personal endings which is used *only* for the perfect tense. These endings are:

|  | SINGULAR | PLURAL |
|---|---|---|
| 1 | -ī | -imus |
| 2 | -istī | -istis |
| 3 | -it | -ērunt |

The *perfect* tense is formed by adding these endings to the perfect stem. Note that there is no tense sign for the perfect.

4. The *pluperfect* tense is formed by adding the tense sign -erā- to the perfect stem and then adding the personal endings -m, -s, -t, -mus, -tis, -nt. It is perhaps easier, however, to regard the formation of the pluperfect indicative as the perfect stem plus the forms of the imperfect indicative of the verb **sum**.

35

5. The *future perfect* tense is formed by adding the tense sign -eri- to the perfect stem and then the personal endings -ō*, -s, -t, -mus, -tis, -nt. As in the pluperfect, it is easier to regard this formation as the perfect stem plus the forms of the future indicative of the verb **sum** (with -erint in the third person plural instead of -erunt). Thus:

| SINGULAR | | | PLURAL | | |
|---|---|---|---|---|---|
| Perf. | Pluperf. | Fut. Perf. | Perf. | Pluperf. | Fut. Perf. |
| 1 optāvī | optāveram | optāverō | optāvimus | optāverāmus | optāverimus |
| 2 optāvistī | optāverās | optāveris | optāvistis | optāverātis | optāveritis |
| 3 optāvit | optāverat | optāverit | optāvērunt | optāverant | optāverint |

* As with the future tense, the -i- in the first person singular is assimilated into the -ō. Thus, **optābō, optāverō**.

## B. The Subjunctive Mood
The indicative mood is used to make statements of fact or to ask direct questions. The subjunctive mood is connected with notions involving idea, intent, desire, uncertainty, potentiality, anticipation, or the like. There are many uses of the subjunctive which will be encountered as this course progresses. In this unit we shall be concerned with only one of these uses.

## C. Formation of the Subjunctive
While the indicative mood in Latin has six tenses, the subjunctive has only four: present, imperfect, perfect, and pluperfect. A subjunctive verb has no one equivalent in English and can only be translated according to the construction in which it occurs. By the same token, the translations of the tenses in the subjunctive do not necessarily correspond with those in the indicative.

### 1. PRESENT ACTIVE SUBJUNCTIVE OF THE FIRST CONJUGATION
The conjugation of the present subjunctive is very similar to that of the present indicative. Begin with the present stem, change the -ā- to -ē-, and add the personal endings -m, -s, -t, -mus, -tis, -nt.

optā- (stem)
optē- (mutated stem for present subjunctive)

| | |
|---|---|
| optem | optēmus |
| optēs | optētis |
| optet | optent |

### 2. IMPERFECT ACTIVE SUBJUNCTIVE OF ALL CONJUGATIONS
The imperfect subjunctive is easily formed for *all* verbs (including irregular verbs) by taking the full present active infinitive, lengthening the final -e, and

adding the personal endings **-m, -s, -t, -mus, -tis, -nt**. (Note that, as always, a long vowel is shortened before final **-m, -t,** or **-nt**.)

| | | | |
|---|---|---|---|
| optāre/m | implēre/m | incipere/m | sentīre/m |
| optārē/s | implērē/s | inciperē/s | sentīrē/s |
| optāre/t | implēre/t | incipere/t | sentīre/t |
| | | | |
| optārē/mus | implērē/mus | inciperē/mus | sentīrē/mus |
| optārē/tis | implērē/tis | inciperē/tis | sentīrē/tis |
| optāre/nt | implēre/nt | incipere/nt | sentīre/nt |

### 3. PERFECT ACTIVE SUBJUNCTIVE OF ALL CONJUGATIONS

To the perfect stem, add **-eri-** and then the personal endings **-m, -s, -t, -mus, -tis, -nt**.

| | | | |
|---|---|---|---|
| optāv/eri/m | implēv/eri/m | incēp/eri/m | sēns/eri/m |
| optāv/eri/s | implēv/eri/s | incēp/eri/s | sēns/eri/s |
| optāv/eri/t | implēv/eri/t | incēp/eri/t | sēns/eri/t |
| | | | |
| optāv/eri/mus | implēv/eri/mus | incēp/eri/mus | sēns/eri/mus |
| optāv/eri/tis | implēv/eri/tis | incēp/eri/tis | sēns/eri/tis |
| optāv/eri/nt | implēv/eri/nt | incēp/eri/nt | sēns/eri/nt |

### 4. PLUPERFECT ACTIVE SUBJUNCTIVE OF ALL CONJUGATIONS

To the perfect stem, add the tense sign **-issē-** and then the personal endings **-m, -s, -t, -mus, -tis, -nt**.

| | | | |
|---|---|---|---|
| optāv/isse/m | implēv/isse/m | incēp/isse/m | sēns/isse/m |
| optāv/issē/s | implēv/issē/s | incēp/issē/s | sēns/issē/s |
| optāv/isse/t | implēv/isse/t | incēp/isse/t | sēns/isse/t |
| | | | |
| optāv/issē/mus | implēv/issē/mus | incēp/issē/mus | sēns/issē/mus |
| optāv/issē/tis | implēv/issē/tis | incēp/issē/tis | sēns/issē/tis |
| optāv/isse/nt | implēv/isse/nt | incēp/isse/nt | sēns/isse/nt |

## D. Present Subjunctive of the Verb *sum*

While the endings are what we should expect, the stem is irregular:

| | |
|---|---|
| sim | sīmus |
| sīs | sītis |
| sit | sint |

The imperfect, perfect, and pluperfect subjunctives of this verb are formed according to the rules given under C above. The principal parts of the verb, it must be remembered, are **sum, esse, fuī, futūrus**.

## E. Conditional Sentences

The sentence "If he works, he is happy" is a conditional sentence. It is composed of two clauses, the *if* clause (sometimes called the *protasis*) and the *concluding* clause (called the *apodosis*). The protasis is introduced in Latin by **sī**, 'if', or **nisī**, 'unless, if not'.

Conditional sentences may be broken up into three basic categories and are formed in Latin according to a specific formula for each category.

### 1. SIMPLE (GENERAL) CONDITIONS

> If (i.e., whenever) he works, he is happy.

Such conditions may also be expressed in past time:

> If (i.e., whenever) he worked, he was happy.

FORMULA: Indicative in both clauses.

> Sī labōrat, fēlīx est.
> Sī labōrābat, fēlīx erat.

### 2. FUTURE CONDITIONS

#### a. MORE VIVID

> If he works, he will be happy.

This type of condition is expressed in English by the present indicative in the *if* clause and the future in the concluding clause.

FORMULA: Future indicative in both clauses.

> Sī labōrābit, fēlīx erit.

NOTE: Occasionally, when the speaker wishes the implications of his condition to be exceptionally emphatic, the future perfect indicative is used in the protasis instead of the simple future.

> Sī labōrāverit, fēlīx erit.   *If* he works (will have worked), (I am sure that) he will be happy.

In such cases it is emphasized that the action in the protasis *must* be completed in order for the action in the apodosis to occur. Frequently, in English, it is difficult to illustrate the difference between the future and the future perfect in such clauses, except by giving special intonation to the voice, or, in printing, by using italics.

#### b. LESS VIVID

> If he should work, he would be happy.

These conditions, while they refer to future time, conceive of the future act less vividly, or less certainly, than future more vivid conditions.

FORMULA: Present subjunctive in both clauses. (In English, *should* ... *would* ....)

Sī labōret, fēlīx sit.

NOTE: Occasionally the perfect subjunctive is used instead of the present, but this is rare, and so its discussion has been omitted from these materials.

### 3. CONTRARY-TO-FACT CONDITIONS

#### a. PRESENT CONTRARY-TO-FACT

Contrary-to-fact conditions state something which is untrue and hypothesized.

If he were (now) working (but he is not), he would be happy.

FORMULA: Imperfect subjunctive in both clauses. (In English, *were* ——*ing*, ...*would*....)

Sī labōrāret, fēlīx esset.

#### b. PAST CONTRARY-TO-FACT

If he had (in the past) worked (but he did not), he would have been happy.

FORMULA: Pluperfect subjunctive in both clauses. (In English, *had*..., *would have*....)

Sī labōrāvisset, fēlīx fuisset.

### 4. MIXED CONDITIONS

In addition to the strict formulae given above, occasionally one finds a mixed condition where the protasis and the apodosis belong to different categories. Such conditions are constructed as logical thought requires. For example:

If he had (in the past) worked (but he did not), he would (now) be happy.

This sentence is past contrafactual in the protasis, but the apodosis refers to present time. Consequently, the protasis must have its verb in the pluperfect subjunctive, while the verb of the apodosis will be imperfect subjunctive.

Sī labōrāvisset, fēlīx esset.

### F. Genitive with Verbs of Accusing and Condemning

The genitive is used with verbs of accusing and condemning to express the charge or the penalty.

*Genitive of the charge:*

> Puellam **cūrae** culpat.   He blames the girl [*of*] *for* (*her*) *concern.*
> [**culpō** (1), 'blame']

*Genitive of the penalty:*

> Nautam **pecūniae** dāmnāvit.   He sentenced the sailor [*of money*] *to pay money.*

# UNIT TWO — VOCABULARY

| | |
|---|---|
| **ā, ab** (prep. + abl.) | (away) from; by (only with living beings) [1] |
| **ad** (prep. + acc.) | to, toward |
| **anima, -ae,** F. | soul, spirit, life force |
| **āra, -ae,** F. | altar |
| **capiō, -ere, cēpī, captus** | take, capture |
| **cella, -ae,** F. | storeroom, (small) room |
| **cēlō** (1) | hide, conceal |
| **cōgitō** (1) | think, ponder, consider |
| **culpa, -ae,** F. | guilt, fault |
| **dāmnō** (1) | condemn, sentence |
| **dubitō** (1) | doubt, hesitate |
| **glōria, -ae,** F. | glory, renown |
| **incipiō, -ere, incēpī, inceptus** | begin |
| **incola, -ae,** M. (occasionally F.) | inhabitant |
| **incolō, -ere, -uī, --** | inhabit |
| **īnsidiae, -ārum,** F. (used only in pl.) | ambush, plot, treachery |
| **invidia, -ae,** F. | envy, jealousy |
| **labōrō** (1) | work |
| **lacrima, -ae,** F. | tear (*as in* 'teardrop') |
| **lūna, -ae,** F. | moon, moonlight |
| **moneō, -ēre, monuī, monitus** | warn, remind |
| **mora, -ae,** F. | delay |
| **mūtō** (1) | change, exchange |
| **nātūra, -ae,** F. | nature |
| **neque** or **nec** (conj.) | and not, nor |
| **neque (nec)...neque (nec)** | neither...nor |
| **nihil** or **nīl,** N. (indeclinable noun) | nothing |
| **nisī** (conj.) | unless, if...not; except |

---

[1] **ā** before a word beginning with a consonant; **ab** before a vowel or **h**

| noxa, -ae, F. | harm, injury |
|---|---|
| nunc (adv.) | now |
| pellō, -ere, pepulī, pulsus | push, drive (off) |
|   expellō, -ere, expulī, expulsus | push out, drive out |
| per (prep. + acc.) | through |
| prōvincia, -ae, F. | province |
| puella, -ae, F. | girl |
| semper (adv.) | always |
| sententia, -ae, F. | feeling, thought, opinion |
| sentiō, -īre, sēnsī, sēnsus | feel, perceive |
| sī (conj.) | if |
| sub (prep. + acc.) | under (i.e., going to a place under) |
|   (prep. + abl.) | under (i.e., at *or* in a place under) |
| superō (1) | overcome, conquer |
| taceō, -ēre, tacuī, tacitus | be (*or* keep) silent |
| teneō, -ēre, tenuī, tentus | hold, keep, possess |
| terra, -ae, F. | earth, land |
| unda, -ae, F. | wave |
| veniō, -īre, vēnī, ventus | come |
| vīta, -ae, F. | life |

# UNIT TWO — NOTES ON VOCABULARY

The preposition ā (ab) is used only with the ablative case. It has two different meanings, 'away from' and 'by' ('through the agency of', *not* 'near'). It means 'by' only when it is used with words representing living beings, for example, ā nautā, 'by the sailor', ā rēgīnā, 'by the queen'; 'by tears' or 'by delay' would not use ā (ab), but simply the ablative case without a preposition.

Since ad means 'to' or 'toward', it governs the accusative case (the case which expresses movement toward). The preposition per, 'through', also provides the idea of motion toward and so takes the accusative.

Incipiō, incipere, incēpī, inceptus is a compound of the preposition in-, 'on', plus the verb capiō, capere, cēpī, captus. The -a- of the uncompounded verb changes to -i- in compounds; this is always the case in Latin. It is very common for the -a- in a perfect passive participle to change to -e- when the verb is compounded. Incipiō means literally 'take on', thus, 'begin'. (Cf. He *takes on* a new task. He *begins* a new task.)

There are many compounds of capiō: ad + capiō is accipiō, 'take to (oneself), receive'. The prefix re- has the meaning 'back'; thus, recipiō, 'take back'. The imperative form recipe 'take back', is our English word "recipe". The Romans used a line to indicate an abbreviation, and so the sign for a prescription ℞ is not Rx, but an abbreviation for **recipe**, 'take back'. **Repellō (re-** + **pellō**, 'drive') means 'drive back'. A water-repellent raincoat drives back the rain so that it does not go through the coat. **Excipiō (ex** + **capiō)** means 'take out', and **suscipiō (sub**, 'under' + **capiō)** means 'undertake'.

**Cōgitō**, a first conjugation verb, means 'think, ponder, consider'. To *think about* something is **cōgitāre dē** (+ ablative) or **cōgitāre** (+ accusative).

**Dubitō** (1) means 'hesitate' when it is used with an infinitive, otherwise 'doubt'.

**Incolō, incolere, incoluī**, 'inhabit', is obviously related to **incola, incolae**, M. or F., 'inhabitant'; it lacks a fourth principal part.

**Īnsidiae, īnsidiārum**, F., 'ambush, plot, treachery', although plural in Latin and governing a plural verb, is translated as singular in English.

There is no distinction between **neque** and **nec**; either spelling may be used. **Neque...neque** means 'neither...nor': **Rēgīnam neque videt neque timet**, 'He neither sees nor fears the queen'. The sentence could also be written **Rēgīnam nec videt nec timet**.

In the same way, the spellings of the word 'nothing', **nihil** and **nīl**, are interchangeable.

**Pellō, pellere, pepulī, pulsus**, 'push, drive off', forms its third principal part by the process of reduplication. Some verbs have such reduplicated third principal parts, which are formed by prefixing the word with the initial consonant, followed either by -**e**- or the vowel of the root. Some other examples of reduplicated perfects are:

| | |
|---|---|
| canō, canere, **cecinī**, cantus | sing (of) |
| currō, currere, **cucurrī**, cursus | run |
| poscō, poscere, **poposcī**, –– | beg, demand |

**Expellō, expellere, expulī, expulsus** is a compound of **pellō (ex** + **pellō)** and so it means 'push out, drive out'. Often a verb that is compounded will lose its reduplicated form in the perfect (cf. **pepulī, expulī**).

Very frequently, first declension nouns that end in -**tia** come over into English with the spelling -*ce* or -*cy* (cf. **sententia**, 'sentence'; **grātia**, 'grace'; **dīligentia**, 'diligence'; **beneficentia**, 'beneficence'; **cōnstantia**, 'constancy').

The perfect forms of **sentiō, sentīre, sēnsī, sēnsus**, 'feel, perceive', have a long -ē- because of the -**ns**- which follows.

**Sub** takes either the accusative or the ablative case depending upon whether the idea of movement toward or location is involved. In other words, if one were drilling down under the earth, in Latin **sub terram** would be used, but if one were to speak of the rock lying under the earth, **sub terrā** would be used.

Again notice the lengthening of the -**e**- in **veniō, venīre** to -ē- in the perfect active, **vēnī**.

A good way of remembering the principal parts of verbs is to associate both the present stem and the perfect passive stem with English words. For example:

| incipiō | *incipi*ent | *incept*ion |
| expellō | *expel* | *expuls*ion |
| sentiō | *sent*ient | *sens*ual |
| veniō | con*vene* | con*vent*ion |

## UNIT TWO — DRILL

**I.**

Verb identification: Translate indicatives; identify subjunctives by so labeling them, and appending information as to person, number, tense, and voice.

1. ambulat, ambulāret, ambulāvit, ambulāverat
2. clāmābunt, clāmant; clāment, clāmāvērunt
3. vīdērunt, vīderant, vīderint (two possibilities), vīdissent
4. optāverās, optāveris (two possibilities), optēmus, optāvimus
5. timērēmus, timēmus, timuimus, timēbāmus
6. dedissem, dem, dabam, dedī

**II.**

Translate:

1. Sī in īnsulā eritis, pecūniam habēre optābitis.
2. Sī in īnsulā sītis, aquam optētis.
3. Sī in patriā essētis, fēminās vidērētis.
4. Sī in patriā fuissētis, clāmāre dubitāvissētis.
5. Sī fēminam vidēbit, clāmābit.
6. Sī fēminam vīderit, clāmābit.
7. Sī fēminam vidēret, clāmāret.
8. Sī fēminam vīdisset, clāmāvisset.
9. Sī fēminam optet, clāmet.
10. Sī taedam nautae det, portam vidēbō.
11. Sī taedam nautae dabit, portam vidēbō.
12. Sī taedam nautae dederit, portam vidēbō.
13. Sī taedam nautae dedisset, portam vīdissem.
14. Sī taedam nautae daret, portam vidērem.

**III.**

Ellipsis. Note the following progression, and how the verb "to be" is omitted.

| Est fāma fēminīs.   Est fōrma fēminīs. |
| Est fāma fēminīs et est fōrma fēminīs. |
| Est fāma fēminīs et      fōrma. |
| Fāma fēminīs et      fōrma. |

## UNIT TWO — PRELIMINARY EXERCISES
## (SECTIONS A, B, C, D)

**I.**

1. Incolaene dē glōriā patriae tacuērunt?
2. Rēgīnam dē incolārum īnsidiīs monuī.
3. Glōriam enim optāverint.
4. Nīl nisī glōriam optāverō.
5. Puellae neque lacrimās neque culpam cēlāverant.
6. Sententiās dē animā mūtāre incēperāmus sed sententiās nōn mūtāverātis.
7. Invidiamne ex animā expulistī?
8. Noxam ab incolīs pepulerimus.
9. Per undās ad terram vēnistis, sed in patriā semper fuimus.
10. Pecūniam rēgīnae ē terrā cēperat.

**II.**

A *synopsis* is a summary outline of a given verb that shows at a glance the major inflectional variations of that verb. In Latin, a synopsis gives all the forms of a given verb in a specified person and number. Writing synopses is an excellent way to solidify one's knowledge of the verbal system in Latin.

The following example is a synopsis of **cēlō** (1) in the third person singular:

**cēlō, cēlāre, cēlāvī, cēlātus,** 'hide, conceal'

| | ACTIVE VOICE | |
|---|---|---|
| | INDICATIVE MOOD | SUBJUNCTIVE MOOD |
| Present | cēlat | cēlet |
| Imperfect | cēlābat | cēlāret |
| Future | cēlābit | —— |
| Perfect | cēlāvit | cēlāverit |
| Pluperfect | cēlāverat | cēlāvisset |
| Future Perfect | cēlāverit | —— |

Write synopses of the following verbs:

1. dubitō (1), second person plural; third person singular
2. labōrō (1), third person plural; first person singular

## UNIT TWO — EXERCISES

**I.**

1. cum puellā; dē lūnā; ē cellīs; in āram; in turbā; ab incolā; ā prōvinciā; ad undam; per terrās; sub portam; sub undīs.

2. Sententiam mūtābit. Sententiam mūtāre dubitat. Sententiam mūtāre incēperat. Sententiam mūtāvit.

3. Nisī fēminae nautās sententiārum dē incolīs dāmnābunt (dāmnāverint), incolae in prōvinciā nōn labōrābunt.

4. Incolae sī fēminās īnsulae dāmnārent, nautae ad terram venīre nōn dubitārent.

5. Incolae sī īnsulae fēminās dāmnāvissent, nautae ad terram venīre nōn dubitāvissent.

6. Incolae sī īnsulae fēminās īnsidiārum dāmnent, nautae ad prōvinciam venīre nōn dubitent.

7. Incolae sī fēminās in turbā dāmnābunt, nautae ad īnsulam venīre nōn dubitābunt.

8. Incolae sī fēminās invidiae dāmnāverint, nautae sententiam dē fāmā incolārum mūtāre nōn dubitābunt.

9. Sī nautae undās timēbunt, in terrā semper erunt.

10. Puella dē glōriā et fāmā poētārum cōgitat.

11. Nautae noxās ā puellīs pepulerant (pepulērunt).

12. Sī nautae noxās ā puellīs pepulissent, et glōriam et fāmam cēpissent.

13. Dē nātūrā animae neque cum poētā sēnseram neque sententiam mūtāre optāveram. [sentiō cum, 'agree with']

14. Terram sī poētae incoluissent, nautās ē prōvinciā expulissent et nātūram patriae mūtāvissent.

15. Sī nautās rēgīnae superāvissem, prōvinciam tenērem.

16. Undae ārās cēlāre incēpērunt.

17. Sī undae ārās cēlāre inciperent, incolās monērem.

18. Nautārum fāma sententiam dē īnsulārum incolīs mūtāverit.

19. Nisī in cellā labōrāvissētis, nautae ē prōvinciā puellās nōn pepulissent.

20. Sī Hannibal ad portās prōvinciae vēnisset, incolās taediīs monuissem. [Hannibal, nom., the name of a Carthaginian general]

21. Nisī pecūniam in cellā cēlāvissēs, rēgīna nautās nec dāmnāvisset nec ē prōvinciā expelleret.

22. Et glōria incolīs prōvinciae et culpa, sed poēta dē nātūrā incolārum tacuit.

23. Nisī pecūniam optāvissent, nautae neque per prōvinciam vēnissent neque īnsulam nunc superārent.

24. Sub lūnā labōrāverāmus.

25. Sub portās ambulāre dubitābam.

26. Puella tacēbat, neque lacrimās cēlāvit.

27. Vīta rēgīnae nihil dedit nisī glōriam fāmamque.

28. Puellāsne dē morā nautārum monuistī? Puellās monuī, sed nīl timent.

29. Nisī īnsidiās incolārum nunc sentīrent, incolās ē prōvinciā nōn expellerent.

## II.

1. If I had changed (my) opinion about the nature of the soul, I would have kept silent.
2. If they were changing (their) opinion about the nature of the soul, they would keep silent.
3. If you are silent, I shall work.
4. You [pl.] had driven the poets from the island.
5. You [pl.] have filled the altar with (your) tears.
6. If they should hide the money, the queen would condemn the inhabitants for treachery.

## III. Reading

Aenēās,[1] id[2] enim nōmen[3] nautae fuit, dum[4] incoluit Africam cum rēgīnā incolās rēxit.[5] Patriam aedificāvērunt.[6] Tum,[7] subitō,[8] deus[9] vēnit et nautam monuit: "Nāvigā[10] nunc," nārrāvit,[11] "antequam[12] rēgīnae sit[13] īra.[14] Sī nunc manēbis,[15] tē[16] semper manēre[15] optet." Nautam terruit et sub lūnā Aenēās[1] turbam monuit, "Sententiam mūtāvī. Parābimus[17] et ab Africā nāvigābimus."[10] Nōn fuit mora. Aenēae[1] pāruērunt[18] et nāvigāvērunt.[10] Rēgīna māne[19] lacrimāvit[20] quod[21] Aenēās[1] cum turbā incolārum patriam relīquerat.[22] Rēgīnam īra[14] implēvit. "Nisī manēre[15] optāverit, nīl habēbō," Annae[23] nārrat.[11] "Vītam nōn optō sine[24] Aenēā.[1] Nisī mē[25] amat, esse nōn optō." Sīc[26] nārrāvit[11] et sē[27] necāvit.[28] Anima rēgīnae discessit.[29] Incolae Africae dē culpā nautae cōgitāvērunt et lacrimāvērunt.[20] Nautam noxae rēgīnae dāmnāvērunt. Dē īnsidiīs cōgitābant. Ad ārās vēnērunt et deōs[30] poenās Aenēae[1] turbaeque ōrāvērunt.[31]

[1] Aenēās, -ae, M., 'Aeneas', a Greek name in the first declension  [2] id, pronoun in the neuter sing., 'this', referring to Aenēās and agreeing with nōmen  [3] nōmen (nom.), 'name'  [4] dum (conj.), 'while'  [5] regō, -ere, rēxī, rēctus, 'rule'  [6] aedificō (1), 'build, establish'  [7] tum (adv.), 'then'  [8] subitō (adv.), 'suddenly'  [9] deus (nom.), 'god'  [10] nāvigō (1), 'sail, set sail'. Nāvigā is the command (i.e., imperative), 'set sail!'  [11] nārrō (1), 'tell, speak'  [12] antequam (conj.), 'before'  [13] sit, 'is'. This form is the 3rd person sing. present subjunctive because of the anticipation of the queen's anger.  [14] īra, -ae, F., 'anger'  [15] maneō, -ēre, mānsī, mānsus, 'remain'  [16] tē (acc.), 'you'  [17] parō (1), 'get ready'  [18] pāreō, -ēre, -uī, -itus, 'obey' (+ dat.)  [19] māne (adv.), 'early in the morning'  [20] lacrimō (1), 'cry, weep, shed tears'  [21] quod (conj.), 'because'  [22] relinquō, -ere, relīquī, relictus, 'leave behind'  [23] Anna, -ae, F., 'Anna', the queen's sister  [24] sine (prep. + abl.), 'without'  [25] mē (acc.), 'me'  [26] sīc (adv.), 'in this way'  [27] sē (acc.), 'herself'  [28] necō (1), 'kill'  [29] discēdō, -ere, -cessī, -cessus, 'withdraw'  [30] deōs (acc.), 'gods'  [31] ōrō (1), 'beg for' (with two accusatives: i.e., one begs someone in the accusative for something in the accusative)

## A. Nouns of the Second Declension

Nouns of the second declension are distinguished by the genitive singular ending -ī.

| | |
|---|---|
| nātus, -ī, M. | son, child |
| puer, puerī, M. | boy |
| saxum, -ī, N. | rock, stone |

While most nouns of the first declension are feminine, most of the second declension are masculine or neuter.

In order to decline a noun of the second declension, add the case endings for this declension to the stem. As usual, the stem is found by dropping the ending from the full genitive singular form. The endings are:

| | SINGULAR | | PLURAL | |
|---|---|---|---|---|
| | MASCULINE | NEUTER | MASCULINE | NEUTER |
| Nom. | -us* | -um | -ī | -a |
| Gen. | -ī | -ī | -ōrum | -ōrum |
| Dat. | -ō | -ō | -īs | -īs |
| Acc. | -um | -um | -ōs | -a |
| Abl. | -ō | -ō | -īs | -īs |

\* The -us ending occurs for the masculine singular in most instances. Occasionally, however, nouns ending in -r or -er will occur, as will be seen in the vocabularies (e.g., **vir, puer**).

NOTE CAREFULLY:

1. The neuter differs from the masculine of the second declension in three places:
   a. nominative singular
   b. nominative plural
   c. accusative plural
2. In all neuter nouns in the language, the nominative and accusative forms of each number are *always* identical.

3. In all neuter nouns in the language, the nominative and accusative plural
end in **-a**.

By applying these rules we can decline **nātus, puer**, and **saxum** as follows:

| | SINGULAR | | | PLURAL | | |
|------|--------|--------|--------|---------|----------|---------|
| Nom. | nātus  | puer   | saxum  | nātī    | puerī    | saxa    |
| Gen. | nātī   | puerī  | saxī   | nātōrum | puerōrum | saxōrum |
| Dat. | nātō   | puerō  | saxō   | nātīs   | puerīs   | saxīs   |
| Acc. | nātum  | puerum | saxum  | nātōs   | puerōs   | saxa    |
| Abl. | nātō   | puerō  | saxō   | nātīs   | puerīs   | saxīs   |

## B. First-Second Declension Adjectives

An adjective is a word which describes or modifies a noun. In Latin, adjectives
must *agree* with the nouns they modify in *gender*, *number*, and *case*, and so
adjectives, like nouns, are *declined*.

First-second declension adjectives utilize the case endings of the first two declensions. When the endings of the first declension are used, the adjective is said to
be feminine and will modify feminine nouns; when the endings of the second
declension are used, the adjective is said to be masculine or neuter and will
modify masculine or neuter nouns respectively.

In the dictionary, the adjectival forms given are the nominative singular masculine, feminine, and neuter (in that order):

magnus, -a, -um   large, big, great

The full forms are

magnus, magna, magnum

The entire declension is:

| | SINGULAR | | | PLURAL | | |
|------|--------|--------|--------|----------|----------|----------|
| | M. | F. | N. | M. | F. | N. |
| Nom. | magnus | magna  | magnum | magnī    | magnae   | magna    |
| Gen. | magnī  | magnae | magnī  | magnōrum | magnārum | magnōrum |
| Dat. | magnō  | magnae | magnō  | magnīs   | magnīs   | magnīs   |
| Acc. | magnum | magnam | magnum | magnōs   | magnās   | magna    |
| Abl. | magnō  | magnā  | magnō  | magnīs   | magnīs   | magnīs   |

Some first-second declension adjectives exhibit the **-er** ending in the masculine
nominative singular (e.g., **dexter, dextra, dextrum**, 'right' [as opposed to left],
'favorable'). The stem in such words may be derived from the feminine nominative form by dropping its ending:

dextr/a

The entire declension will be formed on this stem:

|      | M.      | F.       | N.       |
|------|---------|----------|----------|
| Nom. | dexter  | dextra   | dextrum  |
| Gen. | dextrī  | dextrae  | dextrī   |
| Dat. | dextrō  | dextrae  | dextrō   |
|      |         | ...etc.  |          |

## C. Noun-Adjective Agreement

As noted under B above, an adjective must agree with the noun it modifies in *gender*, *number*, and *case*.

'of a rock' (genitive) = saxī
'of a large rock' = magnī saxī
(The noun is neuter, singular, genitive; the adjective must be neuter, singular, genitive.)
'to/for a woman' (dative) = fēminae
'to/for a wretched woman' = fēminae miserae
(The noun is feminine, singular, dative; the adjective must be feminine, singular, dative.)

At first glance it may seem needless to go through the considerations of gender, number, and case, for agreement appears to be achieved simply by matching endings. But this is generally not true. Consider the following example:

poēta, -ae, M., 'poet'
'great poet' (nominative): The noun is masculine, singular, nominative; thus, the adjective must be *masculine*, singular, nominative.
Thus: poēta magnus
'great poets' (nominative): The noun is masculine, plural, nominative; thus, the adjective must be masculine, plural, nominative.
Thus: poētae magnī

More often than not, the endings of words which go together are *not* identical; therefore, one should not look for such correspondence.

## D. Adjectives Used As Nouns

As in English, an adjective may be used without a noun if that noun can be understood. Cf.:

The good (men) and the just (men) voted for freedom. Fortune favors the brave (men). Examples:

| | |
|---|---|
| magnus (masculine) | a great man |
| magna (feminine) | a great woman |
| magnum (neuter) | a great thing |
| Magna optō. | I desire great things. |
| Multa bona habet. | He has many good things; he has many goods; he has much property. |
| Rōmānōs timet. | He fears the Romans. |

## E. Ablative of Means (Instrument)

The ablative *without* a preposition is used to express the *means* or *instrument* by which something is done.

| | |
|---|---|
| Nautae **gladiīs** pūgnant. | The sailors fight *with (by means of) swords.* |
| **Oculīs** vidēmus. | We see *with (by means of)* [*our*] *eyes.* |
| Fēminās **taedā** terruit. | He frightened the women *with (by means of) a torch.* |

## F. Ablative of Manner (Modal Ablative)

The ablative case may be used *with* or *without* the preposition **cum** to denote the *way* or *manner* in which something is done. The **cum** is required in this construction when the noun in the ablative is *not* modified by an adjective; when it is modified, **cum** is optional.

| | |
|---|---|
| Verba misera **cum veniā** audīvistī. | You heard (my) wretched words *with indulgence (indulgently).* |
| Verba misera **magnā (cum) veniā** audīvistī. | You heard (my) wretched words *with great indulgence (very indulgently).* |

Note that phrases of this type can usually be translated by an English adverb ending in *-ly*.

## G. Clauses of Purpose; Sequence of Tenses

In the sentence "I fight to overcome the sailor," "to overcome the sailor" expresses the *purpose* for which the subject is fighting. Purpose is frequently expressed in English by the infinitive; in Latin a subordinate clause is normally required: "I fight in order that I may overcome the sailor". Purpose clauses are frequently introduced by the subordinating conjunctions **ut** (in this case, meaning 'in order that') or **nē** ('in order that...not'); they have their verbs in the subjunctive.

In Unit One the various tenses of the indicative were divided into two categories: primary and secondary. The tenses of the subjunctive, as well, may be so divided. The scheme follows:

|  | INDICATIVE | SUBJUNCTIVE |
|---|---|---|
| PRIMARY TENSES | Present | Present |
|  | Future | Perfect |
|  | Perfect ("have" or "has") |  |
|  | Future Perfect |  |
| SECONDARY TENSES | Imperfect | Imperfect |
|  | Perfect (English past) | Pluperfect |
|  | Pluperfect |  |

In most subordinate clauses in which the subjunctive is used, a system called *sequence of tenses* occurs. That is, if the verb of the main (independent) clause is in a primary tense, the verb of the subordinate (dependent) subjunctive clause must be primary. This is called *primary sequence*. Likewise, if the verb of the main clause is in a secondary tense, the verb of the subordinate clause must be secondary. This is called *secondary sequence*.

In primary sequence, the *present subjunctive* regularly denotes an action which occurs at the *same time* as that of the main verb or will occur at some time *subsequent* to that of the main verb. The *perfect subjunctive* denotes an action which occurred *prior* to the time of the main verb.

In secondary sequence, the *imperfect subjunctive* regularly denotes an action which occurs at the *same time* as that of the main verb or will occur at some time *subsequent* to that of the main verb. The *pluperfect subjunctive* denotes an action which occurred *prior* to the time of the main verb.

Thus:

Present and Imperfect Subjunctive — contemporaneous or subsequent action (with reference to the main verb)

Perfect and Pluperfect Subjunctive — prior action (with reference to the main verb)

It will be observed, then, that the tenses of the subjunctive frequently have no specific English tense values of their own but are *relative* to the tense of the main verb of a given sentence.

Since purpose clauses must logically refer to an action which will occur subsequent to the main verb, only the present and imperfect subjunctives are used in this construction.

PRIMARY SEQUENCE:

| | |
|---|---|
| Pūgnō **ut** nautam **superem**. | I fight *in order that I may overcome* the sailor; I fight *to overcome* the sailor. |
| Pūgnābō **ut** nautam **superem**. | I shall fight *in order that I may overcome* the sailor; I shall fight *to overcome* the sailor. |
| Pūgnāvī **ut** nautam **superem**. | I have fought *in order that I may overcome* the sailor; I have fought *to overcome* the sailor. |
| Pūgnāverō **ut** nautam **superem**. | I shall have fought *in order that I may overcome* the sailor; I shall have fought *to overcome* the sailor. |

SECONDARY SEQUENCE:

| | |
|---|---|
| Pūgnābam **ut** nautam **superārem**. | I was fighting *in order that I might overcome* the sailor; I was fighting *to overcome* the sailor. |
| Pūgnāvī **ut** nautam **superārem**. | I fought *in order that I might overcome* the sailor; I fought *to overcome* the sailor. |
| Pūgnāveram **ut** nautam **superārem**. | I had fought *in order that I might overcome* the sailor; I had fought *to overcome* the sailor. |

Negative purpose clauses are introduced by the subordinating conjunction **nē** instead of **ut**.

| | |
|---|---|
| Pūgnō **nē** nauta fēminam **superet**. | I fight *in order that* the sailor *may not overcome* the woman; I fight *so that* the sailor *will not overcome* the woman. |
| Pūgnābam **nē** nauta fēminam **superāret**. | I was fighting *in order that* the sailor *might not overcome* the woman; I was fighting *so that* the sailor *would not overcome* the woman. |

## H. Indirect Commands

Consider the sentence, "I beg you to overcome the sailor". "To overcome the sailor" is an indirect command and represents a direct imperative: "I beg you. Overcome the sailor!" In reality, it is an extension of a purpose construction: "I beg (in order) that you overcome the sailor". Many verbs of *ordering, warning, begging, urging, asking,* and the like, take such a construction.

| | |
|---|---|
| Ōrō **ut** nautam **superēs**. | I beg *in order that you may overcome* the sailor; I beg *you to overcome* the sailor. |
| Ōrābam **ut** nautam **superārēs**. | I begged (was begging) *in order that you might overcome* the sailor; I begged *you to overcome* the sailor. |
| Ōrāvī **ut** verba cum veniā **audīrēs**. | I begged *in order that you might hear* (my) words with indulgence; I begged *you to hear* (my) words with indulgence. |
| Ōrābam **nē** verba nautae **audīrēs**. | I begged *in order that you not hear the* words of the sailor; I begged *you not to hear* (*listen to*) the words of the sailor. |

# UNIT THREE — VOCABULARY

| | |
|---|---|
| **acerbus, -a, -um** | bitter, harsh |
| **ager, agrī**, M. | field |
| **audiō, -īre, -īvī, -ītus** | hear, listen (to) |
| **bellum, -ī**, N. | war |
| **bonus, -a, -um** | good |
| **caecus, -a, -um** | blind, hidden, secret |
| **campus, -ī**, M. | plain, level surface |
| **clārus, -a, -um** | bright, clear, famous |
| **dexter, dextra, dextrum** | right (as opposed to left), favorable |
|    **dextra, -ae**, F. | right hand |
|     **ad dextram** | to the right |
| **dīligentia, -ae**, F. | diligence |
| **dōnum, -ī**, N. | gift |
| **gerō, -ere, gessī, gestus** | conduct, manage, wage |
| **gladius, -ī**, M. | sword |
| **laetus, -a, -um** | happy |
| **līber, lībera, līberum** | free |
| **magnus, -a, -um** | large, big, great |
| **malus, -a, -um** | evil, bad, wicked |
| **Marcus, -ī**, M. | Marcus (proper name) |
| **miser, misera, miserum** | miserable, unhappy, wretched |
| **multus, -a, -um** | much, many |
| **nātus, -ī**, M. | son, child |
| **nē** (conj.) | (in purpose clauses) in order that...not |
| **oculus, -ī**, M. | eye |
| **ōrō** (1) | beg (for) |

| | |
|---|---|
| **petō, -ere, petīvī, petītus** | seek (with **ā** + abl.), ask (for) (cf. 'I ask for [seek] money from my son', **Pecūniam ā nātō petō.**) |
| **portō** (1) | carry |
| **puer, puerī**, M. | boy; child |
| **pūgnō** (1) | fight; (with **cum** + abl.), fight with (i.e., against) |
| **pulcher, pulchra, pulchrum** | beautiful |
| **Rōmānus, -a, -um** | Roman |
| **saxum, -ī**, N. | rock, stone |
| **scrībō, -ere, scrīpsī, scrīptus** | write |
| **servus, -ī**, M. | slave |
| **spectō** (1) | look at |
| **ut** (conj.) | (in purpose clauses) in order that |
| **validus, -a, -um** | strong, healthy |
| **vēlum, -ī**, N. | cloth, covering, sail |
|    **vēla dare** | to set sail |
| **venia, -ae**, F. | indulgence, favor, kindness, (obliging) disposition |
| **ventus, -ī**, M. | wind |
| **verbum, -ī**, N. | word |
| **vir, virī**, M. | man |

# UNIT THREE — NOTES ON VOCABULARY

Associating an English word with the Latin will be helpful in remembering when the -e- of a second declension masculine word remains and when it drops out: e.g., a*gri*culture (**ager, agrī**, M., 'field'), pul*chri*tude (**pulcher, pulchra, pulchrum**, 'beautiful'), li*ber*al (**līber, lībera, līberum**, 'free').

**Gerō, gerere, gessī, gestus** means 'conduct, manage'; when it is used with **bellum**, it means 'wage (war)'; **Rōmānī multa bella gessērunt**, 'The Romans waged many wars'.

**Gladius, gladiī**, M., 'sword' has a diminutive **gladiōlus**, 'little sword', which gives the name of the flower whose leaf looks like a little sword. The diminutive endings will be discussed later.

**Multus, multa, multum** usually means 'much' in the singular and 'many' in the plural. However, one can say in Latin: **Multus Rōmānus gladiō pūgnāvit**, 'Many a Roman fought with a sword'.

**Nātus, nātī**, M. is really the passive form of the perfect participle of a verb meaning 'to be born'; thus **nātus** is 'the one having been born, the son, child'.

**Ōrō, ōrāre, ōrāvī, ōrātus**, 'beg (for)' may govern two accusatives: the thing begged for and the person begged: **Rēgīnam pecūniam ōrāvit**, 'He begged the queen for money'.

**Petō, petere, petīvī, petītus** means 'ask' or 'ask for'. If one asks someone for

something in Latin using the verb **petō**, he asks something from somebody:
**Nātus dōnum ā Marcō petīvit**, '(His) son asked Marcus for a gift'.

**Pūgnō, pūgnāre, pūgnāvī, pūgnātus**, 'fight' is used with **cum** to mean 'fight against': **Multī cum Rōmānīs pūgnāvērunt**, 'Many (men) fought with the Romans'. (Note that "with" in this sense means 'against', *not* 'on the side of'.) **Repūgnō** is a compound of **pūgnō** (re- + **pūgnō**) and means 'fight back, resist'.

**Scrībō, scrībere, scrīpsī, scrīptus** means 'write'; thus, **īnscrībō**, 'write in *or* on'; **rescrībō**, 'write back'.

**Spectō**, a first conjugation verb, 'look at' has many compounds:

| | |
|---|---|
| aspectō (**ad** + **spectō**) | look toward, face |
| exspectō | look out for, await |
| respectō | look back |
| | ...etc. |

There is another verb in Latin closely related to **spectō**: **speciō, specere, spēxī**, --, which also means 'look at' and has many compounds:

| | |
|---|---|
| aspiciō | look at *or* toward |
| dēspiciō | look down upon |
| īnspiciō | look into, examine |
| respiciō | look back, consider |

**Vēlum, vēlī**, N. is a 'cloth' or 'covering'; it can also mean a 'sail'. The idiom **vēla dare** means 'to set sail': **Vēla ab īnsulā dedērunt**, 'They set sail from the island'.

## UNIT THREE — DRILL

**I.**

Change these noun forms to the plural. In some cases there may be several possibilities.

| | | |
|---|---|---|
| 1. bellum | 3. oculum | 5. veniae |
| 2. nātī | 4. saxō | |

**II.**

Change these noun forms to the singular:

| | | |
|---|---|---|
| 1. bellōrum | 3. saxa | 5. fēminās |
| 2. puerōs | 4. virīs | |

**III.**

A. Decline **caecus, -a, -um** in the singular.

Decline **bonus, -a, -um** in the plural.

B. For each of the following, supply the proper form of **magnus, -a, -um**:

| | | | |
|---|---|---|---|
| 1. fēmina | 3. puerō | 5. campus | 7. nautārum |
| 2. bellum | 4. poētae | 6. aquam | 8. ager |

## IV.

Translate the following sentences, all of which contain clauses of purpose or indirect commands:

1. Puella dē noxā tacet ut cum nautā ambulet.
2. Puella cūram fāmae cēlāvit ut pecūniam habēret.
3. Poēta tacet ut dē nātūrā animae cōgitet.
4. Poēta tacuit ut dē nātūrā animae cōgitāret.
5. Fēminae pecūniam optābant ut ad prōvinciam venīrent.
6. Tacuērunt incolae nē rēgīna sententiam mūtāret.
7. Tacent incolae nē rēgīna sententiam mūtet.
8. Monēmus ut dē vītā cōgitētis.
9. Cum lacrimīs monuit nē dē vītā cōgitārēmus.
10. Nīl clāmāvit nē incolās terrēret.
11. Nīl clāmāvit nē fēminae oculōs lacrimīs implērent.
12. Nīl clāmāvit nē fēminae oculōs lacrimīs implēre inciperent.
13. Cum cūrā labōrābāmus ut nautās ē prōvinciā pellerēmus.
14. Dē morā nautārum clāmāre dubitābat nē fēminae timērent.
15. Monēbimus ut sententiam mūtētis.
16. Monuistis ut pecūniam cēlem.

## V.

Translate the following sentences which contain adjectives used as nouns and/or ablatives of means or manner.

1. Nōtus cum cūrā labōrat.
2. Nōtōs taedīs pepulērunt.
3. Pecūniamne nōtae cēlāvistī?
4. Nōta cum invidiā cēlāvimus.
5. Nōta magnā (cum) invidiā cēlāvimus. [**magnus, -a, -um**, 'great']
6. Puellās monēbāmus nē nōtās taedīs terrērent.

# UNIT THREE — PRELIMINARY EXERCISES
## (SECTIONS A, B, C, D, E, F)

1. Puer laetus dōna multa ā servīs petīvit.
2. Multa ā servīs petīvistī sed dōna virō bonō veniā bonā dedērunt.

3. Saxum magnum in aquā erat sed in terrā erant saxa magna et multa.
4. Sī nauta miser ventōs bonōs ōrāvisset, laetusne fuisset?
5. Sī līberī magnā cum dīligentiā in agrō pūgnābunt, malōs superābunt.
6. Sī pulchrae poētam caecum audīrent, sententiās malās dē vītā mūtārent.
7. Verba acerba poētae caecī audīvistis et miserī esse incēpistis.
8. Nātīs servōrum gladiōs magnōs dedimus.
9. Rōmānī bella multa acerbaque gessērunt.
10. Malumne est bellum gerere?
11. Sī virī malī in campīs clārīs Marcī pūgnent, incolās bonōs terrae superent.
12. Cum glōriā puerī gladiīs pūgnābant.

# UNIT THREE — EXERCISES

**I.**

1. Nautae validī magnā cum cūrā pūgnābant ut incolās īnsulae superārent.
2. Saxīs pūgnāverāmus nē nautae acerbī fēminās poētārum clārōrum spectārent.
3. Virī magnā dīligentiā labōrant nē cum puerīs malīs in prōvinciā pūgnent.
4. Rēgīna magnum gladium virō bonō dabit ut cum Rōmānīs in campō pūgnet.
5. Marcus, vir magnus et bonus, corōnam ad poētam portāvit.
6. Nautae Rōmānī vēla ventīs dextrīs dabant nē virī malī campōs tenērent.
7. Virī līberī bellum cum dīligentiā gessērunt ut līberī semper essent.
8. Līberī malōs multīs gladiīs superābunt nē servī miserī sint.
9. Rēgīna pulchra poētae caecō dōnum bonum dederat ut verba clāra semper audīret.
10. Turba magna rēgīnam bonam gladiīs terruit ut et prōvinciam et īnsulam superāret.
11. Virī validī nautās ōrāvērunt ut incolās prōvinciae bellō et gladiīs superārent.
12. Sī dōnum bonum poētae Marcō darētis, magna verba cum dīligentiā scrīberet.
13. Sī verba mala puerōrum audīvistis, laetī nōn erātis.
14. Līberī prōvinciae servī fuissent, nisī nautae Rōmānī bellum in patriā gessissent.
15. Nisī tacuisset, miserum monuissem ut lacrimās cēlāret.
16. Nisī tacuerint, miserōs monēbō ut lacrimās cēlent.
17. Sententiās rēgīna prōvinciae mūtāvit nē poētae timērent.
18. Rēgīna virōrum sententiās mūtāvit ut nātī in agrīs labōrāre optent.
19. Poētae bonō sī pecūniam dedissēs, multa dē agrīs prōvinciae scrīpsisset ut incolīs magna fāma esset.
20. Validī incolae patriam et fāmam in dextrīs tenent. Per dextram ōrāmus ut magnā dīligentiā cum malīs pūgnent ut semper Rōmānī sīmus līberī. [**per**, 'by' (in oaths)]

21. Puerī ad dextram spectāverant ut gladiōs malōrum oculīs vidērent.
22. Vīdistisne magnum bellum in campīs? Fēminae sī bellum vīdissent, nātōs magnīs cum lacrimīs monuissent ut malōs ex agrīs patriae expellerent.
23. Nisi verba poētārum audīvissēs, nihil dē nātūrā animae et vītae nunc sentīrēs et vītam miseram nōn mūtāvissēs.
24. Nisī malōs saxīs gladiīsque ē cellā pepulissēmus, patriam cum glōriā nōn tenuissēmus, et nunc servī essēmus.
25. Ā rēgīnā petīvistī ut veniam incolīs daret.
26. Poēta validōs in agrīs monuit ut clārum gladium sub saxō peterent.

## II.

1. The Romans conquered the inhabitants of the island in order to frighten the free men of the province.
2. The wretched child desires to listen to the words of the poet in order to be happy.
3. The strong men were silent in order not to frighten the beautiful children.
4. The Romans very diligently (with great diligence) conquered the free men with swords and the slaves with kindness.
5. If you had looked at the girl with (your) eyes, she would have begged you very tearfully (with many tears) not to set sail.
6. The great queen had given swords to the strong sailors in order that they might fight with the wicked inhabitants of the island.

## III. Reading

Postquam[1] Aenēās ab Africā vēla dederat, sub terram īvit[2] ut patrem[3] mortuum[4] vidēret. Ut in Orcum[5] venīret, dōnum rēgīnae Orcī[5] dedit. In Orcō[5] animōs[6] et laetōs et miserōs multōrum mortuōrum[4] oculīs vīdit. Ibi[7] rēgīnam mortuam[4] vīdit et ōrāvit nē sē[8] īnsidiārum damnāret, sed rēgīna neque spectāvit neque Aenēan[9] audīvit. Aenēās viā[10] ambulāvit; ad dextram erat ager laetōrum, sed ad laevam[11] erant animī[6] malōrum. In agrum laetōrum vēnit et patrem[3] vīdit. Pater[12] nātō verba multa dē vītā et dē Rōmānīs cum veniā dīxit.[13] Aenēās patrem[3] audīvit laetus. Posteā[14] ad Italiam[15] vēla dedit et ibi[7] bellum cum incolīs gessit. Et gladiīs et saxīs magnā cum dīligentiā pūgnāvērunt. Aenēās cum turbā incolās Italiae[15] superāvit et ab Aenēā pācem[16] petīvērunt.

---

[1] postquam (conj.), 'after'   [2] eō, īre, īvī, itus, 'go'   [3] patrem (acc.), 'father'   [4] mortuus, -a, -um, 'dead'   [5] Orcus, -ī, M., 'the land of the dead'   [6] animus, -ī, M., 'soul'   [7] ibi (adv.), 'there'   [8] sē (acc.), 'him'   [9] Aenēan (acc.), 'Aeneas'   [10] viā, 'along the road'   [11] laevus, -a, -um, 'left'   [12] pater (nom.), 'father'   [13] dīcō, -ere, dīxī, dictus, 'say'   [14] posteā (adv.), 'afterward'   [15] Italia, -ae, F., 'Italy'   [16] pācem (acc.), 'peace'

# UNIT FOUR

## A. The Present Active System of All Four Conjugations

### 1. PRESENT ACTIVE INDICATIVE

In order to illustrate the inflections of the entire verbal system, we shall use the following verbs:

1. optō, -āre, -āvī, -ātus — desire
2. impleō, -ēre, -ēvī, -ētus — fill
3. { dūcō, -ere, dūxī, ductus — lead
     incipiō, -ere, -cēpī, -ceptus — begin
4. sentiō, -īre, sēnsī, sēnsus — feel

Note that *two* verbs have been listed for the third conjugation. These differ from one another in the -i- which appears before the final -ō in the first person singular form of one of them. This -i- will appear in various other places throughout the conjugation. Such verbs are called *i-stems*. It will be observed that all verbs of the fourth conjugation also have an -i- before the ending, and so i-stems of the third conjugation will have something in common with verbs of the fourth conjugation. (The major difference is the length of the vowel: in the third conjugation it is short; in the fourth it is generally long.)

The conjugation of the present indicative can best be illustrated by the following table:

| 1 | 2 | 3 | 3 i-stem | 4 | Ending |
|---|---|---|---|---|---|
| optō | impleō | dūcō | incipiō | sentiō | **-ō** |
| optās | implēs | dūcis | incipis | sentīs | **-s** |
| optat | implet | dūcit | incipit | sentit | **-t** |
| | | | | | |
| optāmus | implēmus | dūcimus | incipimus | sentīmus | **-mus** |
| optātis | implētis | dūcitis | incipitis | sentītis | **-tis** |
| optant | implent | dūcunt | incipiunt | sentiunt | **-nt** |

The personal endings are identical for all four conjugations. The difficulty

in the third conjugation lies in the stem vowel: we should expect it to be -e-
(dūce/re), but it appears as -i- or, in the third person plural, -u-. Also, note
that for i-stem verbs, the -i- appears in the first person singular and the third
person plural.

2. PRESENT ACTIVE SUBJUNCTIVE
The sign for the present subjunctive of the first conjugation is the vowel -ē-;
for the second, third, and fourth conjugations, it is -ā-, but this -ā- in some
conjugations appears in conjunction with another vowel. It will be easiest
to form the present subjunctive for all conjugations as follows:
   a. Arrive at the stem.
   b. Drop the stem vowel.
   c. In place of the original stem vowel, substitute -ē- for the first conjugation,
      -eā- for the second,-ā- for the third, -iā- for i-stems of the third, and -iā-
      for the fourth.
   d. Add the endings -m, -s, -t, -mus, -tis, -nt.
The following will illustrate:

| 1 | 2 | 3 | 3 i-stem | 4 |
|---|---|---|----------|---|
| optem | impleam | dūcam | incipiam | sentiam |
| optēs | impleās | dūcās | incipiās | sentiās |
| optet | impleat | dūcat | incipiat | sentiat |
| optēmus | impleāmus | dūcāmus | incipiāmus | sentiāmus |
| optētis | impleātis | dūcātis | incipiātis | sentiātis |
| optent | impleant | dūcant | incipiant | sentiant |

These forms should now be compared to those of the present indicative, so
that the differences may be discerned readily.

One will observe at once some difficulties in the recognition of forms and will
understand how important it is to know the principal parts of verbs, particularly the second part which indicates to which conjugation the verb belongs.
Dūcat, for example, looks dangerously like optat. Only by knowing that dūcō
belongs to the third conjugation, while optō belongs to the first, can one tell
that the -a- in dūcat is the sign of the present subjunctive, while in optat it is
the sign of the present indicative.

3. IMPERFECT ACTIVE INDICATIVE
The sign for the imperfect indicative of all conjugations is -bā-. In the third
conjugation, the stem vowel lengthens (from -e- to -ē-). In i-stem verbs of
the third conjugation and in all verbs of the fourth conjugation, -iē- appears
before the tense sign throughout:

| 1 | 2 | 3 | 3 i-stem | 4 |
|---|---|---|---|---|
| optābam | implēbam | dūcēbam | incipiēbam | sentiēbam |
| optābās | implēbās | dūcēbās | incipiēbās | sentiēbās |
| optābat | implēbat | dūcēbat | incipiēbat | sentiēbat |
| optābāmus | implēbāmus | dūcēbāmus | incipiēbāmus | sentiēbāmus |
| optābātis | implēbātis | dūcēbātis | incipiēbātis | sentiēbātis |
| optābant | implēbant | dūcēbant | incipiēbant | sentiēbant |

## 4. IMPERFECT ACTIVE SUBJUNCTIVE

The imperfect active subjunctive for all conjugations has been illustrated in section C2 of Unit 2 (page 36 above).

## 5. FUTURE ACTIVE INDICATIVE

The sign for the future of the first two conjugations is -bi- (with -bō- in the first person singular and -bu- in the third person plural). The sign for the future of the third and fourth conjugations is -ē- (with -a- in the first person singular). This vowel replaces the original vowel of the stem. I-stems show the -i- throughout.

| 1 | 2 | 3 | 3 i-stem | 4 |
|---|---|---|---|---|
| optābō | implēbō | dūcam | incipiam | sentiam |
| optābis | implēbis | dūcēs | incipiēs | sentiēs |
| optābit | implēbit | dūcet | incipiet | sentiet |
| optābimus | implēbimus | dūcēmus | incipiēmus | sentiēmus |
| optābitis | implēbitis | dūcētis | incipiētis | sentiētis |
| optābunt | implēbunt | dūcent | incipient | sentient |

Again, some possible difficulties in interpretation will be noted:

dūcet; optet; implet

**Dūcō, -ere** is a third conjugation verb; -e- in this conjugation is the sign of the future; therefore, **dūcet** is third person singular future active indicative.

**Optō, -āre** is a first conjugation verb; -e- in this conjugation is the sign of the present subjunctive; therefore, **optet** is third person singular present active subjunctive.

**Impleō, -ēre** is a second conjugation verb; -e- in this conjugation is the vowel of the present stem; therefore, **implet** is third person singular present active indicative.

Frequently, however, the syntactical structure of a sentence will help determine the form of the verb, even if the conjugation to which the verb belongs is not known.

Ōrō ut urnam impleās.

The **ōrō ut** indicates that a subjunctive clause is being introduced; hence, the -ā- in **impleās** must be the sign of the present subjunctive and not the vowel of the present indicative of the first conjugation. Therefore:

Ōrō ut urnam impleās.   I beg you to fill the urn.

## B. The Present Passive System of All Four Conjugations

If one can conjugate a verb in the active voice, he can do it easily in the passive. Instead of appending the personal endings -ō (-m), -s, -t, -mus, -tis, -nt to the appropriate stem or tense sign, he will append a special set of *passive* personal endings. These are:

| -or, -r | -mur |
|---------|------|
| -ris (-re) | -minī |
| -tur | -ntur |

The active and passive forms are placed side by side in the following paradigms to illustrate this formation.

1. PRESENT INDICATIVE

**1**

| ACTIVE | | PASSIVE | |
|--------|--|---------|--|
| optō | I desire | optor* | I am desired |
| optās | you desire | optāris (optāre) | you are desired |
| optat | he desires | optātur | he is desired |
| optāmus | we desire | optāmur | we are desired |
| optātis | you desire | optāminī | you are desired |
| optant | they desire | optantur* | they are desired |

* Note that a long vowel is shortened before final -r and -ntur.

**2**

| ACTIVE | PASSIVE |
|--------|---------|
| impleō | impleor |
| implēs | implēris (implēre) |
| implet | implētur |
| implēmus | implēmur |
| implētis | implēminī |
| implent | implentur |

**3**

| ACTIVE | PASSIVE |
|--------|---------|
| dūcō | dūcor |
| dūcis | dūceris (dūcere)* |
| dūcit | dūcitur |
| dūcimus | dūcimur |
| dūcitis | dūciminī |
| dūcunt | dūcuntur |

**3 i-stem**

| ACTIVE | PASSIVE |
|--------|---------|
| incipiō | incipior |
| incipis | inciperis (incipere)* |
| incipit | incipitur |

**4**

| ACTIVE | PASSIVE |
|--------|---------|
| sentiō | sentior |
| sentīs | sentīris (sentīre) |
| sentit | sentītur |

* Note that the short -i- becomes short -e- before the -ris (-re) ending.

| incipimus | incipimur | | sentīmus | sentīmur |
|-----------|-----------|---|----------|----------|
| incipitis | incipiminī | | sentītis | sentīminī |
| incipiunt | incipiuntur | | sentiunt | sentiuntur |

## 2. IMPERFECT INDICATIVE

### 1

| ACTIVE | | PASSIVE | |
|--------|--|---------|--|
| optābam | I was desiring | optābar | I was being desired |
| optābās | you were desiring | optābāris | you were being desired |
| | | (optābāre) | |
| . . .etc. | | . . .etc. | |

### 2 | | 3

| ACTIVE | PASSIVE | ACTIVE | PASSIVE |
|--------|---------|--------|---------|
| implēbam | implēbar | dūcēbam | dūcēbar |
| implēbās | implēbāris | dūcēbās | dūcēbāris (dūcēbāre) |
| | (implēbāre) | | |
| . . .etc. | . . .etc. | . . .etc. | . . .etc. |

### 3 i-stem | | 4

| ACTIVE | PASSIVE | ACTIVE | PASSIVE |
|--------|---------|--------|---------|
| incipiēbam | incipiēbar | sentiēbam | sentiēbar |
| incipiēbās | incipiēbāris | sentiēbās | sentiēbāris |
| | (incipiēbāre) | | (sentiēbāre) |
| . . .etc. | . . .etc. | . . .etc. | . . .etc. |

## 3. FUTURE INDICATIVE

### 1

| ACTIVE | | PASSIVE | |
|--------|--|---------|--|
| optābō | I shall desire | optābor | I shall be desired |
| optābis | you will desire | optāberis (optābere)* | you will be desired |
| optābit | he will desire | optābitur | he will be desired |
| optābimus | we shall desire | optābimur | we shall be desired |
| optābitis | you will desire | optābiminī | you will be desired |
| optābunt | they will desire | optābuntur | they will be desired |

### 2 | | 3

| ACTIVE | PASSIVE | ACTIVE | PASSIVE |
|--------|---------|--------|---------|
| implēbō | implēbor | dūcam | dūcar |
| implēbis | implēberis (implēbere)* | dūcēs | dūcēris (dūcēre) |
| implēbit | implēbitur | dūcet | dūcētur |

* Note that the short **-i-** becomes short **-e-** before the **-ris** (**-re**) ending.

| | | | |
|---|---|---|---|
| implēbimus | implēbimur | dūcēmus | dūcēmur |
| implēbitis | implēbiminī | dūcētis | dūcēminī |
| implēbunt | implēbuntur | dūcent | dūcentur |

| 3 i-stem | | 4 | |
|---|---|---|---|
| ACTIVE | PASSIVE | ACTIVE | PASSIVE |
| incipiam | incipiar | sentiam | sentiar |
| incipiēs | incipiēris (incipiēre) | sentiēs | sentiēris (sentiēre) |
| incipiet | incipiētur | sentiet | sentiētur |
| incipiēmus | incipiēmur | sentiēmus | sentiēmur |
| incipiētis | incipiēminī | sentiētis | sentiēminī |
| incipient | incipientur | sentient | sentientur |

### 4. PRESENT AND IMPERFECT SUBJUNCTIVES

As one would expect, the present and imperfect subjunctives are formed in the same way as the active, except that the *passive* personal endings are used instead of the active ones. For an illustration of this, see the review chart on page 66.

### C. The Perfect Passive System of All Four Conjugations

All verbs in Latin, regardless of the conjugation to which they belong, are conjugated identically in the perfect system.

In the perfect system the passive is a *compound* form; that is, it is composed of two words: a participle and a helping verb, **sum**. The perfect passive participle is the fourth principal part of most verbs. This form, while given in the vocabularies with a -**us** ending (**optātus**), is, in fact, an adjective and so can be declined. It might be written **optātus, -a, -um** just like the adjective **magnus, -a, -um**.

### 1. PERFECT PASSIVE INDICATIVE

The perfect passive indicative is composed of the fourth principal part of the verb (perfect passive participle) and a form of the present indicative of the verb **sum**. The ending of the participle is declined to show the number and gender of the subject. Since it refers to the subject, it is in the nominative case.

| | |
|---|---|
| optātus sum | I (masc.) have been desired, I was desired |
| optāta sum | I (fem.) have been desired, I was desired |
| optātus est | he has been desired, he was desired |
| optāta est | she has been desired, she was desired |
| optātum est | it has been desired, it was desired |
| optātī sunt | they (masc.) have been desired, they were desired |

The paradigm for the perfect passive indicative is:

optātus (-a, -um) sum    optātī (-ae, -a) sumus
optātus (-a, -um) es     optātī (-ae, -a) estis
optātus (-a, -um) est    optātī (-ae, -a) sunt

2. PLUPERFECT PASSIVE INDICATIVE

FORMATION: Perfect passive participle plus imperfect of the verb **sum**.

optātus (-a, -um) eram   optātī (-ae, -a) erāmus
optātus (-a, -um) erās   optātī (-ae, -a) erātis
optātus (-a, -um) erat   optātī (-ae, -a) erant

3. FUTURE PERFECT PASSIVE INDICATIVE

FORMATION: Perfect passive participle plus future of the verb **sum**.

optātus (-a, -um) erō    optātī (-ae, -a) erimus
optātus (-a, -um) eris   optātī (-ae, -a) eritis
optātus (-a, -um) erit   optātī (-ae, -a) erunt

4. PERFECT PASSIVE SUBJUNCTIVE

FORMATION: Perfect passive participle plus present subjunctive of the verb **sum**.

optātus (-a, -um) sim    optātī (-ae, -a) sīmus
optātus (-a, -um) sīs    optātī (-ae, -a) sītis
optātus (-a, -um) sit    optātī (-ae, -a) sint

5. PLUPERFECT PASSIVE SUBJUNCTIVE

FORMATION: Perfect passive participle plus imperfect subjunctive of the verb **sum**.

optātus (-a, -um) essem  optātī (-ae, -a) essēmus
optātus (-a, -um) essēs  optātī (-ae, -a) essētis
optātus (-a, -um) esset  optātī (-ae, -a) essent

## D. Review of Verb Conjugations

The chart on page 66 will illustrate the forms of all the tenses of the indicative and the subjunctive of all four conjugations.

## E. Ablative of Personal Agent

The *agent* (**agō, -ere, ēgī, āctus**, 'do') or *person* who performs the action of a passive verb is regularly expressed in the ablative case preceded by the preposition **ā** or **ab**, 'by'.

Puella **ā rēgīnā** terrētur.    The girl is frightened *by the queen*.

# Review of Verb Conjugations

(Shown in each box are the *active* forms of the 1st and 2nd person singular, followed by the *passive* forms.)

| | 1st Conjugation | 2nd Conjugation | 3rd Conjugation | 3rd Conjugation: i-stem | 4th Conjugation |
|---|---|---|---|---|---|
| Present Indic. | optō, optās<br>optor, optāris<br>(optāre) | impleō, implēs<br>impleor, implēris<br>(implēre) | dūcō, dūcis<br>dūcor, dūceris (dūcere)<br> | incipiō, incipis<br>incipior, inciperis<br>(incipere) | sentiō, sentis<br>sentior, sentiris<br>(sentire) |
| Imperfect Indic. | optābam, optābās<br>optābar, optābāris<br>(optābāre) | implēbam, implēbās<br>implēbar, implēbāris<br>(implēbāre) | dūcēbam, dūcēbās<br>dūcēbar, dūcēbāris<br>(dūcēbāre) | incipiēbam, incipiēbās<br>incipiēbar, incipiēbāris<br>(incipiēbāre) | sentiēbam, sentiēbās<br>sentiēbar, sentiēbāris<br>(sentiēbāre) |
| Future Indic. | optābō, optābis<br>optābor, optāberis<br>(optābere) | implēbō, implēbis<br>implēbor, implēberis<br>(implēbere) | dūcam, dūcēs<br>dūcar, dūcēris<br>(dūcēre) | incipiam, incipiēs<br>incipiar, incipiēris<br>(incipiēre) | sentiam, sentiēs<br>sentiar, sentiēris<br>(sentiēre) |
| Perfect Indic. | optāvī, optāvistī<br>optātus (-a, -um) sum,<br>optātus (-a, -um) es | implēvī, implēvistī<br>implētus (-a, -um) sum,<br>implētus (-a, -um) es | dūxī, dūxistī<br>ductus (-a, -um) sum,<br>ductus (-a, -um) es | incēpī, incēpistī<br>inceptus (-a, -um) sum,<br>inceptus (-a, -um) es | sēnsī, sēnsistī<br>sēnsus (-a, -um) sum,<br>sēnsus (-a, -um) es |
| Pluperf. Indic. | optāveram, optāverās<br>optātus (-a, -um) eram,<br>optātus (-a, -um) erās | implēveram, implēverās<br>implētus (-a, -um) eram,<br>implētus (-a, -um) erās | dūxeram, dūxerās<br>ductus (-a, -um) eram,<br>ductus (-a, -um) erās | incēperam, incēperās<br>inceptus (-a, -um) eram,<br>inceptus (-a, -um) erās | sēnseram, sēnserās<br>sēnsus (-a, -um) eram,<br>sēnsus (-a, -um) erās |
| Fut. Perf. Indic. | optāverō, optāveris<br>optātus (-a, -um) erō,<br>optātus (-a, -um) eris | implēverō, implēveris<br>implētus (-a, -um) erō,<br>implētus (-a, -um) eris | dūxerō, dūxeris<br>ductus (-a, -um) erō,<br>ductus (-a, -um) eris | incēperō, incēperis<br>inceptus (-a, -um) erō,<br>inceptus (-a, -um) eris | sēnserō, sēnseris<br>sēnsus (-a, -um) erō,<br>sēnsus (-a, -um) eris |
| Present Subj. | optem, optēs<br>opter, optēris<br>(optēre) | impleam, impleās<br>implear, impleāris<br>(impleāre) | dūcam, dūcās<br>dūcar, dūcāris<br>(dūcāre) | incipiam, incipiās<br>incipiar, incipiāris<br>(incipiāre) | sentiam, sentiās<br>sentiar, sentiāris<br>(sentiāre) |
| Imperfect Subj. | optārem, optārēs<br>optārer, optārēris<br>(optārēre) | implērem, implērēs<br>implērer, implērēris<br>(implērēre) | dūcerem, dūcerēs<br>dūcerer, dūcerēris<br>(dūcerēre) | inciperem, inciperēs<br>inciperer, inciperēris<br>(inciperēre) | sentirem, sentirēs<br>sentirer, sentirēris<br>(sentirēre) |
| Perfect Subj. | optāverim, optāveris<br>optātus (-a, -um) sim,<br>optātus (-a, -um) sīs | implēverim, implēveris<br>implētus (-a, -um) sim,<br>implētus (-a, -um) sīs | dūxerim, dūxeris<br>ductus (-a, -um) sim,<br>ductus (-a, -um) sīs | incēperim, incēperis<br>inceptus (-a, -um) sim,<br>inceptus (-a, -um) sīs | sēnserim, sēnseris<br>sēnsus (-a, -um) sim,<br>sēnsus (-a, -um) sīs |
| Pluperf. Subj. | optāvissem, optāvissēs<br>optātus (-a, -um) essem,<br>optātus (-a, -um) essēs | implēvissem, implēvissēs<br>implētus (-a, -um) essem,<br>implētus (-a, -um) essēs | dūxissem, dūxissēs<br>ductus (-a, -um) essem,<br>ductus (-a, -um) essēs | incēpissem, incēpissēs<br>inceptus (-a, -um) essem,<br>inceptus (-a, -um) essēs | sēnsissem, sēnsissēs<br>sēnsus (-a, -um) essem,<br>sēnsus (-a, -um) essēs |

Ablative of personal agent should not be confused with the ablative of means, which has no preposition, and which refers to a thing, not a person (see section E of Unit Three).

Puella **fāmā** rēgīnae terrētur. The girl is frightened *by* (*means of*) *the reputation* of the queen.

## UNIT FOUR — VOCABULARY

| | |
|---|---|
| **aeternus, -a, -um** | eternal |
| **agō, -ere, ēgī, āctus** | do, drive, discuss, spend (time), conduct |
| **altus, -a, -um** | high, tall, deep |
| **amīcus, -a, -um** | friendly (+ dat.) |
| **inimīcus, -a, -um** | unfriendly, hostile (+ dat.) |
| **caelum, -ī, N.** | heaven, sky |
| **cārus, -a, -um** | dear (+ dat.) |
| **cibus, -ī, M.** | food |
| **circum** (prep. + acc.) | around |
| **dēleō, -ēre, -ēvī, -ētus** | destroy |
| **deus, -ī, M.** | a god, deity |
| nom. pl. **dī** | |
| gen. pl. **deōrum** or **deum** | |
| dat., abl. pl. **dīs** | |
| **dea, -ae, F.** | goddess |
| **dūcō, -ere, dūxī, ductus** | lead; consider |
| **faciō, -ere, fēcī, factus** | make, do |
| **factum, -ī, N.** | deed |
| **fīlius, -ī, M.** | son |
| **fīlia, -ae, F.** | daughter |
| **honestus, -a, -um** | respected, honorable, distinguished |
| **intellegō, -ere, intellēxī, intellēctus** | understand |
| **legō, -ere, lēgī, lēctus** | choose, select; read |
| **liber, librī, M.** | book |
| **littera, -ae, F.** | letter (of the alphabet); pl., letter (epistle) |
| **mēnsa, -ae, F.** | table |
| **mittō, -ere, mīsī, missus** | send |
| **mōnstrō** (1) | show, point out, demonstrate |
| **oppidum, -ī, N.** | town |
| **perdō, -ere, perdidī, perditus** | destroy, lose, waste |
| **perīculum, -ī, N.** | danger |

| pōnō, -ere, posuī, positus | put, place, set aside |
| quod (conj.) | because |
| rēgnum, -ī, N. | realm, kingdom |
| respondeō, -ēre, respondī, respōnsus | answer |
| studium, -ī, N. | enthusiasm, zeal |
| tegō, -ere, tēxī, tēctus | cover, conceal |
| tēctum, -ī, N. | roof, house |
| trādō, -ere, trādidī, trāditus | hand over, betray |
| umbra, -ae, F. | shadow |
| urna, -ae, F. | urn |
| vērus, -a, -um | true, real |
| vērē or vērō (adv.) | truly, indeed |
| videō, -ēre, vīdī, vīsus | see; (in passive) seem, *as well as* be seen |
| vīlla, -ae, F. | country house; farmhouse |

## UNIT FOUR — NOTES ON VOCABULARY

**Agō, agere, ēgī, āctus** is an important verb which has many meanings: 'do, drive, discuss, spend time, conduct (life)'. When a speaker **agit**, he is 'pleading (a case)'; when an actor **agit**, he is 'acting'. Note that the **a-** in the present stem lengthens to **ē-** in the perfect active stem, and to **ā-** in the perfect passive form. **Grātiās agere** with the dative means 'to thank' someone: **Grātiās rēgīnae ēgī**, 'I thanked the queen'.

The preposition **cum**, when it is used as a prefix, is spelled **com-** or sometimes **co-**. The verb **cōgō, cōgere, coēgī, coāctus** means 'drive together, collect, compel' (compounded from **cum + agō**).

**Altus, -a, -um** describes something measured up or down; thus, it has both meanings, 'high' and 'deep'.

The adjective **amīcus, -a, -um**, 'friendly', and its opposite **inimīcus, -a, -um**, 'unfriendly', are very often used substantively (as many adjectives are). Thus **amīcus**, 'a friendly (man)' is a 'friend', and **amīca**, a 'girlfriend' as well as a 'prostitute'; **inimīcus** as a noun refers to a personal 'enemy' as opposed to a public enemy.

The plural forms of **deus, deī**, M., 'god', are: **dī, deōrum** or **deum, dīs, deōs, dīs**. Just as **deus, deī** is 'god' and **dea, deae**, 'goddess', so **fīlius, fīliī** is 'son' and **fīlia, fīliae**, 'daughter'.

**Dūcō, dūcere, dūxī, ductus** not only means 'lead' but also 'consider'.

Just as the **a-** of **agō** lengthens to **ē-** in the perfect active stem, so the **-a-** of **faciō, facere**, 'make, do', lengthens in **fēcī**, the perfect active form; however, it remains short in **factus**, the perfect passive participle. There are many compounds of this verb:

| | |
|---|---|
| afficiō (**ad** + **faciō**) | do (something) to (someone), affect |
| cōnficiō (where the prefix **con-** has the meaning 'completely') | do completely, accomplish |
| perficiō (**per**, 'thoroughly') | do thoroughly, complete, accomplish |
| reficiō (**re-** can also mean 'again' as well as 'back') | make again, renew |
| praeficiō (**prae**, 'in front of') | make (someone) in front of (others); put in charge |

**Factum, factī**, N., is 'the thing which has been done', thus, 'deed'.

**Honestus, -a, -um** does *not* mean 'honest', but 'honorable, respected, distinguished'.

**Legō, legere, lēgī, lēctus** basically means 'gather, choose'; it then extends its meaning to 'read'. **Intellegō** is a compound of **legō** (**inter-** [intel-], 'between, among'). When one chooses among other ideas, he understands. Some of the compounds of **legō** keep the -g- in the perfect active stem; others, like **intellegō**, change the -g- to -x-. There is no rule to indicate which compound will take which spelling.

Be careful not to confuse **liber, librī**, M., 'book', with **līber, lībera, līberum**, 'free'.

**Littera, litterae**, F., is a letter of the alphabet; the plural is used for an epistle. Thus **litterae, litterārum** is a 'letter': **Litterās Marcī vīdī**, 'I saw Marcus' letter'. If one wants to speak of 'letters', an adjective must be used: "several letters", "many letters", "two letters", etc. As in English, the plural may be used for "literature"; cf. in English, "a man of letters".

**Mittō, mittere, mīsī, missus** means 'send'. In Latin, one sends something to someone or someplace using **ad** with the accusative, not the dative case alone:

| | | |
|---|---|---|
| Litterās ad amīcum mīsī. | I sent a letter to (my) friend. | [motion stressed] |
| Litterās amīcō mīsī. | I sent a letter for (my) friend. | [the person referred to is stressed] |

Do not confuse the form **mīseris** with its long -ī- with the dative and ablative plural of **miser, misera, miserum** (**miserīs**) which has a short -i- in its root.

An indirect object is often found with **mōnstrō**, a first conjugation verb, 'show, point out, demonstrate'. One points something out to someone in the dative case: **Rēgīnam virō mōnstrābō**, 'I shall point out the queen to the man'.

**Pōnō, pōnere, posuī, positus** means 'put, place, set aside'. Thus:

| | |
|---|---|
| compōnō (**com-**, 'together') | put together |
| dēpōnō | put down, deposit |
| impōnō (**im-** for **in-**) | place in *or* on |
| praepōnō (**prae**, 'in front of') | put in front of, place at the head |
| prōpōnō (**prō-**, 'forward') | put forth |
| repōnō (**re-**, 'back') | put back |

**Tegō, tegere, tēxī, tēctus**, 'cover, conceal', is related to two nouns of interest. **Tēctum, tēctī**, N., is a 'covering' and so 'roof'; the meaning is then extended to 'house'. With a slight vowel change in the root of this verb there is produced the famous covering or garment for which the Romans are known, **toga, togae**, F.

**Trādō, trādere, trādidī, trāditus** is a compound of **trāns-**, 'across' and **dō**, 'give', but note that although **dō** is a first conjugation verb, this compounded form belongs to the third conjugation. Literally it means 'give across' and so the meaning is 'hand over' or 'betray'.

The adverb from **vērus, -a, -um** is either **vērē** or **vērō**; there is no difference between them.

The passive of **videō** means 'seem': **Marcus honestus vidētur**, 'Marcus seems honorable'. It can also mean 'be seen': **Marcus in tēctō vīsus est**, 'Marcus was seen in the house'.

**Vīlla, vīllae**, F.,' is a 'country house, farmhouse'. It was not necessarily a villa in our sense of the word, but a simple dwelling in which countryfolk lived.

# UNIT FOUR — DRILL

**I.**

A. Translate indicatives; identify subjunctives.

B. Change the forms to the passive.

| | | |
|---|---|---|
| 1. spectās | 8. capiētis | 15. dāmnābās |
| 2. corōnāmus | 9. capiātis | 16. dāmnāvistī |
| 3. dētis | 10. capitis | 17. incēpisset |
| 4. dōnent | 11. cēlābāmus | 18. incēpissent |
| 5. habeam | 12. cōgitāret | 19. labōrāverit (2 possibilities) |
| 6. impleat | 13. cōgitet | 20. monuerātis |
| 7. vidēbitis | 14. cōgitat | |

**II.**

A. Translate indicatives; identify subjunctives.

B. Change the forms to the active.

| | | |
|---|---|---|
| 1. mūtātī sumus | 8. pulsa essem | 15. tenēris |
| 2. mūtātī sīmus | 9. pulsae sumus | 16. audītum sit |
| 3. mūtātī erimus | 10. sentiāminī | 17. audiāmur |
| 4. mūtātī erāmus | 11. sentīminī | 18. audiēbāmur |
| 5. pelleris | 12. sentiēminī | 19. gesta sunt |
| 6. pellēris | 13. tenēberis | 20. geruntur |
| 7. pellāris | 14. tenēbāris | |

**III.**

1. Identify **agere** (2 possibilities).
2. Identify **agēre**.
3. Distinguish between:
   (a) dāmnētis, vidētis, mittētis
   (b) mōnstrant, dēleant, faciant
   (c) scrībam, scrībēbam, scrībit, scrībet, scrībēbat

**IV.**

1. Fēminae per portās venient ut rēgīnam videant.
   a) Change **venient** to the perfect tense and make any other necessary change(s).
2. Monēmur nē multa verba amīcīs servōrum scrībāmus.
   a) Change **monēmur** to the pluperfect tense and make any other necessary change(s).
3. Oppidum ā nautīs dēlētum erat; oppidum undīs dēlētum est.
4. Sī oppidum dēlētum esset, tacuissēmus.
   a) Rewrite as a present contrary-to-fact condition.
5. Semper monitus eram nē ab incolīs vidērer, sed nōn audīvī.

## UNIT FOUR — PRELIMINARY EXERCISES
## (SECTION A)

1. Multa vērō dē dīligentiā virī clārī scrībam (scrībō, scrībēbam).
2. Ā līberīs petēmus ut oppida inimīca dēleant.
3. Sī malōs incolīs prōvinciae trādant, dē īnsidiīs taceāmus.
4. Honestī oppidī ad vīllam veniunt ut incolam ē perīculō dūcant.
5. Rōmānī ad ārās deum multīs cum dōnīs veniēbant ut veniam ōrārent.
6. Intellegisne librum poētae clārī?
7. Dē factīs acerbīs aeternōrum deum audiēmus (audīmus, audiēbāmus).
8. Vīllamne cum fīliīs incolēbātis?
9. Sī virum honestum in prōvinciā sentiās, laetus esse incipiam.
10. Multās litterās amīcīs scrībit ut multās legat.

# UNIT FOUR — EXERCISES

**I.**

1. Nautae malī ab incolīs līberīs in viam āctī sunt.
2. Incolae līberī nautās Rōmānōs in viam ēgērunt quod nautae missī erant ut oppidum dēlērent.
3. Sī oppidum validum superābitur, līberī erunt servī.
4. Liber ā poētā cum dīligentiā scrīptus est ut magnum perīculum bonīs mōnstrārētur.
5. Sī litterae ā rēgīnā pulchrā ad honestōs missae essent, monitī essent ut bellum gererent, et oppidum ab amīcīs malōrum nōn superātum esset.
6. Urna pulchra in mēnsā ā fēminīs rēgīnae pōnētur ut cibō aquāque impleātur.
7. Sī umbrīs magnīs aqua alta ā dīs tēcta esset, nautae Rōmānī vēla nōn darent.
8. Magnō cum studiō fīliī rēgīnae respondēre incēpērunt; ōrāvērunt ut perīculum incolīs prōvinciārum magnā dīligentiā dūcerētur.
9. Nisī nautae ad aquam dūcantur, vēla nōn dent.
10. Magnā cum dīligentiā bellum gestum est nē ab incolīs prōvinciae Rōmānae malīs rēgnum superārētur.
11. Sī verba vēra magnō studiō ā virīs bonīs honestīsque legentur et intellegentur, perīculum bellī dēlēbitur.
12. Virī līberī et honestī semper ōrābant nē bellō et gladiīs oppidum dēlērētur; incolās enim monuērunt ut vītam bonam agerent.
13. Litterae ad oppidum clārum ā rēgīnā prōvinciae missae sunt ut incolae veniam vēram vidērent et intellegerent.
14. Fēminae pulchrae virōs miserōs ē prōvinciā Rōmānā ad amīcum oppidum cum magnā turbā mittunt nē incolae prōvinciae esse videantur.
15. Fīlia rēgīnae bonae ad āram ā nautīs Rōmānīs ducta est ut honesta dīs agerentur.
16. Perīculum rēgnō magnum fīliīs līberōrum vidētur.
17. Circum oppidum dūcēbāris ut ā bonīs malīsque vidērēre.
18. Nisī poēta verba honesta vēraque dē factīs bonōrum scrībet, pecūniam nōn faciet.
19. Bonā veniā honesta audiēs; honesta bonā veniā audiuntur; ōrō ut honestum bonā veniā audiātur.
20. Sī litterae fīliō honestō mittantur, respondeatne?
21. Ōrābimus ut urnae aquā ā puellā impleantur.
22. Sī magna bella ab incolīs gerentur, rēgnum vērē dēlēbitur.
23. Sī āra umbrīs tēcta esset, incolae cibum deōrum nōn vīdissent.
24. Multa vērō pecūnia in mēnsā pōnitur ut honestī pecūniam capiant et magnum tēctum fīliīs faciant.
25. Nisī ab amīcīs trāditus esset, vītam nōn perdidisset.

26. Monuerat ut litterās amīcō trāderētis quod vēra dē perīculīs rēgnō legere nōn optāvistis.
27. Āra aeterna ab incolīs oppidī facta est ut dōna dīs cāra darentur.
28. Oppidum enim dēlētum erat quod servī portās magnīs cum īnsidiīs patriae inimīcīs trādiderant.
29. Deās in caelō ōrāvimus ut vīllam pulchram habeāmus.

## II.

1. Very tearfully (with many tears) the queen demonstrated the dangers of war to the inhabitants of the island in order that they might not be overcome by the swords of the strong Roman sailors.
2. If the town is destroyed, the queen, with great kindness, will send both food and money to (ad) the wretched inhabitants.
3. The Romans always will wage wars very zealously (with great zeal) in order that they may not be placed in danger by (their) enemies.
4. If many urns had been made by the children, gifts of money would have been given by the queen.
5. If the evil men should be led around the towns of the queen's realm, the inhabitants would not be betrayed by (their) treachery.

## III. Reading

Liber aeternus, honestīs virīs cārus, ā Vergiliō[1] scrīptus est. In librō vir, fīlius ē deā, ā dīs missus est ut oppidum in Italiā[2] conderet.[3] Vir ā dīs lēctus erat ut factum faceret quod honestus bonam vītam ageret.[4] Patriam, Trōiam,[5] ab inimīcō trāditam[6] relīquit.[7] Trōia[5] dēlēta erat postquam[8] incolae longum[9] bellum cum Graecīs[10] gesserant; īnsidiīs perdita est. Multī inimīcī in altō equō[11] ligneō[12] tēctī erant; Graecus[10] vir incolīs oppidī amīcus ductus,[6] magnō cum studiō amīcōs, Trōiānīs[5] inimīcōs, ex equō[11] dūxit et tēcta mōnstrāvit ut accenderentur[13] et incolās ut interficerentur.[14] Trōia[5] magnō in perīculō posita est; nē[15] fīlius quidem[15] deae cum amīcīs oppidum servāre[16] potuit.[17] Cum parvā[18] turbā amīcōrum patriam relīquit[7] et vēla ad Italiam[2] dedit.

[1] **Vergilius, -ī,** M., 'Vergil', the author of the Roman epic poem *The Aeneid*     [2] **Italia, -ae,** F., 'Italy'     [3] **condō, -ere, -didī, -ditus,** 'found'     [4] **ageret.** The subjunctive is used to express someone else's reason for doing a thing, not a reason one knows for sure. Subjunctive = mood of possibility.     [5] **Trōia, -ae,** F., 'Troy', a city in Asia Minor; **Trōiānus, -a, -um,** 'Trojan'     [6] **trāditam** (**trāditus, -a, -um**) and **ductus** (**ductus, -a, -um**) come from the fourth principal part of the verb and are perfect passive participles. Since a participle is an adjective, it must agree with the noun which it modifies in gender, number, and case. Translate **trāditus, -a, -um** 'having been betrayed, betrayed', and **ductus, -a, -um** 'having been considered, considered'.     [7] **relinquō, -ere, relīquī, relictus,** 'abandon'     [8] **postquam** (conj.), 'after'     [9] **longus, -a, -um,** 'long'     [10] **Graecus, -a, -um,** 'Greek'     [11] **equus, -ī,** M., 'horse'     [12] **ligneus, -a, -um,** 'wooden'     [13] **accendō, -ere, -cendī, -cēnsus,** 'set on fire'     [14] **interficiō, -ere, -fēcī, -fectus,** 'kill'     [15] **nē...quidem,** 'not even'     [16] **servō (1),** 'save'     [17] **possum, posse, potuī, --,** 'be able'     [18] **parvus, -a, -um,** 'small'

# REVIEW: UNITS ONE TO FOUR

### Review of Syntax

1. Dāmnor semper ab acerbīs malōrum factōrum, sed fāma nōn perdita est.
   (ablative of personal agent; adjective used as a noun; genitive with verbs of accusing and condemning)

2. Librī malī ab honestīs dāmnor, sed magnā cum invidiā ab amīcīs legitur et bonus esse dūcitur.
   (genitive with verbs of accusing and condemning; ablatives of personal agent; adjectives used as nouns; ablative of manner; predicate adjective)

3. Sī multa mala dē factīs deōrum audīta essent, incolae ad ārās nōn vēnissent.
   (adjective used as a noun; past contrary-to-fact condition)

4. Sī ad īnsulam clāram mittēmur nē in patriā videāmur, multās litterās amīcīs cārīs scrībēmus nē ab inimīcīs trādāmur.
   (future more vivid condition; two purpose clauses in primary sequence; adjectives used as nouns; ablative of personal agent)

5. Cārusne dīs videāris sī dōna cibī in ārīs pōnās?
   (dative with a special adjective; future less vivid condition)

6. Sī oppidum īnsidiīs dēlērētur, facta mala inimīcōrum ab incolīs intellegerentur.
   (present contrary-to-fact condition; ablative of means; adjective used as a noun; ablative of personal agent)

7. Fēminae lacrimās cēlāre nōn dubitant. Fēminās ōrāmus nē lacrimās cēlent. Tacēmus nē fēminae lacrimās cēlent.
   (indirect command in primary sequence; purpose clause in primary sequence)

8. Petēbāmus ā nātīs ut saxa clāra in cellam neque cum morā neque cum noxā portārentur, nē in campīs cēlārentur et perderentur.
   (ā + abl. with petō; indirect command in secondary sequence; ablatives of manner; purpose clause in secondary sequence)

### Synopsis of Verbs

A synopsis (refer to Preliminary Exercises for Unit Two) should include the active and passive forms of the verb in the indicative and subjunctive moods.

74

The following synopsis of **dūcō, -ere, dūxī, ductus** in the first person plural will serve as a model:

**dūcō, dūcere, dūxī, ductus,** 'lead, consider'

INDICATIVE

|  | ACTIVE | PASSIVE |
|---|---|---|
| Present | dūcimus | dūcimur |
| Imperfect | dūcēbāmus | dūcēbāmur |
| Future | dūcēmus | dūcēmur |
| Perfect | dūximus | ductī (-ae, -a) sumus |
| Pluperfect | dūxerāmus | ductī (-ae, -a) erāmus |
| Future Perfect | dūxerimus | ductī (-ae, -a) erimus |

SUBJUNCTIVE

|  | | |
|---|---|---|
| Present | dūcāmus | dūcāmur |
| Imperfect | dūcerēmus | dūcerēmur |
| Perfect | dūxerimus | ductī (-ae, -a) sīmus |
| Pluperfect | dūxissēmus | ductī (-ae, -a) essēmus |

# UNITS 1–4: Self-Review A

While long marks appear below only in places where confusion might arise, they should appear in your answers.

**I.**

A. Change these forms to the passive, retaining mood, person, number, and tense:

1. impleverunt
2. terrueritis (2 possibilities)
3. viderat
4. spectes
5. sentiebam

B. Change these forms to the active, retaining mood, person, number, and tense:

1. monitus esses
2. teneremur
3. capiemini
4. gesta sit
5. mittitur

**II.**

Fully describe each of the following as to *form*, giving all possibilities of interpretation, and then give the dictionary forms (principal parts) for each:

1. positae sunt
2. gladii (2 possibilities)
3. tegere (3 possibilities)
4. audiverit (2 possibilities)
5. villae (3 possibilities)

**III.**

Translate each sentence into English and then do whatever is required by any questions which follow:

1. Incolae miseri verba filiorum audiverunt ut multa intellegant.
   a) Change **intellegant** to the imperfect subjunctive and show how this would alter your translation of **audiverunt**.
   b) Change the form **audiverunt** to the imperfect tense.
2. Nisi laetus esse videberis, aquā urnam non implebo; regina enim monuit ut urnam laeto impleam.
   a) Rewrite in Latin completely in the plural.
   b) Give the syntax of **videberis**.
   c) Give the case of **laeto**.
   d) Rewrite **Nisi laetus esse videberis, aquā urnam non implebo** as a simple present condition.
   e) Rewrite as a present contrary-to-fact condition.
   f) Rewrite as a past contrary-to-fact condition.
3. Si insidiarum damnatus esset, nauta ab incolis oppidi honestis petivisset ut audiretur ne in periculo poneretur.
   a) Explain the syntax of **insidiarum**.
   b) Explain the syntax of **audiretur**.
4. Magnae turbae servorum ex agris ad portas oppidi venerunt ut multis cum lacrimis viros validos orarent ut de natura belli tacerent.
   a) Explain the syntax of **orarent**.
   b) Explain the syntax of **tacerent**.
5. Multum enim de periculo ab honesto actum et lectum et scriptum est ne regnum a malo deleretur.
   a) Explain the syntax of **malo**.
   b) Rewrite the entire sentence in Latin in the plural.
6. Si bellum gladiis saxisque magnā cum diligentiā gestum esset, viri nunc vela ad insulam non darent.
   a) Give syntax of **gestum esset**.

b) Give syntax of **darent**.

c) Give syntax of **gladiis**.

d) Give syntax of **diligentiā**.

e) Rewrite in Latin as a future less vivid condition.

f) Translate the Latin sentence you wrote under 6e.

7. Si amica facta deorum ducentur magnā cum curā, vitam bonam agere optabimus.

## IV.

Translate into Latin:

1. If they think about the danger, the inhabitants will begin to place big rocks around the island in order that the town may be free.

2. The book had indeed been read zealously by the boy.

# Answer Key — UNITS 1–4: Self-Review A

## I.

A. 1. implētī, -ae, -a sunt

2. territī, -ae, -a sītis
   territī, -ae, -a eritis

3. vīsus, -a, -um erat

4. spectēris (spectēre)

5. sentiēbar

B. 1. monuissēs

2. tenērēmus

3. capiētis

4. gesserit

5. mittit

## II.

1. 3rd pl. fem. perfect passive indicative: **pōnō, pōnere, posuī, positus**

2. genitive sing.; nominative pl.: **gladius, -ī, M.**

3. present active infinitive; 2nd sing. future passive indicative (when -e- is long); 2nd sing. present passive indicative (when -e- is short): **tegō, tegere, tēxī, tēctus**

4. 3rd sing. future perfect active indicative; 3rd sing. perfect active subjunctive: **audiō, audīre, audīvī, audītus**

5. genitive sing.; dative sing.; nominative pl.: **vīlla, -ae, F.**

## III.

1. The wretched inhabitants have heard (have listened to) the words of their sons so that they may understand many things (...in order to understand...).
   a) intellegerent
      'listened to, heard'
   b) audiēbant

2. If you do (will) not seem to be happy (unless you (will) seem...), I shall not fill the urn with water; indeed the queen has warned (has advised) me to fill the urn for a (the) happy man (...that I should fill...).
   a) Nisī laetī esse vidēbiminī, aquīs urnās nōn implēbimus; rēgīnae enim monuērunt ut urnās laetīs impleāmus.
   b) 2nd sing. future passive indicative in protasis of a future more vivid condition
   c) dative sing.
   d) Nisī laetus esse vidēris (vidēre), aquā urnam nōn impleō.
   e) Nisī laetus esse vidērēris (vidērēre), aquā urnam nōn implērem.
   f) Nisī laetus esse vīsus essēs, aquā urnam nōn implēvissem.

3. If he had been condemned for treachery, the sailor would have asked the honorable inhabitants of the town to be heard (that he be heard) so that he might (would) not be placed (put) in danger.
   a) genitive pl. with a verb of condemning
   b) 3rd sing. imperfect passive subjunctive in an indirect command in secondary sequence

4. Large crowds of slaves came out of the fields to the gates of the town so that they might beg ([in order] to beg) the strong men very tearfully (with many tears) to be silent (that they be silent) about the nature of (the) war.
   a) 3rd pl. imperfect active subjunctive in secondary sequence — in a clause of purpose
   b) 3rd pl. imperfect active subjunctive in secondary sequence — in an indirect command

5. Indeed much was done and read and written by the (an) honorable man about the danger so that the kingdom might not be destroyed by the (an) evil man.
   a) ablative of personal agent
   b) Multa enim dē perīculīs ab honestīs ācta et lēcta et scrīpta sunt nē rēgna ā malīs dēlērentur.

6. If the war had been waged very diligently (with great diligence) with swords and rocks, the men would not now be setting sail to the island.
   a) 3rd sing. pluperfect subjunctive passive in the protasis of a mixed contrary-to-fact condition
   b) 3rd pl. imperfect subjunctive active in the apodosis of a mixed contrary-to-fact condition

   c) ablative of means
   d) ablative of manner
   e) Sī bellum gladiīs saxīsque magnā cum dīligentiā gerātur, virī vēla ad īnsulam nōn dent.
   f) If the war should be waged very diligently (with great diligence) with swords and rocks, the men would not set sail to the island.

7. If the friendly deeds of the gods are (will be) considered very carefully (with great care), we shall desire (choose) to conduct a good life.

## IV.

1. Sī dē perīculō cōgitābunt, incolae magna saxa circum īnsulam pōnere incipient ut oppidum līberum sit.
2. Liber enim ā puerō cum studiō lēctus erat.

# UNITS 1–4: Self-Review B

While long marks appear below only in places where confusion might arise, they should appear in your answers.

## I.

A. Identify the form of each of the following, giving *all* possibilities and listing principal parts for verbs and the nominative, genitive singular, and gender for nouns:

   1. gesseritis    3. nautis    5. studia
   2. mitterere    4. sentiar

B. Change the following verb forms to the passive, retaining mood, person, number, and tense:

   1. superamus    3. egeratis    5. perdiderim
   2. terrebis    4. intellegant

C. Change the following verb forms to the active voice, retaining mood, person, number, and tense:

   1. audiebatur    3. positi estis    5. visae essemus
   2. pulsa erunt    4. donaremini

## II.

Translate each of the following and then do whatever is required by the questions which follow:

1. Si nautae validi poenas dedissent, magno studio regina aras deorum donis implevisset.

    a) Explain the ending of **validi**.

    b) Give the syntax of **studio**.

    c) Explain the syntax of **implevisset**.

    d) Change the above condition to the negative.

    e) Rewrite the above as a future less vivid condition.

    f) Rewrite as a future more vivid condition.

    g) Rewrite as a contrary-to-fact condition in present time.

2. Si bellum in provinciā geretis, magnum regnum perdetis.

    a) Give the syntax of **geretis**.

3. Marcus, vir honestus clarusque, servos miseros monuit ut naturam animae intellegerent ut laeti essent.

    a) Explain the syntax of **intellegerent**.

    b) Explain the syntax of **essent**.

    c) Change the subordinate clauses to the negative.

    d) Change **monuit** to the simple present and make any additional change(s) necessary.

4. Multa verba acerba de periculo belli magnā cum diligentiā a poetis scripta sunt ne boni bellum gerere optarent.

    a) Explain the syntax of **diligentia**.

    b) Explain the syntax of **poetis**.

    c) Change the verb in the subordinate clause to primary sequence. How would this alter your translation of **scripta sunt**?

5. Nautae villas insulae gladiis saxisque delere inciperent nisi regina litteras incolis misisset ut multa bona amicis nautarum darentur.

    a) Explain the syntax of **gladiis**.

    b) Explain the syntax of **misisset**.

6. Venia vera deorum aeternorum in caelo natis monstrata est ut vitam bonam agant.

    a) Change **monstrata est** to the simple future tense and make any other necessary change(s).

7. Si incola inimicus a viris visus esset, feminas e villis ad aras duxissent ut a dis peterent ne oppidum periculo et villae lacrimis implerentur.


## III.

Translate the following sentences into Latin:

1. We came to the town very zealously in order to warn the sailors not to betray (their) friends.

2. If we should be seen by the men of the town, we would be considered hostile and would be driven from the province.

# Answer Key — UNITS 1–4: Self-Review B

**I.**

A. 1. 2nd pl. future perfect active indicative; 2nd pl. perfect active subjunctive: **gerō, gerere, gessī, gestus**
   2. 2nd sing. imperfect passive subjunctive: **mittō, mittere, mīsī, missus**
   3. dative/ablative pl.: **nauta, -ae, M.**
   4. 1st sing. future passive indicative; 1st sing. present passive subjunctive: **sentiō, sentīre, sēnsī, sēnsus**
   5. nominative/accusative pl.: **studium, -ī, N.**

B. 1. superāmur
   2. terrēberis (terrēbere)
   3. āctī, -ae, -a erātis
   4. intellegantur
   5. perditus, -a, -um sim

C. 1. audiēbat
   2. pepulerint
   3. posuistis
   4. dōnārētis
   5. vīdissēmus

**II.**

1. If the strong sailors had paid the penalty, very zealously (with great zeal) the queen would have filled the altars of the gods with gifts.
   a) nominative pl. M. adjective agreeing with **nautae, M.**
   b) ablative of manner
   c) 3rd sing. pluperfect active subjunctive in the apodosis of a past contrary-to-fact condition
   d) Nisī nautae validī poenās dedissent, magnō studiō rēgīna ārās deōrum dōnīs nōn implēvisset.
   e) Sī nautae validī poenās dent, magnō studiō rēgīna ārās deōrum dōnīs impleat.
   f) Sī nautae validī poenās $\left\{\begin{array}{l}\text{dabunt}\\\text{dederint}\end{array}\right\}$ magnō studiō rēgīna ārās deōrum dōnīs implēbit.
   g) Sī nautae validī poenās darent, magnō studiō rēgīna ārās deōrum dōnīs implēret.

2. If you (pl.) (will) wage war in the province, you (pl.) will destroy a great kingdom.

a) 2nd pl. future active indicative in the protasis of a future more vivid condition

3. Marcus, an honorable and famous man, warned the wretched slaves to understand (that they should understand) the nature of the soul so that they might be (in order to be) happy.

   a) 3rd pl. imperfect active subjunctive in an indirect command in secondary sequence

   b) 3rd pl. imperfect subjunctive in a purpose clause in secondary sequence

   c) ...servōs miserōs monuit nē nātūram animae intellegerent nē laetī essent.

   d) monet ut...intellegant ut...sint

4. Many harsh (bitter) words about the danger of war were written very diligently (with great diligence) by poets so that good men might (would) not choose (desire) to wage war.

   a) ablative of manner

   b) ablative of personal agent

   c) optent

   'have been written'

5. The sailors would (now) begin to destroy the country houses of the island with swords and rocks if the queen had not (unless the queen had) sent a letter to (for) the inhabitants so that many good things might be given to the sailors' friends.

   a) ablative of means

   b) 3rd sing. pluperfect active subjunctive in the protasis of a mixed contrary-to-fact condition

6. The true favor (kindness) of the eternal gods in the sky (heaven) has been shown (pointed out) to the children (sons) so that they may conduct a good life.

   a) mōnstrābitur

   no other changes necessary

7. If the unfriendly inhabitant had been seen by the men, they would have led the women out of the country houses to the altars to ask the gods (so that they might/would ask the gods) that (in order that) the town not be filled (might not be filled) with danger and the country houses (not be filled) with tears.

## III.

1. Ad oppidum magnō cum studiō vēnimus ut nautās monērēmus nē amīcōs trāderent.

2. Sī ā virīs oppidī videāmur, inimīcī habeāmur (dūcāmur) et ē prōvinciā pellāmur (expellāmur).

# UNIT FIVE

## A. Participles: Definition and Formation

If we wish to take a verb and make an adjective out of it, we construct a *verbal adjective* or *participle*.

> The *shouting* woman departed.
> The men saw the *destroyed* town.

A participle, like any other adjective, must agree with the noun it qualifies in gender, number, and case. In the sentences given as examples above, "shouting" is feminine, singular, nominative to agree with "woman"; "destroyed" is neuter, singular, accusative to agree with "town". The participle also has the attributes of tense and voice: "shouting" is present active; "destroyed" (i.e., "having been destroyed") is perfect passive.

The participle, although an adjective, still retains its verbal powers and accordingly, for example, can take an object:

> The men *destroying the town* were sailors.

The formation of participles is illustrated below:

|         | ACTIVE                                          | PASSIVE                                                   |
|---------|-------------------------------------------------|----------------------------------------------------------|
| Present | optāns<br>desiring                              | --                                                       |
| Perfect | --                                              | optātus, -a, -um<br>having been desired, desired         |
| Future  | optātūrus, -a, -um<br>going to desire, about to desire | optandus, -a, -um<br>having to be desired, to be desired* |

1. PRESENT ACTIVE PARTICIPLE. To form the present active participle, add **-ns** to the present stem. In the case of i-stem verbs, -ie- will appear in the present participle:

> optā/ns  implē/ns  dūcē/ns  incipiē/ns  sentiē/ns

---

* The future passive participle regularly carries the accessory notion of obligation, necessity, or propriety.

The form given is the nominative singular for all three genders. The present participle declines, but according to a scheme which differs from that which you have already learned. This will be discussed in Unit Eight. (Note that a vowel lengthens before **-ns**.)

2. PERFECT PASSIVE PARTICIPLE. The perfect passive participle is the fourth principal part of the verb:

> optātus, -a, -um    implētus, -a, -um    ductus, -a, -um    inceptus, -a, -um
> ,sēnsus, -a, -um

3. FUTURE ACTIVE PARTICIPLE. To form the future active participle, take the fourth principal part of the verb, drop the **-us** ending and add in its place **-ūrus, -a, -um**:

> optātūrus, -a, -um    implētūrus, -a, -um    ductūrus, -a, -um
> inceptūrus, -a, -um    sēnsūrus, -a, -um

4. FUTURE PASSIVE PARTICIPLE. To form the future passive participle, add **-ndus, -a, -um** to the present stem. In i-stem verbs, **-ie-** will appear:

> optandus, -a, -um    implendus, -a, -um    dūcendus, -a, -um
> incipiendus, -a, -um    sentiendus, -a, -um

Note that a long vowel shortens before **-nd**.

## B. Some Uses of the Participle

The tense of the participle is *relative* to that of the main verb. A *present* participle refers to an action *contemporaneous* with that of the main verb; a *perfect* participle refers to an action *prior* to that of the main verb; a *future* participle refers to an action *subsequent* to that of the main verb. There are some problems which arise in this system because of the lack of certain participial forms (i.e., present passive and perfect active), but these may be circumvented easily, as will be seen later.

Multiple interpretations of a participle are possible in English:

1. PRESENT ACTIVE PARTICIPLE

Fēmina **clāmāns** discessit.     The *shouting* woman departed.

The woman departed *shouting*.

*Shouting*, the woman departed.

The woman *who was shouting* departed.

The woman, *since she was shouting*, departed.

The woman, *although she was shouting*, departed.

*When* (*while*) *she was shouting*, the woman departed.

*If she was shouting*, the woman departed.

OBSERVATIONS:

a) In each case, the present participle **clāmāns** refers to an action which was going on at the same time as that of the main verb.

b) The participle can be translated into English with causal ("since"), concessive ("although"), temporal ("when, while"), or conditional ("if") force. The participle alone, then, can stand for the if-clause (protasis) of a conditional sentence. It can also stand for a relative clause. The interpretation of a participle must depend upon the requirements of the *context* of each specific passage.

c) Frequently when a participle is meant to be taken as concessive, the word **tamen**, 'nevertheless', is inserted to qualify the main verb.

Fēmina clāmāns tamen discessit.    Although the woman was shouting, nevertheless she departed.

2. PERFECT PASSIVE PARTICIPLE

Fēmina **territa** clāmāvit.    The *having-been-frightened* woman shouted.
The woman, *having been frightened*, shouted.
*Having been frightened*, the woman shouted.
The *frightened* woman shouted.
The woman *who had been frightened* shouted.
*Since she had been frightened*, the woman shouted.
*Although she had been frightened*, the woman shouted.
*When (after) she had been frightened*, the woman shouted.
*If she had been frightened*, the woman shouted.

OBSERVATIONS:

a) The perfect passive participle refers to an action which occurred prior to the time of the main verb.

b) The absence of the perfect active participle in Latin makes it impossible at this stage of our study to express a verbal idea in the active voice as having occurred prior to the time of the main verb.

The woman, having shouted (after she had shouted), departed.

A subordinate clause, introduced perhaps by the subordinating conjunction **postquam**, 'after', would have to be used in this case:

Postquam clāmāvit, fēmina discessit.    After she shouted, the woman departed.

## 3. FUTURE ACTIVE PARTICIPLE

Fēmina **discessūra** virum vīdit.
The *about-to-depart* woman saw (her) husband.

The woman, *about to depart*, saw (her) husband.

*About to depart*, the woman saw (her) husband.

The woman *who was about (going) to depart* saw (her) husband.

*Since* the woman *was going to depart*, she saw (her) husband.

*Although* the woman *was going to depart*, she saw (her) husband.

*When* (*as*) the woman *was going to depart*, she saw (her) husband.

*If* the woman *was going to depart*, she saw (her) husband.

OBSERVATION: The future active participle refers to an action which will occur or has occurred subsequent to that of the main verb.

## 4. FUTURE PASSIVE PARTICIPLE

Librōs **legendōs** in mēnsā posuit.
He placed *having-to-be-read* books on the table.

He placed books *to be read* on the table.

He placed books *which had to be read* on the table.

OBSERVATIONS:

a) The future passive participle refers to an action which will occur or has occurred subsequent to that of the main verb.

b) The future passive participle (sometimes called the *gerundive*) carries with it the notion of obligation, necessity, or propriety.

These participial constructions may occur in any grammatical case:

Fēminae discessūrae pecūniam dedit.
He gave money to the about-to-depart woman.

He gave money to the woman who was about to depart.

## C. Periphrastics

The future participles (active and passive) are compounded with the verb **sum** to form the active and passive periphrastic conjugations.

### 1. ACTIVE PERIPHRASTIC

The active periphrastic is translated by the English 'about to, going to, ready to'.

INDICATIVE:

| | | |
|---|---|---|
| Pres. | optātūrus (-a, -um) sum | I am about to desire |
| Impf. | optātūrus (-a, -um) eram | I was about to desire |
| Fut. | optātūrus (-a, -um) erō | I shall be about to desire |
| Perf. | optātūrus (-a, -um) fuī | I have been (was) about to desire |
| Plupf. | optātūrus (-a, -um) fueram | I had been about to desire |
| Fut. Pf. | optātūrus (-a, -um) fuerō | I shall have been about to desire |

SUBJUNCTIVE:

| | |
|---|---|
| Pres. | optātūrus (-a, -um) sim |
| Impf. | optātūrus (-a, -um) essem |
| Perf. | optātūrus (-a, -um) fuerim |
| Plupf. | optātūrus (-a, -um) fuissem |

### 2. PASSIVE PERIPHRASTIC

The passive periphrastic is translated by 'have (has) to, should, ought to', or 'must'.

INDICATIVE:

| | | |
|---|---|---|
| Pres. | optandus (-a, -um) sum | I am having-to-be desired, I have to be desired, I should (ought to) be desired, I must be desired |
| Impf. | optandus (-a, -um) eram | I had to be desired |
| Fut. | optandus (-a, -um) erō | I shall have to be desired |
| Perf. | optandus (-a, -um) fuī | I had to be desired |
| Plupf. | optandus (-a, -um) fueram | I had had to be desired |
| Fut. Pf. | optandus (-a, -um) fuerō | I shall have had to be desired |

SUBJUNCTIVE:

| | |
|---|---|
| Pres. | optandus (-a, -um) sim |
| Impf. | optandus (-a, -um) essem |
| Perf. | optandus (-a, -um) fuerim |
| Plupf. | optandus (-a, -um) fuissem |

These compound periphrastic forms should not be confused with the compound passives of the perfect system which have been met earlier. Distinguish:

| | | |
|---|---|---|
| optātus est | he has been desired | (passive) |
| optātūrus est | he is about to desire | (active periphrastic) |
| optandus est | he is (has) to be desired | (passive periphrastic) |

### D. Dative of Agent with the Passive Periphrastic

Personal agent is regularly expressed by the ablative case preceded by the preposition ā (ab). With the passive periphrastic, however, the personal agent is normally expressed by the dative case without a preposition. In fact, this use of the dative is purely referential; the action of the verb is viewed as necessary with reference to the agent.

> Poēta rēgīnae videndus est.   The poet must be seen *by the queen.*

(Note that the -**us** ending on **videndus** agrees with the subject **poēta** which is masculine.)

### E. Dative of the Possessor

With forms of the verb **sum**, the dative is sometimes used to show possession. The *possessor* is put into the dative case.

> Corōna est rēgīnae.   A crown is *to the queen*; *the queen* has a crown; the crown is *the queen's.*
>
> Liber est amīcō.   A book is *to the friend*; *the friend* has a book; the book is *the friend's.*

### F. The Verb *possum,* 'be able'

This verb is a compound of **sum**. In the present system, when the form of **sum** begins with s, the prefix **pos-** is added to conjugate **possum**; when the form of **sum** begins with e, the prefix **pot-** is added. The imperfect subjunctive is constructed, as usual, on the full present infinitive, and the perfect system is formed as one might expect.

**possum, posse, potuī, ——**

| Present | Imperfect | Future | Perfect | Pluperfect | Future Perfect |
|---|---|---|---|---|---|
| INDICATIVE | | | | | |
| pos*sum* | pot*eram* | pot*erō* | potuī | potueram | potuerō |
| pot*es* | pot*erās* | pot*eris* | potuistī | potuerās | potueris |
| pot*est* | ...etc. | ...etc. | ...etc. | ...etc. | ...etc. |
| pos*sumus* | | | | | |
| pot*estis* | | | | | |
| pos*sunt* | | | | | |

| Present | Imperfect | Perfect | Pluperfect |
|---------|-----------|---------|------------|
| SUBJUNCTIVE | | | |
| pos*sim* | possem | potuerim | potuissem |
| pos*sis* | possēs | potueris | potuissēs |
| pos*sit* | ...etc. | ...etc. | ...etc. |
| pos*simus* | | | |
| pos*sitis* | | | |
| pos*sint* | | | |

## G. Complementary Infinitive

There are verbs in Latin which frequently require an infinitive to complete their meaning. Some of these are verbs which express ability, will, desire, and the like.

| Amīcum **vidēre** optō. | I desire *to see* (my) friend. |
| Amīcum **vidēre** possum. | I am able *to see* (my) friend. |
| Bonus **esse** vidētur. | He seems *to be* good. |

Such infinitives are called *complementary* infinitives because they *complete* the idea of the verb.

# UNIT FIVE — VOCABULARY

| | |
|---|---|
| **ante** (prep. + acc.) | before, in front of |
| (adv.) | before, previously |
| **antīquus, -a, -um** | ancient |
| **ardeō, -ēre, arsī, arsus** | burn, be on fire; desire |
| **arma, -ōrum,** N. (pl.) | arms, weapons |
| **aurum, -ī,** N. | gold |
| **aureus, -a, -um** | golden, of gold |
| **autem** (postpositive conj.) | however, moreover |
| **bene** (adv.) | well |
| **canō, -ere, cecinī, cantus** | sing (of) |
| **cēdō, -ere, cessī, cessus** | go, move, yield |
| **accēdō, -ere, -cessī, -cessus** | go to, approach |
| **discēdō, -ere, -cessī, -cessus** | go from, depart, leave |
| **dēbeō, -ēre, dēbuī, dēbitus** | owe, ought |
| **dominus, -ī,** M. | master, lord |
| **dūrus, -a, -um** | hard, harsh |
| **ferrum, -ī,** N. | iron, sword |
| **flamma, -ae,** F. | flame, fire |
| **imperium, -ī,** N. | authority, power, empire |

| | |
|---|---|
| **imperō** (1) | give (an) order(s), give (a) command(s) (The person ordered is in the dative case; the thing ordered is expressed by an **ut** clause [negative **nē**] of indirect command.) |
| **interficiō, -ere, -fēcī, -fectus** | kill |
| **invādō, -ere, -vāsī, -vāsus** | go into, invade, attack |
| **magister, magistrī, M.** | superior, director, master, teacher |
| **medius, -a, -um** | middle of, middle |
| **moveō, -ēre, mōvī, mōtus** | move |
| **removeō, -ēre, -mōvī, -mōtus** | remove, take away, set aside |
| **mox** (adv.) | soon |
| **nōscō, -ere, nōvī, nōtus** | learn, (in perfect) know |
| **cognōscō, -ere, -nōvī, -nitus** | learn, (in perfect) know |
| **novus, -a, -um** | new, strange |
| **numquam (nunquam)** (adv.) | never |
| **umquam (unquam)** (adv.) | ever |
| **pius, -a, -um** | loyal, dutiful, pious |
| **impius, -a, -um** | irreverent, wicked, impious |
| **populus, -ī, M.** | people (use only in singular) |
| **possum, posse, potuī, ––** | be able, can |
| **post** (prep. + acc.) | after, behind |
| (adv.) | afterwards, after, behind |
| **postquam** (conj.) | after (+ indicative) |
| **quamquam** (conj.) | although (+ indicative) |
| **ruīna, -ae, F.** | fall, downfall, ruin, destruction |
| **ruō, -ere, ruī, rutus** | fall, go to ruin, rush |
| **sine** (prep. + abl.) | without |
| **socius, -a, -um** | allied |
| **socius, -ī, M.** | ally |
| **tamen** (adv.) | nevertheless |
| **vīvō, -ere, vīxī, vīctus** | be alive, live |
| **vocō** (1) | call |

## UNIT FIVE — NOTES ON VOCABULARY

The prepositions **ante**, 'before', and **post**, 'after', are well known, since one speaks of the ante-bellum South, or the post-bellum South, for example, in reference to the Civil War. These expressions will serve as reminders that both prepositions govern the accusative case. Both words can be used adverbially as well: **ante**, 'previously, before'; **post**, 'afterwards, after, behind'. And so, one might say either **Urna ante mēnsam posita est**, 'The urn was placed in front of the table', or **Litterās ante scrīpsimus**, 'We wrote the letter before'.

The word **arma, armōrum** has no singular; it is a neuter word found only in the plural.

**Aurum, aurī**, N., 'gold', has as its adjective **aureus, -a, -um**, 'golden, of gold'. The chemical symbol for gold, $Au$, comes from the first two letters of **aurum**.

**Autem**, 'however, moreover', like **enim**, 'indeed', is a postpositive conjunction; it cannot be the first word in a clause.

**Cēdō, cēdere, cessī, cessus** is another verb with many compounds. It means 'go, move, yield', and so **accēdō** (**ad** + **cēdō**) is 'go to, approach'; **discēdō** (**dis-**, 'apart' + **cēdō**), 'go from, depart, leave'; **excēdō**, 'go out'; **recēdō**, 'go back', etc.

**Dēbeō, dēbēre, dēbuī, dēbitus**, when used with an infinitive, means 'ought'; otherwise it means 'owe'.

**Ferrum, ferrī**, N., is the word for 'iron' (chemical symbol $Fe$); it can also mean 'sword'.

**Imperō, imperāre, imperāvī, imperātus**, 'order, command', may govern the dative case. One gives a command to someone that he do something (**ut** or [negative] **nē** + subjunctive): **Fēminae ut canat imperō**, 'I order the woman to sing'.

**Interficiō** is another compound of **faciō** and means 'kill'.

**Magister, magistrī**, M., is the person in charge of something, 'superior, director, master, teacher'.

**Medius, -a, -um** means 'the middle of'; it is an adjective like any other adjective, taking the case of the noun which it modifies: **in mediō oppidō**, 'in the middle of the town'; **ad medium oppidum**, 'toward the middle of the town'.

**Moveō, movēre**, 'move', lengthens its -o- in the perfect tenses: **mōvī, mōtus**. **Removeō**, a compound of **re-** + **moveō**, means 'move back, remove, take away, set aside'.

**Nōscō, nōscere, nōvī, nōtus** and **cognōscō, cognōscere, cognōvī, cognitus** both mean 'learn' in the present, imperfect, and future tenses. However, once one has learned something, he knows it; therefore, the perfect tenses mean 'know'.

**Umquam** (sometimes spelled **unquam**) means 'ever'; its opposite, **numquam** (sometimes spelled **nunquam**) means 'never'.

**Pius, -a, -um**, 'loyal, dutiful, pious', has as its negative counterpart **impius, -a, -um**, 'irreverent, wicked, impious'; the prefix **in-** may have the meaning 'not'.

**Populus** with a short -o- means 'people' and is masculine; with a long -ō- it means 'poplar tree' and is feminine. Obviously, a careful pronunciation is needed to make a distinction between these two words. **Populus, populī**, M., 'people', is a collective noun and since it is singular, any adjective modifying it or verb used with it must also be singular. In the plural, it means 'peoples'.

**Possum, posse, potuī** has no fourth principal part; it means 'be able, can'. If the meaning 'be able' is used, it will be easy to remember that a complementary infinitive is used with **possum**. A complementary infinitive completes the meaning of the verb. "I am able" or "I ought" does not mean anything until an infinitive is used to complete the meaning: **Canere possum**, 'I am able to sing'; **Ferrum removēre dēbeō**, 'I ought to remove the sword'.

The conjunction **postquam**, 'after', is sometimes cut up into two parts (**post**... **quam**); this is called *tmesis*. By dividing the word, one gives the sentence a greater cohesion: **Dominus post interfectus est quam trāditus erat**, 'The master was killed after he had been betrayed'.

The present stem of **ruō, ruere, ruī, rutus**, 'fall, go to ruin, rush', is the same as the perfect active stem; thus, **ruit**, 'he rushes', or 'he has rushed'.

The adjective **socius, -a, -um**, 'allied', when used substantively means 'ally': **Multī sociī Rōmānīs in magnō bellō pūgnāvērunt**, 'Many (men) allied to the Romans fought in the great war' *or* 'Many men fought in the great war as allies to the Romans'. Often adding the English word "as" makes for a smoother translation of a Latin sentence: **Et dominī et servī piī ad ārās deōrum vēnērunt**, 'Both the dutiful masters and slaves came to the altars of the gods' *or* 'Both the masters and slaves came to the altars of the gods as dutiful men'.

# UNIT FIVE — DRILL

## I.

Translate these phrases:

1. puer intellegēns
2. poēta respondēns
3. oppidum pūgnāns
4. fīlius dubitāns
5. deus monēns
6. amīcus audiēns
7. incola capiēns
8. a) incola captus  b) incolae captō  c) incolārum captōrum
9. a) litterae missae  b) litterīs missīs
10. a) inimīcus expulsus  b) inimīcī expulsī  c) inimīcō expulsō
11. a) liber lēctus  b) librōrum lēctōrum
12. a) urna facta  b) urnīs factīs
13. a) rēgnum perdendum  b) rēgna perdenda  c) rēgnō perdendō
14. a) servī spectandī  b) servōrum spectandōrum
15. a) librī scrībendī  b) librīs scrībendīs  c) librōrum scrībendōrum
16. a) dōna danda  b) dōnōrum dandōrum

17. a) puella respōnsūra   b) puellae respōnsūrae
18. a) vir pūgnātūrus   b) virīs pūgnātūrīs
19. a) rēgīnae dāmnātūrae   b) ā rēgīnā dāmnātūrā
20. a) fēmina vīsūra   b) fēminārum vīsūrārum

## II.

Translate these sentences: (participles)

1. Īnsula ā virō capta dēlēbitur (dēlēta est).
2. Vir īnsulam capiēns pecūniam incolīs dabit (dedit).
3. Vir īnsulam captūrus pecūniam incolīs dabit (dedit).
4. Vir īnsulam captam dēlēre poterit (poterat).
5. Īnsula capienda est magna.
6. Nautae oppidum perditūrī fēminās incolārum terrent (terruērunt).
7. Nauta oppidum perdēns fēminās incolārum terret (terruit).
8. Oppidum dē perīculō ab amīcīs monitum ab inimīcīs tamen perditum est.
9. Oppidum perdendum ab amīcīs monitum erat.
10. Dōnum virīs librum lēctūrīs dedistī.
11. Glōria nautārum superātōrum erat magna.
12. Incolīs īnsulam superātūrīs pecūniam dare potuit (potest).
13. Nautae incolās trāditūrō erat mala fāma.
14. Caecō dōna dīs datūrō nōn erat pecūnia.
15. Caecus cibum ā virō ad oppidum missō petere optat.
16. Sī virōs oppidum dēlētūrōs vidēre possim, laetus esse possim.

## III.

Translate the following: (periphrastics, etc.)

1. missūrī sunt
2. missūrī erant
3. missūrī erunt
4. trādendum est
5. Oppidum trādendum erat.
6. Oppidum incolīs trādendum erit.
7. Sententiae puellārum mūtandae sunt.
8. Sententiae puellīs mūtandae sunt.
9. Puellae sententiās mūtātūrae sunt.
10. Venia petenda est.
11. Malī veniam petītūrī erant.
12. Nautae ad oppidum missī erant ut inimīcōs ē prōvinciā pellerent.
13. Nautae ad oppidum mittendī sunt ut inimīcōs ē prōvinciā pellant.
14. Nautae ad oppidum mittendī erant ut inimīcōs ē prōvinciā pellerent.

15. Rēgīna nautās ad oppidum missūra est (erat).
16. Bellum ab acerbīs gestum timēbātur.
17. Acerbus bellum gerēns ab incolīs timētur.
18. Sī sententiae dē bellō virīs mūtandae sint, incolae nōn intellegant.
19. Sī sententiae dē bellō virīs mūtandae essent (fuissent), incolae nōn intellegerent (intellēxissent).
20. Sī sententiam dē bellō mūtātūrus sīs, amīcī nōn taceant.
21. Sī sententiam dē bellō mūtātūrus essēs (fuissēs), amīcī nōn tacērent (tacuissent).

**IV.**
Translate: (datives of the possessor)

1. Nautīs gladiī sunt.
2. Fēminae est mēnsa pulchra.
3. Fīliīs poētae erant pulchrī oculī.
4. Nautae multa pecūnia est; poētae nihil.

# UNIT FIVE — PRELIMINARY EXERCISES
## (SECTIONS A, B)

1. Dominus vocātus ad campum accessit.
2. Aurum ē cellā removēns, magister imperāvit ut in mediā mēnsā pōnerētur.
3. Piōs ad āram cessūrōs vīdimus.
4. Sociīs in perīculum rutūrīs imperāvit.
5. Arma movenda spectāvimus.
6. Impiōs interficiendōs mōnstrāvērunt.
7. Patriam populī territī invādere nōn dēbētis.
8. Poēta autem virōs cognitōs cecinit.
9. Ruīnae oppidōrum arsōrum ā nautīs vīsae sunt.
10. Multam pecūniam capiēns, servus ā dominī tēctō discessit.

# UNIT FIVE — EXERCISES

**I.**

1. Vīlla alta, flammīs ardēns, in ruīnam ante oculōs populī territōs ruit.
2. Magister magnus ab agrō discessūrōs ōrāvit ut oppidum sociōrum captōrum dēlērent.
3. Postquam virīs ab agrō discessūrīs imperāvit ut multa dē nātūrā populī inimīcī cognōscerent, ē mediō sine morā discessit.

4. a) Medium oppidum armīs cum studiō tentum ab impiīs tamen captum est.

   b) Medium oppidum armīs cum studiō tentum piīs tamen capiendum est
   ut sine perīculō bene vīvant.

   c) Piī medium oppidum armīs cum studiō tentum capere dēbent nē ā
   patriā removeantur et ab inimīcīs interficiantur.

5. Magister honestus dōna multa et pulchra servīs bellō captīs dāns imperāvit
   ut cum dīligentiā studiōque labōrārent ut līberī mox essent et ē rēgnō
   cēderent. Servī autem magistrum nōn audīvērunt; ē rēgnō numquam
   cessērunt, sed ē vītā mox cessūrī erant.

6. Rōmānī arma capta superātōrum dēlēbant ut imperium sine perīculō
   tenēre possent.

7. Nōn sine glōriā vītam ēgī; et multa ē librīs nōvī, et magna populō et rēgnō
   fēcī. Mala autem in vītam invāsērunt et nunc inimīcīs interficiendus sum
   ut ē mediō removear. Lācrimīs fēminās inimīcōrum movēre optāvī ut virōs
   ōrent nē pium bonōrum factōrum dāmnent, sed nōn potuī. Sī malam vītam
   ēgissem, nunc interficiendus nōn essem.

8. Impiōrum arma capta sunt ā turbā tēctum invāsūrā.

9. Nautārum Rōmānōrum turba invādēns arma capta līberōrum dēlēvit.

10. Poēta vīvēns in imperiō arma virumque cecinit.

11. a) Sī nauta cum turbā sociōrum oppida nōta capere possit, clārus sit.

    b) Sī nauta cum turbā sociōrum oppida nōta capiat, clārus sit.

    c) Nauta cum turbā sociōrum oppida nōta capiēns clārus sit.

12. Urna antīqua et aurea, in mediā mēnsā posita, ā puerō malō dēlēta est ut
    novam habēret.

13. Fēmina clāmāns servum ē vīllā discessūrum monuit ut urna cāra ā mēnsā
    removenda esset.

14. Multa dūra dē rēgīnā clāmāns, populus tamen ā patriā nōn discessūrus
    est (erat, erit).

15. Postquam ad tēctum sociōrum accessērunt, servīs imperāvērunt ut dē
    patriā multa canerent.

16. Numquam ē patriā cēdam vīvēns. Numquam ē patriā cēdere poterō.

17. Sī nautās ē mediō oppidō vocētis, mox veniant ut īnsulam invādant.

18. Quamquam incolae miserī sunt, bellum tamen gerētur.

19. Quamquam poēta magnum librum scrībet, clārus tamen nōn erit.

20. Poēta magnum librum scrībēns clārus tamen nōn erit.

21. Bene cōgitāta nōn perduntur.

22. Bene perdit pecūniam amīcīs dāns.

23. Socius inimīcōs nec ferrō potuit superāre nec aurō.

24. Sī bellum dūrum sociīs nunc gerendum esset, pūgnātūrī arma caperēmus.

25. Poēta bella gerenda canere potest (poterat, poterit).

26. Novōs librōs legendōs in mēnsā nātō posuissētis sī legere potuisset.

27. Ruīnamne in vītā unquam vīdistis? Sī ruīnam in vītā vīdissēmus, in perīculum caecī nōn ruissēmus.
28. Ante portās pūgnāns interficiētur.
29. Ōrātūrī sumus ut dē vītā ante āctā dominī cōgitētis nē īnsidiārum dāmnētur.
30. Faciam nōn nova, sed multa ante facta.
31. Sī perīculum veniat, ruīna post sit; post perīculum erit ruīna.
32. Impiī vīvunt et vīctūrī sunt; piī semper malīs interficiendī erunt sī imperium tenēre optābunt.

## II.

1. The poet ought to write a book. (translate two ways)
2. The master will have to be overcome by the men who have been betrayed (i.e., the betrayed men) if they are going to drive evil from the land.
3. While the poet was singing of ancient empires destroyed by the sword, he was killed by the men who had been seen previously in the town.
4. A war must be fought by the captured allies in order that they may be free men.
5. After the war, those who had been conquered had neither money nor food. (use dative of the possessor)

## III. Reading

Antequam[1] pius Aenēās oppidum condere[2] potuit, bellum Aenēae pūgnandum fuit. Arma autem Aenēae nōn fuērunt. Fīlius deae mātrem[3] arma ōrāvit ut inimīcōs interficeret. Māter[3] deō imperāvit ut arma historiā[4] populī Rōmānī īnscrīpta[5] faceret. Arma accipiēns[6] Aenēās mox pūgnāre incēpit quamquam historiam[4] populī Rōmānī intellegere nōn potuit. Inimīcus erat impius Turnus, vir dūrus, pūgnāre ardēns. Mediā nocte[7] dea ad Turnum vēnit ut eī[8] imperāret ut cum Aenēā pūgnāret. Ruēns ad bellum Turnus sociōs Aenēae invāsit et amīcum Aenēae interfēcit. Populus socius bellum gestūrus deōs auxilium[9] ōrāvit. "Auxilium[9] cārīs ā dīs[10] dandum est," sēnsit; "sī dī auxilium[9] dabunt, dōna multa ārīs deōrum dare dēbēbimus." Cum Aenēā sociī magnō cum studiō pūgnāvērunt. Turnō parsūrus,[11] Aenēās tamen eum[12] interfēcit. Turnus interficiendus erat ut pius impium superāns oppidum conderet.[2]

---

[1] antequam (conj.), 'before'    [2] condō, -ere, condidī, conditus, 'found'    [3] māter (nom.), mātrem (acc.), 'mother'    [4] historia, -ae, F., 'history'    [5] īnscrībō, -ere, -scrīpsī, -scrīptus, 'inscribe'    [6] accipiō, -ere, -cēpī, -ceptus, 'receive'    [7] nocte (abl.), 'in the night'    [8] eī (dat.), 'him'    [9] auxilium, -ī, N., 'aid'    [10] The ablative of agent with a passive periphrastic is regularly used instead of the dative of agent in order to avoid confusion when another dative is closely associated with the verb.    [11] parcō, -ere, pepercī, parsus, 'spare' (+ dat.)    [12] eum (acc.), 'him'

## A. Nouns of the Third Declension

Nouns of the third declension occur very frequently in Latin and are distinguished by the genitive singular ending -is. This declension admits of all three genders, and while there are several minor variations within the system, all nouns in this declension can be dealt with easily according to the observations which follow.

In order to decline a noun of the third declension, determine the *stem* by dropping the genitive singular ending and then add the specified endings for this declension.

THIRD DECLENSION ENDINGS

|  | MASCULINE & FEMININE | | NEUTER | |
|  | *Sing.* | *Pl.* | *Sing.* | *Pl.* |
|---|---|---|---|---|
| Nom. | –– | -ēs | –– | -a (-ia) |
| Gen. | -is | -um (-ium) | -is | -um (-ium) |
| Dat. | -ī | -ibus | -ī | -ibus |
| Acc. | -em | -ēs (-īs) | –– | -a (-ia) |
| Abl. | -e | -ibus | -e (-ī) | -ibus |

OBSERVATIONS:

1. As is the case with all neuter nouns in Latin, the nominative and accusative forms of each number are identical.
2. There is no specific nominative singular ending for this declension. It must be learned for each noun as a vocabulary item.
3. The alternate endings in parentheses above belong to a class of nouns called *i-stems*. In this book, nouns which are i-stems will be signaled in the vocabulary by the addition of the genitive plural ending -ium to the regular principal parts: **māter, mātris**, *F.*, 'mother'; but **urbs, urbis, -ium**, *F.*, 'city'. Those who care to learn rules for determining which nouns are i-stems may find the notes at the end of this section helpful.

4. Masculine and feminine i-stems frequently have -īs as an alternate for -ēs in the accusative plural.

It will be easy to decline the following nouns according to the observations above.

rūmor, -ōris, M.                    rumor, gossip
nox, noctis, -ium, F.              night
sīdus, -eris, N.                    star, constellation
moenia, -ium, N. (only in pl.)     (city) walls

| MODEL FOR MASC.– FEM. NON-I-STEMS | | MODEL FOR MASC.– FEM. I-STEMS | |
|---|---|---|---|
| rūmor | rūmōrēs | nox | noctēs |
| rūmōris | rūmōrum | noctis | noctium |
| rūmōrī | rūmōribus | noctī | noctibus |
| rūmōrem | rūmōrēs | noctem | noctēs (noctīs) |
| rūmōre | rūmōribus | nocte | noctibus |

| NEUTER NON-I-STEM | | NEUTER I-STEM | |
|---|---|---|---|
| sīdus | sīdera | (moene | moenia |
| sīderis | sīderum | moenis | moenium |
| sīderī | sīderibus | moenī | moenibus |
| sīdus | sīdera | moene | moenia |
| sīdere | sīderibus | moenī) | moenibus |

NOTES: RULES FOR DETERMINING WHICH THIRD DECLENSION NOUNS ARE I-STEMS
A third declension noun will generally be an i-stem if:

1. the nominative and genitive singular have the same number of syllables:

    ignis, ignis, -ium, M.   fire

2. The stem of the noun ends in two consonants *except* if the second consonant is an **l** or **r**:

    nox, noctis, -ium, F.       night
    mōns, montis, -ium, M.   mountain

BUT:

    pater, patris, M.    father
    māter, mātris, F.   mother

(even though the first rule applies also)

3. The nominative singular of a neuter noun ends in -e, -al, or -ar:

> mare, maris, -ium*, N.          sea
> animal, animālis, -ium, N.      animal
> exemplar, exemplāris, -ium, N.  model

These neuter words end in -ī in the ablative singular (instead of -e) and in -ia in the nominative and accusative plural.

* Although this form is not found in extant literature, it has been reconstructed here.

## B. Infinitives

Although the Latin verb has six infinitives — present active, present passive, perfect active, perfect passive, future active, and future passive — only five are in common use. In addition, the future active and future passive participles combined with an infinitive of the verb **sum** yield the infinitives of the active and passive periphrastic conjugations.

1. Present Infinitive
    a) ACTIVE. The present active infinitive is the second principal part of the verb:

    > optāre   to desire
    > dūcere   to lead

    b) PASSIVE. To form the present passive infinitive for the first, second, and fourth conjugations, replace the final -e of the active infinitive with -ī. For the third conjugation, replace the entire -ere with -ī:

    > optārī    to be desired
    > implērī   to be filled
    > dūcī      to be led
    > incipī    to be begun
    > sentīrī   to be felt

2. Perfect Infinitive
    a) ACTIVE. The perfect active infinitive is formed for all verbs by adding -isse to the stem of the third principal part:

    > optāvisse    to have desired
    > implēvisse   to have filled
    > dūxisse      to have led
    > incēpisse    to have begun
    > sēnsisse     to have felt

b) PASSIVE. The perfect passive infinitive is formed with the fourth principal part (perfect passive participle) plus the infinitive of **sum (esse)**.

| | |
|---|---|
| optātus, -a, -um esse | to have been desired |
| implētus, -a, -um esse | to have been filled |
| ductus, -a, -um esse | to have been led |
| inceptus, -a, -um esse | to have been begun |
| sēnsus, -a, -um esse | to have been felt |

3. FUTURE INFINITIVE
   a) ACTIVE. The future active participle plus **esse** are the ingredients for the future active infinitive.

| | |
|---|---|
| optātūrus, -a, -um esse | to be going to desire |
| implētūrus, -a, -um esse | to be going to fill |
| ductūrus, -a, -um esse | to be going to lead |
| inceptūrus, -a, -um esse | to be going to begin |
| sēnsūrus, -a, -um esse | to be going to feel |

   b) PASSIVE. The future passive infinitive occurs so rarely in Latin that its discussion has been omitted from this text.

4. PERIPHRASTIC INFINITIVES
   The periphrastic conjugations also have infinitives formed by compounding the present or perfect infinitives of the verb **sum** with the future active and future passive participles. In the active periphrastic conjugation, this infinitive (with **esse**) merges with, and is in fact one and the same thing as, the future active infinitive. The infinitive of the passive periphrastic carries with it the notion of obligation, necessity, or propriety, just as the finite passive periphrastic forms do.
   a) ACTIVE.

| | |
|---|---|
| optātūrus esse | to be going to desire |
| optātūrus fuisse | to have been going to desire |

   b) PASSIVE.

| | |
|---|---|
| optandus esse | to have to be desired |
| optandus fuisse | to have had to be desired |

## C. Indirect Statement: Subject Accusative and Infinitive

The statement "Dawn is sprinkling the lands with a new light (day)" is a *direct* statement.

Aurōra terrās novō lūmine spargit.

After words which express or imply actions that take place in the head, such as saying, thinking, seeing, perceiving, knowing, and the like, we are able to express statements *indirectly*; that is, the essence of the original speaker's ideas is reported by someone else, although not necessarily in his exact words.

He says that dawn is sprinkling the lands with a new light (day).

In English an indirect statement is generally introduced by the subordinating conjunction *that*, for which there is no equivalent in classical Latin. Instead, a construction with the subject in the accusative case and the verb in the infinitive is used.

In order to change a statement from direct to indirect, take the subject of the direct one and make it accusative; take the finite verb and change it to an infinitive. The rest of the sentence remains unchanged.

Dīcit **aurōram** terrās novō lūmine **spargere**.    He says *dawn to sprinkle* the lands with a new light (day); He says *that dawn is sprinkling* the lands with a new light (day).

The tense of the infinitive in this construction is relative to that of the main verb (much like the tense of participles discussed in the previous unit). The *present* infinitive expresses an action which is or was going on at the *same time* as that of the main verb; the *perfect* infinitive refers to an action which occurred *prior* to that of the main verb; and the *future* infinitive signals one which will occur *subsequent* to that of the main verb.

### PRESENT INFINITIVE

| | |
|---|---|
| Dīcit aurōram terrās novō lūmine spargere. | He says (i.e., now) that dawn is sprinkling the lands with new light (i.e., now). |
| Dīxit aurōram terrās novō lūmine spargere. | He said (i.e., yesterday) that dawn was sprinkling the lands with new light (i.e., yesterday). |
| Dīcet aurōram terrās novō lūmine spargere. | He will say (i.e., tomorrow) that dawn is sprinkling the lands with new light (i.e., tomorrow) |

### PERFECT INFINITIVE

| | |
|---|---|
| Dīcit aurōram terrās novō lūmine sparsisse. | He says (i.e., now) that dawn has sprinkled (sprinkled) the lands with new light (i.e., yesterday). |
| Dīxit aurōram terrās novō lūmine sparsisse. | He said (i.e., yesterday) that dawn had sprinkled (sprinkled) the lands with new light (i.e., the day before yesterday). |
| Dīcet aurōram terrās novō lūmine sparsisse. | He will say (i.e., tomorrow) that dawn has sprinkled (sprinkled) the lands with new light (i.e., today). |

FUTURE INFINITIVE

| | |
|---|---|
| Dīcit aurōram terrās novō lūmine sparsūram* esse. | He says (i.e., now) that dawn will sprinkle the lands with new light (i.e., tomorrow). |
| Dīxit aurōram terrās novō lūmine sparsūram esse. | He said (i.e., yesterday) that dawn would sprinkle the lands with new light (i.e., today). |
| Dīcet aurōram terrās novō lūmine sparsūram esse. | He will say (i.e., tomorrow) that dawn will sprinkle the lands with new light (i.e., the day after tomorrow). |

* Since the future active, perfect passive, and the periphrastic infinitives are composed of a participle and the infinitive of **sum**, the participle is, in effect, a predicate adjective and must agree with its noun (the subject of the indirect statement) in gender, number, and case.

## D. The Irregular Noun *vis*

In the singular this noun regularly means 'force' or 'power'. In the plural it means 'strength'.

| | |
|---|---|
| vīs | vīrēs |
| –– | vīrium |
| –– | vīribus |
| vim | vīrēs (vīrīs) |
| vī | vīribus |

## E. Ablative of Separation

Some verbs which express or imply separation or deprivation are accompanied by the ablative case. The prepositions **ā (ab)**, 'away from', **ē (ex)**, 'from, out of', or **dē**, 'from, down from', are sometimes used with this construction, but more usually the ablative occurs alone.

| | |
|---|---|
| Hominēs incolās īnsulae **servitūte** līberāvērunt. | The men freed the inhabitants of the island *from slavery*. |
| Oedipus, quod līber (ē) **cūrā** nōn erat, sē **oculīs** prīvāvit. | Oedipus, because he was not free *from care*, deprived himself *of (his) eyes*. |

The word **careō, -ēre**, 'lack, be wanting', takes an ablative of separation:

**Pecūniā** careō.     I lack *money*.

Allied with this construction are the following:

1. ABLATIVE OF ORIGIN

   The ablative, with or without a preposition, expresses the origin or descent of a person or thing.

   Aenēās (ē) **deā** nātus est.     Aeneas was born *of a goddess*.

2. ABLATIVE OF PLACE FROM WHICH

   In order to express place from which, the ablative is used with the prepositions **ā** (**ab**), **ē** (**ex**), or **dē**. But with names of towns, cities, and small islands, and the words **domus**, 'home', and **rūs**, 'country', no preposition is used.

> **Ab Italiā** vēnit.　　He came *from Italy*.

BUT:

> **Rōmā** vēnit.　　　He came *from Rome*.

## F. Accusative of Place To Which

Place to which is expressed by the accusative case with the preposition **ad**. With names of towns, cities, and small islands, and the words **domus**, 'home', and **rūs**, 'country', no preposition is used.

> **Ad Italiam** vēnit.　　He came *to Italy*.
> **Ad urbem** vēnit.　　He came *to the city*.

BUT:

> **Rōmam** vēnit.　　He came *to Rome*.
> **Domum** vēnit.　　He came *home*.

## G. The Locative Case (*locus, -ī*, M., 'place')

The names of towns, cities, and small islands, and the words **domus** and **rūs** require a special case to express *place in which* or *place where*, which for other nouns is expressed by the ablative with the preposition **in**. This case is called the *locative*.

For nouns of the first and second declensions, the locative singular is identical to the genitive singular. In the plural for these two declensions, it is identical in form to the ablative plural.

For nouns of the third declension, the locative ends in either **-e** or **-ī** in the singular, in **-ibus** in the plural.

> | | | |
> |---|---|---|
> | *Rōmae* | at Rome | (Rōma, -ae, F.) |
> | *Athēnīs* | at Athens | (Athēnae, -ārum, F.) |
> | *domī* | at home | (domus, -ī, F.) |
> | *Carthāgine* | at Carthage | (Carthāgō, -inis, F.) |
> | *rūrī* | in the country | (rūs, rūris, N.) |

# UNIT SIX — VOCABULARY

| | |
|---|---|
| **animal, -ālis, -ium**, N. | animal |
| **Athēnae, -ārum**, F. (pl.) | Athens |

| | |
|---|---|
| atque or ac (conj.) | and |
| aurōra, -ae, F. | dawn |
| careō, -ēre, -uī, -itus | lack, be without (+ abl.) |
| corpus, corporis, N. | body |
| dīcō, -ere, dīxī, dictus | say, tell, speak |
| diū (adv.) | for a long time |
| domus, -ī, F. | house, home |
| exemplar, -āris, -ium, N. | copy, model, example |
| exemplum, -ī, N. | example |
| frāter, frātris, M. | brother |
| homō, hominis, M. | human being, man |
| ignis, ignis, -ium, M. (abl. sing. igne or ignī) | fire |
| Italia, -ae, F. | Italy |
| Iūnō, Iūnōnis, F. | Juno (sister and wife of Jupiter) |
| Iuppiter, Iovis, M. | Jupiter (god of the sky) |
| līberō (1) | free |
| lūmen, lūminis, N. | light |
| mare, maris, -ium, N. | sea |
| māter, mātris, F. | mother |
| mēns, mentis, -ium, F. | mind, disposition, intellect |
| mīles, mīlitis, M. | soldier |
| moenia, moenium, N. (pl.) | (city) walls |
| mōns, montis, -ium, M. | mountain |
| nōn sōlum...sed etiam | not only...but also |
| nox, noctis, -ium, F. | night |
| oppūgnō (1) | attack, fight against |
| pater, patris, M. | father |
| regō, -ere, rēxī, rēctus | rule |
| rēx, rēgis, M. | king |
| Rōma, -ae, F. | Rome |
| rūmor, -ōris, M. | rumor, gossip |
| rūs, rūris, N. | country (as opposed to city) |
| sānus, -a, -um | sound, healthy, sane |
| sciō, -īre, -īvī, -ītus | know |
| servitūs, servitūtis, F. | slavery |
| sīdus, sīderis, N. | constellation, star; heaven |
| soror, -ōris, F. | sister |
| spargō, -ere, sparsī, sparsus | scatter, sprinkle, distribute |
| timor, timōris, M. | fear, dread |
| urbs, urbis, -ium, F. | city |
| vigor, -ōris, M. | liveliness, activity, vigor |
| vīs; (pl.) vīrēs, vīrium, F. | force, power; (pl.) strength |

# UNIT SIX — NOTES ON VOCABULARY

**Athēnae, Athēnārum,** 'Athens', is a feminine plural word.

The verb **careō, carēre, caruī, caritus,** 'lack, be without', governs the ablative case: **Lūmine carēmus,** 'We are without light'. The mark ^, a caret, shows that something is lacking.

**Dīcō, dīcere, dīxī, dictus,** 'say, tell, speak', often governs an object and an indirect object. Verbs of giving, telling, and showing take an indirect object. **Rūmōrem audītum frātrī dīcam,** 'I shall tell my brother a rumor that I've heard'.

The word **domus** is sometimes considered a second declension noun and sometimes a fourth declension noun. In this book it is presented in Unit Six as second declension, and again in Unit Eight as second or fourth. Note that it is a feminine word even though it has the same endings as a masculine noun in the second declension.

**Exemplar, exemplāris,** N., and **exemplum, exemplī,** N., may be used interchangeably. The abbreviation *e.g.,* *exemplī grātiā* (*grātiā*, with preceding genitive, 'for the sake of'), means 'for the sake of an example'.

**Moenia, moenium** is a neuter plural word of the third declension; these are protective (city) walls as opposed to the walls of a house.

**Nōn sōlum . . . sed etiam** means 'not only . . . but also': **Nōn sōlum sorōre sed etiam frātre careō,** 'I am without not only a sister but also a brother'.

Notice that **māter, mātris,** F., 'mother', **pater, patris,** M., 'father', and **frāter, frātris,** M., 'brother', are not i-stems and that **pater** has a short -a-.

**Regō, regere, rēxī, rēctus,** 'rule', lengthens its -e- in the perfect tenses. **Rēx, rēgis,** M., 'king', and **rēgnum, rēgnī,** N., 'kingdom', are connected with this verb.

The ending **-tūs, -tūtis** is a feminine ending of abstract nouns that indicates a quality or state of being. **Servus** is 'slave' and so **servitūs, servitūtis,** F., is the 'state of being a slave', that is, 'slavery'.

Students often have difficulty with the irregular noun **vīs.** In the singular, which lacks a genitive and dative form, the meaning is 'force, power' and in the plural, it means 'strength'. There is no reason to confuse it with **vir,** 'man', which has a short -i- and belongs to the second declension, since **vīs** has a long -ī- and is a third declension noun. The accusative plural of 'men' is **virōs,** of 'strength', **vīrēs** or **vīrīs.** The dative and ablative plural of 'men' is **virīs,** of 'strength', **vīribus.**

# UNIT SIX — DRILL

**I.**

Supply forms of the adjective **bonus, -a, -um** to modify the following nouns.

| | | | |
|---|---|---|---|
| mīles, mīlitis, M. | | soldier | |
| soror, sorōris, F. | | sister | |
| corpus, corporis, N. | | body | |
| mēns, mentis, -ium, F. | | mind | |
| exemplar, -āris, -ium, N. | | example, model | |

| | | | |
|---|---|---|---|
| 1. mīles | 11. mīlitī | 21. mīlite | 31. mīlitum |
| 2. soror | 12. sorōrī | 22. sorōre | 32. sorōrum |
| 3. corpus | 13. corporī | 23. corpore | 33. corporum |
| 4. mēns | 14. mentī | 24. mente | 34. mentium |
| 5. exemplar | 15. exemplārī | 25. exemplārī | 35. exemplārium |
| 6. mīlitis | 16. mīlitem | 26. mīlitēs | 36. mīlitibus |
| 7. sorōris | 17. sorōrem | 27. sorōrēs | 37. sorōribus |
| 8. corporis | 18. corpus | 28. corpora | 38. corporibus |
| 9. mentis | 19. mentem | 29. mentēs | 39. mentibus |
| 10. exemplāris | 20. exemplar | 30. exemplāria | 40. exemplāribus |

## II.

A. Rewrite these sentences in indirect statement after **sentit**, 'he feels':

1. Puella incolās dē perīculō monet (monēbit, monuit).
2. Fēminae sententiās semper mūtant (mūtābunt, mūtāvērunt).
3. Tēcta in mediō oppidō flammīs dēlentur (dēlēta sunt).
4. Sociī ē terrā discēdere nōn possunt (potuērunt).
5. Amīcus vītam sine culpā agit (aget, ēgit).
6. Vīta bona ab amīcō agitur (ācta est).
7. Honestī in perīculō nōn pōnendī sunt (pōnendī erant).
8. Litterae ad magistrum mittuntur (mittēbantur).
9. Nōtī dē malīs cōgitant (cōgitābunt, cōgitābant).
10. Oppidum ab inimīcīs trāditur (trāditum est).
11. Amīcō est (erat, erit) multa pecūnia.
12. Sine cūrā rēgīna vīvere nōn potest (potuit).

B. Translate the indirect statements you wrote above, first after **sentit**, 'he feels', then after **sēnsit**, 'he felt'.

## III.

Omit the initial verbs of the head and rewrite the indirect statements as direct ones:

1. Vīdimus fāmam rēgīnae esse (fuisse, futūram esse) magnam.
2. Cognōverātis incolās rēgīnae multam pecūniam dēbēre (dēbuisse).
3. Respondit bellum cum dīligentiā pūgnātum esse (pūgnārī).

4. Intellegō nautās vīllam perdidisse (perdere, perditūrōs esse).
5. Intellēxī vīllam ā nautīs perditam esse (perdī).
6. Sentiunt honestōs malum ē terrā pellere nōn posse (potuisse).

**IV.**
Translate the following sentences which contain "place" constructions or ablatives of separation or source:

1. Multōs familiā honestā nātōs ab oppidō ad īnsulam mīsimus. [**familia, -ae,** F., 'family']
2. Multōs Syrācūsīs Tarentum mīsimus. [**Syrācūsae, -ārum,** F. pl., 'Syracuse', a city in Sicily; **Tarentum, -ī,** N., 'Tarentum', a town in Sicily]
3. Ruīnae Syrācūsīs vidērī potuērunt, sed neque Tarentō neque in patriā.
4. Ē viā in cellam ambulāvērunt.
5. Līberī invidiā vītam agimus.
6. Malōs magnā vī dē saxō altō iactāverant. [**iactō** (1), 'throw, hurl']

# UNIT SIX — PRELIMINARY EXERCISES (SECTION A)

1. Rēx mīlitibus imperāvit nē discēderent.
2. Multa lūmina urbis ab hominibus captīs vīsa sunt.
3. Flammae ignium multōrum nōn sōlum in monte sed etiam in marī vīsae sunt.
4. Multa animālia sorōribus frātribusque mōnstrāvimus.
5. Patrī erat magnus timor maris.
6. Sī mentēs mīlitum timōre implēbuntur, hominēsne pūgnāre poterunt?
7. Līberī servitūtem timent et cum vigōre pūgnābunt nē servī sint.
8. Rūmōrēsne novōs dē moenibus ignī dēlētīs audīvistis?
9. Mīlitēs domōs mātrum patrumque vidēre optāvērunt.
10. a) Corpora multōrum hominum vigōre carent.
    b) Corpora multōrum animālium valida sunt.

# UNIT SIX — EXERCISES

**I.**
1. Populus ruēns in viam frātrēs cum frātribus pūgnāre in bellō clāmābat.
2. Poēta dīcit mentem sānam in corpore sānō optandam esse.
3. Rūmor est urbem ā mīlitibus oppūgnātam vī dēlētam esse.

4. Pater māterque audīvērunt fīliōs ante moenia Rōmae ignī et ferrō pūgnāvisse.
5. Populus antīquus dīcēbat Iovem esse patrem deōrum atque hominum rēgem et terram esse mātrem hominum animāliumque.
6. Dīcēbātur Iūnō esse soror Iovis.
7. Vidēmus novam aurōram lūmine mare, terram, et caelum spargere.
8. Postquam antīquum exemplar positum est, poētae Rōmānī nova scrībere incēpērunt.
9. Mīlitēs in mediā urbe nōn mentis sōlum vigōre sed etiam corporis vīribus bellum gessērunt.
10. Noctem mox tēctūram esse terrās umbrīs intellegimus.
11. Noctem ruere dē montibus mox vidēre poterimus.
12. Erant novī rūmōrēs corpora mīlitum esse sāna et mīlitēs validīs vīribus pūgnāre.
13. Hominēs urbium semper pūgnābant ut urbēs essent līberae.
14. Ā frātre dictum est animālia ā marī in terram vī ducta esse.
15. Postquam urbs oppūgnāta est, mātrī imperāvimus nē timēret quod sēnsimus sorōrem frātremque pecūniam ac cibum incolīs datūrōs esse nē in perīculō essent.
16. Respondistī nova perīcula validīs hominibus oppidī mōnstrāta esse.
17. Postquam urbs superāta est, multus mīles patrem mātremque vidēre ardēbat.
18. Rēx populō dīxit terram, montēs, mare animāliaque esse cāra Iovī Iūnōnīque.
19. Quamquam sīdera clāra in caelō vidērī nōn poterant, nautae vēla dedērunt ut rēx esset laetus.
20. Bonum est scīre multum populum ā piō homine, ē deā nātō, ē patriā ad Italiam dūcī potuisse.
21. Ut urbem timōre līberēmus, imperābimus mīlitibus ut discēdant.
22. Sī īnsulam servitūte līberēmus, timor incolārum removeātur.
23. Sī vēra scīvissēmus, dīxissēmus incolās in multīs īnsulīs nōn sōlum aquā sed etiam pecūniā carēre.
24. Rōmae diū fuerant rēgēs, numquam Athēnīs.
25. Rūrī atque in urbe incolīs erant multa perīcula.
26. Rēx rēgnum cum vigōre et magnā veniā regit ut novīs sit rēgibus exemplum.
27. Urbs capta dēlenda est (dēlenda erat, dēlenda fuit); scīmus urbem captam dēlendam esse (dēlendam fuisse).
28. Aureae urnae servīs pōnendae erant in mēnsīs ut amīcīs dominī ad vīllam ventūrīs mōnstrārent deōs multa bona piīs dōnāre.
29. Nox sī terrās mox umbrīs tegat, nōn sōlum moenia inimīcōrum sine perīculō oppūgnāre possīmus sed etiam amīcōs servitūte līberēmus.
30. Hominēs honestī in Italiā magnīs cum vīribus semper pūgnātūrī erant ut urbēs cūrā essent līberae et fēminae perīculō et timōre carērent.

31. Domum sine morā venient.
32. Incolae sentiunt rēgem mala ex urbe pellere dēbēre.

## II.

1. We understood that the city, after it had been attacked, was being destroyed by the strength of the soldiers.
2. Did you hear the rumors that the soldiers were rushing into the cities?
3. We understand that a model of the city walls has been shown to the men (who are) about to attack the city with fire and sword.
4. They told the father of the brothers that the sons had been chosen to fight around the city walls.
5. We shall say that poets should write books not only about Jupiter and Juno but also about the sea and about the animals of the mountains.
6. We know that a war cannot be waged forcefully on the sea by the soldiers without great danger.

### III. Reading

Cicero warns the Roman senators about men plotting against the state (*In Catilīnam** I.2.4–5, liberally adapted):

Optō, patrēs cōnscrīptī,[1] mē[2] esse pium, optō in tantīs[3] urbī perīculīs mē[2] nōn sine cūrā vidērī, sed nunc mē[2] inertiae[4] nēquitiaeque[5] dāmnō. Castra[6] sunt in Italiā contrā[7] populum Rōmānum in Etrūriae[8] montibus conlocāta,[9] crēscit[10] semper inimīcōrum numerus;[11] castrōrum[6] autem imperātōrem[12] ducemque[13] inimīcōrum intrā[14] moenia atque adeō[15] in patrum cōnscrīptōrum[1] numerō[11] vidētis, et intellegere dēbētis illōs[16] dē perīculō et magnīs malīs urbī nostrae[17] cōgitāre.

* Catilīna, -ae, M., 'Catiline', the name of the leader of a conspiracy that Cicero was eager to put down

[1] cōnscrībō (com- + scrībō), 'enroll'. (The "enrolled fathers" were the senators.)　[2] mē (acc.), 'me, myself'　[3] tantus, -a, -um, 'so much, so great'　[4] inertia, -ae, F., 'laziness'　[5] nēquitia, -ae, F., 'worthlessness'　[6] castra, -ōrum, N. pl., 'camp'　[7] contrā (prep. + acc.), 'against'　[8] Etrūria, -ae, F., 'Etruria', a district north of Rome　[9] conlocō (1), 'locate'　[10] crēscō, -ere, crēvī, crētus, 'grow'　[11] numerus, -ī, M., 'number'　[12] imperātor, -ōris, M., 'commander'　[13] dux, ducis, M., 'leader'　[14] intrā (prep. + acc.), 'within'　[15] adeō (adv.), 'even'　[16] illōs (acc. pl.), 'those (men)'　[17] noster, nostra, nostrum, 'our'

## A. Demonstrative Adjectives

Demonstrative (**dēmōnstrō** (1), 'point out') adjectives *point out* the word with which they agree. There are three demonstrative adjectives of extreme importance:

   (1) **hic, haec, hoc,** 'this'
   (2) **ille, illa, illud,** 'that'
   (3) **is, ea, id,** 'this' or 'that' (unemphatic)

### hic, haec, hoc 'this'

|      | SINGULAR | | | PLURAL | | |
|------|------|------|------|------|------|------|
|      | M. | F. | N. | M. | F. | N. |
| Nom. | hic | haec | hoc | hī | hae | haec |
| Gen. | huius | huius | huius | hōrum | hārum | hōrum |
| Dat. | huic | huic | huic | hīs | hīs | hīs |
| Acc. | hunc | hanc | hoc | hōs | hās | haec |
| Abl. | hōc | hāc | hōc | hīs | hīs | hīs |

### ille, illa, illud, 'that'

|      | SINGULAR | | | PLURAL | | |
|------|------|------|------|------|------|------|
|      | M. | F. | N. | M. | F. | N. |
| Nom. | ille | illa | illud | illī | illae | illa |
| Gen. | illīus | illīus | illīus | illōrum | illārum | illōrum |
| Dat. | illī | illī | illī | illīs | illīs | illīs |
| Acc. | illum | illam | illud | illōs | illās | illa |
| Abl. | illō | jllā | illō | illīs | illīs | illīs |

### is, ea, id, 'this' or 'that' (unemphatic)

|      | SINGULAR | | | PLURAL | | |
|------|------|------|------|------|------|------|
|      | M. | F. | N. | M. | F. | N. |
| Nom. | is | ea | id | eī, iī | eae | ea |
| Gen. | eius | eius | eius | eōrum | eārum | eōrum |
| Dat. | eī | eī | eī | eīs, iīs | eīs, iīs | eīs, iīs |
| Acc. | eum | eam | id | eōs | eās | ea |
| Abl. | eō | eā | eō | eīs, iīs | eīs, iīs | eīs, iīs |

| | |
|---|---|
| **Hunc (illum, eum)** virum vidēs. | You see *this* (*that, this* or *that*) man. |
| Cum **hōc (illō, eō)** virō ambulās. | You walk with *this* (*that, this* or *that*) man. |
| Vidēsne **hoc (illud, id)** dōnum? | Do you see *this* (*that, this* or *that*) gift? |

The connotative distinctions between **hic, ille,** and **is** can be gauged from the following:

| | |
|---|---|
| Hunc librum optās? | Do you want this book (i.e., here, as opposed to that book there)? [Emphatic Demonstrative] |
| Illum librum optās? | Do you want that book (i.e., there, as opposed to this book here)? [Emphatic Demonstrative] |
| Eum librum optās? | Do you want this (that) book (i.e., the one just referred to, e.g.)? [Unemphatic Demonstrative] |

As is the case with other adjectives, **hic, ille,** and **is** are often found used substantively:

| | |
|---|---|
| **Hunc (illum, eum)** vidēs. | You see *this* (*that, this* or *that*) man. |
| Cum **hōc (illō, eō)** ambulās. | You walk with *this* (*that, this* or *that*) man. |
| Vidēsne **hoc (illud, id)**? | Do you see *this* (*that, this* or *that*) thing? |

In English it is often more convenient to translate **is, ea, id** when used substantively as a pronoun or, as in the last two examples below, as a possessive adjective:

| | |
|---|---|
| **Eum** vidēs. | You see *this* (*that*) man; you see *him*. |
| Cum **eō** ambulās. | You walk with *this* (*that*) man; you walk with *him*. |
| Vidēsne **id**? | Do you see *this* (*that*) thing? Do you see *it*? |
| **Eius** librum habeō. | I have the book *of this* (*that*) man (woman); I have the book *of him* (*her*); I have *his* (*her*) book. |
| Patrem **eārum** vidēmus. | We see the father *of these* (*those*) women; we see the father *of them*; we see *their* father. |

## B. Personal Pronouns

Since the endings of a Latin verb already indicate the subject of that verb, personal pronouns are not required. However, pronouns in the nominative case are sometimes used for *emphasis*.

| | |
|---|---|
| Clāmō. | I shout. |
| **Ego** clāmō. | It is *I* who shout; *I* am the one who shouts. |

The other cases of the personal pronouns are used as they are in English, i.e., as substitutes for nouns.

| | |
|---|---|
| Librum **mihi** dat. | He gives the book *to me*. |
| **Mē** videt. | He sees *me*. |

> **Mēcum ambulās.**   You are walking with *me*. (Note that, with personal
> pronouns, the **cum** is regularly attached as a suffix to
> the pronoun instead of preceding it.)

1. FIRST PERSON

| ego | I | nōs | we |
|---|---|---|---|
| meī | of me | nostrum⎱<br>nostrī ⎰ | of us |
| mihi | to/for me | nōbīs | to/for us |
| mē | me | nōs | us |
| mē | from/with/in/by me | nōbīs | from/with/in/by us |

2. SECOND PERSON

| tū | you | vōs | you |
|---|---|---|---|
| tuī | of you | vestrum⎱<br>vestrī ⎰ | of you |
| tibi | to/for you | vōbīs | to/for you |
| tē | you | vōs | you |
| tē | from/with/in/by you | vōbīs | from/with/in/by you |

NOTE: **Nostrum** and **vestrum** are used as *partitive* genitives (page 154):

> multī **nostrum**   many *of us*   ("many" is the part, "us" is the whole)

**Nostrī** and **vestrī** are used as *objective* genitives; that is, they function as the
*object* of the word on which they depend (pages 178–9):

> Odium **nostrī** est magnum.   The hatred *of (for) us* is great.
>
> (**nostrī** is the *object* or recipient of the
> hatred)

3. THIRD PERSON

There is no third person personal pronoun as such. As indicated in section
A above, the forms of **is, ea, id** are frequently used without a noun as a substitute for the third person pronoun. However, a third person *reflexive* pronoun
does occur.

4. REFLEXIVE PRONOUNS

A *reflexive* (**reflectō**, **-ere**, **-flexī**, **-flectus**, 'bend back, reflect') pronoun
generally refers to or *reflects* the subject of its own clause; therefore, it cannot
have a nominative case.

In the first and second persons, there is no separate reflexive pronoun; one
uses simply the correct case of **ego** or **tū**, and whether the usage is reflexive
or not can be determined from the relationship of the pronoun to the subject:
If they are the same person or thing, then the pronoun is reflexive; if they are
different, then the pronoun is not reflexive.

Mē videō.   I see *myself*.        (Reflexive)
Mē videt.   He sees *me*.         (Not Reflexive)
Tē vidēs.   You see *yourself*.   (Reflexive)
Tē videt.   He sees *you*.        (Not Reflexive)

In the third person, however, a separate form is used.

SINGULAR AND PLURAL

| Nom. | -- |
|------|------|
| Gen. | suī |
| Dat. | sibi |
| Acc. | sē |
| Abl. | sē |

Sē videt.    He (she, it) sees *himself* (*herself*, *itself*).
Sē vident.   They see *themselves*.

Note the following examples, which illustrate reflexive and nonreflexive usage:

Eum videt.    He (person A) sees *him* (person B).
Sē videt.     He sees *himself*.
Eōs videt.    He sees *them*.
Sē vident.    They see *themselves*.
Mē videt.     He sees *me*.
Mē videō.     I see *myself*.

## C. Possessive Adjectives

The possessive adjectives for the first person are **meus, -a, -um**, 'my', and **noster, nostra, nostrum**, 'our'. For the second person, they are **tuus, -a, -um**, 'your', and **vester, vestra, vestrum**, 'your'. Since they are adjectives, they must agree with the thing possessed in gender, number, and case.

**Tuum** frātrem videō.      I see *your* brother.
**Nostram** mātrem vidēmus.  We see *our* mother.
**Meum** imperium ōdit.      He hates *my* authority.

As has been seen throughout this text, the possessive adjective need not be expressed in Latin when its sense can be inferred easily from the context. When the adjective is used in Latin, it is strictly emphatic or is used to clarify a point which the context would otherwise leave obscure.

Patrem videō.       I see (my) father.

BUT:

Patrem **meum** videō.   I see *my* father.
                    (the adjective is emphatic or elucidative, i.e., as opposed to "your" father, "their" father, etc.)

The possessive adjective for the third person is **suus, -a, -um** (singular and plural), but this word is used only *reflexively*; that is, the thing possessed belongs to the subject. When reflexive possession is not desired in the third person, a form of **is, ea, id** in the genitive case is used.

| | |
|---|---|
| **Suum** imperium ōdit. | He/she hates *his/her* (*own*) authority. |
| **Suum** imperium ōdērunt. | They hate *their* (*own*) authority. |

BUT:

| | |
|---|---|
| **Eius** imperium ōdit. | He/she hates the authority *of him* (*her/it/this one/that one*); he/she (person A) hates *his/her/its* (person B's or something's) authority. |
| **Eōrum** imperium ōdērunt. | They hate the authority *of them* (*of these/those men*); they (group A) hate *their* (group B's) authority. |

OBSERVATION: The genitive of the personal pronouns is *never* used to show possession. In order to express possession in the first and second persons, the *possessive adjectives* must be used.

## D. Relative Pronoun

The relative pronoun introduces an adjectival clause which modifies the antecedent (**ante + cēdō**, 'go before'; thus, 'that which goes before') of that pronoun.

The man *whom* you see is my friend.

*The relative pronoun "whom" agrees in gender and number with its antecedent,* "man", *but its case is determined by its use in its own clause.* Consequently in Latin the pronoun is masculine singular because of its antecedent, but accusative because it is the object of the verb "you see".

The forms of the relative pronoun follow:

| SINGULAR | | | PLURAL | | |
|---|---|---|---|---|---|
| M. | F. | N. | M. | F. | N. |
| quī | quae | quod | quī | quae | quae |
| who | who | which (that) | | | |
| cuius | cuius | cuius | quōrum | quārum | quōrum |
| of whom, whose | | | | | |
| cui | cui | cui | quibus | quibus | quibus |
| to/for whom | | | | | |
| quem | quam | quod | quōs | quās | quae |
| whom | | | | | |
| quō | quā | quō | quibus | quibus | quibus |
| from/with/in/by whom | | | | | |

Note these examples:

> Poēta **cuius** amīcus erat
> caecus puerum audiēbat.
>
> The poet *of whom* the friend was blind was listening to the boy; the poet *whose* friend was blind was listening to the boy.

(**cuius**: masculine singular because of its antecedent **poēta** which is masculine singular; genitive because of its dependence on **amīcus** in its own clause)

> Fēminās **quae** in viā clāmant ōdimus.
>
> We hate the women who shout in the street.

(**quae**: feminine plural because of its antecedent **fēminās** which is feminine plural; nominative because it is the subject of the verb **clāmant**)

THE RELATIVE PRONOUN AT THE BEGINNING OF A SENTENCE

The relative pronoun is frequently used in Latin to begin a sentence where the English would use a demonstrative or a personal pronoun. Since the antecedent of the relative pronoun is a word or idea in the previous sentence, this usage makes for greater cohesion between sentences and thoughts.

> Fīlius dīxit urbem in perīculō magnō esse. **Quae** postquam audīvī, vērō timēbam.
>
> My son said that the city was in great danger. After I heard *which things* (*these things*), I was truly afraid.

> Mīles mē monuerat ut ex oppidō discēderem. **Quem** postquam mē interfectūrum esse sēnsī, mox discessī.
>
> The soldier had warned me to depart from the town. After I perceived that *whom* (*he*) was going to kill me, I soon (i.e., thereupon) departed.

### E. Interrogative Adjective

The interrogative adjective (which? what?) is identical in form to the relative pronoun.

> **Quem** virum vidēs?
> *Which* (*what*) man do you see?
>
> Cum **quō** virō ambulās?
> With *which* (*what*) man are you walking?
>
> **Quod** dōnum vidēs?
> *Which* (*what*) gift do you see?

### F. Interrogative Pronoun

The interrogative pronoun is identical to the interrogative adjective in the *plural*; in the *singular*, the following forms are used:

| M. F. | N. |
|-------|------|
| quis | quid |
| cuius | cuius |
| cui | cui |
| quem | quid |
| quō | quō |

**Quem** vidēs?　　　　　*Whom* do you see?
**Quōcum*** ambulās?　With *whom* are you walking?
**Quid** vidēs?　　　　　*What* do you see?

* Note that with the interrogative pronouns, as with personal pronouns, **cum** is regularly attached as a suffix to the pronoun instead of preceding it.

IN REVIEW — Note the following comparisons between pronominal and adjectival usage:

Pronoun:　**Cui** taedam dedistī?　　　　*To whom* (*to which one*) did you give the torch?

Adjective:　**Cui** fēminae taedam dedistī?　*To which* (*what*) woman did you give the torch?

Pronoun:　**Quis** taedam tibi dedit?　　*Who* gave you the torch?

Adjective:　**Quae** fēmina taedam tibi dedit?　*Which* (*what*) woman gave you the torch?

## G. Ablative of Accompaniment

The ablative is used with the preposition **cum** to denote accompaniment.

Ad urbem **cum amīcō** venit.　He comes to the city *with* (*his*) *friend.*
Ad urbem **mēcum** venit.　　He comes to the city *with me.*

## H. Ablative of Time When or Within Which

Time when or within which is expressed by the ablative. A preposition is not regularly used.

**Illō tempore** miser erat.　　　　*At that time* he was unhappy.
**Quīnque annīs** hoc opus perficiet.　*Within five years* he will complete this task.

## I. Accusative of Duration of Time and Extent of Space

The accusative, usually without a preposition, is used to express duration of time or extent of space. It answers the question "for how long?", whether it be of time or distance.

**Quīnque annōs** miser erat.　　　　*For five years* he was unhappy.
**Quīnque pedēs** ad dextram ambulāvit.　He walked *five feet* to the right.

## J. Subjunctive in Subordinate Clauses in Indirect Statement

Subordinate clauses within an indirect statement (subject accusative and infinitive) normally have their verbs in the subjunctive, the tense of which is determined according to the rules of tense sequence (Unit Three, section G) after the verb or phrase of the head which introduces the indirect statement.

Vir quem vidēs pecūniam optat.        The man whom you see desires
                                                        money.

Dīcō virum quem **videās** pecūniam   I say that the man whom *you see*
optāre.                                               (*may see*) desires money.
    (present subjunctive, primary sequence, simultaneous
        action after **dīcō**)

Dīxī virum quem **vidērēs** pecūniam   I said that the man whom *you saw*
optāre.                                               (*might be seeing*) desired money.
    (imperfect subjunctive, secondary sequence,
      simultaneous action after **dīxī**)

Vir quem vīdistī (vidēbās) pecūniam   The man whom you saw desires
optat.                                                money.

Dīcō virum quem **vīderis** pecūniam   I say that the man whom *you saw*
optāre.                                               (*may have seen*) desires money.
    (perfect subjunctive, primary sequence,
      prior action after **dīcō**)

Dīxī virum quem **vīdissēs** pecūniam   I said that the man whom *you had
optāre.                                               seen* (*might have seen*) desired
                                                        money.
    (pluperfect subjunctive, secondary sequence,
      prior action after **dīxī**)

The development of this usage is logical, for the subjunctive is the mood of *idea,
intention, possibility,* etc., as opposed to *fact,* and the person reporting the statement (in this case, "I") does not claim responsibility that the subject of the
relative clause (in this case, "you") *actually* sees the man. The indicative might
have been used in this case, but the tone would then be:

Dīcō virum quem **vidēs**       I say that the man whom *you actually see* (and I
pecūniam optāre.                 accept responsibility for this statement) desires
                                 money.

## UNIT SEVEN — VOCABULARY

**amō** (1)                                    love
  **amor, amōris,** M.             love
**annus, -ī,** M.                              year
**Asia, -ae,** F.                              Asia
**auctor, -ōris,** M.                         producer, founder, author

| | |
|---|---|
| cīvis, cīvis, -ium, M. *or* F. | citizen |
| cōnficiō, -ere, -fēcī, -fectus | complete |
| ego, meī (pron.) | I |
| fīnis, fīnis, -ium, M. | end, boundary, limit |
| genus, generis, N. | descent, origin, race, sort |
| hic, haec, hoc | this, the latter |
| hōra, -ae, F. | hour, season |
| hostis, hostis, -ium, M. | enemy, public enemy |
| ille, illa, illud | that, the former |
| inveniō, -īre, -vēnī, -ventus | come upon, discover, find |
| is, ea, id | this, that; he, she, it |
| locus, -ī, M. | place, spot |
| meus, -a, -um | my, mine, my own |
| mors, mortis, -ium, F. | death |
| noster, nostra, nostrum | our, ours, our own |
| ōdī, ōdisse (defective verb lacking in the present system; perfect forms have present meanings) | hate |
| opus, operis, N. | work |
| opus est (+ nom. or abl. [instrumental] of thing needed; less frequently + gen.) | there is need of |

**Pecūnia mihi opus est.** Money exists for me (as a) need; there is need of money to me; I need money.

**Opus est mihi pecūniā.** The need exists to me by means of money; there is need to me of money; I need money.

| | |
|---|---|
| perficiō, -ere, -fēcī, -fectus | accomplish, complete, finish |
| pēs, pedis, M. | foot |
| placeō, -ēre, placuī, placitus | be pleasing to, please (+ dat.) |
| premō, -ere, pressī, pressus | press, press upon, press hard |
| opprimō, -ere, -pressī, -pressus | press upon, overwhelm, suppress, oppress |
| quī, quae, quod (rel. pron.) | who, which, that |
| quī, quae, quod (interrogative adj.) | which, what |
| quīnque (indeclinable adj.) | five |
| quis, quid (interrogative pron.) | who, what |
| salūs, -ūtis, F. | health, safety |
| salūtem dīcere | say hello, greet |
| spērō (1) | hope (for) |
| ––, suī (reflexive pron.) | himself, herself, itself, themselves |

| | |
|---|---|
| suus, -a, -um | his own, her own, its own, their own |
| tempus, -oris, N. | time, period, season |
| tū, tuī (pron.) | you |
| tuus, -a, -um | your, yours, your own (sing.) |
| vester, vestra, vestrum | your, yours, your own (pl.) |
| vōx, vōcis, F. | voice |

# UNIT SEVEN — NOTES ON VOCABULARY

**Cōnficiō** and **perficiō** are both compounds of **faciō** with an intensive prefix and mean 'do completely, accomplish'. The -ō- of **cōnficiō** is long because it precedes -**nf**. A vowel is lengthened before -**ns**, -**nf**, and -**nct**.

**Genus, generis**, N., not only means 'descent, origin, race', but also 'sort': **Est homō illīus generis**, 'He is a man of that sort'.

**Hic, haec, hoc** and **ille, illa, illud** are emphatic words which point out the word they modify: this book as opposed to that one; **hic liber**...**ille**. Since **ille** points to something further away, it can also mean the thing mentioned previously, 'the former', as opposed to the last thing said (**hic**, 'the latter').

**Inveniō** is a compound of **veniō**, 'come'; it means 'come upon, find'.

**Is, ea, id** is a weaker word; it does not point out so strongly as **hic** and **ille** and so it can mean either 'this' or 'that'. Of course, when it is used substantively, 'this man', 'this woman', 'this thing' are more easily expressed as 'he', 'she', 'it'. The abbreviation *i.e.*, **id est**, means 'that is'.

**Locus, locī**, 'place', is masculine in the singular, but, most often, neuter in the plural, **loca, locōrum**, 'places'. **Locī, locōrum**, masculine, when it does occur, usually refers to passages of literature or the points of an argument.

**Ōdī** is a defective verb. It has only perfect tenses and so the perfect infinitive is given. The perfect tense is translated as present, the pluperfect as imperfect, and the future perfect as future: **ōdī**, 'I hate', **ōderam**, 'I hated', **ōderō**, 'I shall hate'.

**Opus** and **tempus**, like **corpus**, are neuter words whose nominative singular ends in -**us**. **Opus est** is an idiom meaning 'there is need of'. What is needed is put into the nominative case or the ablative, less frequently the genitive; the person who is in need is in the dative case: **Opus tibi est mēnsa?** or **Opus tibi est mēnsā?** or **Opus tibi est mēnsae?**, 'Do you need a table?'

**Opprimō** is a compound of **premō**. Once again, the vowel in the uncompounded verb weakens when the verb is compounded.

**Quī, quae, quod** can be either the relative pronoun 'who, which, that' or the interrogative adjective 'which, what'. The relative pronoun will have an antecedent; the interrogative adjective will not, but, since it is an adjective, it will be used with a noun: **Vir quem vīdimus nōs ōdit**, 'The man whom we saw hates us'; **Quem librum legis?**, 'What book are you reading?'

**Quis, quid** is the interrogative pronoun, 'who, what': **Quem vidēs?**, 'Whom do you see?'

**Salūs, salūtis**, F., means 'health, safety'; the idiom **salūtem dīcere** means 'to greet, say hello': **Pater tuus nōbīs salūtem dīxit**, 'Your father said hello to us'.

Reflexive pronouns refer to the subject of the sentence or clause in which they occur (for exceptions, see Unit Fourteen, section E) and so there is no nominative case. The same forms are used for the singular and plural and for all three genders. The possessive adjective **suus, -a, -um** refers to something owned by the subject: **Rēgīna nautīs suīs imperāvit ut vēla darent**, 'The queen ordered her sailors to set sail'.

The pronoun **tū** is 'you', referring to one person; **vōs** is the plural 'you'. The plural is never used as a polite form of 'you' in Latin as is the case in many modern languages. The possessive adjective **tuus, -a, -um** is used to indicate possession by a singular 'you'; **vester, vestra, vestrum**, by the plural 'you': **tuus pater**, 'your (singular 'you') father'; **tuī librī**, 'your (singular 'you') books'; **vester fīlius**, 'your (plural 'you') son'; **vestrae sorōrēs**, 'your (plural 'you') sisters'.

**Vōx, vōcis**, F., 'voice', is associated with **vocō**, 'call'.

## UNIT SEVEN — DRILL

### I.

Give the gender, number, and case of the pronouns or adjectives in italics in the following sentences. Then, referring to the paradigms in the Unit, translate only those words into Latin.

1. Is *this your* book? Is *it his*?
2. With *whom* were *you* walking at *that* time? Not with *your* mother, but with *his*.
3. *What* do *you* think about the voice of *this* man?
4. *I* hate *those* men, but *I* love *these*.
5. To *whom* did *you* give the gifts *which I* sent *to you* from *that* island?
6. *This* man knew that *he* hated the voice of *that* man.
7. *I* completed the work, not *you*.
8. *Whose* book is *this which* was placed on *your* table?
9. The women *whom we* saw at *that* time were the mothers of *those* boys *to whom we* had given money.
10. (At) *what* time shall *we* see *them*?
11. *His* friends will love *him* and the woman *whom he* loves.

12. *Whose* right hand has written *that* book about *which* people say many good things?
13. The unhappy man sent gifts neither to *his* sister nor to *his* brother, but *his* friend sent gifts to *his* (i.e., the unhappy man's) mother.
14. The soldier hates *his* country's enemies and *he* desires to conquer *them*.
15. *We* lived in *their* country for five years and *they* did not consider *us* enemies.

## II.

Translate the following sentences:

1. Scīmus tē domum quae ardeat multōs mēnsēs incoluisse. [**mēnsis, mēnsis, -ium**, M., 'month']
2. Dīxērunt sē per oppida in quibus sociī vidērī potuissent trēs noctēs ambulāvisse. [**trēs**, fem. acc. pl. adj., 'three']

# UNIT SEVEN — PRELIMINARY EXERCISES
## (SECTIONS A, B, C)

1. Hunc locum scīmus; illum locum nōn scīmus.
2. Hunc scīmus; illum nōn scīmus.
3. Nōs patrem nostrum vīdimus; is nōs nōn vīdit.
4. Patrem eius vīdit; patrem suum vīdit.
5. Mē sciō; tēne scīs?
6. Eum scit; sēne scit?
7. Sē scit; sēne sciunt?
8. Hī nōbīs salūtem dīxērunt.
9. Multī vestrum mortem timent.
10. Auctor opus suum cōnfēcit quamquam id ōdit.
11. Opus suum ōdērunt.
12. Opus nostrum ōdimus.
13. Opusne vestrum ōdistis?
14. Mors nōs premit.
15. Mors nōbīs nōn placet.
16. Eīs multus amor nostrī est.
17. Mihi opus est vōce magnā.
18. Pēs mātris tuae est magnus; pēs meus est parvus.
19. Vōcem eārum audīvērunt.
20. Vōcem suam audīvērunt.

# UNIT SEVEN — EXERCISES

## I.

1. Ad quem mīsistī librōs quōs noster clārus auctor illō tempore scrīpsit ut populō tuō placēret?
2. Hunc librum cuius auctor scītur ā vestrīs cīvibus amāmus, sed illum librum quī est in mēnsā ōdimus.

3. Dīcit fēminās quās vīderimus in illō locō esse matrēs eōrum puerōrum quī Rōmam ex Asiā vēnērunt ut sibi laetās vītās petant.

4. Hī ab illā īnsulā quae est in nostrō marī vēnērunt, sed illī in hōc locō semper vīxērunt.

5. Ego illum librum lēgī, tūne hunc lēgistī?

6. Cui dedistī librum quem magister dīxit mihi legendum esse?

7. Quī liber tibi legendus est?

8. Quid (tū) agis? Ego litterās scrībō. Ego litterās meīs scrībō.

9. In quibus terrīs servitūs vidērī potest?

10. Quibuscum ambulāvistī ē vīllā in viam quae populō implēta est? Cum quibus fēminīs? Cum quibus virīs? Cum tuīs?

11. Fīlius meī amīcī vīdit vōs, sed nōs neque tē neque tuōs sociōs vīdimus.

12. a) Ōdimus eōs quibus patria nōn placet, sed nōbīs est amor honestōrum piōrumque.
    b) Dīcimus nōs ōdisse eōs quibus patria nōn placeat.

13. Librī quōs ad nōs mīsistī ab hominibus quī amant suum opus scrīptī sunt.

14. Scrībisne in tuō librō dē generibus animālium quae scīs?

15. Dīxērunt dōna quae petītūrī essēmus pulchra futūra esse.

16. Isne est vir quem tua māter vīdit?

17. Cui fēminae dōna dedit quae optāverāmus?

18. Iī quī piō genere nātī sunt nōn sōlum amant patriam quam incolunt sed etiam ōdērunt hostēs quī eam invāsērunt.

19. Hic amat quod ille ōdit.

20. Quis est haec? Quis nostrārum fuit?

21. Dīcam servitūtem quae opprimat hōs quōs vīderitis malam esse.

22. Quī locus est? Ad quem locum vēnī et quōcum?

23. "Quis fuit?" "Marcus." "Quī Marcus?" "Is quī urbem hostibus quī multum tempus genus nostrum oppressissent invādendam esse dīxit."

24. Quae patria est tua?

25. Quem quīnque hōrīs vidēbō? Tē et tuōs.

26. Ille vir, cui patriae salūs est cāra, pius habētur ā populō quī eum scit, sed nōn sē amat.

27. Quod opus ante tempus perfēcistī? Quod opus eō tempore perfēcistī?

28. Tempore careō ut perficiam opus quod scrībō.

29. a) Cīvēs illārum urbium quae habuērunt rēgēs dāmnābātis.
    b) Sēnsit cīvēs illārum urbium quae rēgēs habērent dāmnandōs esse.

30. Quīnque hōrīs vidēbimus amīcōs quibuscum vīvēbāmus.

31. a) Rēx cuius soror Rōmae vīvit bene sē gessit.
    b) Scīmus rēgem cuius soror Rōmae vīvat bene sē gessisse.
    c) Scīmus rēgem cuius soror Rōmae diū vīxerit bene sē gerere.

32. Cuius liber quīnque annōs petītus est?

33. Tibine ea quibus opus est invēnistī? Quod nōn opus est, nōn est cārum.

34. Māter fīliō dīxit multam salūtem quem multōs annōs nōn vīderat.

35. Dīxit et sē et suōs amīcōs et vōs invidiā populī perīculīsque bellī premī; sē autem spērāre nec suōs nec vōs miserōs futūrōs esse. "Nisī malō premerēmur, numquam nātūram vītae intellegerēmus."

36. Tibi imperō ut sciās mortem nōn esse timendam: quae bona sī nōn est, fīnis tamen illa malōrum est.

37. Quīnque annīs bellum cum nostrīs hostibus gerere poterimus ex quibus spērāmus nōs multam pecūniam et magnum imperium captūrōs esse.

38. Dīcit illud opus tibi cōnfectum ā populō lēctum esse.

39. Ut laetī nōs sīmus, nōbīs amōre opus est.

40. Magnā vōce clāmāvimus multa eius generis inventa esse.

41. Sentīs vōcēs eōrum quī clāment eī hominī nōn placēre.

42. Quīnque pedēs ad dextram nōs mōvimus ut verba magistrī audīrēmus.

43. Illī vēnērunt ut quīnque hōrās tēcum agant. Quibuscum in oppidō ambulārēs nisī fessus essēs. [fessus, -a, -um, 'tired']

44. Cīvēs illīus oppidī spērābant nōs mox discessūrōs esse. Quī quamquam nōbīs erant amīcī, nōs nōn amāvērunt.

45. Rēx dīxit rūmōrēs in urbe audītōs esse pellendōs. Quae (eī) quī audiēbant probābant. [probō (1), 'approve (of)']

46. Eō tempore tuus ad nōs vēnit ut salūtem dīceret. Cui respondimus "Et nōs tibi salūtem dīcimus!"

**II.**

Rewrite sentences 11, 13, and 28 in indirect statement after **dīcit** and **dīcēbat**. Translate each of the sentences you wrote.

**III.**

1. What book is this which has been sent to us by our friends (by his friends) with whom we were walking?

2. The man whom you saw at that time is the sailor to whom I gave those gifts.

3. For five years he hoped that he would complete this, his own work, but now he hates it.

4. We said that we would move five feet to the right in order to see your king with his queen and their sons.

5. Those wretched people not only hate themselves, but they also say that we hate them.

**IV. Readings**

A. The poet Catullus, after renouncing his love for Lesbia, addresses her (Catullus 8.15–19):

...Quae tibi manet[1] vīta?
Quis nunc tē adībit?[2] Cui vidēberis bella?[3]
Quem nunc amābis? Cuius esse dīcēris?
Quem bāsiābis?[4] Cui labella[5] mordēbis?[6]

[1] **maneō, -ēre, mānsī, mānsus,** 'remain'    [2] **adībit** (3rd person sing. future indicative),
'will approach'    [3] **bellus, -a, -um,** 'beautiful'    [4] **bāsiō** (1), 'kiss'    [5] **labellum, -ī,** N.,
'little lip'    [6] **mordeō, -ēre, momordī, morsus,** 'bite'

NOTE: For some observations on the rhythm of this and subsequent selections from verse which will appear in the readings, see *A Note on Quantitative
Rhythm*, p. 401.

B. Martial 12.73:

Herēdem[1] tibi mē, Catulle,[2] dīcis.
Nōn crēdam,[3] nisi[4] lēgerō, Catulle.[2]

[1] **herēs, herēdis,** M., 'heir'    [2] **Catullus, -ī,** M., a man's name; here, it is in the vocative
case (the case of direct address; see Unit Eight, Section G)    [3] **crēdō, -ere, crēdidī, crēditus,**
'believe'    [4] **nisi** (for **nisī**): occasionally, certain metrical necessities cause a long vowel
to shorten in verse.

C. Catullus 58:

Caelī,[1] Lesbia nostra, Lesbia illa,
illa Lesbia, quam Catullus ūnam[2]
plūs[3] quam[4] sē atque suōs amāvit omnēs,[5]
nunc in quadriviīs[6] et angiportīs[7]
glūbit[8] magnanimī[9] Rēmī[10] nepōtēs.[11]

[1] **Caelius, -ī,** M., a man's name; here, in the vocative case (the case of direct address; see
Unit Eight, section G)    [2] **ūnus, -a, -um,** 'alone'    [3] **plūs** (adv.), 'more'    [4] **quam** (adv.),
'than'    [5] **omnēs** (acc. pl. M.), 'all'    [6] **quadrivium, -ī,** N., 'crossroads'    [7] **angiportum,
-ī,** N., 'alley'    [8] **glūbō, -ere,** 'bark, peel, skin'    [9] **magnanimus, -a, -um,** 'great-souled'
[10] **Rēmus, -ī,** M., 'Remus', the brother of Romulus, the founder of Rome    [11] **nepōs,
nepōtis,** M., 'descendant'

D. Martial 1.38:

Quem recitās[1] meus est, Ō Fīdentīne,[2] libellus:[3]
sed male[4] cum[5] recitās,[1] incipit esse tuus.

[1] **recitō** (1), 'recite'    [2] **Fīdentīnus, -ī,** M., a man's name; here, in the vocative case (the
case of direct address; see Unit Eight, section G)    [3] **libellus, -ī,** M., 'little book'    [4] **male**
(adv.), 'badly'    [5] **cum** (conj.), 'when'

E. Martial 1.32:

> Nōn amo tē, Sabidī,[1] nec possum dīcere quārē:[2]
>
> hoc tantum[3] possum dīcere, nōn amo tē.

[1] **Sabidius, -ī,** M., a man's name; here, in the vocative case (the case of direct address; see Unit Eight, section G)     [2] **quārē** (adv.), 'why'     [3] **tantum** (adv.), 'only'

F. Martial 5.43:

> Thāïs[1] habet nigrōs,[2] niveōs[3] Laecānia[1] dentēs.[4]
>
> Quae ratiō[5] est? Ēmptōs[6] haec habet, illa suōs.

[1] **Thāïs** and **Laecānia** are names of women in the nominative case.     [2] **niger, nigra, nigrum,** 'black'     [3] **niveus, -a, -um,** 'snowy white'     [4] **dēns, dentis,** M., 'tooth'     [5] **ratiō, -ōnis,** F., 'reason'     [6] **emō, -ere, ēmī, ēmptus,** 'buy'

G. Martial 12.80:

> Nē laudet[1] dīgnōs,[2] laudat[1] Callistratus[3] omnēs.[4]
>
> Cui malus est nēmō,[5] quis bonus esse potest?

[1] **laudō** (1), 'praise'     [2] **dīgnus, -a, -um,** 'worthy'     [3] **Callistratus, -ī,** M., a man's name     [4] **omnēs** (acc. pl. M.), 'all' (i.e., 'everyone')     [5] **nēmō** (nom. sing.), 'no one'

H. Martial 7.3:

> Cūr[1] nōn mitto meōs tibi, Pontiliāne,[2] libellōs?[3]
>
> Nē mihi tū mittās, Pontiliāne,[2] tuōs.

[1] **cūr** (adv.), 'why'     [2] **Pontiliānus, -ī,** M., a man's name; here, in the vocative case (the case of direct address; see Unit Eight, section G)     [3] **libellus, -ī,** M., 'little book'

I. Cicero, *In Catilīnam* II.12.27:

Nunc illōs quī in urbe remānsērunt[1] atque adeō[2] quī contrā[3] urbis salūtem omniumque[4] vestrum in urbe ā Catilīnā relictī sunt,[5] quamquam sunt hostēs, tamen, quia[6] nātī sunt[7] cīvēs, monitōs etiam atque etiam[8] volō.[9]

[1] **remaneō, -ēre, remānsī, remānsus,** 'remain'     [2] **adeō** (adv.), 'thus far'     [3] **contrā** (prep. + acc.), 'against'     [4] **omnium** (gen. pl.), 'all'     [5] **relinquō, -ere, relīquī, relictus,** 'leave behind'     [6] **quia** (conj.), 'because'     [7] **nātī sunt,** 'they were born'     [8] **etiam atque etiam,** 'again and again'     [9] **volō, velle, voluī, ––,** 'want'

# UNIT EIGHT

**A. Adjectives of the Third Declension; Present Participles**
There are two types of adjectives in Latin:

1. those which have the endings of the first and second declensions;
2. those which have the endings of the third declension.

First-second declension adjectives have already been learned. Most third declension adjectives are declined largely like i-stem nouns of the third declension. The important features are:

> ablative singular: **-ī**
> genitive plural: **-ium**
> accusative plural (M. and F.): **-īs** as well as **-ēs**
> nominative and accusative plural (N.): **-ia**

Adjectives of the first and second declension have three terminations; that is, there is a separate nominative singular form for each of the three genders (**bonus, -a, -um**). Adjectives of the third declension can have either three, two, or one termination. These varieties are illustrated below.

1. ADJECTIVES OF THREE TERMINATIONS
   Adjectives of three terminations are given in the vocabulary in the masculine, feminine, and neuter nominative: **ācer, ācris, ācre**, 'sharp'.

|  | SINGULAR | | | PLURAL | |
|---|---|---|---|---|---|
| M. | F. | N. | M. | F. | N. |
| ācer | ācris | ācre | ācrēs | ācrēs | ācria |
| ācris | ācris | ācris | ācrium | ācrium | ācrium |
| ācrī | ācrī | ācrī | ācribus | ācribus | ācribus |
| ācrem | ācrem | ācre | ācrēs(-īs) | ācrēs(-īs) | ācria |
| ācrī | ācrī | ācrī | ācribus | ācribus | ācribus |

The stem for such adjectives will be found by dropping the ending from the feminine singular nominative form.

126

## 2. ADJECTIVES OF TWO TERMINATIONS

Adjectives of two terminations are given in the vocabulary in the masculine-feminine and neuter nominative: **omnis, omne**, 'every, all'.

| SINGULAR | | PLURAL | |
|---|---|---|---|
| M., F. | N. | M., F. | N. |
| omnis | omne | omnēs | omnia |
| omnis | omnis | omnium | omnium |
| omnī | omnī | omnibus | omnibus |
| omnem | omne | omnēs(-īs) | omnia |
| omnī | omnī | omnibus | omnibus |

## 3. ADJECTIVES OF ONE TERMINATION

Adjectives of one termination are given in the vocabulary in the masculine-feminine-neuter nominative and the genitive singular: **ingēns, ingentis**, 'huge'.

| SINGULAR | PLURAL |
|---|---|
| M., F., N. | M., F., N. |
| ingēns | ingentēs, ingentia (neut.) |
| ingentis | ingentium |
| ingentī | ingentibus |
| ingentem, ingēns (neut.) | ingentēs(-īs), ingentia (neut.) |
| ingentī | ingentibus |

The genitive singular for adjectives of one termination is given so that the stem on which the declension is built may be known.

## 4. PRESENT PARTICIPLES

Present participles are declined like third declension adjectives of one termination.

| SINGULAR | PLURAL |
|---|---|
| M., F., N. | M., F., N. |
| optāns | optantēs, optantia (neut.) |
| optantis | optantium |
| optantī | optantibus |
| optantem, optāns (neut.) | optantēs(-īs), optantia (neut.) |
| optantī(-e) | optantibus |

NOTE: For the moment, the following distinction between the -ī and -e endings of the ablative singular should be remembered:

-ī generally occurs when the participle is used as an attributive adjective
-e generally occurs when the participle is used as a noun

## B. Fourth Declension Nouns

The genitive singular ending for the fourth declension is -ūs. While there are three genders of nouns in this declension, the neuter is rare.

frūctus, -ūs, M., 'enjoyment'

|       | SINGULAR | PLURAL     |
|-------|----------|------------|
| Nom.  | frūctus  | frūctūs    |
| Gen.  | frūctūs  | frūctuum   |
| Dat.  | frūctuī  | frūctibus  |
| Acc.  | frūctum  | frūctūs    |
| Abl.  | frūctū   | frūctibus  |

*Most* nouns ending in -us in this declension are *masculine*; the others are feminine. Neuter nouns differ from this paradigm in these places:

1. the nominative and accusative singular end in -ū
2. the dative singular ends in -ū
3. the nominative and accusative plural end in -ua

## C. Fifth Declension Nouns

The genitive singular ending is -eī, but when the stem ends in a vowel, the ending is -ēī. Most nouns of the fifth declension are *feminine*.

rēs, reī, F., 'thing'

|       | SINGULAR | PLURAL   |
|-------|----------|----------|
| Nom.  | rēs      | rēs      |
| Gen.  | reī      | rērum    |
| Dat.  | reī      | rēbus    |
| Acc.  | rem      | rēs      |
| Abl.  | rē       | rēbus    |

NOTE: This completes our discussion of the declensional system in Latin. There are no adjectives which have the endings of the fourth and fifth declensions. Also, the number of nouns which belong to these two declensions is limited; the great bulk of Latin nouns belongs to the third declension.

## D. Ablative of Respect (Specification)

The *respect* in which a statement is true is expressed by the *ablative without a preposition.*

Haec fēmina **speciē** pulchra est.    This woman is beautiful *in (respect to) appearance.*

**Meā sententiā** nihil perficient.    *In (respect to) my opinion,* they will accomplish nothing.

## E. The Irregular Verb *eō, īre,* 'go'

The verb **eō, īre, iī** (or **īvī**), **itus**, 'go', exhibits some irregularities in the present system. The rest of the verb is regular, except as follows:

1. In the perfect active indicative, the second person singular is **istī** (for **iistī**), and the second person plural is **īstis** (for **iistis**).
2. The perfect active infinitive is **īsse** (for **iisse**), which provides the stem for the pluperfect active subjunctive. For the full conjugation, see Appendix, pp. 354–355.

| PRESENT INDICATIVE | | PRESENT SUBJUNCTIVE | |
|---|---|---|---|
| eō | īmus | eam | eāmus |
| īs | ītis | eās | eātis |
| it | eunt | eat | eant |

| IMPERFECT INDICATIVE | | FUTURE INDICATIVE | |
|---|---|---|---|
| (conjugates according to normal rules for the imperfect, but with no -iē-) | | (conjugates like first-second conjugation verbs with -bi-) | |
| ībam | ībāmus | ībō | ībimus |
| ībās | ībātis | ibis | ībitis |
| ībat | ībant | ībit | ībunt |

PRESENT PARTICIPLE
iēns, euntis

## F. The Present Imperative (imperō (1), 'command')

The *imperative* is the mood of *command*. The present imperative is formed for the four conjugations as follows:

1. ACTIVE

For all conjugations, the *singular* imperative active is the present stem:

| optā! | desire! | incipe! | begin! |
|---|---|---|---|
| implē! | fill! | sentī! | feel! |

For the first, second, and fourth conjugations, the *plural* imperative is formed by adding -te to the present stem; for the third conjugation, the stem vowel is changed from -e- to -i- before adding -te:

| optāte! | desire! | incipite! | begin! |
|---|---|---|---|
| implēte! | fill! | sentīte! | feel! |

EXCEPTIONS: The following third conjugation verbs do not have the -e in the singular of the present imperative active: **dīcō**, 'say'; **dūcō**, 'lead'; **faciō**, 'make, do'; **ferō**, 'carry'.

| dīc! | BUT | dīcite! |
|------|-----|---------|
| dūc! |     | dūcite! |
| fac! |     | facite! |
| fer! |     | ferte! (note absence of stem vowel -i-) |

## 2. PASSIVE

The singular imperative passive is identical to the second person singular of the present passive indicative with the -re ending:

| optāre! | be desired! |
|---------|-------------|
| implēre! | be filled! |
| incipere! | be begun! |
| sentīre! | be felt! |

It will be noted that these forms look like those of the present active infinitive.

The plural imperative passive is identical to the second person plural of the present passive indicative:

| optāminī! | be desired! |
|-----------|-------------|
| implēminī! | be filled! |
| incipiminī! | be begun! |
| sentīminī! | be felt! |

## 3. NEGATIVE IMPERATIVES, ACTIVE AND PASSIVE

Negative imperatives are expressed by the command words **nōlī** (singular) and **nōlīte** (plural), 'be unwilling', followed by the present infinitive of the verb:

| Nōlī optāre! | Don't (sing.) desire! |
|--------------|------------------------|
| Nōlī optārī! | Don't (sing.) be desired! |
| Nōlī implēre! | Don't (sing.) fill! |
| Nōlī implērī! | Don't (sing.) be filled! |
| Nōlī dūcere! | Don't (sing.) lead! |
| Nōlī dūcī! | Don't (sing.) be led! |
| Nōlīte dūcere! | Don't (pl.) lead! |
| Nōlīte dūcī! | Don't (pl.) be led! |

Negative imperatives may also be expressed with the present or perfect subjunctive (with no obvious distinction in meaning) introduced by **nē**:

| Nē optēs. | May you not desire; (I hope that you) don't desire. |
|-----------|------------------------------------------------------|
| Nē dūcātis. | May you not lead; (I hope that you) don't lead. |
| Nē dūxeritis. | May you not lead; (I hope that you) don't lead. |

[Another imperative form, the so-called *future imperative*, appears rarely in Latin, generally in formal or legal documents and as a regular imperative for a few verbs. It has been omitted from the exercises in this book, but it is discussed in the Appendix, p. 362.]

**G. The Vocative Case (*vocō* (1), 'call')**
The *vocative* is the case of *direct address*. It is generally identical to the nominative, except for second declension nouns ending in **-us** or **-ius**:

Nouns ending in **-us** have a vocative singular in **-e**:

> Marcus venit.   Marcus is coming.
> **Marce**, venī!   *Marcus*, come!

Nouns ending in **-ius** have a vocative singular in **-ī**:

> Vergilius carmen scrīpsit.   Vergil wrote a poem.
> **Vergilī**, scrībe carmen!   *Vergil*, write a poem!

The adjective **meus, -a, -um**, 'my', has the masculine singular vocative **mī**:

> Meus fīlius venit.   My son is coming.
> **Mī fīlī**, venī!   *My son*, come!

All plural vocatives are identical to the nominative plural.

**H. Datives of Purpose (Service) and Reference: The Double Dative Construction**
Two datives frequently appear in close proximity, one denoting the *purpose* (*service*) with reference to which the action or idea expressed in the clause occurs, the other denoting the person or thing with reference to whom or which the action or idea occurs or is relevant.

> Fīliī **mātrī frūctuī** sunt.   The sons are (*for the purpose of*) *an asset* (*with reference*) *to their mother*; the sons serve *as an asset to* (*for*) *their mother*; the sons are *an asset to their mother*.
>
> Ad urbem **salūtī mihi** vēnit.   He came to the city *for* (*the purpose of*) *a salvation* (*with reference*) *to* (*for*) *me*; he came to the city *to save me*.
>
> Opīniō malī **perīculō** erat **cīvitātī**.   The opinion of the evil (man) was (*for the purpose of*) *a danger* (*with reference*) *to the state*.

# UNIT EIGHT — VOCABULARY

| | |
|---|---|
| **ācer, ācris, ācre** | sharp, keen, fierce |
| **carmen, -inis**, N. | song, poem, incantation |
| **cīvitās, cīvitātis**, F. | citizenship; state |

| | |
|---|---|
| diēs, -ēī, M. | day |
| domus, -ūs and -ī, F. | house, home |
| dulcis, -e | sweet, pleasant |
| eō, īre, iī (or īvī), itus | go |
| fēlīx, fēlīcis | happy, fortunate |
| īnfēlīx, -īcis | unhappy, unfortunate |
| fidēs, -eī, F. | faith, trust, trustworthiness |
| fortis, -e | strong, brave |
| frīgidus, -a, -um | cold |
| frūctus, -ūs, M. | enjoyment; fruit; profit |
| frūctuī esse | to be (for [the purpose of]) a profit, be an asset to (+ dat.) |
| fulgeō, -ēre, fulsī, –– | flash, shine |
| gravis, -e | heavy, severe, important |
| iaciō, -ere, iēcī, iactus | throw |
| iactō (1) | throw, scatter, shake; boast |
| ingēns, ingentis | huge |
| īra, -ae, F. | wrath, anger |
| iubeō, -ēre, iussī, iussus | order, command (+ inf., not **ut** clause of indirect command) |
| lībertās, lībertātis, F. | freedom |
| lītus, lītoris, N. | shore, beach |
| longus, -a, -um | long |
| longē (adv.) | far off, at a distance, far and wide |
| lūx, lūcis, F. | light |
| prīmā lūce | at the first light, at daybreak |
| manus, -ūs, F. | hand; band, troop |
| memor, memoris | mindful, remembering (+ gen.) |
| metus, -ūs, M. | fear, dread |
| mōtus, -ūs, M. | motion, movement |
| nōmen, nōminis, N. | name |
| nūmen, nūminis, N. | divinity, divine spirit |
| ob (prep. + acc.) | on account of |
| quam ob rem | on account of which thing, for what reason, why |
| omnis, -e | every, all |
| opīniō, -ōnis, F. | opinion |
| pectus, -oris, N. | heart, breast |
| prō (prep. + abl.) | in front of, for, on behalf of, instead of, in return for |
| profugus, -a, -um | fugitive, banished, exiled |
| pūblicus, -a, -um | public |

| | |
|---|---|
| quaerō, -ere, quaesīvī, quaesītus | look for, search for, seek, ask |
| rēs, reī, F. | thing, matter, affair, situation |
|   rēs pūblica | state, republic |
| saevus, -a, -um | cruel |
| sēnsus, -ūs, M. | sensation, feeling |
| speciēs, -ēī, F. | appearance |
| spēs, -eī, F. | hope |
| superus, -a, -um | above, upper |
|   superī, -ōrum, M. pl. | the gods above |
| vertex, verticis, M. | head, top, summit; whirlpool, whirlwind |

## UNIT EIGHT — NOTES ON VOCABULARY

The suffix -tās, -tātis is a feminine ending of abstract nouns which indicates a quality or state. Cīvis is a citizen; cīvitās, cīvitātis, F., is the 'state of being a citizen', thus, 'citizenship, state'. Līber, 'free', thus becomes the stem of the abstract noun lībertās, lībertātis, F., 'the state of being free', i.e., 'freedom'.

Diēs, diēī is one of the two masculine nouns in the fifth declension (the other is a compound of diēs). Sometimes it occurs in the singular as feminine, especially when a specific day is meant or when the reference is to time in general: longa diēs, 'a long day'.

Domus, 'house, home', has some forms which belong to the second declension and others which belong to the fourth declension; therefore, it is given in this book as both a second and fourth declension noun. The most common forms are:

| | |
|---|---|
| domus | domūs |
| domūs | domuum |
| domuī | domibus |
| domum | domōs |
| domō | domibus |

The locative is domī.

The verb eō, īre, iī or īvī, itus, 'go', in the perfect active stem may shorten from -īv- to -i-. There are many compounds of this verb:

| | |
|---|---|
| adeō | go to, approach |
| abeō | go away, depart |
| circumeō | go around, surround |
| ineō | go in, enter |
| exeō | go out, depart |
|     ...etc. | |

Fēlīx, fēlīcis, 'happy, fortunate', takes the negative prefix in- to form the word for 'unhappy, unfortunate', īnfēlīx, īnfēlīcis.

Frūctus, frūctūs, M., 'enjoyment, fruit, profit', is used in the dative case with the verb sum to form the idiom frūctuī esse, 'to be an asset to': Nauta rēgīnae frūctuī erat, 'The sailor was an asset to the queen'.

Iaciō, iacere, iēcī, iactus, 'throw', produces the frequentative verb iactō. A frequentative verb is usually a first conjugation verb formed from the fourth principal part of another verb and which, originally, had the idea of the action being repeated; in many verbs, this idea became lost in time and no discernible difference in meaning is seen in the two verbs. However, iactō does have the additional meaning 'boast'.

Iubeō, iubēre, iussī, iussus, 'order', is the only verb of ordering in Latin that does not regularly use the construction for an indirect command (ut or nē with the subjunctive), but rather an infinitive with subject accusative: Rēgīna nautās vēla dare iussit, 'The queen ordered the sailors to set sail'.

The word manus, manūs is feminine even though, in addition to the meaning 'hand', it means 'a band (of men)'.

Mōtus, mōtūs, M., is a noun of the fourth declension made from the perfect passive participle of moveō; it means 'motion, movement'. In the same way, sēnsus, sēnsūs, M., 'sensation, feeling', is formed from the perfect passive participle of sentiō.

The verb quaerō, quaerere, quaesīvī, quaesītus, 'seek, ask (for)', may introduce an indirect command: Quaesīvimus nē domum īrēs, 'We asked that you not go home'. If one seeks something from someone, either ā (ab), dē, or ex is used: Pecūniam ab (dē, ex) amīcīs quaesīvimus, 'We sought money from our friends'.

Rēs, reī, F., is an abstract word with many meanings, e.g., 'thing, matter, affair, situation, business, lawsuit, event, property'; rēs pūblica is the 'public thing, the public matter', therefore, 'state, republic'.

# UNIT EIGHT — DRILL

## I.

Give a form of the adjectives magnus, -a, -um, gravis, -e, and ingēns, ingentis to go with each of the following noun forms. In some cases, there may be several possible interpretations.

| | | | |
|---|---|---|---|
| 1. frāter | 8. sīdera | 15. manūs | 22. perīculōrum |
| 2. noctis | 9. rēgum | 16. manuī | 23. dōnō |
| 3. sīdus | 10. rūmōribus | 17. diēs | 24. bella |
| 4. mātrī | 11. frātrum | 18. frūctibus | 25. gladiō |
| 5. sorōrem | 12. servitūtem | 19. spem | 26. nautae |
| 6. homine | 13. corporis | 20. manuum | |
| 7. hominēs | 14. reī | 21. prōvinciae | |

## II.

Translate and give the syntax of the words in boldface type:

1. Hic homō **mente** est validus.
2. Haec fēmina pulchra est **fōrmā**.
3. Ille cīvis sānus est **corpore**.
4. Illī īnfēlīcēs sunt **salūte**.
5. Superātī mīlitēs **vītā** et **vigōre** sunt miserī.
6. Sī Rōmam **eat**, amīcīs nōn careat.
7. Nisī mīlitēs **urbī salūtī ībunt**, magnus erit timor.
8. Sī ad īnsulam **isset** (**īret**), fēlīx fuissem (essem).
9. Rōmam **it**; Athēnās **eunt**; Eīs imperō ut Athēnās **eant**; Ad urbem **ībant**; Eīs imperābam nē ad urbem **īrent**.
10. Homō ad prōvinciam **iēns** erat intellegēns.
11. Quae est fīlia hominis ad prōvinciam **euntis**?
12. Dīcō hominī ad prōvinciam **euntī** esse fīliam **speciē** pulchram.
13. **Discēde** ē prōvinciā!
14. **Oppūgnāte** urbem cum vigōre!
15. **Nōlī discēdere** ē prōvinciā! **Nē discesseris** (**discēdās**) ē prōvinciā!
16. **Nōlīte oppūgnāre** urbem! **Nē oppūgnāveritis** (**oppūgnētis**) urbem!
17. **Nōlī, amīce, spectāre** montem; **spectā** campum!
18. **Mī fīlī, nōlī** timōre **opprimī**! **Nē** timōre **oppressus sīs** (**opprimāris**)!
19. Morsne erit bonō **fīnī vītae** nostrae?
20. Mīlitēs **timōrī** cīvibus missī sunt.

# UNIT EIGHT — PRELIMINARY EXERCISES
## (SECTIONS A, B, C)

1. Haec cīvitās īnfēlīx metū gravī dēlētur.
2. Sēnsūs omnīs dē lībertāte mūtāvimus.
3. Sēnsūs gravēs nōbīs mūtandī erant.
4. Sēnsūs nostrī dē fidē eōrum prō lībertāte pūgnantium mūtandī sunt.
5. Ācrēs sunt opīniōnēs oppressōrum dē rē pūblicā.
6. Quam ob rem īnfēlīcēs domum īre iussī sunt?
7. Nōbīs est metus nūminum omnium.
8. In hāc cīvitāte omnibus est magna spēs lībertātis.
9. Memorēs metuum suōrum, profugī prīmā lūce discessērunt.
10. Carmina dulcia dē frūctū vītae audīvērunt.
11. Mihi quaerentī opus est mente ācrī ut haec intellegam.

12. Semper erimus rērum omnium memorēs dē reī pūblicae spēbus.
13. Sīdera fulgentia in caelō vīdimus.
14. Opus est reī pūblicae manūs fortium.


# UNIT EIGHT — EXERCISES

## I.

1. Intellegitur pectus rēgīnae dulcis in cuius terrā vīvāmus flammīs ācribus amōris saevī ardēre.

2. Rēx ācer, salūtem sociīs quaerēns, iussit mīlitēs fortēs cīvitātem patrum nostrōrum gravem ignibus gladiīsque superāre ut nostra bona sibi frūctuī essent.

3. a) Lūx aurea aurōrae sīdera quae flammīs frīgidīs nocte fulgent vertice caelī removet.
   b) Lūx aurea aurōrae sīdera flammīs frīgidīs nocte fulgentia vertice caelī removet.

4. Nautae oppressī in mediō marī ventīs ācribus et frīgidīs iactātī clāmāvērunt: "Ō fēlīcēs dī, nostrī memorēs, pellite ventōs ā nōbīs. Removēte noxam. Nōs sumus frīgidī atque miserī. Pōnite īram vestram et iubēte mare magnīs undīs carēre. Haec quaerimus prō omnibus dulcibus quae vōbīs dedimus."

5. Sī puerī fēlīcēs, Rōmā discēdentēs, Athēnās eant, carmina pulchra poētae caecī audiant.

6. Mīlitēs fortēs sociōs Rōmānōrum gladiīs et armīs suīs oppūgnāvērunt ut moenia ingentia urbis īnfēlīcis caperent.

7. Pater meus mihi dīxit Rōmānōrum manum, factīs fēlīcem, omnem rem pūblicam sine morā captūram esse; nūminibus enim deōrum salūtem eōrum cūrae futūram esse.

8. Illud perīculum gravī rēgī superandum est ut cum oppūgnantī manū mīlitum sociōrum prō lībertāte pūgnet. Rēx, ī et pūgnā cum oppūgnante! Nōlī timēre! Sī metus tibi erit, nīl perficiēs.

9. Hominēs fortēs quōs in nōmine rēgis mīsistī ut nōbīs cibum pecūniamque darent mīlitibus nostrīs captīs frūctuī fuērunt.

10. Omnēs mīlitēs spem fidemque rēgīnae dedērunt cuius oppidum ab invādentibus profugīs superātum erat. Nē dūxeris, rēgīna, invādentēs oppidum dēlētūrōs esse. Meā opīniōne, omnēs vī superōrum in salūte pōnēmur.

11. Iacite magna saxa in mare ut in lītore sine perīculō ambulēmus.

12. Ō Marce! Dūc ad lībertātem patriam tuam! Quaere virōs impiōs et malōs! Iace illōs ē rē pūblicā nōn sōlum prō cīvibus līberīs sed etiam prō tē!

13. Opus est mihi mente ācrī ut haec intellegam.

14.         Arma virumque canō, Trōiae[1] quī prīmus[2] ab ōrīs[3]
            [ad] Ītaliam, fātō[4] profugus, Lāvīnaque[5] vēnit [ad]
            lītora, multum[6] ille et [in] terrīs iactātus et [in] altō
            vī super[ōr]um, saevae memorem Iūnōnis ob īram.
                             (Vergil, *Aeneid* I.1–4)

     [1] **Trōia, -ae,** F., 'Troy'     [2] **prīmus, -a, -um,** 'first'     [3] **ōra, -ae,** F., 'shore'
[4] **fātum, -ī,** N., 'fate'     [5] **Lāvīnus, -a, -um,** 'Lavinian', refers to Lavinium, a city of
Latium founded by Aeneas     [6] **multum** (used adverbially), 'a great deal, a lot'

15. Profugō, lībertātis rutae memorī et salūtem sorōribus frātribusque quaerentī,
metus opprimentium saevōrum ingēns multōs diēs erat.

16. Quam ob rem domūs illīus manūs nōs in perīculō pōnentis dēlētae sunt?
Prō salūte reī pūblicae!

17. Scīmus metum rūmōris per oppida euntis magnum esse; Ō rūmōrēs dīcentēs,
īte in malam rem!

18. Deō scrībe carmina, cuius nūminī placent omnia pia.

19. Nōlīte ārās deōrum fulgentēs flammīs ingentibus dēlēre, nisī ab eīs opprimī
optētis.

20. Postquam manum mīlitum suam superātam vīdit sēque lībertātem mox
perditūrum, memor generis amīcōrumque et vīrium, in bellum ruit atque
pūgnāns interfectus est.

21. Rōma enim vertex omnium est cīvitātum. Quam ob rem ex urbe cēdis?

22. Sēnsus eōrum dē rē pūblicā mihi placeat nisī genus suum et nōmen semper
populō dīcentēs iactent.

23. Nisī rēgīna īnfēlīx amōre perdita esset, patriam ingentem numquam
trādidisset et nunc omnēs eam populum bene regentem canerent. Multa enim
amīcīs salūtem quaerentibus semper fēcerat; lībertās salūsque omnium
semper eī cūrae fuerant. Haec autem omnia mala eī ob amōrem sunt.

24. Vir fāmā ingēns glōriāque et vīribus sua iēcit in lītus arma dīcēns sē
numquam prō patriā pūgnātūrum esse nisī ingentia facta rēgī ā cīvibus
mōnstrārentur.

25. Ovidius poēta dīcit dūrum hominum genus saxīs in terram iactātīs nātum
esse. [**Ovidius, -ī,** M., 'Ovid', a poet of the Augustan Age]

26. Helena, speciē pulchra, salūtem petēbat iēns longē sub lūnā per oppidum
ardēns. Incolentibus oppidum neque spēs erat neque frūctus. Dī superī,
prīmā lūce post longum tempus domibus in oppidō discessērunt et novās
quaesīvērunt. [**Helena -ae,** F., 'Helen', the name of the Greek woman over
whom the Trojan war was fought]

27. Nē longum sit, cīvēs, vōbīs omnia dīcam ut dē sententiīs huius rēgis sciātis.

28. Cīvēs, intellegite spem omnium in vestrīs manibus positam esse; pōnite
vestram spem in armīs et pūgnāte magnā cum fidē et vigōre.

29. Ille est homō sine rē, sine fidē, sine spē.

30. a) Socius nōs iussit corpora lūce carentium ā campō removēre.

    b) Socius nōbīs imperāvit ut corpora lūce carentium ā campō removērēmus.

31. Magister nōbīs dē mōtibus sīderum in pūblicō dīxit.

## II.

1. He felt that the enemy was serving as the author of evil for that city which had been oppressed for many years by all sorts of destruction.
(use double dative construction)

2. Soldiers! Destroy the republic! Overcome all free men! Throw liberty, hope, and faith out of the state! Know that all men are your slaves!

3. At daybreak the fugitives, unfortunate in appearance, going hopefully through all the streets of the town, were sought far and wide by the soldiers.

4. Mindful of all dangers, the fugitives went from home, throwing cares from their breasts and seeking Rome as the summit to their hopes.

5. Marcus, my son, don't look at the arms of the invaders shining in the light of the moon.

## III. Readings
### A. Martial 5.57:

> Cum[1] voco tē dominum, nōlī tibi, Cinna,[2] placēre:
> saepe[3] etiam[4] servum sīc[5] resalūto[6] tuum.

[1] cum (conj.), 'when'   [2] Cinna, -ae, M., a man's name   [3] saepe (adv.), 'often'
[4] etiam (adv.), 'even'   [5] sīc (adv.), 'thus, in this way'   [6] resalūtō (1), 'greet in return'

### B. Martial 5.58:

> Crās[1] tē vīctūrum, crās[1] dīcis, Postume,[2] semper.
> Dīc mihi, crās[1] istud,[3] Postume,[2] quando[4] venit?
> Quam[5] longē crās[1] istud,[3] ubi[6] est? Aut[7] unde[8] petendum?
> Numquid[9] apud[10] Parthōs[11] Armeniōsque[12] latet?[13]
> Iam[14] crās[1] istud[3] habet Priamī[15] vel[16] Nestoris[17] annōs.
>
>    . . .
>
> Crās[1] vīvēs? Hodiē[18] iam[14] vīvere, Postume,[2] sērum[19] est:
> ille sapit[20] quisquis,[21] Postume,[2] vīxit heri.[22]

[1] crās (adv.), 'tomorrow'   [2] Postumus, -ī, M., a man's name   [3] istud (nom. sing. N.), 'that (of yours)'; here, modifying crās, which is being used as a noun   [4] quandō (interrogative adv.), 'when'   [5] quam (adv.), 'how'   [6] ubi (adv.), 'where'   [7] aut (conj.), 'or'   [8] unde (adv.), 'from which place, from where'   [9] numquid (interrogative adv.), introduces a question; do not translate   [10] apud (prep. + acc.), 'at, with, among'   [11] Parthus, -ī, M., 'a Parthian'   [12] Armenius, -ī, M., 'an Armenian'   [13] lateō, -ēre, latuī, −−, 'lie hidden'   [14] iam (adv.), 'now, already'   [15] Priamus, -ī, M., 'Priam', aged king of Troy   [16] vel (conj.), 'or'   [17] Nestor, -oris, M., 'Nestor', an aged Greek   [18] hodiē (adv.), 'today'   [19] sērus, -a, -um, 'late, too late'   [20] sapiō, -ere, -īvī, −−, 'be wise'   [21] quisquis (nom. sing. M.), 'whoever'   [22] heri (adv.), 'yesterday'

C. A selection from Terence, *Eunuch* 130–135 (very slightly adapted). Thais explains how she came into the ownership of one of her slave women, Pamphila, supposed to be her sister.

> Hoc audīte amābō.[1] Māter mea illīc[2] mortua est[3]
> nūper,[4] cuius frāter aliquantum[5] ad[6] rem[7] est avidus.[8]
> Is ubi[9] esse hanc fōrmā[10] videt honestā virginem[11]
> et fidibus[12] scīre,[13] pretium[14] spērāns[15] īlicō[16]
> prōdūcit,[17] vendit.[18] Forte[19] fortūnā[19] adfuit[20]
> hic meus amīcus: emit[21] eam dōnō mihi,
> imprūdēns[22] hārum rērum īgnārusque[23] omnium.

[1] **amābō**, the idiomatic way of saying "please"    [2] **illīc** (adv.), 'there'    [3] **mortua est**, '(she) died'    [4] **nūper** (adv.), 'recently'    [5] **aliquantum** (adv.), 'somewhat'    [6] **ad** (prep. + acc.), *here* 'for (the purpose of)'    [7] **rēs**, *here* 'material gain, profit'    [8] **avidus, -a, -um**, 'eager'    [9] **ubi** (conj.), 'when'    [10] **fōrmā...honestā**: the ablative is here used to describe **hanc...virginem**, this maiden 'of distinguished beauty' (see Unit Ten, section D)    [11] **virgō, -inis**, F., 'maiden'    [12] **fidēs, -ium**, F. (pl.), 'a lyre, stringed instrument'    [13] **sciō**, *here* 'be knowledgeable, skilled'    [14] **pretium, -ī**, N., 'price'    [15] **spērō** (1), 'hope (for)'    [16] **īlicō** (adv.), 'right there, on the spot'    [17] **prōdūcō** (prō + dūcō), 'lead forth, put up (for auction)'    [18] **vendō, -ere, vendidī, venditus**, 'sell'    [19] **forte fortūnā**, 'by great good luck', **Fors Fortūna**, a goddess whom the Romans associated with great strokes of good luck    [20] **adsum** (ad + sum), 'be present'    [21] **emō, -ere, ēmī, ēmptus**, 'buy'    [22] **imprūdēns, imprūdentis**, 'unaware (of)' (+ gen.)    [23] **īgnārus, -a, -um**, 'ignorant (of)' (+ gen.)

D. A WEALTHY MAN DESCRIBES HIS TOMBSTONE (Petronius, *Satyricon* 71.9):

> Tē rogō[1] ut nāvēs[2] etiam[3] in monumentō[4] meō faciās plēnīs[5] vēlīs euntēs, et mē in tribūnālī[6] sedentem[7] praetextātum[8] cum ānulīs[9] aureīs quīnque et nummōs[10] in pūblicō dē sacculō[11] effundentem.[12]

[1] **rogō** (1), 'ask'    [2] **nāvis, nāvis**, F., 'ship'    [3] **etiam** (adv.), 'even'    [4] **monumentum, -ī**, N., 'monument'    [5] **plēnus, -a, -um**, 'full'    [6] **tribūnal, -ālis**, N., 'raised platform' (on which magistrates sat)    [7] **sedeō, -ēre, sēdī, sessus**, 'sit'    [8] **praetextātus, -a, -um**, 'wearing the toga worn by magistrates'    [9] **ānulus, -ī**, M., 'ring'    [10] **nummus, -ī**, M., 'coin'    [11] **sacculus, -ī**, M., 'purse'    [12] **effundō, -ere, -fūdī, -fūsus**, 'pour out'

# REVIEW: UNITS FIVE TO EIGHT

**Review of Syntax**

1. Amīce, nē mihi illud dīxeris; nōlī mihi illud dīcere; dīc illud mihi.
   (vocative; negative and positive imperatives; complementary infinitive)

2. Illīs vītam male agentibus sunt multae cūrae. [**male**, 'badly']
   (dative of the possessor)

3. Bellum prō patriā gestūrī et sociīs dīcentēs mortis timōrem ex animō pellendum esse, ā locō nostrī cessērunt nōn sōlum ut ad campum hostium īrent sed etiam ut exemplum mīlitibus pōnerent.
   (subject accusative and passive periphrastic infinitive in indirect statement; ablative of separation; ablative of place from which; accusative of place to which with **ad**; dative of reference)

4. Cēnantī mihi cum fēminā et fīliīs liber ā servō semper legitur. [**cēnō** (1), 'dine']
   (ablative of accompaniment)

5. Meā opīniōne, illī profugī sentiunt lībertātem cīvium dēlendam esse (fuisse).
   (ablative of respect; subject accusative and passive periphrastic infinitive in indirect statement)

6. Eō tempore rēx spērāvit sē urbem timōre et servitūte līberātūrum esse. Illā autem nocte interfectus est. Nunc cīvitās rēge bonō caret.
   (ablatives of time when; subject accusative and infinitive in indirect statement; ablatives of separation)

7. Populus nōn sōlum ab īnsulā sed etiam Rōmā salūtī cīvitātī vēnit.
   (ablative of place from which, with and without a preposition; double dative construction)

8. Hominibus semper est cūra dē pecūniā; dīs numquam.
   (datives of possessor)

9. Rōmae Athēnīsque et multīs in urbibus populus līber semper pūgnābit ut multa bona habeat. In hāc autem urbe lībertās populī ā rēge ācrī dēlēta est; opus est fortī ut cīvēs līberī sint.
   (locatives; place where with **in**; **opus est** with the ablative)

10. Dē caelō, terrā, maribus montibusque magister multa dīxit ut dē nātūrā intellegāmus.

11. Quīnque annīs eius corpus vigōre caruit quī semper ante fuerat.
    (ablative of time within which; possession with the pronoun **is, ea, id**; ablative of separation)

12. Dīxistis illum multōs vestrum eō diē domum quae ab invādentibus dēlērētur sine morā missūrum esse ut hostēs rūre pellerētis.
    (ablative of time when; accusative of place to which without a preposition with the word **domus**; subject accusative and infinitive in indirect statement; subjunctive in a subordinate clause within an indirect statement; ablative of place from which without a preposition with the word **rūs**)

13. Omnēs frūctūs ē sē iēcērunt ut validī corporibus essent.
    (ablative of separation; ablative of respect)

14. Poteritne cīvitās perīculum temporum nostrōrum superāre?
    (complementary infinitive)

15. Rūmor per Asiam ruerat et ad Italiam magnā cum vī ierat.
    (accusative of place to which with **ad**)

16. Amōre carētis sine quō vīta nōn potest esse fēlīx.
    (ablative of separation; complementary infinitive)

17. Fidēs valida opus est in rēbus gravibus illīus generis.
    (**opus est** with nominative)

18. Sciō eōs malōs quī in urbe vīvant (quī Rōmae vīvant) amōre pecūniae multōs annōs rēctōs esse.
    (subject accusative and infinitive in indirect statement; ablative of place where with **in**; subjunctive in a subordinate clause within an indirect statement; locative case; accusative of duration of time)

19. Bellum pūgnandum est sociīs captīs ut sint līberī.
    (passive periphrastic and dative of agent)

20. Post bellum superātīs neque pecūnia neque cibus erat.
    (dative of the possessor)

21. Liber ā poētā scrīptus est; liber poētae scrībendus est; poēta librum scrībere dēbet.
    (passive periphrastic; dative of agent; complementary infinitive)

22. Poēta canēns imperia antīqua ferrō dēlēta interfectus est ā virīs in oppidō ante vīsīs.

23. Quibuscum in oppidō vīsus es? Cum quibus amīcīs in oppidō vīsus es? Quibuscum ambulābāmus amīcī sunt.
    (ablatives of accompaniment)

24. Ē quā deā ille nātus est?
    (ablative of origin)

25. Lībertās cīvium erat rēgī cūrae. Cui dīcēbās tē auxiliō futūrum. [**auxilium, -ī**, N., 'aid']
    (double dative construction)

## Synopsis of Verbs

A full synopsis should include the active and passive forms of the verb in the indicative and subjunctive moods, as well as all the participles and infinitives. The following synopsis of **inveniō, -īre, -vēnī, -ventus** in the second person singular will serve as a model:

**inveniō, invenīre, invēnī, inventus**, 'come upon, find'

|  | ACTIVE | PASSIVE |
|---|---|---|
| **INDICATIVE** | | |
| Present | invenīs | invenīris (invenīre) |
| Imperfect | inveniēbās | inveniēbāris (inveniēbāre) |
| Future | inveniēs | inveniēris (inveniēre) |
| Perfect | invēnistī | inventus (-a, -um) es |
| Pluperfect | invēnerās | inventus (-a, -um) erās |
| Future Perfect | invēneris | inventus (-a, -um) eris |
| **SUBJUNCTIVE** | | |
| Present | inveniās | inveniāris (inveniāre) |
| Imperfect | invenīrēs | invenīrēris (invenīrēre) |
| Perfect | invēneris | inventus (-a, -um) sīs |
| Pluperfect | invēnissēs | inventus (-a, -um) essēs |
| **PARTICIPLES** | | |
| Present | inveniēns | —— |
| Future | inventūrus, -a, -um | inveniendus, -a, -um |
| Perfect | —— | inventus, -a, -um |
| **INFINITIVES** | | |
| Present | invenīre | invenīrī |
| Future | inventūrus (-a, -um) esse | —— |
| Perfect | invēnisse | inventus (-a, -um) esse |

# UNITS 5–8: Self-Review A

## I.

A. Give all possibilities for the following forms, remembering to take into account long and short quantities:

1. sensus
2. res
3. ingenti animali
4. spebus

B. Fully describe the *form* of each of the following, giving all possibilities of interpretation, and then give the dictionary forms (principal parts) for each:

1. arsurus esse
2. tecta
3. spargere (give three possibilities when the -e- of the penult is short, and one additional possibility when the -e- is long)
4. petenda sunt
5. vocatae erant
6. quaeratis
7. iecisse
8. cani

## II.

Translate these sentences and then do whatever is required for each one:

1. Socii si hostium urbem media nocte ferro flammisque capere potuissent, hoc genus belli nunc militibus nostris non pugnandum esset.
   a) Give the syntax of **militibus**.
   b) Give the syntax of **pugnandum esset**.
2. Sciebat auctores horum operum omnium quae omnes cives legissent multa de civitatis nostrae libertate cecinisse.
   a) Give the syntax of **legissent**.
   b) Give the syntax of **auctores**.
   c) Change **sciebat** to the future tense and make any other necessary change(s), explaining why you made them.
3. Verba illorum hominum se multis carere dicentium sed nihil tamen optare vos non solum servitute pecuniae liberabunt sed etiam felices facient.
   a) Syntax of **se**?
   b) Syntax of **dicentium**?
   c) Syntax of **servitute**?
   d) Rewrite in indirect statement after **scit**.
   e) Rewrite the original sentence, changing the participial construction to a relative clause.
4. Quis hoc imperium, quis hunc timorem optare potest?
   a) Rewrite completely in the plural.
   b) Change **potest** to the *imperfect* tense.
5. Quibus manibus prima luce cives huius rei publicae opprimendi erant?
   a) Syntax of **luce**?
6. Cape oppidum! Amici nostri ex urbe discedentes bellum in provincia gladiis gesturi sunt.
   a) Syntax of **urbe**?

7. Pueris, carmina auctorum cum diligentia audire iussis, multi libri novi
   scripti erant ut mens sana in corpore sano eis esset.
   a) Syntax of **eis**?

**III.**

Translate into Latin:

1. His sister said to her (own) friend that she (herself) had to destroy the severe
   rumor about her (own) father.
   (Translate two ways: first, with a passive periphrastic; second, with **debeo**.)
2. Don't hate those men; for much time they have been oppressed by the soldiers, strong in body, who had attacked these walls.

# Answer Key — UNITS 5–8: Self-Review A

**I.**

A. 1. nominative sing., genitive sing., nominative pl., accusative pl. of **sēnsus,
     -ūs**, M.
     OR masculine nominative sing. of the perfect passive participle of **sentiō,
     -īre, sēnsī, sēnsus**
   2. nominative sing., nominative or accusative pl. of **rēs, reī**, F.
   3. dative or ablative sing. of **ingēns animal**
   4. dative or ablative pl. of **spēs, speī**, F.

B. 1. nominative masculine sing. of the future active infinitive: **ardeō, -ēre,
     arsī, arsus**
   2. nominative or accusative pl. of **tēctum, -ī**, N.
     OR nominative or accusative neuter pl. or feminine nominative sing. of
     the perfect passive participle of **tegō, tegere, tēxī, tēctus**
   3. short -**e**-: present active infinitive, 2nd sing. present passive indicative,
     2nd sing. passive imperative
     long -**ē**-: 2nd sing. future passive indicative: **spargō, spargere, sparsī,
     sparsus**
   4. 3rd pl. neuter present indicative passive periphrastic: **petō, -ere, -īvī, -ītus**
   5. 3rd pl. feminine pluperfect passive indicative: **vocō** (1)
   6. 2nd pl. present active subjunctive: **quaerō, -ere, quaesīvī, quaesītus**
   7. perfect active infinitive: **iaciō, -ere, iēcī, iactus**
   8. present passive infinitive: **canō, -ere, cecinī, cantus**

**II.**

1. If the allies had been able to capture the enemies' city in the middle of the
   night with sword and flames, this kind of war would not now have to be
   fought by our soldiers.

a) dative of agent with passive periphrastic
b) passive periphrastic 3rd sing. imperfect subjunctive in a mixed contrary-to-fact condition

2. He knew that the authors of all these works, which all the citizens had read, had sung many things about the freedom of our state.
   a) 3rd pl. pluperfect active subjunctive subordinate clause in indirect statement in secondary sequence. *Pluperfect* subjunctive because action occurs *before* that of **sciēbat**
   b) accusative pl., subject of **cecinisse**, infinitive in indirect statement
   c) **sciet...lēgerint**
      perfect subjunctive, primary sequence

3. The words of those men who say (saying) that they lack many things, but nevertheless desire (wish for) nothing, will not only free you from the slavery of money but also will make you happy.
   a) accusative pl. subject of **carēre**, infinitive in indirect statement
   b) genitive pl. present participle in agreement with **hominum**
   c) ablative of separation
   d) Scit verba illōrum hominum sē multīs carēre dīcentium sed nihil tamen optāre, vōs nōn sōlum servitūte pecūniae līberātūra esse sed etiam fēlīcēs factūra esse.
   e) Verba illōrum hominum quī dīcunt sē multīs carēre...

4. Who can (is able to) desire (wish for) this power, who can (is able to) desire (wish for) this fear?
   a) Quī haec imperia, quī hōs timōrēs optāre possunt?
   b) poterat

5. By what hands had the citizens of this republic to be oppressed at dawn?
   a) ablative of time when

6. Capture the town! Our friends departing (who are departing) from the city are about (going/ready) to wage war in the province with (their) swords.
   a) ablative of place from which

7. Many new books had been written for the boys ordered (who had been ordered) to listen diligently (with diligence) to the authors' poems so that they might have a sound mind in a sound body.
   a) dative of possessor with **esset**

**III.**
1. Soror eius amīcō suō dīxit rūmōrem gravem sibi dē patre suō dēlendum esse. Soror eius amīcō suō dīxit sē rūmōrem gravem dē patre suō dēlēre dēbēre.
2. Nē ōderis (OR nōlī ōdisse) illōs; multum tempus ā mīlitibus, fortibus (validīs) corpore, quī oppūgnāverant haec moenia oppressī sunt.

# UNITS 5–8: Self-Review B

## I.

A. Identify each of the following forms, giving *all* possibilities and listing principal parts for verbs and the nominative singular, genitive singular, and gender for nouns:

| | | | | |
|---|---|---|---|---|
| 1. arsis | 3. invadendi | 5. rebus | 7. manuum | 9. vocaturus |
| 2. imperans | 4. iturae | 6. vertice | 8. removisse | 10. iaci |

B. Change each of the following from the singular to the plural:

| | | |
|---|---|---|
| 1. illius lucis | 3. eo tempore | 5. meam vim |
| 2. huic fructui | 4. cuius sensus | |

C. List all infinitives, participles, and imperatives (active and passive) of **dico**.

## II.

Translate each of the following and complete whatever is required in addition:

1. Si cives verba auctorum clarorum audivissent, viris infelicibus magna bella non pugnanda essent.
   a) Explain the syntax of the phrase **viris infelicibus**.
   b) Explain the syntax of **pugnanda essent**.
   c) Rewrite the sentence completely in the singular.
2. Dicit regem, qui oppida Romanorum bello oppugnet, milites validos superare posse.
   a) Syntax of **regem**?
   b) Syntax of **oppugnet**?
   c) Syntax of **superare**?
   d) Syntax of **posse**?
   e) Write the sentence as a direct statement.
   f) If **dicit** is changed to **dixit**, how will the translation be different? What change will have to be made in the subordinate clause?
3. Quibus viris, oppida Romanorum deleturis, gladii dati erant, ut cum hostibus eorum bellum gererent?
   a) Explain the form of **deleturis**.
4. Eo tempore femina quae formā pulchra erat ab auctore librum novum scripturo amabatur.
   a) Explain the syntax of **tempore**.
   b) Syntax of **formā**?
   c) Syntax of **scripturo**?
   d) Rewrite as an indirect statement after **dixit**.

5. Magister superandus erit traditis si malum e terra pulsuri erunt.

   a) Give the syntax of **traditis.**

**III.**

Translate into Latin:

1. They say that the mountain on which the gods are found is always covered with golden light.
2. That man's mother told him that the great works of Roman authors had to be read by all who wished to complete their lives with glory.

   Translate "who wished..." in two ways:

   a) with a relative clause

   b) with a participle

# Answer Key — UNITS 5–8: Self-Review B

**I.**

A.  1. all genders dative or ablative pl. of the perfect passive participle: **ardeō, -ēre, arsī, arsus**

    2. all genders nominative sing. or neuter accusative sing. of the present participle: **imperō (1)**

    3. masculine or neuter genitive sing. *or* nominative masculine pl. of the future passive participle: **invādō, invādere, invāsī, invāsus**

    4. feminine nominative pl., genitive sing., dative sing. of the future active participle: **eō, īre, iī (īvī), itus**

    5. dative or ablative pl.: **rēs, reī,** F.

    6. ablative sing.: **vertex, verticis,** M.

    7. genitive pl.: **manus, manūs,** F.

    8. perfect active infinitive: **removeō, -ēre, remōvī, remōtus**

    9. nominative masculine sing. of the future active participle: **vocō (1)**

    10. present passive infinitive: **iaciō, iacere, iēcī, iactus**

B.  1. illārum lūcum

    2. hīs frūctibus

    3. eīs temporibus

    4. quōrum sēnsuum

    5. meās vīrēs (-īs)

C. Infinitives:

|         | ACTIVE                 | PASSIVE              |
| ------- | ---------------------- | -------------------- |
| Present | dīcere                 | dīcī                 |
| Perfect | dīxisse                | dictus, -a, -um esse |
| Future  | dictūrus, -a, -um esse | --                   |

Participles:

| | |
|---|---|
| Present active | dīcēns |
| Perfect passive | dictus, -a, -um |
| Future active | dictūrus, -a, -um |
| Future passive | dīcendus, -a, -um |

Imperatives:

| | SINGULAR | PLURAL |
|---|---|---|
| Active | dīc | dīcite |
| Passive | dīcere | dīciminī |

## II.

1. If the citizens had heard (listened to) the words of the famous authors, great wars would not have to be fought by the unhappy men.
   a) dative of agent with passive periphrastic
   b) passive periphrastic 3rd pl. imperfect subjunctive in a mixed contrary-to-fact condition
   c) Sī cīvis verbum auctōris clārī audīvisset, virō īnfēlīcī magnum bellum nōn pūgnandum esset.

2. He says that the king, who attacks (is attacking) the towns of the Romans in (by means of) war, is able to overcome the strong soldiers.
   a) accusative sing., subject of infinitive **posse** in indirect statement
   b) 3rd sing. present active subjunctive in a subordinate relative clause in indirect statement, primary sequence depending on **dīcit**
   c) complementary infinitive
   d) present infinitive in indirect statement
   e) Rēx, quī oppida Rōmānōrum bellō oppūgnat, mīlitēs validōs superāre potest.
   f) He said...; was attacking...; was able to overcome...; **oppūgnāret**; but if **dīxit** is translated as an English present perfect, i.e., 'he has said', then no change has to be made in the rest of the translation or in the subordinate clause.

3. To which (what) men about to destroy (who were about to destroy) the towns of the Romans had the swords been given so that they might wage war with their enemies?
   a) dative pl. future active participle, agreeing with **virīs**

4. At that time a (the) woman who was beautiful in form was loved by an (the) author about (who was about) to write a new book.
   a) ablative of time when
   b) ablative of respect
   c) ablative masculine sing., future active participle modifying **auctōre**

   d) Dīxit eō tempore fēminam quae fōrmā pulchra esset ab auctōre librum novum scrīptūrō amārī.

5. The master (director) will have to be conquered by the men who have been betrayed if they are (will be) about to drive evil out of the land.

   a) dative pl. masculine of the perfect passive participle; dative of agent with passive periphrastic construction

## III.

1. Dīcunt montem in quō dī inveniantur lūce aureā semper tegī.
2. Māter illīus eī dīxit magna opera auctōrum Rōmānōrum omnibus legenda esse quī vītās (suās) cum glōriā cōnficere (perficere) optārent.

   *or* ...omnibus optantibus vītās cum glōriā cōnficere (perficere).

# UNIT NINE

## A. Comparison of Adjectives

Adjectives in Latin occur in three *degrees*: positive (e.g., "brave"), comparative (e.g., "braver, rather brave, too brave"), and superlative (e.g., "bravest, most brave, very brave"). Adjectives appear in the vocabularies in the positive degree.

Note the following observations for the formation of the comparative and superlative degrees of adjectives.

1. COMPARATIVE

    Find the stem of the adjective by dropping the genitive singular ending from the positive form, and to this stem add **-ior** for the masculine and feminine, **-ius** for the neuter.

    | | | |
    |---|---|---|
    | validus, -a, -um | valid/ī | validior, validius |
    | fortis, -e | fort/is | fortior, fortius |

    The comparative adjective is declined like third declension adjectives, but with **-um** in the genitive plural instead of **-ium** and with **-a** in the neuter nominative and accusative plural instead of **-ia** (that is, it is not an i-stem). The stem for adjectives in the comparative degree is the full nominative singular masculine-feminine form, with the **-o-** lengthened.

    | SINGULAR | | PLURAL | |
    |---|---|---|---|
    | M. & F. | N. | M. & F. | N. |
    | fortior | fortius | fortiōrēs | fortiōra |
    | fortiōris | fortiōris | fortiōrum | fortiōrum |
    | fortiōrī | fortiōrī | fortiōribus | fortiōribus |
    | fortiōrem | fortius | fortiōrēs(-īs) | fortiōra |
    | fortiōre(-ī) | fortiōre(-ī) | fortiōribus | fortiōribus |

2. SUPERLATIVE

    Most adjectives form the superlative by adding **-issimus, -a, -um** to the stem of the positive form.

validissimus, -a, -um
fortissimus, -a, -um

These are declined like first-second declension adjectives.

Adjectives which end in -er in the masculine nominative singular of the positive degree form the superlative by adding -rimus, -a, -um directly to the masculine nominative form.

ācer, ācris, ācre     ācerrimus, -a, -um

Six adjectives which end in -lis in the masculine and feminine nominative singular of the positive degree form the superlative by adding -limus, -a, -um to the stem of the positive degree.

similis, -e     simillimus, -a, -um

These adjectives are:

facilis, -e        easy
difficilis, -e     difficult
similis, -e        similar
dissimilis, -e     unlike
gracilis, -e       slender
humilis, -e        humble, low

3. **Quam** PLUS THE SUPERLATIVE

**Quam** followed by an adjective (or adverb) in the superlative degree gives the meaning 'as...as possible'.

**Quam fortissimus** est.   He is *as brave as possible*; he is *as brave as can be*.

B. **Irregular Comparison of Adjectives**

Five common adjectives have irregular comparisons and must be learned.

| | | |
|---|---|---|
| bonus, -a, -um | melior, melius | optimus, -a, -um |
| good | better | best |
| malus, -a, -um | peior, peius | pessimus, -a, -um |
| bad | worse | worst |
| magnus, -a, -um | maior, maius | maximus, -a, -um |
| great | greater | greatest |
| parvus, -a, -um | minor, minus | minimus, -a, -um |
| small | smaller | smallest |
| multus, -a, -um | plūs (neuter only in sing.) | plūrimus, -a, -um |
| much | pl., plūrēs, plūra | most |
| | more | |

NOTE: The masculine plural comparative of **magnus, maiōrēs**, is frequently used to mean 'ancestors', (i.e., 'those greater [in respect to age]').

## C. Comparison with *quam*; Ablative of Comparison
Comparisons can be made in two ways in Latin:

1.          Pater eius est altior **quam hospes**.   His father is taller *than the guest*.

The conjunction **quam** is here equivalent to the English 'than'. As in English, **quam**, 'than', has the same case after it as it has before it.

Dīxit patrem esse altiōrem **quam hospitem**.   He said that his father was
                                                taller *than the guest*.

Pater est altior **quam ego**.   The father is taller *than I*.

2.          Pater eius est altior **hospite**.   His father is taller *than the guest*.

Here the ablative, without a preposition, is used with the comparative adjective to denote comparison. The ablative of comparison and the construction with **quam** may be used interchangeably with no distinction in meaning.

## D. Ablative of Degree of Difference
The ablative, without a preposition, is used with comparatives to express the degree in which the two things being compared differ. Less frequently, this kind of ablative is also found with a superlative in statements in which there is an implicit comparative judgment made.

| | |
|---|---|
| Pater eius est **pede** altior hospite (quam hospes). | His father is taller than the guest *by a foot*; his father is *a foot* taller than the guest. |
| Nunc **multō** fēlīcior est. | Now he is happier *by much*; he is *much* happier now. |
| **Multō** optimus ex omnibus pūgnantibus est. | He is *by far* (*much*) the best of all who are fighting. |

## E. Adverbs and Their Comparison

1. Most adverbs are formed from adjectives. Two of the more frequent formations of the positive degree are noted below:
   a) From adjectives of the first and second declensions, adverbs are frequently formed by adding the ending -ē to the stem of the adjective.

   | | |
   |---|---|
   | miser, misera, miserum | miserē |
   | poor | poorly |

b) Adverbs formed from adjectives of the third declension frequently exhibit the ending **-iter**.

| | |
|---|---|
| fortis, -e | fortiter |
| strong | strongly, bravely |

There is no way to determine that a given adverb will not be formed according to these rules; adverbs formed differently will be given as vocabulary items.

2. The comparative degree of an adverb is formed by adding the ending **-ius** to the stem of the positive degree of the *adjective*. It will be noted that the comparative is really the neuter accusative singular of the comparative of the adjective.

| | |
|---|---|
| fortiter | fortius |
| bravely | more bravely, rather bravely, too bravely |
| facile | facilius |
| easily | more easily, rather easily, too easily |
| misere | miserius |
| poorly | more poorly, rather poorly, too poorly |

3. The superlative is formed with the ending **-issimē** (or **-rimē**, **-limē** when the adjective would be thus formed; see section A above) added to the stem of the positive degree of the *adjective*.

| | |
|---|---|
| fortissimē | most bravely |
| facillimē | most easily |
| miserrimē | most poorly |
| quam miserrimē | as poorly as possible |

## F. Irregular Comparison of Adverbs

| | | |
|---|---|---|
| bene | melius | optimē |
| well | better | best |
| male | peius | pessimē |
| badly | worse | worst |
| magnopere | magis | maximē |
| greatly | more | most, especially |
| parum | minus | minimē |
| not enough | less | least |
| multum | plūs | plūrimum |
| much | more | most |
| diū | diūtius | diūtissimē |
| long (in time), for a long time | longer | longest |

| | | |
|---|---|---|
| saepe | saepius | saepissimē |
| often | more often | very often |
| -- | prius | prīmum |
| | before | first |
| prope | propius | proximē |
| near | nearer | nearest, next |

## G. Partitive Genitive

The genitive is sometimes used in Latin to express the *whole* group or unit of which the word on which the genitive depends expresses the *part*. This usage is called the *partitive genitive* or the *genitive of the whole*.

Fortissimus **omnium mīlitum** ad mē vēnit.     The bravest *of all the soldiers* came to me.

Multī **hominum** opīniōnēs sapientium laudant.     Many *of the men* praise the opinions of the wise.

The ablative, preceded by the prepositions **ē (ex)**, or **dē** is used as an alternative to the partitive genitive with some words. This is especially frequent when the word denoting the *part* is a cardinal numeral.

Quīnque **ex mīlitibus** domum vēnērunt.     Five *of* (*out of*) *the soldiers* came home.

Some words used substantively in Latin require a partitive genitive to render an idea which in English would be expressed with a noun and adjective.

Satis **pecūniae** habet.     He has enough (*of*) *money*.

Plūs **pecūniae** habet quam tū.     He has more (*of*) *money* than you.

In the singular, the word **plūs** is used substantively and is generally indeclinable; in the plural, it is used attributively and is declined.

**Plūs** hominum ad sē vocāvit.     He called *more* (of) men to him.

**Plūrēs** hominēs ad sē vocāvit.     He called *more* men to him.

## UNIT NINE — VOCABULARY

**aiō** (defective verb)          say, affirm
    [pres.: **aiō, ais, ait, --, --, aiunt**
    imperf.: **aiēbam**, etc. (complete)
    pres. subjunctive: --, **aiās, aiat,**
    --, --, **aiant**]
**amīcitia, -ae, F.**          friendship

| | |
|---|---|
| cadō, -ere, cecidī, cāsus | fall |
| cāsus, -ūs, M. | fall, accident, occurrence, chance |
| cōnsilium, -ī, N. | counsel, plan, advice |
| crūdēlis, -e | cruel |
| dēmēns, dēmentis | mad, raving |
| facilis, -e | easy |
| facile (adv.) | easily |
| difficilis, -e | difficult |
| gracilis, -e | slender, unadorned, simple |
| hospes, -itis, M. | guest, host |
| humilis, -e | humble, lowly |
| laudō (1) | praise |
| laus, laudis, F. | praise |
| magnopere (adv.) | greatly |
| maiōrēs, -um, M. pl. | ancestors |
| male (adv.) | badly |
| Mārs, Mārtis, M. | Mars (god of war) |
| multum (adv.) | much, very |
| mūniō, -īre, -īvī, -ītus | fortify |
| nam (conj.) | for |
| odium, -ī, N. | hatred |
| parum (adv. and indeclinable adj.) | too little, not enough |
| parvus, -a, -um | little, small |
| prius (adv.) | before, previously |
| quam prīmum | as soon as possible |
| proximus, -a, -um | nearest, next |
| quam (conj.) | than (used in comparisons) |
| saepe (adv.) | often |
| sapiēns, -ntis | wise |
| sapientia, -ae, F. | wisdom |
| satis (adv. and indeclinable adj.) | enough |
| serēnus, -a, -um | serene, calm |
| similis, -e | like, similar (to) (+ gen. or dat.) |
| dissimilis, -e | dissimilar, unlike (+ gen. or dat.) |
| solvō, -ere, solvī, solūtus | loosen, free, untie |
| summus, -a, -um | highest, top (of) |
| supplex, supplicis | suppliant, humble |
| tam (adv.) | so |
| tam...quam | so ... as, as ... as |
| templum, -ī, N. | temple |
| tūtus, -a, -um | safe |

# UNIT NINE — NOTES ON VOCABULARY

The easiest way to memorize the irregular comparisons of adjectives is to associate the forms with the English derivatives:

> **bonus, melior** (*ameliorate* is to make *better*), **optimus** (an *optimist* is a person who looks at the *best* side of things)
>
> **malus, peior** (a *pejorative* meaning of a word is a *worse* one), **pessimus** (a *pessimist* is a person who looks at the *worst* side of things)
>
> **magnus, maior** (a *major* problem is a *rather great* one), **maximus** (the *maximum* penalty is the *largest* one)
>
> **parvus, minor** (a *minor* problem is a *rather small* one; eight *minus* (*smaller* [*by*]) two is six), **minimus** (the *minimum* penalty is the *smallest* one)
>
> **multus, plūs** (six *plus* (*more* [*by*]) two is eight; *plural* means *more* than one), **plūrimum** does not have an English derivative.

**Maiōrēs, maiōrum**, M. pl. means 'ancestors' because they are the ones 'greater (in age)' than we are.

**Quam** with the superlative means 'as...as possible'; with the comparative it means 'than'. **Quam** can mean 'how' in an exclamatory sense: **Quam pulchra est!**, 'How beautiful she is!' And, of course, **quam** can be the feminine accusative singular of the relative pronoun or interrogative adjective.

**Aiō** is a defective verb with not many forms; the present tense of the indicative is found in four persons, of the subjunctive in three. The imperfect indicative is complete. The verb means 'say' or 'say yes'.

The suffix **-tia**, sometimes with a connecting vowel, or the suffix **-ia** is added to the stem of an adjective to produce an abstract noun; thus, **amīcitia** is 'friendship'. **Sapiēns**, 'wise', produces **sapientia**, 'wisdom'.

**Cadō, cadere, cecidī, cāsus**, 'fall', has many compounds; it must not be confused with **caedō, caedere, cecīdī, caesus**, 'fell, cut', which also has many compounds. **Incidō**, 'fall into, happen', is a compound of **in** + **cadō**; **incīdō**, 'cut into, engrave', is from **in** + **caedō**; the -ae- diphthong becomes -ī- in compounds. Once again it is clear that it pays to be attentive to long and short vowels. The last principal part of **cadō** produces the fourth declension noun **cāsus, cāsūs**, M., 'fall, accident, occurrence, chance'.

**Dēmēns** (dē + mēns) describes someone who is '(down, away) from his mind', thus, 'mad, raving'.

Note the irregular adverbs **facile**, 'easily'; **male**, 'badly'; **multum**, 'much, very'; and **magnopere** (uncontracted, **magnō opere**), 'with great work', thus, 'greatly'.

Remember that the six adjectives ending in -lis — **facilis, difficilis, similis, dissimilis, gracilis**, and **humilis** — form their superlatives by doubling the -l- and adding **-imus**.

The noun **laus, laudis, F.,** 'praise', is related to the first conjugation verb **laudō,** 'praise'.

**Nam** is a *conjunction* meaning 'for': **Nam omnis populus rēgem timuit,** 'For all the people feared the king'.

The neuter second declension noun **odium,** 'hatred', is related to the verb **ōdī,** 'hate'. The English word *annoy* comes from **in odiō.**

Sometimes an adjective is more easily translated as an adverb: **Humilēs in tēctum dominī vēnimus,** 'We came humbly into the master's house'; literally, 'We, humble, came into the master's house'; **Prīmī accessērunt,** 'They were the first to approach' or 'They approached first'.

**Proximus, -a, -um** is often found with the dative: **Proximus turbae fuit,** 'He was nearest the crowd'.

**Similis** and **dissimilis** may govern either the genitive or the dative without distinction: **Patris similis est** and **Patrī similis est** both mean 'He is like his father'.

**Summus, -a, -um** means 'top (of)': **Animal in summō monte vīdimus,** 'We saw the animal on the top of the mountain'.

**Tam...quam** means 'so...as': **Quid est tam dulce quam habēre amīcum cārissimum?,** 'What is so sweet as having (*literally,* 'to have') a very dear friend?'

## UNIT NINE — DRILL

### I.

Give the positive, comparative, and superlative forms of the following adjectives to go with each of the following nouns. Several interpretations of the cases of the nouns may be possible.

> **miser, misera, miserum,** 'wretched, unhappy, poor'
> **saevus, -a, -um,** 'cruel'
> **humilis, -e,** 'humble, low'

| | | | |
|---|---|---|---|
| 1. manuī | 3. spērum | 5. hominibus | 7. carmen |
| 2. profugī | 4. cīvitātēs | 6. amīcum | 8. corpora |

### II.

Translate:

1. Hoc opus difficilius est illō.
2. Hoc opus difficilius est quam illud.
3. Hoc opus difficilius est parvō quam illud.
4. Hoc opus multō difficilius est illō.
5. Hae fēminae sāniōrēs sunt illīs.
6. Hae fēminae multō sāniōrēs sunt quam illae.
7. Dīcimus hās fēminās multō sāniōrēs esse quam illās.

8. Dīcimus hās fēminās multō sāniōrēs esse illīs.
9. Hī hominēs fortiōrēs plūs pecūniae optant.
10. Multa pecūnia hominibus meliōribus optanda est; parum pecūniae hominibus peiōribus optandum est.
11. Plūs pecūniae hominibus meliōribus optandum est peiōribus.
12. Plūs pecūniae hominibus meliōribus optandum est quam peiōribus.
13. Studium mihi dulcius est bellō.
14. Studium mihi dulcius est quam bellum.
15. Verba vēra mihi dīxērunt.
16. Verba vēriōra mihi dīxērunt.
17. Verba vērissima mihi dīxērunt.
18. Verba quam vērissima mihi dīxērunt.
19. Mīlitēs ācerrimī rēgī ācriōrī dīxērunt sē sententiās ācrēs magistrōrum petītūrōs esse.
20. Scīmus sententiās ācerrimās magistrōrum meliōrēs esse quam arma ācerrima.
21. Scīmus sententiās ācerrimās magistrōrum meliōrēs esse armīs ācerrimīs.
22. Hic puer multō facilius quam frāter legit.
23. Mīlitēs quam ācerrimē et fortissimē pūgnāvērunt.
24. Rēx novus melius patre rēxit.
25. Honestē et fēlīciter vītam agere optāmus.

# UNIT NINE — PRELIMINARY EXERCISES
## (SECTIONS A, B, C, D)

1. Domī quam tūtissimī esse dēbēmus.
2. a) Puer frātrī est simillimus, nam est tam sapiēns quam frāter.
   b) Puer est sorōris dissimilis.
3. Multō facilius est laudāre amīcum quam inimīcum.
4. Sapientēs aiunt amīcitiam esse summum bonum.
5. Maiōribus fuisse odium bellī dīcitur.
6. Dōna cāriōra darī fīliō sapientissimō iussit.
7. Tēcta domuum altiōrum (altissimārum) fulgēbant lūmine clāriōre (clārissimō).
8. Hic hospes multō serēnior est illō.
9. Supplicēs humillimī miserrimīque timōre mōtī urbem regentēs magnopere laudāvērunt.
10. Multae urbēs antīquae pulcherrimaeque cāsū crūdēlissimō dēlētae sunt.
11. Auctor clārior erat frātre clārō.
12. Dīcimus Mārtem saepe crūdēliōrem esse multīs dīs.
13. Hic ager est quīnque pedibus longior quam ille.
14. Nam cōnsilium dēmentis est multō crūdēlissimum.

# UNIT NINE — EXERCISES

**I.**

1. Urbs pulcherrima nōn sōlum umbrā maiōre timōris tegitur, sed etiam rūmōribus crūdēlibus (crūdēliōribus, crūdēlissimīs) dē populō dēlētur.

2. Lūx discēdere incipit atque nox venit; maiōrēsque cadunt altīs dē montibus umbrae.

3. Plūs studiī in cūrīs animae pōnendum est quam in cūrīs corporis; nam anima est aeterna, sed corpus dēlēbitur.

4. Nihil est bellō tam simile quam ruīna.

5. Numquam, nisī mē saepius ōrāveris, servitūte amīcum miserrimum facile solvēs.

6. Quam ob rem maxima dēbētur mīlitibus fortissimīs venia? Bellum diūtissimē et fortiter ab eīs gestum est.

7. Bellum grave et crūdēlissimum mīlitibus fortiōribus gerendum est nē nātī incolārum gladiīs flammīsque superentur.

8. Audiēbāmus multōs supplicēs validiōrēs ad templum magnō cum studiō ventūrōs esse ut deōs ōrārent ut perīculum ab oppidō removērētur.

9. Quid īnfēlīcī servō dulcius cūrīs solūtīs?

10. Manū supplicī dōna gravia portāns ad rēgēs pessimōs et crūdēliōrēs humilis vēnit ut ab eīs veniam prō illīs multō īnfēlīciōribus sē quaereret.

11. Summōs virōs dēmentiōrēs esse dīcēbās; nunc eōs quam dēmentissimōs dīcis.

12. Sed nīl dulcius est, bene quam mūnīta tenēre opīniōnibus sapientium templa serēna.

13. Hanc vīllam nātūrā et opere mūnītam incolae humilēs quam prīmum capient.

14. Bellum est grave Mārtis opus; vītam quam serēnissimam optantibus nihil bellō saepe est peius.

15. Auctor dīxit illum hospitem opus magnum in manibus habēre; opus simillimum esse librō ab īnfēlīciōre poētā quī Rōmā pulsus esset scrīptō.

16. Incipit rēs melius īre quam spērāveram.

17. Plūrēs tibi dabō, quī nōn amīcō, sed amīcitiā caruērunt.

18. Facilius genus vītae hominibus quaerendum est.

19. Eō diē mihi dīxit sē audīvisse fēminam altiōre vōce clāmantem satis sibi pecūniae nōn esse ut Rōmam sine morā īret; proximō autem diē sē invenīre eam nōn posse.

20. Aiunt plūs dōnōrum pessimīs servīs nōn optandum esse quam optimīs.

21. Cīvēs honestissimī, spectāte meum hunc cāsum tam gravem, tam malum.

22. Illa cīvitās multō plūris quam nostra cāsūs mortis habet.

23. Oppidum parvum quam optimē mūniēbātur nē hostēs id diūtius oppūgnārent.

24. Maximē maiōrēs laudant quī cum dīligentiā sē prō rē pūblicā gessērunt.
25. Aiēbat sē facillimē lēgisse librōs quōs mīsissēs.
26. Supplex intellēxit amōrem esse difficiliōrem sibi multō quam odium.
27. Nihil est mortis tam simile quam vīta sine salūte, sine pecūniā, sine maximō studiō rērum bonārum.
28. Mors animam cārissimam corpore solvit.
29. Cum omnibus tuīs laudibus, haec, meā opīniōne, est maxima: sapientia tua cīvēs metū solvit quō magnopere atque diūtius territī sunt.
30. Bona opīniō hominum tūtior pecūniā est. Nam pecūnia sine cōnsiliō saepe perditur; fāma nōbīscum semper vīvit.
31. Quae rēs in sē parum cōnsiliī neque multum sapientiae habet, eam cōnsiliō regere nōn potes.
32. Cognōvimus virōs līberōs vītam difficillimam agere quod illīs opus est studiō et dīligentiā quibus rem pūblicam bene gerant. [quibus = ut hīs (introducing a clause of purpose)]
33. Amīcō bonō nihil tenērī melius potest.
34. Cōnsiliīs optimīs vītam agere dēbēbimus, sī quam fēlīcissimē vīvere optābimus.
35. Crūdēliōrem imperium tenentem ōrāvit supplex nē odium profugōrum eī dē poenā cōgitantī esset cūrae.
36. Poēta dīxit sē librum sententiīs gracilibus atque quam dulcissimīs implētūrum esse.
37. Rōmae satis odiī, laudis parum erat.
38. Maiōrēs enim vestrī bella saepe quaesīvērunt ob maximum glōriae amōrem. Male quaesīvērunt.
39. Noster amātissimus auctor dīxit, "Verbum sapientī sat (*i.e.*, satis) est."
40. Hostem crūdēlissimum sī vīdisset, arma manū cecidissent.
41. Rēgem saeviōrem cīvēs prius Rōmā, post et ex Italiā pepulērunt.
42. Multum laudātur quod vīta cōnsiliīs sapientium mūnītur.

## II.

1. The rather humble guest, who had been attacked by the raving inhabitants in the middle of the city, had to fortify the temple as well as possible in order to be safe.
2. It is said that gossip is a much more evil thing than cruel war.
3. The king's very healthy brother feels that the constellations are brighter than the fires in the streets of this city.
4. These soldiers are much better in strength than those.
5. At that time he would very easily have overcome the brave soldiers if (his) rather heavy arms had not fallen from (his) very strong hands.

## III. Reading

Pliny writes about his sorrow over the death of Fundanus' daughter on the night before her wedding (Pliny 5.16, slightly adapted):

Trīstissimus[1] haec tibi scrībō dē morte Fundānī[2] nostrī fīliae minōris. Quā puellā nihil umquam fēstīvius,[3] amābilius[4] nec modo[5] longiōre vītā, sed prope[6] immortālitāte[7] dignius[8] vīdī. Nōndum[9] annōs quattuordecim[10] implēverat, et iam[11] illī anīlis[12] sapientia, fēminae gravitās[13] erat, et tamen suāvitās[14] puellae cum virginis[15] verēcundiā.[16] Ut[17] illa patris cervīcibus[18] inhaerēbat![19] Ut[17] nōs amīcōs patris et amanter[20] et modestē[21] complectēbātur![22] Ut[17] nūtrīcēs,[23] ut[17] paedagōgōs,[24] ut[17] magistrōs prō suō quemque[25] officiō[26] dīligēbat![27] Quam[28] studiōsē,[29] quam[28] intellegenter[30] legēbat! Ut[17] parcē[31] custōdītēque[32] lūdēbat![33] Quā illa temperantiā,[34] quā patientiā,[35] quā cōnstantiā[36] novissimam[37] valētūdinem[38] tulit![39] Medicīs[40] pārēbat,[41] sorōrem, patrem adhortābātur[42] sēque dēstitūtam[43] corporis vīribus vigōre mentis sustinēbat.[44] Dūrāvit[45] hic illī ūsque[46] ad mortem nec aut[47] spatiō[48] valētūdinis[38] aut[47] metū mortis īnfrāctus est,[49] quō plūrēs graviōrēsque nōbīs causās[50] relinqueret[51] et dēsīderiī[52] et dolōris.[53] Ō trīste[1] plānē[54] acerbumque fūnus![55] Ō morte ipsā[56] mortis tempus indīgnius![57]

---

[1] trīstis, -e, 'sad'  [2] Fundānus, -ī, M., a man's name  [3] fēstīvus, -a, -um, 'gay, pleasing'  [4] amābilis, -e, 'lovable'  [5] modo (adv.), 'only'  [6] prope (adv.), 'nearly'  [7] immortālitās, -tātis, F., 'immortality'  [8] dignus, -a, -um, 'worthy' (+ abl.)  [9] nōndum (adv.), 'not yet'  [10] quattuordecim (indeclinable adj.), 'fourteen'  [11] iam (adv.), 'already'  [12] anīlis, -e, 'of an old woman'  [13] gravitās, -tātis, F., 'seriousness'  [14] suāvitās, -tātis, F., 'charm, agreeableness'  [15] virgō, -inis, F., 'maiden'  [16] verēcundia, -ae, F., 'modesty'  [17] ut (adv.), 'how'  [18] cervīx, -īcis, F., 'neck'; here, used in the pl., but with sing. meaning  [19] inhaereō, -ēre, inhaesī, inhaesus, 'cling'  [20] amanter (adv.), from amāns  [21] modestus, -a, -um, 'modest'  [22] complectēbātur, translate as active: 'she used to embrace'  [23] nūtrīx, -īcis, F., 'nurse'  [24] paedagōgus, -ī, M., a slave in charge of escorting a child to and from school  [25] quemque (acc. sing., M. & F.), 'each (one)'  [26] officium, -ī, N., 'duty, service'  [27] dīligō, -ere, -lēxī, -lēctus, 'esteem highly'  [28] quam (adv.), 'how'  [29] studiōsus, -a, -um, 'studious, busy'  [30] intellegenter (adv.), from intellegēns  [31] parcus, -a, -um, 'sparing'  [32] custōdītē (adv.), 'cautiously'  [33] lūdō, -ere, lūsī, lūsus, 'play'  [34] temperantia, -ae, F., 'self-restraint'  [35] patientia, -ae, F., 'patience'  [36] cōnstantia, -ae, F., 'self-possession'  [37] novus, -a, -um, 'recent'  [38] valētūdō, -inis, F., 'bad health'  [39] ferō, ferre, tulī, lātus, 'endure'  [40] medicus, -ī, M., 'doctor'  [41] pāreō, -ēre, pāruī, pāritus, 'be obedient to' (+ dat.)  [42] adhortābātur, translate as active: 'she used to encourage'  [43] dēstituō, -ere, -uī, -ūtus, 'desert'; in perfect participle, 'deprived of'  [44] sustineō (sub + teneō), 'sustain'  [45] dūrō (1), 'last, continue'  [46] ūsque (adv.), 'all the way'  [47] aut...aut (conj.), 'either...or'  [48] spatium, -ī, N., 'length of time'  [49] īnfringō, -ere, -frēgī, -frāctus, 'break up, bring down'  [50] causa, -ae, F., 'reason, cause'  [51] relinquō, -ere, relīquī, relictus, 'leave'; quō...relinqueret = ut...relinqueret  [52] dēsīderium, -ī, N., 'regret' (for the loss of anything)  [53] dolor, -ōris, M., 'pain, sorrow'  [54] plānē (adv.), 'plainly, certainly'  [55] fūnus, -eris, N., 'funeral, death'  [56] ipsā (abl. sing. F.), 'itself' (modifies morte)  [57] indīgnus, -a, -um, 'unworthy' (+ abl.)

## A. Ablative Absolute

The word "absolute" comes from the fourth principal part of the verb **absolvō, -ere, -solvī, -solūtus,** 'untie, loosen'. Grammatically, it refers to a part of the sentence which has no close syntactical connection with the rest; it is "untied" or "detached" from the main clause.

English has a *nominative absolute*:

> *This being the case,* I shall now help you.

Note that the nominative absolute in English utilizes a subject, "this" and a participle, "being". The subject of the absolute construction is different from the subject (or object) of the main clause. In the broadest sense, the absolute functions as an adverb giving the circumstances in which the action of the main clause occurs.

The Latin absolute construction requires the ablative, not the nominative, case. All tenses of the participle may occur, according to the observations stated in the unit on participles above, although the future is very rare in classical Latin.

| | |
|---|---|
| **Coniuge veniente,** | *With her husband coming,* the woman will depart. |
| fēmina discēdet. | *When her husband is coming* (*comes*), the woman will depart. |
| | *Since her husband is coming,* the woman will depart. |
| | *If her husband is coming* (*comes*), the woman will depart. |
| | *Although her husband is coming,* the woman will depart. |
| | . . . etc. |

[NOTE that when the present participle is used in an ablative absolute, the -e ending for the ablative singular occurs rather than -ī.]

OBSERVATIONS:

1. The subject of the ablative absolute, **coniuge,** is different from the subject of the main clause, **fēmina.** Hence, **coniuge veniente** is a true absolute.
2. The present participle refers to an action which occurs at the *same time* as that of the main verb.

3. Because of the absence of a perfect *active* participle, it will be impossible to express an active idea in the absolute as having occurred *prior* to the time of the main verb without recasting it in the passive voice. Another construction would have to be used (e.g., **Sī coniūnx vēnit, postquam coniūnx vēnit, quamquam coniūnx vēnit**, etc.).

| **Coniuge vīsō,** | *With her husband having been seen*, the woman |
|---|---|
| fēmina discessit. | departed. |
| | *When she saw (had seen) her husband*, the woman departed. |
| | *Since she saw (had seen) her husband*, the woman departed. |
| | *If she saw her husband*, the woman departed. |
| | *Although she saw (had seen) her husband*, the woman departed. |
| | ...etc. |

OBSERVATIONS:

1. Note that in the last four translations above, the subordinate clause has been changed from the passive to the active voice. The subject "she" of the subordinate clause is the same as the subject of the main clause *in English*. In the Latin, however, the subject of the perfect passive participle is *not* the same as that of the main verb (**coniuge** is the subject of the ablative absolute; **fēmina** is the subject of the main clause; note the first English translation above).
2. The perfect participle refers to an action which occurred *prior* to the time of the main verb.

NOTE: If we wish to render "When she was departing, the woman saw her husband" into Latin, we *cannot* use the ablative absolute because the subject of each clause ("she" and "woman") is the same. A simple participle must be used instead:

Fēmina discēdēns coniugem vīdit.

| **Illā fēminā rēgīnā,** | *With that woman (being) queen*, the inhabitants |
|---|---|
| incolae fēlīcēs erant. | were happy. |
| | *When that woman was queen*, the inhabitants were happy. |
| | ...etc. |

OBSERVATION:

Since there is no present participle for the verb **sum**, two nouns are sometimes used in an ablative absolute construction with an *implied* participle connecting them. The second noun is in effect a predicate ablative.

**Custōde amīcum vocante,**     *With the guardian calling his friend,* the sailors
nautae fūgērunt.                    fled.

*When the guardian was calling his friend,* the
sailors fled.

...etc.

OBSERVATION:
The participle, since it is a verbal adjective, retains its verbal functions. Consequently it can control an object, as in the case of **amīcum** above.

## B. Adjectives with Genitive Singular in *-ius*

There is a group of adjectives which are like first-second declension adjectives
except that they have **-īus** in the genitive singular of all genders and **-ī** in the
dative singular. One of these is **tōtus, -a, -um**, 'whole, all'.

| SINGULAR | | | PLURAL |
|---|---|---|---|
| M. | F. | N. | |
| tōtus | tōta | tōtum | |
| tōtīus | tōtīus | tōtīus | |
| tōtī | tōtī | tōtī | the plural is identical to that of **magnus, -a, -um** |
| tōtum | tōtam | tōtum | |
| tōtō | tōtā | tōtō | |

The other adjectives of this class are:

| | |
|---|---|
| alius, -a, -ud | other |
| alter, altera, alterum | the other (of two) |
| ūllus, -a, -um | any |
| nūllus, -a, -um | no, none |
| uter, utra, utrum | which (of two) |
| neuter, neutra, neutrum | neither |
| sōlus, -a, -um | only |
| ūnus, -a, -um | one, alone |

## C. Ablative of Cause

The ablative, generally without a preposition, is sometimes used to express
*cause.*

Clāmāre **gaudiō** coepit.     She began to shout *because of joy.*
**Fōrmā** laudābantur.         They were praised *because of (their) beauty.*

Sometimes cause is expressed by **ob** or **propter**, 'on account of', followed by the
accusative case.

**Propter metum** fēminās interfēcit.     He killed the women *on account of fear.*

## D. Ablative and Genitive of Description

A noun in the ablative or genitive case, when modified by an adjective, may be used to describe or express a quality of another noun.

Vir magnā sapientiā  
Vir magnae sapientiae  
} a man of great wisdom

## E. The Irregular Verb *ferō* and Its Compounds

**Ferō, ferre, tulī, lātus**, 'bring, carry, bear, endure', exhibits certain peculiarities in the present indicative, present infinitive, and present imperative. The other forms are exactly what we would expect for a third conjugation verb.

PRESENT INDICATIVE

| ACTIVE | | PASSIVE | |
|--------|--------|--------|--------|
| ferō | ferimus | feror | ferimur |
| fers | fertis | ferris | feriminī |
|  |  | (ferre) |  |
| fert | ferunt | fertur | feruntur |

IMPERATIVE

| SING. | PL. |
|-------|-----|
| fer! | ferte! |

There are several compounds of **ferō** which occur frequently and should be learned. Some are:

**ad** + **ferō** = **afferō, afferre, attulī, allātus**, 'bring to, present'  
**ab** + **ferō** = **auferō, auferre, abstulī, ablātus**, 'carry away'  
**com** + **ferō** = **cōnferō, cōnferre, contulī, collātus**, 'bring together, collect; compare;' reflexive **sē cōnferre** = 'take oneself' (i.e., to a place), 'go'  
**dē** + **ferō** = **dēferō, dēferre, dētulī, dēlātus**, 'bring away, bring down, offer; report'  
**dis** + **ferō** = **differō, differre, distulī, dīlātus**, 'differ'  
**ex** + **ferō** = **efferō, efferre, extulī, ēlātus**, 'carry out; bring forth'  
**in** + **ferō** = **īnferō, īnferre, intulī, illātus**, 'carry into; inflict'  
**ob** + **ferō** = **offerō, offerre, obtulī, oblātus**, 'bring before; offer; expose'  
**re** + **ferō** = **referō, referre, rettulī, relātus**, 'bring back, report'  
**sub** + **ferō** = **sufferō, sufferre, sustulī, sublātus**, 'undergo, endure'

It will be easy to form other compounds of this verb by the addition of other prefixes.

# UNIT TEN — VOCABULARY

| | |
|---|---|
| **alius, -a, -ud** (note that the neuter nom. and acc. end in **-ud**, not **-um**) | other, another |
| **alius...alius** | one...another |
| **aliī...aliī** | some...others |
| **alter, altera, alterum** | the other (of two) |
| **apud** (prep. + acc.) | at, near, among; at the house of |
| **ars, artis, -ium**, F. | skill, art |
| **audācia, -ae**, F. | boldness, courage |
| **audāx, audācis** | bold, courageous |
| **auxilium, -ī**, N. | aid |
| **certus, -a, -um** | certain, sure |
| **incertus, -a, -um** | uncertain, unsure |
| **coepī, coepisse, coeptus** | began (defective verb; it occurs only in the perfect system) |
| **custōs, -ōdis**, M. | guardian |
| **doceō, -ēre, docuī, doctus** | teach |
| **errō** (1) | wander, err |
| **ferō, ferre, tulī, lātus** (for compounds of **ferō**, see section E of this Unit) | bring, carry, bear, endure |
| **figūra, -ae**, F. | figure, form, shape |
| **foedus, foederis**, N. | pact, treaty, agreement |
| **fugiō, -ere, fūgī, fugitus** | flee |
| **fuga, -ae**, F. | flight |
| **gaudium, -ī**, N. | joy |
| **gēns, gentis, -ium**, F. | race, people |
| **iam** (adv.) | now, by this time, already |
| **iter, itineris**, N. | journey, route |
| **iungō, -ere, iūnxī, iūnctus** | join |
| **coniūnx, coniugis**, M. *or* F. | husband, wife, spouse |
| **mōs, mōris**, M. | custom; pl., character |
| **negō** (1) | deny, say no |
| **neuter, neutra, neutrum** | neither |
| **nūllus, -a, -um** | no, none |
| **orbis, orbis, -ium**, M. | ring, orb, circle |
| **orbis terrārum** | circle of lands; the world |
| **pars, partis, -ium**, F. | part |

| | |
|---|---|
| **propter** (prep. + acc.) | on account of, because of |
| **quantus, -a, -um** | how much, how great |
| **quot** (indeclinable adj.) | how many |
| **signum, -ī, N.** | signal, sign |
| **sōl, sōlis, M.** | sun |
| **sōlus, -a, -um** | alone, only |
| **tantus, -a, -um** | so much, so great |
| **tantus...quantus**⎱<br>**quantus...tantus**⎰ | as (so) much (great)...as |
| **temptō** (1) | try, attempt |
| **tot** (indeclinable adj.) | so many |
| **tot...quot**⎱<br>**quot...tot**⎰ | as many...as |
| **tōtus, -a, -um** | all, whole |
| **ūllus, -a, -um** | any |
| **ūnus, -a, -um** | one, alone |
| **uter, utra, utrum** | which (of two) |
| **virtūs, -tūtis, F.** | manliness, courage, excellence, virtue |

## UNIT TEN — NOTES ON VOCABULARY

There are nine adjectives in Latin which end in -**īus** in the genitive singular and -**ī** in the dative singular: **alius, alter, ūllus** ('any'), **nūllus** ('none'), **uter, neuter** ('neither'), **sōlus** ('alone'), **tōtus** ('whole'), and **ūnus** ('one'). **Alius** means 'other, another', **alter**, 'the other (of two)', and **uter**, 'which (of two)'. **Alterīus** was used as the genitive singular of **alius** (see Appendix, page 322). **Alius...alius** means 'one...another': **Alius in tēctō alius in viā erat**, 'One man was in the house, another in the street'. When two forms of the adjective **alius** are found in the same sentence, they are translated twice:

Aliī aliud mihi dīxērunt.   Some men told me one thing; others told me another.

Alia dōna ad aliōs amīcōs mīsērunt.   They sent some gifts to some friends, other gifts to others (other friends).

**Apud** is like the French **chez**; it means 'at, near, among, at the house of, in the works of'.

The adjective **audāx, audācis**, 'bold, courageous', is related to the abstract noun **audācia, audāciae**, F., 'boldness, courage'.

**Coepī, coepisse, coeptus**, 'began', is a defective verb which has only perfect tenses. **Incipiō** may be used if a present, imperfect, or future tense of 'begin' is needed.

The verb **doceō, docēre, docuī, doctus**, 'teach', may govern two accusatives. In other words, one teaches something in the accusative case to someone in the accusative: **Multa nātōs docēre optāmus**, 'We wish to teach many things to our children'.

**Errō**, a first conjugation verb, means 'wander'. If one wanders from the true path, one errs; thus, **errō** also means 'err'.

**Ferō, ferre, tulī, lātus**, 'bear, bring, carry, endure', is sometimes used, usually in the third person, to mean 'say, report': **Auctōrem clārissimum in illō tēctō ferunt vīxisse**, 'They say that the very famous author lived in that house'. Also, **Auctor clārissimus in illō tēctō vīxisse fertur**, 'The very famous author is said to have lived in that house'.

**Ferō** is one of the four verbs (**dīcō, dūcō**, and **faciō** are the others) which drop the ending in the present active singular imperative: **dīc, dūc, fac, fer**.

Connected with **fugiō, fugere, fūgī, fugitus**, 'flee', is the noun **fuga, fugae**, F., 'flight'.

**Iungō, iungere, iūnxī, iūnctus**, 'join', has a compound **coniungō**, 'join together'; the person with whom one is joined, **coniūnx**, is one's 'spouse'; therefore, this word can be either masculine or feminine.

**Iam** is an adverb which relies on the tense of the verb for its meaning; with the present tense, it means 'now', with a past tense, 'up to now, already, by this time', and with the future, 'soon'.

**Mōs, mōris**, M., in the singular means 'custom', but in the plural, 'character', since it is our customs or habits which make up our character.

**Negō**, a first conjugation verb, is the opposite of **aiō**; it means 'say no, deny'.

**Orbis, orbis**, M., is 'ring, circle'; **orbis terrārum**, 'circle of lands', is the way of saying 'the world'.

There is no difference between **propter** with the accusative and **ob** with the accusative.

**Quantus, -a, -um**, 'how much, how great', is often used correlatively with **tantus, -a, -um**, 'so much, so great'. There is no difference in meaning between **quantus...tantus** and **tantus...quantus**: **Quantōs librōs in mēnsā vīdimus tantōs in cellā**, 'We saw as many books on the table as (we saw) in the storeroom'; **Tantum gaudium in urbe erat quantum in prōvinciā**, 'There was as much joy in the city as in the province'.

**Quot**, 'how many', may be correlative with **tot**, 'so many'. There is no difference in meaning between **quot...tot** and **tot...quot**: **Quot puellae tot puerī in tēctō erant**, 'There were as many girls as boys in the house'; **Tot dominōs quot servōs in templō vīdimus**, 'We saw as many masters as slaves in the temple'.

**Virtūs, virtūtis**, F., is an abstract noun meaning 'the state of being a man, *or* the quality of a man'; it is what makes a man a man, namely, 'manliness, courage, excellence, virtue'.

# UNIT TEN — DRILL

**I.**

Translate each of the following ablatives absolute literally; then give at least four smoother translations:

1. hostibus oppressīs
2. opere perfectō
3. timōre superante
4. rēgibus cīvēs servitūte līberantibus
5. imperiō ruente

6. sociīs interfectīs
7. perīculō remōtō
8. urbe ā hostibus invāsā
9. sociō magistrō
10. mīlitibus rūs euntibus

**II.**

Rewrite the subordinate clauses in Latin as ablatives absolute:

1. Postquam oppidum arsum est, mīlitēs discessērunt.
2. Sī Marcus erit magister, superābimus.
3. Sī pater sānus esset, mortem nōn timērēmus.
4. Quamquam nox terrās umbrīs tegit, sociī tamen vidēre possunt.
5. Quamquam perīcula intellēxit, in vīllam tamen ardentem ruit.
6. Incolae timēbant quod urbs ā sociīs trādita erat.
7. Quamquam opīniōnem dē amīcō mūtāverat, crūdēlis esse nōn optāvit.
8. Sī discēdētis, poēta nōn canet.
9. Mīlitēs per campōs īre nōn possunt quod saxa ingentia dē viā nōn removēbantur.
10. Postquam supplex domum missus est, populus omnem spem perdidit.

**III.**

Translate, explaining the syntax of the words in boldface type:

1. Fēmina **magnae fideī** mihi imperāvit ut Rōmam īrem.
2. Mōtibus sīderum **intellēctīs**, poēta librum dē illīs rēbus scrīpsit.
3. Profugō **poenam timente**, amīcī rēgem interficient.
4. **Oppidō** trāditō, incolae tamen spērāvērunt amīcōs sibi frūctuī futūrōs esse.
5. Sententiā dē hospitibus mūtātā, vir magnā **veniā** ad nōs vēnit ut dē īnsidiīs monēret.
6. Ille puer quem magister ad rēgnum vocāvit minimā est **dīligentiā**, maximā sapientiā.
7. **Illō dominō**, nōn timēmus.
8. Hostibus **pulsīs**, mīles fēlīx erat.
9. **Bellō** cōnfectō, diūtius pūgnātis?
10. **Amōre** patriae pūgnāvit.
11. Omnibus hostibus ab urbe **remōtīs**, incolae **gaudiō** clāmābant.

**IV.**

Note the following uses of participles and ablatives absolute:

1. Puerōs scrībentēs vīdī.
2. Hominēs in bellō superātī discessērunt.
3. Mīles erat pūgnātūrus.
4. Poēta, sub caelō legēns, sīdera spectāvit.
5. Puella hōs librōs lēctūra est.
6. Opere cōnfectō, virī domum missī sunt.
7. Mediā nocte ad socium litterās portantēs vēnērunt.
8. Hīs rēbus gestīs, omnēs discessērunt.
9. Audiēns virōs magnae sapientiae dē bellō clāmantēs, maximē timēbam.
10. Audiēns virōs magnae sapientiae dē bellō clāmāre, maximē timēbam.
11. Servīs līberātīs, dominus suōs fīliōs labōrāre in agrīs iussit.
12. Homō miser, vīllā arsā, nūllam domum habēbat.
13. Clārum multās hōrās sociīs vēra dīcentem audīvī; minimō tempore discessit. Illō discēdente, mīlitēs gaudiō clāmāvērunt.
14. Multa dōna ūnī virō cibum ad hospitēs ferentī dabimus.
15. Taedamne ad profugōs nocte ambulantēs ferēs?

**V.**

1. Puer fert librōs.
2. Puer ferēbat librōs.
3. Is est puer quī ferēbat librōs.
4. Puer fertur esse bonus. [**fertur**, '(he) is said...']
5. Puer fertur librōs ferre.
6. Puer fertur librōs tulisse.
7. Librōs nōn feram.
8. Librī ā puerō feruntur.
9. Librī ā mē nōn lātī sunt.
10. Dīcō puerum quī librōs ferat bonum esse.
11. Dīcēbam puerum quī librōs ferret bonum esse.
12. Dīxī puerum quī librōs tulisset bonum esse.
13. Intellegit librōs frūctuī esse hominibus sapientibus.
14. Librī ad nōs feruntur ut sapientiōrēs sīmus.

# UNIT TEN — PRELIMINARY EXERCISES
## (SECTIONS A, B)

1. Fugā temptātā, audācēs per prōvinciam itinere errāre coepērunt.
2. Audācia custōdis sōlīus auxilium gentī tōtī tulit.

3. Gaudiō positō, aliī vītam tulērunt, aliī negāvērunt.
4. Omnibus fortibus mōrēs supplicis alterīus laudantibus, opīniō nostra nōn petīta est.
5. Librō aliō scrīptō, auctor alium scrībere coepit.
6. Sōle auxiliō, viīs incertīs fūgimus ut nōs sociīs quam prīmum iungerēmus.
7. Quot artēs sunt aliī tot aliī.
8. Omnī spē fugae dēlētā, locus nūllus salūtis ā profugīs inventus est.
9. Itinere incertō et nūllō signō ā magistrō datō, in neutram viam sine timōre perīculī ruere iam possumus.
10. Nūllus homō quī apud nōs vīvit tanta gaudia quantōs metūs tulit.

## UNIT TEN — EXERCISES

**I.**

1. Mīlitibus foedere iūnctīs, haec urbs sōla nōn dēlēbitur; multa gravia iam sustulit.
2. Aliō bellō in prōvinciam illātō, hostēs tēctīs et templīs tōtīus urbis ignēs īnferre temptāvērunt.
3. Tōtam diem illae gentēs socium magnae audāciae invenīre temptābant quem vī abstulerant saeviōrēs servī.
4. Sōle multīs partibus maiōre quam terrā tōtā, ōrō ut mē dē illō plūs doceās.
5. Sorōrī meae nōmen est magnā apud omnēs glōriā; eam oculīs tuīs in lītore errantem saepe vīdistī.
6. Pectoribus mōrēs tot sunt quot in orbe figūrae.
7. Negat sē mōre et exemplō populī Rōmānī posse iter ūllī per prōvinciam dare.
8. Dīs nūllam mihi culpam esse scientibus, audāx metū carēbō.
9. Patriā līberā, mē ad mortem nōn offeram.
10. Hīs ā sociō dictīs, rēx prīmā lūce respondit lībertātem cīvibus ā dīs oblātam et datam esse.
11. Quot hominēs tot sententiae.
12. Tot mīlitibus urbem oppūgnantibus, rēgīnae coniūnx pecūniae quam rēgnī melior custōs erat.
13. Quam ob rem per tōtum oppidum rūmor huius generis ībit?
14. Rēx prōvinciae fūgisse cum multā pecūniā dīcitur ac sē contulisse Rōmam.
15. a) Rēge crūdēlī Rōmam fugiente, aliī cīvēs gaudiō clāmant, aliī timōre tacent.
    b) Rēge crūdēlī Rōmam fugiente, aliī cīvēs gaudiō clāmābant, aliī timōre tacēbant.
16. Amīcitia ex sē et propter sē petenda est.
17. Illō discēdente, rēs agī coepta est.

18. Mīlitibus sē in fugam dantibus, utrum dūcentium laudāre coeperās? Neutrum!

19. Ūnō signō datō, cum gaudiō invēnimus cīvibus quantum audāciae tantum satis esse.

20. Suffer! Multō graviōra tulistī.

21. Nūllī servitūtem sī dēfers, honestus habēris.

22. Multī mōre illō atque exemplō vīvunt.

23. Quī nihil sciunt timent fortūnam; sapientēs ferunt. [**fortūna, -ae**, F., 'chance, fortune']

24. Hostēs maximārum vīrium, cum suīs sociīs iūnctī, oppidum oppūgnāvērunt.

25. Multīs prō oppidō pūgnantibus, incolae nōn timēbant.

26. Vir bonus optimīsque artibus clārus cīvibus auxiliō fuit.

27. Custōdibus maiōre opus erit et arte et dīligentiā sī malōs ex urbe pellent.

28. Amīcus certus in rē incertā vidētur.

29. Mōrēs cōnferte et artēs sī fīliōs maximae virtūtis esse optābitis. [**cōnferte**, *here*, 'apply, bestow']

30. Cōnsiliīs certiōribus factīs, dōna ā rēge abstulit et ea ad suam patriam attulit.

31. Mīles mīlitī iūnctus amīcitiā bellum magnā cum virtūte gessit.

32. Illī custōdī, virō magnā audāciā et mōribus clārō, coniūnx auxiliō vēnit, nē urbis īnsidiīs hostium dēlētae damnārētur. Eum enim monuit cōnsilia hostium urbī mala esse.

33. Pars gentis domum cum sapientiā fūgit; pars propter audāciam bellum gessit.

34. In tōtō orbe terrārum numquam vīdimus tot errantēs quot in hāc urbe vīvunt. Alius bellum gentibus fortiōribus īnferre optat, alius sine arte et auxiliō tōtum orbem terrārum superāre; nūllus homō negat sē omnia (facere) posse.

35. Hostibus foedere iūnctīs, ūnus ex pūgnantibus negābat sē bellum gerere umquam optāvisse; sibi gerendum fuisse vīribus atque mōribus malīs rēgis.

36. Quam ob rem magister docuit errantem verbīs sapientium in lūcem dūcendum esse?

37. Signō datō, fēminae maximā fōrmā sē in fugam contulērunt.

38. Bellō cōnfectō, multa nōbīs superātīs relāta sunt.

39. Tantō perīculō in urbem illātō, lacrimae incolārum mātrem certiōrem fēcērunt ruīnae. Māter fēmina erat clārā virtūte, sed tanta mala sufferre nōn poterat.

40. Ferrum ē manibus interfectī cēpit, ēlātumque dēferēbat in pectus alterīus inimīcī ā dextrā ad sē venientis.

41. Quantā maximē poterat vī superāvit.

42. Hominibus ācriter pūgnantibus, rēx ardentēs oculōrum orbēs in moenia torsit. [**torqueō, -ēre, torsī, tortus**, 'turn, turn away, twist']

## II.

1. Because the people of this city have been conquered by the Roman soldiers, the woman's husband, bold in character, is going to try to flee in order to seek (ask for) aid from the guardians of other towns.
2. On account of the treaty by which they were joined to the Romans, the husband learned that the guardians did not desire to give aid to any people.
3. He alone will not be able to flee to the shore because of fear; the others have already boldly set sail.
4. In the whole world I have never seen with my eyes a man of such (so) great skill.
5. Since he has done these things, his name will be borne by the winds to all lands in order that people may praise him.

## III. Readings

A. THE LOVE OF DAPHNE AND APOLLO (selections slightly adapted from Ovid, *Metamorphoses* I, taken from lines 452–3, 495, 502–3, 533–4, 539)

Prīmus amor Phoebī[1] Daphnē[2] quem dedit saeva Cupīdinis[3] īra. Sīc[4] deus in flammās abiit;[5] fugit ōcior[6] aurā[7] illa levī.[8] Ut[9] canis[10] in vacuō[11] leporem[12] arvō[13] cum[14] vīdit, et ille praedam[15] pedibus petit, hic salūtem; sīc[4] deus et virgō.[16] Est hic spē celer,[17] illa timōre.

[1] **Phoebus, -ī,** M., the god Apollo  [2] **Daphnē** (nom. sing. F.), 'Daphne', a girl's name  [3] **Cupīdō, -inis,** M., 'Cupid'  [4] **sīc** (adv.), 'in this way'  [5] **abeō (ab + eō),** 'go away'  [6] **ōcior, ōcius,** 'swifter'  [7] **aura, -ae,** F., 'breeze'  [8] **levis, leve,** 'light'  [9] **ut** (adv.), 'as' (here, correlative with sīc below)  [10] **canis, canis,** M. or F., 'dog'  [11] **vacuus, -a, -um,** 'empty'  [12] **lepus, leporis,** M., 'rabbit'  [13] **arvum, -ī,** N., 'field'  [14] **cum** (conj.), 'when'  [15] **praeda, -ae,** F., 'loot'  [16] **virgō, virginis,** F., 'maiden'  [17] **celer, celeris, celere,** 'swift'

B. Dido, after berating Aeneas for intending to abandon her, falls silent and leaves him to think about her plight (Vergil, *Aeneid* IV.388–91):

His medium dictīs sermōnem[1] abrumpit[2] et aurās[3]
aegra[4] fugit sēque ex oculīs āvertit[5] et aufert,
linquēns[6] multa metū cūnctantem[7] et multa parantem[8]
dīcere.

[1] **sermō, -ōnis,** M., 'speech'  [2] **abrumpō, -ere, -rūpī, -ruptus,** 'break off'  [3] **aura, -ae,** F., 'air, breeze, outdoors'  [4] **aeger, aegra, aegrum,** 'sick, wretched'  [5] **āvertō, -ere, -vertī, -versus,** 'turn away'  [6] **linquō, -ere, līquī, lictus,** 'desert'  [7] **cūnctor, -ārī, -ātus sum,** 'delay' (this is a verb of the first conjugation; the finite forms are all passive, but with active meanings; see Unit Eleven, section A, "Deponent Verbs")  [8] **parō** (1), 'prepare'

C. Catullus 87:

> Nūlla potest mulier[1] tantum[2] sē dīcere amātam
> Vērē, quantum[2] ā mē Lesbia[3] amāta mea es:
> Nūlla fidēs ūllō fuit unquam in foedere tanta
> Quanta in amōre tuō ex parte reperta meā est.[4]

[1] mulier, mulieris, F., 'woman'    [2] tantum...quantum (adv.), 'so much...as'    [3] Lesbia, -ae, F., 'Lesbia', the literary name of Catullus's mistress    [4] reperiō, -īre, repperī, repertus, 'find, discover'

D. Seneca speaks about the advantages of clemency and about the difference between the king and the tyrant (Seneca, *Dē Clēmentiā* I.xi.4–xii.2, slightly adapted):

Clēmentiā[1] ergō[2] hominēs nōn tantum[3] honestiōrēs sed tūtiōrēs sunt. Clēmentia[1] ōrnāmentum[4] imperiōrum est simul[5] et certissima salūs. Metū hostium sublātō,[6] hominēs maximae clēmentiae[1] sine cūrā possunt vīvere. Cūr[7] enim rēgēs cōnsenēscunt[8] fīliīsque trādunt rēgna, tyrannōrum[9] exsecrābilis[10] ac brevis[11] potestās[12] est? Quid interest[13] inter[14] tyrannum[9] ac rēgem?—Tyrannī[9] voluptāte[15] saeviunt,[16] rēgēs nōn nisī ex causā[17] ac necessitāte.[18]

"Quid ergō?[2] Nōn rēgēs quoque[19] interficere solent?"[20] Sed ubi[21] id fierī[22] pūblica ūtilitās[23] persuadet;[24] tyrannīs[9] saevitia[25] cordī[26] est. Tyrannus[9] autem ā rēge factīs distat,[27] nōn nōmine; nam et Dionȳsius[28] maior iūre[29] meritōque[30] praeferrī[31] multīs rēgibus potest. Et L. Sullam[32] tyrannum[9] appellārī[33] quid prohibet,[34] cui factōrum malōrum fīnem fēcit inopia[35] hostium? Quī umquam tyrannus[9] avidius[36] hūmānum[37]

[1] clēmentia, -ae, F., 'clemency'    [2] ergō (adv.), 'therefore'    [3] tantum (adv.), 'only'    [4] ōrnāmentum, -ī, N., 'decoration, ornament'    [5] simul (adv.), 'at the same time'    [6] tollō, -ere, sustulī, sublātus, 'remove'    [7] cūr (adv.), 'why'    [8] cōnsenēscō, -ere, cōnsenuī, ––, 'grow old'    [9] tyrannus, -ī, M., 'absolute ruler, tyrant'; tyrannōrum exsecrābilis...est: the clause is antithetical to the previous one; assume the ellipsis of sed, 'but'    [10] exsecrābilis, -e, 'deserving punishment, deadly'    [11] brevis, -e, 'brief'    [12] potestās, -tātis, F., 'power'    [13] interest (impersonal verb), '(it) is different'; quid interest?, 'what is the difference?'    [14] inter (prep. + acc.), 'between'    [15] voluptās, -tātis, F., 'pleasure'    [16] saeviō, -īre, -iī, -ītus, 'rage, be fierce'    [17] causa, -ae, F., 'cause, reason'    [18] necessitās, -tātis, F., 'necessity'    [19] quoque (adv.), 'also'    [20] soleō, -ēre, solitus sum, 'be accustomed'    [21] ubi (adv.), 'when'    [22] fīō, fierī, factus sum, 'happen, be done'    [23] ūtilitās, -tātis, F., 'advantage'    [24] persuadeō, -ēre, -suāsī, -suāsus, 'persuade'    [25] saevitia, -ae, F., 'cruelty'    [26] cor, cordis, N., 'heart'; cordī, 'for the purpose of the heart,' i.e., 'dear'    [27] distō (1), 'differ, be distinct'    [28] Dionȳsius, -ī, M., a man's name; Dionysius was the famous tyrant of Sicily    [29] iūs, iūris, N., 'right, law'    [30] meritum, -ī, N., 'merit, desert'    [31] praeferō, -ferre, -tulī, -lātus, 'prefer (to)' (+ dat.)    [32] L. Sulla, -ae, M., 'Lucius Sulla', the name of a Roman dictator whose policy it was to have all his enemies killed    [33] appellō (1) ,'call, name'; appellārī, the infinitive is used here with prohibet to express prevention: 'What prohibits L. Sulla to be called...'; 'What keeps L. Sulla from being called...'    [34] prohibeō, -ēre, -uī, -itus, 'prohibit'    [35] inopia, -ae, F., 'lack'    [36] avidē (adv.), 'eagerly'    [37] hūmānus, -a, -um, 'human'

sanguinem [38] bibit [39] quam ille, quī septem [40] mīlia [41] cīvium Rōmānōrum interficī iussit et, ubi [21] in vīcīnō [42] sedēns [43] audīvit conclāmātiōnem [44] tot mīlium [41] sub gladiō gementium, [45] exterritō [46] senātū, [47] "Nē haec conclāmātiō," [44] ait, "vobīs sit cūrae, patrēs cōnscrīptī; [48] sēditiōsī [49] pauculī [50] meō iussū [51] interficiuntur"? Hoc vērum erat; paucī [52] Sullae [32] vidēbantur.

[38] sanguis, -inis, M., 'blood'   [39] bibō, -ere, bibī, ––, 'drink'   [40] septem (indeclinable adj.), 'seven'   [41] mīlia, -ium, N., 'thousands'   [42] vīcīnum, -ī, N., 'vicinity'   [43] sedeō, -ēre, sēdī, sessus, 'sit'   [44] conclāmātiō, -ōnis, F., 'loud shouting'   [45] gemō, -ere, -uī, -itus, 'groan, lament'   [46] exterreō (ex + terreō), 'frighten thoroughly'   [47] senātus, -ūs, M., 'senate'   [48] cōnscrībō (com- + scrībō), 'enroll'; patrēs cōnscrīptī, 'senators'   [49] sēditiōsus, -a, -um, 'seditious, turbulent'   [50] pauculī, -ae, -a, 'a very few'   [51] iussū (abl. sing.), 'by order'   [52] paucī, -ae, -a, 'few'

## A. Deponent Verbs

Many verbs in Latin have only passive forms, but active meanings. These verbs are called *deponents* (**dē** + **pōnō**, 'put aside'; i.e., they *put aside* their active forms).

| | |
|---|---|
| precor, -ārī, precātus sum | beg, request |
| vereor, -ērī, veritus sum | fear |
| ingredior, -ī, ingressus sum | enter, proceed |
| experior, -īrī, expertus sum | try, experience |

PRESENT TENSE

| INDICATIVE | SUBJUNCTIVE |
|---|---|
| precor | precer |
|   I entreat | |
| precāris (-re) | precēris (-re) |
|   you entreat | |
| precātur | precētur |
|   he entreats | |
| | |
| precāmur | precēmur |
|   we entreat | |
| precāminī | precēminī |
|   you entreat | |
| precantur | precentur |
|   they entreat | |

IMPERFECT TENSE

| INDICATIVE | SUBJUNCTIVE |
|---|---|
| precābar | precārer |
|   I used to entreat | |
| precābāris (-re) | precārēris (-re) |
|   you used to entreat | |
|   ...etc. | ...etc. |

NOTE that the imperfect subjunctive is built onto what would have been the entire

176

present *active* infinitive. This is especially important for third conjugation verbs where the present passive infinitive looks so different from the active one. Thus:

ingred**erer**
ingred**erēris** (-re)
...etc.

FUTURE TENSE

| INDICATIVE | SUBJUNCTIVE |
|---|---|
| precābor | |
| I shall entreat | *None* |
| precāberis (-re) | |
| you will entreat | |
| ...etc. | |

PERFECT TENSE

| INDICATIVE | SUBJUNCTIVE |
|---|---|
| precātus sum | precātus sim |
| I have entreated | |
| precātus es | precātus sīs |
| you have entreated | |
| ...etc. | ...etc. |

PLUPERFECT TENSE

| INDICATIVE | SUBJUNCTIVE |
|---|---|
| precātus eram | precātus essem |
| I had entreated | |
| precātus erās | precātus essēs |
| you had entreated | |
| ...etc. | ...etc. |

FUTURE PERFECT TENSE

| INDICATIVE | SUBJUNCTIVE |
|---|---|
| precātus erō | *None* |
| I shall have entreated | |
| ...etc. | |

INFINITIVES

| | ACTIVE | PASSIVE |
|---|---|---|
| Present | precārī | -- |
| | to entreat | |
| Perfect | precātus esse | -- |
| | to have entreated | |
| Future | precātūrus esse | -- |
| | to be going to entreat | |

NOTE that, while the present and perfect infinitives have *passive forms* but *active meanings*, the future infinitive is *active* in *form* and *meaning*.

## PARTICIPLES

|          | ACTIVE                | PASSIVE                |
|----------|-----------------------|-----------------------|
| Present  | precāns<br>entreating | ──                    |
| Perfect  | precātus, -a, -um<br>having entreated | ── |
| Future   | precātūrus, -a, -um<br>going to entreat | precandus, -a, -um<br>having to be entreated |

NOTE that the following irregularities occur in the participial system:

1. Deponents *do have* a present participle which is active in *form* and *meaning*.
2. Deponent verbs have a perfect *active* participle; other verbs have only a perfect *passive* participle.
3. Deponent verbs have *both* a future *active* and a future *passive* participle in *form* and *meaning*.

The present and future participles and the future infinitive, then, pose the only problem in the deponent system. In all other instances, remember: DEPONENTS HAVE PASSIVE FORMS, BUT ACTIVE MEANINGS.

## B. Semi-Deponent Verbs

Several verbs have active forms and meanings in the present system, but passive forms with active meanings in the perfect system. These are called *semi-deponents*.

### audeō, -ēre, ausus sum, 'dare'

| audeō      | I dare              |
|------------|---------------------|
| audēbam    | I used to dare      |
| audēbō     | I shall dare        |
| ausus sum  | I have dared        |
| ausus eram | I had dared         |
| ausus erō  | I shall have dared  |

## C. Subjective and Objective Genitive

There is a verbal idea understood in nouns and adjectives of feeling or action. The noun that is the object of this verbal idea is called the *objective genitive*, and the noun that is its subject is called the *subjective genitive*.

OBJECTIVE GENITIVE:

| | |
|---|---|
| amor **patriae** | love *of the native land* (i.e., what is loved is the native land; **patriae** is the object of the verbal idea understood in **amor**) |
| metus **bellī** | fear *of war* (i.e., what is feared is war) |
| cupidus (-a, -um) **pecūniae** | desirous of money (i.e., what the subject desires is money) |

SUBJECTIVE GENITIVE:

| | |
|---|---|
| **fēminae** amor patriae | the *woman's* love of her native land (i.e., the woman is doing the loving and therefore **fēminae** is the *subjective genitive*; the woman [subject] loves her native land [object]) |

## D. Predicate Genitive (Genitive of Characteristic)

A noun in the genitive case which stands alone (or modified by an adjective) in the predicate denotes a characteristic or a class.

| | |
|---|---|
| **Hominis sapientis** est librōs legere. | It is (*the mark*) *of a wise man* to read books. Reading books is *the mark of a wise man.* |
| **Bonī** est deōs laudāre. | It is (*the mark*) *of a good* [*man*] to praise the gods. |

## E. Infinitive As Subject

The infinitive is, in fact, a neuter noun. In the sentences given as examples under section D above, **legere** and **laudāre** are the subjects of the verb **est**.

**Vidēre** est crēdere.   *To see* is to believe; *seeing* is believing.

Infinitives used in this way may be modified by adjectives which will appear in the neuter.

| | |
|---|---|
| Librōs legere **bonum** est. | To read books is (*a*) *good* (*thing*); reading books is *good*; it is *a good thing* to read books. |
| Scīmus **bonum** esse librōs legere. | We know that to read books is (*a*) *good* (*thing*); we know that reading books is (*a*) *good* (*thing*). |

In the last example, the infinitive **legere** is the subject accusative of the infinitive **esse**.

## F. The Irregular Verbs *volō, nōlō, mālō*

| | |
|---|---|
| volō, velle, voluī -- | wish, want, be willing |
| nōlō, nōlle, nōluī, -- | be unwilling (contracted from **nōn volō**) |
| mālō, mālle, māluī, -- | prefer (contracted from **magis volō**) |

All three verbs actually belong to the third conjugation. The only irregularities which occur are in the present tense, as illustrated below. The imperfect subjunctive is formed on the irregular infinitives **velle, nōlle, mālle**. The imperfect and future indicatives as well as the present participle (except for **mālō**, which lacks one) are formed on the stems **vole-, nōle-**, and **māle-**, as if the verbs had regular infinitives (★**volere,** ★**nōlere,** ★**mālere**).

PRESENT TENSE

| | INDICATIVE | SUBJUNCTIVE | PRESENT PARTICIPLE |
|---|---|---|---|
| **volō** | volō | velim | volēns |
| | vīs | velīs | |
| | vult | velit | |
| | volumus | velīmus | |
| | vultis | velītis | |
| | volunt | velint | |
| **nōlō** | nōlō (= nōn volō) | nōlim (= nōn velim) | nōlēns |
| | nōn vīs | nōlīs (= nōn velīs) | |
| | nōn vult | nōlit (= nōn velit) | |
| | nōlumus (= nōn volumus) | nōlīmus (= nōn velīmus) | |
| | nōn vultis | nōlītis (= nōn velītis) | |
| | nōlunt (= nōn volunt) | nōlint (= nōn velint) | |
| | IMPERATIVE: nōlī (sing.); nōlīte (pl.) | | |
| **mālō** | mālō (= magis volō) | mālim (= magis velim) | —— |
| | māvīs (= magis vīs) | mālīs (= magis velīs) | |
| | māvult (= magis vult) | mālit (= magis velit) | |
| | mālumus (= magis volumus) | mālīmus (= magis velīmus) | |
| | māvultis (= magis vultis) | mālītis (= magis velītis) | |
| | mālunt (= magis volunt) | mālint (= magis velint) | |

## UNIT ELEVEN — VOCABULARY

| | |
|---|---|
| **arbitror, arbitrārī, arbitrātus sum** | think, believe, judge |
| **audeō, -ēre, ausus sum** | dare |
| **cēna, -ae, F.** | dinner |
| **cōnor, cōnārī, cōnātus sum** | try, attempt |
| **cōnsul, cōnsulis, M.** | consul |
| **crēdō, -ere, crēdidī, crēditus** | be credulous, believe; be trusting, trust (+ dat.) |
| **cupidus, -a, -um** | desirous, eager, fond of (+ gen.) |

| | |
|---|---|
| dīvitiae, -ārum, F. pl. | riches, wealth |
| dux, ducis, M. *or* F. | leader, guide |
| experior, experīrī, expertus sum | try, put to the test, experience |
| familia, -ae, F. | household, family |
| fateor, fatērī, fassus sum | confess |
| cōnfiteor, cōnfitērī, cōnfessus sum | confess |
| flūmen, -inis, N. | river, running water |
| forum, -ī, N. | open space, market place, public square |
| gradior, gradī, gressus sum | step, walk |
| aggredior, -ī, -gressus sum | go to, approach |
| ēgredior, -ī, -gressus sum | go out, go away |
| ingredior, -ī, -gressus sum | go into, enter, advance, begin |
| prōgredior, -ī, -gressus sum | go forth, advance, proceed |
| hortor, hortārī, hortātus sum | urge, encourage (+ **ut** *or* **nē** and subjunctive) |
| imperātor, -ōris, M. | commander, general |
| iuvenis, -is, M. *or* F. | youth, young person |
| loquor, loquī, locūtus sum | speak, talk |
| mālō, mālle, māluī, — | prefer, choose rather |
| minor, minārī, minātus sum | jut forth, threaten |
| morior, morī, mortuus sum | die |
| nāscor, nāscī, nātus sum | be born, descend from |
| nāvis, -is, -ium, F. | ship |
| neglegō, -ere, neglēxī, neglēctus | disregard, neglect |
| nōlō, nōlle, nōluī, — | be unwilling, wish...not |
| ōrātor, -ōris, M. | speaker |
| parēns, parentis, M. *or* F. | parent |
| patior, patī, passus sum | suffer, endure, allow |
| pauper, pauperis | poor |
| praemium, -ī, N. | reward |
| precor, precārī, precātus sum | beg, request |
| proficīscor, proficīscī, profectus sum | set forth, set out, start |
| scelus, sceleris, N. | wicked deed, crime |
| sequor, sequī, secūtus sum | follow |
| servō (1) | save, preserve, rescue, keep |
| soleō, -ēre, solitus sum | be accustomed, be customary |
| statua, -ae, F. | statue |
| ut (conj. + indicative) | as, when |
| ūtor, ūtī, ūsus sum | use, enjoy, experience (+ abl.) |
| vereor, verērī, veritus sum | reverence, fear, dread |
| volō, velle, voluī, — | wish, want, be willing |

# UNIT ELEVEN — NOTES ON VOCABULARY

**Audeō, audēre, ausus sum,** 'dare', and **soleō, solēre, solitus sum,** 'be accustomed', are semi-deponents. In other words, in the present, imperfect, and future tenses, the forms are active with active meanings, but in the perfect tenses, the forms are passive with active meanings: **audēbis,** 'you will dare'; **ausus erat,** 'he had dared'.

**Crēdō, crēdere, crēdidī, crēditus** is really an intransitive verb which means 'be trusting' and governs the dative case; however, we often translate it as 'believe, trust': **Cui crēdis?** 'To whom are you trusting?; Whom do you trust?'

The adjective **cupidus, -a, -um,** 'desirous, eager, fond of', governs an objective genitive: **Cupidus imperiī erat,** 'He was desirous of power'.

**Dīvitiae, dīvitiārum** is a feminine plural noun meaning 'riches, wealth'.

**Dux, ducis,** 'leader, guide', may be either masculine or feminine; it is related to the verb **dūcō,** 'lead'.

**Fateor, fatērī, fassus sum** and its compound **cōnfiteor, cōnfitērī, cōnfessus sum** both mean 'confess' and may be used interchangeably.

There is a third conjugation verb **fluō, fluere, flūxī, flūxus,** 'flow'; when the abstract noun ending **-men, -minis** is added to the stem, the noun **flūmen, flūminis,** N., 'the result of flowing', that is, 'river', results.

**Gradior, gradī, gressus sum,** 'step, walk', when compounded gives the stem **-gredior.** Thus, **aggredior (ad + gradior),** 'go to, approach'; **ēgredior,** 'go out'; **ingredior,** 'go into, enter, advance, begin'; **prōgredior,** 'go forth, proceed, advance'.

The verb **hortor, hortārī, hortātus sum,** 'urge, encourage', can introduce an indirect command: **Amīcōs hortātī sumus nē huic hominī crēderent,** 'We urged our friends not to believe this man'.

**Imperātor, imperātōris,** M., is 'the one who does the ordering', namely, 'commander, general'; **ōrātor, ōrātōris,** M., is 'one who does the begging *or* pleading', and then, 'speaker'.

**Iuvenis, iuvenis,** M. *or* F., 'youth, young man', is not an i-stem; neither is **parēns, parentis,** M. *or* F., 'parent', although according to the rules for i-stems, one would expect them to be.

**Loquor, loquī, locūtus sum** is 'speak, talk'; **dīcō, dīcere, dīxī, dictus** is 'say, tell'.

**Volō, velle, voluī, —,** 'wish, want, be willing', is an irregular verb of the third conjugation. It has two compounds: **(nōn + volō) nōlō, nōlle, nōluī, —,** 'be unwilling, wish...not', and **(magis + volō) mālō, mālle, māluī, —,** 'prefer, choose rather'. Literally **mālō** means 'want more'; it may govern an accusative and an ablative of comparison: **Virtūtemne fōrmā māvīs?,** 'Do you want courage more than beauty?; Do you prefer courage to beauty?'

**Minor, minārī, minātus sum** means 'jut forth'. Since something that juts forth may be threatening, this verb also means 'threaten' and when it does it may govern the dative case. One can either threaten something in the accusative case to the person or thing in the dative or threaten the person or thing in the dative with something in the ablative case:

Dux mortem impiīs minātus est.   The leader threatened the impious men
*or*                              with death.
Dux impiīs morte minātus est.

**Morior, morī, mortuus sum**, 'die', has as its future participle **moritūrus, -a, -um**.

**Nāscor, nāscī, nātus sum**, 'be born, descend from', has as its past participle **nātus**. Thus, **nātus, nātī**, M., is 'the one born *or* descended', thus, 'son'.

**Neglegō** is a compound of **legō** (nec + legō, 'not choose'); it means 'disregard, neglect'. Like **intellegō**, **neglegō** has an -x- in the perfect active stem, **neglēxī**.

**Patior, patī, passus sum** has the meanings 'suffer, endure, allow'. The English word "patient" is a good reminder of the meanings of this verb: a patient in a hospital may be suffering and a person who is patient endures the things that happen to him; when one speaks of Christ's passion, he means His suffering. The words "patient" and "passion" are also good reminders of the stems of this verb.

**Servō**, a first conjugation verb, does *not* mean 'serve' (**serviō, servīre** does); it means 'save, preserve, rescue, keep'.

Notice that **ut** may be used with the indicative; when it is so used, it means 'as' or 'when'.

**Ūtor, ūtī, ūsus sum**, 'use, enjoy, experience', is one of several deponents which govern the ablative case: **Ferrō ūsus es?**, 'Did you use your sword?' The most common of the other deponents which govern the ablative are: **fruor, fruī, frūctus sum**, 'enjoy'; **fungor, fungī, fūnctus sum**, 'perform'; **potior, potīrī, potītus sum**, 'gain possession of'; and **vēscor, vēscī, --**, 'eat'.

## Noun Suffixes

The suffixes -tor (M.), -trīx (F.) added to the stem of a verb produce a noun. Each means 'one who'. Thus:

**inceptor, -ōris**, M., 'one who begins, beginner'
**audītor, -ōris**, M., 'one who hears, hearer'
**scrīptor, -ōris**, M., 'one who writes, writer'
**spectātor, -ōris**, M., and **spectātrīx, -trīcis**, F., 'one who looks on, spectator'
**āctor, -ōris**, M., 'one who does, doer, performer'

līberātor, -ōris, M., 'one who frees, liberator'
amātor, -ōris, M., and **amātrīx, amātrīcis**, F., 'one who loves, lover'
inventor, -ōris, M., and **inventrīx, inventrīcis**, F., 'one who finds, discoverer'
cantor, -ōris, M., and **cantrīx, cantrīcis**, F., 'one who sings, singer'
victor, -ōris, M., and **victrīx, victrīcis**, F., 'one who conquers, conqueror'
petītor, -ōris, M., 'one who seeks, seeker', also, 'a candidate for office'

By analogy, there are **viātor**, -ōris, M., and **viātrīx**, **viātrīcis**, F., 'traveler' (from **via**, 'way' + -**tor** or -**trīx**).

The endings -**ulus**, -**a**, -**um**; -**ōlus**, -**a**, -**um** (after a vowel); -**culus** -**a**, -**um**; -**ellus**, -**a**, -**um**; -**illus**, -**a**, -**um** are diminutive endings which may also be used to show affection, pity, or contempt.

puellula, -ae, F., 'a little girl'
fīliōlus, -ī, M., 'a little son'
homunculus, -ī, M., 'a little man; a poor, weak man'
libellus, -ī, M., 'a little book'
ocellus, -ī, M., 'a little eye'
Graeculus, -ī, M. (**Graecus, -a, -um**, 'Greek'), 'a no-good Greek'
sigilla, -ōrum, N. pl. (**signum, -ī**, N., 'sign'), 'little figures, little images'

## ADJECTIVAL SUFFIXES ADDED TO THE STEMS OF NOUNS

The suffixes -**eus**, -**ius**, -**ānus**, -**ēnus**, -**īnus**, -**ēius**, -**cus**, -**ticus** added to the stem of a noun (or, sometimes, an adjective) mean 'made of' or 'belonging to':

fēmineus, -a, -um, 'belonging to a woman, feminine'
aureus, -a, -um, 'made of gold, golden'
patrius, -a, -um, 'belonging to a father, paternal'
rēgius, -a, -um, 'belonging to a king, royal'
montānus, -a, -um, 'belonging to a mountain, mountain-'
urbānus, -a, -um, 'belonging to the city, city-'
terrēnus, -a, -um, 'made of earth, earthen'
aliēnus, -a, -um, 'belonging to another, strange'
dīvīnus, -a, -um, (**dīvus, -ī**, M., 'god'), 'belonging to a deity, divine'
marīnus, -a, -um, 'belonging to the sea, marine'
plēbēius, -a, -um (**plēbs, plēbis**, F., 'common people'), 'belonging to the common people, plebeian'
cīvicus, -a, -um, 'belonging to *or* of a citizen, civic'
bellicus, -a, -um, 'belonging to *or* of war, war-'
domesticus, -a, -um,' belonging to the house, domestic'
viāticus, -a, -um, 'belonging to a road, belonging to a journey'

The suffixes -**ālis**, -**āris**, -**īlis** added to the stem of a noun mean 'pertaining to':

> **aquālis**, -e, 'pertaining to water'
> **corporālis**, -e, 'pertaining to the body, corporeal'
> **populāris**, -e, 'pertaining to the people'
> **cōnsulāris**, -e, 'pertaining to a consul, consular'
> **hostīlis**, -e, 'pertaining to an enemy, hostile'
> **cīvīlis**, -e, 'pertaining to citizens, civil, civic'

The suffixes -**ter** (-**tris**), -**ester** (-**estris**), -**timus**, -**nus**, -**urnus**, -**ternus** mean 'belonging to' (especially of times and places):

> **equester, equestris, equestre** (**eques**, 'horseman, knight'), 'belonging to a horseman, equestrian'
> **campester, campestris, campestre**, 'of *or* pertaining to a level field'
> **terrestris**, -e, 'of *or* belonging to the earth'
> **maritimus**, -a, -**um**, 'of *or* belonging to the sea'
> **fīnitimus**, -a, -**um**, 'bordering upon, neighboring'
> **meridiānus**, -a, -**um** (**meridiēs**, 'noon'), 'of *or* belonging to mid-day'
> **nocturnus**, -a, -**um**, 'of *or* belonging to the night'
> **diūturnus**, -a, -**um**, 'of long duration, lasting'
> **hesternus**, -a, -**um** (**heri**, 'yesterday'), 'of *or* pertaining to yesterday'

# UNIT ELEVEN — DRILL

## I. Deponent Verbs

Translate indicatives, participles, infinitives, and imperatives; fully identify subjunctives.

| | |
|---|---|
| cōnor, -ārī, cōnātus sum | try, attempt |
| fateor, -ērī, fassus sum | confess |
| sequor, sequī, secūtus sum | follow |
| experior, -īrī, expertus sum | try, experience |

1. cōnātur; fatētur; sequitur; experītur
2. cōnābātur; fatēbātur; sequēbātur; experiēbātur
3. cōnābitur; fatēbitur; sequētur; experiētur
4. cōnāta est; fassa est; secūta est; experta est
5. cōnāta erat; fassa erat; secūta erat; experta erat
6. cōnāta erit; fassa erit; secūta erit; experta erit
7. cōnētur; fateātur; sequātur; experiātur
8. cōnārētur; fatērētur; sequerētur; experīrētur
9. cōnāta sit; fassa sit; secūta sit; experta sit

10. cōnāta esset; fassa esset; secūta esset; experta esset
11. cōnāre; fatēre; sequere; experīre
12. cōnāminī; fatēminī; sequiminī; experīminī
13. cōnārī; fatērī; sequī; experīrī
14. cōnātus esse; fassus esse; secūtus esse; expertus esse
15. cōnātūrus esse; fassūrus esse; secūtūrus esse; expertūrus esse
16. cōnāns; fatēns; sequēns; experiēns
17. cōnātus; fassus; secūtus; expertus
18. cōnātūrus; fassūrus; secūtūrus; expertūrus
19. cōnandus; fatendus; sequendus; experiendus
20. capit
21. sequitur
22. cēpērunt
23. secūtī sunt
24. iubētis
25. fatēminī
26. iubēminī
27. fassī estis
28. iussī estis
29. iussus, -a, -um
30. fassus, -a, -um
31. laudāns
32. cōnāns
33. laudās
34. laudāris
35. cōnāris

## II.

Translate the following sentences and give the syntax of the words in boldface type:

1. Fuga **servōrum** eō tempore relāta est.
2. Timōrem **supplicis** intellegere temptāvimus.
3. Laus **maiōrum** nostrōrum maxima erat.
4. Nātōs amōrem **virtūtis** docēbant.
5. **Gentis** crūdēlis est bellum gentī amīcae **īnferre**.
6. **Virī** pessimī semper fuit patriam **trādere**.
7. Amōrem **coniugis** amōre fēminae alterīus māluērunt.
8. Factumne crūdēle negāre vīs?
9. Virī īnfēlīcis est **velle** plūs quam satis.
10. Custōs **templī** fugere nōlet.

## UNIT ELEVEN — PRELIMINARY EXERCISES
## (SECTIONS A, B)

1. Arbitror cōnsulem morī; Arbitror cōnsulem mortuum esse; Arbitror cōnsulem moritūrum esse.
2. Scelusne cōnfitērī ausus es?
3. Ōrātōremne loquī patiēminī?
4. Imperātor mīlitēs hortābātur ut prōgrederentur.
5. Sī iuvenēs nōbīs noxam minentur, eōs magnopere vereāmur.
6. Auxilium precāns, supplex ad āram ruit.
7. Flūmen secūtī, ad oppidum maximum vēnimus.
8. Crēdidistīne parentēs quam prīmum profectūrōs esse?
9. Ducēs nāvibus nōn ūsī erant.
10. Pauperēs hortātī sumus nē ē prōvinciā ēgredī cōnārentur.

## UNIT ELEVEN — EXERCISES

**I.**

1. Sī ūtāmur nāvibus sociōrum, quam prīmum fugere possīmus.
2. Nōlī arbitrārī nostra scelera esse peiōra tuīs.
3. Imperātor sequentēs hortātus est nē odium iuvenum verērentur.
4. Fatēbāmur nōs proficīscī cōnātōs esse ut iungerēmus manum hostium.
5. Patientēs multās poenās quam prīmum Rōmam prōgredī voluimus.
6. Ēgrediēns prīmā lūce, familia ad flūmen quod erat altissimum prōgressa sē ulterius gradī nōlle dīxit. [**ulterius,** comparative adv., 'farther']
7. Dux fassus est sibi esse metum cōnsulum.
8. Dominī servīs ut sibi labōrārent maximā cum dīligentiā minārī solitī sunt.
9. Est fortis virī neglegere perīcula quae minantur.
10. Est cōnsulis velle morī prō patriā.
11. Bonum est velle prō amātīs patī.
12. Sī cōnāns servāre vītam cōnsulis moriāris, tuī cīvēs fortissimum factum laudent et ut statua pōnātur in forō hortentur.
13. Sapientēs crēdere ausī sunt hominem cupidum dīvitiārum saepe errāre.
14. Datūrus cēnam iuvenibus sequentibus sē, imperātor deōs precārī coepit ut familiam servārent. Dīxit sē quam prīmum domum prōgressūrum esse.
15. Fassus est sē nātum esse pauperibus parentibus quibus amor suī esset maximus.
16. Aenēās ē deā nātus est, ut aiunt, et multa proficīscēns Troiā ad Italiam expertus est. [**Aenēās,** proper name of a Roman hero]
17. Amor patriae est bonī cīvis.

18. Dulce est scīre amīcōs mala nōn patī, ut scīs.

19. Cupidus magnōrum praemiōrum ōrātor dē sceleribus cum duce proficīscentium nōn loquētur.

20. Imperātor sequentibus nē vereantur hostēs minantēs ignī et ferrō imperāre solet.

21. Nōn est patī meum.

22. Audē gradī cum virtūte et audāciā, omnibus cūrīs neglēctīs.

23. Iuvenēs in vīllam nocte ingredī māluērunt nē ā paupere familiā eam incolentī vidērentur.

24. Servāre pecūniam nōn est facile ūllō tempore.

25. Aliī dīvitiīs bene ūtī volunt, aliī ob mōrēs nōlunt.

26. Saxa ingentia ē flūmine minantia perīculō fuērunt nāvibus.

27. Servī nōs aggredientēs viam ad vīllam mōnstrāvērunt.

28. Sī in hāc cūrā vīta mihi pōnenda sit, pōnam spem salūtis in amōre fidēque tuī.

29. Quid tibi pecūniā opus est, sī ūtī nōn potes? [**quid**, *here*, 'why']

30. Quod vult habet quī velle quod satis est potest.

31. Antīquus populus sōlem esse deum maximum arbitrāns eum precātus est auxilium. Cōnfessus est sibi auxilium multum opus esse.

32. Satis est superāre inimīcum, pessimum est perdere.

33. Ūnus deus poenam affert, ut multī cōgitant.

34. Virī bonī est nōlle facere noxam.

35. Quī superārī sē patitur prō tempore superat.

36. Sine morā ex urbe ēgrediminī! Nōlīte vōs ūnā hōrā in urbe invenīrī patī!

37. Quam ob rem scelera illīus generis ferre solēbās? Nōs in hāc familiā neque tanta mala ferre solitī sumus neque ferēmus.

38. Imperātōre multa locūtō, mīlitēs fassī sunt sē parum mortem verērī sed bene scīre sē omnēs morī nōn posse; sibi opus esse mala atque perīcula patī ut omnis orbis terrārum sē cum gaudiō laudāret dīcēns malum propter audāciam hōrum virōrum ē terrā pulsum esse.

39. Crēdidistis iuvenēs quōs ad vōs vocāvissētis maximā esse dīligentiā et omnibus rēbus ūsūrōs esse ut Rōmam sē cōnferrent. Nihil eīs autem fideī erat; male crēdidistis.

40. Cupidī dīvitiārum et prīmā lūce Rōmam proficīscentēs, pauperēs deōs precābantur nē salūte, pecūniāque et omnibus bonīs in urbe caritūrī essent. Spēs hominibus est saepe caecissima!

41. Parentum malōrum est iuvenēs neglegere; sapientēs semper illum parentem hortātī sunt ut fīliī eī cūrae sint.

42. Tot mala sum passus, quot in caelō sīdera sunt.

43. Fatēmur scelera maximae audāciae in nostrā rē pūblicā hōc annō facta esse. Quōrum quod simile in tōtō orbe terrārum factum?

**II.**

1. Having dared to enter the neglected house, the children fled as soon as possible when the guardian approached.
2. Desirous of money, the young men attempted crimes, nor did they fear the punishment which threatened.
3. Famous consuls, don't use all your wealth to fill the forum with statues of impious men.
4. The soldiers confessed that the commander's hope of safety had saved lives in a time of great danger.
5. Loving both (one's) enemies and (one's) friends is the mark of a distinguished man.

**III. Readings**

A. Cicero, *In Catilīnam* I.5.10, 6.15, 8.20, 11.27

In Marcus Tullius Cicero's consulship, Lucius Catiline planned a conspiracy. Cicero found out about it and, after exposing Catiline's plans to the senate, drove him into exile.

Quae cum[1] ita[2] sint, Catilīna,[3] perge[4] quō[5] coepistī, ēgredere aliquandō[6] ex urbe; patent[7] portae: proficīscere. Nōbīscum versārī[8] iam diūtius nōn potes; nōn feram, nōn patiar, nōn sinam.[9] Quotiēns[10] tū mē dēsīgnātum,[11] quotiēns[10] vērō cōnsulem interficere cōnātus es! Nihil agis, nihil adsequeris[12] neque tamen cōnārī ac velle dēsistis.[13] Ēgredere ex urbe, Catilīna,[3] līberā rem pūblicam metū, in exsilium[14] sī hanc vōcem exspectās,[15] proficīscere. Etenim[16] sī mēcum patria, quae mihi vītā meā multō est cārior, sī cūncta[17] Italia, sī omnis rēs pūblica sīc[18] loquitur: "Marce Tullī, quid agis? Tūne eum quem esse hostem comperistī,[19] quem ducem bellī futūrum vidēs, quem exspectārī[15] imperātōrem in castrīs[20] hostium sentīs, auctōrem sceleris, principem[21] coniūrātiōnis,[22] ēvocātōrem[23] servōrum et cīvium perditōrum, exīre[24] patiēre, ut abs[25] tē nōn ēmissus[26] ex urbe sed immissus[27] in urbem esse videātur?"

[1] **cum** (conj. + subjunctive), 'since'   [2] **ita** (adv.), 'so'   [3] **Catilīna, -ae,** M., a man's name   [4] **pergō, -ere, perrēxī, perrēctus,** 'continue'   [5] **quō** (adv.), '(to) where'   [6] **aliquandō** (adv.), 'now at last'   [7] **pateō, -ēre, -uī, --,** 'stand open'   [8] **versor** (1), 'live'   [9] **sinō, -ere, sīvī, situs,** 'allow'   [10] **quotiēns** (adv.), 'how many times'   [11] **dēsīgnātus, -a, -um,** 'elect' (understand **cōnsulem**)   [12] **adsequor** (**ad** + **sequor**), 'gain'   [13] **dēsistō, -ere, dēstitī, dēstitus,** 'stop (from)' (+ infinitive)   [14] **exsilium, -ī,** N., 'exile'   [15] **exspectō** (1), 'wait for'   [16] **etenim** (conj.), 'and indeed'   [17] **cūnctus, -a, -um,** 'all'   [18] **sīc** (adv.), 'in this way'   [19] **comperiō, -īre, comperī, compertus,** 'learn'   [20] **castra, -ōrum,** N. pl., 'camp'   [21] **princeps, principis,** M., 'the leading man'   [22] **coniūrātiō, -ōnis,** F., 'conspiracy'   [23] **ēvocātor, -ōris,** M., 'a summoner, one who calls out (to arms)'   [24] **exeō, -īre, -īvī, -itus,** 'go out'   [25] **abs = ab**   [26] **ēmittō** (**ē** + **mittō**), 'send out'   [27] **immittō** (**in** + **mittō**), 'send against' (+ **in** and the accusative)

B.  Martial 2.21:

> Bāsia[1] dās aliīs, aliīs dās, Postume,[2] dextram.
> Dīcis, 'Utrum māvīs? Ēlige.'[3] Mālo manum.

[1] **bāsium, -ī, N.**, 'kiss'    [2] **Postumus, -ī, M.**, a man's name    [3] **ēligō, -ere, -lēgī, -lēctus,** 'choose'

C.  Martial 10.8:

> Nūbere[1] Paula[2] cupit[3] nōbīs, ego dūcere[4] Paulam[2]
> nōlō: anus[5] est. Vellem, sī magis esset anus.[5]

[1] **nūbō, -ere, nūpsī, nuptus,** 'marry' (+ dat.); used for a *woman* marrying    [2] **Paula, -ae, F.**, a woman's name    [3] **cupiō, -ere, -īvī, -ītus,** 'wish'    [4] **dūcō,** *here*, 'marry'; used for a *man* marrying (understand **in mātrimōnium**)    [5] **anus, -ūs, F.**, 'an old woman'; here, used as an adjective, 'old'; **magis** is used with it to give a comparative force

D.  Martial 9.10:

> Nūbere[1] vīs Prīscō:[2] nōn mīror,[3] Paula;[4] sapīstī.[5]
> Dūcere[6] tē nōn vult Prīscus:[2] et ille sapit.[5]

[1] **nūbō, -ere, nūpsī, nuptus,** 'marry' (+ dat.); used for a *woman* marrying    [2] **Prīscus, -ī, M.**, a man's name    [3] **mīror (1),** 'wonder'    [4] **Paula, -ae, F.**, a woman's name    [5] **sapiō, -ere, -īvī, --,** 'be sensible'; **sapīstī** is a contraction for **sapīvistī** (see Unit Eighteen, Section D)    [6] **dūcō,** *here*, 'marry'; (understand **in mātrimōnium**); used for a *man* marrying.

E.  Martial 8.27:

> Mūnera[1] quī tibi dat locuplētī,[2] Gaure,[3] senīque,[4]
> sī sapis[5] et sentīs, hoc tibi ait 'Morere'.

[1] **mūnus, mūneris, N.**, 'gift'    [2] **locuplēs, locuplētis,** 'wealthy'    [3] **Gaurus, -ī, M.**, a man's name    [4] **senex, senis,** 'old'    [5] **sapiō, -ere, sapīvī, --,** 'be sensible'

F.  Martial 2.87:

> Dīcis amōre tuī bellās[1] ardēre puellās,
> quī faciem[2] sub aquā, Sexte,[3] natantis[4] habēs.

[1] **bellus, -a, -um,** 'beautiful'    [2] **faciēs, -ēī, F.**, 'face'    [3] **Sextus, -ī, M.**, a man's name    [4] **natō (1),** 'swim'

G.  Martial 12.78:

> Nīl in[1] tē scrīpsī, Bīthȳnice.[2] Crēdere nōn vīs
> et iūrāre[3] iubēs? Mālo satisfacere.[4]

[1] **in,** *here*, 'against'    [2] **Bīthȳnicus, -ī, M.**, a man's name    [3] **iūrō (1),** 'swear'    [4] **satisfaciō (satis + faciō),** 'make amends'

H. Martial 5.83:

> Īnsequeris,[1] fugiō; fugis, īnsequor;[1] haec mihi mēns est:
> velle tuum nōlō, Dindyme,[2] nōlle, volō.

[1] īnsequor (in + sequor), 'pursue'    [2] **Dindymus, -ī, M.**, a man's name

I. Cicero, *Dē Amīcitiā* 2.10 (adapted):

> Amīcō mortuō, graviter angī[1] nōn amīcī est, sed sē ipsum[2] amantis est.

[1] angī (present passive infinitive), 'to suffer torment'    [2] **ipsum** (acc. sing. M.), intensifies **sē**, translate **sē ipsum** 'his very self'

J. Cicero, *Dē Officiīs* I.24.83:

> In tranquillō[1] tempestātem[2] adversam[3] optāre dēmentis est.

[1] **tranquillum, -ī, N.**, 'calm'    [2] **tempestās, -tātis, F.**, 'weather'    [3] **adversus, -a, -um**, 'unfavorable'

K. Vergil, *Aeneid* I.198–9 and 202–3:

> Ō sociī (neque enim īgnārī[1] sumus ante malōrum),
> Ō passī graviōra, dabit deus hīs quoque[2] fīnem.
>
> . . .
>
> . . . revocāte[3] animōs[4] maestumque[5] timōrem
> mittite; forsan[6] et haec ōlim[7] meminisse[8] iuvābit.[9]

[1] **īgnārus, -a, -um**, 'unaware (of)' (+ gen.)    [2] **quoque** (adv.), 'also'    [3] **revocō** (re- + vocō), 'call back, recover'    [4] **animus, -ī, M.**, 'spirit'    [5] **maestus, -a, -um**, 'gloomy'    [6] **forsan** (adv.), 'perhaps'    [7] **ōlim** (adv.), 'at some time'    [8] **meminī, meminisse** (defective verb), 'remember'    [9] **iuvō, -āre, iūvī, iūtus**, 'please, help, delight'

L. Cicero, *Dē Officiīs* I.6.18:

> Omnēs enim trahimur[1] et dūcimur ad cognitiōnis[2] et scientiae[3] cupiditātem,[4] in quā excellere[5] pulchrum putāmus,[6] lābī[7] autem, errāre, nescīre,[8] dēcipī[9] et malum et turpe[10] dūcimus.

[1] **trahō, -ere, trāxī, tractus**, 'attract'    [2] **cognitiō, -ōnis, F.**, 'knowledge'    [3] **scientia, -ae, F.**, 'knowing'    [4] **cupiditās, -tātis, F.**, 'desire'    [5] **excellō, -ere, excelluī, excelsus**, 'excel'    [6] **putō** (1), 'think'    [7] **lābor, lābī, lāpsus sum**, 'slip'    [8] **nesciō** (ne + sciō), 'not know'    [9] **dēcipiō** (dē + capiō), 'deceive'    [10] **turpis, -e**, 'disgraceful'

# REVIEW: UNITS NINE TO ELEVEN

**Review of Syntax**

1. Custōdis ācerrimī est hospitēs monēre dē illīs oppidō ignem minantibus ut sē in fugam quam prīmum cōnferant.
(predicate genitive; infinitive as subject; **quam** with superlative)
2. Imperium illīus ducis nunc minus est quam prius; nec habet apud hās gentēs satis auctōritātis. [**auctōritās, -tātis**, F., 'influence']
(comparison with **quam**; partitive genitive)
3. Timentī auxilium ferre solēmus nē metū male ūtātur. Hominēs enim clārissimae fāmae metū saepe scelera crūdēliōra faciunt.
(instrumental ablative with **ūtor**; genitive of description; ablative of cause)
4. Multī virī suā sententiā sunt fēlīcēs; illī autem multōrum saepe dominī sunt, sed plūrium servī.
(objective genitive)
5. Multīs ante diēbus, lūce erant clāriōra nōbīs tua cōnsilia; nunc ea intellegere nōn possumus.
(ablative of degree of difference; ablative of comparison)
6. Oppidō captō, ōrātōrem, virum clārissimō patre maiōribusque, superantēs interficere ausī sunt (audēbunt).
(ablative absolute; ablative of description; semi-deponent verb)
7. Hīs dictīs, hoc genus verbōrum patī nōlēbant, sed magnus eīs metus erat eōrum loquentium.
(ablative absolute; objective genitive)
8. Dīs inimīcīs, multō maxima pars cīvium bellum tamen gessit.
(ablative absolute; ablative of degree of difference; partitive genitive)
9. Sī in hāc cūrā auxilium opus erit, pōnam spem salūtis totīus in amōre fidēque vestrī.
(objective genitives)
10. Omnibus bonīs optimum est plūs glōriae quam dīvitiārum habēre.
(partitive genitive; comparison with **quam**; infinitive as subject)
11. Servī ē vīllīs ēgrediuntur, noctemque tōtam itinere factō, in alterum oppidum prīmā lūce venient.
(ablative absolute)

12. Nam arbitrātī sunt sē dīs superīs cūrae esse.
13. Cognitīs imperātōris rēbus, Rōmae gaudium magnum erat.
    (ablative absolute)
14. Nostrā ūtere amīcitiā ut volēs.
    (instrumental ablative with **ūtor**)
15. Tū hortāris ut fidē sim magnā et spem habeam salūtis.
    (ablative of description; objective genitive)
16. Amōre Iovis multae fēminae īram Iunōnis passae sunt.
    (ablative of cause; subjective genitives)
17. Aliī huic sōlī crēdidērunt, aliī ūllī crēdere nōluērunt.
18. Quīnque ē supplicibus erant simillimī virīs quōs sciō.
19. Virī magnae virtūtis saepe laudābuntur ā populō honestīs mōribus.
    (genitive of description; ablative of description)
20. Mihi nihil est tam cārum quam amīcus amātus.
21. Quam prīmum nāvēs ācerrimōs mīlitēs facillimē auferent.
    (**quam** with superlative)
22. Quid cōnsulī est cārius quam patria? Cōnsulī nihil est cārius patriā.
    (comparison with **quam**; ablative of comparison)
23. Tibi ūnī, nōn eī, loquī mālō.
24. Quid cōnsiliī cēpistī?
    (partitive genitive)
25. Multō melius frātre legit.
    (ablative of degree of difference; ablative of comparison)

# UNITS 9–11: Self-Review A

## I.
Change to the plural, giving all possibilities:

| | | |
|---|---|---|
| 1. difficiliori | 3. nullius | 5. loqueris |
| 2. maius | 4. offert | |

## II.
Translate indicative forms; identify subjunctives. Then change each form to the simple future tense, retaining person, number, and voice.

| | | | |
|---|---|---|---|
| 1. passi sunt | 3. neglexeris | 5. solitus es | 7. malim |
| 2. hortantur | 4. proficiscebar | 6. volumus | |

## III.
Translate, and then do whatever else is required:

1. Sentio illum virum omnibus temporibus fortiter vivere cui timor mortis gravissimus non sit.
   a) What is the syntax of **mortis**?

2. Ullusne nostrum dicere potest se suam vitam quam sapientissimē egisse?
   a) Syntax of **nostrum**?

3. Illi cives qui sunt multo fortiores quam nos corpore credunt se hostes e sua
   civitate expellere vi posse.
   a) Give an alternative construction in Latin for **quam nos**.

4. Imperator militi dicit bellum quo urbem servaverint longius multis diebus
   fuisse quam illud in monte.
   a) Syntax of **diebus**?

5. Dicit maiores multo maiora et meliora fecisse quam ea quae iuvenes facturi
   sint.

6. Fassi sunt hunc consulem multo melius se civitati gessisse quam illum.
   a) Change **fassi sunt** to the future tense.

7. Dis volentibus, consilia iuvenum crudeliorum nostrae saluti minari
   conantium delebuntur.
   a) Syntax of **volentibus**?

8. Cupidi divitiarum est bonos mores invidiā et audaciā neglegere et in scelera
   se conferre.
   a) Syntax of **cupidi**?
   b) Syntax of **divitiarum**?
   c) Syntax of **neglegere**?

9. Bello illato, hospes magni studii et minimi timoris ad moenia venit et homines
   portas servantes hortatus est ut quam primum proficiscerentur. "Nisi,"
   ait, "profecti eritis, magna scelera patiemini."
   a) Syntax of **studii**?
   b) Change **venit** to the future tense and make any other necessary change(s)
      in the sentence.
   c) Rewrite the conditional sentence in Latin as a present contrary-to-fact
      condition.

10. Matris odio belli, filius, iuvenis bonis moribus, pugnare neque vult neque
    audet.
    a) Syntax of **matris**?
    b) Syntax of **odio**?
    c) Syntax of **moribus**?
    d) Change **vult** and **audet** to the future perfect tense.

## IV.

Translate:

Noli arbitrari me alii longiores litteras scribere, nisi unus ex amicis ad me multa
scripsit ad quem arbitror me respondere debere; nihil enim habeo quod scribere
possum, et hōc tempore nihil difficilius facio. Ad te et ad nostram filiam non

possum sine plurimis lacrimis et magnā curā scribere; vos video miserrimas esse, quae mihi cariores vitā sitis.

(part of a letter written by Cicero to his wife; adapted)

## Answer Key — UNITS 9–11: Self-Review A

**I.**

1. difficiliōribus
2. maiōra
3. nūllōrum, nūllārum
4. offerunt
5. loquiminī (present tense); loquēminī (future tense, if the original -e- was long)

**II.**

1. they have suffered, they suffered, they did suffer; **patientur**
2. they encourage, they are encouraging, they do encourage; **hortābuntur**
3. you will have neglected; perfect subjunctive second person singular active; **neglegēs**
4. I was setting forth, I used to set forth, I kept on setting forth; **proficīscar**
5. you were accustomed, you have been accustomed; **solēbis**
6. we wish, we are wishing, we do wish; **volēmus**
7. present subjunctive, first person singular active; **mālam**

**III.**

1. I feel that that man to whom the fear of death is not very severe lives bravely at all times.
   a) objective genitive
2. Is anyone of us able to say that he has conducted his own life as wisely as possible?
   a) partitive genitive
3. Those citizens who are far (much) stronger (stronger by far/much) than we in body believe that they are able to (can) drive the enemies out of their state by force.
   a) nōbīs (ablative of comparison)
4. The general says to the soldier that the war by means of which they saved the city has been (was) many days longer than that (war) on the mountain.
   a) ablative of degree of difference (longer by many days)
5. He says that his ancestors did (have done) (much) greater and better things (by far) than those which the young men are about to do.

6. They confessed that this consul had conducted himself for the state (much) better (by far) than that (consul).
   a) fatēbuntur
7. With the gods willing, the plans of the rather cruel young men (youths) trying (who are trying) to threaten our safety will be destroyed.
   a) ablative absolute (with present participle)
8. It is the mark of a man (characteristic of one) desirous of wealth (riches) to neglect (his) good character because of envy and boldness and to take himself into (resort to) crimes.
   a) predicate genitive (genitive of characteristic)
   b) objective genitive
   c) infinitive, subject of **est** ('neglecting good character is [the mark] of one desiring riches')
9. When the war had been (was) brought on (inflicted), the host of great eagerness and very little fear came to the walls and urged the men saving (who were saving) the gates to set out as soon as possible. "If you do not set out," he says, "you will suffer (endure) great crimes."
   a) genitive of description
   b) Bellō...moenia veniet et...hortābitur ut...proficīscantur.
   c) "Nisī," ait, "proficīscerēminī, magna scelera paterēminī." (imperfect subjunctives)
10. Because of the hatred of his mother (his mother's hatred) for war, the son, a young man of good character, neither wishes nor dares to fight.
    a) subjective genitive
    b) ablative of cause
    c) ablative of description
    d) voluerit; ausus erit (Since this is a semi-deponent verb, the perfect system has passive forms but active meanings.)

**IV.**

Do not think that I write a longer letter (a rather long letter) to another unless one of my friends, (to) whom I think that I ought to answer, has written many things to me; indeed, I have nothing which I am able to write, and at this time I do nothing more difficult (with more difficulty). I am not able to write to you and to our daughter without very many tears and great anxiety; I see that you are very wretched, you who are dearer to me than life.

## UNITS 9–11: Self-Review B

**I.**

A. Give the comparative and superlative forms of each of the following adjectives and adverbs:

| 1. crudelis | 3. validus | 5. magnopere | 7. diu | 9. bene |
|-------------|------------|--------------|--------|---------|
| 2. bonus | 4. malus | 6. magnus | 8. parvus | 10. multum |

B. Change the following from the singular to the plural, retaining person, mood, and voice:

| 1. ferris | 3. contuli | 5. volebat |
|-----------|------------|------------|
| 2. offers | 4. malit | |

## II.
Translate, and then do whatever else is required:

1. Magister plus boni in vita quam mali esse nos credere voluit.
   a) Give the syntax of **boni**.
2. Milites multo fortius in hoc bello quam in illo pugnaverunt quod quam optimis consiliis usi sunt.
   a) Syntax of **multo**?
   b) Syntax of **consiliis**?
3. Spem gloriae esse consulis bonis moribus nostri maiores crediderunt.
   a) Syntax of **gloriae**?
   b) Syntax of **consulis**?
   c) Syntax of **moribus**?
4. Cupidior divitiarum pio, impius malae familiae scelera quam facta honesta maluit.
   a) Syntax of **pio**?
   b) Give an alternate way of phrasing the first three words of the sentence.
   c) Syntax of **familiae**?
5. Melius est laudare quam laudari.
   a) Syntax of **laudare**?
6. Litteris quam primum scriptis, unus ex amicis nos curā laudari detulit.
   a) Syntax of **scriptis**?
   b) Syntax of **curā**?
   c) Give an alternate way of expressing **curā**.
7. Unius invidiā tota gens magnopere passa est.
   a) Syntax of **unius**?
8. Postquam dulciores hospites parum laudatos esse sensimus, nos eis maximas gratias acturos esse arbitrati sumus. [**gratias agere**, 'to thank']

## III. Translate:

1. How many days after me do you want to set out to Rome?
2. When the general died, the young people, raving and very unlike (their) cruel enemies, fell because of their boldness and because no aid was offered.

# Answer Key — UNITS 9–11: Self-Review B

**I.**

A.  1. crūdēlior, crūdēlius; crūdēlissimus, -a, -um
    2. melior, melius; optimus, -a, -um
    3. validior, validius; validissimus, -a, -um
    4. peior, peius; pessimus, -a, -um
    5. magis; maximē
    6. maior, maius; maximus, -a, -um
    7. diūtius; diūtissimē
    8. minor, minus; minimus, -a, -um
    9. melius; optimē
   10. plūs; plūrimum

B.  1. feriminī
    2. offertis
    3. contulimus
    4. mālint
    5. volēbant

**II.**

1. The teacher wished us to believe that there was more good in life than bad.
   a) partitive genitive

2. The soldiers fought more bravely by far (much more bravely) in this war than in that one because they used the best possible plans (as good plans as possible).
   a) ablative of degree of difference
   b) ablative of instrument after the verb **ūtor**

3. Our ancestors believed that hope of glory was the mark of a consul of good character.
   a) objective genitive
   b) predicate genitive (genitive of characteristic)
   c) ablative of description

4. More desirous of riches than a pious man, the impious man of bad family preferred crimes rather than honorable deeds.
   a) ablative of comparison
   b) cupidior dīvitiārum quam pius
   c) genitive of description

5. To praise is better than to be praised (praising is better than being praised; it is better to praise than to be praised).
   a) infinitive as subject

6. When (since, after) the letter had been written as soon as possible, one of

our friends reported that we were (being) praised because of (our) concern.

a) ablative absolute; the participle modifies the subject **litterīs**

b) ablative of cause

c) propter cūram *or* ob cūram

7. Because of the envy of one man, the entire race suffered greatly.

   a) subjective genitive

8. After we perceived that the rather sweet (pleasant) guests had not been praised enough, we thought that we would give very great thanks to them.

## III.

1. Quantīs diēbus post mē Rōmam proficīscī vīs?

2. Imperātōre mortuō iuvenēs, dēmentēs et crūdēlium hostium (crūdēlibus hostibus) dissimillimī audāciā (ob audāciam/propter audāciam) cecidērunt et quod nūllum auxilium oblātum est (offerēbātur).

# UNIT TWELVE

## A. Independent Uses of the Subjunctive

The subjunctive occurs most frequently in ~~Latin~~ in subordinate clauses, but some independent uses are found. All of these express notions connected with the basic definition of the subjunctive given in Unit One.

1. JUSSIVE (**iubeō, -ēre, iussī, iussus**, 'command') AND HORTATORY (**hortor** (1), 'urge') SUBJUNCTIVES

   The present subjunctive is used to express a command or an exhortation.

   veniat!     let him come!   command (JUSSIVE)
   veniāmus!  let's come!     exhortation (HORTATORY)

   The jussive sense occurs mainly in the third person; the hortatory in the first. The negative is introduced by **nē**.

   Nē hoc faciat!   Let him not do this!

2. POTENTIAL SUBJUNCTIVE

   The subjunctive may be used independently to express an action which might possibly or conceivably occur.

   Haec crēdās.   You would (could, might) believe these things; one might believe this.

   For present or future potentiality, the present (sometimes the perfect) subjunctive is used. This type of subjunctive is allied to future less vivid conditions (see Unit Two); in fact, one might conceive of it as the apodosis (concluding clause) of such a condition, the protasis (if-clause) of which has been suppressed:

   Frātrem meī miserērī nōlim   I would not wish (my) brother to pity me
   (sī mē videat).                (if he should see me).

   OBSERVATION:
   The verb **misereor** takes the genitive case to express its object; hence the objective genitive **meī**.

200

| Dīcas eum hominem bonum esse. | You would say (i.e., if you could) that he is a good man; you might say that he is a good man. |

Past potentiality is expressed with the imperfect subjunctive.

| Crēderēs eum hominem bonum esse. | You would have believed that he was a good man; you might have believed that he was a good man. |

The negative of the potential subjunctive is introduced by **nōn**.

3. DELIBERATIVE SUBJUNCTIVE

The present and imperfect subjunctives may be used to *deliberate* about a course of action. This is frequently used in a rhetorical question (i.e., a question which is asked for effect, but which does not demand an answer).

| Quid faciam? | What am I to do?  What should I do? |
| Quid facerem? | What was I to do?  What should I have done? |

The negative is introduced by **nōn**.

4. OPTATIVE (**optō** (1), 'desire, wish') SUBJUNCTIVE

A wish for the future which is capable of fulfillment is expressed by the present subjunctive alone or is introduced by **utinam** or **ut** (negative **utinam nē** or **nē**).

| Utinam veniat! | Would that he may come; I wish he would come; if only he would come! |
| Utinam nē veniat! | Would that he may not come; I wish he would not come; if only he would not come! |

Wishes incapable of fulfillment utilize the imperfect subjunctive for present time (cf. present contrary-to-fact conditions) and the pluperfect for past time (cf. past contrary-to-fact conditions).

| Utinam venīret! | Would that he were coming; I wish he were coming; if only he were coming! (but he is not; the wish is incapable of fulfillment, or contrafactual) |
| Utinam vēnisset! | Would that he had come; I wish he had come; if only he had come! (but he did not; the wish is incapable of fulfillment, or contrafactual) |

## B. Direct Questions

Questions are sometimes introduced by interrogative words: **quis**?, 'who?'; **quid**?, 'what?'; **quandō**?, 'when?'; **quō**?, **quō modō**?, 'how?'; **cūr**?, **quam ob rem**?, 'why?'; **unde**?, 'from where?'; etc. If no interrogative word is used, the enclitic -ne is frequently attached to the introductory word in order to indicate that a question is approaching.

Venīsne mēcum?   Are you coming with me?

When the answer "yes" is expected, the question is introduced by the word nōnne.

Nōnne venīs mēcum?   You are coming with me, aren't you? (answer "yes" expected)

When the answer "no" is expected, the question is introduced by the word num.

Num venīs mēcum?   You aren't coming with me, are you? (answer "no" expected)

Double questions are introduced by the particles utrum (or -ne or no introductory particle at all) ...an, 'whether...or'.

| | |
|---|---|
| Utrum mēcum venīs an cum eō manēs? | (Whether) are you coming with me or staying with him? |
| Servusne es an nōn? | Are you a slave or not? |
| Servus es an nōn? | Are you a slave or not? |

## C. Indirect Questions

Indirect questions are subordinate noun clauses which serve as the object (and, less frequently, the subject) of the words on which they depend. These words usually, but not always, express or imply actions that take place in the head, such as saying, thinking, seeing, perceiving, knowing, asking, and the like. Indirect questions are introduced by an interrogative word and have their verbs in the subjunctive.

I know *who you are.*   Direct Question: Who are you?

The noun clause "who you are" serves as the object of the word ("know") on which it depends. It is introduced by an interrogative word ("who") and, in Latin, its verb ("you are") would be in the subjunctive.

We wondered *what gifts you brought.*   Direct Question: What gifts did you bring?

The noun clause "what gifts you brought" serves as the object of the word ("wondered") on which it depends. It is introduced by an interrogative word ("what") and, in Latin, its verb ("you brought") would be in the subjunctive.

*What you are doing* bothers me.   Direct Question: What are you doing?

The noun clause "what you are doing" serves as the subject of the word ("bothers") on which it depends. It is introduced by an interrogative word ("what") and, in Latin, its verb ("you are doing") would be in the subjunctive.

In direct speech, these clauses would have been direct questions with their verbs in the indicative or the deliberative subjunctive.

DIRECT QUESTIONS:

| | |
|---|---|
| Quid sentiō? | What do I feel? |
| Quid agēs? | What will you do? |
| Unde vēnistī? | Where have you come from? |
| Quam ob rem mē spectās? | Why are you looking at me? |
| Spectāsne mē? | Are you looking at me? |
| Venīsne mēcum an cum eō manēs? | Are you coming with me or staying with him? |
| Servusne es an nōn? | Are you a slave or not? |
| Quid faciam? | What am I to do? What should I do? |

In order to turn these direct questions into the indirect form, we must review the rules for sequence of tenses (Unit Three, section G). The primary tenses in the indicative are the present, future, future perfect, and perfect (when translated using the English auxiliary verbs "has, have"). The secondary tenses in the indicative are the imperfect, perfect, and pluperfect. The subjunctive tenses in each sequence are illustrated in the examples below.

NOTE: While indirect questions follow the rules for sequence of tenses, a periphrastic form is frequently used to denote future time.

| MAIN CLAUSE | | SUBORDINATE CLAUSE | |
|---|---|---|---|
| PRIMARY SEQUENCE: | PRESENT TIME | FUTURE TIME | PAST TIME |
| Dīcō, Rogō | quid faciam | quid factūrus sim | quid fēcerim |
| I say, I ask | what I am doing | what I shall do | what I did |
| SECONDARY SEQUENCE: | | | |
| Dīxī, Rogāvī | quid facerem | quid factūrus essem | quid fēcissem |
| I said, I asked | what I was doing | what I would do | what I had done |

Now, we shall turn the direct questions above into the indirect form:

| | |
|---|---|
| Quid sentiō? | What do I feel? |
| Rogō quid sentiam. | I ask what I feel. |
| Rogāvī quid sentīrem. | I asked what I felt (was feeling). |
| Expōnam quid sentiam. | I shall explain what I feel. |
| Sciō quid sentiam. | I know what I feel. |
| ...etc. | |

| | |
|---|---|
| Quid agēs? | What will you do? |
| Rogō quid āctūrus sīs. | I ask what you will do. |
| Rogāvī quid āctūrus essēs. | I asked what you would do. |
| Expōnam quid āctūrus sīs. | I shall explain what you will do. |
| Sciō quid āctūrus sīs. | I know what you will do. |
| ...etc. | |

| | |
|---|---|
| Unde vēnistī? | Where have you come from? |
| Rogō unde vēneris. | I ask where you have come from. |
| Rogāvī unde vēnissēs. | I asked where you came (had come) from. |
| ...etc. | |

| | |
|---|---|
| Quam ob rem mē spectās? | Why are you looking at me? |
| Rogō quam ob rem mē spectēs. | I ask why you are looking at me. |
| Exposuī quam ob rem mē spectārēs. | I explained why you were looking at me. |
| Exposuī quam ob rem mē spectāvissēs. | I explained why you had looked at me. |
| ...etc. | |

| | |
|---|---|
| Spectāsne mē? | Are you looking at me? |
| Rogō num (*here* = 'whether') mē spectēs. | I ask whether you are looking at me. |
| ...etc. | |

| | |
|---|---|
| Utrum venīs mēcum (venīsne mēcum) an cum eō manēs? | Are you coming with me or staying with him? |
| Nescīvērunt utrum venīrēs mēcum (venīrēsne mēcum) an cum eō manērēs. | They did not know whether you were coming with me or staying with him. |
| ...etc. | |

| | |
|---|---|
| Servusne es an nōn? | Are you a slave or not? |
| Rogō servusne sīs necne. | I ask whether you are a slave or not. |
| ...etc. | |

| | |
|---|---|
| Quid faciam? | What should I do? |
| Rogō quid faciam. | I ask what I should do. |
| ...etc. | |

OBSERVATION: In double indirect questions, when the second question is negative, **necne** is used more frequently than the **an nōn** of the direct question.

**D. The Adjective** *īdem, eadem, idem,* 'same'

The forms are essentially those of **is, ea, id,** with **-dem** added as a suffix. The differences are as follows:

1. In the nominative masculine singular, the **s** of **is** drops out and the **i** becomes long.
2. In the nominative and accusative neuter singular, the **d** of **id** disappears.
3. A final **-m** is changed to **-n** before **-dem.**

Thus, the paradigm:

|  | SINGULAR |  |  | PLURAL |  |
|---|---|---|---|---|---|
| **M.** | **F.** | **N.** | **M.** | **F.** | **N.** |
| īdem | eadem | idem | eīdem (īdem) | eaedem | eadem |
| eiusdem | eiusdem | eiusdem | eōrundem | eārundem | eōrundem |
| eīdem | eīdem | eīdem | eīsdem (īsdem) | eīsdem (īsdem) | eīsdem (īsdem) |
| eundem | eandem | idem | eōsdem | eāsdem | eadem |
| eōdem | eādem | eōdem | eīsdem (īsdem) | eīsdem (īsdem) | eīsdem (īsdem) |

As with the demonstrative adjectives you have learned, the forms may also be used as pronouns.

**E. The Pronoun and the Adjective** *quīdam,* 'certain'

The pronoun **quīdam, quaedam, quiddam,** and the adjective **quīdam, quaedam, quoddam** are essentially the same in declension as the relative pronoun, with **-dam** added as a suffix. The only exceptions are:

1. The pronoun has **quid-** for the neuter singular, nominative and accusative.
2. **-m** before **-dam** becomes **-n.**

|  | SINGULAR |  |  | PLURAL |  |
|---|---|---|---|---|---|
| **M.** | **F.** | **N.** | **M.** | **F.** | **N.** |
| quīdam | quaedam | quiddam (quoddam) | quīdam | quaedam | quaedam |
| cuiusdam | cuiusdam | cuiusdam | quōrundam | quārundam | quōrundam |
| cuidam | cuidam | cuidam | quibusdam | quibusdam | quibusdam |
| quendam | quandam | quiddam (quoddam) | quōsdam | quāsdam | quaedam |
| quōdam | quādam | quōdam | quibusdam | quibusdam | quibusdam |

**F. The Intensive Adjective** *ipse, ipsa, ipsum,* 'self, very'

This adjective, which may also be used as a pronoun, declines like **ille,** except in the neuter nominative and accusative singular which have **-um** instead of **-ud.**

| SINGULAR | | | PLURAL | | |
|---|---|---|---|---|---|
| **M.** | **F.** | **N.** | **M.** | **F.** | **N.** |
| ipse | ipsa | ipsum | ipsī | ipsae | ipsa |
| ipsīus | ipsīus | ipsīus | ipsōrum | ipsārum | ipsōrum |
| ipsī | ipsī | ipsī | ipsīs | ipsīs | ipsīs |
| ipsum | ipsam | ipsum | ipsōs | ipsās | ipsa |
| ipsō | ipsā | ipsō | ipsīs | ipsīs | ipsīs |

**Ipse** is used to *intensify* the word it modifies or stands for.

| | |
|---|---|
| **Ipse** veniam. | I *myself* shall come. |
| Virum **ipsum** vīdit. | He saw the man *himself*; he saw the *very* man. |
| Expōnam quid **ipse** sentiam. | I shall explain what I *myself* feel. |
| **Ipse** sēcum loquitur. | He *himself* speaks with (to) himself. |

**G. The Demonstrative Adjective** *iste, ista, istud,* 'that (of yours)'
This adjective (also used as a pronoun) declines like **ille**. It frequently carries a pejorative or derogatory tone.

| | |
|---|---|
| **Iste** amīcus venīre nōn potest. | *That* friend (*of yours*) can't come; *that damned* friend can't come. |

# UNIT TWELVE — VOCABULARY

| | |
|---|---|
| **accipiō, -ere, -cēpī, -ceptus** | receive, accept; hear |
| **recipiō, -ere, -cēpī, -ceptus** | take back, regain, recover |
| **sē recipere** | withdraw, take oneself |
| **an** (conj.) | or (introducing the second part of a double question); whether (introducing a single indirect question) |
| **aura, -ae**, F. | breeze, wind, air |
| **comes, comitis**, M. or F. | companion |
| **cōpia, -ae**, F. | abundance, supply; pl., troops |
| **cūr** (adv.) | why, for what reason |
| **dēligō, -ere, dēlēgī, dēlēctus** | select, choose, gather |
| **exorior, -īrī, exortus sum** | rise, arise, appear, start |
| **expōnō, -ere, -posuī, -positus** | set forth, expose, explain |
| **horridus, -a, -um** | horrible, rough |
| **hostīlis, -e** | of an enemy, hostile |
| **ibi** (adv.) | there, then |
| **īdem, eadem, idem** | same |
| **immortālis, -e** | immortal, everlasting |

| | |
|---|---|
| **ipse, -a, -um** | self, very |
| **iste, ista, istud** | that (of yours), that (with pejorative sense) |
| **iussum, -ī, N.** | command, order (the abl. sing. is **iussū**, 'by order') |
| **maneō, -ēre, mānsī, mānsus** *or* | |
| **remaneō, -ēre, -mānsī, -mānsus** | remain |
| **misereor, -ērī, miseritus sum** | pity (+ gen.) |
| **modus, -ī, M.** | way, manner, limit; kind |
| **quō modō** | in what way, how |
| **necne** (conj.) | or not (generally used as the second part of a double indirect question, representing **an nōn** in the direct question) |
| **nesciō, -īre, -īvī (-iī), -ītus** | not know, be ignorant |
| **nōnne** (adv.) | (in a direct question, anticipates the answer "yes") |
| **num** (adv.) | (in a direct question, anticipates the answer "no"); whether (in an indirect question) |
| **occultē** (adv.) | secretly |
| **ops, opis, F.** | power, strength; pl., resources, wealth |
| **paucī, -ae, -a** | few |
| **poscō, -ere, poposcī, ——** | beg, demand |
| **quamdiū** (adv.) | how long |
| **quandō** (adv.) | when; since |
| **quārē** (adv.) | by what means, why; and therefore |
| **quia** (conj.) | because |
| **quīdam, quaedam, quiddam** (pron.) | a certain one, a certain thing |
| **quīdam, quaedam, quoddam** (adj.) | certain |
| **rogō** (1) | ask (for) |
| **sors, sortis, -ium, F.** | lot, destiny |
| **tamquam** (adv.) | as if, as, as it were |
| **tandem** (adv.) | at last, at length |
| **ubi** (adv.) | where, when |
| **unde** (adv.) | from where |
| **utinam** (adv.) | I wish!, would that!, if only |
| **utrum** (conj.) | whether |
| **utrum...an**<br>**-ne...an**<br>**——...an** | whether...or |
| **utrum...an nōn**<br>**-ne...an nōn**<br>**——...an nōn** | whether...or not (in direct double questions) |

| utrum...necne ⎫ | |
|---|---|
| -ne...necne ⎬ | whether...or not (in indirect double |
| --...necne ⎭ | questions) |

# UNIT TWELVE — NOTES ON VOCABULARY

**Accipiō** (**ad** + **capiō**) in addition to meaning 'receive, accept' means 'hear', that is, to receive information through the ears.

**Sē recipere** means 'to take oneself, withdraw' to a place: **Servī sē ad deōrum ārās recēpērunt**, 'The slaves took themselves to the altars of the gods'.

**Comes, comitis**, M. or F., is formed as though from **comeō** (**com-** + **eō**), 'go with'; **comes** is the person who goes with someone, 'companion'.

**Cōpia, cōpiae**, F., means 'abundance, supply' in the singular, but in the plural, it means 'troops'.

**Dēligō**, 'select, choose, gather', is a compound of **legō**; it has **dēlēgī** for the third principal part.

**Exorior** is a compound of **orior, orīrī, ortus sum**, 'rise'. **Exorior** in addition to meaning 'rise, arise' means 'appear, start'. The East is called the Orient because that is where the sun rises.

**Expōnō** is a compound of **pōnō**; it means 'set forth, expose, explain'.

**Horridus, -a, -um** is derived from a verb meaning 'to bristle'; therefore, it means 'rough, shaggy', and thus, 'horrible'.

**Īdem, eadem, idem** is simply a compound of **is, ea, id** plus **-dem**, 'exactly'; it means 'same'. The abbreviation *ibid.* stands for **ibīdem**, 'exactly there'.

**Immortālis, -e** means literally 'not' (**im-**) 'pertaining to' (**-ālis**) 'death' (**-mort-**), thus, 'immortal, everlasting'.

**Ipse, -a, -um**, declined like **ille, -a, -ud** (except for the neuter singular nominative and accusative) intensifies the word it modifies and means 'self, very'. As in Irish literature one is accustomed to read "Oh, 'tis himself" or "Himself is coming", so in Latin one may find **Ipse venit**, 'He himself is coming', or **Ipsum voluī!**, 'The very man I wanted!'

**Iste, -a, -ud** (declined like **ille, -a, -ud**) frequently (but not always) has a pejorative sense and means 'that (of yours)' or 'that rotten no-good'.

**Iussum** is simply the fourth principal part of the verb used as a noun, 'the ordered thing' or 'order, command'. Note that the ablative singular is **iussū**.

**Maneō, manēre, mānsī, mānsus** and **remaneō, remanēre, remānsī, remānsus**, may be used interchangeably; the **-a-** lengthens in the perfect stem before **-ns-**. Both verbs mean 'remain'. Do not confuse the singular present active imperative **manē**, 'remain', with **māne** (adverb), 'early in the morning'.

The deponent verb **misereor, miserērī, miseritus sum**, 'pity', governs the genitive case: **Meī miserēris?**, 'Do you pity me?'

**Nesciō** is simply **ne** + **sciō**, 'not know, be ignorant'.

**Nōnne** and **num** introduce a question. **Nōnne** is used when the answer "yes" is expected, **num** when the answer expected is "no". **Num** may also introduce an indirect question and then it means 'whether'.

**Ops, opis**, F., in the singular means 'power, strength, help', but in the plural it means 'resources, wealth'.

**Paucī, paucae, pauca** is an adjective found in the plural; it means 'few'.

**Quia** and **quod**, 'because', may be used interchangeably.

**Quīdam, quaedam, quiddam** is the pronoun, 'a certain'; **quīdam, quaedam, quoddam** is the adjective, 'certain': **Sī quiddam mihi dīcās, dē eō taceam**, 'If you should tell me a certain thing, I would be silent about it'; **Quoddam dōnum quod placēbit tibi habeō**, 'I have a certain gift which will please you'.

**Rogō**, 'ask', a first conjugation verb, means not only to ask a question, but also to make a demand on someone: **Tē rogāvī nē id facerēs**, 'I asked you not to do that'. Note that this verb can take two objects: **Tē pecūniam rogō**, 'I ask you for money'.

**Tamquam** means 'as if, as, as it were', and **tandem** means 'at last, at length'. In order not to confuse these two words, it might be helpful to remember that a bicycle built for two is called a tandem (humorously, from the idea of length: the second person sits behind, not next to, the other.)

ADJECTIVAL SUFFIXES ADDED TO THE STEMS OF VERBS

The suffixes **-āx, -idus, -ulus**, or **-īvus** added to the stem of a verb express the action of the verb as a quality or tendency.

> **audāx, -ācis**, 'bold, courageous'
> **efficāx, -ācis** (**efficiō**, 'effect, bring about'), 'effectual, efficient'
> **fugāx, -ācis**, 'apt to flee, swift'
> **loquāx, -ācis**, 'talkative'
> **pūgnāx, -ācis**, 'fond of fighting, combative, warlike'
>
> **timidus, -a, -um**, 'fearful, afraid'
> **vīvidus, -a, -um**, 'containing life, living'
>
> **bibulus, -a, -um** (**bibō, -ere**, 'drink'), 'drinking readily'
> **crēdulus, -a, -um**, 'easy of belief, credulous'
> **garrulus, -a, -um** (**garriō, -īre**, 'chatter'), 'chattering, talkative'
> **querulus, -a, -um** (**queror, querī**, 'complain'), 'full of complaints, complaining'
> **tremulus, -a, -um** (**tremō, -ere**, 'tremble'), 'shaking, trembling'
> **āctīvus, -a, -um**, 'active, practical'

captīvus, -a, -um, 'taken prisoner, captive'
fugitīvus, -a, -um, 'fleeing away, fugitive'
nātīvus, -a, -um, 'imparted by birth, innate'

The suffixes -ilis and -bilis added to the stem of a verb express passive qualities, and occasionally active ones.

agilis, -e, 'easily moveable, nimble'
docilis, -e, 'easily taught'
amābilis, -e, 'worthy of love, lovely'
crēdibilis, -e, 'worthy of belief, credible'
mīrābilis, -e (mīror, -ārī, 'wonder at, admire'), 'wonderful, admirable'
mūtābilis, -e, 'changeable'
spectābilis, -e, 'visible, worth seeing'

The suffixes -bundus and -cundus added to the stem of a verb denote a continuance of the act or quality expressed by the verb.

errābundus, -a, -um, 'wandering about'
furibundus, -a, -um (furō, -ere, 'be mad'), 'raging, mad'
moribundus, -a, -um, 'dying'
īrācundus, -a, -um (īrāscor, īrāscī, 'be angry'), 'irritable, angry'
fācundus, -a, -um (for, fārī, fātus sum, 'speak'), 'speaking with ease, eloquent'

This verb for contains the stem fā- which is found in such words as fāma, 'talk, report, reputation'; fābula, -ae, F., 'narration, story, play'; fātum, -ī,N., 'prediction, destiny, fate'; fās, indeclinable, 'right, proper, allowable (according to divine dictate)'; nefās, indeclinable, 'unlawful, abominable', in other words, so bad it cannot be talked about. The Romans divided their calendar between fāstī and nefāstī — days (lucky and unlucky) on which business was allowed or not allowed to be conducted. An infant, literally, is a child who does not (in-) speak; once he begins speaking he is no longer technically an infant.

## UNIT TWELVE — DRILL

1. Respondeāmus!
2. Utinam dominī respondeant (respondissent)!
3. Ad quem locum accēdāmus?
4. Intellegēbat quam ob rem nōn respondissēmus.
5. Utrum iubēbis eum fortem esse an ego iubēbō?
6. Opprimarne ab hostibus an in fugam mē cōnferam?
7. Nōnne tibi hoc opus placet? Num illud opus clārissimum tibi placet?
8. Sine morā ille auctor librum cōnficiat!

9. Nē ōderimus malum nōs opprimentem. Nōn sentiō eum scīre quid agat.
10. Pater scit quantā pecūniā nōbīs opus sit.
11. Frāter ā nōbīs quaesīvit quanta sīdera in caelō essent.
12. Omnia superat amor: et nōs cēdāmus amōrī.
13. Omnēs intellegere voluērunt quid hominēs illīus temporis tanta mala passī essent. [**quid**, 'in respect to what thing, why']
14. Sciunt hunc ōrātōrem cupidissimum dīvitiārum esse.
15. Sciunt quam ob rem hic ōrātor cupidissimus sit (fuerit) dīvitiārum.
16. Cognōscēbātis ducem mortem minātūrum esse illīs patriam neglegentibus.
17. Cognōscēbātis quam ob rem dux mortem minātūrus esset illīs patriam neglegentibus.
18. Cognōscēbāmus quō tempore dux mortem illīs patriam neglegentibus minātus esset; numquam intellegēmus quam ob rem patriam neglēxerint.
19. Utrum nostram patriam servāre cōnāberis an nōn?
20. Quaerimus utrum nostram patriam servāre cōnātūra sīs necne.
21. Quīdam homō habēbat ferrum quoddam. Dedit cuidam. Is post dedit aliī. Is erat īdem quī prīmus habēbat.
22. Nē iuvenī cupidō dīvitiārum crēdant.
23. Utinam scelus nē cōnfitērēris.
24. Perīculum eō tempore neglegāmus.
25. Nāvēs eius generis nōn vidērēs.
26. Domum hōc tempore ingrediantur?
27. Iste amīcus mē ōdit.
28. Īdem amīcus mē ōdit.
29. Amīcus ipse mē ōdit.
30. Istum frātrem vīdī.
31. Eundem frātrem vīdī.
32. Frātrem ipsum vīdī.
33. Frātrem ipse vīdī.

# UNIT TWELVE — PRELIMINARY EXERCISES
## (SECTIONS A, B)

1. Comitēs nostrī iussa tandem expōnant.
2. Utinam cōpiae hostīlēs sē ex patriā recipiant.
3. Parentum iuvenis occultē miserear?
4. Nē domī maneāmus.
5. Pauca eius modī acciperēs.
6. Num negās tē haec nescīvisse?
7. Utrum melius est haec dēligere an illa?

8. Nōnne comitēs vestrī opēs recipient?
9. Tē sequī velīmus an hortēmur ut dux sine nōbīs proficīscātur?
10. Utinam nē hoc audeās; magnopere patiāris.

# UNIT TWELVE — EXERCISES

## I.

1. Omnēs eīdem mīlitēs quī prō rē pūblicā pūgnāvērunt magna pecūniae praemia ā cīvibus accipiant.
2. Rogāvimus quaedamne cibum an pecūniam an auxilium posceret.
3. Dī immortālēs salūtem, opēs et imperium cīvibus comitibusque dent!
4. Iuppiter! Mihi vītam longam sine gravī mortis timōre dēs!
5. Crēdāsne oppidum, ā cōpiīs fortibus per tōtam diem nōn captum, nocte ā parvā īnfēlīcium cīvium manū occultē dēlētum esse?
6. Quārē iste tandem meī misereātur?
7. Nōn vellem istōs hominēs, omnēs agrōs dēlentēs, nōbīscum remanēre.
8. Quid faciam, cīvēs? Quid dīcam istīs quī cīvitātem dēlēre volunt? Quō modō rem pūblicam servāre possim? Quandō exoriēminī? Ubi cīvitās oppūgnābitur? Exoriāminī! Rem pūblicam et cīvēs servāte!
9. Scīsne Marcum? Num cum eō venīs? Nōnne cibum fers?
10. Utinam mīlitēs hostīlēs nē veniant ut oppidum dēleant!
11. Utinam eī, quōrum cōpiae fortiōrēs quam illae hostium oppūgnantium sunt, patriam nostram servent!
12. Utinam dux ipse paucīs hōrīs veniat ut hostēs moenia ā cīvibus mūnīta oppūgnantēs et capientēs dēleat.
13. Iste comes cīvēs rogāvit unde vēnissent, et quam ob rem ad ārās deōrum īrent.
14. Nescīvērunt utrum manus mīlitum superāvisset an superāta esset.
15. Expōne quid urnās pulchrās manibus servōrum factās dēlēveris. [quid, 'in respect to what thing, why']
16. Semper intellegēbam quam ob rem omnēs hominēs līberī servōrum miserērentur.
17. Expōnere nōn potuerim quam ob rem rēx dōna ā turbā supplicī nōn accēperit.
18. Quīdam nōbīs dīcere possunt quamdiū cōnsulēs ipsī in urbe remānsūrī sint.
19. Hīs tantīs in rēbus est tuum vidēre quid agātur.
20. Ā vōbīs quaerō utrum pecūniam accēperitis necne.
21. Quid dīcam dē servitūte quae opprimit hōs quōs vidēmus?
22. Multōrum cognōsce exemplō, quae facta sequāris, quae fugiās: vīta est nōbīs magister.

23. Paucōrum est intellegere quid dōnet deus.
24. Ducēs dēlēctī nesciunt cūr magnus mortis timor inter cīvēs exoriātur. Utinam incolae fortiōrēs essent! [**inter**, prep. + acc., 'among']
25. Paucī tandem imperātōris iussū exposuērunt cūr horrida bella hominibus saepe pūgnanda essent: hominum est semper velle plūs imperiī quam habent.
26. Nē misereāmur ipsōrum comitum quī nōbīs noxae fuērunt et quōs nostrī amīcī ōdērunt.
27. Sapiēns scit quid sorte sibi datum sit, quid nōn. Utinam omnēs sapientēs essēmus!
28. Scīre volēbātis quamdiū in illā urbe vīxissem. Quīnque annōs ibi mānsī, sed mihi nunc tempus nōn est vōbīs expōnere quārē mē rūs recēperim.
29. Nōnne intellegis quantō in perīculō sīs (fueris; futūrus sīs)?
30. Vestrī comitēs verba mīlitum accipientēs nesciēbant quam ob rem expōnere nōllent quid ducēs dē salūte cōgitārent.
31. Omnēs sē in tēcta recēpērunt, nescientēs quandō sociī ventūrī essent, ut sē timōre et perīculō līberārent.
32. Nesciō quō modō iste ā cīvibus dux dēlēctus sit; vir pessimus est.
33. Rogātis ut opibus bene ūtāmur; rogāmus num ipsī opibus bene ūtāminī.
34. Quaedam mē rogāvit unde vēnissem; dīxī mē Rōmā occultē profectum esse; sortem esse ad hanc urbem mē cōnferre ut multa huic populō tamquam magister dīcerem.
35. PLINY TRIES TO HANDLE THE CHRISTIANS (selected and adapted from Pliny, *Letters* x.96):
Interim in eīs quī ad mē tamquam Christiānī dēferēbantur hoc ēgī. Rogāvī ipsōs an essent Christiānī. Dīxērunt sē Christiānōs esse. Sī negāvissent, imperāvissem ut eī ipsī līberārentur; persevērantēs autem dūcī ad poenam iussī. Fuērunt aliī similis āmentiae quōs, quia cīvēs Rōmānī erant, dīxī in urbem mittendōs. Quid aliud in rēbus huius modī facerem? Magnum perīculum cīvitātī atque populō Rōmānō erat.
[**āmentia, -ae**, F., 'madness, folly'; **Christiānus, -a, -um**, 'Christian'; **in** (prep. + abl.), *here*, 'in the case of'; **interim** (adv.), 'meanwhile'; **persevērō** (1), 'persevere']
36. Amīcus optimus mortuus est. Cōgitō quō amīcō, quō virō caream.
37. Quaerō utrum Brūtī similem mālīs an Antōniī. [**Brūtus, -ī**, M., proper name; **Antōnius, -ī**, M., proper name]
38. Hoc quaerāmus, immortālis sit ille hospes necne: Esne immortālis an nōn?
39. Unde quoddam dōnum dē quō diū audīvimus recipiēmus? Scīsne an nōn?
40. Ubi estis? Quandō veniam ut vōs videam? Nisī domī eritis, quō modō sciam quid mihi faciendum sit?
41. Eīdem parentēs iuvenēs ipsōs audentēs loquī cum audāciā ōderint.
42. "Moriēmur sine culpā, sed moriāmur," ait.

43. Sed ubi diēs coepit, et incolae, nihil hostīle verentēs, multī oppidō ēgressī, aliī ibi manentēs, imperātor cōpiās portās oppūgnāre iussit.

44. Nōs ipsī morī velīmus an mortem vereāmur (timeāmus)? Quae sit nostra sententia rogāre vīs.

45. Dāmnātus cuiusdam sceleris, mē quae esset poena nōn accēpisse fassus sum.

46. Quārē discēdant impiī!

47. Vidē nunc quid agās, quid ferre possīs, neque quamdiū vīxerit Caesar sed quam nōn diū rēxerit cōgitā! [Note how **nōn** splits **quamdiū** for effect. **Caesar, Caesaris**, M., proper name]

48. Utinam minus vītae cupidī fuissēmus! Certē nihil aut nōn multum in vītā malī vīdissēmus. [**aut** (conj.), 'or']

49. Ad tē quid scrībam nesciō.

50. Utinam nē tōtam opīniōnem parva nōn numquam mūtāvisset aura rūmōris.

51. Rogābās quam ob rem somnus ad mē illā nocte nōn vēnisset; magnopere timēbam; omnēs mē terrēbant aurae. [**somnus, -ī**, M., 'sleep']

52. Omnibus modīs miser sum.

## II.

1. Let all citizens in a free state be dutiful and willing to fight for their country.
2. If only we could always be free from care!
3. All men know why the enemy must be overcome.
4. What are we to do to remain free men?
5. He might believe that you are all good and honorable men.
6. He explained how the enemy would attack and destroy the fortified walls at Rome.

## III. Readings

A. Cicero speaks of the disadvantages of knowing one's future (*Dē Dīvīnātiōne* II.9.22, slightly adapted):

Atque ego nē ūtilem[1] quidem[2] arbitror esse nōbīs futūrārum rērum scientiam.[3] Quae enim vīta fuisset Priamō,[4] sī ab adulēscentiā[5] scīvisset, quōs ēventūs[6] senectūtis[7] esset habitūrus? Abeāmus[8] ā fābulīs,[9] propiōra[10] videāmus. Clārissimōrum hominum nostrae cīvitātis dē gravissimīs mortibus in aliō librō scrīpsī. Quid igitur?[11] ut omittāmus[12] superiōrēs,[13] Marcōne

---

[1] **ūtilis, -e**, 'advantageous'    [2] **nē...quidem**, 'not...even' (enclosing the word or words they qualify)    [3] **scientia, -ae**, F., 'knowledge'    [4] **Priamus, -ī**, M., 'Priam', the aged king of Troy    [5] **adulēscentia, -ae**, F., 'youth'    [6] **ēventus, -ūs**, M., 'issue, end, catastrophe'    [7] **senectūs, -tūtis**, F., 'old age'    [8] **abeō (ab + eō)**, 'depart'    [9] **fābula, -ae**, F., 'story, myth'    [10] **propior, -ius**, 'nearer, more closely affecting'    [11] **igitur** (postpositive conj.), 'therefore'    [12] **omittō (ob + mittō)**, 'leave out, omit'; translate **ut** 'granted that, although' (see Appendix, p. 392, Concessive Clauses #5)    [13] **superior, -ius**, comparative of **superus, -a, -um**, *here*, 'prior, former, earlier'

Crassō[14] putās ūtile[1] fuisse tum,[15] cum[16] maximīs opibus flōrēbat,[17] scīre sibi interfectō Pūbliō[18] fīliō exercitūque[19] dēlētō trāns[20] Euphrātem[21] cum īgnōminiā[22] esse moriendum?[23]

[14] **Marcus Crassus, -ī,** M., a man's name      [15] **tum** (adv.), 'then, at that time'      [16] **cum** (conj. + indicative), 'when'      [17] **flōreō, -ēre, -uī, --,** 'prosper'      [18] **Pūblius, -ī,** M., a man's name      [19] **exercitus, -ūs,** M., 'army'      [20] **trāns** (prep. + acc.), 'across, beyond' [21] **Euphrātes, -is,** M., 'the Euphrates', a river in western Asia      [22] **īgnōminia, -ae,** F., 'disgrace'      [23] **esse moriendum:** The neuter indicates that the verb is used impersonally: '. . . that it had to be died by him', i.e., 'that he had to die' (see Unit Thirteen, section C).

## B. Martial 2.7:

> Dēclāmās[1] bellē,[2] causās[3] agis, Attice,[4] bellē,[2]
> historiās[5] bellās,[2] carmina bella[2] facis,
> compōnis[6] bellē[2] mīmōs,[7] epigrammata[8] bellē,[2]
> bellus[2] grammaticus,[9] bellus[2] es astrologus,[10]
> et bellē[2] cantās[11] et saltās,[12] Attice,[4] bellē,[2]
> bellus[2] es arte lyrae,[13] bellus[2] es arte pilae.[14]
> Nīl bene cum[15] faciās, faciās tamen omnia bellē,[2]
> vīs dīcam[16] quid sīs? Magnus es ardeliō.[17]

[1] **dēclāmō** (1), 'declaim'      [2] **bellē** (adv.), 'beautifully'; **bellus, -a, -um,** 'beautiful' [3] **causa, -ae,** F., *here*, 'lawsuit'; **causās agere,** 'to plead cases'      [4] **Atticus, -ī,** M., a man's name      [5] **historia, -ae,** F., 'history'      [6] **compōnō (com- + pōnō),** 'compose, arrange' [7] **mīmus, -ī,** M., 'a mime' (a type of stage entertainment)      [8] **epigramma, -atis,** M., 'an epigram'      [9] **grammaticus, -ī,** M., 'grammarian'      [10] **astrologus, -ī,** M., 'astronomer' [11] **cantō** (1), 'sing'      [12] **saltō** (1), 'dance'      [13] **lyra, -ae,** F., 'lyre' (a stringed instrument) [14] **pila, -ae,** F., 'ball, a game of ball'      [15] **cum** (conj. + subjunctive), 'although'      [16] **vīs dīcam = vīs ut dīcam**      [17] **ardeliō, -ōnis,** M., 'busybody'

## C. Martial 8.12:

> Uxōrem[1] quārē locuplētem[2] dūcere[3] nōlim
> quaeritis? Uxōrī[1] nūbere[4] nōlo meae.
> Īnferior[5] mātrōna[6] suō sit, Prīsce,[7] marītō:[8]
> nōn aliter[9] fīunt[10] fēmina virque parēs.[11]

[1] **uxor, -ōris,** F., 'wife'      [2] **locuplēs, -plētis,** 'wealthy'      [3] **dūcere (in mātrimōnium** understood), 'marry' (of a man to a woman)      [4] **nūbō, -ere, nūpsī, nuptus,** 'marry' (+ dat.) (of a woman to a man)      [5] **inferior, -ius,** comparative of **inferus, -a, -um,** 'low'      [6] **mātrōna, -ae,** F., 'a married woman'      [7] **Prīscus, -ī,** M., a man's name      [8] **marītus, -ī,** M., 'husband'      [9] **aliter** (adv.), 'otherwise'      [10] **fīunt,** '(they) become' (3rd person pl. pres. indic. of **fīō, fierī, factus sum**)      [11] **pār, paris,** 'equal'

## D. Martial 12.20:

> Quārē nōn habeat, Fabulle,[1] quaeris
> uxōrem[2] Themisōn?[3] Habet sorōrem.

[1] **Fabullus, -ī,** M., a man's name      [2] **uxor, -ōris,** F., 'wife'      [3] **Themisōn, -ōnis,** M., a man's name

E. Martial 12.92:

> Saepe rogāre solēs quālis[1] sim, Prīsce,[2] futūrus,
> sī fīam[3] locuplēs[4] simque repente[5] potēns.[6]
> Quemquam[7] posse putās mōrēs nārrāre[8] futūrōs?
> Dīc mihi, sī fīās[9] tū leo,[10] quālis[1] eris?

[1] quālis, -e, 'what kind (of)'  [2] Prīscus, -ī, M., a man's name  [3] fīam, 1st person sing., pres. subj. of fīō, fierī, factus sum, 'become'  [4] locuplēs, -plētis, 'wealthy'  [5] repente (adv.), 'suddenly'  [6] potēns, potentis, 'powerful'  [7] quemquam (acc. sing. M.), 'anyone'  [8] nārrō (1), 'tell, relate'  [9] fīās, 2nd person sing., pres. subj. of fīō, fierī, factus sum, 'become'  [10] leō, leōnis, M., 'lion'

F. Horace, *Odes* i.11:

> Tū nē quaesieris[1] — scīre nefās[2] — quem mihi, quem tibi
> Fīnem dī dederint, Leuconoē,[3] nec Babylōniōs[4]
> Temptāris[5] numerōs.[6] Ut[7] melius, quicquid[8] erit, patī!
> Seu[9] plūrēs hiemēs,[10] seu[9] tribuit[11] Iuppiter ultimam,
> Quae nunc oppositīs[12] dēbilitat[13] pūmicibus[14] mare
> Tyrrhēnum.[15] Sapiās,[16] vīna[17] liquēs,[18] et spatiō[19] brevī[20]
> Spem longam resecēs.[21] Dum[22] loquimur, fūgerit invida[23]
> Aetās:[24] carpe[25] diem, quam minimum crēdula[26] posterō.[27]

[1] quaesieris = quaesīveris  [2] nefās, N. (indeclinable), 'unlawful, wrong'  [3] Leuconoē (vocative), a woman's name  [4] Babylōnius, -a, -um, 'Babylonian' (The Babylonians were noted for their astrological calculations.)  [5] temptō (1), *here*, 'consult'; temptāris is a syncopated or contracted form of temptāveris (see Unit Eighteen, Section D)  [6] numerus, -ī, N., *here*, 'calculation'  [7] ut (adv.), 'how'  [8] quicquid (nom. sing. N., indefinite pron.), 'whatever'  [9] seu...seu (conj.), 'whether...or'  [10] hiems, hiemis, F., 'winter'  [11] tribuō, -ere, tribuī, -ūtus, 'assign'  [12] oppōnō (ob, 'against' + pōnō), 'oppose'  [13] dēbilitō (1), 'weaken, break'  [14] pūmex, -icis, M., '(porous) rock'  [15] Tyrrhēnus, -a, -um, 'Tyrrhenian'  [16] sapiō, -ere, -iī, ––, 'be sensible'  [17] vīnum, -ī, N., 'wine'  [18] liquō (1), 'strain'  [19] spatium, -ī, N., 'time'  [20] brevis, -e, 'brief'  [21] resecō, -āre, -secuī, -sectus, 'remove'  [22] dum (conj.), 'while'  [23] invidus, -a, -um, 'envious'  [24] aetās, -tātis, F., 'life'  [25] carpō, -ere, carpsī, carptus, 'pluck, take advantage of'  [26] crēdulus, -a, -um, 'trusting (in)' (+ dat.)  [27] posterus, -a, -um, 'future'; here, used as a neuter noun

# UNIT THIRTEEN

## A. The Indefinite Pronouns *aliquis, quis, quisquam, quisque*

*Indefinite* pronouns represent *some* person or thing without designating exactly *which* one. **Quīdam**, 'a certain', met in the previous unit, is also an *indefinite* pronoun.

### 1. aliquis

The pronoun **aliquis, aliquid** is declined like the interrogative pronoun **quis, quid** with **ali-** added as a prefix; the forms for the adjective, **aliquī, aliqua, aliquod**, are identical to those of the relative pronoun **quī, quae, quod** with the prefix **ali-**, with the exception of the feminine nominative singular (as noted in the three parts given), and the neuter nominative and accusative plural, which are **aliqua**.

The pronoun means 'someone, something, anyone, anything'; the adjective means 'some, any'.

> **Aliquis** ad mē heri vēnit.    *Someone* came to me yesterday.
>
> Nōn sine **aliquō** metū cum    We fought with the inhabitants not without incolīs pūgnāvimus.    *some* fear.
>
> Vīdistīne **aliquem**?    Did you see *anyone* (*someone*)?

### 2. quis

**Quis, quid** (adjective **quī, qua, quod**) is essentially identical to **aliquis, aliquid** (adjective, **aliquī, aliqua, aliquod**), although it perhaps has a greater degree of indefiniteness about it. It is most frequently used instead of **aliquis** after the words **sī, nisī, num**, and **nē**.

REMEMBER: After **sī, nisī, num**, and **nē**, all the **ali-**'s drop away.

> Sī **quis** ad mē veniat, fēlīx sim.    If *anyone* (*someone*) should come to me, I would be happy.
>
> Nisī **quem** videās, fēlīx nōn sīs.    If you should not see *anyone* (*someone*), you would not be happy.
>
> Num **quem** vidēs?    You don't see *anyone* (*someone*), do you?

217

Hoc fēcit nē **quis** īrātus esset.         He did this in order that (so that) not *anyone* would be angry; he did this so that no *one* would be angry (so that *someone* would not be angry).

### 3. quisquam

**Quisquam, quidquam** (sometimes written **quicquam**) is declined like **quis, quid** with the suffix **-quam**. It means 'someone (something), anyone (anything)' and is used mainly in sentences which are negative or imply negation. The adjective for **quisquam** is supplied by the word **ūllus, -a, -um**, 'any'.

Vix **quisquam** hoc negāre potest.        Hardly *anyone* can deny this.

Fortior fuit lēgātus quam **quisquam** mīlitum.        The envoy was braver than *any(one)* of the soldiers. (The implied negation here is that no one of the soldiers was braver than the envoy.)

Sōlis lūx clārior est quam lūx **ūllīus** ignis.        The light of the sun is brighter than that of *any* fire.

### 4. quisque

The pronoun **quisque, quidque** (sometimes written **quicque**) (adjective, **quīque, quaeque, quodque**) is declined like **quis, quid** (adjective like **quī, quae, quod**) with the suffix **-que** and means 'each one (each), everyone (every)'.

Haec optimus **quisque** sentit.        *Each* (*every*) very good man perceives these things.

**Quīque** vir hanc puellam amat.        *Each* (*every*) man loves this girl.

**Cuique** hominī multa pecūnia est.        There is much money to *each* (*every*) man; *each* (*every*) man has much money.

## B. Dative with Certain Intransitive Verbs

There are certain intransitive verbs in Latin which govern the dative case. For example, while in English the verb "persuade" is transitive and governs an object, in Latin **persuādeō** is intransitive (it means 'I am persuasive') and takes a dative of reference.

**Tibi** persuādeō.        I am persuasive (*with reference*) *to you*; I persuade *you.*

Some of the more common verbs of this variety are:

| | |
|---|---|
| crēdō, crēdere, crēdidī, crēditus | be credulous, believe; be trusting, trust |
| faveō, -ēre, fāvī, fautus | be favorable, favor |
| īgnōscō, īgnōscere, īgnōvī, īgnōtus | be forgiving, forgive, pardon |
| imperō (1) | give orders, command |
| noceō, nocēre, nocuī, nocitus | be harmful, harm |
| parcō, parcere, pepercī, parsus | be sparing, spare |
| pāreō, -ēre, pāruī, pāritus | be obedient, obey |
| placeō, -ēre, placuī, placitus | be pleasing, please |
| persuādeō, -ēre, persuāsī, persuāsus | be persuasive, persuade |
| studeō, -ēre, -uī, — | be zealous, study |

## C. Impersonal Passives

Like all intransitive verbs, the verbs introduced in B above cannot logically be used in the passive. When a passive idea is desired, an *impersonal* construction must be used. An *impersonal* verb form appears in the third person singular and has no personal subject. The pronoun "it" may be used in English to give a literal translation.

| | |
|---|---|
| Tibi parcō. | I spare (am sparing to) you. |
| Tibi ā mē **parcitur**. | *It is spared* (*there is sparing*) to you by me; you are spared by me. |
| Mihi ā tē **parcitur**. | *It is spared* (*there is sparing*) to me by you; I am spared by you. |
| Mihi ā tē **parsum est**. | *It was* (*has been*) *spared* (*there was/has been sparing*) to me by you; I was (have been) spared by you. |

When such verbs are used in the passive periphrastic construction, the ablative of agent generally occurs instead of the more usual dative of agent in order to avoid confusion with the dative that is governed by the intransitive verb.

| | |
|---|---|
| Tibi **ā nōbīs** parcendum est. | It must be spared to you *by us*; *we* must spare you. |

The impersonal passive construction sometimes occurs with other verbs which do not take the dative when particular attention is called to the verbal action itself rather than to the ones performing the action.

| | |
|---|---|
| Domī **pūgnātur**. | *It is* (*being*) *fought* at home; *there is fighting* at home; *fighting is going on* at home; a battle is being fought at home. |

| | |
|---|---|
| Ācriter **pūgnātum est.** | *It was fought* fiercely; *there was* fierce *fighting*; the battle was fiercely fought. |
| Ad vīllam **curritur.** | *It is* (*being*) *run* to the villa; *there is* (*a*) *running* to the villa; people are running to the villa. |

## D. Dative with Compound Verbs
Many verbs compounded with prefixes such as the following govern the dative case.

| | | | |
|---|---|---|---|
| **ad-** | **con-** | **ob-** | **prō-** |
| **ante-** | **in-** | **post-** | **sub-** |
| **circum-** | **inter-** | **prae-** | **super-** |

It will be noted that such verbs cannot stand alone or, if transitive, simply with an accusative object; they require another word to complete the sense. For example,

| | |
|---|---|
| praesum | I am at the head of... (Another word is required to complete the sense; it will be in the dative.) |
| **Nautīs** praesum. | I am at the head of *the sailors*; I command *the sailors*. |
| praeficiō | I make at the head of, I place in command of... (Two additional words are required to complete the sense. Since the basic verb in this compound (-ficiō from **faciō**) is transitive, the root **-ficiō** will govern the accusative, and the prefix **prae-** will govern the dative.) |
| Tē **nautīs** praeficiō. | I place you in command of *the sailors*. |

These datives, like all datives, are basically referential.

| | |
|---|---|
| Nautīs praesum. | I am at the head with reference to the sailors; I am at the head of the sailors. |
| Tē nautīs praeficiō. | I make you in command with reference to the sailors; I place you in command of the sailors. |

## E. The Verb *fīō*, 'be made, be done, happen, become'
**Fīō, fierī, factus sum** is used as the passive for the verb **faciō, -ere, fēcī, factus.** The perfect system poses no problem, for it is identical to that formed from **faciō** (the last principal part of both verbs is the same). The present system functions like an i-stem verb of the third conjugation, except that it has active forms with passive meanings, and the quantity of the -i- is long in the present (except for the third person singular), the imperfect, and future indicative, the imperative, and the present subjunctive.

NOTE that the imperfect subjunctive is formed on the hypothetical active infinitive for this verb:

    fiere/m
    fierē/s
    ...etc.


**F. The Numerical Adjective *duo, duae, duo*, 'two'**

The plural adjective **duo**, 'two', has its own set of endings (shared also by **ambo, ambae, ambo**, 'both').

| M. | F. | N. |
|---|---|---|
| duo | duae | duo |
| duōrum | duārum | duōrum |
| duōbus | duābus | duōbus |
| duōs (-o) | duās | duo |
| duōbus | duābus | duōbus |


# UNIT THIRTEEN — VOCABULARY

| | |
|---|---|
| **admīrātiō, -ōnis, F.** | admiration |
| **adulēscēns, -entis** | young, youthful |
| **aliquis, aliquid** (pron.) | someone, something; anyone, anything |
| **aliquī, aliqua, aliquod** (adj.) | some, any |
| **celer, celeris, celere** | swift |
| **cōnstituō, -ere, -stituī, -stitūtus** | set, establish, decide |
| **currō, -ere, cucurrī, cursus** | run |
| **duo, duae, duo** | two |
| **faveō, -ēre, fāvī, fautus** | be favorable, favor (+ dat.) |
| **fīō, fierī, factus sum** | be made, be done, happen, become (passive for **faciō**) |
| **heri** (adv.) | yesterday |
| **hīc** (adv.) | here |
| **ignōscō, -ere, -nōvī, -nōtus** | be forgiving, forgive, pardon (+ dat.) |
| **illīc** (adv.) | there |
| **īrātus, -a, -um** | angry |
| **iūs, iūris, N.** | right, law |
| **lēgātus, -ī, M.** | legate, envoy |
| **mīror, -ārī, -ātus sum** | wonder (at), be amazed (at), admire |
| **moror, -ārī, -ātus sum** | delay, stay, hinder |

| | |
|---|---|
| nēmō, nēminis, M. *or* F. | no one |
| noceō, -ēre, -uī, -itus | be harmful, harm (+ dat.) |
| ōrātiō, -ōnis, F. | oration, speech |
| paene (adv.) | almost |
| parcō, -ere, pepercī, parsus | be sparing, spare (+ dat.) |
| pāreō, -ēre, -uī, -itus | be obedient, obey (+ dat.) |
| persuādeō, -ēre, -suāsī, -suāsus | be persuasive, persuade (+ dat.) |
| plēbs, plēbis, F. | common people |
| praeferō, -ferre, -tulī, -lātus | bring (place) before, prefer |
| praeficiō, -ere, -fēcī, -fectus | make before (at the head of), put in command of |
| praesum, praeesse, -fuī, –– | be before (at the head of), be in command of |
| quis, quid (pron.) | someone, something; anyone, anything |
|   quī, qua, quod (adj.) | some, any |
| quisquam, quidquam or | someone, something; anyone, anything (used |
|   quicquam (pron.) | with a negative or a virtual negative) |
| quisque, quidque or | each one, each thing, every one, every thing |
|   quicque (pron.) | |
|   quīque, quaeque, quodque (adj.) | each, every |
| quō (adv.) | (to) where |
| sollers, sollertis | skilled, expert |
| studeō, -ēre, -uī, –– | be zealous, study (+ dat.) |
| ūsus, -ūs, M. | use, advantage, enjoyment |
| vix (adv.) | hardly, scarcely |

# UNIT THIRTEEN — NOTES ON VOCABULARY

**Aliquis, aliquid** is the pronoun, 'someone, anyone, something, anything'; it is declined like **quis, quid** with the prefix **ali-**. **Aliquī, aliqua, aliquod** is the adjective 'some, any', declined like the relative pronoun (except that the **quae** forms become **-qua**) with the prefix **ali-**. But the feminine plural remains **-quae**.

Note that the verb **cōnstituō, cōnstituere, cōnstituī, cōnstitūtus**, 'set, establish, decide', has the same stem in the present and perfect active. Therefore, **cōnstituit** may be either present or perfect, for example.

**Currō, currere, cucurrī, cursus**, 'run', duplicates the **cu** in the perfect active stem in the same way that **pellō**, for instance, duplicates the **pe** in its perfect active stem **pepul-**.

**Duo, duae, duo**, 'two', and **ambo, ambae, ambo**, 'both', are declined in the same way. They are the only remains of the *dual* number in Latin; the dual was used for two objects only, as the singular is used for one object, and the plural for several objects.

The verb **fīō, fierī, factus sum**, 'be made, be done, happen, become', is used as the passive of **faciō**. In a way, it is the opposite of a deponent verb since its forms are active in appearance, but passive in meaning: **Hoc fīēbat**, 'This was done'.

**Hīc**, 'here', is an adverb and should not be confused with the adjective **hic**; **illīc** is the adverb 'there'.

**Īgnōscō** is a compound of **nōscō**; it means 'be forgiving, forgive, pardon' and governs the dative case.

There is a deponent verb **īrāscor, īrāscī, īrātus sum**, 'become angry', which is derived from **īra**, 'anger'. Its participle **īrātus** is used as an adjective, 'angry'.

**Iūs, iūris**, N., is 'right, law', as in our Bill of Rights. There is another word **iūs, iūris**, N., which means 'soup, sauce'.

**Lēgātus, lēgātī**, M., is an 'envoy, legate'; the legate was an official assistant of a general or governor of a province.

**Mīror** is a first conjugation deponent meaning 'wonder (at), be amazed (at), admire'; it has a compound, **admīror**, with the same meanings. Related to this compound is the noun **admīrātiō, admīrātiōnis**, F., 'admiration'.

The first conjugation deponent **moror**, 'delay, stay, hinder', is related to the noun **mora, -ae**, F., 'delay'.

Four Latin verbs are frequently confused with one another; a careful memorization of the principal parts of each of them would eliminate such confusion:

> **parcō, parcere, pepercī, parsus**, 'be sparing, spare' (+ dative)
> **pāreō, pārēre, pāruī, pāritus**, 'be obedient, obey' (+ dative)
> **parō** (1), 'prepare, make ready, provide, get'
> **pariō, parere, peperī, partus**, 'bear, give birth to, produce'

**Persuādeō, persuādēre, persuāsī, persuāsus** is a compound of **suādeō**, 'urge, persuade'. This verb and **suēscō, suēscere, suēvī, suētus**, 'be accustomed', have many compounds and derivatives; in these words, **su** is pronounced as **sw** (compare the English word "suave"). **Persuādeō**, therefore, has four syllables.

**Plēbs, plēbis**, F., 'common people', is a collective noun and so it takes a singular verb: **Plēbs ducī crēdit**, 'The common people trust the leader'.

**Praeferō**, 'bring before, place before, prefer', and **praeficiō**, 'make before, make at the head of, put in command of', govern both an object in the accusative case and a dative with compounds: **Dux lēgātum cōpiīs praefēcit**, 'The leader put the legate in command of the troops'.

After **sī, nisī, num**, and **nē, quis** means 'someone, anyone', and **quid** means 'something, anything'. The adjective **quī, qua, quod**, 'some, any', has **qua** forms instead of **quae**.

The spelling **quicquam**, 'something, anything', may be used instead of **quid-quam**, as **quicque**, 'each thing, everything', may be used instead of **quidque**.

**Quō** is an adverb meaning '(to) where'. A summary of these "place" adverbs might be helpful at this point:

| | | |
|---|---|---|
| **ubi**, 'where' | **quō** '(to) where' | **unde**, 'from where' |
| **hīc**, 'here' | **hūc**, '(to) here' | **hinc**, 'from here' |
| **illīc**, 'there' | **illūc** '(to) there' | **illinc**, 'from there' |
| **ibi**, 'there' | **eō**, '(to) there' | **inde**, 'from there' |

Obviously, **studium, studiī**, N., 'zeal', and **studeō, studēre, studuī**, --, 'be zealous, study' (+ dative), are related.

**Ūsus** is a fourth declension noun from **ūtor**; it means 'use, advantage, enjoyment'.

## ADJECTIVAL SUFFIXES ADDED TO THE STEMS OF NOUNS

The suffixes **-ōsus** and **-lentus** added to the stem of a noun mean 'full of'.

| | |
|---|---|
| **animōsus, -a, -um** | full of courage, bold, spirited |
| **annōsus, -a, -um** | of many years, aged |
| **aquōsus, -a, -um** | abounding in water, moist |
| **bellicōsus, -a, -um** | warlike, martial |
| **fāmōsus, -a, -um** | much talked of, famous |
| **glōriōsus, -a, -um** | full of glory, famous, renowned |
| **sententiōsus, -a, -um** | full of meaning, pithy |
| **corpulentus, -a, -um** | corpulent, fleshy, fat |
| **opulentus, -a, -um** | rich, wealthy |
| **turbulentus, -a, -um** | full of commotion, confused, disturbed |

The suffixes **-fer** and **-ger** (the roots of **ferō** and **gerō**) added to the stem of a noun mean 'bearing'.

| | |
|---|---|
| **armifer, -a, -um**<br>**armiger, -a, -um** } | bearing weapons, armed, warlike |
| **aurifer, -a, -um** | bearing, producing *or* containing gold |
| **belliger, -a, -um** | waging war, warlike, martial |
| **flammifer, -a, -um**<br>**flammiger, -a, -um** } | flame-bearing, flaming, fiery |
| **lūcifer, -a, -um** | light-bringing |
| **mortifer, -a, -um** | death-bringing |

## ABSTRACT NOUN SUFFIXES

The suffixes **-ia (-iēs), -tia (-tiēs), -tās, -tūs, -tūdō** added to the stems of adjectives (usually) produce feminine abstract nouns.

| | |
|---|---|
| dēmentia, -ae, F. | insanity, madness |
| memoria, -ae, F. | memory, recollection |
| pauperiēs, -ēī, F. | poverty |
| saevitia, -ae, F. | a raging, rage, fierceness |
| laetitia, -ae, F. | joy, gladness, pleasure |
| cānitiēs, -ēī, F. (cānus, -a, -um, 'white') | a grayish-white color |
| crūdēlitās, -tātis, F. | harshness, severity, cruelty |
| gravitās, -tātis, F. | weight, heaviness |
| iuventūs, -tūtis, F. | the age of youth, youth |
| senectūs, -tūtis, F. (senex, senis, 'old') | old age |
| magnitūdō, -inis, F. | greatness, size |
| multitūdō, -inis, F. | a great number, multitude |

The suffixes -ium and -tium added to noun stems (usually) produce neuter abstract nouns.

| | |
|---|---|
| augurium, -ī, N. (augur, -uris, M. or F., 'soothsayer') | the observation and interpretation of omens, augury |
| magisterium, -ī, N. | the office of a president, chief, director, superintendent, etc. |
| hospitium, -ī, N. | hospitality |
| servitium, -ī, N. | the condition of a slave, slavery |

# UNIT THIRTEEN — DRILL

## I.

Give the following forms:

1. gen. sing. quaeque aura
2. nom. pl. aliquod iussum
3. acc. sing. quisquam, aliquis
4. dat. sing. quisque
5. abl. pl. quīque modus

## II.

Translate:

1. Amōremne iussīs praepōnis?
2. In forō clāmātur.
3. Vōbīs imperāvimus nē iussa amōrī postpōnātis.
4. Ducī placet moenia oppidō circumpōnere.
5. Īra fit ruīnā nostrōrum bonōrum.
6. Crēdāmus imperātōrī ā regentibus honestīs dēlēctō.
7. Quisque pessimus poenās det!

8. Utinam quisque patriam amet!
9. Nōlī crēdere alicui maiōrī quam tibi.
10. Duōbus imperāvit nē cui maiōrī quam eīs crēdant.
11. a) Duo cōnsulēs exposuērunt quōsdam ducēs nāvibus praefectōs esse.
    b) Duo cōnsulēs exposuērunt sē quōsdam ducēs nāvibus praefectūrōs esse.
    c) Duo cōnsulēs exposuērunt sē quōsdam ducēs nāvibus praefectūrōs.
12. Dux ipse hortātus est ut hostīlēs cōpiae flammās oppidō circumdarent.
13. Per viās oppidī errātum est.
14. Tibi ab omnibus audientibus crēditum est.
15. Sī quis domī maneat, quid fīat in orbe terrārum nesciat.
16. Aliquisne tē timet? Num quis timēret tē rogāvimus.
17. Aliquī amīcus mihi dōnum aliquod mīsit.
18. Illud flūmen erat longius quam ūllum in Graeciā.
19. Marcus sē esse sapientiōrem quam quemquam amīcōrum arbitrātus est.
20. In bellō magnopere timētur.
21. Hoc difficilius est quam quidquam.

## UNIT THIRTEEN — PRELIMINARY EXERCISES (SECTIONS A, B)

1. Cūr aliquī adulēscēns per forum heri currere cōnstituit?
2. Cūr aliquis per forum heri currere cōnstituit?
3. Nescīvī num quis per forum currere cōnstitueret.
4. Sī quī adulēscēns per forum currere cōnstituat, īrātissimus sim.
5. Vix quisquam virtūtem illīc mōnstrāre voluit.
6. Ōrātiōnem lēgātī mīrātī sumus plūs quam ūllam ōrātiōnem quam audīvimus.
7. Cuique persuāsērunt ut quam honestissimus esset.
8. Plēbī quodque iūs nōn datum est.
9. Rogāvimus quārē aliqua admīrātiō adulēscentibus offerrētur reī pūblicae nocēre cōnantibus.
10. a) Nēmō intellēxit cūr dux aliqua scelera eō tempore fassus esset.
    b) Cīvēs ducī malō nōn fāvērunt.

## UNIT THIRTEEN — EXERCISES

**I.**

1. Quō quisque est sollertior, hōc docet facilius. [**quō**...**hōc**, 'by the degree in which...by this degree; the more...the']
2. Quō maius quodque animal, eō magis timendum est. [**quō**...**eō** = **quō**...**hōc**]

3. Sī quisquam est īrātus, is ego sum.

4. Vix ūllī crēdit, nec quisquam ex omnibus gentibus ad eum accēdere audet.

5. Hārum sententiārum quae vēra sit, deus aliquī videat.

6. Aliquid ā nōbīs invenītur; nescīmus quid sit. Quīdam crēdunt id malum esse. Illīs nōn crēdimus.

7. Nisī cui imperābis ut illī servō īgnōscat, mox moriētur.

8. Ignōscite mihi, adulēscentēs, sī vōbīs quid dīcam: cūrae vōbīs sit ut mōribus multārum gentium maximā cum cūrā studeātis.

9. Imperātōrī quodque sit bellum laudī.

10. Lēgātī illīus virtūs omnibus cīvibus admīrātiōnī fuit.

11. Cui bonō fuit? Nēminī bonō fuit.

12. Hoc vōbīs sit exemplō!

13. Hic mihi magnō ūsuī erit lēgātus, iste parvō.

14. Quem ūnī ē nōbīs saepe praetulit?

15. Pecūnia amīcitiae nōn praeferenda est.

16. Imperātōrī quī oppidō praeerat pārendum erat.

17. Dīxī imperātōrī quī oppidō praeesset pārendum esse.

18. Hīc vīvitur; illīc nēminī vīta placet.

19. Mihi ā quāque fēminā in urbe favētur.

20. Quaeque fēmina respondit hanc esse partem ōrātiōnis quae rem cōnstitueret paene ante oculōs cuiusque audientis.

21. Rogāmus quid fīat (quid factum sit, quid factūrus sit).

22. Omnia nātūrae nūminī, caelum, ignēs, terrae, maria pārent.

23. Aliquis hominī cuidam heri dīxit omnibus vīventibus animum datum esse ex illīs aeternīs ignibus, quae sīdera et stellās vocārētis. [animus, -ī, M., 'mind, soul'; stella, -ae, F., 'star']

24. Homō quīdam rogāvit quō modō haec fierī possint; alius respondit fierī nōn posse.

25. Quisque suam opīniōnem habet.

26. Signō datō, celeriter Rōmam curritur.

27. Lūx fīat.

28. Rogat num cui magnopere placuerit.

29. Quī amābant hunc, illī favēbunt.

30. Vix cuiquam persuādēbātur ē Graeciā omnī cessūrōs (esse) Rōmānōs.

31. Sī qua mihi virtūs esset, in bellum sine metū ruerem.

32. Dī in caelō, parcite nōbīs! Nātūram optimam ducem tamquam deum sequimur eīque pārēmus.

33. Crēdō ego vōs mīrārī quō ferat nātūra sua quemque.

34. Sī quisque suā manū captum ex hoste domum rettulisset, multī servī nōbīs nunc domī essent.

35. a) Gladium ēdūcere cōnantī dextram morātur manum. [**ēdūcere** = **ē** + **dūcere**]

    b) Mē interficere cōnantī dextram morātus sum manum.

36. Sī nēmō nēminī similis est, nōbīs opus est mōrēs cuiusque hominis intellegere et in quōque quaerere aliquid virtūtis.

37. Eō vītae tempore, dux sēnsit scelera quam pessima in orbe terrārum fierī.

38. Quid fīet sī quis cōnstituet nōs rogāre unde vēnerimus? Cōnfitērī nōn possumus nōs Rōmā herī profectōs esse, urbe hīs gentibus inimīcissimā.

39. Mōrēs istīus aliquam mihi admīrātiōnem movērent nisī opibus semper male ūterētur (nisī opēs amīcōrum dēlēre occultē cōnārētur).

40. Hīc saxō, liquidīs ille colōribus
    sollers nunc hominem pōnere, nunc deum.  (Horace, *Odes* IV.8.7–8)
    Quisque artem suam habet.

    [**liquidus, -a, -um**, 'liquid'; **color, -ōris**, M., 'color'; **pōnō**, *here*, 'portray, fashion']

41. Imperātūrus es hominibus, quī nec tōtam servitūtem patī possunt nec tōtam lībertātem. Aliquid tibi cōnsiliī atque mentis opus est.

42. Amīcī fīāmus et sine bellō atque odiō vīvāmus. Huicne cōnsiliō favētis an nōn?

43. Mē herī rogāvistī num quem vīdissem. Dīxī mē aliquem vīdisse, sed nescīre quis esset. Nihil novī nunc tibi afferre possum.

44. Intellegī potest nōn sōlum hominēs solēre dubitāre, bonumne aliquod cōnsilium an malum sit, sed etiam ē duōbus cōnsiliīs bonīs utrum melius sit.

45. Quō plūs custōdum fortissimōrum imperātōrī est, hōc tūtior; nam plēbs, alterīus ducis cupida, nihil audāciae agere audēbit.

46. Dīxitne aliquid? Nōn dīxit quicquam.

47. Hominī pepercērunt quem dux manuī fortium praefēcerat.

48. Mihi nōn ab istīs nocērī potest.

49. Mōtus celer flūminis intellegendus erit nē cui trānseuntī noceātur. [**trānseō** from **trāns**, 'across' + **eō**]

50. Parva magnīs cōnferantur.

51. THE COMMON PEOPLE AND THE DRUIDS IN GAUL (adapted from Caesar, *The Gallic Wars* VI.13):

    In omnī Galliā eōrum hominum quī aliquō sunt honōre genera sunt duo; nam plēbs paene servōrum habētur locō, quae nihil audet per sē, ad nūllum cōnsilium [*here*, 'council'] īre potest. Multī, pecūniā carentēs aut vīribus aliōrum fortiōrum pressī, sē in servitūtem trādunt nōbilibus; quibus in [*here*, 'over'] hōs eadem omnia sunt iūra quae dominīs in ['over'] servōs. Sed dē hīs duōbus generibus alterum est druidum, quibus ūnus fortissimus praeest, alterum equitum. Illī rēbus dīvīnīs intersunt; sacrificia pūblica et prīvāta faciunt. Ad eōs magnus adulēscentium numerus disciplīnae causā currit, magnōque hī sunt apud eōs honōre. Nam paene dē omnibus contrōversiīs pūblicīs prīvātīsque cōnstituunt, et, sī quod est scelus factum, sī quis interfectus est, sī dē fīnibus contrōversia est, īdem cōnstituunt quid faciendum sit. Hī dīcunt quae poenae, quae praemia quibus danda sint. Sī quī aut prīvātus aut populus eōrum iussīs nōn pāret, sacrificiīs prohibent. Haec poena apud eōs est gravissima. Quibus ita est prohibitum, hī numerō impiōrum habentur, hīs omnēs discēdunt nē quid ex eīs malī accipiant, neque iīs petentibus iūs datur neque honor ūllus.

[**aut** (conj.), 'or'; **causā** (used prepositionally + gen. — placed after the genitive which it governs), 'for the sake of'; **contrōversia, -ae,** F., 'controversy'; **disciplīna, -ae,** F., 'training'; **dīvīnus, -a, -um,** 'divine'; **druidēs, -um,** M., 'the druids' (the priests and wise men of Gaul); **eques, equitis,** M., 'horseman, knight'; **Gallia, -ae,** F., 'Gaul', a country in the ancient world corresponding roughly to modern France; **honor, honōris,** M., 'honor, respect'; **intersum, -esse, -fuī, ——,** 'be between, be concerned'; **ita** (adv.), 'in this way'; **nōbilis, -e,** 'noble'; **numerus, -ī,** M., 'number'; **prīvātus, -a, -um,** 'private'; **prohibeō, -ēre, -uī, -itus,** 'prohibit, keep from'; **sacrificium, -ī,** N., 'sacrifice']

## II.

1. Will anyone pardon him? He will not be pardoned by anyone.
2. I don't prefer anyone to her. She is a great aid to me.
3. What was happening yesterday on land and sea?
4. He said that he would please each man whom he had praised.
5. If anyone should shout that there is danger here, there would be a great running in the streets; the consul would put the legate in command of the people so that the ruler will be obeyed.

## III. Readings

A. Cicero, *Dē Amīcitiā* 5.17:

Ego vōs hortārī tantum[1] possum, ut amīcitiam omnibus rēbus hūmānīs[2] antepōnātis;[3] nihil est enim tam nātūrae aptum,[4] tam conveniēns[5] ad rēs vel[6] secundās[7] vel[6] adversās.[8]

---

[1] tantum (adv.), 'only'    [2] hūmānus, -a, -um, 'human'    [3] antepōnō (ante + pōnō), 'put (place) before, prefer'    [4] aptus, -a, -um, 'suited to'    [5] conveniēns, -entis, 'appropriate'    [6] vel...vel (adv.), 'either...or'    [7] secundus, -a, -um, 'favorable'    [8] adversus, -a, -um, 'adverse'

B. Cicero, *Dē Amīcitiā* 6.20:

Amīcitiae dīvitiās aliī praepōnunt,[1] bonam aliī valētūdinem,[2] aliī potentiam,[3] aliī honōrēs,[4] multī etiam[5] voluptātēs.[6]

[1] **praepōnō (prae + pōnō)**, 'place before, prefer'     [2] **valētūdō, -inis**, F., 'health'     [3] **potentia, -ae**, F., 'power'     [4] **honor, -ōris**, M., 'honor, distinction'     [5] **etiam** (adv.), 'even'     [6] **voluptās, -tātis**, F., 'pleasure'

C. Cicero *Dē Dīvīnātiōne* I.25.52:

Est apud[1] Platōnem[2] Sōcratēs,[3] cum[4] esset in custōdiā[5] pūblicā, dīcēns Critōnī,[6] suō familiārī,[7] sibi post tertium[8] diem esse moriendum;[9] vīdisse enim sē in somnīs[10] pulchritūdine[11] eximiā[12] fēminam, quae sē nōmine appellāns,[13] dīceret Homēricum[14] quendam eius modī versum:[15]

tertia[8] tē Phthīae[16] tempestās[17] laeta[18] locābit.[19]

Quod, ut est dictum, sīc[20] scrībitur contigisse.[21]

[1] **apud** (prep. + acc.), *here*, 'in the works of'     [2] **Platō, -ōnis**, M., 'Plato', the Greek philosopher     [3] **Sōcratēs, -is**, M., 'Socrates', the Greek philosopher     [4] **cum** (conj. + subjunctive), 'when'     [5] **custōdia, -ae**, F., 'custody'     [6] **Critōn, -ōnis**, M., 'Crito', a friend of Socrates     [7] **familiāris, -is**, M., 'friend'     [8] **tertius, -a, -um**, 'third'     [9] The neuter participial form indicates that the verb is used impersonally; see section C of this Unit.     [10] **somnus, -ī**, M., 'dream'     [11] **pulchritūdō, -inis**, F., 'beauty'     [12] **eximius, -a, -um**, 'exceptional'     [13] **appellō** (1), 'call'     [14] **Homēricus, -a, -um**, 'of Homer, Homeric'     [15] **versus, -ūs**, M., 'a line of poetry, verse'     [16] **Phthīa, -ae**, F., 'Phthia', a town in Thessaly. [The line echoes Homer, *Iliad* IX.363. Phthia, the homeland of Achilles, is used here to suggest that Socrates is going home.]     [17] **tempestās, -tātis**, F., 'period of time, season, day'     [18] **laetus, -a, -um**, *here*, 'felicitous'     [19] **locō** (1), 'locate, place'     [20] **sīc** (adv.), 'in this way'     [21] **contingō, -ere, -tigī, -tāctus**, 'happen'

D. Cicero, *In Catilīnam* I.4.8:

Videō enim esse hīc in senātū[1] quōsdam quī tēcum ūnā[2] fuērunt.

[1] **senātus, -ūs**, M., 'senate'     [2] **ūnā** (adv.), 'together'

E. Cicero, *In Catilīnam* I.9.23:

Sīn[1] autem servīre[2] meae laudī et glōriae māvīs, ēgredere cum importūnā[3] scelerātōrum[4] manū, cōnfer tē ad Manlium,[5] concitā[6] perditōs[7] cīvēs, sēcerne[8] tē ā bonīs, īnfer patriae bellum, exsultā[9] impiō latrōciniō,[10] ut ā mē nōn ēiectus[11] ad aliēnōs,[12] sed invītātus[13] ad tuōs īsse videāris.

[1] **sīn** (conj.), 'but if'     [2] **serviō, -īre, -īvī, -ītus**, 'serve, be a slave to' (+ dat.)     [3] **importūnus, -a, -um**, 'rude, savage'     [4] **scelerātus, -a, -um**, 'polluted, profaned by guilt'     [5] **Manlius, -ī**, M., a man's name     [6] **concitō** (1), 'arouse'     [7] **perditus, -a, -um**, *here*, 'desperate, corrupt, infamous, degenerate'     [8] **sēcernō, -ere, -crēvī, -crētus**, 'separate'     [9] **exsultō** (1), 'rejoice, triumph'     [10] **latrōcinium, -ī**, N., 'criminality'     [11] **ēiciō (ē + iaciō)**, 'throw out'     [12] **aliēnus, -a, -um**, 'strange, foreign'     [13] **invītō** (1), 'invite'

F.  Cicero, *In Catilīnam* II.5.11:

Cum lūxuriā[1] nōbīs, cum āmentiā,[2] cum scelere certandum est.[3]

[1] **lūxuria, -ae,** F., 'luxury, excess'    [2] **āmentia, -ae,** F., 'madness'    [3] **certō** (1), 'fight'

G. Cicero, *In Catilīnam* II.12.27:

Quod[1] reliquum[2] est, iam nōn possum oblīvīscī[3] meam hanc esse patriam, mē hōrum esse cōnsulem, mihi aut[4] cum hīs vīvendum aut[4] prō hīs esse moriendum.

[1] **quod,** *here,* '(with respect to) what...; as far as what...'    [2] **reliquus, -a, -um,** 'remaining'    [3] **oblīvīscor, oblīvīscī, oblītus sum,** 'forget'    [4] **aut...aut,** 'either...or'

# UNIT FOURTEEN

## A. Clauses of Result

Clauses which express the result of an action or a quality are introduced by **ut** for the positive, **ut nōn** (**nēmō, nihil, numquam,** etc.) for the negative, and have their verbs in the subjunctive.

The approach of a result clause is often indicated by the presence of an adjective or adverb of degree in the main clause.

ADJECTIVES:
- **tantus, -a, -um,** 'so great'
- **tālis, -e,** 'such, of such a sort'
- **tot** (indeclinable), 'so many'

ADVERBS:
- **ita,** 'so'
- **tam,** 'so'
- **sīc,** 'in this way'
- **adeō,** 'so'

| | |
|---|---|
| **Tanta** est tempestās **ut** omnēs nāvēs **dēleantur.** | *So great* is the storm *that* all the ships *are being destroyed.* |
| **Tam** celeriter currit **ut nēmō** eum vincere **possit.** | He runs *so* fast *that no one can* beat him. |

The rules for sequence of tenses are generally observed. However, the perfect subjunctive is sometimes found in secondary sequence instead of the imperfect in order to lay stress on the fact that the action is completed.

| | |
|---|---|
| **Tam** īrātus erat **ut** hoc **dīceret.** | He was *so* angry *that he said* this. |
| **Tam** īrātus erat **ut** hoc **dīxerit.** | He was *so* angry *that he* (actually) *said* this. (emphasis on completion of the action) |
| **Tanta** erat tempestās **ut** omnēs nāvēs **dēlērentur.** | *So great* was the storm *that* all the ships *were* (*being*) *destroyed.* |
| **Tanta** erat tempestās **ut** omnēs nāvēs **dēlētae sint.** | *So great* was the storm *that* all the ships *were* (actually) *destroyed.* (emphasis on completion of the action) |

Note the following similarities and distinctions between purpose and result clauses:

| PURPOSE | RESULT |
|---|---|
| Positive introduced by **ut**. | Positive introduced by **ut**. |
| Negative introduced by **nē**. | Negative introduced by **ut...nōn**. |
| | An adverb or adjective of degree in the main clause frequently signals the approach of a clause of result. |
| Vēnit **ut** turbam vinceret. | **Tam** fortis erat **ut** turbam vinceret (vīcerit). |
| He came *to* overcome the crowd. | He was *so* brave *that* he overcame the crowd. |
| Nōn vēnit **nē** turbam vinceret. | **Tam** fortis erat **ut** ā turbā **nōn** vincerētur (victus sit). |
| He didn't come *so that* he would *not* overcome the crowd. | He was *so* brave *that* he was *not* overcome by the crowd. |

## B. Substantive Clauses of Result

Certain verbs and expressions have result clauses either as their object or subject. Of these, the most important are:

**efficere ut**, 'to bring it about that'
**facere ut**, 'to see to it that'
} + object clause

**accidit ut**, 'it happens that'
**fit ut**, 'it comes about that, it happens that'
**fierī potest ut**, 'it is able to happen that, it is possible that'
} + subject clause

| | |
|---|---|
| **Effēcit ut** nautae inter sē **pūgnārent**. | *He brought it about that* the sailors *fought* among themselves; *he brought it about that* the sailors *fought* one another. |
| **Accidit ut** ego ipse illīc **manērem**. | *It happened that* I myself *remained* there. |
| **Fit ut** nēmō **sit** laetior quam ego. | *It happens that* no one *is* happier than I. |

The verbs **efficere** and **facere** are frequently followed by **nē** instead of **ut...nōn** to introduce a negative clause, particularly when there is an implicit notion of command in the sentence.

Fac **nē** cui noceās.   See to it *that* you do *not* harm anyone.

## C. Relative Clauses of Characteristic (Generic [*genus, generis*, N., 'sort']
   Relative Clauses)

The relative pronoun **quī, quae, quod** plus the subjunctive can be used to describe its antecedent in terms of the general qualities or characteristics of the group to which the antecedent belongs.

> **Is est quī** celeriter **ambulet.**   *He is the (kind of) man who walks* fast; *he is a man who walks* fast.

(The relative clause with its verb in the subjunctive characterizes its antecedent in terms of the general qualities of the larger group to which the antecedent belongs.)

COMPARE:

> Is est quī celeriter ambulat.   He is the (actual) man who walks fast.

(The relative clause with its verb in the indicative describes a particular antecedent.)

> **Sunt quī** eī **crēdant.**   *They are the (kind of) men who trust* him; *there are men (of the kind) who trust* him; *there are those who trust* him.

COMPARE:

> Hī sunt quī eī crēdunt.   These are the (actual) ones who trust him.
> **Quis erat quī** hoc **crēderet?**   *Who was there (of the kind) who believed* this?

In many instances, these clauses have general or indefinite antecedents, of which the following are common:

| | |
|---|---|
| sunt quī | there are those who |
| est quī | he is one who |
| nēmō est quī | there is no one who |
| nihil est quod | there is nothing that |
| quis est quī? | who is there who? |
| quid est quod? | what is there that? |

But these generic clauses are also found with less vague and even with precise antecedents when they are felt to characterize or generalize rather than denote a specific attribute of the antecedent:

| | |
|---|---|
| sōlus est quī | he is the only (kind of) man who |
| is est quī | he is the (kind of) man who |
| Cicerō est quī | Cicero is the (kind of) man who |
| dīgnus est quī | he is the (kind of) man worthy who (to) |

Relative clauses of characteristic are best translated into English using the indicative; the generic idea is carried over into English by the formulae which introduce such clauses — i.e., 'there is *no one* who', 'he is the *sort of* man who'. Sometimes, however, the context requires that the subjunctive be rendered with potential force:

| | |
|---|---|
| Sōlus est quī hoc nesciat. | He is the only one who does not know this. OR He is the only one who would not know this. (potential force) |
| Quid erat quod agerēmus? | What was there that we could do? (potential force) |
| Quis est quī hoc faciat? | Who is the (kind of) one who does this?; Who is there who does this? OR Who is there who would do this? (potential force) |
| Nēmō erat quī eum rīdēret. | There was no one (the kind) who laughed at him. OR There was no one who would laugh at him. (potential force) |
| Dignus est quī nautīs praesit. | He is the kind of worthy man (i.e., he belongs to the class of worthy men) who is (would be) in command of the sailors; he is worthy to be in command of the sailors. |

Frequently, negative relative clauses of characteristic are introduced by **quīn** (= **quī [quae, quod] nōn**):

| | |
|---|---|
| Nēmō est **quīn** haec intellegat. | There is no one *who* does *not* understand these things. OR There is no one *who would not* understand these things. |

### D. Relative Clauses of Result
Very closely allied to the relative clause of characteristic is the relative clause of result.

| | |
|---|---|
| Nihil est tam malum **quod** mūtārī nōn **possit**. | There is nothing so bad *with the result that it cannot* be changed; there is nothing so bad *that it cannot* be changed. |
| Nēmō est tam caecus **quī** haec nōn **videat**. | There is no one so blind *who* does not *see* these things; there is no one so blind *that he does* not *see* these things. |

Here there is a fusion of both a relative clause of characteristic and a result clause to produce a relative clause of result. The relative pronoun is standing for the **ut** which would normally introduce the clause of result.

### E. Relative Clauses of Purpose and Purpose Clauses Introduced by Adverbs

Purpose clauses were presented in Unit Three as having their verbs in the subjunctive and as being introduced by **ut** for the positive and **nē** for the negative. However, there are other ways of expressing purpose with the subjunctive in Latin:

1. **Quō** (ablative, 'by which') introduces a purpose clause which contains a comparative.

> Properātis **quō** celerius **adveniātis**.
>
> You hasten *by which you may arrive* more quickly; you hasten (in order) to arrive more quickly.
>
> (= Properātis ut celerius adveniātis.)

2. Purpose clauses may be introduced by a relative pronoun when its antecedent, usually not the subject of the main verb, is clearly expressed in the main clause. They may also be introduced by an adverb (**ubi**, 'where'; **unde**, 'from where'; **quō**, '(to) where').

> Nūntium mittit **quī** dē mōribus incolārum **roget**.
>
> He sends a messenger *who may ask* about the customs of the inhabitants; he sends a messenger *in order that he* (i.e., *the messenger*) *may ask* about the customs of the inhabitants; he sends a messenger *to ask* about the customs of the inhabitants.
>
> (= Nūntium mittit ut dē mōribus incolārum roget.)

> Domum cucurrī **ubi** mē **cēlārem**.
>
> I ran home *where I might hide*; I ran home *to hide there*.
>
> (= Domum cucurrī ut ibi mē cēlārem. I ran home in order that I might hide there.)

> Scrībēbat librōs **quōs** aliī **legerent**.
>
> He wrote books *which* others might *read*; he wrote books *in order that* others *might read* them; he wrote books for others to read.
>
> (= Scrībēbat librōs ut eōs aliī legerent.)

## F. Indirect Reflexives

It has been pointed out in Unit Seven, section B4, that reflexives refer to the subject of the verb of their own clause. A reflexive so used is called a *direct reflexive.*

> Senex multam pecūniam **sibi** parāvit.  The old man got much money *for himself.*

However, in subordinate subjunctive clauses, the reflexive usually refers to the subject of the *main* clause and not to that of the clause in which it appears. This use is called the *indirect reflexive.*

> Dux lēgātum mittit quī **sibi** multam pecūniam paret.  The leader sends a legate to get much money *for him(self)* (i.e., the leader.)

> Plēbs ōrat ut **sibi** parcāmus.  The common people beg that we spare *them.*

> Dīcit illōs īrātōs **sē** interficere velle.  He says that those angry men want to kill *him.*

> Vir rogāvit quam ob rem iste adulēscēns ad **sē** vēnisset.  The man asked why that young man of yours had come to *him* (i.e., to the man).

If, in the third example above, the author had wished to take the less frequent course and have his reflexive refer to the subject of the verb in its own clause (here, the infinitive **velle**), clarity could have been achieved by inserting the appropriate form of the intensive pronoun, **ipse, ipsa, ipsum**:

> Dīcit illōs īrātōs sē **ipsōs** interficere velle.  He says that those angry men want to kill *themselves* (i.e., their *very* selves).

# UNIT FOURTEEN — VOCABULARY

**accidō, -ere, -cidī, --**  fall upon; happen, occur
**adeō** (adv.)  so, so much, so far
**adveniō, -īre, -vēnī, -ventus**  come to, arrive
**animus, -ī,** M.  mind, rational spirit, soul
**auctōritās, -tātis,** F.  authority
**aut** (conj.)  or
  **aut...aut**  either...or
**Carthāgō, -inis,** F.  Carthage, a city on the coast of North Africa
**colloquor, -loquī, -locūtus sum**  speak, talk, converse with
**dignus, -a, -um**  worthy, deserving, suitable (+ abl.)
  **indignus, -a, -um**  unworthy, unsuitable (+ abl.)

| | |
|---|---|
| **dolor, -ōris,** M. | pain, grief, sorrow |
| **efficiō, -ere, -fēcī, -fectus** | effect, bring about |
| **etiam** (adv.) | even |
| **hūc** (adv.) | to this place |
| **illūc** (adv.) | to that place, up to that time |
| **intendō, -ere, -tendī, -tentus** | stretch out, extend, aim, exert |
| **inter** (prep. + acc.) | between, among |
| **ita** (adv.) | so, in this way |
| **modo** (adv.) | only |
| **nōtus, -a, -um** | known, well-known, customary |
| **nūntiō** (1) | report, announce |
|    **nūntius, -ī,** M. | messenger, message |
| **nūper** (adv.) | recently |
| **ōs, ōris,** N. | mouth, expression |
| **ostendō, -ere, -tendī, -tentus** | show, expose, make plain |
| **parō** (1) | prepare, make ready, provide, get |
| **paulus, -a, -um** | little, small (compares irregularly: **minor, minus;** **minimus, -a, -um**) |
| **pāx, pācis,** F. | peace |
| **polliceor, -ērī, -itus sum** | promise |
| **properō** (1) | hasten |
| **quālis, -e** | of what kind, what kind of |
| **rīdeō, -ēre, rīsī, rīsus** | laugh (at) |
| **senex, senis** | old |
| **sīc** (adv.) | so, in this way |
| **tālis, -e** | such, of such a sort |
|    **tālis...quālis** | such...as |
| **tempestās, -tātis,** F. | weather, storm, season |
| **trāns** (prep. + acc.) | across, on the other side of |
| **tum** or **tunc** (adv.) | then, at that time |
| **ubīque** (adv.) | everywhere, anywhere, wherever |
| **vēritās, -tātis,** F. | truth |
| **vincō, -ere, vīcī, victus** | conquer, beat, overcome |

# UNIT FOURTEEN — NOTES ON VOCABULARY

**Accidō, accidere, accidī,** 'fall upon, happen, occur', is a compound of **ad** and **cadō**; it lacks a fourth principal part and the perfect active stem loses the redu-plication of the uncompounded form.

**Adveniō** is obviously a compound of **ad** and **veniō** and so it means 'come to, arrive'. From the fourth principal part there is formed a fourth declension noun, **adventus, adventūs,** M., 'arrival'.

**Anima** (Unit Two) was defined as 'soul, spirit, life-force'; **animus, animī,** M., is 'mind, rational spirit, soul'.

**Auctōritās, auctōritātis,** F., is the abstract noun from **auctor**; it means 'authority'.

**Colloquor,** a compound of **com-** and **loquor,** means 'speak, talk, converse with'.

**Dīgnus, -a, -um,** 'worthy', and its opposite **indīgnus, -a, -um,** 'unworthy', both govern the ablative case: **Multīs dōnīs est dīgna,** 'She is worthy of many gifts'.

**Intendō, intendere, intendī, intentus** and **ostendō, ostendere, ostendī, ostentus,** both have the same stem in the present and in the perfect active: **intendimus,** 'we stretch out', 'we have stretched out'; **ostendit,** 'he shows', 'he has shown'.

**Nōtus, -a, -um** is simply the perfect passive participle of **nōscō** used as an adjective meaning 'known, well-known, customary'. The original root of **nōscō** began with the letter **g- (gnōscō).** The Latin **g** is represented by the **k** in the German "kennen" and the English "know".

**Nūntiō** and **nūntius** are obviously related; **nūntiō,** a first conjugation verb, is 'report, announce', and **nūntius, nūntiī,** M., is the one bringing the report, 'messenger', or the report itself, 'message'. There is also an adjective **nūntius, -a, -um,** 'announcing'.

**Ōs, ōris,** N., is 'mouth, expression'. The diminutive **ōsculum, ōsculī,** N., is both 'little mouth' and 'kiss'.

**Parō,** a first conjugation verb already mentioned (vocabulary notes in Unit Thirteen) means 'prepare, make ready, provide, get'. From the last principal part there is formed a fourth declension noun **parātus, parātūs,** M., 'preparation'.

The root of **senex, senis,** 'old', is found in the words **senātor, senātōris,** M., 'senator', and **senātus, senātūs,** M., 'senate'. The senators originally were the older men who through their wisdom and experience were thought capable of guiding the state.

**Quālis, -e,** 'what kind of, of what kind', and **tālis, -e,** 'such, of such a sort', are correlatives: **Tālis dux erat quālis pater fuerat,** 'He was such a leader as his father had been; as a leader, he was of the same character as his father'.

**Tempestās, tempestātis,** F., is 'weather', good or bad, as well as 'storm, season'.

**Vēritās, vēritātis,** F., 'truth', is the abstract noun from **vērus, -a, -um,** 'true'.

**Vincō, vincere, vīcī, victus** is 'conquer, beat, overcome'. Remember Caesar's expression, **Vēnī, vīdī, vīcī,** 'I came, I saw, I conquered', for the third principal part of this verb. Do not confuse the last principal part **victus** with the last principal part of **vīvō,** 'live', which is **vīctus.**

## Suffixes Added to Produce Nouns

The suffixes -iō, -tiō, -tūra, and -tus added to the root or stem of a verb produce abstract nouns and names of actions.

> **opīniō, -ōnis**, F. (**opīnor, -ārī, -ātus sum**, 'suppose, imagine'), 'opinion, supposition'
> **āctiō, -ōnis**, F., 'doing, performing, action, act'
> **mūnītiō, -ōnis**, F., 'defending, fortifying, protecting'
> **iactūra, -ae**, F., 'a throwing, a throwing away'
> **iūnctūra, -ae**, F., 'a joining, uniting, juncture'
> **arbitrātus, -ūs**, M., 'judgment, free-will, decision'
> **vīctus, -ūs**, M., 'way of life'

The suffixes -men, -mentum, -mōnium, and -mōnia added to the root or stem of a verb produce nouns denoting acts, or means and results of acts.

> **agmen, agminis**, N., 'a collected multitude in motion or moving forward, a line of battle, march'
> **cōnāmen, -inis**, N., 'effort, exertion, struggle'
> **hortāmen, -inis**, N., 'incitement, encouragement, exhortation'
> **experimentum, -ī**, N., 'proof, test, trial'
> **mōmentum, -ī**, N., 'movement, motion'
> **mūnīmentum, -ī**, N., 'defense, fortification, protection'
> **alimōnium, -ī**, N., (**alō, alere, aluī, altus**, 'nourish, support'), 'nourishment, support'
> **parsimōnia, -ae**, F. (**parcō**), 'sparingness, frugality, thrift'

The suffix -tōrium added to the stem or root of a verb produces a noun meaning the place of the action.

> **auditōrium, -ī**, N., 'the place where something is heard, lecture room, hall of justice'
> **dormitōrium, -ī**, N., (**dormiō, -īre, -īvī (-iī), -ītus**, 'sleep'), 'sleeping room, dormitory'

The suffix -ārius added to the stem of a noun produces a noun meaning 'the person belonging to *or* the person engaged in *or* the person concerned with'.

> **argentārius, -ī**, M., (**argentum, -ī**, N., 'silver'), 'a money changer, banker'
> **apiārius, -ī**, M., (**apis, apis**, F., 'bee'), 'beekeeper'

The suffix -ārium added to the stem of a noun produces a noun meaning 'place for'.

> **apiārium, -ī**, N., (**apis, apis**, F., 'bee'), 'beehive'
> **aviārium, -ī**, N., (**avis, avis**, F., 'bird'), 'a place where birds are kept, aviary'
> **librārium, -ī**, N., 'a place in which to keep books, bookcase'

# UNIT FOURTEEN — DRILL

**I. Relative Clauses of Characteristic, Indefinite Pronouns, Questions, etc.**

1. a) Ea est quae pecūniam mīrātur.
   b) Ea est quae pecūniam mīrētur.
   c) Quis est quī pecūniam nōn mīrētur?
   d) Nēmō est quī pecūniam nōn mīrētur.
   e) Nēmō est quīn pecūniam mīrētur.
   f) Homō quīdam nōn vult mīrārī pecūniam.
   g) Nōn tam stultus ('foolish') est ut pecūniam mīrētur.
   h) Mīrātur eam quae pecūniam mīrētur.

2. a) Illī sunt quī Horātium maiōrem esse Vergiliō arbitrantur.
   b) Sunt quī Horātium maiōrem esse Vergiliō dīcant.
   c) Quīdam dīcunt Horātium maiōrem esse Vergiliō.
   d) Horātius dīcitur ā quibusdam maior esse Vergiliō.
   e) Aliī rogant num Horātius maior sit Vergiliō; aliī rogant cūr Horātius maior sit Vergiliō; quisque opīniōnem suam habet. Quot hominēs, tot sententiae.

3. a) Quis est quī tantum malum facere possit?
   b) Is est quī tantum malum facere possit.
   c) Quis crēdat eum tantum malum facere posse?
   d) Quis scit cūr tantum malum fēcerit?
   e) Dīcitur hoc fēcisse prō fēminā quādam.
   f) Nēmō scit quis sit fēmina.

4. a) Aliquis dīxit quendam vīcisse Caesarem. [**vincō, -ere, vīcī, victus,** 'conquer']
   b) Aliquis dīxit Caesarem ā quōdam victum esse.
   c) Quīdam dīxit aliquem vīcisse Caesarem.
   d) Quīdam dīxērunt aliquōs vīcisse Caesarem.
   e) Quis est quī dīxit Caesarem victum esse?
   f) Quis est quī dīxerit Caesarem victum esse?
   g) Quis est quīn dīxerit Caesarem victum esse?
   h) Sunt quī dīcant eum bonum esse.
   i) Nēmō est quī dīcat eum bonum esse.
   j) Nēmō est quīn huic faveat.

5. a) Hominēs quīdam mīrantur verenturque Caesarem.
   b) Rogant quālis vir sit.
   c) Negant quidquam maius ab ūllō factum esse.
   d) Caesar tālis est quālem omnēs verentur.
   e) Caesar est quem omnēs vereantur.
   f) Dīcunt Caesarem tālem esse quālem omnēs vereantur.
   g) Quisque dīcit idem.

    h) Dīcunt Caesarem esse verendum.

    i) Dīcunt tālem virum quālem Caesarem esse verendum.

    j) Caesar dīgnus est quī timeātur.

6. a) Nōnne sum īdem quī fuī?

    b) Num sum īdem quī fuī?

    c) Possum iterum fierī īdem quī fuī? [**iterum**, adv., 'again']

    d) Quis est quī possit fierī īdem quī fuit?

    e) Negō quemquam posse fierī eundem quī fuerit.

    f) Iuvenis fuī, senior fīēbam, mox nihil fīam.

    g) Utinam iuvenis nunc fierem.

    h) Quī senēs fīunt, iuvenēs esse volunt.

    i) Quis est quīn sē senem fierī neget?

7. a) Rogat quis sibi dōnum dederit.

    b) Rogant num quis sibi dōnum dederit.

    c) Rogant num quis sibi ipsī dōnum dederit.

    d) Dīcit nēminem sibi dōnum dedisse.

    e) Negat quemquam sibi dōnum dedisse.

    f) Dīcit quendam sibi dōnum dedisse.

    g) Dīcit dōnum sibi ā nūllō datum esse.

    h) Crēdet vix cuiquam.

    i) Crēdit nēminem in hāc urbe memorem esse suī.

    j) Crēdit custōdem sē neglēctūrum esse.

## II. Purpose and Result Clauses

1. a) Parvā vōce loquor, ut audīs.

    b) Parvā vōce loquor ut audiās.

    c) Tālī vōce loquor ut nōn audiar.

    d) Tālī vōce loquor ut nōn audiās.

    e) Tālis vōx mihi est quae audiātur.

    f) Parvā vōce loquor nē audiar.

    g) Magnā vōce locūtus sum ut audīrēs.

    h) Magnā vōce locūtus sum ut audīrer.

    i) Tantā vōce locūtus sum ut audīrer.

    j) Tantā vōce locūtus sum ut nōn audīrer.

    k) Quae vōx nōn erat tanta quae audīrī nōn posset?

2. a) Mittunt mīlitēs quī hostēs superant.

    b) Mittunt mīlitēs quī hostēs superent.

    c) Mittent mīlitēs quī hostēs superent.

    d) Mīsērunt mīlitēs quī hostēs superārent.

    e) Pūgnāvērunt mīlitēs ut hostēs superārent.

    f) Pūgnāvērunt mīlitēs tantā virtūte ut hostēs superārent.

g) Pūgnāvērunt mīlitēs magnā virtūte ut hostēs superārent.

h) Pūgnāvērunt hostēs tantā virtūte ut nōn superārentur.

i) Pūgnāvērunt hostēs magnā virtūte nē superārentur.

j) Pūgnāvērunt mīlitēs magnā virtūte ut hostēs superārentur.

3. a) Morātus sum ut hominī placērem.

   b) Tam diū morātus es ut hominī placērēs.

   c) Morātus est nē hominī placēret.

   d) Morātī sumus ut hominī placērēmus.

   e) Tam diū morātī sumus ut hominī placērēmus.

   f) Tam diū morātī estis ut hominī nōn placērētur.

   g) Morātī sunt nē hominī placērent.

4. a) Hortor ut veniat.

   b) Hortātus sum ut venīret.

   c) Verbīs multīs hortātus sum nē venīret.

   d) Verbīs tālibus hortātus sum ut nōn venīret.

   e) Verbīs tālibus hortātus sum ut venīret.

   f) Sīc hortābor ut nōn veniat.

   g) Cum audāciā hortābor nē veniat.

   h) Efficiāmus ut hortēmur nē veniat.

5. a) Curris quō celerius praemia accipiātis.

   b) Cucurristis quō celerius praemia acciperētis.

   c) Tam cucurristis ut celerius praemia acciperētis.

   d) Nōn cucurristis quō tardius praemia acciperētis. [**tardē**, adv., 'late, tardily']

   e) Cucurristis quō praemia acciperētis.

   f) Domum currō ubi praemia accipiam.

   g) Adulēscēns effēcit ut praemia sibi acciperēmus.

   h) Adulēscēns malus effēcit nē praemia acciperēmus.

   i) Facite nē tam caecī fīātis ut haec nōn intellegātis.

   j) Quis erat tam caecus quīn haec intellegeret?

# UNIT FOURTEEN — PRELIMINARY EXERCISES (SECTIONS A, B)

1. Tam celeriter cucurrit ut quisque eum admīrārētur (admīrātus sit).

2. Senī nūper erat tantus dolor ut rīdēre nōn posset.

3. Tālis pāx est ut bellum ubīque parētur.

4. Accidit ut tempestās sīc mala esset ut nōs omnēs magnopere timērēmus.

5. Ita dīgnus laude erat ut omnēs eī īgnōscerent.

6. Fit ut nēmō plūs umquam pollicitus sit quam ille.

7. Efficiāmus ut ōra nostra vēritātem ostendant.

8. a) Facite ut vēritātem semper loquāminī.
   b) Efficite nē indīgnī auctōritāte sītis.
9. Tot nūntiōs tum advenientēs vīdimus ut scīre vellēmus quid accideret.
10. Fierī potest ut hostēs vincāmus.

## UNIT FOURTEEN — EXERCISES

1. Nēmō est tam senex quī sē annum nōn arbitrētur posse vīvere.
2. Nūntiātum erat ducem hostium mīsisse Carthāginem lēgātum quī cum imperātōre sociōrum colloquerētur.
3. Nūllus est dolor quem tempus nōn auferat.
4. Semper sīc vīvāmus ut nātūram optimam ducem sequī videāmur.
5. Quis est tam dēmēns quī patriam servitūte oppressam incolere mālit?
6. Tanta est vīs vēritātis ut ubīque videātur.
7. Cōpiae tam bene vīcērunt ut hostēs nunc hūc nunc illūc fugerent.
8.         "Nīl (here, 'in no way') opus est tē īrātum fierī:
               quendam volō vidēre nōn tibi
            nōtum — trāns flūmen longē incolit is."
            "Nīl habeō quod agam et nōn sum piger: sequar tē."
   [piger, pigra, pigrum, 'lazy, slow']
9. Nēmō est quī sciat cūr cōnsul auctōritāte suā ūtī dubitet.
10. Sōlus est quī nōbīs mittendus sit ad Asiam ubi rēs cognōscat.
11. Omnibus parātīs, lēgātī ad Asiam advēnērunt quī pācem peterent.
12. Erant tam cupidī laudis, ut sē rīdēre ōrātiōnem cōnsulis ostendere nōllent.
13.         Tanta tibi est animī probitās ōrisque, Safrōnī,
               ut mīrer fierī tē potuisse patrem.
                                        (Martial 11.103)
   [probitās, -tātis, F., 'modesty'; Safrōnius, -ī, M., a proper name]
14. In forō audīvimus ōrātōrem sīc sollertem ut eum locūtūrum esse diū spērārēmus.
15. Aliquid invēnī modo quod amēs. [modo, adv., 'just, now']
16. a) Adeō dīgna rēs est ut efficiās ut omnibus nūntiētur.
    b) Adeō dīgna rēs est ut fierī nōn possit ut ab incolīs neglegātur.
17. Sunt quī mortem meliōrem vītā esse dīcant.
18. Tum pūgnābātur in viīs ita ācriter ut omnēs domum sē recipere properārent.
19. Ūsī sumus tālī tempestāte ut omnēs mortem timentēs nautās precātī sint ut peterent ubi tūtī essent.
20. Nīl tam difficile est quīn intellegī possit.
21. Sī tanta vīs virtūtis est, ut eam nōn sōlum in eīs, quōs numquam vīdimus, sed, quod maius est, in hoste etiam mīrēmur, quid mīrum est, sī animī

hominum moveantur, videntēs eōrum, quibuscum ūsū iūnctī esse possunt, virtūtem et vēritātem? [**mīrus, -a, -um**, 'wonderful, strange'; **ūsus**, *here*, 'familiarity']

22. Neque enim quisquam est tam inimīcus Mūsīs quī nōn trādī versibus aeternam suōrum factōrum fāmam facile patiātur. [**Mūsa, -ae**, F., 'Muse'; *here*, a goddess who inspires poets; **versus, -ūs**, M., 'a line of poetry']

23. Hīc sunt nūntiī nōn parvae auctōritātis. Hīc sunt nūntiī tantae auctōritātis ut multī in urbe diūtius mānsūrī sint quō cum eīs plūs colloquantur.

24. Cīvēs cīvitātum quae habuissent rēgēs sīc rīdēbātis ut īrātissimī fierent.

25. Quis nostrum tam animō dūrō fuit ut poētae morte nūper nōn movērētur?

26. Tanta illīus bellī fāma ad nostram cīvitātem dēlāta est ut duo virī maximae virtūtis mitterentur lēgātī ut vēritātem dē eius nātūrā cognōscerent.

27. Modo fac nē quid aliud hōc tempore agās nisī ut hunc dolōrem ex animō quam celerrimē pellās.

28. Neque is sum quī mortis perīculum timeam. Sunt autem quī dē hōc timōre cōgitāre nōlint.

29. Sapientia est ūna quae tālem timōrem pellat ex animīs.

30. Sī sapientia esset ūna quae timōrem pelleret ex animīs, tam cupidī sapientiae essēmus ut multōs librōs legerēmus.

31. Fierī nōn potest ut eum tū nōn cognōveris.

32. Tam dēmēns erat ut nihil nisī dē ruīnā populī Rōmānī cōgitāret.

33. Omnibus parātīs, tantīs vīribus ubīque pūgnātum est ut nēmō urbem ingredī atque vincere posset; nisī quī sapiēns dē pāce loquī voluisset, multō diūtius pūgnātum esset.

34. Litterās tuās lēgimus simillimās eārum quās heri lēgimus, minimē dīgnās quae ā tē ad nōs mitterentur. Numquam tibi nocuimus; quam ob rem tālēs litterās mittis?

35. Ita efficitur ut omnis rēs pūblica in magnō perīculō sit.

36. Accidit ut omnēs in nāve sē aut mortis aut servitūtis perīculō trāderent.

37. Imperātor adeō īrātus erat ut comitēs mentēs studiīs et rēbus honestīs intenderent quō melius sibi placērent.

38. Inventī sunt duo equitēs Rōmānī quī tē istā cūrā līberārent et sē illā ipsā nocte paulō ante lūcem mē in meō lectō interfectūrōs esse pollicērentur. [**eques, equitis**, M., 'knight'; **lectus, -ī**, M., 'bed']

39. Quid est enim quod tibi iam in hāc urbe placēre possit? in quā nēmō est extrā istam turbam impiōrum hominum quī tē nōn timeat, nēmō quī nōn ōderit. [**extrā**, prep. + acc., 'outside']

40. Tunc tālis vir quālis dux iste indīgnus laude habēbātur; quam ob rem neque praemia neque glōriam parāvit.

41. Fierī nōn potest ut cognōscās unde vēnerit iste senex, quālis sit. Est tamen tam nōtae fāmae ut in ōre omnium semper sit.

42. Quālis vir scelera huius modī facere audeat?

43. Fēcit ut amīcī nihil aliud eō tempore agerent nisī ut dolōrem ex sē ipsīs quam prīmum expellerent.

44. Dīgnī erant quī cīvitāte dōnārentur.

45. Fierī nūllō modō poterat quīn victīs parcerētur.

46. Nēmō tam impius est quīn hoc iūre factum esse fateātur.

47. Quae rēs efficiēbat ut cibus sine perīculō portārī posset.

48. Tālis est quaeque rēs pūblica, quālis eius nātūra aut voluntās, quī illam regit. [**voluntās, -tātis,** F., 'desire, inclination']

49. Hīc, hīc sunt inter nōs, amīce, in hōc orbis terrārum gravissimō cōnsiliō, quī dē nostrum omnium ruīnā, quī dē huius urbis atque adeō dē orbis terrārum ruīnā cōgitent. [**cōnsilium, -ī,** N., *here,* 'the people who deliberate, a council'; **adeō,** adv., *here,* 'indeed']

## II.

1. They ran across the fields so quickly that they arrived home faster than their friends.

2. There is no one who does not know that the commander of the allies has been in charge of the troops for many years. ["has been in charge": Latin requires the present infinitive here to denote the present perfect idea. The fact that the action began in the past is represented by the adverbial "for many years".]

3. The storm was so great that everyone wondered why the ships had not been destroyed.

4. They so wanted to get help that they ran as quickly as possible to where they could get it.

5. He was the only one in Rome who did not know what his daughter was doing.

6. It is possible that the old men have suffered more sorrow than we know.

## III. Readings

A. Petronius, *Satyricon* 111.1:

Mātrōna[1] quaedam Ephesī[2] tam nōtae erat pudīcitiae,[3] ut vīcīnārum[4] quoque[5] gentium fēminās ad spectāculum[6] suī ēvocāret.[7]

[1] **mātrōna, -ae,** F., 'a married woman'   [2] **Ephesus, -ī,** M., a town in Asia Minor   [3] **pudīcitia, -ae,** F., 'purity, chastity'   [4] **vīcīnus, -a, -um,** 'neighboring'   [5] **quoque** (adv.), 'also'   [6] **spectāculum, -ī,** N., 'sight, spectacle'   [7] **ēvocō** (1), 'call forth, summon'

B. Cicero chides the senate for their inaction regarding Catiline and his fellow conspirators and urges those who wish ill to the state to depart at once (*In Catilīnam* I, selections from sections 12 and 13):

Nōnnūllī[1] sunt in hōc ōrdine[2] quī aut ea quae imminent[3] nōn videant aut ea quae vident dissimulent;[4] quī spem Catilīnae mollibus[5] sententiīs aluērunt;[6] auctōritātem secūtī multī nōn sōlum[7] improbī,[8] vērum etiam[7] imperītī,[9] sī in hunc animadvertissem,[10] crūdēliter factum esse dīcerent. Nunc intellegō, sī iste, quō intendit, in Manliāna[11] castra[12] ierit, nēminem tam stultum[13] futūrum esse quī nōn videat coniūrātiōnem[14] esse factam, nēminem tam improbum[8] quī nōn fateātur. Hōc autem ūnō interfectō, intellegō hanc reī pūblicae pestem[15] paulīsper[16] reprimī,[17] nōn in perpetuum[18] comprimī[19] posse. Quod sī[20] sē ēiēcerit[21] sēcumque suōs ēdūxerit,[22] dēlēbitur nōn modo[23] haec tam adulta[24] reī pūblicae pestis,[15] vērum etiam[23] stirps[25] ac sēmen[26] malōrum omnium.

Quārē sēcēdant[27] improbī,[8] sēcernant[28] sē ā bonīs, mūrō[29] dēnique,[30] id quod saepe iam dīxī, discernantur[31] ā nōbīs. Polliceor hoc vōbīs, patrēs cōnscrīptī,[32] tantam in nōbīs cōnsulibus futūram esse dīligentiam, tantam in vōbīs auctōritātem, tantam in equitibus[33] Rōmānīs virtūtem, tantam in omnibus bonīs cōnsēnsiōnem,[34] ut Catilīnae profectiōne[35] omnia patefacta,[36] inlūstrāta,[37] oppressa, vindicāta esse[38] videātis.

---

[1] **nōnnūllī, -ae, -a**, 'some'  [2] **ōrdō, -inis**, M., 'order, class, body of men'  [3] **immineō, -ēre, -uī, --**, 'threaten, be imminent'  [4] **dissimulō** (1), 'conceal, leave unnoticed'  [5] **mollis, -e**, 'gentle, mild'  [6] **alō, -ere, aluī, altus**, 'nourish, support'  [7] **nōn sōlum...vērum etiam** (adv.), 'not only...but also'  [8] **improbus, -a, -um**, 'bad, wicked'  [9] **imperītus, -a, -um**, 'inexperienced, ignorant'  [10] **animadvertō, -ere, -vertī, -versus**, 'turn one's attention to, notice' (often with **in** + accusative)  [11] **Manliānus, -a, -um**, 'of Manlius (a Roman name)'  [12] **castra, -ōrum**, N. pl., 'camp'  [13] **stultus, -a, -um**, 'foolish'  [14] **coniūrātiō, -ōnis**, F., 'conspiracy'  [15] **pestis, -is**, F., 'infectious disease, pestilence'  [16] **paulīsper** (adv.), 'for a short time'  [17] **reprimō (re- + premō)**, 'hinder, repress'  [18] **in perpetuum** (adverbial phrase), 'forever'  [19] **comprimō (com- + premō)**, 'suppress, subdue'  [20] **quod sī**, 'but if'  [21] **ēiciō (ē + iaciō), -ere, -iēcī, -iectus**, 'throw out'  [22] **ēdūcō (ē + dūcō)**, 'lead out'  [23] **nōn modo...vērum etiam** (adv.), 'not only...but also'  [24] **adultus, -a, -um**, 'grown up, adult, advanced'  [25] **stirps, stirpis**, F., 'root'  [26] **sēmen, -inis**, N., 'seed'  [27] **sēcēdō, -ere, -cessī, -cessus**, 'withdraw'  [28] **sēcernō, -ere, -crēvī, -crētus**, 'separate'  [29] **mūrus, -ī**, M., 'wall'  [30] **dēnique** (adv.), 'finally, at last'  [31] **discernō, -ere, -crēvī, -crētus**, 'set apart'  [32] **cōnscrībō (com- + scrībō)**, 'enroll'; **patrēs cōnscrīptī**, 'senators'  [33] **eques, -itis**, M., 'knight'  [34] **cōnsēnsiō, -ōnis**, F., 'agreement, harmony'  [35] **profectiō, -ōnis**, F., 'departure'  [36] **patefaciō, -ere, -fēcī, -factus**, 'disclose'  [37] **inlūstrō** (1), 'elucidate, explain'  [38] **vindicō** (1), 'avenge, punish'

# UNIT FIFTEEN

**A.** *cum* **Clauses**

**Cum** is not only a preposition meaning 'with', but it occurs also as a subordinating conjunction with the meanings 'when', 'after', 'since', and 'although'. The verb in such clauses is most often in the subjunctive, its tense determined by the rules for sequence of tenses after the main verb. The meaning of **cum** in such clauses must be determined from the context of the sentence.

1. TEMPORAL AND CIRCUMSTANTIAL CLAUSES

When the **cum** clause refers strictly to *time* and its action is coordinate with that of the main verb, it is a *temporal* **cum** *clause* and **cum** is translated 'when'. Such clauses have their verbs in the *indicative*.

> **Cum** tē **vidēbō**, fēlīx erō.   (*At the very time*) *when I see* you, I shall be happy.
> **Cum** tē **vīdī**, fēlīx eram.   (*At the very time*) *when I saw* you, I was happy.

If the **cum** clause states the *circumstances* in which the action of the main verb takes place, it is called a *circumstantial* **cum** *clause* and **cum** is translated 'when' or 'after'. When the action in such **cum** clauses refers to *present* or *future* time, the *indicative* is used.

> **Cum** tē **vidēbō**, fēlīx erō.   *Under the circumstances of my seeing* you, I shall be happy; *when I see* you, I shall be happy.

When the action in the circumstantial **cum** clause is in *past* time, the *subjunctive* is used.

> **Cum** tē **vidērem**, fēlīx eram.   *When I saw* you (i.e., not at a point of time, but under these circumstances), I was happy.

2. CAUSAL CLAUSES

When **cum** translates as 'since' or 'because', the **cum** clause is *causal*. The verb in *causal* **cum** *clauses* is *always* in the *subjunctive*.

| Cum tē **videam**, fēlīx sum. | *Since I see* you, I am happy. |
| Cum tē **vīderim**, fēlīx sum. | *Since I saw* you, I am happy. |
| Cum tē **vidērem**, fēlīx eram. | *Since I saw* you, I was happy. |
| Cum tē **vīdissem**, fēlīx eram. | *Since I had seen* you, I was happy. |

3. CONCESSIVE CLAUSES

When **cum** translates 'although', the **cum** clause is *concessive*. Frequently **tamen**, 'nevertheless', in the main clause indicates that **cum** is to be taken as 'although', but the **tamen** is not always there. *Concessive* **cum** *clauses always* have their verbs in the *subjunctive*.

| Cum tē **videam**, fēlīx (tamen) sum. | *Although I see* you, (nevertheless) I am happy. |
| Cum tē **vīderim**, fēlīx (tamen) sum. | *Although I saw* you, (nevertheless) I am happy. |
| Cum tē **vidērem**, fēlīx (tamen) eram. | *Although I saw* you, (nevertheless) I was happy. |
| Cum tē **vīdissem**, fēlīx (tamen) eram. | *Although I had seen* you, (nevertheless) I was happy. |

THUS:

| | PRIMARY SEQUENCE | SECONDARY SEQUENCE |
|---|---|---|
| **cum** Temporal | indicative | indicative |
| **cum** Circumstantial | indicative | subjunctive |
| **cum** Causal | subjunctive | subjunctive |
| **cum** Concessive | subjunctive | subjunctive |

4. *cum*, 'whenever'

If **cum** means "whenever", it takes a *perfect* indicative when the main verb is present, a *pluperfect* indicative when the main verb is imperfect.

| Cum tē **vīdī**, fēlīx sum. | *Whenever I see* you, I am happy. |
| Cum tē **vīderam**, fēlīx eram. | *Whenever I saw* you, I was happy. |

B. *cum* Clauses and Ablatives Absolute

The sentences used to illustrate the ablative absolute construction in Unit Ten might also have been expressed with **cum** clauses with no change in meaning:

| Coniuge veniente, fēmina discēdet. <br> Cum coniūnx veniet, fēmina discēdet. | When her husband comes, the woman will depart. |
| Coniuge veniente, fēmina discēdet. <br> Cum coniūnx veniat, fēmina discēdet. | Since (although) her husband is coming, the woman will depart. |
| Coniuge vīsō, fēmina discessit. <br> Cum coniugem vīdisset, fēmina discessit. | When (after, since, although) she saw (had seen) her husband, the woman departed. |

It will be noted in this last example that, whereas the ablative absolute with the perfect participle must be expressed in the passive because of the lack of a perfect active participle (since **videō, -ēre** is not a deponent verb) and also in order to avoid concordance of subjects in both clauses, the **cum** clause may use the active voice.

## C. Other Words Introducing Temporal, Causal, and Concessive Clauses

### 1. TEMPORAL

**ut**
**ubi**    $\Big\}$ + indicative
**postquam**
**quandō**

> Ut (ubi, postquam, quandō) mē rīsit,    When (after) he laughed at me, I
> īrātus fīēbam.                           became angry.

### 2. CAUSAL

**quoniam**  $\Big\}$ almost always with indicative
**quandō**

**quod**  $\Big\}$ + indicative or subjunctive; see section D1
**quia**

> Quoniam (quandō) mē rīsit,    Since (because) he laughed at me, I became
> īrātus fīēbam.                angry.

### 3. CONCESSIVE

**quamquam**  $\Big\}$ + indicative
**etsī**
**quamvīs** + subjunctive
  (**quam vīs**, 'as you wish')

> Quamquam (etsī) mē rīsit, īrātus    Although he laughed at me, I did not
> (tamen) nōn fīēbam.                 (nevertheless) become angry.
> Quamvīs mē rīsisset, īrātus         Although he laughed (had laughed)
> (tamen) nōn fīēbam.                 at me, I did not (nevertheless) be-
>                                     come angry.

## D. Conjunctions with Indicative or Subjunctive

Several conjunctions take either the indicative or the subjunctive. The distinction is based on the difference between these two moods, which was stated in Unit One: The indicative is the mood of fact, while the subjunctive is the mood of probability, intention, or idea.

1. **quod** OR **quia**, 'because'

> Abest **quod (quia)** corpore    He is absent *because he is* (*actually*) not
> validus nōn **est**.            healthy in body (i.e., the speaker believes
>                             and accepts responsibility for the excuse).
>
> Abest **quod (quia)** corpore    He is absent *because he is* (*allegedly*) not
> validus nōn **sit**.            healthy in body (i.e., the speaker does not
>                             accept responsibility for the excuse and so
>                             does not express it as a fact; it is within the
>                             realm of probability or idea).

2. **dum** OR **dōnec**, 'while, as long as, until'

**Dum** or **dōnec** meaning 'while, as long as' or 'until', when referring merely to a temporal idea, takes the indicative.

> Exspectāvit **dum (dōnec) vēnī**.    He waited *until I* (*actually*) *came.*
> Exspectāvit **dum (dōnec)** rēgīnae    He waited *until* (*while*) *I greeted* the
> **salūtem dīxī**.                    queen.
> Exspectāvit **dum (dōnec) voluit**.    He waited *as long as he wished.*

NOTE: **Dum**, 'while', normally uses the present indicative (the so-called historical present) to denote continued action in past time.

> **Dum** haec **geruntur**, nūntius ad    *While* these things *were* (*are*) *going on*, a
> mē vēnit.                     messenger came to me.

When a notion of purpose, intention, or a future idea is involved, the subjunctive is used.

> Exspectāvit **dum (dōnec) venīrem**.    He waited *until I should come*; he
>                             waited *for me to come.* (i.e., there
>                             is nothing in the sentence to say
>                             that "I" actually *did* come; the
>                             clause is expressed as an idea or
>                             an intention, not a fact)
>
> Exspectāvit **dum (dōnec)** rēgīnae    He waited *until I should greet* the
> **salūtem dīcerem**.           queen; he waited *for me to greet*
>                             the queen.

3. **antequam** OR **priusquam**, 'before'

When **antequam** and **priusquam** refer strictly to time, they take the indicative.

> **Antequam (Priusquam) vēnī**,    *Before I came*, he went away. (stated as a
> discessit.                    fact)

When purpose, intention, or idea is involved, the subjunctive is used in secondary sequence.

> **Antequam (Priusquam) venīrem,** *Before I could come,* he went away. (i.e.,
> discessit.                          nothing in the sentence states that,
>                                     as a fact, "I" actually did come)

In primary sequence, the present or future perfect indicative is generally used (less frequently, the present subjunctive).

> **Antequam (Priusquam) vēnerō,** *Before I (shall have) come,* he will leave.
> discēdet.

Frequently **ante/quam** or **prius/quam** is split (tmesis) so as to give the sentence a greater degree of cohesion:

> **Ante** discessit **quam** venīrem.  He went away *before* I could come.
> **Prius** clāmāvit **quam** mē vīdit.  He shouted *before* he saw me.

### E. Clauses of Proviso

**Dum, modo,** and **dummodo** (all meaning 'if only, provided that') are used to express conditional wishes with the present and imperfect subjunctives. The negative uses **nē.**

> Ōderint, **dum (modo, dummodo) timeant.**  Let them hate, *provided that they*
>                                            *fear.*
> Id saepe faciat, **dum (modo, dummodo)**  Let him do this often, *provided that*
> **nē** miser **fīat.**                     *he does not become* unhappy.

### F. Accusative of Exclamation

The accusative case is sometimes used in exclamations.

> Ō tempora! Ō mōrēs!  Oh, the times, oh, the customs!, What times (these
>                       are), what customs!
> Patriam perditam!     Oh wasted land!
> Puerum miserum!       Unhappy boy!

## UNIT FIFTEEN — VOCABULARY

| | |
|---|---|
| **absum, abesse, āfuī, āfutūrus** | be away, be absent |
|   **absēns, absentis** | absent |
| **adsum, adesse, adfuī, --** | be present |
| **agitō** (1) | disturb, stir up |
| **antequam** (conj.) | before |
| **appāreō, -ēre, -uī, -itus** | appear, come in sight, be apparent |

| | |
|---|---|
| **calamitās, -tātis,** F. | disaster, calamity |
| **contrā** (prep. + acc.; adv.) | against, facing; opposite, in opposition, in turn |
| **cum** (conj.) | when, after, since, although |
| **dēsinō, -ere, dēsiī, --** | stop, cease (frequently with infinitive or ablative: **pūgnāre dēsiit,** 'he stopped fighting'; **inimīcitiā dēsiit,** 'he stopped (his) hostility') |
| **dōnec** (conj.) | while, until, as long as |
| **dum** (conj.) | while, until, as long as; if only, provided that |
| **dummodo** (conj.) | if only, provided that |
| **etsī** (conj.) | although, even if (+ indicative) |
| **exiguus, -a, -um** | small |
| **exspectō** (1) | wait (for), expect |
| **fore** | = **futūrus, -a, -um esse** (future infinitive of **sum**) |
| **fors, fortis, -ium,** F. | chance |
| **fulgor, -ōris,** M. | lightning, flash, brightness |
| **grātus, -a, -um** | pleasing (+ dat.) |
| **igitur** (postpositive conj.) | therefore |
| **ingenium, -ī,** N. | nature, talent, disposition, natural quality |
| **inimīcitia, -ae,** F. | hostility |
| **interdum** (adv.) | sometimes |
| **iūdex, iūdicis,** M. | judge; jury (pl.) |
|    **iūdicium, -ī,** N. | trial, judgment, decision |
| **memoria, -ae,** F. | memory |
| **misceō, -ēre, -uī, mixtus** | mix, intermingle, blend |
| **modo** (conj.) | if only, provided that |
| **nusquam** (adv.) | nowhere |
| **nūtrīx, nūtrīcis,** F. | nurse |
| **occidō, -ere, -cidī, -cāsus** | fall, set, die |
| **omnīnō** (adv.) | all in all, as a whole, entirely |
| **pereō, -īre, -iī (-īvī), -itus** | die, perish |
| **priusquam** (conj.) | before |
| **prōsum, prōdesse, prōfuī, --** | be useful, do good, benefit, profit (+ dat.) |
| **putō** (1) | think |
| **quamvīs** (conj.) | although (+ subjunctive) |
| **quasi** (adv.) | as if, as it were |
| **quidem** (adv.) | indeed |
|    **nē...quidem** (enclosing the word or words they emphasize) | not even |
| **quōad** (conj.) | as long as, as far as, until (takes same construction as **dum** and **dōnec**) |

| | |
|---|---|
| **quoniam** (conj.) | since (+ indicative) |
| **redeō, -īre, -iī, -itus** | return, go back |
| **simul ac** (*or* **atque**) (conj.) | as soon as (+ indicative) |
| **somnus, -ī,** M. | sleep, dream |
| **supersum, -esse, -fuī, --** | be left over, survive |
| **ubi** (conj.) | when |

## UNIT FIFTEEN — NOTES ON VOCABULARY

**Absum, abesse, āfuī, āfutūrus,** a compound of **ab** and **sum** meaning 'be away, be absent', has a present participle **absēns,** 'absent'; **adsum, adesse, adfuī, --,** 'be present', has no fourth principal part. (Note that although **ab** as a prefix may be shortened to **ā-,** **ad** does not shorten except in such instances as **adspiciō,** 'look at', which is usually spelled **āspiciō.** This normally happens before **gn, sp, sc,** and **st.**)

**Prōsum,** another compound of **sum,** uses **-d-** as a connecting consonant between **prō** and **esse, prōdesse, prōfuī, --,** 'be useful, do good, benefit, profit'. This connecting **-d-** is used to prevent hiatus (a pause between vowels).

**Supersum,** also lacking a fourth principal part, means 'be left over, survive.'

**Antequam** and **priusquam,** both meaning 'before', may be cut into two parts, **ante...quam, prius...quam** for greater cohesion in the sentence. This is called tmesis: **Ante (Prius) discessimus quam tē vidēre potuimus,** 'We left before we could see you'.

**Appāreō** is a compound of **ad** and **pāreō;** it means 'appear, come in sight, be apparent'.

**Dēsinō, dēsinere, dēsiī, --** is a compound of **dē** and **sinō** which originally meant 'let, set', but later was used exclusively as 'allow, permit'. **Dēsinō,** literally 'set down', means 'stop, cease'.

**Exspectō,** a compound of **ex** and **spectō,** 'look out for', means 'wait (for), expect'.

**Fore** is often used instead of **futūrus (-a, -um) esse,** the future infinitive of **sum. Āfore, affore (adsum), prōfore** also are used.

**Fors, fortis,** F., is a noun meaning 'chance'. Notice that the genitive singular looks like the adjective **fortis** and that the ablative singular **forte,** 'by chance', looks like the neuter adjective **forte.**

**Igitur,** 'therefore', is a postpositive conjunction; it cannot be the first word in a clause.

We have already learned **amīcitia** and so **inimīcitia** is clearly 'hostility'.

**Iūdex, iūdicis,** M., and **iūdicium, iūdiciī,** N., both have the same root; **iūdex** is 'judge', and in the plural, 'jury', and **iūdicium** is 'trial, judgment, decision'.

Nusquam, 'nowhere', is the opposite of usquam, 'anywhere', and should not be confused with numquam, 'never'.

Nūtrīx, nūtrīcis, F., is 'she who suckles, nourishes, brings up' (nūtriō, nūtrīre, nūtrīvī (nūtriī), nūtrītus), thus 'nurse'.

Occidō, a compound of ob and cadō, means 'fall, set, die', and in this last meaning it is synonymous with pereō (a compound of per and eō, 'go through [life]', thus 'die, perish'). It gives the stem of "occident", the place of the falling (i.e., setting) sun, thus, the West.

Redeō is another compound of eō (re- and eō, with a connecting -d- to avoid hiatus); it means 'return, go back'.

Quidem is an adverb, 'indeed'; nē...quidem, 'not even', surround the word or words they emphasize: Cum nūllā nē sorōre quidem collocūta est, 'She spoke with no woman, not even her sister'.

Simul is an adverb meaning 'at the same time, together', but simul ac or simul atque is a conjunction introducing a verb in the indicative and meaning 'as soon as'.

PREFIXES (from prepositions)

ā-, ab- (abs-, au-, as- [before -p-, very rare]), 'away'
    abdūcō, 'lead away'
    aberrō, 'wander away'
    absolvō, 'loosen from, set free'
    abstineō, 'keep off *or* away; abstain from'
    asportō, 'carry off *or* away'
    aufugiō, 'flee, run away; flee from'
    āvertō (vertō, -ere, vertī, versus, 'turn'), 'turn away'

ad- (ac-, af-, ag-, al-, ap-, ar-, as-, at-), 'to, toward'
    accingō (cingō, -ere, cīnxī, cīnctus, 'gird'), 'gird to'
    addūcō, 'lead to'
    affor (for, fārī, fātus sum, 'speak'), 'speak to'
    aggerō, 'bring *or* bear to *or* toward'
    alloquor, 'speak to'
    appōnō, 'apply to, add'
    arrīdeō, 'smile toward'
    assiliō (saliō, -īre, --, -ītus, 'leap'), 'leap to *or* upon'
    attrahō (trahō, -ere, trāxī, tractus, 'draw, drag'), 'draw to *or* toward; attract'

ante-, 'before'
    antecurrō, 'run before'
    anteeō, 'go before'
    anteferō, 'carry before, prefer, anticipate'

circum-, 'around, on all sides'
    circumagō, 'drive around'
    circumdūcō, 'lead around'
    circumspectō, 'look around'
(cum, preposition) com- (col-, con-, co-, cor-), 'together (with), completely'
    collaudō, 'praise very much'
    collocō (locō (1), 'place'), 'place together'
    comedō (edō, -ere, ēdī, ēsus, 'eat'), 'eat entirely'
    conveniō, 'come together'
    cooperiō (operiō, -īre, -uī, -tus, 'cover'), 'cover wholly'
    corrīvō (rīvō (1), 'lead, draw off'), 'conduct streams of water together'
dē-, 'down, utterly, from'
    dēcēdō, 'go away, withdraw, depart'
    dēcidō, 'fall down'
    dērelinquō (relinquō, -ere, relīquī, relictus, 'leave behind, abandon')
        'forsake wholly'
ē-, ex- (ef-), 'out'
    ēdormiō (dormiō, -īre, -īvī (-iī), -ītus, 'sleep'), 'sleep out, sleep away'
    effundō (fundō, -ere, fūdī, fūsus, 'pour'), 'pour out'
    exeō, 'go out'
in- (il-, im-, ir-), 'in, on, against'
    illigō (ligō (1), 'bind'), 'bind on'
    immittō, 'send into, send against'
    ineō, 'go in'
    irrigō (rigō (1), 'wet, water'), 'lead (water) to (a place), irrigate'
inter-, 'between'
    interpōnō, 'put *or* place between *or* among'
    intersum, 'be between'
    interveniō, 'come between'
ob- (oc-, of-, op-), 'toward, to meet, against'
    obveniō, 'come to meet'
    occurrō, 'run up to, run to meet'
    offulgeō, 'shine against *or* upon'
    oppōnō, 'set *or* place against'
per-, 'through, thoroughly'
    pererrō, 'wander through'
    perfluō (fluō, fluere, flūxī, flūxus, 'flow'), 'flow through'
    permoveō, 'move thoroughly, stir up thoroughly'
    permūniō, 'fortify completely'
    permūtō, 'change completely'
post-, 'after'

**postferō**, 'put after'
**postpōnō**, 'put after, postpone'
**prae-**, 'before, previous'
    **praemittō**, 'send forward, send before'
    **praemōnstrō**, 'show beforehand'
    **praescrībō**, 'write before *or* in front *or* previously'
**prō-**, 'in front of, forth'
    **prōcēdō**, 'go forth, proceed'
    **prōcidō**, 'fall forward'
    **prōmoveō**, 'move forward'
    **prōscrībō**, 'write before *or* in front of'
**sub-** (**suc-, suf-, sum-, sup-, sur-, sus-**), 'under, up from under'
    **subiciō**, 'throw under, place under'
    **subigō**, 'bring under, turn up from beneath'
    **succurrō**, 'run under, run to the aid of'
    **suffundō** (**fundō, fundere, fūdī, fūsus**, 'pour'), 'pour below *or* underneath'
    **summittō**, 'set *or* put under *or* below; send below *or* from below'
    **suppōnō**, 'put, place, *or* set under'
    **surrepō** (**repō, repere, repsī, reptus**, 'creep'), 'creep under, creep along'
    **sustineō**, 'hold up, support, sustain'
**super-**, 'over and above'
    **superpōnō**, 'put *or* place over *or* upon'
    **supertegō**, 'cover above, cover over'
**trāns-** (**trā-, trān-**), 'across'
    **trānseō**, 'go across, cross over, pass over'
    **trānsmittō**, 'send *or* carry across *or* over *or* through'
    **trādūcō**, 'lead *or* bring across, transfer'
    **trānsiliō** (**saliō, -īre, ––, salītus**, 'leap, jump'), 'leap *or* jump across *or* over, hasten'

## UNIT FIFTEEN — DRILL

**I. *cum* Clauses**
1. Cum verba tua audīvissem, rem intellēxī.
2. Cum verba mea nōn audīvisset, rem tamen intellēxit.
3. Cum verba vestra audīvissēmus, rem intellēximus.
4. Ego cum ā tē monitus essem, nihil tamen fēcī.
5. Tū cum ā mē monitus sīs, tamen nihil facis.
6. Cum ā vōbīs monitī essēmus, aliquid fēcimus.
7. Cum ā nōbīs moneāminī, aliquid facitis.
8. Cum urbs capta esset, mīlitēs tamen mānsērunt.

9. Cum oppidum captum sit, mīlitēs tamen manent.
10. Cum urbs capiētur, fēminae clāmābunt.
11. Cum oppida capiantur, fēminae clāmābunt.
12. Cum perīculum timeam, ex urbe proficīscor.
13. Cum tē videō, fēlīx sum.
14. Cum perīculum timuerim, ex urbe proficīscor.
15. Cum perīculum timērem, ex urbe proficīscēbar.
16. Cum perīculum timuissem, ex urbe profectus sum.
17. Cum perīculum timuī, clāmō.
18. Cum perīculum timueram, clāmābam.

II. **Exercises in Conjunctions with Indicative or Subjunctive, etc.**
1. Dum Lesbiam amābat Catullus, Lesbia amābat alium.
2. Quamvīs Lesbia amāret alium, Catullus eam amāvit.
3. Cum īnfēlīx esset Catullus, tamen amābat Lesbiam.
4. Catullus domī manēbat dum Lesbia alium amābat.
5. Catullus domī manēbat dum Lesbia eum amāret.
6. Catullus quamquam domī mānserat, tamen Lesbiam amābat.
7. Catullus ā Lesbiā discessit antequam eum ōdisse incēpit illa.
8. Catullus ā Lesbiā discessit antequam eum ōdisse inciperet illa.
9. Dum Cicerō est cōnsul, nōn timeō.
10. Dum Cicerō in urbe maneat, nōn timēbō.
11. Nōn discēdam dum Cicerō veniat.
12. Antequam Cicerō venīret, discessit turba.
13. Turba laudāvit Cicerōnem, quod rem pūblicam servāvisset.
14. Turba laudāvit Cicerōnem, nōn quod inimīcum superāvisset, sed quia rem pūblicam servāvit.
15. Turba laudāvit Cicerōnem quod cōnsul optimus esset.
16. Quamvīs turba laudāverit Cicerōnem, cōnsilia eius nōn cēpit.
17. Nē Cicerōnem turba laudet, dummodo cōnsilia eius capiat.
18. Domum cucurrit quia timuit.
19. Indīgnum senem! Domum cucurrit quia timēret.
20. Morātī sunt dōnec tempestās erat serēna.
21. Morātī sunt dōnec tempestās esset serēna.
22. Morārī cōnstituērunt modo tempestās nōn esset serēna.
23. Morārī cōnstituērunt dum tempestās nōn esset serēna.
24. Morārī cōnstituērunt dummodo tempestās nōn esset serēna.

III. **Other Words Introducing Temporal, Causal, and Concessive Clauses**
1. Ubi hostēs victī sunt, laetī erāmus.
2. Postquam hostēs victī sunt, laetī erāmus.

3. Quandō hostēs victī sunt, laetī erāmus.
4. Ut ad patriam advēnimus, laetī erāmus.
5. Quoniam ad patriam advēnimus, laetī erāmus.
6. Etsī ad patriam advēnimus, laetī nōn erāmus.
7. Quamquam ad patriam advēnimus, laetī nōn erāmus.
8. Dum ea accidunt, mīlitēs trāns flūmen quam celerrimē properāvērunt.
9. Dum nūntius multōs diēs morātur, lēgātus cum eīs cōpiīs quās ā rēge accēperat ad fīnēs sociōrum advēnit.

## UNIT FIFTEEN — PRELIMINARY EXERCISES
## (SECTIONS A, B)

1. Cum āfuistī, misera sum.
2. Cum āfuerās, misera eram.
3. Cum nūper perierit, tamen memoria factōrum bonōrum manet.
4. Cum fulgor appāret, multī quidem timent.
5. Cum fulgor appāruit, multī timuērunt.
6. Cum inimīcitia inter eōs maxima esset, iūdex cōnstituit ut numquam inter sē miscēre dēbērent.
7. Cum pūgnāre dēsinerent, hostēs tamen mānsērunt.
8. Cum animus agitārētur, multa pūtāre nōn potuī.
9. Cum ingenium tuum mihi omnīnō grātum sit, tē semper adesse volō.
10. Interdum cum calamitās exspectātur, somnus ā nōbīs longē abest.

## UNIT FIFTEEN — EXERCISES

1. a) Dē futūrīs rēbus etsī semper difficile est dīcere, tamen interdum coniectūrā possīs accēdere. [**coniectūra, -ae**, F., 'guess, conjecture']
   b) Dē futūrīs rēbus cum semper difficile sit dīcere, tamen interdum coniectūrā possīs accēdere.
2. Quae cum ita essent, dīxit sē quam celerrimē domum receptūrum esse.
3. Saepe magnum ingenium virtūtis priusquam reī pūblicae prōdesse posset dēlētum est.
4. a) Rēx cum Rōmā redīret mortuus est.
   b) Rēx ubi Rōmā redierat mortuus est.
5. Rēge Rōmā redeunte, cīvēs dēmentēs effēcērunt ut servī inter sē inimīcitiam agitantēs miscērent.
6. Ō rēs horridās! Ō cīvitātem malam! Quis caelum terrīs miscēre velit, quis mare caelō?

7. Quae cum ita sint, effectum est ut nihil sit malum quod mūtārī nōn possit.

8. Perīre artem putāmus nisī appāret, cum dēsinat ars esse, sī appāret.

9. Animus, nec cum adest nec cum discēdit, appāret.

10. Longum illud tempus cum nōn erō magis mē movet quam hoc exiguum.

11. Ex rēgnō prius ēgressus est quam rēx eum in fidem reciperet.

12. Ibi manēbat dum rēx eum in fidem reciperet (recēpit).

13. Ante vidēmus fulgōrem quam sonum audiāmus. [**sonus, -ī**, M., 'sound']

14. Antequam ad sententiam redeō, dē mē pauca dīcam.

15. a) Mē omnia expertūrum esse certum est priusquam perībō.
    b) Eum omnia expertum esse certum est priusquam periit.
    c) Mē omnia prius expertūrum esse certum est quam perierō.

16. Vīta dum superest, bene est.

17. Ille imperātor tam diū laudābitur dum memoria rērum Rōmānārum manēbit.

18. Dōnec grātus eram tibi, Persārum vīxī rēge laetior. [**Persae, -ārum**, M., 'the Persians']

19. Morātus est dum frāter imperātōrem rogāret in quantā calamitāte essent.

20. Dummodo somnus celeriter accēdat, nūtrīcem nōn vocābimus.

21. Ībam forte viā sacrā, ut meus est mōs. [**sacer, sacra, sacrum**, 'sacred']

22. Postquam ē tantā tempestāte lūx rediit, nautae Rōmam sē recēpērunt.

23. Cum bene vīvās, nē cōgitēs dē verbīs malōrum; sapientī nē sit cūrae quid quisque loquātur.

24. Multa ante cōnēris quam virum inveniās bonum.

25. a) Cum (quamvīs) exigua pars iūdiciī superesset dum rēs cōnstituerētur, nēmō tamen ex iūdicibus manēre voluit quod magnum futūrum esset perīculum eīs dē istō pessimō male loquentibus.
    b) Quamquam exigua pars iūdiciī supererat, nēmō tamen manēre voluit.

26. Magnopere timētur quod ducēs in forō appāruerint ut culpam in omnēs inimīcitiam inter sē agitantēs iacerent.

27. Cum somnō solūtus erō tibi dīcam quid heri fēcerim.

28. Dīxit sē somnō mox datūrum esse; eō modō fēlīciōrem fore.

29. Ex eō bellō quod iam ā cīvibus domī timērī dēsierat, nē duo quidem ē mīlitibus prius tūtī rediērunt quam pāx cōnstituerētur.

30. Cum rūmōrēs pulsī sunt, hominēs multō sunt fēlīciōrēs.

31. Cūrārum maxima nūtrīx est nox, dummodo nōs somnō celeriter dēmus.

32. a) Cum senex iūdicium meae virtūtis fēcisset, omnēs cōnstituērunt mē nēminī nocēre potuisse. Imperāvērunt igitur ut domum īrem.
    b) Postquam (ubi) senex iūdicium meae virtūtis fēcit, omnēs cōnstituērunt mē nēminī nocēre potuisse.

33. Tē iūdice, nōn ego calamitātem timeam dummodo mea verba contrā

imperātōrem cīvibus līberīs prōsint; priusquam tū iūdex fīēbās, magnopere timuī.

34. Dum cōnāmur, laudāmur. Homō nihil agēns nēminī placet.

35. Nē exigua quidem pars cīvitātis exspectāvit dum cōpiae sociōrum advenīrent; dēsiērunt autem nihil agere et cum audāciā hostēs ex urbe pepulērunt.

36. Cum ego loquī velim, nihil tamen dīcam.

37. Illum absentem diū exspectāvimus, sed nusquam appāruit quod validus nōn fuit. Quoniam quidem validus nōn est, absit. Sī occidat, miserī quasi perditī omnīnō sīmus.

38. Imperātor contrā cōnstituit exspectandam nāvem; quae ubi advēnit, omnibus prōfuit.

39. Cicero, *Dē Senectūte* 22, adapted:

Sophoclēs ad summam senectūtem tragoediās fēcit; quod propter studium cum rem neglegere familiārem vidērētur, ā fīliīs in iūdicium vocātus est, ut, quia nostrō mōre solet male rem gerentēs patrēs ē bonīs removērī, sīc illum quasi dēsipientem ā rē familiārī removērent iūdicēs. Tum senex dīcitur eam tragoediam quam in manibus habēbat et nūperrimē scrīpserat, *Oedipum Colōnēum*, lēgisse iūdicibus quaesīvisseque num illud carmen dēsipientis vidērētur. Ille cum id lēgisset, sententiīs iūdicum est līberātus. Quamquam Sophoclēs ā iūdicibus līberātus erat, fīliī tamen īrātissimī erant quod eius bona capere nōn poterant.

[**dēsipiēns, -entis**, 'foolish, insane'; **familiāris, -e**, 'pertaining to the family'; **Oedipus Colōnēus**, 'Oedipus at Colonus' (a tragedy by Sophocles); **senectūs, -tūtis**, F., 'old age'; **Sophoclēs, -is**, M., proper name; **tragoedia, -ae**, F., 'tragedy']

40. Cicero, *Dē Senectūte* 79-80, adapted slightly:

Moriēns Cȳrus maior haec dīcit: "nōlīte arbitrārī, ō mihi cārissimī fīliī, mē, cum ā vōbīs discesserō, nusquam aut nūllum fore. Nec enim, dum eram vōbīscum, animum meum vidēbātis, sed eum esse in hōc corpore ex hīs rēbus quās gerēbam intellegēbātis. Eundem igitur esse crēdite, etiam sī nūllum vidēbitis. Nec vērō clārōrum virōrum post mortem honōrēs manērent, sī nihil eōrum ipsōrum animī efficerent, quō diūtius memoriam suī tenērēmus. Mihi quidem numquam persuādērī potuit animōs dum in corporibus essent mortālibus vīvere, cum excessissent ex eīs morī.

[**Cȳrus, -ī**, M., proper name; **excēdō (ex + cēdō)**, 'depart, withdraw'; **honor, -ōris**, M., 'honor, distinction'; **mortālis, -e**, 'mortal']

41. Cicero, *Dē Senectūte* 76, adapted:

Omnīnō, ut mihi quidem vidētur, studiōrum omnium satietās vītae facit satietātem. Sunt pueritiae studia certa: num igitur ea optant adulēscentēs? Quoad puerī sumus, illa studia nōbīs cāriōra sunt; simul ac adulēscentēs fīmus, alia studia nōbīs placent. Sunt incipientis adulēscentiae studia: num ea iam vult aetās, quae media dīcitur? Sunt etiam eius aetātis: nē ea quidem quaeruntur in senectūte. Sunt extrēma quaedam studia senectūtis: ut igitur aliārum aetātum studia occidunt, sīc occidunt etiam senectūtis; quod cum fit, satietās vītae tempus bonum mortis affert.

[adulēscentia, -ae, F., 'young manhood'; aetās, -tātis, F., 'age, time of life'; extrēmus, -a, -um, 'last, outermost'; pueritia, -ae, F., 'boyhood, childhood'; satietās, -tātis, F., 'satiety, fullness'; senectūs, -tūtis, F., 'old age']

42.                   Nīl recitās et vīs, Māmerce, poēta vidērī.
               Quidquid vīs estō, dummodo nīl recitēs.
                    (Martial 2.88)

[estō, 2nd person sing. future imperative of sum, 'you shall be' (see Appendix, pp. 353, 381); Māmercus, -ī, M., a proper name; quidquid (pron.), 'whatever'; recitō (1), 'recite']

43. Manent ingenia senibus, modo maneat studium et industria. [industria, -ae, F., 'diligence, activity']

44. Simul atque dē Caesaris adventū cognitum est, lēgātus ad eum vēnit. [adventus, -ūs, M., 'arrival'; Caesar, -aris, M., 'Caesar']

45. Dum ea Rōmānī parant, Saguntum summā vī oppūgnābātur. [Saguntum, -ī, N., 'Saguntum', a town in Spain; summā, here, 'very great']

46. Dum ea geruntur, eī Caesarī nūntiāvērunt pulverem in eā parte vidērī. [pulvis, pulveris, M., 'dust']

## II.

1. Since someone is approaching, we shall bring it about that your friend does not harm anyone.
2. Although he delayed a long time, he could not wait for the nurse to approach.
3. When the people fear you, they hate you.
4. Let him come, provided that my opinions profit him.
5. He withdrew to his home because (he claimed) he was going to die soon.

## III. Readings

A. Cicero, Dē Amīcitiā 7.24:

Facile indicābat[1] ipsa nātūra vim suam, cum hominēs, quod facere ipsī nōn possent, id rēctē[2] fierī in alterō iūdicārent.[3]

[1] indicō (1), 'disclose, show'    [2] rēctē (adv.), 'rightly'    [3] iūdicō (1), 'judge'

B. Cicero, Dē Dīvīnātiōne I.20.39:

Dionȳsiī[1] māter, eius quī Syrācosiōrum[2] tyrannus[3] fuit, ut scrīptum apud[4]

[1] Dionȳsius, -ī, M., 'Dionysius', tyrant of Sicily    [2] Syrācosius, -a, -um, 'Syracusan'    [3] tyrannus, -ī, M., 'tyrant, absolute ruler'    [4] apud (prep. + acc.), here, 'in the works of'

Philistum[5] est, et doctum hominem et dīligentem[6] et aequālem[7] temporum illōrum, cum praegnāns[8] hunc ipsum Dionȳsium[1] alvō[9] continēret,[10] somniāvit[11] sē peperisse[12] Satyriscum.[13] Huic interpretēs[14] portentōrum,[15] quī Galeōtae[16] tum in Siciliā[17] nōminābantur,[18] respondērunt, ut ait Philistus,[5] eum, quem illa peperisset,[12] clārissimum Graeciae diūturnā[19] cum fortūnā[20] fore.

[5] **Philistus, -ī,** M., 'Philistus', a Greek historian from Syracuse   [6] **dīligēns, -entis,** 'diligent'   [7] **aequālis, -e,** 'contemporary with' (+ gen.)   [8] **praegnāns, -antis,** 'pregnant'   [9] **alvus, -ī,** F., 'womb'   [10] **contineō** (**com-** + **teneō**), 'contain'   [11] **somniō** (1), 'dream'   [12] **pariō, -ere, peperī, partus,** 'bring forth, give birth to'   [13] **Satyriscus, -ī,** M., 'a little satyr'   [14] **interpres, -pretis,** M. & F., 'interpreter, seer'   [15] **portentum, -ī,** N., 'portent'   [16] **Galeōtae, -ārum,** M., 'Galeotae', a group of Sicilian seers   [17] **Sicilia, -ae,** F., 'Sicily'   [18] **nōminō** (1), 'name'   [19] **diūturnus, -a, -um,** 'of long duration'   [20] **fortūna, -ae,** F., 'fortune'

C. Cicero, *Dē Dīvīnātiōne* I.25.54:

Adiungāmus[1] philosophīs[2] doctissimum hominem, poētam quidem dīvīnum,[3] Sophoclem;[4] quī cum ex aede[5] Herculis[6] patera[7] aurea gravis subrepta esset,[8] in somnīs vīdit ipsum deum dīcentem, quī id fēcisset. Quod semel[9] ille iterumque[10] neglēxit. Ubi īdem saepius āscendit[11] in Arēopagum,[12] dētulit rem; Arēopagītae[13] comprehendī[14] iubent eum, quī ā Sophocle[4] erat nōminātus;[15] is, quaestiōne[16] adhibitā,[17] cōnfessus est pateramque[7] rettulit. Quō factō fānum[18] illud Indicis[19] Herculis[6] nōminātum est.[15]

[1] **adiungō** (**ad-** + **iungō**), 'join, add'   [2] **philosophus, -ī,** M., 'philosopher'   [3] **dīvīnus, -a, -um,** 'divine, divinely inspired'   [4] **Sophoclēs, -is,** M., 'Sophocles', the Greek tragic poet   [5] **aedēs, -is,** F., 'temple'   [6] **Herculēs, -is,** M., 'Hercules'   [7] **patera, -ae,** F., 'dish' (from which libations were poured)   [8] **subripiō, -ere, -ripuī, -reptus,** 'steal'   [9] **semel** (adv.), 'once, a single time'   [10] **iterum** (adv.), 'again'   [11] **āscendō, -ere, -scendī, -scēnsus,** 'ascend, go up'   [12] **Arēopagus, -ī,** M., a hill in Athens, upon which the court called the 'Areopagus' held sessions   [13] **Arēopagītēs, -ae,** M., a member of the Areopagus   [14] **comprehendō, -ere, -prehendī, -prehēnsus,** 'seize'   [15] **nōminō** (1), 'name'   [16] **quaestiō, -ōnis,** F., 'trial, inquiry'   [17] **adhibeō** (**ad** + **habeō**), 'employ, hold'   [18] **fānum, -ī,** N., 'temple, holy place'   [19] **index, indicis,** M., 'informer'

D. Martial 12.12:

Omnia prōmittis[1] cum tōtā nocte bibistī;[2]

māne[3] nihil praestās,[4] Pollio,[5] māne[3] bibe.[2]

[1] **prōmittō** (**prō** + **mittō**), 'promise'   [2] **bibō, -ere, bibī, --,** 'drink'   [3] **māne** (adv.), 'in the morning'   [4] **praestō, -āre, -stitī, -stitus,** 'perform'   [5] **Polliō, -ōnis,** M., a man's name

E. A DREAM COMES TRUE (Cicero, *Dē Dīvīnātiōne* I.24.50):

Apud[1] Agathoclem[2] scrīptum in historiā[3] est Hamilcarem[4] Karthāginiēnsem,[5]

[1] **apud** (prep. + acc.), here, 'in the works of'   [2] **Agathoclēs, -is,** M., the name of an historian   [3] **historia, -ae,** F., 'history, work of history'   [4] **Hamilcar, -caris,** M., a Carthaginian general, father of Hannibal   [5] **Karthāginiēnsis, -e,** 'Carthaginian'

cum oppūgnāret Syrācūsās,[6] vīsum esse audīre vōcem, sē postrīdiē[7] cēnātūrum[8] Syrācūsīs;[6] cum autem is diēs illūxisset,[9] magnam sēditiōnem[10] in castrīs[11] eius inter Poenōs[12] et Siculōs[13] mīlitēs esse factam; quod cum sēnsissent Syrācūsānī,[14] inprōvīsō[15] eōs in castra[11] irrūpisse,[16] Hamilcaremque[4] ab eīs vīvum[17] esse sublātum.[18] Ita rēs somnium[19] comprobāvit.[20]

[6] Syrācūsae, -ārum, F., 'Syracuse', the chief town of Sicily  [7] postrīdiē (adv.), 'the next day'  [8] cēnō (1), 'dine'  [9] illūcēscō, -ere, -lūxī, --, 'become light, dawn'  [10] sēditiō, -ōnis, F., 'uprising'  [11] castra, -ōrum, N. pl., 'camp'  [12] Poenus, -a, -um, 'Carthaginian' [13] Siculus, -a, -um, 'Sicilian'  [14] Syrācūsānus, -a, -um, 'Syracusan'  [15] inprōvīsō (adv.), 'unexpectedly'  [16] irrumpō, -ere, -rūpī, -ruptus, 'rush in'  [17] vīvus, -a, -um, 'alive' [18] tollō, -ere, sustulī, sublātus, 'carry off'  [19] somnium, -ī, N., 'dream'  [20] comprobō (1), 'verify'

# UNIT SIXTEEN

### A. The Gerund

It has been said that the infinitive is a neuter *verbal noun* and that it may be used as the subject of a verb.

**Legere** est difficile.    *To read* is (a) difficult (thing); *reading* is difficult.

Yet, the infinitive retains its character as a verb by taking an object or by being modified by an adverb.

**Ducem dēligere** est difficile.    It is (a) difficult (thing) *to choose a leader*; *choosing a leader* is difficult.

When the verbal noun is not functioning as the subject of a verb, a specific form, called the *gerund*, is used. The infinitive supplies the nominative of the gerund. The other cases are formed by adding **-nd-** to the present stem of the verb (for i-stems of the third conjugation and for all fourth conjugation verbs, an **-ie-** will appear before the **-nd-**), plus the neuter endings of the second declension. These forms are in fact the same as the neuter singular of the future passive participle, except that there is no nominative.

The gerund has no plural.

Therefore, the forms of the gerund of **dēligō, -ere**, 'choose', are:

| | | |
|---|---|---|
| (Nom. | dēligere | choosing) |
| Gen. | dēligendī | of choosing |
| Dat. | dēligendō | to/for choosing |
| Acc. | dēligendum | choosing |
| Abl. | dēligendō | from/with/in/by choosing |

The gerund functions in the various grammatical cases like any other noun, but it still retains its verbal force and so may control an object and may be modified by an adverb. Intransitive verbs which govern the dative case will do so in the gerund form as well.

265

| | | |
|---|---|---|
| **Legendō** legere discimus. | We learn to read *by* (*means of*) *reading*. | (ABLATIVE OF MEANS) |
| Cupidus **legendī** est. | He is desirous *of reading*. | (OBJECTIVE GENITIVE WITH **cupidus**) |
| Ducī libenter **pārendō** fortiōrēs fīēmus. | *By obeying the leader willingly*, we shall become stronger. | (ABLATIVE OF MEANS; INTRANSITIVE VERB GOVERNING DATIVE) |

## B. The Gerundive

The gerundive is a verbal adjective and is sometimes called the future passive participle. The forms for the gerundive of **dēligō, -ere**, 'choose', are **dēligendus, -a, -um**.

Although the gerund may govern an object, in such instances Latin frequently prefers to use a gerundive construction instead, except when that object is a neuter adjective or pronoun. Observe:

| | | |
|---|---|---|
| GERUND: | **Librōs legendō** legere discimus. | *By reading books* we learn to read. |
| GERUNDIVE: | **Librīs legendīs** legere discimus. | *By means of books to-be-read* we learn to read; *by reading books* we learn to read. |
| GERUND: | Cupidus **librōs legendī** est. | He is desirous *of reading books*. |
| GERUNDIVE: | Cupidus **librōrum legendōrum** est. | He is desirous *of books-to-be-read*; he is desirous *of reading books*. |

## C. The Gerund and Gerundive Used to Express Purpose

Purpose may be expressed by the gerund and gerundive in two common ways:

1. **Ad** + THE ACCUSATIVE

   **Ad** + the accusative of the gerund may express purpose.

   > **Ad legendum** venit.   He comes *to* (*towards*) *reading, for the purpose of reading, in order to read*.

   The gerund, as always, may take a direct object:

   > **Ad legendum librōs** venit.   He comes to read books.

   But when the gerund would take an object, the gerundive construction is preferred in Latin:

   > **Ad librōs legendōs** venit.   He comes *to* (*towards*) *books to-be-read*; he comes *for the purpose of reading books*; he comes *to read books*.

2. GENITIVE FOLLOWED BY **causā**, 'for the sake of'
The genitive of the gerund, followed by **causā**, may be used to express purpose.

| | |
|---|---|
| **Legendī causā** venit. | He comes *for the sake of reading*; he comes *to read.* |
| Librōs **legendī causā** venit. | He comes *for the sake of reading* books; he comes *to read* books. |

Again, when the gerund would govern an object (except in the case of neuter adjectives or pronouns), the gerundive construction is preferred:

| | |
|---|---|
| **Librōrum legendōrum causā** venit. | He comes *for the sake of books to-be-read*; he comes *for the sake of reading books*; he comes *to read books.* |

The reason for the exception in the case of neuter adjectives or pronouns is the confusion in gender which might arise. Consider:

Multa videndī causā venit.   He comes to see many things.

BUT:

Multōrum videndōrum causā venit.   He comes to see many things (or) men.

It is unclear in the latter case whether the gender is masculine or neuter.

The constructions discussed above are alternate ways of expressing the same idea as purpose clauses:

Venit **ut** librōs **legat**.   He comes *to read* books.

### D. Impersonal Verbs
A small number of verbs in Latin are found only in the third person singular, the infinitive, and sometimes the participle because of their peculiar meanings. Such verbs are called *impersonal* verbs because of their lack of a personal subject and require in English the word "it" to function as the subject. Some verbs of this type are:

| | |
|---|---|
| licet, licēre, licuit | it is permitted |
| oportet, oportēre, oportuit | it is necessary, it is proper |
| miseret, miserēre, miseruit | it pities; it moves to pity |
| piget, pigēre, piguit | it disgusts |
| taedet, taedēre, taeduit | it bores, it disgusts |
| paenitet, paenitēre, paenituit | it repents |
| pudet, pudēre, puduit | it shames |
| necesse est | it is necessary |

The constructions with these verbs are as follows:

1. WITH ACCUSATIVE AND INFINITIVE

oportet; necesse est; licet

| | |
|---|---|
| Oportet **mē abīre.** | It is necessary (proper) *that I go away*; It is necessary (proper) *for me to go away*; I must go away. |
| Necesse est **mē abīre.** | It is necessary *that I go away*; I must go away. |
| Licet **mē abīre.** | It is permitted *that I go away*; I can (am permitted to) go away. |

2. WITH DATIVE AND INFINITIVE

necesse est; licet

| | |
|---|---|
| Necesse est **mihi abīre.** | It is necessary *for me to go away*; I must go away. |
| Licet **mihi abīre.** | It is permitted *for me to go away*; I can (am permitted to) go away. |

3. WITH SUBJUNCTIVE CLAUSE INTRODUCED BY **ut** (EXPRESSED OR IMPLIED)

necesse est; licet

| | |
|---|---|
| Necesse est **(ut) abeam.** | It is necessary *that I go away*; I must go away. |
| Licet **(ut) abeam.** | It is permitted *that I go away*; I can (am permitted to) go away. |

NOTE that there is *no* distinction in meaning in the three uses of **necesse est** and of **licet.**

4. WITH OBJECTIVE GENITIVE AND ACCUSATIVE

miseret; piget; taedet; paenitet; pudet

These impersonals take the genitive of the thing which arouses the feeling and the accusative of the person concerned.

| | |
|---|---|
| Miseret **mē dolōris.** | It pities *me of (his) grief*; *I* pity *(his) grief.* |
| Paenitet **mē sceleris.** | It repents *me of (my) crime*; *I* am sorry *for (my) crime.* |

Instead of a genitive, an infinitive, a **quod** clause, or a neuter pronoun is sometimes used to express the source of the feeling. When this occurs, the infinitive, the **quod** clause, or the neuter pronoun is the subject of the verb.

| | |
|---|---|
| **Legere** mē taedet. | *Reading* bores me. |
| Mē paenitet **quod tanta scelera in hāc cīvitāte facta sunt.** | *The fact that* (see p. 294) *such great crimes have been committed in this state* repents me; I am sorry *that such great crimes have been committed in this state.* |
| **Hoc** mē pudet. | *This* shames me; I am ashamed *of this.* |

### E. The Impersonals *interest* and *rēfert*

These two impersonals, which mean 'it concerns, it is of interest, it is in the interest of', take the genitive of the person concerned and an infinitive, an **ut** clause, or a demonstrative pronoun in the neuter singular to express the thing which is of concern. But instead of the genitive of the personal pronouns, the following adjectival forms in the ablative case are used: **meā, tuā, suā, nostrā, vestrā.**

| | |
|---|---|
| **Ducis** interest (rēfert) opus **cōnficere.** | It is in the interest *of the leader to complete* (his) work. |
| **Ducis** interest (rēfert) **ut** celeriter **abeās.** | It is in the interest *of the leader that you go away* quickly; it concerns *the leader that you go away* quickly. |
| **Hoc ducis** interest (rēfert). | *This* is in the interest *of the leader.* |
| BUT: | |
| **Meā** interest (rēfert) ut celeriter **abeās.** | It is of interest (*with respect to my* [*affair*]) *to me* that you go away quickly; it concerns *me* that you go away quickly. |

In the latter case, **meā** is in fact modifying the noun **rē**, which is the first part of the verb **rēfert**. The use of the ablative **meā** with **interest** is on analogy with **rēfert.**

# UNIT SIXTEEN — VOCABULARY

| | |
|---|---|
| **abeō, -īre, -iī, (-īvī), -itus** | go away, depart |
| **adversus, -a, -um** | opposite, hostile, adverse |
| **aliēnus, -a, -um** | belonging to another, strange, out of place |
| **āmittō, -ere, -mīsī, -missus** | let go, lose |
| **aperiō, -īre, -uī, apertus** | open |
| **causa, -ae,** F. | cause, reason |
| **causā** (preceded by the genitive) | for the sake of |

| | |
|---|---|
| cottīdiē or cotīdiē (adv.) | daily |
| decōrus, -a, -um | fitting, suitable; handsome |
| dēsum, dēesse, dēfuī, -- | be missing, fail (often + dat.) |
| discō, -ere, didicī, -- | learn |
| frūstrā (adv.) | in vain |
| īnfirmus, -a, -um | weak, unhealthy |
| īnstituō, -ere, -uī, -ūtus | set (up), establish, arrange |
| interest, -esse, -fuit, -- | it is of importance, it concerns, it is of interest |
| lābor, lābī, lāpsus sum | slip, glide, fall |
| lēx, lēgis, F. | law |
| libenter (adv.) | freely, willingly, gladly |
| licet, -ēre, -uit (licitum est) | it is permitted |
| miseret, -ēre, -uit (miseritum est) | it pities, it moves to pity |
| necesse (indeclinable adj.) | necessary |
| oportet, -ēre, -uit, -- | it is necessary, it is proper |
| paenitet, -ēre, -uit, -- | it repents |
| piget, -ēre, -uit (pigitum est) | it disgusts |
| pudet, -ēre, -uit (puditum est) | it shames |
| rēfert, -ferre, -tulit, -- | it is of importance |
| scrīptor, -ōris, M. | writer |
| stō, stāre, stetī, stātus | stand |
| studiōsus, -a, -um | fond of, partial to, studious (+ gen.) |
| sustineō, -ēre, -tinuī, -tentus | support, maintain |
| taedet, -ēre, -uit (taesum est) | it bores, it disgusts |
| ūtilis, -e | useful, beneficial |
| vel (conj.) | or |
|    vel...vel | either...or |
| vetus, -eris | old |
| violō (1) | do violence to, break (an agreement, the law) |

## UNIT SIXTEEN — NOTES ON VOCABULARY

Aliēnus, -a, -um has the stem of alius, -a, -ud as its base, with the adjectival ending -ēnus, -a, -um, 'belonging to', added; thus, aliēnus means 'belonging to another, strange, out of place'.

The ablative of the noun causa, 'cause, reason', is used as a preposition governing the genitive case; causā is placed after the genitive it governs: Mīlitēs ex oppidō pācis causā discessērunt, 'The soldiers withdrew from the town for the sake of peace'.

Īnfirmus, -a, -um means literally 'not strong', therefore 'weak, unhealthy'.

Stō, stāre, stetī, stātus is the verb 'stand'. There is also a verb sistō, sistere, stitī, stātus meaning 'cause to stand, make stand, place, set up, establish'. Connected with these two verbs is another, statuō, statuere, statuī, statūtus, 'cause to stand, set up, establish'. These verbs have many compounds:

astō, astāre, astitī, --, 'stand at or near'
circumstō, circumstāre, circumstetī, --, 'stand around'
īnstō, īnstāre, īnstitī, īnstātus, 'stand on or upon, insist, threaten'
obstō, obstāre, obstitī, obstātus, 'stand before or against; hinder'
dēsistō, dēsistere, dēstitī, dēstitus, 'set down, stand off, stop'
īnsistō, īnsistere, īnstitī, --, 'stand upon, pursue'
obsistō, obsistere, obstitī, obstitus, 'set or place before; set oneself against, oppose, resist'
persistō, persistere, perstitī, --, 'continue steadfastly'
resistō, resistere, restitī, --, 'stand back, stand still, stop'
cōnstituō, cōnstituere, cōnstituī, cōnstitūtus, 'cause to stand, set up, establish; decide'
dēstituō, dēstituere, dēstituī, dēstitūtus, 'set down, leave alone, abandon'
īnstituō, īnstituere, īnstituī, īnstitūtus, 'put or place into; set up, establish, arrange'
restituō, restituere, restituī, restitūtus, 'set up again, restore'

Studiōsus, -a, -um, literally 'full of zeal', means 'fond of, partial to, studious,' and governs the genitive case.

Ūtilis, -e has the same root as ūtor and thus means 'useful, beneficial'.

PREFIXES (not from prepositions)

dis- (dī-, dif-), 'apart'
dīdūcō, 'draw apart, separate, divide'
diffugiō, 'flee in different directions, scatter'
dispellō, 'drive apart, scatter, disperse'
dispōnō, 'place here and there, distribute regularly, arrange'

in- (il-, im-, ir-), 'not'
illiterātus, -a, -um, 'unlettered, uneducated'
immemor, immemoris, 'unmindful, forgetful'
inaudītus, -a, -um, 'unheard (of), strange'
irrevocābilis, -e, 'not to be called back, irrevocable, uncontrollable'

re-, 'back, again'
recēdō, 'go back, withdraw, retire'
recidō, 'fall back'
reficiō, 'make again, remake, restore, renew'

**sē-**, 'apart'

> **sēcēdō,** 'go apart, go away, withdraw'
> **sēdūcō,** 'lead apart, draw aside'

## DENOMINATIVE VERBS

Many verbs in Latin were formed from nouns or adjectives; although these denominative verbs are found in all conjugations, most of them are in the first conjugation.

> **bellō** (1), 'wage, carry on war, fight in war' (from **bellum**)
> **corōnō** (1), 'crown' (from **corōna**)
> **culpō** (1), 'reproach, blame, condemn' (from **culpa**)
> **custōdiō,** -īre, -īvī (-iī), -ītus, 'watch, protect, defend, preserve' (from **custōs**)
> **dīgnor** (1), 'deem worthy' (from **dīgnus**)
> **dominor** (1), 'be lord and master, rule, domineer' (from **dominus**)
> **dūrō** (1), 'make hard, harden, last' (from **dūrus**)
> **fīniō,** -īre, -īvī (-iī), -ītus, 'limit, restrain, check' (from **fīnis**)
> **flōreō,** -ēre, -uī, ––, 'bloom, blossom, flower' (from **flōs, flōris**, M., 'blossom, flower')
> **locō** (1), 'place, lay, set' (from **locus**)
> **metuō,** -ere, metuī, ––, 'fear, be afraid' (from **metus**)
> **saeviō,** -īre, -iī, -ītus, 'be fierce, rage' (from **saevus**)

# UNIT SIXTEEN — DRILL

1. a) Legere est bonum.
   b) Amor legendī est bonus.
   c) Legendō praefuistī.
   d) Ad legendum omnibus adfuit.
   e) Legendō multum cognōvimus.
2. a) Rōmam īvimus ad Caesarem videndum.
   b) Rōmam īvimus Caesaris videndī causā.
3. a) Impiī plēbem agitābant ad pūgnandum.
   b) Impiī plēbem agitābant pūgnandī causā.
4. a) Omnēs patī necesse est.
   b) Omnibus patī necesse est.
   c) Necesse est (ut) omnēs patiantur.
5. a) Rēgis rēfert rēgnum regere.

    b) Rēgis rēfert ut rēgnum regat.

    c) Meā rēfert rēgī pārēre.

6. a) Cōnsulis intererat malōs perīre.

    b) Cōnsulis intererat ut malī perīrent.

    c) Meā intererat ut malī perīrent.

7. Et meā et urbis interfuit quid agerēs.

8. Estne perīculum in currendō per viās urbis?

9. Magna sunt gaudia docendī.

10. Cicerō clārus erat arte loquendī.

11. a) Iuvenēs cupidī fuērunt puellās pulchrās videndī.

    b) Iuvenēs gaudium cēpērunt ē puellīs pulchrīs videndīs.

12. Studium plūra habendī pectora multōrum implet.

13. a) Rōmae adfuimus ad magnās dīvitiās parandās.

    b) Parāre magnās dīvitiās est difficillimum.

    c) Quid agerēs magnārum dīvitiārum parandārum causā?

14. Nostrā patriā discessimus ad vīvendum sine inimīcitiā.

15. Diūtissimē exspectandō īnfēlīcēs sumus.

16. Morandō domī placuistis vestrīs parentibus; domī morātī estis vestrīs parentibus placendī causā.

# UNIT SIXTEEN — PRELIMINARY EXERCISES
## (SECTIONS A, B, C)

1. Celeriter abīre ab hāc terrā est magnum gaudium.

2. Mihi timor abeundī ab hāc terrā est magnus.

3. Eum īnstituendō lēgēs praefēcimus.

4. Mea bona āmittere ōdī.

5. Semper in discendō vītam agere dēbēmus.

6. Cupidus amīcī videndī Rōmam īvī.

7. Mihi timor lēgum violandārum est magnus.

8. Novōrum verbōrum discendōrum studiōsī sumus.

9. Lēgis violandae studiōsī nōn sumus.

10. In novīs rēbus discendīs vītam agere dēbēmus.

11. Ab hāc terrā abīvī ad pecūniam multam faciendam (pecūniae multae faciendae causā).

12. Ab hāc terrā abīvit rēgnī novī īnstituendī causā.

13. Rēgnum novum īnstituērunt fēlīciter vīvendī causā.

14. Multa didicimus ad bene vītam agendam.

15. Hic scrīptor multa ad bene scrībendum didicit.

# UNIT SIXTEEN — EXERCISES

**I.**

1. Tam studiōsus librōrum legendōrum fuit ut omnēs ē vīllā ducis clārī removēret.
2. Rōmam vēnit ad auxilium ā mīlitibus rēgis quaerendum.
3. Cottīdiē currendō salūtem corporis sustineō; numquam ab hōc modō vīvendī lāpsus sum.
4. Carminibus canendīs poēta pecūniam accēpit.
5. Cīvēs fortēs reī pūblicae hostium superandōrum causā oppūgnāre incēpērunt.
6. a) Mē semper necesse erat intellegere illa quae ā duce dicta sunt.
   b) Semper necesse erat ut intellegerem quae ā duce dicta essent.
7. Omnēs oportet vītam quam optimē agere; tempus enim celerrimē lābitur. Nisī quid bonī ēgerimus, frūstrā vīvēmus.
8. Rēgī morī necesse est ut lībertās in hāc rē pūblicā īnstituātur.
9. Pācis temporibus licet ut portae urbis antīquae mūnītae aperiantur.
10. Sī hominibus lēgēs violāre licet, quam ob rem iussīs cōnsulis ā nōbīs pārendum est?
11. Custōdem honestum piumque sceleris parvī tam paenituit ut multa dōna ārīs deōrum immortālium offerret.
12. Nesciō cūr tē gravis dolōris omnium virōrum corporibus īnfirmīs misereat.
13. Bonōs honestōsque taedet pigetque virōrum malōrum quī lēgēs, ā rēge īnstitūtās, violāre volunt.
14. Cuius rēfert ut lēgēs ūtilēs īnstituat salūtis omnium gentium servandae causā?
15. Nostrā interest sapientiam legendīs librīs scrīptōris sapientis discere.
16. Neque cuiquam nostrum licuit istā lēge ūtī.
17. Male imperandō summum imperium āmittitur.
18. Dē cīvitātibus novīs īnstituendīs litterae ad mē mittēbantur.
19. Quamquam studiōsus erat bene regendī, amor populī eī dēerat.
20. Pācis petendae causā, ducem oportēbat pollicērī sē nēminī post bellum nocitūrum esse.
21. Rogāvit num id scelus sit, cuius paenitēre fuerit necesse.
22. Gerenda bella sunt ut sine noxā in pāce vīvātur; hostibus victīs, pāce perfectā, populī nōn rēfert ut tot fortissimī mortuī sint quod prō patriā et omnium lībertāte perierint.
23. Mē paenitet causam reī pūblicae bene nōn sustinendī; sed maximē meā interfuit ut tūtus vīverem.
24. Pudet pigetque meī mē.
25. Nostra mater, tuī nōs miserēret nisī tam cupida coniugis perdendī essēs!

26. a) Ad pācem parandam cīvēs sibi hostēs foedere iūnxērunt.
    b) Pācis parandae causā cīvēs sibi hostēs foedere iūnxērunt.
    c) Ut pācem parārent, cīvēs sibi hostēs foedere iūnxērunt.
27. a) Operis melius cōnficiendī causā, coniūnx auxilium parābat.
    b) Ad opus melius cōnficiendum, coniūnx auxilium parābat.
    c) Quō melius opus cōnficeret, coniūnx auxilium parābat.
28. Bellīs gerendīs patriae validiōrēs fīunt.
29. Bene regendō dux amōrem comitum capit.
30. Sequāmur nātūram optimam bene vīvendī ducem!
31. Istīus vērē ducis hoc rēferre vidētur.
32. Neque rēfert cuiusquam utrum rēx cupidus sit auctōritātis ostendendae necne. Cīvēs eī favent, nec suā interest quō modō vīribus ūtātur, dummodo sibi ipsīs nē noceat.
33. Ac sī quis est tālis quālis esse omnīs oportēbat, quī īrātus fit quod istōs hostēs, cīvitātī inimīcōs, nōn interfēcerim potius quam ex urbe pepulerim, nōn est istud mea culpa, sed temporum. [**potius quam**, 'rather than']
34. Necesse est hominēs adsint vel bellō vel pācī parātī.
35. Adversīs ventīs nautae ad īnsulam accēdere nōn potuērunt; nāvēs adversō flūmine feruntur. Quī proximō in lītore stetērunt nihil auxiliī ferre poterant.
36. Fēlīx est quī libenter potuit rērum cognōscere causās multīs librīs legendīs et multa discendō.
37. Crēdendum erit veteribus sī cupidī erimus bene vīvendī. Exempla optima ante oculōs stant. Necesse est ea videāmus.
38. Quae dōna decōra abeuntibus dedistī?
39. Pepercit dux neque suīs comitibus neque aliēnīs. Nēmō in omnibus prōvinciae urbibus vel in hāc ipsā erat tūtus.
40. Bonus etiam causam dandī cōgitat.
41. Respondit ad cōnsilium capiendum temporis opus esse.
42. A SYLLOGISM PROVING THAT THERE IS SUCH A THING AS DIVINATION (Cicero, *Dē Dīvīnātiōne* 101–2, adapted):

Sī sunt dī neque ante dīcunt hominibus quae futūra sint, aut nōn dīligunt hominēs, aut quid futūrum sit nesciunt; aut arbitrantur nihil interesse hominum scīre quid sit futūrum; aut nōn putant esse suae glōriae praesīgnificāre hominibus quae sunt futūra; aut ea nē ipsī quidem dī sīgnificāre possunt. At neque nōn dīligunt nōs (sunt enim clārissimī bonīque hominum amīcī); neque nesciunt ea quae ab ipsīs cōnstitūta sunt; neque nostrā nihil interest scīre ea quae futūra sunt (erimus enim fēlīciōrēs et tūtiōrēs, certiōrēs dē illō quod accidet, sī sciēmus); neque hoc aliēnum dūcunt glōriā suā (nihil est enim beneficentiā clārius meliusque); neque nōn possunt futūra praenōscere; nōn igitur dī sunt nec sīgnificant nōbīs futūra; sunt autem dī; sīgnificant igitur ad nōs dē rēbus futūrīs monendōs; et nōn, sī sīgnificant futūra, nūllās dant viās nōbīs ad signa intellegenda (frūstrā enim sīgnificārent); nec, sī dant viās, nōn est dīvīnātiō; est igitur dīvīnātiō. [**at** (conj.), 'but'; **beneficentia, -ae,** F., 'kind deed, service'; **dīligō, -ere, dīlēxī, dīlēctus,** 'esteem, be fond of'; **dīvīnātiō, -ōnis,** F., 'divination'; **nihil** (*here*, as adv.), 'not at all'; **praenōscō (prae + nōscō),** 'know beforehand'; **praesīgnificō** (1), 'show beforehand, express beforehand'; **sīgnificō** (1), 'show, report, express']

43. Cicero, *Dē Senectūte* 69, adapted:

Quid est in hominis nātūrā diū? Dā enim summum tempus, exspectēmus longam aetātem, mihi autem nē longum quidem quicquam vidētur, in quō est aliquī fīnis. Cum enim id advēnit, tum illud, quod praeteriit, efflūxit; id sōlum remanet, quod virtūte et bonīs factīs cōnsecūtus sīs; hōrae quidem cēdunt et diēs et mēnsēs et annī, nec praeteritum tempus umquam redit, nec, quid sequātur, scīrī potest; quod cuique temporis ad vīvendum datur, eō dēbet esse contentus. [**aetās, -tātis,** F., 'age, life'; **cōnsequor (com- + sequor),** 'obtain, acquire'; **contentus, -a, -um,** 'content'; **effluō, -ere, -flūxī, --,** 'flow forth, escape'; **mēnsis, -is,** M., 'month'; **praetereō (praeter,** 'beyond', **+ eō),** 'pass by']


## II.

1. The queen was so ashamed of her burning love for the handsome leader that she drove him from her state.
2. In order to terrify the citizens, the legate ordered the troops to attack and destroy their province.
3. The art of writing a poem is so difficult that very few men are desirous of learning how it should be done.
4. After the torches had been carried into the (city) gates, the king was able to show the lofty walls to the guests from the province who had come to learn the art of fortifying towns.
5. Learning about other people's laws bores me; I don't even have time to read our own.


## III. Readings

A. Cicero, *In Catilīnam* II.7.15:

Numquam ego ab dīs immortālibus optābō, Quirītēs,[1] invidiae meae relevandae[2] causā ut Catilīnam dūcere exercitum[3] hostium atque in armīs volitāre[4] audiātis, sed trīduō[5] tamen audiētis.

---

[1] **Quirītēs, -ium,** M., 'fellow citizens'       [2] **relevō** (1), 'diminish'       [3] **exercitus, -ūs,** M., 'army'       [4] **volitō** (1), 'hasten about'       [5] **trīduum, -ī,** N., 'a space of three days'

B. Cicero, *Dē Senectūte* 5.15:

Etenim,[1] cum complector[2] animō, quattuor[3] reperiō[4] causās cūr senectūs[5] misera videātur: ūnam, quod āvocet[6] ā rēbus gerendīs; alteram, quod corpus faciat īnfirmius; tertiam,[7] quod prīvet[8] omnibus ferē[9] voluptātibus;[10] quartam,[11] quod haud[12] procul[13] absit ā morte. Eārum, sī placet, causārum quanta quamque[14] sit iūsta[15] ūna quaeque videāmus.

[1] etenim (adv.), 'truly, and indeed'  [2] complector, -plectī, -plexus sum, 'embrace intellectually, think over'  [3] quattuor (indeclinable adj.), 'four'  [4] reperiō, -īre, repperī, repertus, 'discover'  [5] senectūs, -tūtis, F., 'old age'  [6] āvocō (1), 'call away *or* off'  [7] tertius, -a, -um, 'third'  [8] prīvō (1), 'deprive'  [9] ferē (adv.), 'almost, practically'  [10] voluptās, -tātis, F., 'pleasure'  [11] quartus, -a, -um, 'fourth'  [12] haud (adv.), 'not at all'  [13] procul (adv.), 'at a distance'  [14] quam (adv.), 'how'  [15] iūstus, -a, -um, 'just'

C. Cicero, *Dē Senectūte* 17.59:

Multās ad[1] rēs perūtilēs[2] Xenophontis[3] librī sunt, quōs legite, quaesō,[4] studiōsē, ut facitis. Quam[5] cōpiōsē[6] ab eō agrī cultūrā[7] laudātur in eō librō, quī est dē tuendā[8] rē familiārī,[9] quī *Oeconomicus*[10] īnscrībitur![11]

[1] ad, *here*, 'for'  [2] perūtilis, -e, 'very useful'  [3] Xenophōn, Xenophontis, M., 'Xenophon', a Greek historian  [4] quaesō, -ere, -īvī, -itus, 'beg, entreat'  [5] quam (adv.), 'how'  [6] cōpiōsē (adv.), 'copiously, abundantly'  [7] cultūra, -ae, F., 'cultivation'  [8] tueor, tuērī, tūtus sum, 'care for, protect'  [9] familiāris, -e, 'belonging to the household'  [10] oeconomicus, -a, -um, 'pertaining to domestic economy', here, the title of a book by Xenophon (understand liber)  [11] īnscrībō (in + scrībō), 'entitle, name'

D. Cicero, *Dē Amīcitiā* 26.98:

Nūlla est igitur haec amīcitia, cum alter vērum audīre nōn vult, alter ad mentiendum[1] parātus est.

[1] mentior, mentīrī, mentītus sum, 'lie, tell a falsehood'

E. Martial 12.23:

Dentibus[1] atque comīs[2] — nec tē pudet — ūteris ēmptīs.[3]
Quid faciēs oculō, Laelia?[4] Nōn emitur.[3]

[1] dēns, dentis, M., 'tooth'  [2] coma, -ae, F., 'hair' (of the head)  [3] emō, emere, ēmī, ēmptus, 'buy'  [4] Laelia, -ae, F., a woman's name

F. Seneca writes to his friend, Lucilius, on the subject of masters and slaves (*Epistulae Mōrālēs* XLVII.1–5):

Libenter ex iīs, quī ā tē veniunt, cognōvī familiāriter[1] tē cum servīs tuīs vīvere. Hoc prūdentiam[2] tuam, hoc ērudītiōnem[3] decet.[4] "Servī sunt."

[1] familiāriter (adv.), 'in a friendly way'  [2] prūdentia, -ae, F., 'discretion'  [3] ērudītiō, -ōnis, F., 'erudition, knowledge'  [4] decet, -ēre, decuit, 'it fits, it suits' (impersonal verb)

Immō[5] hominēs. "Servī sunt." Immō[5] contubernālēs.[6] "Servī sunt." Immō[5] humilēs amīcī. "Servī sunt." Immō[5] cōnservī,[7] sī cōgitāveris tantundem[8] in utrōsque[9] licēre fortūnae.[10]

Itaque[11] rīdeō istōs, quī turpe[12] exīstimant[13] cum servō suō cēnāre.[14] Quārē, nisī quia superbissima[15] cōnsuētūdō[16] cēnantī[14] dominō stantium servōrum turbam circumdedit?[17] Ēst[18] ille plūs quam capit, et ingentī avidītāte[19] onerat[20] distentum[21] ventrem[22] ac dēsuētum[23] iam ventris[22] officiō,[24] ut maiōre operā[25] omnia ēgerat[26] quam ingessit;[27] at[28] īnfēlīcibus servīs movēre labra[29] nē in hōc[30] quidem, ut loquantur, licet. Virgā[31] murmur[32] omne compescitur,[33] et nē fortuīta[34] quidem verberibus[35] excepta sunt,[36] tussis,[37] sternūmenta,[38] singultūs.[39] Magnō malō ūllā vōce interpellātum[40] silentium[41] luitur.[42] Nocte tōtā iēiūnī[43] mūtīque[44] perstant.[45]

Sīc fit, ut istī dē dominō loquantur, quibus cōram[46] dominō loquī nōn licet. At[28] illī, quibus nōn tantum[47] cōram[46] dominīs, sed cum ipsīs erat sermō,[48] quōrum ōs nōn cōnsuēbātur,[49] parātī erant prō dominō porrigere[50] cervīcem,[51] perīculum imminēns[52] in caput[53] suum āvertere;[54] in convīviīs[55] loquēbantur, sed in tormentīs[56] tacēbant. Deinde[57] eiusdem arrogantiae[58] prōverbium[59] iactātur, tot hostēs esse quot servōs. Nōn habēmus illōs hostēs, sed facimus.

---

[5] immō (adv.), 'no, but. . .'     [6] contubernālis, -is, M. & F., 'comrade'     [7] cōnservus, -ī, M., 'fellow slave'     [8] tantusdem, tantadem, tantundem, 'just so much'     [9] uterque, utraque, utrumque, 'each (of two), both'; in utrōsque, 'to (for) both (of you)'     [10] fortūna, -ae, F., 'fortune'     [11] itaque (adv.), 'and so'     [12] turpis, -e, 'foul, ugly'     [13] exīstimō (1), 'think'     [14] cēnō (1), 'dine'     [15] superbus, -a, -um, 'haughty'     [16] cōnsuētūdō, -tūdinis, F., 'habit, custom'     [17] circumdō (circum + dō), 'put around'     [18] ēst, 3rd person sing. of edō, edere (esse), ēdī, ēsus, 'eat'     [19] avidītās, -tātis, F., 'greed'     [20] onerō (1), 'burden, load down'     [21] distentus, -a, -um, 'full, distended'     [22] venter, ventris, M., 'belly'     [23] dēsuēscō, -ere, -suēvī, -suētus, 'become unaccustomed'     [24] officium, -ī, N., 'duty, task'     [25] opera, -ae, F., 'effort'     [26] ēgerō (ē + gerō), here, 'vomit' (lit., 'carry out')     [27] ingerō (in + gerō), 'throw in, heap on'     [28] at (conj.), 'but'     [29] labrum, -ī, N., 'lip'     [30] in hōc (understand tempore)     [31] virga, -ae, F., 'rod, whip'     [32] murmur, murmuris, N., 'murmur'     [33] compescō, -ere, -pescuī, —, 'restrain, check'     [34] fortuītus, -a, -um, 'casual, accidental'     [35] verber, verberis, N., 'lash'     [36] excipiō (ex + capiō), 'except'     [37] tussis, -is (acc. -im), F., 'cough'     [38] sternūmentum, -ī, N., 'sneeze'     [39] singultus, -ūs, M., 'sobbing'     [40] interpellō (1), 'interrupt'     [41] silentium, -ī, N., 'silence'     [42] luō, -ere, luī, luitūrus, 'atone for'     [43] iēiūnus, -a, -um, 'hungry, thirsty'     [44] mūtus, -a, -um, 'mute'     [45] perstō, -āre, -stitī, -stātus, 'stand firm'     [46] cōram (prep. + abl.), 'in the presence of, facing'     [47] nōn tantum. . .sed, 'not only. . .but'     [48] sermō, -ōnis, M., 'conversation'     [49] cōnsuō, -ere, -suī, -sūtus, 'sew (stitch) together'     [50] porrigō, -ere, porrēxī, porrēctus, 'offer'     [51] cervīx, -īcis, F., 'neck'     [52] immineō, -ēre, —, —, 'threaten'     [53] caput, capitis, N., 'head'     [54] āvertō, -ere, -vertī, -versus, 'turn off, divert'     [55] convīvium, -ī, N., 'banquet'     [56] tormentum, -ī, N., 'torture'     [57] deinde (adv.), 'finally'     [58] arrogantia, -ae, F., 'arrogance'     [59] prōverbium, -ī, N., 'proverb'

# UNIT SEVENTEEN

## A. Clauses of Fearing

Verbs or expressions of fearing take subjunctive clauses introduced by **nē** for the positive and **ut** for the negative. While this may seem a curious reversal, it is a logical construction. In the earliest stages of the language, the constructions were *paratactic*; *parataxis* is the absence of subordination and the arrangement of several clauses side by side.

> Timeō. I fear.   Ut veniat! I wish he would come!
> Timeō. I fear.   Nē veniat! I wish he would not come!
> (*Veniat* is an optative subjunctive; see Unit Twelve.)

As the language developed, the constructions became *hypotactic*; *hypotaxis* is the subordination of one clause to another. Thus:

> Timeō **ut** veniat.   I fear that he is *not* coming; I fear that he will *not* come.
> (It is logical that one would fear that the *opposite* of his wish might come about.)
> Timeō **nē** veniat.   I fear that he *is* coming (*will* come).

Clauses of fearing follow the normal rules for sequence of tenses. While the present subjunctive may refer to an act that is either contemporaneous with or subsequent to the action of the main verb, when stress is laid on the subsequence (futurity) of the action, the active periphrastic is occasionally used:

> Timeō **ut veniat**.   I fear *that he is not coming*; I fear *that he will not come.*
> Timeō **ut ventūrus**   I fear *that he will not come* (emphasis on futurity).
> **sit**.
> Sometimes, **nē...nōn** are found instead of **ut** to introduce a negative clause of fearing:
> Timeō **nē nōn veniat.**   I fear *that he is not coming (will not come).*

## B. Clauses of Doubting

When **dubitō** (1) means 'hesitate', it takes an infinitive:

> Hoc **facere** dubitō.   I hesitate *to do* this.

When it means 'doubt', it takes the following constructions which are regularly used with words or expressions of doubting:

1. When the word or expression of doubting is positive (as opposed to negative), it introduces an indirect question.

> Dubitō **num abitūrus sit.**    I doubt *whether (that) he will go away.*
> Dubitō **an abeat.**    I doubt *whether (that) he is going away.*

2. When the word or expression of doubting is negative, a subjunctive clause introduced by **quīn** (translated literally 'but that') is used.

> Nōn dubitō **quīn abeat.**    I don't doubt *(but) that he is going away.*
> Nōn dubitō **quīn abitūrus sit.**    I don't doubt *(but) that he will go away.*
> Nōn dubium est **quīn abeat.**    There is no doubt *(but) that he is going away.*
> Quis dubitat **quīn abeat?**    Who doubts *(but) that he is going away?*

In the last sentence, **quis dubitat** is an example of a *virtual negative*; that is, the implication is that *no one doubts* that he is going away.

## C. Clauses of Prevention

To express prohibition or prevention, the following constructions are used:

1. **Vetō, -āre, -uī, -itus**, 'forbid', and **prohibeō, -ēre, -uī, -itus**, 'prohibit', take a simple infinitive.

> Tē vetō **abīre.**    I forbid you *to go away.*
> Tē prohibeō **abīre.**    I prohibit you *to go (from going) away.*

2. The following verbs are among those which take a subjunctive construction:

> **dēterreō, -ēre, -uī, -itus**    deter, prevent
> **impediō, -īre, -īvī (-iī), -ītus**    hinder
> **obstō, -āre, -stitī, -stātus**    hinder, stand in the way of

If the verb of prevention is *positive*, the subjunctive clause will be introduced by **quōminus** (= quō minus, 'by which the less') or **nē**, 'in order that not'. These clauses are analogous to relative clauses of purpose introduced by **quō** (see Unit Fourteen), and **quōminus** in effect is standing for **ut eō minus**, 'in order that by this the less'.

> (Tē) dēterreō **quōminus abeās.**    I deter you *by which the less you go away;* I deter you *from going away.*
> (Tē) dēterreō **nē abeās.**    I deter you *in order that you not go away;* I deter (prevent) you *from going away.*

When the verb of prevention is *negative*, the subjunctive clause is introduced by **quōminus**, 'by which the less', or **quīn**, 'but that'.

| Nōn (tē) dēterreō **quōminus abeās.** | I don't deter you *by which the less you go away*; I don't deter you *from going away*. |
| Nōn (tē) dēterreō **quīn abeās.** | I don't deter you *but that you go away*; I don't deter you *from going away*. |

## D. The Supine

The gerund is a verbal noun. There is another variety of verbal noun in Latin called the *supine*. As we might expect, it is neuter singular, but it has only two cases, the accusative and the ablative, each of which has a specific use. The supine, then, is not nearly as versatile as the gerund and, in fact, occurs infrequently. Declined like a fourth declension noun, it is formed on the fourth principal part of the verb.

|  | I | II | III | IV |
|---|---|---|---|---|
| ACCUSATIVE | optātum | implētum | inceptum | sēnsum |
| ABLATIVE | optātū | implētū | inceptū | sēnsū |

The *accusative* of the supine is used without a preposition after verbs of motion to express *purpose*.

It urbem **captum.**   He goes *to capture* the city.

The *ablative* of the supine is used with some adjectives as an *ablative of respect*.

Hic liber facilis est **lēctū.**   This book is easy *with respect to reading*; this book is easy *to read*.

# UNIT SEVENTEEN — VOCABULARY

| | |
|---|---|
| **aetās, aetātis,** F. | time of life, age, life |
| **celeritās, -tātis,** F. | speed, swiftness |
| **dēfendō, -ere, dēfendī, dēfēnsus** | defend |
| **dēnique** (adv.) | finally, at last |
| **dēsistō, -ere, -stitī, -stitus** | stop, desist |
| **dēterreō, -ēre, -uī, -itus** | deter, prevent, hinder, keep from |
| **dubius, -a, -um** | doubtful |
| **dubium, -ī,** N. | doubt, hesitation |
| **dubitō** (1) | hesitate (with inf.); doubt (with indirect question or **quīn** + subjunctive) |
| **impediō, -īre, -īvī (-iī), -ītus** | deter, impede, prevent |
| **metuō, -ere, metuī, ––** | fear |

| | |
|---|---|
| nemus, nemoris, N. | grove, wood |
| obitus, -ūs, M. | a going down, setting; downfall, ruin |
| obstō, -āre, -stitī, -stātus | stand in the way of, hinder (+ dat.) |
| orior, -īrī, ortus sum | rise, arise, begin |
| ortus, -ūs, M. | rising, source |
| perveniō, -īre, -vēnī, -ventus | arrive (at) (+ **ad**) |
| prohibeō, -ēre, -uī, -itus | keep from, prohibit, prevent |
| quīn (conj.) | but that, that not (used after expressions of prevention, negative doubting, etc.) |
| quōminus (conj.) | by which the less, that not, from (used in positive or negative clauses of prevention) |
| radius, -ī, M. | rod, ray |
| religiō, -ōnis, F. | religious awe, reverence, integrity, sanctity |
| relinquō, -ere, -līquī, -lictus | leave behind, abandon |
| reliquus, -a, -um | remaining; rest of |
| retegō, -ere, -tēxī, -tēctus | uncover, reveal |
| tergum, -ī, N. | back |
| turpis, -e | foul, ugly |
| ūnā (adv.) | together, at the same time |
| vēnor, -ārī, -ātus sum | hunt, go hunting |
| vertō, -ere, vertī, versus | turn |
| animadvertō, -ere, -vertī, -versus | turn one's attention to, notice |
| vetō, -āre, -uī, -itus | forbid |

## UNIT SEVENTEEN — NOTES ON VOCABULARY

**Aetās, aetātis,** F., is 'time of life, age, life'; do not confuse it with **aestās, aestātis,** F., 'summer'.

**Celeritās, celeritātis,** F., is 'the state of being swift', thus, 'speed, swiftness'.

**Dēfendō, dēfendere, dēfendī, dēfēnsus,** has the same stem in the present and perfect active; and so **dēfendimus** is 'we defend' or 'we have defended'.

**Dēterreō,** a compound of **dē** and **terreō,** means 'frighten from', and so 'deter, prevent, hinder, keep from'.

**Dubius, -a, -um** is the adjective 'doubtful'. Its stem comes from **duo** and **habeō,** 'hold two'; its primary meaning is 'moving in two directions alternately, fluctuating'. It then gets to mean 'vacillating in mind, uncertain, doubting, doubtful'.

Another adjective, **anceps, ancipitis,** has a similar history of meaning. Literally, it means 'two-headed' (**ambi-,** shortened to **an-,** 'both', + **ceps** from **caput,**

**capitis**, N., 'head'); the meaning then expands to 'that extends on two opposite sides', and then, 'fluctuating, doubtful'.

The neuter adjective **dubium** used substantively is 'doubt, hesitation'. The verb **dubitō** with an infinitive is 'hesitate'; without an infinitive it means 'doubt' and takes a construction using the subjunctive. **Dubitō** has **habeō** hidden in its stem as **dēbeō** does (**dē** + **habeō**). **Dēbeō** means literally 'hold from'; if one holds something from someone, he owes it to him, or he is under obligation to give it back. From there, the two meanings of **dēbeō** emerge: 'owe' and 'be bound to, ought'. **Dubitō** is a contraction of **duhibitāre** (**duo** + a frequentative of **habeō**), 'to have or hold as two'.

**Impediō** is a fourth conjugation denominative verb from **pēs, pedis**, 'foot'. When one gets something in the way of his foot, he becomes hindered and so the verb means 'deter, impede, prevent'. **Impedīmenta, impedīmentōrum**, N. pl., is the Latin word for 'baggage'.

**Obitus** is the fourth declension noun from **obeō**, 'go to meet, go down, die, travel, perform'; therefore **obitus** means 'visit, going down, setting, downfall, ruin, death'.

**Ortus**, 'rising', is the fourth declension noun from **orior**, 'rise'.

**Perveniō**, a compound of **per** and **veniō**, means 'arrive at'; **ad** is used with this verb: **Ad Italiam heri pervēnimus**, 'We arrived at Italy yesterday'.

**Relinquō, relinquere, relīquī, relictus**, 'leave behind, abandon', has an -**n**- only in the present stem; the English words "relinquish" and "derelict" might be helpful in remembering the roots of the principal parts of this verb.

**Retegō** (re- + tegō) does *not* mean 'cover again' but 'uncover, reveal'.

**Ūnā** is an adverb meaning 'together, at the same time'; often it is used with **cum**: **Ad Italiam ūnā cum sorōre īvī**, 'I went to Italy together with my sister'. Of course, this same sentence could be translated, 'I went to Italy with one sister', but usually this ambiguity does not occur.

**Vertō, vertere, vertī, versus**, has the same stem in the present and perfect active; **vertit** is both 'he turns' and 'he has turned'. Since this verb has many compounds, if one thinks of English derivatives, it is easy to remember the principal parts. For example, consider "convert, conversion; invert, inversion". **Animadvertō** means literally 'turn the mind to', and so 'notice'.

**Vetō**, 'forbid', is one of the few verbs of the first conjugation that do not follow the usual pattern of principal parts: **vetō, vetāre, vetuī, vetitus**.

## FREQUENTATIVE VERBS

Frequentative (sometimes called iterative) verbs are usually first conjugation verbs that are formed from the stem of the perfect passive participle of another verb (of any conjugation) and have the idea of repeated or forcible action, although sometimes this idea is lost.

**captō** (1), 'strive to seize, lay hold with zeal *or* longing; catch at' (from **capiō**)

**clāmitō\*** (1), 'cry out violently *or* aloud' (from **clāmō**)

**cursō** (1), 'run here and there *or* back and forth' (from **currō**)

**dictō** (1), 'say often' (from **dīcō**)

**factitō†** (1), 'make *or* do frequently; be wont to make *or* do' (from **faciō**)

**fugitō** (1), 'flee eagerly *or* in haste; shun' (from **fugiō**)

**habitō** (1), 'have frequently, be wont to have; inhabit' (from **habeō**)

**lectitō†** (1), 'gather *or* collect eagerly *or* often; read often *or* with eagerness *or* with attention' (from **legō**)

**scrīptitō†** (1), 'write often, compose' (from **scrībō**)

\* Frequentatives made from first conjugation verbs end in -**itō** rather than -**ātō**.
† Here -**itō** has been added to the participial stem.

The following, although frequentatives, have lost the frequentative meaning:

**ductō** (1), 'lead, draw, conduct; delude' (from **dūcō**)

**inceptō** (1), 'begin, undertake, attempt' (from **incipiō**)

**gestō** (1), 'bear, carry, have' (from **gerō**)

**Vīsō, vīsere, vīsī, vīsus**, although not a first conjugation verb, is a frequentative meaning 'look at attentively'. From this verb another frequentative is formed, **vīsitō** (1), 'see, go to see, visit'.

## INCHOATIVE VERBS

Inchoative (also called inceptive) verbs add the ending -**scō**, -**scere** either to the present stem of another verb or to the stem of a noun or adjective in order to indicate the beginning of an action. The inchoative verb has no perfect tense of its own, but it may use that of the verb on which it is based.

**ardēscō, -ere, arsī, ––,** 'take fire, kindle, be inflamed, gleam'
    (**ardeō, -ēre, arsī, arsus,** 'be on fire, burn')

**calēscō, -ere, caluī, ––,** 'grow warm'
    (**caleō, -ēre, caluī, ––,** 'be hot')

**candēscō, -ere, canduī, ––,** 'become bright'
    (**candeō, -ēre, canduī, ––,** 'glitter, shine')

**fervēscō, -ere, ––, ––,** 'become boiling'
    (**ferveō, -ēre, ferbuī, ––,** 'be boiling hot, boil')

**liquēscō, -ere, licuī, ––,** 'become fluid *or* liquid, melt'
    (**liqueō, -ēre, līquī** or **licuī, ––,** 'be fluid *or* clear')

**lūcēscō, -ere, ––, ––,** 'begin to shine, grow light'
    (**lūceō, -ēre, lūxī, ––,** 'be light, clear; shine')

**rubēscō, -ere, rubuī, ––,** 'grow red'
    (**rubeō, -ēre, rubuī, ––,** 'be red')

valēscō, -ere, valuī, – –, 'grow strong'
  (valeō, -ēre, -uī, -itus, 'be strong')
īrāscor,* -ī, īrātus sum, 'grow angry'
  (īra, -ae, F., 'anger')
mitēscō,* -ere, – –, – –, 'grow mild'
  (mitis, -e, 'mild')

* Note that a connecting vowel is sometimes added between the stem and the inchoative suffix.

Some verbs although inchoative in form have no inchoative force in their meaning:

crēscō, -ere, crēvī, crētus, 'grow, spring forth'
īgnōscō, -ere, īgnōvī, īgnōtus, 'be forgiving, forgive, pardon'
oblīvīscor, -ī, oblītus sum, 'forget'
proficīscor, -ī, profectus sum, 'set forth, set out, start'

# UNIT SEVENTEEN — DRILL

1. Verēmur nē fulgor domūs dēleat.
2. Timuērunt nē hostēs oppidum oppūgnātūrī essent.
3. Veritī sumus ut iuvenēs lēgibus novīs pārērent.
4. Timuistis nē veterēs in prōvinciā novā ūtilēs nōn essent.
5. Dē hōc tibi dīcere dubitābam.
6. Quis est quī dubitet quīn multō optimus magister sīs?
7. Dubitāvimus an senēs prīmā lūce ventūrī essent.
8. Dubitātis num multum discāmus.
9. Nōn dubitāmus quīn multum discāmus.
10. Īvērunt Rōmam Caesarem vīsum.
11. Dolor erat difficilis lātū.
12. Liber erat facilis lēctū.
13. Nōn est dubium quīn liber facilis lēctū sit.
14. a) Cīvēs verentur ut urbs quam optimē mūniātur.
    b) Lēgātum igitur ad cōnsulem auxilium rogātum mittent.
    c) Dubium est an eīs cum veniā respōnsūrus sit.
15. Tē vetō istud facere.
16. a) Dēterrēbō quōminus istud faciās.
    b) Dēterrēbō nē istud faciās.
    c) Nōn dēterrēbō quōminus istud faciās.
    d) Num dēterreō quīn istud faciās?

17. Tuus pater māterque veniunt.

Rewrite this sentence after each of the following introductory words or phrases:

a) Timeō ut
b) Timeō nē
c) Vetō
d) Dēterreō
e) Nōn dēterreō

18. Soror frātrī dōnum dat.

Rewrite this sentence after the five introductory words or phrases given under 17 above.

## UNIT SEVENTEEN — PRELIMINARY EXERCISES (SECTIONS A, B)

1. Metuō ut ūnā vēnātūrī sīmus.
2. Timuistī nē illō tempore relictus essēs?
3. Verēmur ut adulēscentēs urbem nostram cum celeritāte dēfendant.
4. Metuisne nē facta turpia sociōrum nōn cēlāta sint?
5. Timeō nē reliquī ad urbem nōn perveniant.
6. Dubitō num religiō nōbīs prōfutūra sit.
7. Dubitāsne an nōs ad hās rēs animadvertāmus?
8. Dubium nōn est quīn mihi magnus metus sit.
9. Nōn dubitāvērunt quīn ortum sōlis vidērent.
10. Dubitāre numquam dēsiit num ad āram pervenīrēs.
11. Quis dubitat quīn sōl oriātur?
12. Dubitāvērunt an hostēs patriam invāsissent.

## UNIT SEVENTEEN — EXERCISES

**I.**

1. Vereor ut vincēns tuīs parsūrus sit.
2. Ūnum illud timēbam nē quid turpius facerem, vel dīcam, iam effēcissem.
3. Nōn dubium est quīn uxōrem nōlit fīlius. [uxor, uxōris, F., 'wife']
4. Nōn dubitārī dēbet quīn fuerint ante Homērum poētae. [Homērus, -ī, M., 'Homer', a Greek epic poet]
5. Nōn dēterret sapientem mors quōminus reī pūblicae auxiliō sit.
6. Aetās nōn impedit quōminus sapiēns bene vīvendī cupidus sit.
7. Adest vir summā auctōritāte et religiōne et fidē quī nōs dēterrēre potest nē plūra loquāmur.

8. Tū modo nē mē prohibeās accipere, sī quid det mihi. [modo (adv.), 'just']
9. Dēsinite dubitāre, utrum sit ūtilius.
10. Honestumne factū sit dubitant.
11. Spectātum veniunt, veniunt spectentur ut ipsae.
12. Metuō quid futūrum dēnique sit.
13. Difficile est mihi omnia dē quibus dubitō ad tē referre.
14. Neque enim dubitandum putō quīn aqua dūcenda sit in illam cīvitātem.
15. Opus est quam prīmum aliquō quod aquam in cīvitātem cum celeritāte dūcat.
16. Vērē spērō tē eā quā dēbēbis dīligentiā hoc opus factūrum.
17.             Vēnātum Aenēās ūnāque miserrima Dīdō
                in nemus īre parant, ubi prīmōs crāstinus ortūs
                extulerit Tītān radiīsque retēxerit orbem.
                            (Vergil, *Aeneid* iv.117–119)
   [Aenēās, proper name, a Roman hero; Dīdō, proper name, the queen of Carthage; crāstinus, -a, -um, 'pertaining to tomorrow, tomorrow's'; Tītān, a god, 'the sun']
18. Sapientēs antīquī sōlis et lūnae reliquōrumque sīderum ortūs, obitūs, mōtūsque cognōscere voluērunt.
19. Tū prō tuā sapientiā quid optimum factū sit vidēbis; omnēs multō prius animadvertērunt tē intellegentiōrem esse illīs hanc cīvitātem regentibus. [prō, *here*, 'by virtue of']
20. Omnēs hostēs terga vertērunt, nec prius fugere destitērunt, quam ad flūmen pervēnērunt.
21. Lēgātum suum ad eum mittit rogātum ut sibi mīlitibusque parcat.
22. a) Vōs dēfendere relictam urbem vetāmus.
    b) Dubium est an relictam urbem dēfēnsūrus sit.
    c) Eīs obstat quōminus relictam urbem dēfendant.
23. Ortō sōle, nēmō erat quī dubitāret quīn cōpiae nostrae eō diē omnīnō superārent.
24. Cum tanta scelera fēcissent, omnēs impiī metuērunt ut sōl eō diē horridō orīrētur.
25. Nōn vērō perīculum erat nē nōn mortem optandam putāret.
26. Num est perīculum nē quis putet turpe esse?
27. Veritus est nē vēnārī nōn posset.
28. Nē quod bellum orīrētur metus erat.
29. Vidēsne enim, quae dubia sint, ea crēdī prō certīs?

## II.

1. He was (a man) of such sanctity that he kept the leaders from committing crimes.

2. a) We fear that he will reveal the crimes of this house.

   b) We fear that he revealed the crimes of this house.

   c) We fear that he is revealing the crimes of this house.

   d) We feared that he would reveal the crimes of this house.

3. The honorable men doubted whether his lifetime had been well spent.

4. The honorable men did not doubt that his lifetime had been well spent.

5. Stop hunting! I forbid you to kill more animals.

# UNIT SEVENTEEN — CONNECTED READINGS

Caesar, *Gallic War* VI.11

Quoniam ad hunc locum[1] perventum est, nōn aliēnum esse vidētur dē Galliae Germāniaeque mōribus et quō differant[2] hae nātiōnēs inter sēsē prōpōnere. In Galliā nōn sōlum in omnibus cīvitātibus atque in omnibus pāgīs partibusque, sed paene etiam in singulīs domibus factiōnēs sunt, eārumque factiōnum prīncipēs sunt quī summam auctōritātem eōrum[3] iūdiciō habēre exīstimantur, quōrum ad arbitrium iūdiciumque summa omnium rērum cōnsiliōrumque redeat.[4] Idque eius reī causā antīquitus īnstitūtum vidētur, nē quis ex plēbe contrā potentiōrem auxiliī egēret; suōs enim quisque opprimī et circumvenīrī nōn patitur, neque, aliter sī faciat, ūllam inter suōs habeat auctōritātem. Haec eadem ratiō est in summā[5] tōtīus Galliae; namque omnēs cīvitātēs dīvīsae sunt in duās partēs.

aliter (*adv.*), otherwise
antīquitus (*adv.*), in ancient times, long ago
arbitrium, -ī, *N.*, decision, judgment
circumveniō (circum + veniō), surround
dīvidō, -ere, -vīsī, -vīsus, divide
egeō, -ēre, -uī, --, be in need of (+ *gen.*)
exīstimō (1), think, estimate, judge, deem
factiō, -ōnis, *F.*, faction, (political) party
nātiō, -ōnis, *F.*, nation

pāgus, -ī, *M.*, district
potēns, potentis, powerful
prīnceps, prīncipis, *M.*, leader, chief
prōpōnō (prō + pōnō), set forth, report
ratiō, -ōnis, *F.*, plan, reason, rationale
sēsē, = sē
singulī, -ae, -a, single, one by one
summa, -ae, *F.*, control, main point

[1] **hunc locum:** i.e., in his narrative. Caesar has been writing about his conquests in Gaul and Germany and now pauses to speak about the culture of these countries.
[2] **quō differant:** indirect question dependent on **prōpōnere; quō = quō modō**
[3] **eōrum:** refers to the Gauls
[4] **redeat:** subjunctive in a relative clause of characteristic; translate 'is referred'
[5] **in summā:** 'generally'

Caesar, *Gallic War* VI.12

Cum Caesar in Galliam vēnit, alterīus factiōnis prīncipēs erant Aeduī,[6] alterīus Sēquanī.[6] Hī cum per sē minus valērent, quod summa auctōritās antīquitus erat in Aeduīs[6] magnaeque eōrum erant clientēlae, Germānōs atque Ariovistum[7] sibi adiūnxerant eōsque ad sē magnīs iactūrīs pollicitātiōnibusque perdūxerant. Proeliīs vērō complūribus factīs secundīs atque omnī nōbilitāte Aeduōrum[6] interfectā, tantum[8] potentiā antecesserant ut magnam partem clientium ab Aeduīs[6] ad sē trādūcerent obsidēsque ab hīs prīncipum fīliōs acciperent, et pūblicē iūrāre cōgerent nihil sē contrā Sēquanōs[6] cōnsiliī[9] initūrōs, et partem fīnitimī agrī per vim occupātam possidērent Galliaeque tōtīus prīncipātum obtinērent. Quā necessitāte adductus Dīviciācus[10] auxiliī petendī causā Rōmam ad senātum profectus īnfectā rē redierat. Adventū Caesaris factā commūtātiōne rērum, obsidibus Aeduīs[6] redditīs, veteribus clientēlīs restitūtīs, novīs per Caesarem comparātīs, quod iī quī sē ad eōrum amīcitiam aggregāverant

accipiō (ad + capiō), take over, receive
addūcō (ad + dūcō), lead to, influence
adiungō (ad + iungō), join to, attach
adventus, -ūs, *M.*, arrival
aggregō (1), add, adhere; join
antecēdō (ante + cēdō), go before, excel
antīquitus (*adv.*), in ancient times, long ago
cliēns, clientis, *M.*, dependent
clientēla, -ae, *F.*, dependent, dependency
cōgō, -ere, coēgī, coāctus, compel
commūtātiō, -ōnis, *F.*, change
comparō (1), acquire
complūrēs, -a (-ia), several
dīgnitās, -tātis, *F.*, dignity
factiō, -ōnis, *F.*, faction, (political) party
fīnitimus, -a, -um, nearby, neighboring
grātia, -ae, *F.*, grace, favor
iactūra, -ae, *F.*, loss; expense, cost
ineō (in + eō), go into, begin
īnfectus, -a, -um (in + faciō), not done
iūrō (1), swear
necessitās, -tātis, *F.*, need, necessity

nōbilitās, -tātis, *F.*, nobility
obses, obsidis, *M. + F.*, hostage
obtineō (ob + teneō), obtain
occupō (1), occupy
perdūcō (per + dūcō), lead to, win over, persuade
pollicitātiō, -ōnis, *F.*, promise
possideō, -ēre, -sēdī, -sessus, seize, possess
potentia, -ae, *F.*, power
prīnceps, prīncipis, *M.*, leader, chief
prīncipātus, -ūs, *M.*, leadership
proelium, -ī, *N.*, battle
pūblicē (*adv.*), in public
reddō, -ere, reddidī, redditus, return
restituō, -ere, restituī, restitūtus, set up again, restore
secundus, -a, -um, second; favorable
senātus, -ūs, *M.*, senate
trādūcō (trāns + dūcō), lead over, win over
valeō, -ēre, -uī, valitus, be well, be strong, be influential

[6] Aeduī, Sēquanī: Gallic tribes
[7] Ariovistus: a German king
[8] tantum: *here*, as adverb, 'so much, to such a degree'
[9] cōnsiliī: the partitive genitive is dependent on nihil
[10] Dīviciācus: a chief of the Aedui who was a friend of Caesar

meliōre condiciōne atque aequiōre imperiō sē ūtī vidēbant, reliquīs rēbus
eōrum grātiā dīgnitāteque amplificātā, Sēquanī⁶ prīncipātum dīmīserant. In
eōrum locum Rēmī¹¹ successerant; quōs¹² quod adaequāre apud Caesarem¹³
grātiā intellegēbātur, iī quī propter veterēs inimīcitiās nūllō modō cum Aeduīs⁶
coniungī poterant sē Rēmīs¹¹ in clientēlam dīcābant.¹⁴ Hōs illī dīligenter
tuēbantur; ita et novam et repente collēctam auctōritātem tenēbant. Eō tamen
statū rēs erat, ut longē prīncipēs Aeduī⁶ habērentur, secundum locum dīgnitātis
Rēmī¹¹ obtinērent.

adaequō (l), be equal (to)
aequuus, -a, -um, equal; level; equitable, just
amplificō (l), make bigger, amplify
clientēla, -ae, F., dependent, dependency
colligō (com- + legō), gather, collect
condiciō, -ōnis, F., condition, terms
coniungō (com- + iungō), join, join together
dīcō (l), declare, proclaim
dīgnitās, -tātis, F., dignity
dīligenter (adv.), diligently
dīmittō (dis- + mittō), dismiss, give up

grātia, -ae, F., grace, favor
obtineō (ob + teneō), obtain
prīnceps, prīncipis, M., leader, chief
prīncipātus, -ūs, M., leadership
repente (adv.), suddenly
secundus, -a, -um, second; favorable
status, -ūs, M., state, condition, situation
succēdō (sub + cēdō), go beneath, approach,
    advance
tueor, -ērī, tūtus sum, watch, protect

¹¹ Rēmī: a Gallic tribe
¹² quōs: subject accusative of the infinitive adaequāre
¹³ apud Caesarem: 'in Caesar's eyes'
¹⁴ Sē...in clientēlam dīcābant: i.e., 'they attached themselves (to)'

# UNIT EIGHTEEN

### A. Subjunctive by Attraction
We have seen earlier (Unit Seven, section J) that relative clauses in indirect statements usually have their verbs in the subjunctive. This is also frequently the case with relative and other subordinate clauses within clauses whose verbs are in the subjunctive, provided that the subordinate clause is an integral part of the idea of the main clause. The verbs in such subordinate clauses are said to be *attracted* into the subjunctive by the sheer force of the verb that governs the larger construction.

> Rōmam profectus est ut illam urbem quō amīcī **issent** perīculō servāret.
>
> He set out for Rome in order that he might save from danger that city where his friends *had gone*.

### B. *futūrum esse ut; fore ut*
Although Latin has a future passive infinitive, it is not commonly found and consequently its form and use have been omitted from this book. When a future passive idea had to be expressed in indirect statement, a periphrasis was used as follows:

> He knows *that* the citizens *will be conquered.*
> He knows *that it will be* (*with the result*) *that* the citizens *be conquered.*
>
> Scit **futūrum esse ut** cīvēs **superentur.**

The futurity is expressed in **futūrum esse**; the verbal idea in the English indirect statement is expressed in an **ut** clause of result (**ut...superentur**).

**Fore** is an alternate way of expressing **futūrum esse**.

> Sentit **fore** ut ipse ā cīvibus laudētur.
>
> He feels *that it will be* that he (himself) be praised by the citizens; he feels that he (himself) will be praised by the citizens.

> Dīxit **fore** ut librī ā poētīs scrīberentur.
>
> He said *that it would be* that books be written by the poets; he said that books would be written by the poets.

This construction is also used to stand for an *active* idea in future time when the verb in question has no fourth principal part and therefore can have no future active infinitive.

Putat **fore ut** ille vir carmen scrībere **possit**.

He thinks *that it will be that* that man *be able* to write a poem; he thinks *that* that man *will be able* to write a poem.

**Possum, posse, potuī** has no fourth principal part and so no future active infinitive; the periphrasis is essential in this case to express the future idea.

### C. The Historical Infinitive

Occasionally an infinitive is used in narrative passages instead of a finite verb where the English demands a finite verb. Such infinitives are called *historical* infinitives and emphasize the pure verbal action rather than the agents of that action.

In viīs urbis heri **currere, clāmāre, fortiter pūgnāre.**

In the streets of the city yesterday (there were) *running, shouting, fighting* bravely; in the streets of the city yesterday (men/they) were *running, shouting, fighting* bravely.

The historical infinitive, in which one can most clearly see the function of the infinitive as a pure verbal noun, is one of the earliest uses of the infinitive.

Yesterday in the streets of the city *running* (occurred), *shouting* (occurred), brave *fighting* (occurred).

The subject of an historical infinitive is in the *nominative* case.

**Homō** ācriter pūgnāre.    *The man* fought fiercely.

### D. Shortened or Syncopated Forms of the Perfect Active System of Verbs

Forms of the perfect tenses which have -**vi**- or -**ve**- in them are sometimes shortened or syncopated by dropping the -**vi**- or -**ve**-. Observe:

| | | |
|---|---|---|
| amāstī | FOR | amāvistī |
| amārunt | | amāvērunt |
| amārim | | amāverim |
| audīsse | | audīvisse |
| audīssem | | audīvissem |
| dēlērunt | | dēlēvērunt |
| dēlēssem | | dēlēvissem |
| laudāssēmus | | laudāvissēmus |
| amāstis | | amāvistis |

### E. -ēre for -ērunt in the Third Person Plural, Perfect Active Indicative

The ending -ēre is sometimes used in poetry and high style prose as an alternate for -ērunt:

| | | |
|---|---|---|
| amāvēre | FOR | amāvērunt |
| dīxēre | | dīxērunt |

### F. The Greek Accusative: Accusative of Respect or Accusative After Verbs in the Middle Voice

The ablative case is regularly used in Latin to express *respect* or *specification* (see Unit Eight, section D). Occasionally in poetry and in late Latin the accusative is found with this function. This is really a Greek construction which has been borrowed by the Latin.

**Ferrum** cingitur.　He is girded *with respect to a sword*; he girds on a sword.

The Greek verb has three voices: active, passive, and middle. The middle voice often has the same forms as the passive, but it is used in a reflexive sense; that is, the subject at the same time performs the action and experiences its effect(s). In the example above, **cingitur** may be explained as the equivalent of a Greek middle, meaning literally 'he girds (a sword) on himself'. If we interpret **cingitur** in this way, then **ferrum** may be explained alternatively as the *object* of the middle verb **cingitur**. Whichever way we choose to interpret the grammar, the construction involved is a Greek one.

The accusative of respect is frequently used to express the *part affected*:

**Caput** vulnerātus est.　He was wounded *with respect to his head*; he was wounded *in the head*.

**Ōs** pallōre suffūsa est.　She was suffused *with respect to her face* with pallor; she was suffused with pallor *in her face*.

### G. Adverbial Accusative

Closely allied to the accusative of respect is the so-called *adverbial accusative*. What is in fact an accusative of respect functions adverbially:

**Maximam partem** ille vir sapientissimus est.　*With respect to the greatest part*, that man is very wise; *for the most part* that man is very wise.

**Id** temporis magnus numerus lēgātōrum ad urbem vēnit.　*With respect to that* of time, a great number of legates came to the city; *at that* time a great number of legates came to the city.

**Multum** labōrat ut ā cīvibus laudētur.    He works *with respect to much* in order to be praised by the citizens; he works *a lot* in order to be praised by the citizens.

## H. Genitive with Expressions of Remembering and Forgetting

The genitive is frequently used with verbs and expressions of remembering and forgetting.

**Mātris** et **patris** bene meminī.    I remember *my mother* and *father* well.
**Dolōris** nūper oblītus eram.    I had recently forgotten *my grief.*
**Virtūtis** eōrum nōn oblīvīscor.    I do not forget their *courage.*

Note that the accusative is also found with verbs and expressions of remembering and forgetting.

## I. Genitive of Indefinite Value

A few neuter adjectives and some nouns implying utter worthlessness, such as **as, assis**, M., 'as' (a small denomination of money), **floccus, -ī**, M., 'a lock of wool', and **nihilum, -ī**, N., 'nothing', are sometimes used in the genitive case to express the value of a person, thing, or situation when that value is not specifically determined or is indefinite. This use of the genitive is generally found with verbs meaning 'consider', 'reckon', and 'value'.

**Magnī** mē hàbet.    He considers me *of great (value).*
**Parvī** suam cīvitātem facit.    He reckons (makes) his state *of little (value).*
Familiam suam **floccī** dūcit.    He considers his family *of a lock of wool*; he doesn't care *at all* for his family; he doesn't give *a damn* for his family.

## J. Ablative of Price

The instrumental ablative (ablative of means) is used with some expressions to express the price of something.

Vīllam suam **magnō (pretiō)** vendidit.    He sold his country house *by means of a great price*; he sold his country house *at a great price.*

Nēmō est quī **pāce** bellum mūtet.    There is no one who would (ex)change war *by means of peace*; there is no one who would exchange war *for peace.*

## K. *quod*, 'the fact that'

A substantive clause introduced by **quod**, 'the fact that', and with its verb in the indicative is sometimes used as the subject or object of another verb, or in apposition to the subject of that other verb.

**Quod** ille coniugem tantum amat mē movet.

*The fact that* he loves (his) wife so much moves me. (subject of main verb)

Alterum est perīculum, **quod** iste plūs imperiī vult.

The other danger is *the fact that* that man wants more power. (in apposition to subject of main verb)

Neglēxērunt **quod** ego cīvitātī multōs annōs prōsum.

They have neglected *the fact that* I have been useful to the state for many years. (object of main verb)

## UNIT EIGHTEEN — VOCABULARY

| | |
|---|---|
| **aestimō** (1) | estimate, reckon |
| **as, assis, -ium,** M. | as (a small denomination of money) |
| **cingō, -ere, cīnxī, cīnctus** | surround, gird |
| **emō, -ere, ēmī, ēmptus** | buy |
| **honor, honōris,** M. | honor, distinction, office |
| **meminī, meminisse** (defective verb) | remember |
| **nihilum, -ī,** N. | nothing |
| **numerus, -ī,** M. | number |
| **oblīvīscor, oblīvīscī, oblītus sum** | forget |
| **pretium, -ī,** N. | price; value |
| **pūgna, -ae,** F. | battle, fight |
| **quod sī** | but if |
| **vendō, -ere, vendidī, venditus** | sell |
| **vulnerō** (1) | wound |

## UNIT EIGHTEEN — NOTES ON VOCABULARY

**Cingō, cingere, cīnxī, cīnctus,** 'surround, gird', lengthens the -i- in the perfect active stem since it is followed by -nx- and in the perfect passive stem since it is followed by -nct-.

In the perfect forms of **emō, emere, ēmī, ēmptus,** 'buy', the e- is long. **Ēmptor,** 'buyer', is a well-known word because of the famous expression, **Caveat ēmptor,** 'Let the buyer beware' (**caveō, cavēre, cāvī, cautus,** 'be on guard, take care, beware').

**Meminī,** 'remember', is a defective verb like **ōdī**; it is found only in the perfect tenses and the perfect tense is translated as present, the pluperfect as past, and the future perfect as future. Often this verb governs the genitive: **Patriae meministī?** 'Do you remember your native land?'

**Numerus, numerī,** M., is not only 'number' but can also mean 'a group': **Iste in numerō nostrō nōn est,** 'That (awful) man is not in our group (crowd)'.

**Oblīviscor, oblīviscī, oblītus sum,** 'forget', often governs the genitive case: **In mediō bellō metūs oblītus est,** 'In the midst of the war he forgot his fear'.

**Pūgna, pūgnae,** F., 'battle, fight', is related to **pūgnō**; they both have the same root.

**Quod sī** means 'but if'. Remember that **quod** has several different meanings: 'because', 'which' (the neuter relative pronoun), 'which?, what?' (interrogative adjective), and 'the fact that'.

**Vendō, vendere, vendidī, venditus,** is a contraction of **vēnum dō**, 'give a sale', and so it means 'sell'.

**Vulnerō,** a first conjugation verb, 'wound' is a denominative verb from **vulnus, vulneris,** N., 'wound'.

## COMPOUND WORDS

In addition to using prefixes and suffixes to compound words, Latin may combine a noun stem with a verb or verb stem, an adverb with a verb, or an adjective with a noun. Other combinations also exist.

> **manumittō, -ere, -mīsī, -missus,** 'set at liberty, free a slave'
> **armiger, -a, -um,** 'bearing weapons, armed, warlike'
>    (used substantively, **armiger, -ī,** M., 'armor-bearer, shield-bearer')
> **benedīcō, -ere, -dīxī, -dictus,** 'commend, praise'
> **caelicola, -ae,** M. (**caelum + colō, ere, coluī, cultus,** 'dwell'), 'god'
> **magnanimus, -a, -um** 'great-souled, magnanimous'
> **avipēs, -pedis** (**avis, avis,** F., 'bird'), 'bird-footed, swift-footed'

Some of the principles of Latin word formation are illustrated in the accompanying diagram of the verb **amō**.

## Latin Word Formation

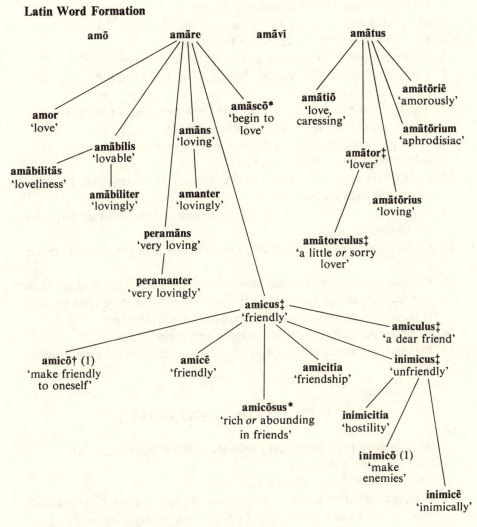

amō amāre amāvi amātus

amor 'love'

amābilitās 'loveliness'

amābilis 'lovable'

amābiliter 'lovingly'

amāns 'loving'

amanter 'lovingly'

peramāns 'very loving'

peramanter 'very lovingly'

amāscō* 'begin to love'

amātiō 'love, caressing'

amātōriē 'amorously'

amātōrium 'aphrodisiac'

amātor‡ 'lover'

amātōrius 'loving'

amātorculus‡ 'a little *or* sorry lover'

amicus‡ 'friendly'

amiculus‡ 'a dear friend'

amicō† (1) 'make friendly to oneself'

amicē 'friendly'

amicitia 'friendship'

inimicus‡ 'unfriendly'

amicōsus* 'rich *or* abounding in friends'

inimicitia 'hostility'

inimicō (1) 'make enemies'

inimicē 'inimically'

\* Word found only in an old grammarian.
† Word found once.
‡ Feminine forms are also possible, with the addition of feminine suffixes (-a, -trīx).

# UNIT EIGHTEEN — DRILL

1. Multī hominēs familiam parvī habuēre.
2. Cottīdiē multum studēmus ut multa discāmus.
3. Dīxit futūrum esse ut dux ā mīlitibus nōn metuerētur.
4. Populus tōtus spērat fore ut hostēs vincantur.
5. Memorēs perīculī magnā cum cūrā in nemus ingressī sunt.
6. Remānsit Aenēās clārāque in lūce refulsit ('gleamed') ōs umerōsque ('shoulders') deō similis.
7. Signum Iūnō mōnstrārat; sīc nam fore bellō ēgregiam et facilem vīctū per aetātēs gentem. [**ēgregius, -a, -um,** 'outstanding']
8. Quod populus tōtus eum timet ducī saevō magnopere placet.
9. Ōdit quod populus tōtus eum timet.
10. Cum vīllam amīcī relinquere properārent, statuās tamen plūrimā pecūniā ēmptās ('bought') animadvertēre.
11. Cum multum laudāssent fortiōra facta ducis, omnēs dīxērunt eum nōn diū vīctūrum.
12. Cēlāta corpus umbrīs, fēmina saeva cui nōn erat fidēs per ardēns oppidum errāvit.
13. Postquam in tēctum ingressī sunt, aliī rēgem quaerere; aliī aliōs vīsōs interficere; quaerere loca cēlāta; clausa ('closed') aperīre; strepitū ('noise') et tumultū ('confusion') omnia miscēre dum rēx invenīrētur.
14. Nēmō est cui quotquot ('however much') sit pecūniae placeat.
15. Relinquāmus omnēs terram quam incolāmus ut lībertātem vītamque novam petāmus.

# UNIT EIGHTEEN — EXERCISES

I.

1. Ille amīcitiam parvī habet, quī pecūniam amīcīs semper praepōnat.
2. Illud cōnsilium bonī faciō.
3. Quīnque librōs duōbus ferrīs ēmī.
4. Postquam domum multā cum pecūniā rediēre, meministīne quantum istae ā cīvibus suīs laudātae sint? Pecūniane eīs tantī (pretiī) erat?
5. Fāma Caesaris erat plūris cīvibus Rōmānīs quam aliōrum ducum. Vīrium ac virtūtis eius numquam oblītī sunt. Eārum etiam nunc meminērunt.
6. Cum vidērem fore ut cum nūntiō colloquī nōn possem, cōnstituī mē quam celerrimē domum recipere ubi cognōscerem quid in campō nūper accīdisset.
7. Metū mortis neglēctō, cōpiae perīcula pūgnae nihilī aestimārunt.
8. Ille miser virtūtem honōremque pecūniā vendidit. Cīvēs eum nunc parvī dūcunt. Quod iste sē ita gessit, hominēs mōrum bonōrum in omnī orbe terrārum taedet.

9. Quis fāmam dīvitiīs mūtārit? Nēmō est quī crēdat futūrum esse ut tālis esse miser umquam dēsinat.
10. Putant fore ut nēmō ē cīvibus metuat nē plūs imperiī capere velit.
11. Sī carmina illīus poētae audīsset, ea magnī habuisset.
12. Pollicitus est sē Rōmam properātūrum esse; aliōs illūc iam properāsse.
13.                Carmina Paulus emit, recitat sua carmina Paulus.
                   Nam quod emās possīs iūre vocāre tuum.
                                                    (Martial 2.20)
    [**Paulus, -ī**, M., proper name; **recitō** (1), 'recite']
14. Quis autem eum magnī dūcat quem multum metuat vel ā quō sē metuī putet?
15. Ab aliō exspectēs alterī quod fēceris.
16. Mors tam mihi grāta est ut, quō propius ad eam accēdam, quasi terram vidēre videar post longum in nāvī iter.
17. Quod sī quem socium caput vulnerātum in urbe vīdistī, mōnstrā eum mihi sine morā! [**caput, capitis**, N., 'head']
18. Mūtā iam istam mentem, mihi crēde, oblīvīscere timōris atque dubiī!
19.                Vīvāmus, mea Lesbia, atque amēmus,
                   rūmōrēsque senum sevēriōrum
                   omnēs ūnius aestimēmus assis.
                                                    (Catullus 5.1–3)
    [**sevērus, -a, -um**, 'stern, severe']
20. Istōs hominēs, ferrā cīnctōs, populus maximē timet. Nam imperātor omnēs rēs horridās per eōs agere, in amīcīs habēre, eōs maximī aestimat.

## II.

1. Although the man was wounded in the foot, he forgot his pain and, for the most part, fought courageously.
2. He said that he would not be able to sell his sword for much money; in times of peace, others don't value such weapons highly.
3. The fact that he bought his own safety at the price of the freedom of his people disgusts me.
4. I wanted to gird myself with a sword so that I could drive back the soldiers who were rushing into the city.

# UNIT EIGHTEEN — CONNECTED READINGS

Caesar, *Gallic War* VI.14 (For an adaptation of the content of *Gallic War* VI.13, which provides the link between the connected reading in Unit Seventeen and that which follows, see the exercises of Unit Thirteen.)

Druidēs[1] ā bellō abesse cōnsuērunt neque tribūta ūnā cum reliquīs pendunt. Tantīs excitātī praemiīs et suā sponte multī in disciplīnam conveniunt et ā parentibus propinquīsque mittuntur. Magnum ibi numerum versuum ēdiscere dīcuntur. Itaque annōs nōnnūllī XX in disciplīnā permanent. Neque fās esse exīstimant ea litterīs mandāre, cum in reliquīs ferē rēbus, pūblicīs prīvātīsque ratiōnibus, Graecīs litterīs ūtantur. Id mihi duābus dē causīs īnstituisse videntur, quod neque in vulgus disciplīnam efferrī velint, neque eōs quī discunt litterīs cōnfīsōs minus memoriae studēre[2] — quod ferē plērīsque accidit, ut praesidiō litterārum dīligentiam in perdiscendō ac memoriam remittant. In prīmīs hoc volunt persuādēre, nōn interīre animās,[3] sed ab aliīs post mortem trānsīre ad aliōs; atque hōc maximē ad virtūtem excitārī[4] putant, metū mortis neglēctō. Multa praetereā dē sīderibus atque eōrum mōtū, dē mundī ac terrārum magnitūdine, dē rērum nātūrā, dē deōrum immortālium vī ac potestāte disputant et iuventūtī trādunt.

cōnfīdō, -ere, -fīsus sum, trust fully (+ *dat.*)
cōnsuēscō, -ere, -suēvī, -suētus, be accustomed
conveniō (com- + veniō), gather, come together
disciplīna, -ae, *F.*, training
disputō (l), dispute
ēdiscō (ē + discō), learn thoroughly, learn by heart
excitō (l), arouse, excite
exīstimō (l), think, judge, deem
fās, *N.* (*indeclinable*), right, divine right
ferē (*adv.*), almost
intereō (inter + eō), die
iuventūs, -tūtis, *F.*, young manhood, youth
magnitūdō, -tūdinis, *F.*, size, magnitude
mandō (l), entrust
mundus, -ī, *M.*, world
nōnnūllus, -a, -um, not none, *i.e.*, some
pendō, -ere, pependī, pēnsus, weigh out, pay
perdiscō (per + discō), learn thoroughly

permaneō (per + maneō), stay through, continue, persist
plērusque, plēraque, plērumque, most (of), the larger part (of)
potestās, -tātis, *F.*, power
praesidium, -ī, *N.*, help, aid
praetereā (*adv.*), besides
prīmus, -a, -um, first
in prīmīs, especially, first of all
prīvātus, -a, -um, private
propinquus, -a, -um, near, close by
propinquus, -ī, *M.*, relative
ratiō, -ōnis, *F.*, reason, plan; account
remittō (re- + mittō), send back; relax, weaken
sponte (*abl. F.*), of one's own will, voluntarily
trānseō (trāns + eō), cross over
tribūtum, -ī, *N.*, tribute, tax
versus, -ūs, *M.*, a line of poetry, verse
vulgus, -ī, *N.*, common people, crowd

---

[1] **Druidēs, -um, M.**: the Druids, the priests and wise men of Gaul
[2] **studēre**: *here*, 'pay attention to'
[3] **nōn interīre animās, sed...ad aliōs...**: The entire clause is in apposition to **hoc**.
[4] **excitārī**: Supply **hominēs** as the subject.

Caesar, *Gallic War* VI.15

Alterum genus [5] est equitum. Hī, cum est ūsus atque aliquod bellum incidit
(quod ferē ante Caesaris adventum quotannīs accidere solēbat, utī aut ipsī
iniūriās īnferrent aut illātās prōpulsārent), omnēs in bellō versantur, atque
eōrum ut quisque est genere cōpiīsque amplissimus, ita [6] plūrimōs circum sē
ambactōs clientēsque habet. Hanc ūnam grātiam potentiamque nōvērunt.

Caesar, *Gallic War* VI.16

Nātiō est omnis Gallōrum admodum dēdita religiōnibus, atque ob eam causam
quī sunt affectī graviōribus morbīs quīque in proeliīs perīculīsque versantur
aut prō victimīs hominēs immolant aut sē immolātūrōs vovent, administrīsque
ad [7] ea sacrificia druidibus ūtuntur, quod, prō vītā hominis nisī hominis vīta
reddātur, [8] nōn posse deōrum immortālium nūmen plācārī arbitrantur; pūblicēque
eiusdem generis habent īnstitūta sacrificia. Aliī immānī magnitūdine simulācra
habent, quōrum contexta vīminibus membra vīvīs hominibus complent;
quibus succēnsīs circumventī flammā exanimantur hominēs. Supplicia eōrum
quī in fūrtō aut in latrōciniō aut in aliquā noxā sint comprehēnsī grātiōra
dīs immortālibus esse arbitrantur; sed, cum eius generis cōpia dēficit, etiam ad
innocentium supplicia dēscendunt.

administer, administrī, *M.*, attendant
admodum (*adv.*), in a high degree, very much
adventus, -ūs, *M.*, arrival
afficiō (ad + faciō), do to, affect
ambactus, -ī, *M.*, dependent, vassal
amplus, -a, -um, great, ample
circumveniō (circum + veniō), surround
cliēns, clientis, *M.*, dependent
compleō, -ēre, -ēvī, -ētus, fill completely
comprehendō, -ere, -prehendī, -prehēnsus, seize, catch, arrest
contexō, -ere, -texuī, -textus, weave together; plait
dēdō, -ere, dēdidī, dēditus, give up, surrender
dēficiō (dē + faciō), fail, give out
dēscendō, -ere, -scendī, -scēnsus, go down, descend; resort
eques, equitis, *M.*, horseman, knight
exanimō (1), exhaust; take breath from, kill
ferē (*adv.*), almost
fūrtum, -ī, *N.*, theft
grātia, -ae, *F.*, grace, favor
immānis, -e, great, huge, large
immolō (1), sacrifice, immolate
incidō (in + cadō), fall upon; happen
iniūria, -ae, *F.*, injury, wrong; outrage
innocēns, innocentis, innocent

latrōcinium, -ī, *N.*, robbery
magnitūdō, -tūdinis, *F.*, size, magnitude
membrum, -ī, *N.*, limb
morbus, -ī, *M.*, disease
nātiō, -ōnis, *F.*, nation
plācō (1), placate, appease
potentia, -ae, *F.*, power, influence
proelium, -ī, *N.*, battle
prōpulsō (1), drive off
pūblicē (*adv.*), in public
quotannīs (*adv.*), yearly
reddō, -ere, reddidī, redditus, return, give back, give in return
religiō, -ōnis, *F.*, *here*, religion
sacrificium, -ī, *N.*, sacrifice
simulācrum, -ī, *N.*, image, statue
succendō, -ere, -cendī, -cēnsus, ignite from below, burn
supplicium, -ī, *N.*, punishment
utī, = ut
versō (1), keep turning; *in passive*, be engaged, be busy
victima, -ae, *F.*, victim, sacrificial animal
vīmen, -inis, *N.*, pliant twig
vīvus, -a, -um, living, alive
voveō, -ēre, vōvī, vōtus, vow

[5] **alterum genus:** The first class of people mentioned in Gaul was the Druids; now Caesar
turns his attention to the knights. See sentence 51 in Unit Thirteen.

[6] **ut...ita:** used correlatively (e.g., 'As' Maine goes, 'so' goes the nation.)

[7] **ad:** *here*, 'for'

[8] **reddātur:** present subjunctive representing the indicative in a present general condition
in indirect statement. See *Appendix*, pp. 397–399.

Caesar, *Gallic War* VI.17

Deōrum maximē Mercurium colunt; huius sunt plūrima simulācra; hunc omnium inventōrem artium ferunt,[9] hunc viārum atque itinerum ducem, hunc ad [10] quaestūs pecūniae mercātūrāsque habēre vim maximam arbitrantur. Post hunc Apollinem et Mārtem et Iovem et Minervam. Dē hīs eandem ferē quam reliquae gentēs habent opīniōnem: Apollinem morbōs dēpellere, Minervam operum atque artificiōrum initia trādere, Iovem imperium caelestium tenēre, Mārtem bella regere. Huic, cum proeliō dīmicāre cōnstituērunt, ea quae bellō cēperint plērumque dēvovent; cum superāvērunt, animālia capta immolant reliquāsque rēs in ūnum locum cōnferunt. Multīs in cīvitātibus hārum rērum exstrūctōs tumulōs locīs cōnsecrātīs cōnspicārī licet; neque saepe accidit ut neglēctā quispiam religiōńe aut capta apud sē occultāre aut posita tollere audēret, gravissimumque eī reī supplicium cum cruciātū cōnstitūtum est.

Caesar, *Gallic War* VI.18

Gallī sē omnēs ab Dīte [11] patre prōgnātōs praedicant idque ab druidibus prōditum dīcunt. Ob eam causam spatia omnis temporis nōn numerō diērum, sed noctium fīniunt; diēs nātālēs et mēnsium et annōrum initia sīc observant ut noctem diēs subsequātur. In reliquīs vītae īnstitūtīs hōc ferē ab reliquīs differunt, quod suōs līberōs, nisī cum adolēvērunt ut mūnus mīlitiae sustinēre possint, palam ad sē adīre nōn patiuntur, fīliumque puerīlī aetāte in pūblicō in cōnspectū patris assistere turpe dūcunt.

**adeō** (ad + eō), approach
**adolēscō, -ere, adolēvī, adultus,** grow up
**artificium, -ī,** *N.,* handicraft
**assistō, -ere, -stitī, --,** stand near
**caelestis, -e,** heavenly
**colō, -ere, -uī, cultus,** cultivate, worship
**cōnsecrō** (1), consecrate
**cōnspectus, -ūs,** *M.,* view, sight
**cōnspicor, -ārī, -ātus sum,** observe, see
**cruciātus, -ūs,** *M.,* torture
**dēpellō** (dē + pellō), drive away
**dēvoveō, -ēre, -vōvī, vōtus,** vow, dedicate
**dīmicō** (1), fight
**exstruō, -ere, -trūxī, -trūctus,** pile up
**ferē** (*adv.*), almost
**fīniō, -īre, -īvī, -ītus,** set limits to
**immolō** (1), sacrifice, immolate
**initium, -ī,** *N.,* beginning
**īnstitūtum, -ī,** *N.,* practice, custom
**inventor, -ōris,** *M.,* inventor, founder
**līberī, -ōrum,** *M. pl.,* children
**mēnsis, -is, -ium,** *F.,* month
**mercātūra, -ae,** *F.,* trade
**mīlitia, -ae,** *F.,* warfare, military service

**morbus, -ī,** *M.,* disease
**mūnus, -eris,** *N.,* gift; duty, task
**nātālis, -e,** pertaining to birth, of birth
**observō** (1), observe
**occultō** (1), hide
**palam** (*adv.*), openly
**plērumque** (*adv.*), generally, for the most part
**praedicō** (1), proclaim
**prōdō, -ere, -didī, -ditus,** give forth; hand down
**proelium, -ī,** *N.,* battle
**prōgnātus, -a, -um,** descended
**puerīlis, -e,** of a boy, boyish, childish
**quaestus, -ūs,** *M.,* profit, gain
**quispiam, quidpiam** (*indef. pron.*), anyone, anything
**simulācrum, -ī,** *N.,* image, statue
**spatium, -ī,** *N.,* space, distance, period
**subsequor** (sub + sequor), follow closely
**supplicium, -ī,** *N.,* punishment
**sustineō** (sub + teneō), sustain, endure
**tollō, -ere, sustulī, sublātus,** take away, remove
**tumulus, -ī,** *M.,* mound, tomb

[9] **ferunt:** *here,* 'they say, they call'
[10] **ad:** *here,* 'for, in regard to'
[11] **Dīs, Dītis,** M.: Dis, Pluto, Hades (god of the underworld)

Caesar, *Gallic War* VI.19

Virī, quantās pecūniās ab uxōribus dōtis nōmine accēpērunt, tantās ex suīs bonīs aestimātiōne factā cum dōtibus commūnicant. Huius omnis pecūniae coniūnctim ratiō habētur frūctūsque[12] servantur; uter eōrum vītā superāvit,[13] ad eum pars utrīusque cum frūctibus[12] superiōrum temporum pervenit. Virī in[14] uxōrēs, sīcutī in[14] līberōs, vītae necisque habent potestātem; et cum pater familiae illūstriōre locō nātus dēcessit, eius propinquī conveniunt et, dē morte sī rēs in suspīciōnem vēnit, dē uxōribus in servīlem modum[15] quaestiōnem habent et, sī compertum est,[16] ignī atque omnibus tormentīs excruciātās interficiunt. Fūnera sunt prō[17] cultū Gallōrum magnifica et sūmptuōsa; omniaque quae vīvīs cordī fuisse[18] arbitrantur in ignem īnferunt, etiam animālia, ac paulō suprā hanc memoriam[19] servī et clientēs quōs ab iīs dīlēctōs esse cōnstābat, iūstīs fūneribus cōnfectīs, ūnā cremābantur.

aestimātiō, -ōnis, *F.*, value, appraisal
cliēns, clientis, *M.*, dependent
commūnicō (1), join to an equal part, unite
comperiō, -īre, comperī, compertus, find out, discover
coniūnctim (*adv.*), jointly
cōnstat (*impersonal verb*), it is evident, it is agreed (+ *subject acc. and inf.*)
conveniō (com- + veniō), gather, come together
cor, cordis, *N.*, heart
cremō (1), burn, cremate
cultus, -ūs, *M.*, cultivation, refinement
dēcēdō (dē + cēdō), go away from, withdraw; die
dīligō, -ere, dīlēxī, dīlēctus, esteem highly, love
dōs, dōtis, *F.*, dowry
excruciō (1), torment, afflict, vex
fūnebris, -e, pertaining to a funeral (*neuter plural as noun*, funeral rites)
fūnus, -eris, *N.*, funeral
illūstris, -e, illustrious, distinguished
iūstus, -a, -um, just

līberī, -ōrum, *M. pl.*, children
magnificus, -a, -um, magnificent
nex, necis, *F.*, death
perveniō (per + veniō), arrive at, reach
potestās, -tātis, *F.*, power, influence
prō (*prep. + abl.*), in consideration of, in accordance with
propinquus, -a, -um, near, close by
propinquus, -ī, *M.*, relative
quaestiō, -ōnis, *F.*, inquiry
ratiō, -ōnis, *F.*, account
servīlis, -e, pertaining to a slave, servile
sīcutī (*adv.*), just as
sūmptuōsus, -a, -um, sumptuous
superior, superius, former, past
suprā (*prep. + acc.*), above, beyond
suspīciō, -ōnis, *F.*, suspicion
tormentum, -ī, *N.*, torment, torture, anguish, pain
uterque, utraque, utrumque, each of two, both
uxor, uxōris, *F.*, wife
vīvus, -a, -um, alive, living

---

[12] frūctūs: 'profit, interest'
[13] uter eōrum vītā superāvit: i.e., whichever one survives the other
[14] in: *here*, 'over'
[15] in servīlem modum: 'as in the case of slaves'. According to Roman custom, freeborn people could not be tortured; slaves could.
[16] sī compertum est: i.e., that the death of the father of the household was not natural
[17] prō: *here*, 'in keeping with'
[18] vīvīs cordī fuisse: double dative construction; translate 'to have been dear to the heart of the living'
[19] suprā...memoriam: 'shortly before our own time'

Caesar, *Gallic War* VI.20

Quae cīvitātēs commodius suam rem pūblicam administrāre exīstimantur
habent lēgibus sānctum,[20] sī quis quid dē rē pūblicā ā fīnitimīs rūmōre ac fāmā
accēperit, utī ad magistrātum dēferat nēve cum quō[21] aliō commūnicet, quod
saepe hominēs temerāriōs atque imperītōs falsīs rūmōribus terrērī et ad facinus
impellī et dē summīs rēbus cōnsilium capere cōgnitum est. Magistrātūs quae
vīsa sunt[22] occultant, quae esse ex ūsū[23] iūdicāvērunt multitūdinī prōdunt.
Dē rē pūblicā nisī per concilium loquī nōn concēditur.

Caesar, *Gallic War* VI.21

Germānī multum ab hāc cōnsuētūdine differunt. Nam neque druidēs habent
quī rēbus dīvīnīs praesint, neque sacrificiīs student.[24] Deōrum numerō eōs
sōlōs dūcunt quōs cernunt et quōrum apertē opibus iuvantur, Sōlem et
Vulcānum et Lūnam; reliquōs nē fāmā quidem accēpērunt.[25] Vīta omnis in
vēnātiōnibus atque in studiīs reī mīlitāris cōnsistit; ā parvīs[26] labōrī ac dūritiae
student.

administrō (1), serve, provide for; execute
cernō, -ere, crēvī, crētus, see, perceive
commodus, -a, -um, suitable
commūnicō (1), communicate
concēdō (com- + cēdō), yield, allow
concilium, -ī, N., assembly
cōnsistō, -ere, cōnstitī, --, depend upon
cōnsuētūdō, cōnsuētūdinis, F., custom
dīvīnus, -a, -um, divine
dūritia, -ae, F., harshness
exīstimō (1), estimate, judge, deem
facinus, -oris, N., crime
falsus, -a, -um, false
fīnitimus, -a, -um, neighboring, close by
impellō (in + pellō), drive on, impel
imperītus, -a, -um, inexperienced
iūdicō (1), judge

iuvō, -āre, iūvī, iūtus, help; delight
labor, -ōris, M., labor, toil, hardship
magistrātus, -ūs, M., magistracy; public
officer
mīlitāris, -e, pertaining to the military,
military
multitūdō, -tūdinis, F., crowd, multitude
nēve (*conj.*), and not, and lest
occultō (1), hide
prōdō, -ere, prōdidī, prōditus, give forth;
hand down; reveal
sacrificium, -ī, N., sacrifice
sanciō, -īre, sānxī, sānctus, guarantee,
arrange
temerārius, -a, -um, rash, reckless
utī, = ut
vēnātiō, -ōnis, F., hunting

[20] sānctum: explained by utī...commūnicet
[21] quō = aliquō
[22] vīsa sunt: *here*, 'seemed best'
[23] ex ūsū: 'of advantage'
[24] student: *here*, 'attach importance to'
[25] accēpērunt: accipiō here has the force 'hear of'
[26] ā parvīs: 'from childhood'

Caesar, *Gallic War* VI.22

Agricultūrae nōn student, maiorque pars eōrum vīctūs in lacte, cāseō, carne cōnsistit. Neque quisquam agrī modum certum aut fīnēs habet propriōs; sed magistrātūs ac prīncipēs in annōs singulōs[27] gentibus cognātiōnibusque hominum,[28] quīque ūnā coiērunt, quantum et quō locō vīsum est[29] agrī attribuunt atque annō post aliō trānsīre cōgunt. Eius reī multās afferunt causās: nē assiduā cōnsuētūdine captī studium bellī gerendī agricultūrā commūtent; nē lātōs fīnēs parāre studeant potentiōrēs atque humiliōrēs possessiōnibus expellant; nē accūrātius quam ad frīgora atque aestūs vītandōs aedificent; nē qua oriātur pecūniae cupiditās, quā ex rē factiōnēs dissēnsiōnēsque nāscuntur; ut animī aequitāte plēbem contineant, cum suās quisque opēs cum potentissimīs aequārī videat.

**accūrātē** (*adv.*), carefully
**aedificō** (1), build
**aequitās, -tātis,** *F.*, fairness, equality
**aequō** (1), make equal
**aestus, -ūs,** *M.*, heat
**agricultūra, -ae,** *F.*, agriculture
**aliō** (*adv.*), to another place
**assiduus, -a, -um,** continual
**attribuō, -ere, -uī, -ūtus,** allot
**carō, carnis,** *F.*, meat
**cāseus, -ī,** *M.*, cheese
**coeō (com- + eō),** go together, unite
**cognātiō, -ōnis,** *F.*, blood relationship, association, affinity
**cōgō, -ere, coēgī, coāctus,** bring together; compel
**commūtō (com- + mūtō),** cf. mūtō (1)
**cōnsistō, -ere, cōnstitī, --,** depend upon
**cōnsuētūdō, -tūdinis,** *F.*, custom, habit

**contineō (com- + teneō),** keep together, hem in; restrain
**cupiditās, -tātis,** *F.*, desire
**dissēnsiō, -ōnis,** *F.*, dissension
**factiō, -ōnis,** *F.*, faction, (political) party
**frīgus, -oris,** *N.*, cold
**lac, lactis,** *N.*, milk
**lātus, -a, -um,** broad, wide
**magistrātus, -ūs,** *M.*, magistracy, public officer
**possessiō, possessiōnis,** *F.*, possession
**potēns, potentis,** powerful
**prīnceps, prīncipis,** *M.*, leader, chief
**proprius, -a, -um,** special, particular, proper; one's own
**singulī, -ae, -a,** one by one, single
**trānseō (trāns + eō),** go across, cross
**vīctus, -ūs,** *M.*, food, nourishment
**vītō** (1), avoid

[27] **in annōs singulōs:** 'each year'
[28] **cognātiōnibus hominum:** 'groups of relatives'
[29] **vīsum est:** 'it seemed best'

Caesar, *Gallic War* VI.23

Cīvitātibus maxima laus est quam lātissimē circum sē vāstātīs fīnibus sōlitūdinēs habēre. Hoc proprium virtūtis exīstimant, expulsōs agrīs fīnitimōs cēdere, neque quemquam prope sē audēre cōnsistere; simul hōc sē fore tūtiōrēs arbitrantur, repentīnae incursiōnis timōre sublātō. Cum bellum cīvitās aut illātum dēfendit[30] aut īnfert, magistrātūs quī eī bellō praesint et vītae necisque habeant potestātem dēliguntur. In pāce nūllus est commūnis magistrātus, sed prīncipēs regiōnum atque pāgōrum inter suōs iūs dīcunt contrōversiāsque minuunt. Latrōcinia nūllam habent īnfāmiam quae extrā fīnēs cuiusque cīvitātis fīunt, atque ea iuventūtis exercendae ac dēsidiae minuendae causā fierī praedicant. Atque ubi quis[31] ex prīncipibus in conciliō dīxit sē ducem fore, quī sequī velint[32] profiteantur,[33] cōnsurgunt iī quī et causam et hominem probant, suumque auxilium pollicentur, atque ā multitūdine collaudantur; quī ex hīs secūtī nōn sunt in dēsertōrum ac prōditōrum numerō dūcuntur, omniumque hīs rērum posteā fidēs dērogātur. Hospitem violāre fās nōn putant; quī[34] quācumque dē causā ad eōs vēnērunt ab iniūriā prohibent sānctōsque habent, hīsque omnium domūs patent vīctusque commūnicātur.

collaudō (com- + laudō), cf. laudō
commūnicō (1), share, communicate
commūnis, -e, common
concilium, -ī, N., assembly
cōnsistō, -ere, cōnstitī, –, take a stand, halt
cōnsurgō, -ere, -surrēxī, -surrēctus, rise up together
contrōversia, -ae, F., controversy
dērogō (1), take away from
dēsertor, -ōris, M., deserter
dēsidia, -ae, F., sloth, laziness
exerceō, -ēre, -uī, -itus, train, exercise
exīstimō (1), estimate, judge, deem
extrā (prep. + acc.), outside of
fās, N. (indeclinable), right, divinely right
fīnitimus, -a, -um, neighboring, close by
incursiō, -ōnis, F., incursion, attack
īnfāmia, -ae, F., ill repute
iniūria, -ae, F., wrong, injury; injustice
iuventūs, -tūtis, F., youth, young manhood
latrōcinium, -ī, N., robbery
lātus, -a, -um, broad, wide
magistrātus, -ūs, M., public office; public officer; magistrate
minuō, -ere, minuī, minūtus, lessen, diminish

multitūdō, -tūdinis, F., crowd, multitude
nex, necis, F., death
pāgus, -ī, M., district
pateō, -ēre, -uī, –, lie open
posteā (adv.), afterwards
potestās, -tātis, F., power
praedicō (1), proclaim
prīnceps, prīncipis, M., leader, chief
probō (1), approve
prōditor, -ōris, M., traitor
profiteor, -ērī, -fessus sum, declare publicly, acknowledge
prope (prep. + acc.), near, close to
proprius, -a, -um, special, particular, one's own
quīcumque, quaecumque, quodcumque (indefinite pron.), whoever, whatever
regiō, -ōnis, F., region
repentīnus, -a, -um, sudden
sānctus, -a, -um, holy, sacred
simul (adv.), at the same time
sōlitūdō, -tūdinis, F., solitude; empty space
tollō, -ere, sustulī, sublātus, remove
vāstō (1), devastate, lay waste
vīctus, -ūs, M., food

---

[30] dēfendit: here, 'ward off'

[31] quis = aliquis

[32] velint: subjunctive by attraction

[33] profiteantur: subjunctive in an indirect command, dependent on dīxit; assume the ellipsis of et ut after fore.

[34] quī: assume the ellipsis of eōs as the antecedent of quī

Caesar, *Gallic War* VI.24

Ac fuit anteā tempus cum Germānōs Gallī virtūte superārent, ultrō bella īnferrent, propter hominum multitūdinem agrīque inopiam trāns Rhēnum[35] colōniās mitterent. Itaque ea quae fertilissima Germāniae sunt loca, circum Hercyniam silvam,[36] quam Eratosthenī[37] et quibusdam Graecīs fāmā nōtam esse videō, quam illī Orcyniam appellant, Volcae[38] Tectosagēs[39] occupāvērunt atque ibi cōnsēdērunt; quae gēns ad hoc tempus hīs sēdibus sēsē continet summamque habet iūstitiae et bellicae laudis opīniōnem. Nunc, quod in eādem inopiā, egestāte, patientiā quā ante Germānī permanent, eōdem vīctū et cultū corporis ūtuntur, Gallīs autem prōvinciārum[40] propinquitās et trānsmarīnārum rērum nōtitia multa[41] ad[42] cōpiam atque ūsūs lārgītur, paulātim assuēfactī superārī multīsque victī proeliīs nē sē quidem ipsī cum illīs virtūte comparant.

**anteā** (*adv.*), beforehand, formerly
**appellō** (l), call, name
**assuēfaciō**, -ere, -fēcī, -factus, accustom
**bellicus**, -a, -um, warlike, pertaining to war
**colōnia**, -ae, *F.*, settlement
**comparō** (l), compare
**cōnsīdō**, -ere, -sēdī, -sessus, sit, settle
**contineō** (com- + teneō), keep together, keep in, contain
**cultus**, -ūs, *M.*, cultivation
**egestās**, -tātis, *F.*, lack, poverty
**fertilis**, -e, fertile
**inopia**, -ae, *F.*, lack, need
**iūstitia**, -ae, *F.*, justice
**lārgior**, -īrī, -ītus sum, bestow generously

**multitūdō**, -tūdinis, *F.*, crowd, multitude
**nōtitia**, -ae, *F.*, knowledge
**occupō** (l), seize
**patientia**, -ae, *F.*, patience, endurance
**paulātim** (*adv.*), little by little
**permaneō** (per + maneō), cf. **maneō**
**proelium**, -ī, *N.*, battle
**propinquitās**, -tātis, *F.*, nearness, proximity
**sēdēs**, -is, *F.*, seat; settlement
**sēsē**, = **sē**
**silva**, -ae, *F.*, forest
**trānsmarīnus**, -a, -um, pertaining to across the sea; overseas
**ultrō** (*adv.*), of one's own accord
**victus**, -ūs, *M.*, living, way of life

[35] **Rhēnus, -ī, M.**: the Rhine river
[36] **Hercyniam silvam**: the Hercynian forest, a forest in southern Germany
[37] **Eratosthenēs, -is, M.**: a Greek scholar in the Hellenistic period
[38] **Volcae**: a tribe in southern Gaul
[39] **Tectosagēs, -um, M.**: a branch of the Volcae tribe in southern Gaul
[40] **prōvinciārum**: the Roman provinces which were considered civilizing factors in Gaul
[41] **multa**: object of **lārgītur**
[42] **ad**: *here*, 'for the purpose of'

# REVIEW—UNITS TWELVE TO EIGHTEEN

**Review of Syntax**

1. Nē offerāmus nōs perīculīs sine causā.
   (hortatory subjunctive; dative with compound verb)
2. Cōgitat quantum in illō sceleris fuerit.
   (indirect question)
3. Accēdente senectūte, quīdam īrātiōrēs fīunt quod multīs ante annīs plūra agere potuerint: plūs est adulēscentibus vīrium quam senibus. [**senectūs, -tūtis**, F., 'old age']
   (**quod** clause of alleged reason)
4. Nescit plēbs quō modō comitēs servet; numquam ūllī pauperī ab imperātōre parsum est.
   (indirect question; impersonal passive with an intransitive verb governing the dative)
5. Eīs diēbus nēmō erat quī dīvitiās virtūtī praeferret.
   (relative clause of characteristic; dative with compound verb)
6. Quid dē ūsū pācis cōnstituāmus? Utrum aliquid nunc cōnstituāmus an morēmur dum lēgātus adveniat?
   (deliberative subjunctives; double direct question; **dum** with subjunctive expressing anticipation)
7. Magnī est iūdicis cōnstituere quid quemque cuique praestāre oporteat. [**praestō, -āre, -stitī, -stitus**, 'excel, be superior to']
   (adverbial accusative; dative with compound verb; impersonal verb; indirect question)
8. Faciam ut intellegās quid hī dē tē sentiant.
   (substantive clause of result after **faciam ut**; indirect question)
9. Exiguum enim tempus aetātis satis longum est ad bene honestēque vīvendum.
   (**ad** + gerund expressing purpose)
10. Quō dē genere mortis difficile dictū est.
    (ablative of supine — ablative of respect)

11. Exclūsī eōs quōs tū ad mē salūtātum mīserās. [exclūdō, -ere, -clūsī, -clūsus, 'shut out'; salūtō (1), 'greet']
    (accusative of supine expressing purpose)
12. Vīvis, et vīvis nōn ad dēpōnendam sed ad cōnfirmandam audāciam. [cōn-firmō (1), 'confirm, strengthen'; dēpōnō (dē + pōnō), 'set aside']
    (ad + accusative + gerundive expressing purpose)
13. Ō deōs immortālēs! Multōs dolōrēs ipse sufferam, dum modo ā vōbīs huius horridī bellī perīculum dēpellātur. [dēpellō (dē + pellō), 'drive away, off, from']
    (accusative of exclamation; subjunctive clause of proviso)
14. Nūllum est dubium quīn nōs omnēs multa prius mala sufferāmus quam iste ex urbe dēnique pellātur.
    (negative clause of doubting with quīn; priusquam with subjunctive expressing anticipation)
15. Timēmus ut multī ē pūgnantibus superfutūrī sint. Nēmō autem dēterrērī poterit quōminus agat quid putet reī pūblicae prōfutūrum esse.
    (clause of fearing introduced by ut; clause of prevention introduced by quōminus; indirect question; dative with compound verb)
16. Rogantī melius quam imperantī pāreās.
    (dative with intransitive verb; potential subjunctive)
17. Lēgātum mittit quī petat ut vōbīscum loquī liceat.
    (relative clause of purpose; impersonal verb)
18. Tamne parvī animī videāmur omnēs quī reī pūblicae atque hīs vītae perīculīs intersumus ut nōbīscum peritūra omnia arbitrēmur? Anima enim immortālis est; numquam perībit. [intersum (inter + sum), 'be engaged in, be involved in']
    (deliberative subjunctive; dative with compound verb; clause of result)
19. Cum vīta sine amīcīs multōs metūs habeat, amīcitiās maximī aestimāre dēbēmus. Verbōrum illīus sapientis nōlī oblīvīscī: Tālis igitur inter virōs amīcitia tantās opportūnitātēs habet, quantās vix possum dīcere. [oppor-tūnitās, -tātis, F., 'opportunity']
    (cum causal clause; genitive of indefinite value; genitive with expressions of remembering or forgetting)
20. Cum illī ipsī vēnissent quōs ego ad mē id temporis ventūrōs esse praedīxeram, maximē timēbam. [praedīcō (prae + dīcō), 'foretell, predict'] (cum circumstantial clause; adverbial accusative)
21. Nōn dubitat quīn sit māter peritūra.
    (quīn in clause of negative doubting)
22. Ipse negat fore ut vīllam multā pecūniā vendere possit.
    (the periphrasis fore (futūrum) ut + subjunctive to make up for the lack of the future active infinitive in some verbs; ablative of price)

23. Quamdiū quisquam erit quī tē dēfendere audeat, vīvēs, et vīvēs ita ut nunc vīvis, multīs custōdibus circumdatus, nē commovēre tē contrā rem pūblicam possīs. [circumdō (circum + dō), 'surround'; commoveō (com- + moveō), 'move thoroughly, excite']
(relative clause of characteristic or purpose)

24. Quid enim malī vel sceleris fierī vel cōgitārī potest?

25. Hīs et tālibus pūgnīs inter nōs discessum est.
(impersonal use of the passive)

26. Beneficium dandō accēpit, quī dignō dedit. [beneficium, -ī, N., 'good deed']
(ablative of gerund)

27. Sed quam multōs fuisse putātis quī quae ego dēferrem nōn crēderent! [quam, adv., 'how' — in exclamations]
(relative clause of characteristic; subjunctive by attraction)

28. Quamvīs turpis quī monet nūllī nocet.
(dative with special intransitive verb)

29. Haec habuī dē amīcitiā quae dīcerem.
(relative clause of purpose)

30. Num quid malī aut sceleris cōgitārī potest quod nōn iste fēcerit?
(direct question with num; relative clause of characteristic)

31. Quis rēx umquam fuit, quis populus, quī nōn ūterētur signīs ā dīs datīs? neque sōlum in pāce, sed in bellō multō etiam magis, quō maius erat perīculum.
(relative clause of characteristic)

32. Fac ut veniās.
(substantive clause of result)

33. Ō tempora mala! Ō rem pūblicam perditam!
(accusatives of exclamation)

34. Illō tempore omnia in peius ruere, omnēs hominēs maiōribus peiōrēs fierī.
(historical infinitives)

35. Quid nunc rogem tē ut veniās? Nōn rogem! Sine tē igitur sim! (adverbial accusative; deliberative subjunctive; potential subjunctive; hortatory subjunctive)

36. Postquam labōrantēs mūnīvēre moenia oppidī, ūnus pedem vulnerātus est.
(accusative of respect)

37. Cum incolae cōnsulem laudāssent, nihil tamen prō eōrum salūte cōnstituere potuit.
(**cum** concessive clause)

38. Cucurrit quō celerius Caesarem vidēret; cucurrit quō Caesarem vidēret; cucurrit Caesaris videndī causā.
(relative clause of purpose; purpose clause introduced by an adverb; genitive plus gerundive followed by **causā** to express purpose)

39. Hoc amō, quod possum quā mihi placet īre viā.
    (**quod**, 'the fact that')

40. Quīn loquar haec, numquam mē potest dēterrēre.
    (negative clause of prevention introduced by **quīn**)

41. Tantum abest ab eō ut malum mors sit ut verear nē hominī sit nihil bonum aliud.
    (adverbial accusative; substantive clause of result after **tantum abest ut**; clause of result; positive clause of fearing introduced by **nē**)

42. Cum loquī incēpī, vereor nē dum dēfendam meōs, nōn parcam tuīs.
    (**cum** meaning 'whenever'; positive clause of fearing introduced by **nē**... **nōn**; subjunctive by attraction)

43. Dubitāvī, hōs hominēs multā pecūniā emerem an nōn emerem.
    (positive clause of doubting with alternative indirect question; ablative of price)

44. Maximō sum gaudiō affectus cum audīvī cōnsulem tē factum esse. [**afficiō** (**ad + faciō**), 'affect']
    (**cum** temporal clause)

45. Nōnne verētur nē rogātūrī sīmus cūr iūdex sē dāmnāverit?
    (direct question with **nōnne**; positive clause of fearing; indirect reflexive)

46. Meā rēfert ut īdem duo hominēs veniant.
    (impersonal verb)

47. Utinam ille omnīs sēcum suās cōpiās ēduxisset!
    (optative subjunctive)

48. Aeneas replies to Dido's reproaches for leaving her by expressing his concern for her and, afterwards, by stating that he is not leaving of his own accord but out of necessity. (Vergil, *Aeneid* IV.333–6)

    Ego tē, quae plūrima fandō

    ēnumerāre valēs, numquam, rēgīna, negābō
    prōmeritam,[1] nec mē meminisse pigēbit Elissae
    dum memor[2] ipse meī, dum spīritus hōs regit artūs.

    [1] supply **esse**    [2] supply **sum**

    [**artus, -ūs**, M., 'joint, limb'; **Elissa, -ae**, F., 'Dido'; **ēnumerō** (1), 'recount'; **for, fārī, fātus sum**, 'speak, tell'; **prōmereor, -ērī, -itus sum**, 'deserve, earn'; **spīritus, -ūs**, M., 'breath, soul, life'; **valeō, -ēre, valuī, valitus**, 'be able']
    (ablative of gerund; impersonal verb; genitives with verb and expression of remembering, **dum** + indicative)

49. Dum haec geruntur, nostrīs omnibus occupātīs quī erant in agrīs reliquī discessērunt. [**occupō** (1), 'occupy']
    (**dum** with present indicative to denote continued action in past time)

# UNITS 12–18: Self-Review

**I.**

Translate the following passage; the words in boldface type relate to questions in part II.

NOTE: While serving as provincial governor in Cilicia (Asia Minor), Cicero wrote this letter to Marcus Caelius Rufus, an orator and friend who was in Rome serving as an **aedile**, a public official in charge of public works and recreation. Caelius had written repeatedly to Cicero, keeping him abreast of political news from Rome and also requesting that Cicero be on the lookout for exotic animals that he could import and use for sports events. (It has been slightly adapted.)

**Putaresne** umquam fieri posse ut mihi verba omnino **deessent**? Non careo solum istā tuā[1] oratoriā,[2] sed illo etiam ingenio exiguo quo nuper ad litteras **scribendas** utebar. Cum senatus[3] **muneris**[4] mei oblitus sit, vereor ut Romam multos annos rediturus sim et — quod peius est — ne te absente in hāc terrā alienā **peream.**

Magnum desiderium[5] — mirabile **dictu** — urbis me tenet, desiderium meorum atque in primis[6] tui. Rogitant legati comitesque, quoniam provinciae me tantopere taedet, quam ob rem diutius hīc **maneam.** Tanta onera[7] in re publicā sustinere potui et solitus sum ut totum negotium[8] in hoc ultimo[9] loco viribus meis indignum omnibus arbitrandum sit.

Desine quaerere de pantheris;[10] iussu meo diligenter **agitatur** ab eis qui venari solent; sed permagna paucitas est, et eae, quae vere sunt, dicuntur queri[11] quod nihil cuiquam insidiarum in meā provinciā nisi sibi fiat. Itaque plurimae, ut quidam credunt, in Carian[12] ex hac regione[13] horridā se recipere constituerunt. Quicquid[14] erit, tibi erit, sed quot futurae sint plane[15] nescio.

Mihi mehercle[16] magnae curae est aedilitas[17] tua. Meā maxime refert ut ludos[18] quam gratissimos facias.[18] Tu velim ad me de omni rei publicae casu quam celerrime perscribas; ea enim certissima putabo quae ex te **cognoro.**

---

[1] istā tuā: **tuā** added for emphasis    [2] **ōrātōria, -ae,** F., 'oratory, oratorical skill'   [3] **senātus, -ūs,** M., 'the senate'    [4] **mūnus, mūneris,** N., 'duty, office, service'    [5] **dēsī-derium, dēsīderiī,** N., 'ardent desire, longing'    [6] **in prīmīs,** 'especially'    [7] **onus, oneris,** N., 'load, burden'    [8] **negōtium, negōtiī,** N., 'business'    [9] **ultimus, -a, -um,** 'farthest, most distant'    [10] **panthēra, -ae,** F., 'panther'    [11] **queror, querī, questus sum,** 'lament, complain'    [12] **Cārian** (acc. sing. of **Cāria, -ae,** F.), 'Caria', a province in Asia Minor    [13] **regiō, regiōnis,** F., 'district, territory'    [14] **quisquis, quidquid** or **quicquid** (indefinite pron.), 'whoever, whatever'    [15] **plānē** (adv.), 'plainly, clearly'    [16] **mehercle** (an oath), 'by Hercules!'    [17] **aedīlitās, aedīlitātis,** F., 'the office of an aedile, aedileship'    [18] **lūdus, lūdī,** M., 'game, exhibition'; **lūdōs facere,** 'to stage games'

## II.

The questions below refer to the words and phrases in boldface type in the passage you have just translated.

1. Identify the tense and mood of **putares**. How is it used here?
2. Explain the reason for the mood of **deessent**.
3. a) What part of speech is **scribendas**?
   b) What idea does the phrase **ad litteras scribendas** express?
4. What is the case and reason for the case of **muneris**?
5. What is the syntax of **peream**?
6. Identify the form and give the syntax of **dictu**.
7. Identify the mood and give the reason for the mood of **maneam**.
8. Comment on the use of the word **agitatur**.
9. **Cognoro** is a syncopated form. What would the full form be?

## III.

Translate the following sentences. The words in boldface type relate to questions on syntax and form in Part IV.

1. Num metus tibi obstitit quominus **meminisses** quid fieret?
2. Pollicemur fore ut foedus quam primum fiat.
3. Aliquis **videat** utrum consilium de civitatibus instituendis invenire possimus necne.
4. Odioso imperatum est ne **cui** armigerorum in urbe viventium parcatur.
5. His intellectis, erant tamen qui pugnare **desinerent** priusquam amicis **proderant**.
6. Ipsi non dubitemus quin domum vendendo multam pecuniam capere **possit**.
7. Non dubitavere exspectare dum dux **adveniret**. Idem vero **omnibus** praefectus erat quo manus militum **esset** tutior.
8. Cum nuntiassent quid vellent, legati tamen efficere non poterant ut omnes **sibi** parerent.
9. Quod quidam cupidi divitiarum sunt nos non **movet**; speramus autem eos divitiarum tam cupidos non fore ut honoris obliviscantur.
10. **Nihil** metuerunt ne iudices salutem **parvi** aestimaturi sint.

## IV.

The questions below refer to the words in boldface type in the sentences in part III.

1. Explain the tense and mood of **meminisses** (sentence 1).
2. Identify the mood and use of **videat** (sentence 3).

3. What does the form **cui** stand for in sentence 4?
4. What is the mood and the reason for the mood of **desinerent** (sentence 5)?
5. What is the mood and the reason for the mood of **proderant** (sentence 5)?
6. Identify the mood and give the reason for the mood of **possit** (sentence 6).
7. What is the syntax of **adveniret** (sentence 7)?
8. Give the case and the reason for the case of **omnibus** (sentence 7).
9. Identify the mood and give the reason for the mood of **esset** (sentence 7).
10. Write a brief commentary on the use of the reflexive **sibi** in sentence 8.
11. What is the subject of **movet** (sentence 9)?
12. What is the syntax of **nihil** (sentence 10)?
13. Identify the case and give the reason for the case of **parvi** (sentence 10).

## Answer Key — UNITS 12–18: Self-Review

**I.**

Would you have thought that it was ever possible that words entirely failed me? I lack not only that oratorical skill of yours, but also that small talent which I recently used (enjoyed) for writing a letter. Since the senate has forgotten my service, I fear that I will not return to Rome for many years and — what is worse — that, in your absence, I will perish in this foreign land.

A great longing for the city holds me — remarkable (wonderful, able to be wondered at) to say — a longing for my friends and family (my people) and especially for you. Legates and companions keep on asking why I remain here (any) longer, since the province bores me so greatly. I have been able to endure (support) and have been accustomed to so many responsibilities (burdens) in the state that the whole business in this most distant place must be judged by everyone (all) unworthy of my strength.

Stop asking about the panthers; by my order, there is diligent activity (there is a stirring up diligently) by those men who are accustomed to hunt; but there is a very great scarcity (fewness) [of panthers] and those which are actually here (which truly exist) are said to be complaining because (allegedly) no treachery happens to anyone in my province except (if not) to them. And so most, as certain men believe, have decided to withdraw into Caria from this horrible district. Whatever there is (will be), will be for you, but I clearly don't know how many there will be.

By Hercules, your aedileship is a great concern to me. It especially interests me that you stage as pleasing games as possible. I should wish that you write to me thoroughly about every occurrence with reference to the state as quickly as possible; indeed, I shall consider (think) those things which I know (I'll have learned) from you most reliable (most certain).

**II.**

1. Imperfect subjunctive as the main verb in the sentence (an independent usage of the subjunctive) expressing a potential idea in past time
2. Subjunctive in a substantive clause of result
3. a) Gerundive (adjective)
   b) **ad** is used with a noun and a gerundive to express purpose
4. Genitive case with an expression of forgetting
5. Present subjunctive in primary sequence in a clause expressing positive fearing
6. Ablative form of the supine of **dīcere** functioning as an ablative of respect
7. Subjunctive in an indirect question in primary sequence
8. Impersonal passive usage stressing verbal action
9. cognōverō

**III.**

1. Fear did not keep (hinder, stand in your way) you (did it) from remembering what was happening (did it)?
2. We promise that a treaty will be made as soon as possible (that it will be that a treaty be made...).
3. Let someone see whether we can find (discover) a plan about establishing states or not.
4. The hateful man has been ordered (It has been ordered to the hateful man) that no one of the arm bearers living (who live) in the city be spared (that it not be spared to anyone of the arm bearers...).
5. With these things understood (although these things had been understood), there were nevertheless those who (men of the sort who) stopped fighting before they profited (did good to) (their) friends.
6. We ourselves would (could, might) not doubt (but) that by selling (his) home he is able to take (get) much money.
7. They did not hesitate to wait
   - until the leader (guide) should (could) arrive.
   - for the leader (guide) to arrive.
   - provided that the leader (guide) arrive.

   The same one (man), truly (indeed), had been put in command of all (the men) by which (in order that) the band of soldiers might be safer (rather safe).
8. Although they had reported (announced) what they were wanting (wanted), the legates nevertheless were not able to (could not) bring it about (effect) that all (men) obey(ed) them.
9. (The fact) that certain men are desirous of wealth (riches) does not move us; we hope, moreover (however), that they (these/those men) will not be so desirous of wealth (riches) that they are forgetful of (forget) honor (distinction).

10. They have feared not at all that the judges (jurymen) will (are going to) estimate (reckon) health (safety) of small value (worth).

## IV.

1. Pluperfect subjunctive of a defective verb; thus the pluperfect = imperfect. It is in a relative clause of prevention in secondary sequence.
2. Subjunctive; independent use, either jussive, potential, or optative
3. alicui
4. Subjunctive; relative clause of characteristic (secondary sequence)
5. Indicative; to state a fact (temporal clause referring strictly to time)
6. Subjunctive in a negative clause of doubting (primary sequence)
7. Imperfect subjunctive in secondary sequence in a **dum** clause expressing anticipation (The king hasn't arrived yet; there is no certainty that he will ever arrive.) Also possible as a proviso clause
8. Dative with a compound verb
9. Subjunctive; relative clause of purpose (secondary sequence)
10. **Sibi** is dative case because the intransitive verb **pāreō** governs the dative. It is an indirect reflexive since it does not refer to the subject of the clause in which it occurs (**omnēs**), but rather to the subject of the main verb of the sentence (**lēgātī**).
11. The whole clause **quod...sunt**
12. Adverbial accusative
13. Genitive of indefinite value

# APPENDIX

This appendix will be useful as a reference for complete paradigms, explanations, and examples of syntactical structures and as a comprehensive review of the forms and syntax of Latin. In many cases, a greater number of illustrative sentences is provided in the appendix than in the actual text.

In order to enhance the value of the book as a tool for the reading of a wide variety of Latin authors, the appendix also contains some syntactical explanations which have not been included in the main body of the text.

Refer to the alphabetical index for cross-referencing between the text and the appendix.

## NOUNS

**Declension Endings**

SINGULAR

| | I | II | | III | | IV | | V |
|---|---|---|---|---|---|---|---|---|
| | F.* | M. | N. | M. & F. | N. | M. | N. | F.† |
| Nom. | -a | -us (-er, -r) | -um | —— | —— | -us | -ū | -ēs |
| Gen. | -ae | -ī | -ī | -is | -is | -ūs | -ūs | -eī |
| Dat. | -ae | -ō | -ō | -ī | -ī | -uī | -ū | -eī |
| Acc. | -am | -um | -um | -em | —— | -um | -ū | -em |
| Abl. | -ā | -ō | -ō | -e | -e (-ī) | -ū | -ū | -ē |

PLURAL

| | I | II | | III | | IV | | V |
|---|---|---|---|---|---|---|---|---|
| | F.* | M. | N. | M. & F. | N. | M. | N. | F.† |
| Nom. | -ae | -ī | -a | -ēs | -a(-ia) | -ūs | -ua | -ēs |
| Gen. | -ārum | -ōrum | -ōrum | -um(-ium) | -um(-ium) | -uum | -uum | -ērum |
| Dat. | -īs | -īs | -īs | -ibus | -ibus | -ibus | -ibus | -ēbus |
| Acc. | -ās | -ōs | -a | -ēs(-īs) | -a(-ia) | -ūs | -ua | -ēs |
| Abl. | -īs | -īs | -īs | -ibus | -ibus | -ibus | -ibus | -ēbus |

\* Nouns of the first declension are feminine, except for those that denote males, such as **nauta**, 'sailor'.

† Most nouns of the fifth declension are feminine, except for **diēs**, which is generally masculine.

Note that the *vocative* case is the same as the nominative except in nouns of
the second declension whose nominative singular ends in -**us**; their vocative
ends in -**e**. If such a noun has a stem ending in -**i** (before the -**us** ending), the
vocative form ends in a single -**ī**: **Marcus**, vocative **Marce**; **Rōmānus**, vocative
**Rōmāne**; **fīlius**, vocative **fīlī**; **gladius**, vocative **gladī**.

The *locative* case endings for the first two declensions are the same as the
genitive singular if the word is singular, or the ablative plural if the word is
plural: **Rōma**, locative **Rōmae**; **Athēnae**, locative **Athēnīs**. For nouns of the third
declension, the locative ends in -**e** or -**ī** in the singular: **Carthāgō**, locative
**Carthāgine**; **rūs**, locative **rūrī**. In the plural the ending -**ibus** is used.

## First Declension

**SINGULAR**

| Nom. | fēmina | (the/a) woman (subject) |
|------|--------|-------------------------|
| Gen. | fēminae | of the (a) woman, (the/a) woman's |
| Dat. | fēminae | to/for (the/a) woman |
| Acc. | fēminam | (the/a) woman (object) |
| Abl. | fēminā | from/with/in/by (the/a) woman |

**PLURAL**

| Nom. | fēminae | (the) women (subject) |
|------|---------|------------------------|
| Gen. | fēminārum | of (the) women, women's |
| Dat. | fēminīs | to/for (the) women |
| Acc. | fēminās | (the) women (object) |
| Abl. | fēminīs | from/with/in/by (the) women |

Masculine nouns in the first declension are declined like **fēmina**.

## Second Declension

**SINGULAR**

|      | M. | M. | M. | N. |
|------|------|--------|-------|-------|
| Nom. | nātus | puer | liber | saxum |
| Gen. | nātī | puerī | librī | saxī |
| Dat. | nātō | puerō | librō | saxō |
| Acc. | nātum | puerum | librum | saxum |
| Abl. | nātō | puerō | librō | saxō |

**PLURAL**

|      | M. | M. | M. | N. |
|------|--------|----------|---------|---------|
| Nom. | nātī | puerī | librī | saxa |
| Gen. | nātōrum | puerōrum | librōrum | saxōrum |
| Dat. | nātīs | puerīs | librīs | saxīs |
| Acc. | nātōs | puerōs | librōs | saxa |
| Abl. | nātīs | puerīs | librīs | saxīs |

Although none are included in this book, feminine nouns ending in -us in the second declension are declined like **nātus** (except for **domus** which, although primarily fourth declension, has alternate second declension endings in cases other than the nominative, dative, and ablative plural).

## Third Declension

SINGULAR

|      | M.       | M.        | M.        | F.          | N.        |
|------|----------|-----------|-----------|-------------|-----------|
| Nom. | rūmor    | homō      | mīles     | servitūs    | sīdus     |
| Gen. | rūmōris  | hominis   | mīlitis   | servitūtis  | sīderis   |
| Dat. | rūmōrī   | hominī    | mīlitī    | servitūtī   | sīderī    |
| Acc. | rūmōrem  | hominem   | mīlitem   | servitūtem  | sīdus     |
| Abl. | rūmōre   | homine    | mīlite    | servitūte   | sīdere    |

PLURAL

|      | M.         | M.         | M.         | F.            | N.         |
|------|------------|------------|------------|---------------|------------|
| Nom. | rūmōrēs    | hominēs    | mīlitēs    | servitūtēs    | sīdera     |
| Gen. | rūmōrum    | hominum    | mīlitum    | servitūtum    | sīderum    |
| Dat. | rūmōribus  | hominibus  | mīlitibus  | servitūtibus  | sīderibus  |
| Acc. | rūmōrēs    | hominēs    | mīlitēs    | servitūtēs    | sīdera     |
| Abl. | rūmōribus  | hominibus  | mīlitibus  | servitūtibus  | sīderibus  |

Nouns of this declension are i-stem if:

1. the nominative and genitive singular have the same number of syllables.
2. the stem ends in a double consonant or -x (exceptions: **māter, frāter, pater,** even though the first rule also applies).
3. they are neuter nouns whose nominative singular ends in -e, -al, or -ar.

## Third Declension: i-Stems

SINGULAR

|      | M.              | F.        | N.     |
|------|-----------------|-----------|--------|
| Nom. | ignis           | nōx       | mare   |
| Gen. | ignis           | noctis    | maris  |
| Dat. | ignī            | noctī     | marī   |
| Acc. | ignem           | noctem    | mare   |
| Abl. | igne (or ignī)  | nocte     | marī   |

PLURAL

|      | M.             | F.               | N.       |
|------|----------------|------------------|----------|
| Nom. | ignēs          | noctēs           | maria    |
| Gen. | ignium         | noctium          | [marium] |
| Dat. | ignibus        | noctibus         | maribus  |
| Acc. | ignēs,         | noctēs,          | maria    |
|      | ignīs          | noctīs           |          |
| Abl. | ignibus        | noctibus         | maribus  |

### SINGULAR

|      | N.       | N.       | N.         |
|------|----------|----------|------------|
| Nom. | animal   | [moene   | exemplar   |
| Gen. | animālis | moenis   | exemplāris |
| Dat. | animālī  | moenī    | exemplārī  |
| Acc. | animal   | moene    | exemplar   |
| Abl. | animālī  | moenī]   | exemplārī  |

### PLURAL

|      | N.         | N.       | N.          |
|------|------------|----------|-------------|
| Nom. | animālia   | moenia   | exemplāria  |
| Gen. | animālium  | moenium  | exemplārium |
| Dat. | animālibus | moenibus | exemplāribus|
| Acc. | animālia   | moenia   | exemplāria  |
| Abl. | animālibus | moenibus | exemplāribus|

## Third Declension: Irregular Noun *vīs*

|      | SINGULAR | PLURAL      |
|------|----------|-------------|
|      | F.       | F.          |
| Nom. | vīs      | vīrēs       |
| Gen. | --       | vīrium      |
| Dat. | --       | vīribus     |
| Acc. | vim      | vīrēs, vīrīs|
| Abl. | vī       | vīribus     |

## Fourth Declension

|      | SINGULAR | | PLURAL | |
|------|----------|--------|----------|--------|
|      | M.       | N.     | M.       | N.     |
| Nom. | frūctus  | genū*  | frūctūs  | genua  |
| Gen. | frūctūs  | genūs  | frūctuum | genuum |
| Dat. | frūctuī  | genū   | frūctibus| genibus|
| Acc. | frūctum  | genū   | frūctūs  | genua  |
| Abl. | frūctū   | genū   | frūctibus| genibus|

\* **genū**, 'knee' (not included in this book).

Although none are included in this book (with the exception of **domus**), feminine nouns in the fourth declension are declined like **frūctus**.

## Fifth Declension

|       | SINGULAR | PLURAL |
|-------|----------|--------|
|       | F.       | F.     |
| Nom.  | rēs      | rēs    |
| Gen.  | reī      | rērum  |
| Dat.  | reī      | rēbus  |
| Acc.  | rem      | rēs    |
| Abl.  | rē       | rēbus  |

# ADJECTIVES

## First-Second Declension

|       | SINGULAR |         |         |
|-------|----------|---------|---------|
|       | M.       | F.      | N.      |
| Nom.  | magnus   | magna   | magnum  |
| Gen.  | magnī    | magnae  | magnī   |
| Dat.  | magnō    | magnae  | magnō   |
| Acc.  | magnum   | magnam  | magnum  |
| Abl.  | magnō    | magnā   | magnō   |

|       | PLURAL   |          |          |
|-------|----------|----------|----------|
|       | M.       | F.       | N.       |
| Nom.  | magnī    | magnae   | magna    |
| Gen.  | magnōrum | magnārum | magnōrum |
| Dat.  | magnīs   | magnīs   | magnīs   |
| Acc.  | magnōs   | magnās   | magna    |
| Abl.  | magnīs   | magnīs   | magnīs   |

|       | SINGULAR |          |          |
|-------|----------|----------|----------|
|       | M.       | F.       | N.       |
| Nom.  | dexter   | dextra   | dextrum  |
| Gen.  | dextrī   | dextrae  | dextrī   |
| Dat.  | dextrō   | dextrae  | dextrō   |
| Acc.  | dextrum  | dextram  | dextrum  |
| Abl.  | dextrō   | dextrā   | dextrō   |

|       | PLURAL    |           |           |
|-------|-----------|-----------|-----------|
|       | M.        | F.        | N.        |
| Nom.  | dextrī    | dextrae   | dextra    |
| Gen.  | dextrōrum | dextrārum | dextrōrum |
| Dat.  | dextrīs   | dextrīs   | dextrīs   |
| Acc.  | dextrōs   | dextrās   | dextra    |
| Abl.  | dextrīs   | dextrīs   | dextrīs   |

## ADJECTIVES WITH GENITIVE SINGULAR IN -īus

### SINGULAR

|  | M. | F. | N. | M. | F. | N. |
|------|--------|--------|--------|-----------|-----------|-----------|
| Nom. | tōtus | tōta | tōtum | alius | alia | aliud |
| Gen. | tōtīus | tōtīus | tōtīus | alterīus* | alterīus* | alterīus* |
| Dat. | tōtī | tōtī | tōtī | aliī | aliī | aliī |
| Acc. | tōtum | tōtam | tōtum | alium | aliam | aliud |
| Abl. | tōtō | tōtā | tōtō | aliō | aliā | aliō |

* The genitive of **alter** is generally used for the genitive of **alius** in order to avoid confusion between **alius** (nominative) and **alīus** (genitive).

### PLURAL

|  | M. | F. | N. | M. | F. | N. |
|------|---------|---------|---------|---------|---------|---------|
| Nom. | tōtī | tōtae | tōta | aliī | aliae | alia |
| Gen. | tōtōrum | tōtārum | tōtōrum | aliōrum | aliārum | aliōrum |
| Dat. | tōtīs | tōtīs | tōtīs | aliīs | aliīs | aliīs |
| Acc. | tōtōs | tōtās | tōta | aliōs | aliās | alia |
| Abl. | tōtīs | tōtīs | tōtīs | aliīs | aliīs | aliīs |

The other adjectives in this category are: **alter, ūllus, nūllus, uter, neuter, sōlus, ūnus.**

## Third Declension

### ADJECTIVES OF THREE TERMINATIONS

|  | SINGULAR | | | PLURAL | | |
|------|--------|--------|--------|---------------|---------------|---------|
|  | M. | F. | N. | M. | F. | N. |
| Nom. | ācer | ācris | ācre | ācrēs | ācrēs | ācria |
| Gen. | ācris | ācris | ācris | ācrium | ācrium | ācrium |
| Dat. | ācrī | ācrī | ācrī | ācribus | ācribus | ācribus |
| Acc. | ācrem | ācrem | ācre | ācrēs (ācrīs) | ācrēs (ācrīs) | ācria |
| Abl. | ācrī | ācrī | ācrī | ācribus | ācribus | ācribus |

### ADJECTIVES OF TWO TERMINATIONS / ADJECTIVES OF ONE TERMINATION

|  | SINGULAR | | SINGULAR | |
|------|---------|-------|------------------|--------|
|  | M. & F. | N. | M. & F. | N. |
| Nom. | omnis | omne | ingēns | |
| Gen. | omnis | omnis | ingentis | |
| Dat. | omnī | omnī | ingentī | |
| Acc. | omnem | omne | ingentem | ingēns |
| Abl. | omnī | omnī | ingentī | |

| | PLURAL | | PLURAL | |
|---|---|---|---|---|
| | M. & F. | N. | M. & F. | N. |
| Nom. | omnēs | omnia | ingentēs | ingentia |
| Gen. | omnium | omnium | ingentium | |
| Dat. | omnibus | omnibus | ingentibus | |
| Acc. | omnēs (-īs) | omnia | ingentēs (-īs) | ingentia |
| Abl. | omnibus | omnibus | ingentibus | |

## Present Participles

| | SINGULAR | | PLURAL | |
|---|---|---|---|---|
| | M. & F. | N. | M. & F. | N. |
| Nom. | optāns | | optantēs | optantia |
| Gen. | optantis | | optantium | |
| Dat. | optantī | | optantibus | |
| Acc. | optantem | optāns | optantēs (-īs) | optantia |
| Abl. | optantī (-e) | | optantibus | |

## Comparative Degree of Adjectives

| | SINGULAR | | PLURAL | |
|---|---|---|---|---|
| | M. & F. | N. | M. & F. | N. |
| Nom. | fortior | fortius | fortiōrēs | fortiōra |
| Gen. | fortiōris | fortiōris | fortiōrum | fortiōrum |
| Dat. | fortiōrī | fortiōrī | fortiōribus | fortiōribus |
| Acc. | fortiōrem | fortius | fortiōrēs (-īs) | fortiōra |
| Abl. | fortiōre (-ī) | fortiōre (-ī) | fortiōribus | fortiōribus |

## Other Adjectives

### THE NUMERICAL ADJECTIVE duo

| | M. | F. | N. |
|---|---|---|---|
| Nom. | duo | duae | duo |
| Gen. | duōrum | duārum | duōrum |
| Dat. | duōbus | duābus | duōbus |
| Acc. | duōs (-o) | duās | duo |
| Abl. | duōbus | duābus | duōbus |

### THE DEMONSTRATIVE ADJECTIVE hic | THE DEMONSTRATIVE ADJECTIVE ille

| | SINGULAR | | | | SINGULAR | | |
|---|---|---|---|---|---|---|---|
| | M. | F. | N. | | M. | F. | N. |
| Nom. | hic | haec | hoc | | ille | illa | illud |

|        | SINGULAR |       |       | SINGULAR |        |        |
|--------|------|-------|-------|--------|--------|--------|
|        | M.   | F.    | N.    | M.     | F.     | N.     |
| Gen.   | huius | huius | huius | illīus | illīus | illīus |
| Dat.   | huic | huic  | huic  | illī   | illī   | illī   |
| Acc.   | hunc | hanc  | hoc   | illum  | illam  | illud  |
| Abl.   | hōc  | hāc   | hōc   | illō   | illā   | illō   |

|        | PLURAL |       |       | PLURAL |        |        |
|--------|------|-------|-------|--------|--------|--------|
|        | M.   | F.    | N.    | M.     | F.     | N.     |
| Nom.   | hī   | hae   | haec  | illī   | illae  | illa   |
| Gen.   | hōrum | hārum | hōrum | illōrum | illārum | illōrum |
| Dat.   | hīs  | hīs   | hīs   | illīs  | illīs  | illīs  |
| Acc.   | hōs  | hās   | haec  | illōs  | illās  | illa   |
| Abl.   | hīs  | hīs   | hīs   | illīs  | illīs  | illīs  |

### The Intensive Adjective ipse
### The Demonstrative Adjective iste

|        | SINGULAR |       |       | SINGULAR |        |        |
|--------|------|-------|-------|--------|--------|--------|
|        | M.   | F.    | N.    | M.     | F.     | N.     |
| Nom.   | ipse | ipsa  | ipsum | iste   | ista   | istud  |
| Gen.   | ipsīus | ipsīus | ipsīus | istīus | istīus | istīus |
| Dat.   | ipsī | ipsī  | ipsī  | istī   | istī   | istī   |
| Acc.   | ipsum | ipsam | ipsum | istum  | istam  | istud  |
| Abl.   | ipsō | ipsā  | ipsō  | istō   | istā   | istō   |

|        | PLURAL |       |       | PLURAL |        |        |
|--------|------|-------|-------|--------|--------|--------|
|        | M.   | F.    | N.    | M.     | F.     | N.     |
| Nom.   | ipsī | ipsae | ipsa  | istī   | istae  | ista   |
| Gen.   | ipsōrum | ipsārum | ipsōrum | istōrum | istārum | istōrum |
| Dat.   | ipsīs | ipsīs | ipsīs | istīs  | istīs  | istīs  |
| Acc.   | ipsōs | ipsās | ipsa  | istōs  | istās  | ista   |
| Abl.   | ipsīs | ipsīs | ipsīs | istīs  | istīs  | istīs  |

### The Demonstrative Adjective is

|        | SINGULAR |       |       | PLURAL |        |        |
|--------|------|-------|-------|--------|--------|--------|
|        | M.   | F.    | N.    | M.     | F.     | N.     |
| Nom.   | is   | ea    | id    | eī, iī | eae    | ea     |
| Gen.   | eius | eius  | eius  | eōrum  | eārum  | eōrum  |
| Dat.   | eī   | eī    | eī    | eīs, iīs | eīs, iīs | eīs, iīs |
| Acc.   | eum  | eam   | id    | eōs    | eās    | ea     |
| Abl.   | eō   | eā    | eō    | eīs, iīs | eīs, iīs | eīs, iīs |

## THE ADJECTIVE **idem**

### SINGULAR

|      | M.      | F.      | N.      |
|------|---------|---------|---------|
| Nom. | īdem    | eadem   | idem    |
| Gen. | eiusdem | eiusdem | eiusdem |
| Dat. | eīdem   | eīdem   | eīdem   |
| Acc. | eundem  | eandem  | idem    |
| Abl. | eōdem   | eādem   | eōdem   |

### PLURAL

|      | M.              | F.              | N.              |
|------|-----------------|-----------------|-----------------|
| Nom. | eīdem (īdem)    | eaedem          | eadem           |
| Gen. | eōrundem        | eārundem        | eōrundem        |
| Dat. | eīsdem (īsdem)  | eīsdem (īsdem)  | eīsdem (īsdem)  |
| Acc. | eōsdem          | eāsdem          | eadem           |
| Abl. | eīsdem (īsdem)  | eīsdem (īsdem)  | eīsdem (īsdem)  |

## THE INTERROGATIVE ADJECTIVE **quī** / THE INDEFINITE ADJECTIVE **aliquī**

### SINGULAR

|      | M.     | F.     | N.     | M.       | F.       | N.       |
|------|--------|--------|--------|----------|----------|----------|
| Nom. | quī    | quae   | quod   | aliquī   | aliqua   | aliquod  |
| Gen. | cuius  | cuius  | cuius  | alicuius | alicuius | alicuius |
| Dat. | cui    | cui    | cui    | alicui   | alicui   | alicui   |
| Acc. | quem   | quam   | quod   | aliquem  | aliquam  | aliquod  |
| Abl. | quō    | quā    | quō    | aliquō   | aliquā   | aliquō   |

### PLURAL

|      | M.      | F.      | N.      | M.         | F.         | N.         |
|------|---------|---------|---------|------------|------------|------------|
| Nom. | quī     | quae    | quae    | aliquī     | aliquae    | aliqua     |
| Gen. | quōrum  | quārum  | quōrum  | aliquōrum  | aliquārum  | aliquōrum  |
| Dat. | quibus  | quibus  | quibus  | aliquibus  | aliquibus  | aliquibus  |
| Acc. | quōs    | quās    | quae    | aliquōs    | aliquās    | aliqua     |
| Abl. | quibus  | quibus  | quibus  | aliquibus  | aliquibus  | aliquibus  |

# PRONOUNS

**Personal Pronouns**

| FIRST PERSON | SECOND PERSON | THIRD PERSON |
|--------------|---------------|--------------|

### SINGULAR

| FIRST PERSON | SECOND PERSON | THIRD PERSON |
|--------------|---------------|--------------|
| Nom. ego, I | tū, you | The adjective **is, ea,** |
| Gen. meī, of me | tuī, of you | **id** is used for the |

|  | FIRST PERSON | SECOND PERSON | THIRD PERSON |
|---|---|---|---|

**SINGULAR**

| Dat. | mihi, to/for me | tibi, to/for you | personal pronoun |
| Acc. | mē, me | tē, you | of the third person. |
| Abl. | mē, from/with/in/by me | tē, from/with/in/by you |  |

**PLURAL**

| Nom. | nōs, we | vōs, you |
| Gen. | nostrum, nostrī*, of us | vestrum, vestrī*, of you |
| Dat. | nōbīs, to/for us | vōbīs, to/for you |
| Acc. | nōs, us | vōs, you |
| Abl. | nōbīs, from/with/in/by us | vōbīs, from/with/in/by you |

* **Nostrum** and **vestrum** are used as partitive genitives, **nostrī** and **vestrī** as objective genitives.

**Reflexive Pronoun**

Nom. --
Gen. suī, of himself, herself, itself, themselves
Dat. sibi, to/for himself, herself, itself, themselves
Acc. sē (sēsē), himself, herself, itself, themselves
Abl. sē (sēsē), from/with/in/by himself, herself, itself, themselves

| THE INTERROGATIVE PRONOUN **quis** | | | THE INDEFINITE PRONOUN **quīdam** | | |
|---|---|---|---|---|---|

**SINGULAR** | | | **SINGULAR** | | |

|  | M. & F. | N. | M. | F. | N. |
|---|---|---|---|---|---|
| Nom. | quis | quid | quīdam | quaedam | quiddam |
| Gen. | cuius | cuius | cuiusdam | cuiusdam | cuiusdam |
| Dat. | cui | cui | cuidam | cuidam | cuidam |
| Acc. | quem | quid | quendam | quandam | quiddam |
| Abl. | quō | quō | quōdam | quādam | quōdam |

**PLURAL** | | | **PLURAL** | | |

|  | M. | F. | N. | M. | F. | N. |
|---|---|---|---|---|---|---|
| Nom. | quī | quae | quae | quīdam | quaedam | quaedam |
| Gen. | quōrum | quārum | quōrum | quōrundam | quārundam | quōrundam |
| Dat. | quibus | quibus | quibus | quibusdam | quibusdam | quibusdam |
| Acc. | quōs | quās | quae | quōsdam | quāsdam | quaedam |
| Abl. | quibus | quibus | quibus | quibusdam | quibusdam | quibusdam |

# VERBS

## Personal Endings

| ACTIVE | PASSIVE | PERFECT ACTIVE |
|---|---|---|
| SINGULAR | SINGULAR | SINGULAR |
| 1st -ō *or* -m | 1st -or *or* -r | 1st -ī |
| 2nd -s | 2nd -ris *and* -re | 2nd -istī |
| 3rd -t | 3rd -tur | 3rd -it |
| PLURAL | PLURAL | PLURAL |
| 1st -mus | 1st -mur | 1st -imus |
| 2nd -tis | 2nd -minī | 2nd -istis |
| 3rd -nt | 3rd -ntur | 3rd -ērunt (-ēre) |

---

*First Conjugation*: **optō, optāre, optāvī, optātus,** 'desire, wish (for), choose'

## INDICATIVE

| ACTIVE | PASSIVE |
|---|---|

### PRESENT

| | |
|---|---|
| optō, I desire, I am desiring, I do desire, I always desire | optor, I am (being) desired |
| optās, you desire, etc. | optāris, optāre, you are (being) desired |
| optat, he/she/it desires, etc. | optātur, he/she/it is (being) desired |
| optāmus, we desire, etc. | optāmur, we are (being) desired |
| optātis, you desire, etc. | optāminī, you are (being) desired |
| optant, they desire, etc. | optantur, they are (being) desired |

### IMPERFECT

| | |
|---|---|
| optābam, I was desiring, I used to desire, I kept on desiring, I desired (habitually) | optābar, I was (being) desired |
| optābās, you were desiring, etc. | optābāris, optābāre, you were (being) desired |
| optābat, he/she/it was desiring, etc. | optābātur, he/she/it was (being) desired |
| optābāmus, we were desiring, etc. | optābāmur, we were (being) desired |
| optābātis, you were desiring, etc. | optābāminī, you were (being) desired |
| optābant, they were desiring, etc. | optābantur, they were (being) desired |

|                    ACTIVE                    |                    PASSIVE                    |
|:---:|:---:|

## FUTURE

| ACTIVE | PASSIVE |
|---|---|
| optābō, I shall desire, I shall be desiring | optābor, I shall be desired |
| optābis, you will desire, etc. | optāberis, optābere, you will be desired |
| optābit, he/she/it will desire, etc. | optābitur, he/she/it will be desired |
| optābimus, we shall desire, etc. | optābimur, we shall be desired |
| optābitis, you will desire, etc. | optābiminī, you will be desired |
| optābunt, they will desire, etc. | optābuntur, they will be desired |

## PERFECT

| ACTIVE | PASSIVE |
|---|---|
| optāvī, I have desired, I desired, I did desire | optātus (-a, -um) sum, I have been desired, I was desired |
| optāvistī, you have desired, etc. | optātus (-a, -um) es, you have been desired, etc. |
| optāvit, he/she/it has desired, etc. | optātus (-a, -um) est, he/she/it has been desired, etc. |
| optāvimus, we have desired, etc. | optātī (-ae, -a) sumus, we have been desired, etc. |
| optāvistis, you have desired, etc. | optātī (-ae, -a) estis, you have been desired, etc. |
| optāvērunt, optāvēre, they have desired, etc. | optātī (-ae, -a) sunt, they have been desired, etc. |

## PLUPERFECT

| ACTIVE | PASSIVE |
|---|---|
| optāveram, I had desired | optātus (-a, -um) eram, I had been desired |
| optāverās, you had desired | optātus (-a, -um) erās, you had been desired |
| optāverat, he/she/it had desired | optātus (-a, -um) erat, he/she/it had been desired |
| optāverāmus, we had desired | optātī (-ae, -a) erāmus, we had been desired |
| optāverātis, you had desired | optātī (-ae, -a) erātis, you had been desired |
| optāverant, they had desired | optātī (-ae, -a) erant, they had been desired |

| ACTIVE | PASSIVE |
|--------|---------|

### FUTURE PERFECT

| ACTIVE | PASSIVE |
|--------|---------|
| optāverō, I shall have desired | optātus (-a, -um) erō, I shall have been desired |
| optāveris, you will have desired | optātus (-a, -um) eris, you will have been desired |
| optāverit, he/she/it will have desired | optātus (-a, -um) erit, he/she/it will have been desired |
| optāverimus, we shall have desired | optātī (-ae, -a) erimus, we shall have been desired |
| optāveritis, you will have desired | optātī (-ae, -a) eritis, you will have been desired |
| optāverint, they will have desired | optātī (-ae, -a) erunt, they will have been desired |

## SUBJUNCTIVE

| ACTIVE | PASSIVE |
|--------|---------|

### PRESENT

| ACTIVE | PASSIVE |
|--------|---------|
| optem | opter |
| optēs | optēris, optēre |
| optet | optētur |
| optēmus | optēmur |
| optētis | optēminī |
| optent | optentur |

### IMPERFECT

| ACTIVE | PASSIVE |
|--------|---------|
| optārem | optārer |
| optārēs | optārēris, optārēre |
| optāret | optārētur |
| optārēmus | optārēmur |
| optārētis | optārēminī |
| optārent | optārentur |

### PERFECT

| ACTIVE | PASSIVE |
|--------|---------|
| optāverim | optātus (-a, -um) sim |
| optāveris | optātus (-a, -um) sīs |
| optāverit | optātus (-a, -um) sit |
| optāverimus | optātī (-ae, -a) sīmus |
| optāveritis | optātī (-ae, -a) sītis |
| optāverint | optātī (-ae, -a) sint |

| Active | Passive |
|---|---|

**PLUPERFECT**

| | |
|---|---|
| optāvissem | optātus (-a, -um) essem |
| optāvissēs | optātus (-a, -um) essēs |
| optāvisset | optātus (-a, -um) esset |
| optāvissēmus | optātī (-ae, -a) essēmus |
| optāvissētis | optātī (-ae, -a) essētis |
| optāvissent | optātī (-ae, -a) essent |

## PARTICIPLES

| Active | Passive |
|---|---|

**PRESENT**

| | |
|---|---|
| optāns, desiring | — |

**PERFECT**

| | |
|---|---|
| — | optātus, -a, -um, (having been) desired |

**FUTURE**

| | |
|---|---|
| optātūrus, -a, -um, about to desire, going to desire, ready to desire | optandus, -a, -um, to be desired, having to be desired |

## INFINITIVES

| Active | Passive |
|---|---|

**PRESENT**

| | |
|---|---|
| optāre, to desire | optārī, to be desired |

**PERFECT**

| | |
|---|---|
| optāvisse, to have desired | optātus, -a, -um esse, to have been desired |

**FUTURE**

| | |
|---|---|
| optātūrus, -a, -um esse, to be about to desire, to be going to desire, to be ready to desire | optātum īrī, to be about to be desired, to be going to be desired, to be ready to be desired |

## IMPERATIVES

| Active | | Passive | |
|---|---|---|---|
| SINGULAR | PLURAL | SINGULAR | PLURAL |

**PRESENT**

| | | | |
|---|---|---|---|
| optā, desire! | optāte, desire! | optāre, be desired! | optāminī, be desired! |

|                          ACTIVE | | PASSIVE | |

### FUTURE*

| | | |
|---|---|---|
| 2nd optātō, you | optātōte, you | optātor, you shall | — |
| shall desire! | shall desire! | be desired! | |
| 3rd optātō, he/she/it | optāntō, they | optātor, he/she/it | optantor, they |
| shall desire! | shall desire! | shall be desired! | shall be |
| | | | desired! |

\* The formation and use of the future imperative are discussed on pages 362 and 381–382.

## Periphrastics

# INDICATIVE

ACTIVE                                              PASSIVE

### PRESENT

| ACTIVE | PASSIVE |
|---|---|
| optātūrus (-a, -um) sum, I am about to desire, I am going to desire, I am ready to desire | optandus (-a, -um) sum, I am having-to-be desired, I should be desired, I ought to be desired, I must be desired, I have to be desired |
| optātūrus (-a, -um) es, you are about to desire, etc. | optandus (-a, -um) es, you are having-to-be desired, etc. |
| optātūrus (-a, -um) est, he/she/it is about to desire, etc. | optandus (-a, -um) est, he/she/it is having-to-be desired, etc. |
| optātūrī (-ae, -a) sumus, we are about to desire, etc. | optandī (-ae, -a) sumus, we are having-to-be desired, etc. |
| optātūrī (-ae, -a) estis, you are about to desire, etc. | optandī (-ae, -a) estis, you are having-to-be desired, etc. |
| optātūrī (-ae, -a) sunt, they are about to desire, etc. | optandī (-ae, -a) sunt, they are having-to-be desired, etc. |

### IMPERFECT

| ACTIVE | PASSIVE |
|---|---|
| optātūrus (-a, -um) eram, I was about to desire, I was going to desire, I was ready to desire | optandus (-a, -um) eram, I had to be desired |
| optātūrus (-a, -um) erās, you were about to desire, etc. | optandus (-a, -um) erās, you had to be desired |
| optātūrus (-a, -um) erat, he/she/it was about to desire, etc. | optandus (-a, -um) erat, he/she/it had to be desired |
| optātūrī (-ae, -a) erāmus, we were about to desire, etc. | optandī (-ae, -a) erāmus, we had to be desired |

ACTIVE                                    PASSIVE

IMPERFECT

optātūrī (-ae, -a) erātis, you were
about to desire, etc.

optāndī (-ae, -a) erātis, you had to
be desired

optātūrī (-ae, -a) erant, they were
about to desire, etc.

optāndī (-ae, -a) erant, they had to
be desired

FUTURE

optātūrus (-a, -um) erō, I shall be
about to desire, I shall be going to
desire, I shall be ready to desire

optandus (-a, -um) erō, I shall have to
be desired

optātūrus (-a, -um) eris, you will be
about to desire, etc.

optandus (-a, -um) eris, you will
have to be desired

optātūrus (-a, -um) erit, he/she/it
will be about to desire, etc.

optandus (-a, -um) erit, he/she/it
will have to be desired

optātūrī (-ae, -a) erimus, we shall be
about to desire, etc.

optandī (-ae, -a) erimus, we shall
have to be desired

optātūrī (-ae, -a) eritis, you will be
about to desire, etc.

optandī (-ae, -a) eritis, you will have
to be desired

optātūrī (-ae, -a) erunt, they will be
about to desire, etc.

optandī (-ae, -a) erunt, they will
have to be desired

PERFECT

optātūrus (-a, -um) fuī, I have been
(I was) about to desire, going to
desire, ready to desire

optandus (-a, -um) fuī, I had to be
desired

optātūrus (-a, -um) fuistī, you have
been about to desire, etc.

optandus (-a, -um) fuistī, you had to
be desired

optātūrus (-a, -um) fuit, he/she/it has
been about to desire, etc.

optandus (-a, -um) fuit, he/she/it
had to be desired

optātūrī (-ae, -a) fuimus, we have
been about to desire, etc.

optandī (-ae, -a) fuimus, we had to
be desired

optātūrī (-ae, -a) fuistis, you have
been about to desire, etc.

optandī (-ae, -a) fuistis, you had to
be desired

optātūrī (-ae, -a) fuērunt, fuēre, they
have been about to desire, etc.

optandī (-ae, -a) fuērunt, fuēre, they
had to be desired

PLUPERFECT

optātūrus (-a, -um) fueram, I had
been about to desire, I had been
going to desire, I had been ready
to desire

optandus (-a, -um) fueram, I had
had to be desired

| ACTIVE | PASSIVE |
|---|---|

### PLUPERFECT

| | |
|---|---|
| optātūrus (-a, -um) fuerās, you had been about to desire, etc. | optandus (-a, -um) fuerās, you had had to be desired |
| optātūrus (-a, -um) fuerat, he/she/it had been about to desire, etc. | optandus (-a, -um) fuerat, he/she/it had had to be desired |
| optātūrī (-ae, -a) fuerāmus, we had been about to desire, etc. | optandī (-ae, -a) fuerāmus, we had had to be desired |
| optātūrī (-ae, -a) fuerātis, you had been about to desire, etc. | optandī (-ae, -a) fuerātis, you had had to be desired |
| optātūrī (-ae, -a) fuerant, they had been about to desire, etc. | optandī (-ae, -a) fuerant, they had had to be desired |

### FUTURE PERFECT

| | |
|---|---|
| optātūrus (-a, -um) fuerō, I shall have been about to desire, I shall have been going to desire, I shall have been ready to desire | optandus (-a, -um) fuerō, I shall have had to be desired |
| optātūrus (-a, -um) fueris, you will have been about to desire, etc. | optandus (-a, -um) fueris, you will have had to be desired |
| optātūrus (-a, -um) fuerit, he/she/it will have been about to desire, etc. | optandus (-a, -um) fuerit, he/she/it will have had to be desired |
| optātūrī (-ae, -a) fuerimus, we shall have been about to desire, etc. | optandī (-ae, -a) fuerimus, we shall have had to be desired |
| optātūrī (-ae, -a) fueritis, you will have been about to desire, etc. | optandī (-ae, -a) fueritis, you will have had to be desired |
| optātūrī (-ae, -a) fuerint, they will have been about to desire, etc. | optandī (-ae, -a) fuerint, they will have had to be desired |

## SUBJUNCTIVE

| ACTIVE | PASSIVE |
|---|---|

### PRESENT

| | |
|---|---|
| optātūrus (-a, -um) sim | optandus (-a, -um) sim |
| optātūrus (-a, -um) sīs | optandus (-a, -um) sīs |
| optātūrus (-a, -um) sit | optandus (-a, -um) sit |
| optātūrī (-ae, -a) sīmus | optandī (-ae, -a) sīmus |
| optātūrī (-ae, -a) sītis | optandī (-ae, -a) sītis |
| optātūrī (-ae, -a) sint | optandī (-ae, -a) sint |

| ACTIVE | PASSIVE |
|---|---|

### IMPERFECT

| ACTIVE | PASSIVE |
|---|---|
| optātūrus (-a, -um) essem | optandus (-a, -um) essem |
| optātūrus (-a, -um) essēs | optandus (-a, -um) essēs |
| optātūrus (-a, -um) esset | optandus (-a, -um) esset |
| optātūrī (-ae, -a) essēmus | optandī (-ae, -a) essēmus |
| optātūrī (-ae, -a) essētis | optandī (-ae, -a) essētis |
| optātūrī (-ae, -a) essent | optandī (-ae, -a) essent |

### PERFECT

| ACTIVE | PASSIVE |
|---|---|
| optātūrus (-a, -um) fuerim | optandus (-a, -um) fuerim |
| optātūrus (-a, -um) fueris | optandus (-a, -um) fueris |
| optātūrus (-a, -um) fuerit | optandus (-a, -um) fuerit |
| optātūrī (-ae, -a) fuerimus | optandī (-ae, -a) fuerimus |
| optātūrī (-ae, -a) fueritis | optandī (-ae, -a) fueritis |
| optātūrī (-ae, -a) fuerint | optandī (-ae, -a) fuerint |

### PLUPERFECT

| ACTIVE | PASSIVE |
|---|---|
| optātūrus (-a, -um) fuissem | optandus (-a, -um) fuissem |
| optātūrus (-a, -um) fuissēs | optandus (-a, -um) fuissēs |
| optātūrus (-a, -um) fuisset | optandus (-a, -um) fuisset |
| optātūrī (-ae, -a) fuissēmus | optandī (-ae, -a) fuissēmus |
| optātūrī (-ae, -a) fuissētis | optandī (-ae, -a) fuissētis |
| optātūrī (-ae, -a) fuissent | optandī (-ae, -a) fuissent |

(Periphrastics have no participles.)

## INFINITIVES

| ACTIVE | PASSIVE |
|---|---|

### PRESENT

| ACTIVE | PASSIVE |
|---|---|
| optātūrus (-a, -um) esse, to be about to desire, to be going to desire, to be ready to desire | optandus (-a, -um) esse, to have to be desired |

### PERFECT

| ACTIVE | PASSIVE |
|---|---|
| optātūrus (-a, -um) fuisse, to have been about to desire, etc. | optandus (-a, -um) fuisse, to have had to be desired |

### FUTURE

| -- | -- |
|---|---|

(Periphrastics have no imperatives.)

*Second Conjugation*: **impleō, implēre, implēvī, implētus,** 'fill, fill up'

## INDICATIVE

| ACTIVE | PASSIVE |
|--------|---------|

### PRESENT

| impleō | impleor |
| implēs | implēris, implēre |
| implet | implētur |
| implēmus | implēmur |
| implētis | implēminī |
| implent | implentur |

### IMPERFECT

| implēbam | implēbar |
| implēbās | implēbāris, implēbāre |
| implēbat | implēbātur |
| implēbāmus | implēbāmur |
| implēbātis | implēbāminī |
| implēbant | implēbantur |

### FUTURE

| implēbō | implēbor |
| implēbis | implēberis, implēbere |
| implēbit | implēbitur |
| implēbimus | implēbimur |
| implēbitis | implēbiminī |
| implēbunt | implēbuntur |

### PERFECT

| implēvī | implētus (-a, -um) sum |
| implēvistī | implētus (-a, -um) es |
| implēvit | implētus (-a, -um) est |
| implēvimus | implētī (-ae, -a) sumus |
| implēvistis | implētī (-ae, -a) estis |
| implēvērunt, implēvēre | implētī (-ae, -a) sunt |

### PLUPERFECT

| implēveram | implētus (-a, -um) eram |
| implēverās | implētus (-a, -um) erās |
| implēverat | implētus (-a, -um) erat |
| implēverāmus | implētī (-ae, -a) erāmus |
| implēverātis | implētī (-ae, -a) erātis |
| implēverant | implētī (-ae, -a) erant |

| ACTIVE | PASSIVE |
|--------|---------|

### FUTURE PERFECT

| ACTIVE | PASSIVE |
|--------|---------|
| implēverō | implētus (-a, -um) erō |
| implēveris | implētus (-a, -um) eris |
| implēverit | implētus (-a, -um) erit |
| implēverimus | implētī (-ae, -a) erimus |
| implēveritis | implētī (-ae, -a) eritis |
| implēverint | implētī (-ae, -a) erunt |

## SUBJUNCTIVE

| ACTIVE | PASSIVE |
|--------|---------|

### PRESENT

| ACTIVE | PASSIVE |
|--------|---------|
| impleam | implear |
| impleās | impleāris, impleāre |
| impleat | impleātur |
| impleāmus | impleāmur |
| impleātis | impleāminī |
| impleant | impleantur |

### IMPERFECT

| | |
|--------|---------|
| implērem | implērer |
| implērēs | implērēris, implērēre |
| implēret | implērētur |
| implērēmus | implērēmur |
| implērētis | implērēminī |
| implērent | implērentur |

### PERFECT

| | |
|--------|---------|
| implēverim | implētus (-a, -um) sim |
| implēveris | implētus (-a, -um) sīs |
| implēverit | implētus (-a, -um) sit |
| implēverimus | implētī (-ae, -a) sīmus |
| implēveritis | implētī (-ae, -a) sītis |
| implēverint | implētī (-ae, -a) sint |

### PLUPERFECT

| | |
|--------|---------|
| implēvissem | implētus (-a, -um) essem |
| implēvissēs | implētus (-a, -um) essēs |
| implēvisset | implētus (-a, -um) esset |
| implēvissēmus | implētī (-ae, -a) essēmus |
| implēvissētis | implētī (-ae, -a) essētis |
| implēvissent | implētī (-ae, -a) essent |

## PARTICIPLES

| ACTIVE | PASSIVE |
|---|---|
| **PRESENT** | |
| implēns | -- |
| **PERFECT** | |
| -- | implētus, -a, -um |
| **FUTURE** | |
| implētūrus, -a, -um | implendus, -a, -um |

## INFINITIVES

| ACTIVE | PASSIVE |
|---|---|
| **PRESENT** | |
| implēre | implērī |
| **PERFECT** | |
| implēvisse | implētus, -a, -um esse |
| **FUTURE** | |
| implētūrus, -a, -um esse | implētum īrī |

## IMPERATIVES

| | ACTIVE | | PASSIVE | |
|---|---|---|---|---|
| | SINGULAR | PLURAL | SINGULAR | PLURAL |
| | **PRESENT** | | | |
| | implē | implēte | implēre | implēminī |
| | **FUTURE** | | | |
| 2nd | implētō | implētōte | implētor | -- |
| 3rd | implētō | implentō | implētor | implentor |

## PERIPHRASTICS

As in the first conjugation, the future active and passive participles and forms of the verb "to be" make up the periphrastic conjugations. See **optō** for examples.

---

*Third Conjugation*: **dūcō, dūcere, dūxī, ductus,** 'lead; consider'

## INDICATIVE

| ACTIVE | PASSIVE |
|---|---|
| **PRESENT** | |
| dūcō | dūcor |
| dūcis | dūceris, dūcere |
| dūcit | dūcitur |

<table>
<tr><td>ACTIVE</td><td>PASSIVE</td></tr>
</table>

### PRESENT

| ACTIVE | PASSIVE |
|---|---|
| dūcimus | dūcimur |
| dūcitis | dūciminī |
| dūcunt | dūcuntur |

### IMPERFECT

| | |
|---|---|
| dūcēbam | dūcēbar |
| dūcēbās | dūcēbāris, dūcēbāre |
| dūcēbat | dūcēbātur |
| dūcēbāmus | dūcēbāmur |
| dūcēbātis | dūcēbāminī |
| dūcēbant | dūcēbantur |

### FUTURE

| | |
|---|---|
| dūcam | dūcar |
| dūcēs | dūcēris, dūcēre |
| dūcet | dūcētur |
| dūcēmus | dūcēmur |
| dūcētis | dūcēminī |
| dūcent | dūcentur |

### PERFECT

| | |
|---|---|
| dūxī | ductus (-a, -um) sum |
| dūxistī | ductus (-a, -um) es |
| dūxit | ductus (-a, -um) est |
| dūximus | ductī (-ae, -a) sumus |
| dūxistis | ductī (-ae, -a) estis |
| dūxērunt, dūxēre | ductī (-ae, -a) sunt |

### PLUPERFECT

| | |
|---|---|
| dūxeram | ductus (-a, -um) eram |
| dūxerās | ductus (-a, -um) erās |
| dūxerat | ductus (-a, -um) erat |
| dūxerāmus | ductī (-ae, -a) erāmus |
| dūxerātis | ductī (-ae, -a) erātis |
| dūxerant | ductī (-ae, -a) erant |

### FUTURE PERFECT

| | |
|---|---|
| dūxerō | ductus (-a, -um) erō |
| dūxeris | ductus (-a, -um) eris |
| dūxerit | ductus (-a, -um) erit |

ACTIVE                           PASSIVE
FUTURE PERFECT

dūxerimus                        ductī (-ae, -a) erimus
dūxeritis                        ductī (-ae, -a) eritis
dūxerint                         ductī (-ae, -a) erunt


# SUBJUNCTIVE

ACTIVE                           PASSIVE
PRESENT

dūcam                            dūcar
dūcās                            dūcāris, dūcāre
dūcat                            dūcātur

dūcāmus                          dūcāmur
dūcātis                          dūcāminī
dūcant                           dūcantur


IMPERFECT

dūcerem                          dūcerer
dūcerēs                          dūcerēris, dūcerēre
dūceret                          dūcerētur

dūcerēmus                        dūcerēmur
dūcerētis                        dūcerēminī
dūcerent                         dūcerentur


PERFECT

dūxerim                          ductus (-a, -um) sim
dūxeris                          ductus (-a, -um) sīs
dūxerit                          ductus (-a, -um) sit

dūxerimus                        ductī (-ae, -a) sīmus
dūxeritis                        ductī (-ae, -a) sītis
dūxerint                         ductī (-ae, -a) sint


PLUPERFECT

dūxissem                         ductus (-a, -um) essem
dūxissēs                         ductus (-a, -um) essēs
dūxisset                         ductus (-a, -um) esset

dūxissēmus                       ductī (-ae, -a) essēmus
dūxissētis                       ductī (-ae, -a) essētis
dūxissent                        ductī (-ae, -a) essent

## PARTICIPLES

|  | ACTIVE | PASSIVE |
|---|---|---|
| PRESENT | dūcēns | -- |
| PERFECT | -- | ductus, -a, -um |
| FUTURE | ductūrus, -a, -um | dūcendus, -a, -um |

## INFINITIVES

|  | ACTIVE | PASSIVE |
|---|---|---|
| PRESENT | dūcere | dūcī |
| PERFECT | dūxisse | ductus, -a, -um esse |
| FUTURE | ductūrus, -a, -um esse | ductum īrī |

## IMPERATIVES

|  | ACTIVE | | PASSIVE | |
|---|---|---|---|---|
|  | SINGULAR | PLURAL | SINGULAR | PLURAL |
| PRESENT | dūc* | dūcite | dūcere | dūciminī |
| FUTURE | | | | |
| 2nd | dūcitō | dūcitōte | dūcitor | -- |
| 3rd | dūcitō | dūcuntō | dūcitor | dūcuntor |

* **dūcō, dīcō, faciō,** and **ferō** drop the final **-e.**

## PERIPHRASTICS

As in the first conjugation, the future active and passive participles and forms of the verb "to be" make up the periphrastic conjugations. See **optō** for examples.

---

*Third Conjugation i-Stems*: **incipiō, incipere, incēpī, inceptus,** 'begin'

## INDICATIVE

|  | ACTIVE | PASSIVE |
|---|---|---|
| PRESENT | incipiō | incipior |
|  | incipis | inciperis, incipere |
|  | incipit | incipitur |

| ACTIVE | PASSIVE |
|--------|---------|

### PRESENT

| | |
|--------|---------|
| incipimus | incipimur |
| incipitis | incipiminī |
| incipiunt | incipiuntur |

### IMPERFECT

| | |
|--------|---------|
| incipiēbam | incipiēbar |
| incipiēbās | incipiēbāris, incipiēbāre |
| incipiēbat | incipiēbātur |
| incipiēbāmus | incipiēbāmur |
| incipiēbātis | incipiēbāminī |
| incipiēbant | incipiēbantur |

### FUTURE

| | |
|--------|---------|
| incipiam | incipiar |
| incipiēs | incipiēris, incipiēre |
| incipiet | incipiētur |
| incipiēmus | incipiēmur |
| incipiētis | incipiēminī |
| incipient | incipientur |

### PERFECT

| | |
|--------|---------|
| incēpī | inceptus (-a, -um) sum |
| incēpistī | inceptus (-a, -um) es |
| incēpit | inceptus (-a, -um) est |
| incēpimus | inceptī (-ae, -a) sumus |
| incēpistis | inceptī (-ae, -a) estis |
| incēpērunt, incēpēre | inceptī (-ae, -a) sunt |

### PLUPERFECT

| | |
|--------|---------|
| incēperam | inceptus (-a, -um) eram |
| incēperās | inceptus (-a, -um) erās |
| incēperat | inceptus (-a, -um) erat |
| incēperāmus | inceptī (-ae, -a) erāmus |
| incēperātis | inceptī (-ae, -a) erātis |
| incēperant | inceptī (-ae, -a) erant |

### FUTURE PERFECT

| | |
|--------|---------|
| incēperō | inceptus (-a, -um) erō |
| incēperis | inceptus (-a, -um) eris |
| incēperit | inceptus (-a, -um) erit |
| incēperimus | inceptī (-ae, -a) erimus |
| incēperitis | inceptī (-ae, -a) eritis |
| incēperint | inceptī (-ae, -a) erunt |

## SUBJUNCTIVE

| ACTIVE | PASSIVE |
|---|---|

### PRESENT

| | |
|---|---|
| incipiam | incipiar |
| incipiās | incipiāris, incipiāre |
| incipiat | incipiātur |
| incipiāmus | incipiāmur |
| incipiātis | incipiāminī |
| incipiant | incipiantur |

### IMPERFECT

| | |
|---|---|
| inciperem | inciperer |
| inciperēs | inciperēris, inciperēre |
| inciperet | inciperētur |
| inciperēmus | inciperēmur |
| inciperētis | inciperēminī |
| inciperent | inciperentur |

### PERFECT

| | |
|---|---|
| incēperim | inceptus (-a, -um) sim |
| incēperis | inceptus (-a, -um) sīs |
| incēperit | inceptus (-a, -um) sit |
| incēperimus | inceptī (-ae, -a) sīmus |
| incēperitis | inceptī (-ae, -a) sītis |
| incēperint | inceptī (-ae, -a) sint |

### PLUPERFECT

| | |
|---|---|
| incēpissem | inceptus (-a, -um) essem |
| incēpissēs | inceptus (-a, -um) essēs |
| incēpisset | inceptus (-a, -um) esset |
| incēpissēmus | inceptī (-ae, -a) essēmus |
| incēpissētis | inceptī (-ae, -a) essētis |
| incēpissent | inceptī (-ae, -a) essent |

## PARTICIPLES

| ACTIVE | PASSIVE |
|---|---|

### PRESENT

| | |
|---|---|
| incipiēns | –– |

### PERFECT

| | |
|---|---|
| –– | inceptus, -a, -um |

### FUTURE

| | |
|---|---|
| inceptūrus, -a, -um | incipiendus, -a -um |

## INFINITIVES

| ACTIVE | PASSIVE |
|---|---|

### PRESENT

incipere incipī

### PERFECT

incēpisse inceptus, -a, -um esse

### FUTURE

inceptūrus, -a, -um esse inceptum īrī

## IMPERATIVES

| ACTIVE | | PASSIVE | |
|---|---|---|---|
| SINGULAR | PLURAL | SINGULAR | PLURAL |

### PRESENT

| | incipe | incipite | incipere | incipiminī |
|---|---|---|---|---|

### FUTURE

| | SINGULAR | PLURAL | SINGULAR | PLURAL |
|---|---|---|---|---|
| 2nd | incipitō | incipitōte | incipitor | -- |
| 3rd | incipitō | incipiuntō | incipitor | incipiuntor |

## PERIPHRASTICS

As in the first conjugation, the future active and passive participles and forms of the verb "to be" make up the periphrastic conjugations. See **optō** for examples.

---

*Fourth Conjugation*: **sentiō, sentīre, sēnsī, sēnsus,** 'feel, perceive'

## INDICATIVE

| ACTIVE | PASSIVE |
|---|---|

### PRESENT

| sentiō | sentior |
|---|---|
| sentīs | sentīris, sentīre |
| sentit | sentītur |
| sentīmus | sentīmur |
| sentītis | sentīminī |
| sentiunt | sentiuntur |

### IMPERFECT

| sentiēbam | sentiēbar |
|---|---|
| sentiēbās | sentiēbāris, sentiēbāre |
| sentiēbat | sentiēbātur |

| ACTIVE | PASSIVE |
|--------|---------|
| **IMPERFECT** | |
| sentiēbāmus | sentiēbāmur |
| sentiēbātis | sentiēbāminī |
| sentiēbant | sentiēbantur |
| **FUTURE** | |
| sentiam | sentiar |
| sentiēs | sentiēris, sentiēre |
| sentiet | sentiētur |
| sentiēmus | sentiēmur |
| sentiētis | sentiēminī |
| sentient | sentientur |
| **PERFECT** | |
| sēnsī | sēnsus (-a, -um) sum |
| sēnsistī | sēnsus (-a, -um) es |
| sēnsit | sēnsus (-a, -um) est |
| sēnsimus | sēnsī (-ae, -a) sumus |
| sēnsistis | sēnsī (-ae, -a) estis |
| sēnsērunt, sēnsēre | sēnsī (-ae, -a) sunt |
| **PLUPERFECT** | |
| sēnseram | sēnsus (-a, -um) eram |
| sēnserās | sēnsus (-a, -um) erās |
| sēnserat | sēnsus (-a, -um) erat |
| sēnserāmus | sēnsī (-ae, -a) erāmus |
| sēnserātis | sēnsī (-ae, -a) erātis |
| sēnserant | sēnsī (-ae, -a) erant |
| **FUTURE PERFECT** | |
| sēnserō | sēnsus (-a, -um) erō |
| sēnseris | sēnsus (-a, -um) eris |
| sēnserit | sēnsus (-a, -um) erit |
| sēnserimus | sēnsī (-ae, -a) erimus |
| sēnseritis | sēnsī (-ae, -a) eritis |
| sēnserint | sēnsī (-ae, -a) erunt |

## SUBJUNCTIVE

| ACTIVE | PASSIVE |
|--------|---------|
| **PRESENT** | |
| sentiam | sentiar |
| sentiās | sentiāris, sentiāre |
| sentiat | sentiātur |

| ACTIVE | PASSIVE |
|---|---|

### PRESENT

| | |
|---|---|
| sentiāmus | sentiāmur |
| sentiātis | sentiāminī |
| sentiant | sentiantur |

### IMPERFECT

| | |
|---|---|
| sentīrem | sentīrer |
| sentīrēs | sentīrēris, sentīrēre |
| sentīret | sentīrētur |
| sentīrēmus | sentīrēmur |
| sentīrētis | sentīrēminī |
| sentīrent | sentīrentur |

### PERFECT

| | |
|---|---|
| sēnserim | sēnsus (-a, -um) sim |
| sēnseris | sēnsus (-a, -um) sīs |
| sēnserit | sēnsus (-a, -um) sit |
| sēnserimus | sēnsī (-ae, -a) sīmus |
| sēnseritis | sēnsī (-ae, -a) sītis |
| sēnserint | sēnsī (-ae, -a) sint |

### PLUPERFECT

| | |
|---|---|
| sēnsissem | sēnsus (-a, -um) essem |
| sēnsissēs | sēnsus (-a, -um) essēs |
| sēnsisset | sēnsus (-a, -um) esset |
| sēnsissēmus | sēnsī (-ae, -a) essēmus |
| sēnsissētis | sēnsī (-ae, -a) essētis |
| sēnsissent | sēnsī (-ae, -a) essent |

## PARTICIPLES

### PRESENT

| ACTIVE | PASSIVE |
|---|---|
| sentiēns | -- |

### PERFECT

| | |
|---|---|
| -- | sēnsus, -a, -um |

### FUTURE

| | |
|---|---|
| sēnsūrus, -a, -um | sentiendus, -a, -um |

# INFINITIVES

| Active | Passive |
|--------|---------|

### Present

sentīre            sentīrī

### Perfect

sēnsisse          sēnsus, -a, -um esse

### Future

sēnsūrus, -a, -um esse     sēnsum īrī

# IMPERATIVES

| Active | | Passive | |
|--------|--------|---------|--------|
| SINGULAR | PLURAL | SINGULAR | PLURAL |

### Present

| | sentī | sentīte | sentīre | sentīminī |
|---|-------|---------|---------|-----------|

### Future

| 2nd | sentītō | sentītōte | sentītor | — |
|-----|---------|-----------|----------|--------|
| 3rd | sentītō | sentiuntō | sentītor | sentiuntor |

## PERIPHRASTICS

As in the first conjugation, the future active and passive participles and forms of the verb "to be" make up the periphrastic conjugations. See **optō** for examples.

# *Deponent Verbs*

**precor, precārī, precātus sum,** 'beg, request'
**vereor, verērī, veritus sum,** 'fear'
**ingredior, ingredī, ingressus sum,** 'enter, proceed'
**experior, experīrī, expertus sum,** 'try, experience'

## First Conjugation

### INDICATIVE

| Present | Imperfect |
|---------|-----------|
| precor, I beg, I am begging, I do beg, I (always) beg | precābar, I was begging, etc. |
| precāris, precāre, you beg, etc. | precābāris, precābāre, you were begging, etc. |
| precātur, he/she/it begs, etc. | precābātur, he/she/it was begging, etc. |

| PRESENT | IMPERFECT |
|---|---|
| precāmur, we beg, etc. | precābāmur, we were begging, etc. |
| precāminī, you beg, etc. | precābāminī, you were begging, etc. |
| precantur, they beg, etc. | precābantur, they were begging, etc. |

| FUTURE | PERFECT |
|---|---|
| precābor, I shall beg, etc. | precātus (-a, -um) sum, I have begged, etc. |
| precāberis, precābere, you will beg, etc. | precātus (-a, -um) es |
| precābitur, he/she/it will beg, etc. | precātus (-a, -um) est |
| precābimur, we shall beg, etc. | precātī (-ae, -a) sumus |
| precābiminī, you will beg, etc. | precātī (-ae, -a) estis |
| precābuntur, they will beg, etc. | precātī (-ae, -a) sunt |

| PLUPERFECT | FUTURE PERFECT |
|---|---|
| precātus (-a, -um) eram, I had begged | precātus (-a, -um) erō, I shall have begged |
| precātus (-a, -um) erās | precātus (-a, -um) eris |
| precātus (-a, -um) erat | precātus (-a, -um) erit |
| precātī (-ae, -a) erāmus | precātī (-ae, -a) erimus |
| precātī (-ae, -a) erātis | precātī (-ae, -a) eritis |
| precātī (-ae, -a) erant | precātī (-ae, -a) erunt |

## SUBJUNCTIVE

| PRESENT | IMPERFECT |
|---|---|
| precer | precārer |
| precēris, precēre | precārēris, precārēre |
| precētur | precārētur |
| precēmur | precārēmur |
| precēminī | precārēminī |
| precentur | precārentur |

| PERFECT | PLUPERFECT |
|---|---|
| precātus (-a, -um) sim | precātus (-a, -um) essem |
| precātus (-a, -um) sīs | precātus (-a, -um) essēs |
| precātus (-a, -um) sit | precātus (-a, -um) esset |
| precātī (-ae, -a) sīmus | precātī (-ae, -a) essēmus |
| precātī (-ae, -a) sītis | precātī (-ae, -a) essētis |
| precātī (-ae, -a) sint | precātī (-ae, -a) essent |

# PARTICIPLES

## PRESENT

precāns, begging

## PERFECT

precātus, -a, -um, having begged

## FUTURE ACTIVE

precātūrus, -a, -um, about to beg, going to beg, ready to beg

## FUTURE PASSIVE

precandus, -a, -um, to be begged, having to be begged

# INFINITIVES

## PRESENT

precārī, to beg

## PERFECT

precātus (-a, -um) esse, to have begged

## FUTURE

precātūrus (-a, -um) esse, to be about to beg, to be going to beg, to be ready
   to beg

# IMPERATIVES

|  SINGULAR  |  PLURAL  |
|---|---|

## PRESENT

| precāre, beg! | precāminī, beg! |

## FUTURE

| 2nd | precātor, you shall beg! | -- |
| 3rd | precātor, he/she/it shall beg! | precantor, they shall beg! |

**Second, Third, and Fourth Conjugations**

# INDICATIVE

## PRESENT

| vereor | ingredior | experior |
| verēris, verēre | ingrederis, ingredere | experīris, experīre |
| verētur | ingreditur | experītur |
| verēmur | ingredimur | experīmur |
| verēminī | ingrediminī | experīminī |
| verentur | ingrediuntur | experiuntur |

## IMPERFECT

| | | |
|---|---|---|
| verēbar | ingrediēbar | experiēbar |
| verēbāris, verēbāre | ingrediēbāris, ingrediēbāre | experiēbāris, experiēbāre |
| verēbātur | ingrediēbātur | experiēbātur |
| verēbāmur | ingrediēbāmur | experiēbāmur |
| verēbāminī | ingrediēbāminī | experiēbāminī |
| verēbantur | ingrediēbantur | experiēbantur |

## FUTURE

| | | |
|---|---|---|
| verēbor | ingrediar | experiar |
| verēberis, verēbere | ingrediēris, ingrediēre | experiēris, experiēre |
| verēbitur | ingrediētur | experiētur |
| verēbimur | ingrediēmur | experiēmur |
| verēbiminī | ingrediēminī | experiēminī |
| verēbuntur | ingredientur | experientur |

## PERFECT

| | | |
|---|---|---|
| veritus (-a, -um) sum | ingressus (-a, -um) sum | expertus (-a, -um) sum |
| veritus (-a, -um) es | ingressus (-a, -um) es | expertus (-a, -um) es |
| veritus (-a, -um) est | ingressus (-a, -um) est | expertus (-a, -um) est |
| veritī (-ae, -a) sumus | ingressī (-ae, -a) sumus | expertī (-ae, -a) sumus |
| veritī (-ae, -a) estis | ingressī (-ae, -a) estis | expertī (-ae, -a) estis |
| veritī (-ae, -a) sunt | ingressī (-ae, -a) sunt | expertī (-ae, -a) sunt |

## PLUPERFECT

| | | |
|---|---|---|
| veritus (-a, -um) eram | ingressus (-a, -um) eram | expertus (-a, -um) eram |
| veritus (-a, -um) erās | ingressus (-a, -um) erās | expertus (-a, -um) erās |
| veritus (-a, -um) erat | ingressus (-a, -um) erat | expertus (-a, -um) erat |
| veritī (-ae, -a) erāmus | ingressī (-ae, -a) erāmus | expertī (-ae, -a) erāmus |
| veritī (-ae, -a) erātis | ingressī (-ae, -a) erātis | expertī (-ae, -a) erātis |
| veritī (-ae, -a) erant | ingressī (-ae, -a) erant | expertī (-ae, -a) erant |

## FUTURE PERFECT

| | | |
|---|---|---|
| veritus (-a, -um) erō | ingressus (-a, -um) erō | expertus (-a, -um) erō |
| veritus (-a, -um) eris | ingressus (-a, -um) eris | expertus (-a, -um) eris |
| veritus (-a, -um) erit | ingressus (-a, -um) erit | expertus (-a, -um) erit |
| veritī (-ae, -a) erimus | ingressī (-ae, -a) erimus | expertī (-ae, -a) erimus |
| veritī (-ae, -a) eritis | ingressī (-ae, -a) eritis | expertī (-ae, -a) eritis |
| veritī (-ae, -a) erunt | ingressī (-ae, -a) erunt | expertī (-ae, -a) erunt |

## SUBJUNCTIVE

### PRESENT

| | | |
|---|---|---|
| verear | ingrediar | experiar |
| vereāris, vereāre | ingrediāris, ingrediāre | experiāris, experiāre |
| vereātur | ingrediātur | experiātur |
| vereāmur | ingrediāmur | experiāmur |
| vereāminī | ingrediāminī | experiāminī |
| vereantur | ingrediantur | experiantur |

### IMPERFECT

| | | |
|---|---|---|
| verērer | ingrederer | experīrer |
| verērēris, verērēre | ingrederēris, ingrederēre | experīrēris, experīrēre |
| verērētur | ingrederētur | experīrētur |
| verērēmur | ingrederēmur | experīrēmur |
| verērēminī | ingrederēminī | experīrēminī |
| verērentur | ingrederentur | experīrentur |

### PERFECT

| | | |
|---|---|---|
| veritus (-a, -um) sim | ingressus (-a, -um) sim | expertus (-a, -um) sim |
| veritus (-a, -um) sīs | ingressus (-a, -um) sīs | expertus (-a, -um) sīs |
| veritus (-a, -um) sit | ingressus (-a, -um) sit | expertus (-a, -um) sit |
| veritī (-ae, -a) sīmus | ingressī (-ae, -a) sīmus | expertī (-ae, -a) sīmus |
| veritī (-ae, -a) sītis | ingressī (-ae, -a) sītis | expertī (-ae, -a) sītis |
| veritī (-ae, -a) sint | ingressī (-ae, -a) sint | expertī (-ae, -a) sint |

### PLUPERFECT

| | | |
|---|---|---|
| veritus (-a, -um) essem | ingressus (-a, -um) essem | expertus (-a, -um) essem |
| veritus (-a, -um) essēs | ingressus (-a, -um) essēs | expertus (-a, -um) essēs |
| veritus (-a, -um) esset | ingressus (-a, -um) esset | expertus (-a, -um) esset |
| veritī (-ae, -a) essēmus | ingressī (-ae, -a) essēmus | expertī (-ae, -a) essēmus |
| veritī (-ae, -a) essētis | ingressī (-ae, -a) essētis | expertī (-ae, -a) essētis |
| veritī (-ae, -a) essent | ingressī (-ae, -a) essent | expertī (-ae, -a) essent |

## PARTICIPLES

### PRESENT

| | | |
|---|---|---|
| verēns | ingrediēns | experiēns |

### PERFECT

| | | |
|---|---|---|
| veritus, -a, -um | ingressus, -a, -um | expertus, -a, -um |

### FUTURE ACTIVE

| | | |
|---|---|---|
| veritūrus, -a, -um | ingressūrus, -a, -um | expertūrus, -a, -um |

### FUTURE PASSIVE

| | | |
|---|---|---|
| verendus, -a, -um | ingrediendus, -a, -um | experiendus, -a, -um |

# INFINITIVES

## PRESENT

| | | |
|---|---|---|
| verērī | ingredī | experīrī |

## PERFECT

| | | |
|---|---|---|
| veritus (-a, -um) esse | ingressus (-a, -um) esse | expertus (-a, -um) esse |

## FUTURE

| | | |
|---|---|---|
| veritūrus (-a, -um) esse | ingressūrus (-a, -um) esse | expertūrus (-a, -um) esse |

# IMPERATIVES

| SINGULAR | PLURAL | SINGULAR | PLURAL | SINGULAR | PLURAL |
|---|---|---|---|---|---|

### PRESENT

| SINGULAR | PLURAL | SINGULAR | PLURAL | SINGULAR | PLURAL |
|---|---|---|---|---|---|
| verēre | verēminī | ingredere | ingrediminī | experīre | experīminī |

### FUTURE

| | SINGULAR | PLURAL | SINGULAR | PLURAL | SINGULAR | PLURAL |
|---|---|---|---|---|---|---|
| 2nd | verētor | -- | ingreditor | -- | experītor | -- |
| 3rd | verētor | verentor | ingreditor | ingrediuntor | experītor | experiuntor |

---

**sum, esse, fuī, futūrus, 'be'**
**possum, posse, potuī, --, 'be able'**

# INDICATIVE

## PRESENT

| | |
|---|---|
| sum, I am | possum, I am able, I can |
| es, you are | potes, you are able, etc. |
| est, he/she/it/there is | potest, he/she/it is able, etc. |
| sumus, we are | possumus, we are able, etc. |
| estis, you are | potestis, you are able, etc. |
| sunt, they/there are | possunt, they are able, etc. |

## IMPERFECT

| | |
|---|---|
| eram, I was | poteram, I was able, I could |
| erās, you were | poterās, you were able, etc. |
| erat, he/she/it/there was | poterat, he/she/it was able, etc. |
| erāmus, we were | poterāmus, we were able, etc. |
| erātis, you were | poterātis, you were able, etc. |
| erant, they/there were | poterant, they were able, etc. |

## FUTURE

| | |
|---|---|
| erō, I shall be | poterō, I shall be able |
| eris, you will be | poteris, you will be able |
| erit, he/she/it/there will be | poterit, he/she/it will be able |

## FUTURE

erimus, we shall be
eritis, you will be
erunt, they/there will be

poterimus, we shall be able
poteritis, you will be able
poterunt, they will be able

## PERFECT

fuī, I have been, I was

fuistī, you have been, etc.

fuit, he/she/it/there has been, etc.

fuimus, we have been, etc.

fuistis, you have been, etc.

fuērunt, fuēre, they/there have been, etc.

potuī, I have been (was) able, I could

potuistī, you have been (were) able, etc.

potuit, he/she/it has been (was) able, etc.

potuimus, we have been (were) able, etc.

potuistis, you have been (were) able, etc.

potuērunt, potuēre, they have been (were) able, etc.

## PLUPERFECT

fueram, I had been
fuerās, you had been
fuerat, he/she/it/there had been

fuerāmus, we had been
fuerātis, you had been
fuerant, they/there had been

potueram I had been able
potuerās, you had been able
potuerat, he/she/it had been able

potuerāmus, we had been able
potuerātis, you had been able
potuerant, they had been able

## FUTURE PERFECT

fuerō, I shall have been
fueris, you will have been
fuerit, he/she/it/there will have been

fuerimus, we shall have been
fueritis, you will have been
fuerint, they/there will have been

potuerō, I shall have been able
potueris, you will have been able
potuerit, he/she/it will have been able

potuerimus, we shall have been able
potueritis, you will have been able
potuerint, they will have been able

## SUBJUNCTIVE

### PRESENT

| sim | sīmus | possim | possīmus |
|-----|-------|--------|----------|
| sīs | sītis | possīs | possītis |
| sit | sint  | possit | possint  |

### IMPERFECT

| | | | |
|---|---|---|---|
| essem | essēmus | possem | possēmus |
| essēs | essētis | possēs | possētis |
| esset | essent | posset | possent |

### PERFECT

| | | | |
|---|---|---|---|
| fuerim | fuerimus | potuerim | potuerimus |
| fueris | fueritis | potueris | potueritis |
| fuerit | fuerint | potuerit | potuerint |

### PLUPERFECT

| | | | |
|---|---|---|---|
| fuissem | fuissēmus | potuissem | potuissēmus |
| fuissēs | fuissētis | potuissēs | potuissētis |
| fuisset | fuissent | potuisset | potuissent |

## PARTICIPLES

### PRESENT

——  potēns, (being) able, powerful

### PERFECT

——  ——

### FUTURE

futūrus, -a, -um, about to be,  ——
going to be, ready to be

## INFINITIVES

### PRESENT

esse, to be  posse, to be able

### PERFECT

fuisse, to have been  potuisse, to have been able

### FUTURE

futūrus, -a, -um esse (fore), to be  ——
about to be, to be going to be,
to be ready to be

## IMPERATIVES

| | SINGULAR | PLURAL | SINGULAR | PLURAL |
|---|---|---|---|---|
| | | **PRESENT** | | |
| | es, be! | este, be! | —— | —— |
| | | **FUTURE** | | |
| 2nd | estō, you shall be! | estōte, you shall be! | —— | —— |
| 3rd | estō, he/she/it shall be! | suntō, they shall be! | —— | —— |

### eō, īre, iī (īvī), itus, 'go'

## INDICATIVE

| Present | Imperfect | Future |
|---|---|---|
| eō | ībam | ībō |
| īs | ībās | ībis |
| it | ībat | ībit |
| īmus | ībāmus | ībimus |
| ītis | ībātis | ībitis |
| eunt | ībant | ībunt |

| Perfect | Pluperfect | Future Perfect |
|---|---|---|
| iī (īvī) | ieram (īveram) | ierō (īverō) |
| īstī (īvistī) | ierās (īverās) | ieris (īveris) |
| iit (īvit) | ierat (īverat) | ierit (īverit) |
| iimus (īvimus) | ierāmus (īverāmus) | ierimus (īverimus) |
| īstis (īvistis) | ierātis (īverātis) | ieritis (īveritis) |
| iērunt, iēre | ierant (īverant) | ierint (īverint) |
| (īvērunt, īvēre) | | |

## SUBJUNCTIVE

| Present | Imperfect | Perfect | Pluperfect |
|---|---|---|---|
| eam | īrem | ierim (īverim) | īssem (īvissem) |
| eās | īrēs | ieris (īveris) | īssēs (īvissēs) |
| eat | īret | ierit (īverit) | īsset (īvisset) |
| eāmus | īrēmus | ierimus (īverimus) | īssēmus (īvissēmus) |
| eātis | īrētis | ieritis (īveritis) | īssētis (īvissētis) |
| eant | īrent | ierint (īverint) | īssent (īvissent) |

## PARTICIPLES

| Active | Passive |
|---|---|
| **Present** | |
| iēns, *gen.* euntis | -- |
| **Perfect** | |
| -- | itum |
| **Future** | |
| itūrus, -a, -um | eundum |

## INFINITIVES

| ACTIVE | PASSIVE |
|--------|---------|

PRESENT

| ire | -- |

PERFECT

| īsse (īvisse) | -- |

FUTURE

| itūrus (-a, -um) esse | -- |

## IMPERATIVES

| SINGULAR | PLURAL |
|----------|--------|

PRESENT

| | ī | īte |

FUTURE

| 2nd | ītō | ītōte |
| 3rd | ītō | euntō |

---

**ferō, ferre, tulī, lātus, 'bring, carry, bear, endure'**

## INDICATIVE

| ACTIVE | PASSIVE |
|--------|---------|

PRESENT

| ferō | feror |
| fers | ferris, ferre |
| fert | fertur |
| ferimus | ferimur |
| fertis | feriminī |
| ferunt | feruntur |

IMPERFECT

| ferēbam | ferēbar |
| ferēbās | ferēbāris, ferēbāre |
| ferēbat | ferēbātur |
| ferēbāmus | ferēbāmur |
| ferēbātis | ferēbāminī |
| ferēbant | ferēbantur |

| ACTIVE | PASSIVE |
|---|---|

### FUTURE

| feram | ferar |
|---|---|
| ferēs | ferēris, ferēre |
| feret | ferētur |
| ferēmus | ferēmur |
| ferētis | ferēminī |
| ferent | ferentur |

### PERFECT

| tulī | lātus (-a, -um) sum |
|---|---|
| tulistī | lātus (-a, -um) es |
| tulit | lātus (-a, -um) est |
| tulimus | lātī (-ae, -a) sumus |
| tulistis | lātī (-ae, -a) estis |
| tulērunt, tulēre | lātī (-ae, -a) sunt |

### PLUPERFECT

| tuleram | lātus (-a, -um) eram |
|---|---|
| tulerās | lātus (-a, -um) erās |
| tulerat | lātus (-a, -um) erat |
| tulerāmus | lātī (-ae, -a) erāmus |
| tulerātis | lātī (-ae, -a) erātis |
| tulerant | lātī (-ae, -a) erant |

### FUTURE PERFECT

| tulerō | lātus (-a, -um) erō |
|---|---|
| tuleris | lātus (-a, -um) eris |
| tulerit | lātus (-a, -um) erit |
| tulerimus | lātī (-ae, -a) erimus |
| tuleritis | lātī (-ae, -a) eritis |
| tulerint | lātī (-ae, -a) erunt |

## SUBJUNCTIVE

| ACTIVE | PASSIVE |
|---|---|

### PRESENT

| feram | ferar |
|---|---|
| ferās | ferāris, ferāre |
| ferat | ferātur |
| ferāmus | ferāmur |
| ferātis | ferāminī |
| ferant | ferantur |

| ACTIVE | PASSIVE |
|--------|---------|

**IMPERFECT**

| ferrem | ferrer |
| ferrēs | ferrēris, ferrēre |
| ferret | ferrētur |

| ferrēmus | ferrēmur |
| ferrētis | ferrēminī |
| ferrent | ferrentur |

**PERFECT**

| tulerim | lātus (-a, -um) sim |
| tuleris | lātus (-a, -um) sīs |
| tulerit | lātus (-a, -um) sit |

| tulerimus | lātī (-ae, -a) sīmus |
| tuleritis | lātī (-ae, -a) sītis |
| tulerint | lātī (-ae, -a) sint |

**PLUPERFECT**

| tulissem | lātus (-a, -um) essem |
| tulissēs | lātus (-a, -um) essēs |
| tulisset | lātus (-a, -um) esset |

| tulissēmus | lātī (-ae, -a) essēmus |
| tulissētis | lātī (-ae, -a) essētis |
| tulissent | lātī (-ae, -a) essent |

## PARTICIPLES

| ACTIVE | PASSIVE |
|--------|---------|

**PRESENT**

| ferēns | -- |

**PERFECT**

| -- | lātus, -a, -um |

**FUTURE**

| lātūrus, -a, -um | ferendus, -a, -um |

## INFINITIVES

| ACTIVE | PASSIVE |
|--------|---------|

**PRESENT**

| ferre | ferrī |

|                | ACTIVE                |                | PASSIVE |
|----------------|-----------------------|----------------|---------|

### PERFECT

tulisse                         lātus (-a, -um) esse

### FUTURE

lātūrus (-a, -um) esse      lātum īrī

## IMPERATIVES

|          | ACTIVE |        | PASSIVE  |        |
|----------|--------|--------|----------|--------|
|          | SINGULAR | PLURAL | SINGULAR | PLURAL |

### PRESENT

|     | fer   | ferte   | ferre  | feriminī |
|-----|-------|---------|--------|----------|

### FUTURE

|     | fertō | fertōte | fertor | --      |
|-----|-------|---------|--------|---------|
| 2nd | fertō | fertōte | fertor | --      |
| 3rd | fertō | feruntō | fertor | feruntor |

---

**volō, velle, voluī, --,** 'wish, want, be willing'
**nōlō, nōlle, nōluī, --,** 'be unwilling'
**mālō, mālle, māluī, --,** 'prefer'

## INDICATIVE

### PRESENT

| volō     | nōlō      | mālō     |
|----------|-----------|----------|
| vīs      | nōn vīs   | māvīs    |
| vult     | nōn vult  | māvult   |
| volumus  | nōlumus   | mālumus  |
| vultis   | nōn vultis| māvultis |
| volunt   | nōlunt    | mālunt   |

### IMPERFECT

| volēbam   | nōlēbam   | mālēbam   |
|-----------|-----------|-----------|
| volēbās   | nōlēbās   | mālēbās   |
| volēbat   | nōlēbat   | mālēbat   |
| volēbāmus | nōlēbāmus | mālēbāmus |
| volēbātis | nōlēbātis | mālēbātis |
| volēbant  | nōlēbant  | mālēbant  |

### FUTURE

| volam  | nōlam  | mālam  |
|--------|--------|--------|
| volēs  | nōlēs  | mālēs  |
| volet  | nōlet  | mālet  |

| | | |
|---|---|---|
| volēmus | nōlēmus | mālēmus |
| volētis | nōlētis | mālētis |
| volent | nōlent | mālent |

### PERFECT

| | | |
|---|---|---|
| voluī | nōluī | māluī |
| voluistī | nōluistī | māluistī |
| voluit | nōluit | māluit |
| voluimus | nōluimus | māluimus |
| voluistis | nōluistis | māluistis |
| voluērunt, voluēre | nōluērunt, nōluēre | māluērunt, māluēre |

### PLUPERFECT

| | | |
|---|---|---|
| volueram | nōlueram | mālueram |
| voluerās | nōluerās | māluerās |
| voluerat | nōluerat | māluerat |
| voluerāmus | nōluerāmus | māluerāmus |
| voluerātis | nōluerātis | māluerātis |
| voluerant | nōluerant | māluerant |

### FUTURE PERFECT

| | | |
|---|---|---|
| voluerō | nōluerō | māluerō |
| volueris | nōlueris | mālueris |
| voluerit | nōluerit | māluerit |
| voluerimus | nōluerimus | māluerimus |
| volueritis | nōlueritis | mālueritis |
| voluerint | nōluerint | māluerint |

## SUBJUNCTIVE

### PRESENT

| | | |
|---|---|---|
| velim | nōlim | mālim |
| velīs | nōlīs | mālīs |
| velit | nōlit | mālit |
| velīmus | nōlīmus | mālīmus |
| velītis | nōlītis | mālītis |
| velint | nōlint | mālint |

### IMPERFECT

| | | |
|---|---|---|
| vellem | nōllem | māllem |
| vellēs | nōllēs | māllēs |
| vellet | nōllet | māllet |
| vellēmus | nōllēmus | māllēmus |
| vellētis | nōllētis | māllētis |
| vellent | nōllent | māllent |

### Perfect

| voluerim | nōluerim | māluerim |
|----------|----------|----------|
| volueris | nōlueris | mālueris |
| voluerit | nōluerit | māluerit |
| voluerimus | nōluerimus | māluerimus |
| volueritis | nōlueritis | mālueritis |
| voluerint | nōluerint | māluerint |

### Pluperfect

| voluissem | nōluissem | māluissem |
|-----------|-----------|-----------|
| voluissēs | nōluissēs | māluissēs |
| voluisset | nōluisset | māluisset |
| voluissēmus | nōluissēmus | māluissēmus |
| voluissētis | nōluissētis | māluissētis |
| voluissent | nōluissent | māluissent |

## PARTICIPLES

### Present

| volēns | nōlēns | -- |
|--------|--------|----|

### Perfect

| -- | -- | -- |
|----|----|----|

### Future

| -- | -- | -- |
|----|----|----|

## INFINITIVES

### Present

| velle | nōlle | mālle |
|-------|-------|-------|

### Perfect

| voluisse | nōluisse | māluisse |
|----------|----------|----------|

### Future

| -- | -- | -- |
|----|----|----|

## IMPERATIVES

| SINGULAR | PLURAL |
|----------|--------|

### Present

| -- | nōlī | nōlīte | -- |
|----|------|--------|----|

### Future

| -- | 2nd nōlītō | nōlītōte | -- |
|----|-----------|----------|----|
|    | 3rd nōlītō | nōluntō |   |

**fīō, fierī, factus sum**, 'be made, be done, happen, become'

## INDICATIVE

| PRESENT | IMPERFECT | FUTURE |
|---|---|---|
| fīō, I am made, | fīēbam, I was made, | fīam, I shall be made, |
| I become | I became | I shall become |
| fīs | fīēbās | fīēs |
| fit | fīēbat | fīet |
| fīmus | fīēbāmus | fīēmus |
| fītis | fīēbātis | fīētis |
| fīunt | fīēbant | fīent |

| PERFECT | PLUPERFECT | FUTURE PERFECT |
|---|---|---|
| factus (-a, -um) sum | factus (-a, -um) eram | factus (-a, -um) erō |
| factus (-a, -um) es | factus (-a, -um) erās | factus (-a, -um) eris |
| factus (-a, -um) est | factus (-a, -um) erat | factus (-a, -um) erit |
| factī (-ae, -a) sumus | factī (-ae, -a) erāmus | factī (-ae, -a) erimus |
| factī (-ae, -a) estis | factī (-ae, -a) erātis | factī (-ae, -a) eritis |
| factī (-ae, -a) sunt | factī (-ae, -a) erant | factī (-ae, -a) erunt |

## SUBJUNCTIVE

| PRESENT | IMPERFECT | PERFECT | PLUPERFECT |
|---|---|---|---|
| fīam | fierem | factus (-a, -um) sim | factus (-a, -um) essem |
| fīās | fierēs | factus (-a, -um) sīs | factus (-a, -um) essēs |
| fīat | fieret | factus (-a, -um) sit | factus (-a, -um) esset |
| fīāmus | fierēmus | factī (-ae, -a) sīmus | factī (-ae, -a) essēmus |
| fīātis | fierētis | factī (-ae, -a) sītis | factī (-ae, -a) essētis |
| fīant | fierent | factī (-ae, -a) sint | factī (-ae, -a) essent |

## PARTICIPLES

### PRESENT

--

### PERFECT

factus, -a, -um, having been made, having become

### FUTURE

faciendus, -a, -um, having to be made, having to become

## INFINITIVES

### PRESENT

fierī, to be made, to become

PERFECT

factus (-a, -um) esse, to have been made, to have become

FUTURE

factum īrī, to be about (going, ready) to be made, to be about (going, ready) to become

## IMPERATIVES

| SINGULAR | PLURAL |
|---|---|
| **PRESENT** | |
| fī, be made, become! | fīte, be made, become! |

FUTURE

2nd   fītō, you shall be made,     —
       you shall become!

3rd   fītō, he/she/it shall be made,   —
       he/she/it shall become!

## *Formation of the Future Imperative*

The future imperative is a rare form in Latin. It exists in the second and third persons, singular and plural. To form the future *active* imperative, take the present stem and for the second and third persons singular, add the ending **-tō**. For the second person plural, add **-tōte** to the present stem, and for the third person plural, add **-ntō** to the stem.

The future *passive* imperative lacks a second person plural. The endings which are added to the present stem are **-tor** for the second and third persons singular and **-ntor** for the third person plural.

In the third conjugation, the **-e-** of the present stem is changed to **-i-**, but in the third person plural to **-u-**. In i-stems of the third conjugation and in the fourth conjugation, an **-i-** appears before the **-u-**.

Thus:

### ACTIVE

| | | | | | |
|---|---|---|---|---|---|
| SINGULAR | 2nd | optātō | implētō | dūcitō | incipitō | sentītō |
| | 3rd | optātō | implētō | dūcitō | incipitō | sentītō |
| PLURAL | 2nd | optātōte | implētōte | dūcitōte | incipitōte | sentītōte |
| | 3rd | optantō | implentō | dūcuntō | incipiuntō | sentiuntō |

### PASSIVE

| | | | | | |
|---|---|---|---|---|---|
| SINGULAR | 2nd | optātor | implētor | dūcitor | incipitor | sentītor |
| | 3rd | optātor | implētor | dūcitor | incipitor | sentītor |
| PLURAL | 2nd | — | — | — | — | — |
| | 3rd | optantor | implentor | dūcuntor | incipiuntor | sentiuntor |

# REVIEW OF THE SYNTAX OF NOUNS

## Apposition

Apposition may occur in all cases in Latin.

NOMINATIVE: 1. Marcus, **bonus vir**, in agrīs labōrat. Marcus, *a good man,* is working in the fields.
2. **Nūntiī** ad īnsulam īvimus. We went *as messengers* to the island; We, *messengers,* went to the island.
3. **Amīcus tuus** tibi loquor. I speak to you *as your friend*; I, *your friend,* speak to you.

GENITIVE: Memorēs invidiae tuae, **culpae magnae**, ex urbe ībimus. Mindful of your envy, *a great fault,* we shall go out of the city.

DATIVE: Sorōrī **Annae** dōnum dedit. He gave a gift to his sister *Anna.*

ACCUSATIVE: Marcum **ducem** cōpiārum in Italiam mīsērunt. They sent Marcus, *the leader* of the troops, into Italy; They sent Marcus into Italy *as leader* of the troops.

ABLATIVE: Sociī in patriā **Asiā** vīsī sunt. The allies were seen in their native land *of Asia* (literally, their native land, *Asia*).

## Nominative Case

The nominative case is used for the subject of a finite verb and for the predicate nominative.

1. **Nautae** vēla ad īnsulam dedērunt. *The sailors* set sail to the island.
2. Marcus est **vir** honestus. Marcus is a distinguished *man.* (predicate nominative)
3. Marcus **vir** honestus vidētur. Marcus seems a distinguished *man.* (predicate nominative)
4. Marcus **honestus** vidēbātur. Marcus seemed *distinguished.* (predicate adjective)
5. **Puerī puellae**que in tēctum missī sunt. *The boys* and *girls* were sent into the house. (For the masculine verb, see *Additional Rules,* p. 400)
6. **Mare, sīdera, animālia, terra**que ā dīs immortālibus facta est. *The sea, stars, animals* and *land* were made by the immortal gods. (For the singular verb, see *Additional Rules,* p. 400)

## Genitive Case

The genitive case, in general, is used for a noun which is dependent upon another noun. In addition, it may depend upon a verb or an adjective. Thus:

GENITIVE OF POSSESSION (not discussed in the text)

1. Tēctum **meī amīcī** ignī dēlētum est. *My friend's* house was destroyed by fire.

2. Māter **ducis** ab incolīs laudāta est. The mother *of the leader* was praised by the inhabitants.

3. Iuvenis frātrem gladiō **patris** interfēcit. The young man killed his brother with his *father's* sword.

4. Poēta **cuius** liber est nōtus auxilium ā rēge petīvit. The poet *whose* book is well known sought aid from the king.

## PARTITIVE GENITIVE (GENITIVE OF THE WHOLE) (Unit 9G)

The genitive is sometimes used in Latin to express the *whole* group or unit of which the word on which the genitive depends expresses the *part.*

1. Quid **malī** in nostrō oppidō est? What *evil* is in our town?

2. Pars **oppidī** flammīs dēlēta erat. Part *of the town* had been destroyed by flames.

3. Nihil **bonī** in hāc urbe vidēre possumus. We are able to see nothing *good* in this city.

4. Plūs **pecūniae** nōs habēmus quam vōs. We have more *money* than you (do).

BUT:

1. Ūnus **ē librīs** ad nōs missus est. One *of the books* was sent to us.

2. Quīnque **ē mīlitibus** interfectī sunt. Five *of the soldiers* were killed.

3. Quīdam **ex hominibus** in viā ambulābat. A certain one *of the men* was walking in the street.

## GENITIVE OF DESCRIPTION (QUALITY) (Unit 10D)

A noun in the genitive case, when modified by an adjective, may be used to describe or express a quality of another noun.

1. Vir **magnae sapientiae** ab omnibus laudātur. A man *of great wisdom* is praised by all.

2. Verba **eius modī** ā populō omnī audīta sunt. Words *of this kind* have been heard by all the people.

3. Cicerō fuit homō **magnae fāmae.** Cicero was a man *of great reputation.*

## GENITIVE OF MATERIAL (not discussed in the text)

The genitive is used to express the material of which something is composed.

1. Urna **aurī** ā nātīs inventa est. An urn *of gold* was found by the children.

2. Tēlane **ferrī** habēs? Do you have weapons *of iron*?

3. Magnum agrum **frūmentī** vīdimus. We have seen a large field *of grain.* [frūmentum, -ī, N., 'grain']

4. Turba **fēminārum** in viā vīsa est. A crowd *of women* was seen in the street.

## APPOSITIONAL GENITIVE (not discussed in the text)

The genitive is sometimes used instead of a noun in apposition.

1. Nōmen **rēgis** ā populō Rōmānō nōn dīlēctum est. The name *of king* was not esteemed by the Roman people. [**dīligō, -ere, -lēxī, -lēctus,** 'esteem']
2. Difficile est artem **reī mīlitāris** docēre. It is difficult to teach the art *of warfare.* [**rēs mīlitāris, reī mīlitāris,** F., 'warfare']
3. Opportūnitās **librī legendī** nōbīs nōn offertur. The opportunity *of reading a book* is not offered to us. [**opportūnitās, -tātis,** F., 'opportunity']

PREDICATE GENITIVE (GENITIVE OF CHARACTERISTIC) (Unit 11D)
A noun in the genitive case which stands alone (or modified by an adjective) in the predicate denotes a characteristic or a class.

1. Est **bonī imperātōris** bene dūcere. It is *the mark of a good commander* to lead well.
2. **Dignī cīvis** est dē cūrīs patriae cōgitāre. It is *the mark of a worthy citizen* to think about the cares of his native land.
3. Sapienter regere est **honestī rēgis.** Ruling wisely is *the mark of a respected king.*

The genitive serves as the object of a verbal idea of nouns, adjectives, and is used with some verbs. Thus:

GENITIVE WITH VERBS OF ACCUSING AND CONDEMNING (Unit 2F)
The genitive is used with verbs of accusing and condemning to express the charge or penalty.

1. Hostēs **gravium scelerum** dāmnāvērunt. They condemned the enemy *for serious crimes.*
2. Fēminās **īrae** dāmnāmus. We condemn the women *for their anger.*
3. Nautās **īnsidiārum** dāmnābitis. You will condemn the sailors *for their treachery.*

OBJECTIVE GENITIVE (Unit 11C)
There is a verbal idea understood in nouns and adjectives of feeling or action. The noun that is the *object* of this verbal idea is called the objective genitive.

1. Dux **bellī** hortātus est ut mīlitēs quam fortissimē pūgnārent. The leader *of the war* urged that the soldiers fight as bravely as possible.
2. Incolae **oppidī** ruīnam **tēctōrum** timuērunt. The inhabitants *of the town* feared the destruction *of the houses.*
3. Erant multī rūmōrēs dē spē **pācis.** There were many rumors about the hope *of peace.*
4. Multa pecūnia saepe est **invidiae** causa. A lot of money is often the cause of *envy.*
5. Iūnō dē Iovis amōre **pulchrārum fēminārum** monēbātur. Juno was warned about Jupiter's love *of beautiful women.*

6. Iuvenis studiōsus **legendī** multa didicit. The young man, fond *of reading*, learned many things.

BUT NOTE also, in contrast, the SUBJECTIVE GENITIVE (Unit 11C):
There is a verbal idea understood in nouns and adjectives of feeling or action. The noun that is the *subject* of this verbal idea is called the subjective genitive.

1. Iūnō dē **Iovis** amōre pulchrārum fēminārum monēbātur. Juno was warned about *Jupiter's* love of beautiful women.
2. Īra **rēgīnae** populum terret. The *queen's* anger is frightening the people.
3. Mīlitēs īnsidiīs **hostium** superātī sunt. The soldiers were conquered by the treachery *of the enemy*.
4. Ob **rēgis** cūram dē salūte populī urbs quam optimē mūnīta est. On account of the *king's* concern about the safety of the people, the city has been fortified as well as possible.
5. Facta fortissima **mīlitum** ā ducibus laudāta sunt. The very brave deeds *of the soldiers* were praised by the leaders.

OBJECTIVE GENITIVE WITH IMPERSONAL VERBS (Unit 16D4)
Some impersonal verbs take the genitive of the thing which arouses the feeling and the accusative of the person concerned.

1. Mē **invidiae** pudet. I am ashamed *of my jealousy*.
2. Vōs **bellī longī** piget? Are you disgusted *with the long war*?
3. Quōs **superātōrum** miseret? Who pities *the conquered*?
4. **Ducis** interest inimīcōs interficī. It is in *the leader's* interest that his enemies be killed.

GENITIVE WITH EXPRESSIONS OF REMEMBERING AND FORGETTING (Unit 18H)
The genitive is frequently used with verbs and expressions of remembering and forgetting.

1. **Factōrum fortium** ducum nostrōrum semper meminerimus. We shall always remember *the brave deeds* of our leaders.
2. **Veniae nostrae** oblīvīsceris? Are you forgetting *our kindness*?
3. Memorēs **patriae** magnō cum studiō pūgnābimus. Mindful *of our native land* we shall fight with great zeal.

Note that the accusative may also be used in these constructions.

GENITIVE OF INDEFINITE VALUE (Unit 18I)
A few neuter adjectives and some nouns implying utter worthlessness, such as **as, floccus**, and **nihilum**, are sometimes used in the genitive case to express the value of a person, thing, or situation when that value is not specifically determined or is indefinite. This use of the genitive is generally found with verbs meaning 'consider', 'reckon', and 'value'.

1. Tēctum **magnī** habeō. I have a house *of great value.*
2. Inimīcōs **parvī** facimus. We reckon our enemies *of little worth.*
3. Quid **tantī** aestimāmus? What do we estimate *of such great value?*
4. Tē **floccī** dūcō. I don't give *a damn* for you.

GENITIVE OF FULLNESS AND WANT (not discussed in the text)
Words expressing fullness and emptiness often govern the genitive.

1. Servī urnam $\begin{cases} \text{plēnam } \textbf{aquae} \\ \text{inānem } \textbf{aquae} \end{cases}$ in mēnsā posuērunt. The slaves placed on the table the urn $\begin{cases} \text{full } of\ water \\ \text{empty } of\ water \end{cases}$. [**plēnus, -a, -um,** 'full'; **inānis, -e,** 'empty']
2. Mīlitēs fortēs **timōris** semper nōn egent. Brave soldiers do not always lack *fear.* [**egeō, -ēre, -uī, ——,** 'lack, be without']
3. Marcus agrum pauperem **aquae** coluit. Marcus tilled a field poor *in water.* [**colō, -ere, -uī, cultus,** 'till']

GREEK GENITIVE (EPEXEGETICAL GENITIVE) (not discussed in the text)
Following Greek usage, adjectives meaning 'skilled in, having knowledge of' may govern the genitive.

1. Puerum perītum **legendī** laudābāmus. We kept on praising the boy skilled in *reading.* [**perītus, -a, -um,** 'skilled in']
2. Vir doctus **litterārum** fuit. He was a man learned in *literature.* [**doctus, -a, -um,** 'learned']
3. Dux **bellī gerendī** scītus ā cīvibus factus est. A leader skilled in *waging war* was chosen (*literally,* 'made') by the citizens. [**scītus, -a, -um,** 'skilled in']

The genitive is sometimes governed by other words, e.g., **causā** and **grātiā.** Thus:

GENITIVE WITH **causā** AND **grātiā**
**Causā** and **grātiā,** both meaning 'for the sake of', govern the genitive and are placed *after* it.

1. **Glōriae causā (grātiā),** bellum gessimus. We waged war *for the sake of glory.*
2. Gēns hostīlis bella gerēbat **vincendī causā (grātiā).** The hostile people used to wage wars *for the sake of conquering* (i.e., *in order to conquer*).
3. Nātōs ad prōvinciam mīsērunt **auxiliī petendī causā (grātiā).** They sent their sons to the province *for the sake of seeking* (i.e., *in order to seek*) *aid.*

### Dative Case
The basic use of the dative case is referential. The person or thing to whom or which the action or idea refers, is of advantage, or disadvantage, is put into the dative case. Thus:

1. **Vōbīs** Rōmam īre licet. *You* are permitted to go to Rome.
2. Librum **nautae** ēmī. I bought a book *for the sailor*.
3. Dōnum **mātrī nostrae** invēnimus. We have found a gift *for our mother*.
4. Tua facta fortia in **mihi** mentem vēnērunt. Your brave deeds came into *my* mind.
5. Hoc **mihi** āctum est. This was done *for me* (i.e., *for my advantage* or *for my disadvantage*).
6. Cōnsulem **tibi** laudāvistī. You praised the consul *for your advantage*.
7. Pontem **hostibus** dēlēvimus. We destroyed the bridge *for the enemy's disadvantage*. [**pōns, pontis**, M., 'bridge']

The following specialized uses of the referential dative also occur:

DATIVE OF INDIRECT OBJECT (Unit 1H3)
The indirect object occurs with verbs of *giving, telling*, and *showing*. The person to whom something is given, told, or shown is put into the dative case.

1. Librum **magistrō** mōnstrāvimus. We showed the book *to the teacher*.
2. Liber **magistrō** datus est. The book was given *to the teacher*.
3. Rēgīna **poētae** multa respondit. The queen answered many things *to the poet. Or*: The queen gave many answers *to the poet*.
4. Quid **rēgīnae** dictum est? What was said *to the queen*?
5. Nōlī **timōrī** cēdere. Don't yield *to fear*.

DATIVE WITH CERTAIN ADJECTIVES (not discussed in the text)
Adjectives meaning 'near (to), fit (for), friendly (to), pleasing (to), similar (to)', etc., and their opposites take the dative case.

1. Servus **dominō** cārus fuit. The slave was dear *to his master*.
2. Hostēs proximī **oppidō** iam erunt. The enemy by this time will be very near *the town*.
3. Cōnsul amīcus **plēbī** factus est. A consul friendly *to the common people* was chosen.
4. Fīlius simillimus **patrī** vidētur. The son seems very like *his father*.

DATIVE WITH CERTAIN INTRANSITIVE VERBS (Unit 13B)
Certain intransitive verbs in Latin govern the dative case. Some common examples are: **crēdō, faveō, īgnōscō, imperō, noceō, parcō, pāreō, placeō, persuādeō, studeō**.

1. **Quibus** crēdis? *Whom* do you believe?
2. Magister **puellīs** fāvit. The teacher favored *the girls*.
3. Dōnum **frātrī** placuit? Did the gift please *your brother*?
4. Servī **dominō** pārent. The slaves obey *their master*.

5. Imperātor **cōpiīs** imperāvit ut pūgnārent. The commander ordered *the troops* to fight.

### DATIVE OF THE POSSESSOR (Unit 5E)

With forms of the verb **sum**, the dative is sometimes used to show possession. The *possessor* is put into the dative case.

1. **Incolīs** multa tēcta erant. *The inhabitants* had many houses.
2. Cōnsilium bonum fuerat **ducibus**. *The leaders* had had a good plan.
3. **Vōbīsne** est magna cōpia pecūniae? Do *you* have a large supply of money?

### DATIVE OF AGENT (Unit 5D)

With the passive periphrastic the personal agent is normally expressed by the dative case without a preposition.

1. Quid **puellae** agendum est? What must *the girl* do? (*Literally*, What must be done *by the girl*?)
2. Oppidum **mīlitibus** oppūgnandum erat. The town had to be attacked *by the soldiers.*
3. Aliquid magnī **cīvibus** agendum erit. *The citizens* will have to do something great.

### DATIVE WITH COMPOUND VERBS (Unit 13D)

Many verbs compounded with such prefixes as **ad-**, **ante-**, **circum-**, **con-**, **in-**, **inter-**, **ob-**, **post-**, **prae-**, **prō-**, **sub-**, **super-** govern the dative case. When the original verb is transitive, the compounded form governs an accusative as well.

1. Hostēs bellum **prōvinciae** īnferunt. The enemies inflict a war on *the province.*
2. Vir **amīcō** in viā occurrit. The man met *his friend* in the street. [**occurrō, -ere, -currī, -cursus,** 'meet']
3. Dux optimōs **nāvibus** praefēcit. The leader put the best men in command of *the ships.*
4. Marcus **cōpiīs** praeerit. Marcus will be in command of *the troops.*

### ETHICAL DATIVE (not discussed in the text)

The ethical dative is a personal pronoun in the dative case not closely connected with the rest of the sentence; it does not depend on any one word.

1. Nihil bonī **mihi** hīc invenīrī potest. Nothing good can be found here *in my opinion.*
2. Illud **mihi** scelus non est. That is not a crime *as far as I'm concerned.*
3. Quod cōnsilium **tibi** ā ducibus legētur? What plan will be chosen by the leaders *in your opinion?*
4. Illud **tibi** est fortis virī factum! That is the deed of a brave man *for you!*
5. Vīta **mihi** sine spē est mors. Life without hope, *for me* (i.e., *as far as I'm concerned*), is death.

In addition to these basic referential uses, a noun in the dative case can express the purpose for which an action is performed or for which something exists. This is often used in conjunction with another noun in the dative case which is purely referential in nature. Thus:

## DATIVE OF PURPOSE (SERVICE) (Unit 8H)

1. Aurum **auxiliō** oppidō missum est. The gold was sent *as an aid* to the town.
2. Magna cōpia pecūniae est **magnae cūrae.** A large supply of money is *a great concern* (i.e., it serves *as a great concern*).
3. Hostēs fuērunt **timōrī** populō. The enemy were *a fear* to the people (i.e., they served *as a source of fear* for the people).
4. Amīcō librum **dōnō** dedit. He gave his friend a book *for a gift* (i.e., to serve *as a gift*).
5. **Magnō auxiliō** nostrīs amīcīs fuimus. We were *a great aid* to our friends.

## Accusative Case
The accusative case is used as the direct object of a verb or as the object of certain prepositions.

## ACCUSATIVE OF DIRECT OBJECT (Unit 1H4)

1. **Multōsne maiōrēs frātrēs** habēs? Do you have *many older brothers*?
2. **Impiōs** nōn laudābimus. We shall not praise *wicked men.*
3. **Mōtūs** sīderum nōn intellēxit. He did not understand *the movements* of the stars.

## COGNATE ACCUSATIVE (not discussed in the text)
The direct object whose meaning is very closely related to that of the verb is called a cognate accusative (e.g., to dream a dream, dance a dance, sing a song).

1. **Vītam** bonam et fēlīcem vīvit. He lives a good and happy *life.*
2. **Somnium** longum et grātum somniāvī. I dreamed a long and pleasing *dream.*
   [somnium, -ī, N., 'dream'; somniō (1), 'dream']
3. Mīlitēs multa **facta** fortia fēcērunt. The soldiers did many brave *deeds.*

## DOUBLE ACCUSATIVE (not discussed in the text)
Some verbs take two accusatives.

1. **Nōs litterās** docēre volunt. They want to teach *us literature.*
2. Amīcī **nōs pecūniam** ōrāvērunt. Our friends asked *us* for *money.*
3. **Vōs auxilium** rogāmus. We ask *you* for *aid.*
4. **Factum tē** cēlāvī. I have hidden the *deed* from *you.*

GREEK ACCUSATIVE: ACCUSATIVE OF RESPECT OR ACCUSATIVE AFTER VERBS IN THE MIDDLE VOICE (Unit 18F)

Occasionally in poetry and late Latin the accusative is used to express *respect* or *specification*. It is frequently used to express the *part affected*. The accusative is used as the object of a verb which looks passive, but which may be considered the equivalent of a Greek middle voice.

1. Multī **oculōs** vulnerātī sunt. Many men were wounded *in their eyes*.
2. Fēmina **caput** tēcta per viās oppidī sine servīs ambulāvit. The woman having covered *her head* walked through the streets of the town without slaves. [**caput, capitis**, N., 'head']
3. **Caput** cīnctus laurō deus magnum amōrem puellae cecinit. Having bound his *head* with laurel, the god sang of his great love for the girl. [**caput, capitis**, N., 'head'; **laurus, -ī**, F., 'laurel']

SUBJECT OF THE INFINITIVE (not discussed in the text; but see Unit 6C)

The subject of the infinitive is put into the accusative case.

1. **Nōs** īre nōlunt. They are unwilling *for us* to go.
2. **Fēminās** ē tēctīs expulsās esse dīcit. He says that *the women* were driven out of the houses.
3. Dux **mīlitēs** oppidum oppūgnāre iussit. The leader ordered *the soldiers* to attack the town.

BUT: the subject of an historical infinitive is in the nominative case.

4. **Servī** libenter fugere. *The slaves* fled gladly.

ACCUSATIVE OF DURATION OF TIME AND EXTENT OF SPACE (Unit 7I)

The accusative, usually without a preposition, is used to express duration of time or extent of space. It answers the question "for how long?", whether it be of time or distance.

1. In īnsulā **quīnque diēs** manēbimus. We shall remain on the island *for five days*.
2. Nōs **duās hōrās** exspectāvērunt. They waited for us *for two hours*.
3. Rōmam **multōs annōs** incoluērunt. They lived in Rome *for many years*.
4. Puerī parvī saxum magnum **quīnque pedēs** portāvērunt. The small boys carried the large rock *for five feet*.

ACCUSATIVE OF EXCLAMATION (Unit 15F)

The accusative case is sometimes used in exclamations.

1. Ō impiās fēminās! Oh wicked women!
2. Mē miserum! Unhappy me!
3. Īnfēlīcem diem! Unfortunate day!

ADVERBIAL ACCUSATIVE (Unit 18G)
A word in the accusative case may be used adverbially.

1. **Quid** hoc tibi vidētur? *In what way* does this seem best to you? [**videor,** 'seem (best)']
2. **Nihil** hoc meā interest. This is *in no way* of interest to me.
3. **Maximam partem** id mihi nōn placet. *For the most part* this does not please me.

PREPOSITIONS WITH THE ACCUSATIVE (Unit 1H4)
The prepositions **per, trāns, inter, post, intrā** ('within'), **apud, contrā, super** ('above'), etc., govern the accusative case.

1. **Ob/Propter nostram culpam** patria dēlēta est. *Because of our fault* our native land has been destroyed.
2. Mīlitēs **post bellum** ad patriam redībunt. The soldiers will return to their native land *after the war.*
3. Puerī **per multās viās** oppidī cucurrērunt. The boys ran *through many streets* of the town.
4. **Trāns flūmen** fūgimus. We fled *across the river.*

ACCUSATIVE OF PLACE TO WHICH (Unit 6F)
Place to which is expressed by the accusative case with the preposition **ad**. With names of cities, small islands, towns, and the words **domus** and **rūs**, no preposition is used.

1. Nautae vēla **ad īnsulam** dabunt. The sailors will set sail *to the island.*
2. **Ad Italiam** īmus. We are going *to Italy.*

BUT:

3. **Rōmam** īmus. We are going *to Rome.*

ACCUSATIVE OF PLACE INTO WHICH (not discussed in the text)
Place into which is expressed by the accusative case with the preposition **in**, 'into'.

1. Fēminae **in viam** ambulant. The women are walking *into the street.*
2. Incolae **in patriam** rediērunt. The inhabitants went back *into their native land.*
3. Nautae **in aquam** ībunt. The sailors will go *into the water.*

BUT:

4. **In viā** ambulant. They are walking *in the street.* (place where)

**Ablative Case**
The basic function of the ablative case is to answer the questions "from?, where?, how?, when?, by?"; it can frequently be rendered literally by the

prepositions "from, with, in, by". For convenience, the uses are arranged below according to whether or not they require prepositions in Latin.

## WITHOUT PREPOSITIONS

### ABLATIVE OF MEANS (INSTRUMENT) (Unit 3E)

The ablative without a preposition is used to express the *means* or *instrument* by which something is done.

1. Tēcta prōvinciae **ignī** dēlēta sunt. The houses of the province were destroyed *by fire.*
2. Nātī **gladiīs** mīlitum territī erant. The children had been frightened *by the swords* of the soldiers.
3. Urna pulchra **aquā** implētur. The beautiful urn is being filled *with water.*
4. Cōnsul populum **spē** salūtis hortātus est. The consul encouraged the people *with the hope* of safety.

Some additional uses of the ablative of means are:

### ABLATIVE OF ROUTE (not discussed in the text)

Ībam forte **Viā Sacrā**. I was walking by chance *along the Sacred Way.* [**sacer, sacra, sacrum**, 'sacred']

### ABLATIVE OF PRICE (Unit 18J)

The instrumental ablative (ablative of means) is used with some expressions to indicate the price of something.

1. Domum **multā pecūniā** ēmimus. We bought a house *for a lot of money.*
2. Patriam **aurō trādidit**. He handed over his native land *for gold.*
3. Iuvenem **duce seniōre** mūtāre nōlumus. We do not want to exchange a young leader *for an older one.*
4. Servōs **magnō pretiō** vendidit. He sold the slaves *for a great price.*

### ABLATIVE WITH CERTAIN DEPONENT VERBS (not discussed in the text)

**Ūtor** 'use', **fruor** 'enjoy', **fungor** 'perform', **potior** 'gain possession of', and **vēscor** 'eat' take the ablative case.

1. **Auxiliō** amīcōrum ūtitur. He makes use of his friends' *aid.*
2. **Dōnō** frātris frūctus es? Did you enjoy your brother's *gift*? [**fruor, -ī, frūctus sum**, 'enjoy']
3. Miserī **animālibus mortuīs** vēscuntur. The wretched men are eating *dead animals.* [**vēscor, -ī, ––**, 'eat']

**opus est** + ABLATIVE (Vocabulary, Unit 7)

1. Nōbīs **bonō amīcō** opus est. We need *a good friend.*

This idea may also be expressed:

2. **Bonus amīcus** nōbīs opus est. (i.e., with the nominative)

or less frequently:

3. Nōbīs **bonī amīcī** opus est. (i.e., with the genitive)

## ABLATIVE OF DESCRIPTION (Unit 10D)

A noun in the ablative case, when modified by an adjective, may be used to describe or express a quality of another noun.

1. Virum **ūnō oculō** vīdimus. We saw a man *with one eye.*
2. Fēmina **manibus pulchrīs** litterās longās scrīpsit. The woman *with the beautiful hands* wrote a long letter.
3. Patria **maximā fāmā** erat pulcherrima. The country *with a very great reputation* was very beautiful.

## ABLATIVE OF TIME WHEN OR WITHIN WHICH (Unit 7H)

Time when or within which is expressed by the ablative. A preposition is not regularly used.

1. **Paucīs annīs** patriam novam incolēmus. We shall inhabit a new land *in a few years.*
2. **Eō tempore** multōs amīcōs vīdimus. We saw many friends *at that time.*
3. **Proximō mēnse** sociī ad tēctum ducis venient. *Next month* the allies will come to the leader's house. [**mēnsis, mēnsis, -ium**, M., 'month']
4. **Proximā nocte** sociī ad tēctum ducis vēnērunt. *Last night* the allies came to the leader's house. [**proximus, -a, -um**, *here,* 'last']

## ABLATIVE OF COMPARISON (Unit 9C)

The ablative, without a preposition, is used with an adjective or adverb in the comparative degree to denote comparison.

1. Iuvenēs facta fortiōra **patribus** fēcērunt. The young men did braver deeds *than their fathers* (did).
2. Tū fēlīcior **mē** es. You are happier *than I.*
3. Puella pulchrior **mātre pulchrā** est. The girl is more beautiful *than her beautiful mother.*

Note that the same idea may be expressed using **quam**:

4. Iuvenēs facta fortiōra **quam patrēs** fēcērunt.
5. Tū fēlīcior **quam ego** es.
6. Puella pulchrior **quam māter pulchra** est.

## ABLATIVE OF DEGREE OF DIFFERENCE (Unit 9D)

The ablative, without a preposition, is used with comparatives to express the degree in which the two things being compared differ. Less frequently, this kind of ablative is also found with a superlative in statements in which there is an implicit comparative judgment made.

1. Puella **multō** pulchrior mātre pulchrā est. The girl is *much* more beautiful than her beautiful mother.
2. Marcus **duōbus pedibus** altior quam frāter est. Marcus is *two feet* taller than his brother.
3. Hic nūntius Rōmam **quīnque diēbus** post missus est. This messenger was sent to Rome *five days* later.
4. Is **multō** pulcherrimus hīc est. He is *by far* the most handsome man here.

ABLATIVE OF CAUSE (Unit 10C)
The ablative, generally without a preposition, is sometimes used to express *cause*.

1. Rēgīnam **īrā crūdēlī** timēmus. We fear the queen *because of her cruel anger*.
2. Mīlitēs **metū** pūgnāre nōn potuērunt. The soldiers were not able to fight *because of fear*.
3. Imperātor lēgātum **virtūte** laudāvit. The commander praised the legate *because of his courage*.

ABLATIVE OF RESPECT (SPECIFICATION) (Unit 8D)
The *respect* in which a statement is true is expressed by the ablative without a preposition.

1. Puella erat pulchra **vīsū**. The girl was beautiful *to see*.
2. Illa erat pulchra **corpore** et **animō**. She was beautiful *in body* and *mind*.
3. Hostēs nōs **virtūte** vīcērunt. The enemy excelled us *in courage*.

ABLATIVE OF ATTENDANT CIRCUMSTANCE (not discussed in the text)
The ablative case, without a preposition, may be used to express the circumstances in which the action of the sentence occurs.

1. **Ventīs secundīs** multōs diēs nāvigāvimus. We sailed for many days *with favorable winds*. [secundus, -a, -um, 'favorable'; nāvigō (1), 'sail']
2. Sacrificium **bonīs ōminibus** fit. The sacrifice is being made *under good omens*. [sacrificium, -ī, N., 'sacrifice'; ōmen, ōminis, N., 'omen']
3. Flūmen ad lītus **magnō strepitū** ruit. The river rushes to the shore *with a great noise*. [strepitus, -ūs, M., 'noise']

Note that the ablative absolute may be used to express attendant circumstance:

4. Dīs grātiās **manibus** ad caelum **sublātīs** agēmus. We shall give thanks to the gods *with hands raised* to heaven. [grātiās agere, 'to give thanks' + dative; tollō, -ere, sustulī, sublātus, 'lift, raise']
5. Ōrātor turbae **fulgōre** ad dextram **vīsō** locūtus est. The speaker spoke to the crowd *with lightning seen* toward the right.

ABLATIVE ABSOLUTE (Unit 10A)

The ablative absolute composed of a noun and participle in the ablative case (or two nouns, or a noun and adjective, or pronoun and adjective with the participle of the verb "to be" understood) has no close syntactical connection with the rest of the sentence. It functions as an adverb giving the circumstances, time, cause, condition, or concession in which the action of the main verb occurs.

1. **Lēgātō** auxilium **ferente**, cōpiae hostēs superant. *With the legate bringing* aid, the troops overcome the enemy.
2. **Cicerōne cōnsule**, multī fuērunt laetī. *When Cicero was consul,* many men were happy. [**Cicerō, -ōnis,** M., 'Cicero']
3. **Fulgōre vīsō** plēbs territa fūgit. *When the lightning was seen,* the terrified (common) people fled.
4. **Multīs nāvibus dēlētīs**, hostēs victī sunt. The enemy were conquered *after many of their ships had been destroyed.*
5. **Hōc factō**, laetī tamen fuimus. *Although this had happened,* nevertheless we were happy.
6. **Marcō laetō**, laetī tamen nōn fuimus. *Although Marcus was happy,* nevertheless we were not happy.

ADJECTIVES WITH THE ABLATIVE (not discussed in the text)

**Frētus, -a, -um,** 'relying upon, dependent upon', and **dīgnus, -a, -um,** 'worthy', govern the ablative.

1. Senex frētus **nātīs** vīvit. The old man lives dependent upon *his sons.*
2. Frētī **fidē tuā** nōn timēbimus. Relying upon *your trustworthiness,* we shall not fear.
3. Ille est dīgnus **multīs bonīs**. That man is worthy of *many good things.*

## WITH PREPOSITIONS

ABLATIVE OF PERSONAL AGENT (Unit 4E)

The *agent* or *person* who performs the action of a passive verb is regularly expressed in the ablative case preceded by the preposition **ā** or **ab**, 'by'.

1. Illī **ab omnibus** in oppidō vīsī sunt. Those men were seen *by everyone* in town.
2. Rēx **ā populō** timētur. The king is feared *by the people.*
3. Bellum **ab incolīs** prōvinciae gestum est. War was waged *by the inhabitants* of the province.

PREPOSITIONS WITH THE ABLATIVE

The prepositions **cum, in, ā (ab), ē (ex), dē, sine, prō, sub, super** ('above'), etc., govern the ablative case.

1. Sociī **cum hostibus** pūgnāvērunt. The allies fought *with the enemy*.
2. Ducēs **dē multīs** cōgitābant. The leaders thought *about many things*.
3. Nihil **sine pecūniā** emere potest. He can buy nothing *without money*.
4. Hostēs **prō moenibus** pūgnāvērunt. The enemy fought *in front of the city walls*.

ABLATIVE OF ACCOMPANIMENT (Unit 7G)
The ablative is used with the preposition **cum** to denote accompaniment.

1. Fēminae **cum nautīs** ambulābant. The women were walking *with the sailors*.
2. Nautae **cum multīs sociīs** vēla dabunt. The sailors will set sail *with many allies*.
3. Incolae prōvinciae **cum amīcīs** ex oppidō discessērunt. The inhabitants of the province left the town *with their friends*.

ABLATIVE OF PLACE IN WHICH (PLACE WHERE) (Unit 6G)
Place where is expressed by **in** with the ablative, except for the names of small islands, towns and cities, and with the words **domus** and **rūs**.

1. Erant multī montēs **in īnsulā**. There were many mountains *on the island*.
2. Pecūnia **in cellīs** cēlāta est. The money was hidden *in the storerooms*.
3. Plūrimī **in pāce** vīvere volunt. Most men want to live *in peace*.

BUT:

4. **Rōmae** esse volunt. They want to be *in Rome*.

ABLATIVE OF PLACE AWAY FROM WHICH (Unit 6E2)
**Ā (ab)** with the ablative expresses the direction away from a place; however, no preposition is used with the names of small islands, towns and cities, and with the words **domus** and **rūs**.

1. **Ab īnsulā** quam celerrimē discessimus. We went *away from the island* as quickly as possible.
2. Animālia **ab ārīs** pepulimus. We drove the animals *away from the altars*.
3. Turbamne **ā tēctō** cōnsulis dūcēs? Will you lead the crowd *away from the consul's house*?

BUT:

4. **Rōmā** ad Asiam vēnimus. We came *from Rome* to Asia.

ABLATIVE OF PLACE OUT OF WHICH (Unit 6E2)
**Ē (ex)** with the ablative expresses the direction out of a place.

1. Parva animālia **ē marī** in terram vēnērunt. Small animals came *out of the sea* onto land.
2. Servī quī **ex Āfricā** vēnerant in multīs urbibus vīsī sunt. Slaves who had come *out of Africa* were seen in many cities.

3. Puerōs ē tēctō in viam mittis? Are you sending the boys *out of the house* into the street?

### ABLATIVE OF PLACE DOWN FROM WHICH (Unit 6E2)
Dē with the ablative expresses the direction down from a place.

1. Incolae saxa **dē moenibus** iēcērunt. The inhabitants threw rocks *down from the city walls*.
2. **Dē monte** magnā cum cūrā ambulāvērunt. They walked *down the mountain* with great care.
3. Quīdam **dē monte** ad mortem cecidit. A certain man fell *down the mountain* to his death.

# WITH OR WITHOUT PREPOSITIONS

### ABLATIVE OF MANNER (MODAL ABLATIVE) (Unit 3F)
The ablative case may be used *with* or *without* the preposition **cum** to denote the *way* or *manner* in which something is done. **Cum** is required when the noun in the ablative is *not* modified by an adjective; when it is modified, **cum** is optional.

1. Mīlitēs **magnō (cum) studiō** pūgnāvērunt. The soldiers fought *with great zeal* (*very zealously*).
2. Nātī litterās longās **magnā (cum) cūrā** scrīpsērunt. The children wrote a long letter *with great care* (*very carefully*).
3. Nūntiī **cum virtūte** locūtī sunt. The messengers spoke *with courage* (*courageously*).
4. Sociī cōnsilia **cum dīligentiā** fēcērunt. The allies made plans *with diligence* (*diligently*).

### ABLATIVE OF SEPARATION (Unit 6E)
Some verbs which express or imply separation or deprivation are accompanied by the ablative case. The prepositions **ā (ab)**, **ē (ex)**, or **dē** are sometimes used with this construction, but more usually the ablative occurs alone.

1. Multī miserī **spē** carent. Many unhappy men lack *hope*.
2. Virī (**ā**) **cūrīs** līberātī vītam fēlīcem ēgērunt. The men freed *from their cares* lived a happy life.
3. Fāma imperātōrem **ā noxā** nōn solvit. His reputation did not free the commander *from harm*.

### ABLATIVE OF MATERIAL (not discussed in text)
The ablative case may be used, sometimes with the prepositions **dē** or **ex**, to show the material from which an object is made.

1. Urnam **ex aurō** numquam vīdimus. We have never seen an urn *of gold*.

2. Statua **dē marmore** in forō posita est. A statue (made) *of marble* was placed in the forum. [**marmor, -oris**, M., 'marble']
3. Mēnsa minima **ex aurō** facta mihi mōnstrāta est. A very small table made *of gold* was shown to me.
4. Agrī **multīs flōribus pulcherrimīs** cōnstant. The fields consist of *many very beautiful flowers.* [**flōs, flōris,** M., 'flower'; **cōnstō, -āre, cōnstitī, -status,** 'consist of']

ABLATIVE OF ORIGIN (ALLIED WITH ABLATIVE OF SEPARATION) (Unit 6E1)
The ablative, with or without a preposition, expresses the origin or descent of a person or thing.

1. Cōnsul **gente clārā** nātus est. The consul was descended *from a famous race.*
2. Hic **ē mātre pulchrā** nātus est. This man was born *of a beautiful mother.*
3. Flūmen **ā marī** oritur. The river rises *from the sea.*

**Locative Case (Unit 6G)**
The names of towns, cities, and small islands and the words **domus** and **rūs** use the locative case to express *place where*, which for other nouns is expressed by the ablative with the preposition **in.**

1. Aenēās **Carthāgine** nōn diū remānsit. Aeneas did not remain *in Carthage* for a long time.
2. Servī vītam fēlīcem **Rōmae** nōn semper vīxērunt. Slaves did not always live a happy life *in Rome.*
3. Multa aedificia pulchra **Athēnīs** fuērunt. There were many beautiful buildings *in Athens.* [**aedificium, -ī,** N., 'building']

**Vocative Case (Unit 8G)**
The vocative is the case of *direct address.*

1. **Puerī,** nōlīte id facere. *Boys,* don't do this.
2. Librum novum, **scrīptor clāre,** mihi lege. Read me your new book, *famous writer.*
3. Venī, **fīlī mī,** mēcum. Come with me, *my son.*

# REVIEW OF THE SYNTAX OF VERBS

**Infinitives**
The infinitive is an abstract verbal noun. (Unit 1C)

COMPLEMENTARY (Unit 5G)
There are verbs in Latin which frequently require an infinitive to complete

their meaning. Some of these are verbs which express ability, will, desire, and the like. The infinitive completes the idea of the verb.

1. Ad Italiam **īre** volumus. We want *to go* to Italy.
2. Clārissimum virum **vidēre** potes? Can you *see* the very famous man?
3. Honestus vir **esse** vidētur. He seems *to be* an honorable man.
4. Opus difficile **cōnficere** cōnātī sumus. We tried *to complete* the difficult work.
5. Parentēs et amīcōs nōlī **relinquere**. Don't *abandon* your parents and friends.

### INFINITIVE AS SUBJECT (Unit 11E)

The infinitive is, in fact, a neuter noun and thus can be the subject of a verb.

1. **Vidēre** est crēdere. *Seeing* is believing. (*Literally*, 'To see is to believe'. **Crēdere** is a predicate nominative.)
2. Difficile nōn est vītam bene **agere**. It is not difficult *to conduct* life well.
3. Hoc est bonum: bene **agere** et multōs amīcōs **habēre**. This is good: *to do* well and *to have* many friends.
4. Facta fortia **perficere** optimum vidētur. *To accomplish* brave deeds seems best.
5. Est nātī omnibus dictīs parentis **crēdere**. It is the mark of a child *to believe* all the sayings of his parent.
6. Bene **vīvere** oportet. It is proper *to live* well. (This also occurs with other impersonal verbs.)

### OBJECT INFINITIVE (not discussed in the text)

An infinitive with subject accusative may be used as the object of another verb.

1. Rōmam vōs **īre** volumus. We want you *to go* to Rome.
2. Dux mīlitēs oppidum **oppūgnāre** iussit. The leader ordered the soldiers *to attack* the town.
3. Vōs hoc **facere** vetat. He forbids you *to do* this.
4. Dux mīlitēs sē **recipere** prohibuit. The leader prevented the soldiers from *withdrawing*.

A further use of the object infinitive is:

### THE INFINITIVE IN INDIRECT STATEMENT (Unit 6C)

After words which express or imply actions that take place in the head, such as saying, thinking, seeing, perceiving, knowing, and the like, statements are made indirectly. The verb of this indirect statement is in the infinitive and the subject of the infinitive is in the accusative case.

1. Nōs fēlīcēs mox **futūrōs esse (fore)** spērat. He hopes that we *will* soon *be* happy.
2. Tē hoc **fēcisse** pūtāvimus. We thought that you *had done* this.
3. Nōs rūs **īre** scīvit. He knew that we *were going* to the country.

HISTORICAL INFINITIVE (Unit 18C)
The infinitive is used in narrative passages instead of a finite verb to emphasize the pure verbal action rather than the agents of that action. The subject of the historical infinitive is in the nominative case.

1. Multī in oppidō **clāmāre**. Many men in the town *shouted.*
2. Mīlitēs multā cum vī **pūgnāre**. Soldiers *fought* with a lot of force.
3. Aliī per viās oppidī **currere**, aliī apertē **plōrāre**, aliī manūs ad deōs **tollere**. Some *ran* through the streets of the town, others *wept* openly, others *raised* their hands to the gods. [**apertē**, adv., 'openly'; **plōrō** (1), 'weep'; **tollō, -ere, sustulī, sublātus**, 'raise, lift']

EPEXEGETICAL INFINITIVE (not discussed in the text)
An infinitive may be dependent upon an adjective, as happens in Greek.

1. Poēta carmen dīgnum **legī** fēcit. The poet composed a poem worthy *to be read.*
2. Servus erat perītus **docēre**. The slave was skilled in *teaching.* [**perītus, -a, -um**, 'skilled']
3. Hic vir aptus erat **regere**. This man was fit *to rule.* [**aptus, -a, -um**, 'fit']

INFINITIVE IN EXCLAMATIONS (not discussed in the text)
The infinitive with subject accusative may be used as a main verb in exclamations.

1. Tālem scelerātum imperium **obtinuisse**! (To think) that such a scoundrel *has obtained* power!; Such a scoundrel *has obtained* power?! [**scelerātus, -ī**, M., 'scoundrel'; **obtineō** (**ob** + **teneō**), 'get hold of, obtain']
2. Mē ut hunc diem vidērem **vīxisse**! (To think) that I *have lived* to see this day!; I *have lived* to see this day?!
3. Mē tē facere hoc nōn **dare**! I not *grant* you to do this?!

Sometimes the enclitic -ne is added to the emphatic word to lay stress on the interrogative nature of the exclamation:

4. Mēne ā tē **victum esse**! I *beaten* by you?!

**Imperatives (Units 1A5, 8F)**
The imperative mood expresses the action as a command.

1. Timōrem mortis **superā**! *Overcome* your fear of death!
2. Librum hūc **fer**! *Bring* the book here!
3. Verba sapientis **audīte**! *Listen to* the words of the wise man!
4. Noxam **patere**! *Endure* the injury!

The future imperative is used to stress the futurity of the command (particularly when another verb in the sentence is in the future or future perfect tense). It is also used in legal terms.

1. Cum tē vidēbō, respōnsum mihi **dīcitō**. When I see you, *you shall tell* me your answer. [**respōnsum, -ī**, N., 'answer']
2. Mox veniet; poenās **datō**. He will come soon; *he shall pay* the penalty.
3. Rēs pūblica ā duōbus cōnsulibus **regitor**. The republic *shall be ruled* by two consuls.

Some verbs, like **meminī**, 'remember', regularly use the future imperative instead of the present:

4. **Mementōte** hōrum factōrum fortium! *Remember* (pl.) these brave deeds!

**Indicative Mood**
The indicative mood is the mood of fact and is used for making direct statements and asking direct questions. (Unit 1A5)

1. Hās litterās ad amīcum **mittēs**? *Will you send* this letter to your friend?
2. Liber quī ā clārissimō auctōre **scrīptus erat** omnibus praesentibus **lēctus est**. The book which *had been written* by the very famous author *was read* to all who were present. [**praesēns, praesentis**, 'present']
3. Servus ad poenās trāditus scelus **negāvit**. The slave handed over to punishment *denied* his crime.

CONCESSIVE CLAUSES (**quamquam** and **etsī**) (Unit 15C3)

1. **Quamquam** rūs **incolimus**, fēlīcēs nōn sumus. *Although we live* in the country, we are not happy.
2. **Etsī** rūs urbe **māluērunt**, tamen Rōmam incoluērunt. *Although they preferred* the country to the city, nevertheless they lived in Rome.
3. **Quamquam** eōs **vīderāmus**, tamen loquī nōluimus. *Although we had seen* them, nevertheless we did not want to speak.

BUT:

4. **Cum** eōs **vīdissēmus**, tamen loquī nōluimus. *Although we had seen* them, nevertheless we did not want to speak.
5. **Quamvīs** eōs **vīdissēmus**, tamen loquī nōluimus. *Although we had seen* them, nevertheless we did not want to speak.
6. **Eīs** ā nōbīs **vīsīs**, tamen loquī nōluimus. *Although they had been seen* by us, nevertheless we did not want to speak. (Ablative Absolute)

CAUSAL CLAUSES (**quoniam/quandō**, **quod/quia** take the indicative to express actual fact) (Unit 15C2)

1. $\left.\begin{array}{l}\textbf{Quoniam}\\\textbf{Quandō}\end{array}\right\}$ **sumus** amīcī, amīcitiam nōn negābimus. *Since we are* friends, we shall not deny our friendship.

2. $\left.\begin{array}{l}\textbf{Quoniam}\\\textbf{Quandō}\end{array}\right\}$ **labōrāverant,** fēlīcēs erant. *Since they had worked,* they were happy.

3. $\left.\begin{array}{l}\textbf{Quod}\\\textbf{Quia}\end{array}\right\}$ **sumus** amīcī, amīcitiam nōn negābimus. *Because we (actually) are* friends, we shall not deny our friendship.

BUT:

4. **Cum sīmus** amīcī, amīcitiam nōn negābimus. *Since we are* friends, we shall not deny our friendship.

5. $\left.\begin{array}{l}\textbf{Quod}\\\textbf{Quia}\end{array}\right\}$ **labōrāvissent,** fēlīcēs erant. *Because they (allegedly) had worked,* they were happy.

6. **Amīcō meō fēlīcī,** felix sum. *Since my friend is happy,* I am happy. (Ablative Absolute)

CIRCUMSTANTIAL CLAUSES (Unit 15A1)

1. **Cum** parentēs **vidēmus,** fēlīcēs sumus. *When we see* our parents, we are happy.
2. **Cum** parentēs **vidēbimus,** fēlīcēs erimus. *When we (shall) see* our parents, we shall be happy.
3. **Cum** parentēs **vīderimus,** fēlīcēs erimus. *When we shall have seen* our parents, we shall be happy.

BUT:

4. **Cum** parentēs **vidērēmus,** fēlīcēs erāmus. *When we saw* our parents, we were happy. (In past time, the subjunctive is used.)

TEMPORAL CLAUSES (Unit 15A1 and C1)

1. $\left.\begin{array}{l}\textbf{Ut}\\\textbf{Ubi}\\\textbf{Quandō}\\\textbf{Cum} \text{ (}stresses \text{ time)}\end{array}\right\}$ tē **rīdeō,** mē ipsum rīdeō. *When I laugh at* you, I laugh at my very self.

2. $\left.\begin{array}{l}\textbf{Ut}\\\textbf{Ubi}\\\textbf{Quandō}\\\textbf{Cum} \text{ (}stresses \text{ time)}\end{array}\right\}$ in viā **ambulābam,** Marcō occurrī. *When I was walking* in the street, I met Marcus. [**occurrō, -ere, occurrī, occursus,** 'meet']

3. $\left.\begin{array}{l}\textbf{Ut}\\\textbf{Ubi}\\\textbf{Quandō}\\\textbf{Cum} \text{ (}stresses \text{ time)}\end{array}\right\}$ amīcōs **vīdērunt,** fēlīcēs vīsī sunt. *When they saw* their friends, they seemed happy.

4. **Postquam** amīcōs **vīdērunt,** fēlīcēs vīsī sunt. *After they saw* their friends, they seemed happy.

BUT:

5. **Amīcīs vīsīs**, fēlīcēs vīsī sunt. *When their friends had been seen*, they seemed happy. (Ablative Absolute)
6. **Cum** amīcōs **vidērent**, fēlīcēs vīsī sunt. *When they saw* their friends, they seemed happy. (stresses circumstances)

**dum, dōnec**, 'while, until'; **simul ac (atque)**, 'as soon as'; **quōad**, 'as long as, as far as, until' (Unit 15D2)

1. **Simul ac** eum **vīdī**, eum **dīlēxī**. *As soon as I saw* him, I liked him. [**dīligō, -ere, -lēxī, -lēctus**, 'esteem, like']

2.
$$\left.\begin{array}{l}\textbf{Quōad}\\ \textbf{Dum}\\ \textbf{Dōnec}\end{array}\right\}$$
ventī secundī **fuērunt**, nautae vēla dedērunt. *While* the winds *were* favorable, the sailors set sail. [**secundus, -a, -um**, 'favorable']

3.
$$\left.\begin{array}{l}\textbf{Quōad}\\ \textbf{Dum}\\ \textbf{Dōnec}\end{array}\right\}$$
rēx **vīxit**, populus līber nōn erat. *While* the king *lived*, the people were not free.

4. **Dum** paucōs diēs in urbe **morāmur**, amīcī nostrī rūs īvērunt. *While we delayed* in the city for a few days, our friends went to the country.

BUT:

5. Cōnsilia nostra perficere nōn possumus,
$$\left\{\begin{array}{l}\textbf{dum}\\ \textbf{dōnec}\\ \textbf{quōad}\end{array}\right\}$$
**adveniās**. We are not able to complete our plans *until you arrive*. (subjunctive stresses anticipation)

**antequam, priusquam**, 'before' (Unit 15D3)

1. **Antequam** urbem **relīquimus**, eum **vīdimus**. *Before we abandoned* the city, we saw him.
2. Multa cōnsilia **prius** fēcērunt **quam** librum **scrīpsērunt**. They made many plans *before they wrote* the book.
3. Cum cūrā **ante** audī **quam rīdēs**. Listen carefully *before you laugh*.
4. Eum vidēre volō **antequam perierit**. I want to see him *before he dies*.

BUT:

5. Mortuus est **antequam** eum **vidērem**. He died *before I could see* him.

**quod**, 'the fact that' (Unit 18K)
A substantive clause introduced by **quod**, 'the fact that', and with its verb in the indicative is sometimes used as the subject or object of another verb, or in apposition to the subject of that other verb.

1. **Quod fēlīx es**, negāre nōn possumus. *The fact that you are happy* we cannot deny.
2. **Quod tē amō** mē fēlīcem facit. *The fact that I love you* makes me happy.
3. Alia causa timōris est **quod nōs ōdit**. Another cause of fear is *the fact that he hates us.*

**cum**, 'whenever' (perfect indicative when the main verb is present; pluperfect indicative when the main verb is imperfect) (Unit 15A4)

1. **Cum** plēbs ducibus **pāruit**, pāx in rē pūblicā est. *Whenever* the common people *obey* their leaders, there is peace in the republic.
2. Nautae vēla dabant **cum** ventī secundī **fuerant**. The sailors used to set sail *whenever* the winds *were* favorable. [**secundus, -a, -um**, 'favorable']
3. **Cum** parentēs **vīderāmus**, fēlīcēs erāmus. *Whenever we saw* our parents, we were happy.

BUT:

4. **Cum** parentēs **vīdimus**, fēlīcēs erāmus. *When we saw* our parents, we were happy. (stresses time — a single action)
5. **Cum** parentēs **vidērēmus**, fēlīcēs erāmus. *When we saw* our parents, we were happy. (stresses circumstances — a single action)

## CONDITIONS

### SIMPLE OR GENERAL CONDITIONS (indicative in both clauses) (Unit 2E1)

1. Sī in agrō **es**, **labōrās**. If *you are* in the field, *you are working.*
2. Sī in agrō **fuistī**, **labōrāvistī**. If *you were* in the field, *you worked.*
3. Sī in agrō **fuerās**, **labōrāverās**. If *you had been* in the field, *you had worked.*

### FUTURE MORE VIVID CONDITIONS (future indicative in both clauses; for emphasis, future perfect indicative in protasis) (Unit 2E2a)

1. Sī in agrō **eris**, **labōrābis**. If *you are* (*will be*) in the field, *you will work.*
2. Sī in agrō **fueris**, **labōrābis**. If *you are* (*will have been*) in the field, *you will work.* (emphatic)
3. Sī domum **veniet**, statuam **vidēbit**. If *he comes* (*will come*) home, *he will see* the statue.
4. Sī deōs **precātus erit**, **impetrābit**. If *he begs* (*will have begged*) the gods, *he will gain his request.* (emphatic) [**impetrō** (1), 'gain one's request']

## IMPERSONAL PASSIVES (Unit 13C)

1. In oppidō **agitātum est**. *There was a disturbance* in the town.
2. Domō **discēditur**. *There is a departure* from the house; *they are leaving* the house.

3. Hostibus ā duce **parcētur**. The enemy *will be spared* by the leader.
4. Puellīs ā magistrō **favēbātur**. The girls *were favored* by the teacher.

NOTE that this construction may be used with the subjunctive also:

5. In oppidō **agitētur**. *Let there be a disturbance* in the town.
6. Sī puellīs ā magistrō **faveātur**, īnfēlīx sim. If the girls *should be favored* by the teacher, I would be unhappy.

## Subjunctive Mood

The subjunctive mood is the mood used to express idea, intent, desire, uncertainty, potentiality, or anticipation. (Unit 1A5)

## INDEPENDENT USES OF THE SUBJUNCTIVE

### HORTATORY SUBJUNCTIVE (Unit 12A1)

The present subjunctive is used to express an exhortation in the first person. The negative is introduced by **nē**.

1. Tēcum **veniam**. *Let me come* with you.
2. Nē rūs **relinquāmus**. *Let us not abandon* the country.
3. Auxilium ad miserōs **ferāmus**. *Let us bring* aid to the wretched men.

### JUSSIVE SUBJUNCTIVE (Unit 12A1)

The present subjunctive is used to express a command in the second and third persons. The negative is introduced by **nē**.

1. Crūdēlis senem **nē interficiat**. *Let* the cruel man *not kill* the old man.
2. Īram rēgīnae **timeant**. *Let them fear* the queen's anger.
3. Pecūniam oblātam **capiās**. *Take* the offered money.
4. Rēs meliōrēs **nē spērētis**. *Don't hope for* better matters.

In the second person, occasionally, when the verb is negative, the perfect subjunctive is found instead of the present:

5. Rēs meliōrēs **nē spērāveritis**. *Don't hope for* better matters.

### DELIBERATIVE SUBJUNCTIVE (Unit 12A3)

The present and imperfect subjunctive may be used to deliberate about a course of action. This is frequently found in a rhetorical question. The negative is introduced by **nōn**.

1. Rūs **redeam**? *Should I go back* to the country? *Am I to return* to the country?
2. Eum iterum **nōn videam**? *Should I not see* him again? [**iterum**, adv., 'again']
3. Dōnum frātrī eius **darem**? *Should I have given* a gift to his brother?

Oᴘᴛᴀᴛɪᴠᴇ Sᴜʙᴊᴜɴᴄᴛɪᴠᴇ (Unit 12A4)

A wish for the future which is capable of fulfillment is expressed by the present subjunctive alone or is introduced by **utinam** or **ut**. The negative is introduced by **utinam nē** or **nē**.

Wishes incapable of fulfillment utilize the imperfect subjunctive for present time and the pluperfect for past time.

1. (**Utinam**) meliōrēs rēs mihi **sint**! *If only* affairs *will be* better for me!
2. (**Ut**) diūtius vīvere **possēmus**! *If only we could* live longer!
3. (**Utinam**) sapientior **fuisset**! *If only he had been* wiser!
4. (**Utinam**) **nē adesset**! *If only he were not present*!

Pᴏᴛᴇɴᴛɪᴀʟ Sᴜʙᴊᴜɴᴄᴛɪᴠᴇ (Unit 12A2)

The subjunctive may be used independently to express an action which might possibly or conceivably occur. For present or future potentiality, the present subjunctive is used. For past potentiality, the imperfect subjunctive is used. The negative is expressed by **nōn**.

1. Hoc **nōn faciās**. *You wouldn't do* this.
2. Servī in bellō **pūgnent**. The slaves *might fight* in the war.
3. Tēcum **īrēmus**. *We would have gone* with you; *we might have gone* with you.

## USES OF THE SUBJUNCTIVE IN DEPENDENT CLAUSES

### Sᴇǫᴜᴇɴᴄᴇ ᴏꜰ Tᴇɴsᴇs

|  | INDICATIVE | SUBJUNCTIVE |
|---|---|---|
| Primary Tenses | Present<br>Future<br>Perfect ("have" or "has")<br>Future Perfect | Present (*same time as* or *subsequent to* the action of the main verb)<br>Perfect (*prior to* the action of the main verb) |
| Secondary Tenses | Imperfect<br>Perfect<br>(English past)<br>Pluperfect | Imperfect (*same time as* or *subsequent to* the action of the main verb)<br>Pluperfect (*prior to* the action of the main verb) |

Pᴜʀᴘᴏsᴇ Cʟᴀᴜsᴇs (**ut** + subjunctive; negative **nē**) (Unit 3G)

1. Multō cum vigōre lābōrāvimus **ut** magna praemia **acciperēmus**. We worked with much vigor *so that we might receive* great rewards.
2. Nē inimīcī **vidērentur**, dōna pulchra accēpērunt. *So that they might not seem* unfriendly, they accepted the beautiful gifts.
3. Magistrōs laudat **ut** sibi (ipsī) **faveant**. He praises his superiors *so that they will favor* him.

## Relative Clauses of Purpose (Unit 14E)

**Quō** introduces a purpose clause which contains a comparative. A purpose clause may be introduced by a relative pronoun when its antecedent, usually not the subject of the main verb, is clearly expressed in the main clause.

1. **Quō** melius **intellegās**, tōtam rem tibi expōnam. *So that you may understand* better, I shall explain the whole matter for you.
2. Eum hīs cōnsiliīs praefēcimus, **quī** multam fāmam **obtinēret.** We put him in charge of these plans *so that he might gain* much fame. [**obtineō (ob + teneō),** 'get hold of, obtain']
3. Poēta carmen scrīpsit **quod** rēgīnae **placēret.** The poet wrote a poem *in order to please* the queen.

## Purpose Clauses Introduced by Adverbs (Unit 14E)

Purpose clauses may be introduced by an adverb (**ubi, unde, quō**).

1. In tēctō sē cēlāvit **ubi** tūtus **esset.** He hid in the house *so that he might be* safe *there.*
2. Nāvēs in portū parant **unde** vēla **dent.** They are preparing the ships in the harbor *so that they may set* sail *from there.* [**portus, -ūs,** M., 'harbor']
3. Eunt **quō** tūtī **sint.** They are going *where they may be* safe.

By way of review, note the following seven ways of expressing purpose. There is no difference in the meaning of the sentences below:

1. Amīcōs nostrōs Rōmam mīsimus **ut** multa **vidērent.**
2. Amīcōs nostrōs Rōmam mīsimus **quī** multa **vidērent.**
3. Amīcōs nostrōs Rōmam mīsimus **ad videndum** multa.
4. Amīcōs nostrōs Rōmam mīsimus **ad multa videnda.**
5. Amīcōs nostrōs Rōmam mīsimus **videndī** multa **causā (grātiā).** [**grātiā,** preceded by gen., 'for the sake of']
6. Amīcōs nostrōs Rōmam mīsimus **multōrum videndōrum causā (grātiā).** [**grātiā,** preceded by gen., 'for the sake of']
7. Amīcōs nostrōs Rōmam mīsimus multa **vīsum.**

We sent our friends to Rome to see many things.

KEY: (1) **ut** + subjunctive; (2) relative clause of purpose; (3) **ad** + accusative of the gerund; (4) **ad** + accusative + gerundive; (5) **causā** or **grātiā** + genitive of the gerund; (6) **causā** or **grātiā** + genitive + gerundive; (7) supine in **-um** with a verb of motion

## Indirect Commands (Unit 3H)

1. Servōs monet **nē** verba **rīdeant.** He is warning the slaves *not to laugh* at his words.

2. Amīcōs hortātī sumus **nē** opera **neglegant**. We have urged our friends *not to neglect* their works.

3. Nōbīs imperātum est **ut** vīribus ac virtūte **ūterēmur**. We were ordered *to use* our strength and courage.

RESULT CLAUSES (Unit 14A)

Clauses expressing the result of an action are introduced by **ut** for the positive, **ut nōn** (**nēmō, nihil, numquam**, etc.) for the negative, and have their verbs in the subjunctive.

1. Tam crūdēlis est **ut** ab omnibus **timeātur**. He is so cruel *that he is feared* by all.

2. Tantō vigōre discipulī respondent **ut** magistrō **placeant**. The students answer with such great liveliness *that they please* the teacher. [**discipulus, -ī**, M., 'student']

3. Nōn satis celeriter cucurrērunt **ut** perīculum **nōn fugerent** (**fūgerint**). They did not run quickly enough *with the result that they did not flee* the danger.

4. Ventī ita validī erant **ut nēmō** vēla dare **posset** (**potuerit**). The winds were so strong *that no one could* set sail.

SUBSTANTIVE CLAUSES OF RESULT (Unit 14B)

Certain verbs and expressions have result clauses either as their object or subject.

1. Effēcērunt **ut** pāx **fieret** (**facta sit**). They brought it about *that* peace *was made*.

2. Fit **ut** nōs **sīmus** amīcī. It happens *that we are* friends.

3. Fac **ut** hoc quam celerrimē **fīat**. See to it *that* this *is done* as quickly as possible.

With **faciō** and **efficiō**, the negative is often expressed by **nē**, particularly when there is an implicit notion of command in the sentence:

4. Fac **nē** sit mora. See to it *that there isn't* a delay.

RELATIVE CLAUSES OF RESULT (Unit 14D)

A relative clause of characteristic may be fused with a result clause to produce a relative clause of result. The relative pronoun is standing for the **ut** which would normally introduce the clause of result.

1. Quod factum tantum fuit **quod** omnēs **mīrārentur**? What deed was so great *that* everyone *admired it*?

2. Tam clārus est **quem** omnēs **sciant**. He is so famous *that* everyone *knows him*.

3. Tam senex est **quī** morī **velit**. He is so old *that he wants* to die.

**fore ut** + SUBJUNCTIVE (Unit 18B)

**Fore ut** is used with the subjunctive often in place of a future *passive* infinitive in indirect statement or in place of a future *active* infinitive when the verb lacks a fourth principal part.

1. Spērat **fore ut** impiī ex urbe **expellantur**. He hopes that the wicked men *will be driven* out of the city.
2. Scīvit **fore ut** multum ab eīs librīs **discerēmus**. He knew that *we would learn* a lot from those books.
3. Tibi dīximus **fore ut** id **accideret**. We told you that this *would happen*.
4. Putās **fore ut** eī **adsint**? Do you think that they *will be present*?

RELATIVE CLAUSES OF CHARACTERISTIC (GENERIC RELATIVE CLAUSES) (Unit 14C)
The relative pronoun **quī, quae, quod** plus the subjunctive can be used to describe the antecedent of the pronoun in terms of the general qualities or characteristics of the group to which the antecedent belongs. The negative clause is often introduced by **quīn**.

1. **Sunt quī** eum **laudent**. *There are those who praise* him; *There are those who would praise* him.
2. **Nēmō est quī** eum tē **mālit**. *There is no one who prefers* him to you; *There is no one who would prefer* him to you.
3. **Quid erat quod** nōbīs **timendum esset**? *What was there which* we *had to fear*?
4. **Sōlus erit quīn** hoc **faciat**. *He will be the only one who doesn't do* it; *He will be the only one who won't do* it; *He will be the only one who wouldn't do* it.

CLAUSES OF FEARING (Unit 17A)
Clauses of fearing are introduced by **nē** for the positive and **ut** (occasionally, **nē...nōn**) for the negative.

1. Metuunt **ut** hostēs urbem **relīquerint**. They fear *that* the enemy *has not abandoned* the city.
2. Veritī sumus **nē** nōs **ōdissent**. We feared *that they hated* us.
3. Timet **ut** cōpiīs **praesit**. He is afraid *that he will not be in charge of* the troops.
4. Timent **nē nōn** vēritātem sibi **dictūrus sīs**. They fear *that you will not tell* them the truth.

INDIRECT QUESTIONS (Unit 12C)
Indirect questions are subordinate noun clauses which serve as the object (and, less frequently, the subject) of the words on which they depend. These words usually, but not always, express or imply actions that take place in the head, such as saying, thinking, seeing, perceiving, knowing, asking, and the like. Indirect questions are introduced by an interrogative word and have their verbs in the subjunctive.

1. Nōn intellegit **quō modō** hoc **fīat**. He does not understand *how* this *is done*.
2. **Quid sciat** incertum est. It is uncertain *what he knows*.
3. Nōn exposuistī **cūr** hūc **venīrēs**. You did not explain *why you were coming* here.

4. **Quā dē causā** hoc **factūrus sīs** manifestum est. It is clear *for what reason you will do* this. [**manifestus, -a, -um,** 'evident, clear']

CONDITIONS

PRESENT CONTRARY-TO-FACT CONDITIONS (imperfect subjunctive in both clauses) (Unit 2E3a)

1. Sī rēx **essem**, imperium mihi **esset**. If *I were* king, I *would have* power.
2. Nisī frāter meus **essēs**, poenās **darēs**. If *you were* not my brother, *you would pay* the penalty.
3. Sī īnsidiās contrā rem pūblicam **facerent**, cōnsul eōs **opprimeret**. If *they were making* a plot against the state, the consul *would suppress* them.

PAST CONTRARY-TO-FACT CONDITIONS (pluperfect subjunctive in both clauses) (Unit 2E3b)

1. Sī dē nōbīs **cōgitāvissētis**, hoc numquam **fēcissētis**. If *you had thought* about us, *you would* never *have done* this.
2. Sī oppidum moenibus **dēfēnsum esset**, hostēs nōn **invāsissent**. If the town *had been defended* by walls, the enemy *would* not *have invaded* it.
3. Nisī auxilium **tulissētis**, **mortuī essēmus**. If *you had* not *brought* aid, *we would have died*.

FUTURE LESS VIVID CONDITIONS (present subjunctive in both clauses; occasionally perfect subjunctive in protasis) (Unit 2E2b)

1. Sī iuvenem **laudēs**, fēlīx **sit**. If *you should praise* the young man, *he would be* happy.
2. Sī oppidum ab hostibus **vincātur**, incolae servī **fīant**. If the town *should be conquered* by the enemy, the inhabitants *would become* slaves.
3. Nisī auxilium ad incolās **ferātur**, **patiantur**. If aid *should* not *be brought* to the inhabitants, *they would suffer*.

Note that conditions can be mixed as logic requires (Unit 2E4):

1. Sī eum **vīdisset**, fēlīx **esset**. If *she had seen* him, *she would be* happy.
2. Sī perīculum **sit**, **clāmābō**. If *there should be* danger, *I shall shout*.
3. Sī Rōmae **essem**, iter longum **fēcissem**. If *I were* in Rome, *I would have made* a long journey.

SUBJUNCTIVE IN SUBORDINATE CLAUSES IN INDIRECT STATEMENT (Unit 7J)
Subordinate clauses within an indirect statement normally have their verbs in the subjunctive, the tense of which is determined by the verb or phrase of the head introducing the indirect statement.

1. Virum quem **vidērēmus** esse frātrem poētae dīxērunt. They said that the man whom *we saw* was the poet's brother.

2. Deōs praemia populō cui **faveant** datūrōs esse sentit. *He feels that the gods will give rewards to the people whom* they favor.

3. Sē ducibus quī reī pūblicae **praeessent** crēditūrōs esse arbitrātī sunt. *They thought that they would believe the leaders who* were in charge of *the state.*

CAUSAL CLAUSES (**cum** + subjunctive) (Unit 15A2 and D1)
**Quod** or **quia** is used with the subjunctive to give an *alleged* reason.

1. **Cum** cōnsilia eōrum **rīdērēmus**, magistrī nōs ōderant. *Since we laughed at their plans, our superiors hated us.*

2. Haec facere scīvimus, **cum** nōbīs ā tē **exposita essent**. *We knew how to do these things, since they had been explained to us by you.* [sciō, *here,* 'know how']

3. **Cum** in Italiā **sīmus**, Rōmam ībimus. *Since we are in Italy, we shall go to Rome.*

4. Rōmam vēnērunt $\begin{cases} \textbf{quod} \\ \textbf{quia} \end{cases}$ nōs vidēre **vellent**. *They came to Rome because they* (allegedly) *wanted to see us.*

BUT:

5. Quid faciat nescit $\begin{cases} \textbf{quoniam} \\ \textbf{quandō} \end{cases}$ haec nōn **exposita sunt**. *He does not know what to do since these things have* not *been explained.*

6. Quid faciat nescit $\begin{cases} \textbf{quod} \\ \textbf{quia} \end{cases}$ haec nōn **exposita sunt**. *He does not know what to do because these things* (actually) *have* not *been explained.*

7. Quid faciat nescit, **hīs** nōn **expositīs**. *He does not know what to do since these things have* not *been explained.* (Ablative Absolute)

CONCESSIVE CLAUSES (**cum** + subjunctive; **quamvīs** + subjunctive; **ut** + subjunctive) (Unit 15A3 and C3; **ut** + subj. not discussed in the text)

1. **Cum** in Italiā **sīmus**, Rōmam tamen nōn ībimus. *Although we are in Italy, nevertheless we shall not go to Rome.*

2. **Cum** ad rēgem **missī essent**, eum vidēre nōn potuērunt. *Although they had been sent to the king, they were not able to see him.*

3. Tē vidēre volō, **cum** tē hōc tempore nōn **amem**. *I want to see you, although I do not love you at this time.*

4. **Quamvīs** mē ad tē venīre **volueris**, tamen hoc nōn faciam. *Although you wanted me to come to you, nevertheless I shall not do it.*

5. Illūc īvī **ut nōllem**. *I went there* $\begin{cases} \textit{even though} \\ \textit{granted that} \end{cases}$ *I did not want to.*

BUT:

6. $\left.\begin{array}{l}\textbf{Quamquam} \\ \textbf{Etsī}\end{array}\right\}$ mē ad tē venīre **voluistī**, tamen hoc nōn faciam. *Although you wanted* me to come to you, nevertheless I shall not do it.

7. **Hīs expositīs**, tamen quid facerēmus nescīvimus. *Although these things had been explained*, nevertheless we did not know what to do. (Ablative Absolute)

CIRCUMSTANTIAL CLAUSES (**cum** + subjunctive when the action is in past time; **cum** + indicative when the action is in present or future time) (Unit 15A1)

1. **Cum** fulgor **vīsus esset**, multī timuērunt. *When* the lightning *had been seen*, many feared.

2. **Cum** tēctum **ardēret**, omnēs clāmāvērunt. *When* the house *was burning*, everyone shouted.

3. **Cum** hunc cōpiīs **praefēcissent**, mīlitēs hostēs vīcērunt. *When they had put* him *in charge of* the troops, the soldiers conquered the enemy.

BUT:

4. **Hōc** cōpiīs **praefectō**, mīlitēs hostēs vīcērunt. *When this man had been put in charge of* the troops, the soldiers conquered the enemy. (Ablative Absolute)

5. **Cum** fulgor **vīsus erat**, multī timuērunt. *When* the lightning *had been seen*, many feared. (The indicative is used to stress time.)

ANTICIPATION (Unit 15D2 and D3)
One of the basic uses of the subjunctive is to express anticipation.

1. $\left.\begin{array}{l}\textbf{Dōnec} \\ \textbf{Dum} \\ \textbf{Quōad}\end{array}\right\}$ hoc **faciās**, īnfēlīx erō. *Until you do* this, I shall be unhappy.

2. Labōrem neglēxērunt $\left\{\begin{array}{l}\textbf{dōnec} \\ \textbf{dum} \\ \textbf{quōad}\end{array}\right\}$ litterās tuās **acciperent**. They neglected their work *until they could receive* your letter. [labor, -ōris, M., 'work']

3. Hoc faciēmus **antequam** tē **videāmus**. We shall do this *before we see* you.

4. **Ante** aderō **quam adveniās**. I shall be present *before you arrive*.

5. **Prius** eum laudāvērunt **quam** eum **scīrent**. They praised him *before they could know* him.

BUT:

1. Labōrem neglēxērunt **dum** litterās tuās **accēpērunt**. They neglected their work *until they received* your letter. (The indicative is used to express fact, not anticipation.)

2. **Prius** eum laudāvērunt **quam** eum **scīvērunt**. They praised him *before they* (actually) *knew* him.

AND:

3. **Ante** aderō **quam advenīs (advēneris)**. I shall be present *before you arrive*. (The present or future perfect indicative frequently is used with **antequam** and **priusquam** in primary sequence even when there is a notion of anticipation.)

CLAUSES OF PROVISO (**dum, modo,** and **dummodo** + present or imperfect subjunctive; the negative uses **nē**) (Unit 15E)

1. Hoc faciēmus $\begin{Bmatrix} \textbf{dummodo} \\ \textbf{dum} \\ \textbf{modo} \end{Bmatrix}$ auxilium **offerās**. We shall do this *provided that you offer* help.

2. Auxilium offerēmus $\begin{Bmatrix} \textbf{dum} \\ \textbf{modo} \\ \textbf{dummodo} \end{Bmatrix}$ **quaerātur**. We shall offer help *provided it is sought*.

3. Nautae vēla dabunt $\begin{Bmatrix} \textbf{modo} \\ \textbf{dum} \\ \textbf{dummodo} \end{Bmatrix}$ ventī secundī **sint**. The sailors will set sail *provided that* the winds *are* favorable. [**secundus, -a, -um,** 'favorable']

4. $\begin{Bmatrix} \textbf{Dum} \\ \textbf{Dummodo} \\ \textbf{Modo} \end{Bmatrix}$ **nē** tibi **noceam**, faciam quid dēbeam. *Provided that I do not harm* you, I shall do what I must.

SUBJUNCTIVE BY ATTRACTION (Unit 18A)

Frequently relative and other subordinate clauses within clauses whose verbs are in the subjunctive have verbs which are attracted into the subjunctive provided that the subordinate clause is an integral part of the idea of the main clause.

1. Rōmam īre volō ut tēctum in quō **vīxerit** poēta clārissimus videam. I want to go to Rome to see the house in which the very famous poet *lived*.

2. Tam crūdēlis erat ut omnis populus dum **vīveret** eum timēret. He was so cruel that all the people while *he lived* feared him.

3. Quis est quī tēctum in quō **vīvat** poēta clārissimus vidēre velit? Who is there who wants to see the house in which the very famous poet *lives*?

CLAUSES OF DOUBTING (Unit 17B)

**Num** or **an** + subjunctive is used after a positive expression of doubting; **quīn** + subjunctive after a negative one.

1. Dubitō **num veniat**. I doubt *whether* (*that*) *he is coming* (*he will come*).
2. Dubitāvērunt **an** hoc **facerēmus**. They doubted *whether* (*that*) *we were doing* (*would do*) this.
3. Dubitāsne **num** diē cōnstitūtā **adventūrī sint**? Do you doubt *whether* (*that*) *they will arrive* on the day which has been decided?
4. Nōn est dubium **quīn tē timeat**. There is no doubt (*but*) *that he fears* you.
5. Quis dubitet **quīn** impius **sit**? Who would doubt (*but*) *that he is* wicked?

Clauses of Prevention (Unit 17C)
If the verb of prevention is positive, the subjunctive clause will be introduced by **quōminus** or **nē**; if negative, by **quōminus** or **quīn**.

1. Hostēs cōpiās nostrās dēterruērunt $\left\{\begin{array}{l}\text{quōminus}\\\text{nē}\end{array}\right\}$ **advenīrent**. The enemy prevented our troops *from arriving*.
2. Ignis nōn impediet $\left\{\begin{array}{l}\text{quīn}\\\text{quōminus}\end{array}\right\}$ in tēctum **ingrediāmur**. The fire will not hinder *us from entering* the house.
3. Puerī obstant $\left\{\begin{array}{l}\text{nē}\\\text{quōminus}\end{array}\right\}$ opus tuum **perficiās**? Are the children hindering *you from completing* your work?

Subjunctive Clauses with Impersonal Verbs (**ut** or **nē** expressed or implied + subjunctive) (Unit 16D3 and E)

1. Necesse est (**ut**) Marcus nāvibus **praesit**. It is necessary *that* Marcus *be in charge of* the ships.
2. Licet (**ut**) rēgem **videāmus**. It is permitted *for us to see* the king. OR: *We are permitted to see* the king.
3. Patriae interest **ut** hostēs **discēdant**. It is in the interest of the country *that* the enemy *withdraw*.
4. Tuā rēfert **nē** illūc **eās**. It is to (in) your interest *not to go* there.

**Participles (Unit 5B)**
A participle is a verbal adjective.

Participles as Attributive Adjectives

1. Virum ā perīculō **fugientem** vīdimus. We saw the man *fleeing* from danger.
2. Oppidum ab hostibus **captum** incēnsum est. The town *captured* by the enemy was set on fire. [incendō, -ere, -cendī, -cēnsus, 'set on fire']
3. Servus ā tēctō dominī **fugitūrus** timuit. The slave, *about to flee* from his master's house, was afraid.

ABLATIVE ABSOLUTE
See page 376.

### Gerunds (Unit 16A)
The gerund is a verbal noun found only in the singular. It lacks a nominative case which is supplied by the infinitive.

1. Timor **scrībendī** multōs scrībere prohibet. The fear *of writing* keeps many people from writing.
2. Rūs īvimus **venandī** $\left\{ \begin{array}{l} \text{causā} \\ \text{grātiā} \end{array} \right\}$. We went to the country for the sake *of hunting.*

   OR: We went to the country to *hunt.* [**grātiā**, preceded by gen., 'for the sake of']
3. Marcum **canendō** praefēcimus. We put Marcus in charge of *the singing.*
4. Ad **venandum** rūs īvimus. We went to the country to *hunt.*
5. **Eundō** rūs patrī placuimus. *By going* to the country we pleased our father.

   BUT: Rūs īvimus **venandōrum animālium** $\left\{ \begin{array}{l} \text{causā} \\ \text{grātiā} \end{array} \right\}$. We went to the country to *hunt animals.* [**grātiā**, preceded by gen., 'for the sake of'] (The gerundive is used instead of a gerund with an object.)

### Gerundives (Unit 16B)
The gerundive is a verbal adjective. It is frequently used instead of a gerund which governs an object except when the object is a neuter adjective or pronoun.

1. Timor librōrum **scrībendōrum** multōs scrībere prohibet. The fear *of writing* books keeps many people from writing.
2. Multī linguam antīquam **discendam** ōdērunt. Many people hate *learning* an ancient language. [**lingua, -ae**, F., 'tongue, language']
3. Linguā antīquā **discendā** ūtimur. We enjoy *learning* an ancient language. [**lingua, -ae**, F., 'tongue, language']
4. Rōmam ad Caesarem **videndum** īvimus. We went to Rome to *see* Caesar. [**Caesar, -aris**, M., 'Caesar']
5. Rōmam Caesaris **videndī** $\left\{ \begin{array}{l} \text{causā} \\ \text{grātiā} \end{array} \right\}$ īvimus. We went to Rome for the sake of *seeing* (to *see*) Caesar. [**Caesar, -aris**, M., 'Caesar'; **grātiā**, preceded by gen., 'for the sake of']

### Supines (Unit 17D)
The supine is a verbal noun which occurs only in the accusative and ablative singular. The accusative case is used, without a preposition, to express purpose after a verb of motion, and the ablative, with certain adjectives, expresses respect.

1. Rōmam Caesarem **vīsum** īvimus. We went to Rome *to see* Caesar. [**Caesar, -aris**, M., 'Caesar']
2. Ā perīculō **fugitum** cucurrimus. We ran *to flee* from danger.
3. Librum — mīrābile **dictū**! — perfēcimus. We have finished the book — wonderful *to say*! [**mīrābilis, -e**, 'wonderful, marvelous']

# CONDITIONS IN INDIRECT STATEMENT

In order to put a conditional statement into the indirect form after a verb or expression of the head, the apodosis is recast in the subject accusative and infinitive construction; the protasis will have its verb in the subjunctive, regardless of its mood in the direct statement. Observe the following:

### Simple (General) Conditions
APODOSIS: The subject accusative and infinitive construction is used in indirect statement; the tense of the infinitive is relative to that of the main verb of the head.

PROTASIS: The verb is in the subjunctive, the tense of which is determined by sequence relative to the main verb of the head.

Sī īnsidiās contrā rem pūblicam faciunt, cōnsul eōs opprimit.
If they plot against the state, the consul oppresses them.

Dīcit (dīcet) sī īnsidiās contrā rem pūblicam faciant, cōnsulem eōs opprimere.
He says (will say) that, if they plot against the state, the consul oppresses them.

Dīxit sī īnsidiās contrā rem pūblicam facerent, cōnsulem eōs opprimere.
He said that, if they plotted against the state, the consul oppressed them.

Sī īnsidiās contrā rem pūblicam faciēbant, cōnsul eōs opprimēbat.
If they plotted against the state, the consul oppressed them.

Dīcit (dīcet) sī īnsidiās contrā rem pūblicam fēcerint, cōnsulem eōs oppressisse.
He says (will say) that, if they plotted against the state, the consul oppressed them.

Dīxit sī īnsidiās contrā rem pūblicam fēcissent, cōnsulem eōs oppressisse.
He said that, if they had plotted against the state, the consul had oppressed them.

### Future More Vivid Conditions and Future Less Vivid Conditions
Note that no distinction is made between these two kinds of conditions in indirect statement.

APODOSIS: The subject accusative and infinitive construction is used in indirect statement; the tense of the infinitive will always be future.

PROTASIS: The verb is always in the subjunctive, the tense of which is determined by sequence relative to the main verb of the head.

MORE VIVID:

Sī īnsidiās contrā rem pūblicam $\begin{Bmatrix} \text{facient} \\ \text{fēcerint} \end{Bmatrix}$, cōnsul eōs opprimet.

If $\begin{Bmatrix} \text{they plot} \\ \quad \textit{plot} \text{ (will have plotted)} \end{Bmatrix}$ against the state, the consul will oppress them.

LESS VIVID:

Sī īnsidiās contrā rem pūblicam $\begin{Bmatrix} \text{faciant} \\ \text{fēcerint} \end{Bmatrix}$, cōnsul eōs opprimat.

If $\begin{Bmatrix} \text{they should plot} \\ \quad \textit{should plot} \text{ (should have plotted)} \end{Bmatrix}$ against the state, the consul would oppress them.

MORE VIVID:

Dīcit (dīcet) sī īnsidiās contrā rem pūblicam $\begin{Bmatrix} \text{faciant} \\ \text{fēcerint} \end{Bmatrix}$, cōnsulem eōs oppressūrum esse.

He says (will say) that, if $\begin{Bmatrix} \text{they plot} \\ \quad \textit{plot} \text{ (will have plotted)} \end{Bmatrix}$ against the state, the consul will oppress them.

LESS VIVID:

Dīcit (dīcet) sī īnsidiās contrā rem pūblicam $\begin{Bmatrix} \text{faciant} \\ \text{fēcerint} \end{Bmatrix}$, cōnsulem eōs oppressūrum esse.

He says (will say) that, if $\begin{Bmatrix} \text{they should plot} \\ \quad \textit{should plot} \text{ (should have plotted)} \end{Bmatrix}$ against the state, the consul would oppress them.

MORE VIVID:

Dīxit sī īnsidiās contrā rem pūblicam $\begin{Bmatrix} \text{facerent} \\ \text{fēcissent} \end{Bmatrix}$, cōnsulem eōs oppressūrum esse.

He said that, if $\begin{Bmatrix} \text{they plotted} \\ \quad \textit{plotted} \text{ (will have plotted)} \end{Bmatrix}$ against the state, the consul would oppress them.

LESS VIVID:

Dīxit sī īnsidiās contrā rem pūblicam $\begin{Bmatrix} \text{facerent} \\ \text{fēcissent} \end{Bmatrix}$, cōnsulem eōs oppressūrum esse.

He said that, if $\begin{Bmatrix} \text{they should plot} \\ \quad \textit{should plot} \text{ (should have plotted)} \end{Bmatrix}$ against the state, the consul would oppress them.

### Present and Past Contrary-to-Fact Conditions

APODOSIS: The subject accusative and infinitive construction is used in indirect statement; the infinitive is always composed of the future active participle plus **fuisse**.

PROTASIS: The verb is always in the subjunctive, the tense of which is the same as it would have been in the direct statement, *regardless* of the tense sequence relative to the main verb of the head.

PRESENT CONTRARY-TO-FACT:
Sī īnsidiās contrā rem pūblicam facerent, cōnsul eōs opprimeret.
If they were plotting against the state, the consul would oppress them.

PAST CONTRARY-TO-FACT:
Sī īnsidiās contrā rem pūblicam fēcissent, cōnsul eōs oppressisset.
If they had plotted against the state, the consul would have oppressed them.

PRESENT CONTRARY-TO-FACT:
Dīcit (dīcet) sī īnsidiās contrā rem pūblicam facerent, cōnsulem eōs oppressūrum fuisse.
He says (will say) that, if they were plotting against the state, the consul would oppress them.

PAST CONTRARY-TO-FACT:
Dīcit (dīcet) sī īnsidiās contrā rem pūblicam fēcissent, cōnsulem eōs oppressūrum fuisse.
He says (will say) that, if they had plotted against the state, the consul would have oppressed them.

PRESENT CONTRARY-TO-FACT:
Dīxit sī īnsidiās contrā rem pūblicam facerent, cōnsulem eōs oppressūrum fuisse.
He said that, if they were plotting against the state, the consul would oppress them.

PAST CONTRARY-TO-FACT:
Dīxit sī īnsidiās contrā rem pūblicam fēcissent, cōnsulem eōs oppressūrum fuisse.
He said that, if they had plotted against the state, the consul would have oppressed them.

## CONDITIONS IN OTHER SUBORDINATE CLAUSES

In order to put a conditional statement into the indirect form after a verb of commanding, fearing, or the like, the observations made above about the protasis of each type of condition will apply, but the apodosis will be recast in the appropriate construction dependent on the verb of commanding, fearing, or the like.

Sī Caesar veniet, vincet. If Caesar comes, he will conquer.
Timeō, sī Caesar **veniat, nē vincat (victūrus sit)**. I fear that, if Caesar *comes, he will conquer*.

## ADDITIONAL RULES

A collective noun usually takes a verb in the singular, but the plural is found when individuals are thought of: **Quisque domum īre voluērunt**, 'Each one wanted to go home'.

A compound subject, even when the subjects are singular, takes a verb in the plural: **Māterne et pater tuus venient**? 'Will your mother and father come?' When the compound subject is in different persons, the verb is usually in the first person rather than the second person and in the second person rather than the third person: **Sī tū et tuus frāter domum ībitis, ego et mea soror illūc ībimus**, 'If you and your brother go home, my sister and I will go there'. When there is a compound subject in the third person, the verb may agree with the nearest one: **Multī puerī parvī et ūna puella parva aderat**, 'Many little boys and one little girl were present'.

Two negatives are equivalent to an affirmative: **nōn numquam**, 'sometimes'; **nōn nūllī**, 'some'; **Nēmō nōn veniet**, 'Everyone will come'; **Nōn possum nōn venīre**, 'I must come'.

When several nouns of different gender are described by one adjective, the masculine gender predominates over the feminine if *persons* are being described; if *things* of different genders are described by one adjective, the adjective will be neuter: **Meus frāter sororque sunt piī**, 'My brother and sister are pious'; **Virtūs et vigor sunt bona**, 'Courage and vigor are good'. Sometimes the adjective will agree with the nearest noun: **Virtūs et vigor sunt bonus**, 'Courage and vigor are good'.

There is no one word in Latin for "yes" or for "no". Sometimes the verb is repeated for "yes" or repeated with **nōn** for "no": **Venīsne?**, 'Are you coming?' **Veniō**, 'Yes'. **Nōn veniō**, 'No'. There are other ways of saying "yes" including: **aiō, etiam, ita, vērō, certē**. Some ways of saying "no" are: **negō, nōn, minimē, nūllō modō, nōn quidem**.

**Nescio quis** is used as an indefinite pronoun meaning 'someone or other' and **nescio quid**, 'something or other'. **Quis** and **quid** are declined, but **nescio** remains the same: **Nescio quis clāmābat**. 'Someone or other kept shouting'; **Nescio quem dāmnāvērunt**, 'They condemned someone or other'; **Nescio quid dīxit**, 'He said something or other'. Note that this phrase does not introduce an indirect question.

# ROMAN NAMES

Roman citizens usually had three names: the **praenōmen** (or personal name), the **nōmen** (or family name), the **cōgnōmen** (the name designating the branch of the family).

> e.g. Marcus Tullius Cicero
> Gaius Julius Caesar
> Publius Vergilius Maro

The **praenōmina** were relatively few in number and were customarily abbreviated in the following way:

| | | | |
|---|---|---|---|
| A. | = Aulus | P. | = Publius |
| App. | = Appius | Q. | = Quintus |
| C. | = Gaius | Ser. | = Servius |
| Cn. | = Gnaeus | Sex. | = Sextus |
| D. | = Decimus | Sp. | = Spurius |
| L. | = Lucius | T. | = Titus |
| M. | = Marcus | Ti. | = Tiberius |
| M'. | = Manius | | |

# A NOTE ON QUANTITATIVE RHYTHM

Accentual or *qualitative* rhythm in poetry is based on a sequence of stressed and unstressed syllables.

> By brooks too broad for leaping
> The light-foot lads are laid.
> And rose-lipt girls are sleeping
> In fields where roses fade.
>> (A. E. Housman)

The rhythm of classical Latin poetry is *quantitative*, not qualitative. It is based on a sequence of syllables which are *temporally* long or short; that is, a long syllable takes more time to pronounce than a short one. To give a rough illustration, one might say that a long syllable is equivalent to a half note while the short syllable is equivalent to a quarter note. On the most basic level, this rhythmic scheme admits of no stress, although one syllable in each foot does in practice receive a *slight* accent which is called **ictus [ictus, -ūs, M., 'blow, beat'].**

In order to *scan* or construct a schematic representation of a line of verse, the quantitative length of each of the syllables in that line must be determined. In working this out, division into words is disregarded and the entire line is considered as one cluster of sounds. The rules for syllabification and for determining the quantitative length of syllables are the same as those given in the Introduction (pp. 2–3): A syllable is *long by nature* if it contains a long vowel or a diphthong; a syllable is *long by position* if it contains a vowel which is followed by two consonants. The letter **x** (= ks) is said to be a double consonant. The letters **qu** (= kw) function as one sound cluster; the **u** is not a separate syllable. The combination **qu** does not make for length by position. EXCEPTION: When the two consonants following a vowel are a mute (plosive) (**p, b, t, d, c(k), g**) followed by **l** or **r**, the poet has the license to regard the syllable as either long or short.

According to this scheme, the following verses are scanned as shown:

$$— \quad —\,\smile\,— \quad — \qquad — \quad \smile — \smile \quad — \quad — \smile$$

Quem bāsiābis ? Cui labella mordēbis?
(Catullus 8.19; p. 124)

$$— \quad \smile\,\smile\,— \quad \smile\,\smile\,— \quad — \quad — \quad —\,\smile\,\smile\,— \quad —\,\smile$$

Quem recitās meus est, Ō Fīdentīne, libellus:

$$— \quad \smile\,\smile \quad — \quad \smile\,\smile\,— \quad —\,\smile\,\smile \quad —\,\smile \quad \smile\,\smile$$

sed male cum recitās, incipit esse tuus.
(Martial 1.38; p. 124)

$$— \quad —\,— \quad \smile\,\smile\,—\,\smile \quad \smile \quad — \quad \smile\,\smile \quad — \quad \smile \quad \smile \quad —\,\smile$$

Ō passī graviōra, dabit deus hīs quoque fīnem.
(Vergil, *Aeneid* I.199; p. 191)

Note that the symbol — is used for long syllables, and ˘ is used for short syllables. Do not confuse the symbol for long syllables with the macron, which is used to mark long vowels.

Occasionally, *elision*, or the full or partial suppression of a final syllable, occurs in the scansion and reading of poetry. Elision is found in the following instances:

1. When a word ending in a vowel or diphthong is followed by a word which begins with a vowel or diphthong:

$$\smile\,\smile \quad —\,\smile \quad \smile \quad — \quad — \quad — \quad \smile\,\smile \quad —\,\smile$$

...revocāte animōs maestumque timōrem
(Vergil, *Aeneid* I.202; p. 191)

Note that the quantity of the full syllable formed by elision is determined by the length (natural or positional) of the second of the two original syllables. In the example above, the syllable is short because the first syllable of **animōs** is short.

2. When a word ending in a vowel or diphthong is followed by a word which begins with a vowel preceded by **h**:

$$\breve{\phantom{x}} \; \underline{\phantom{x}} \; \underline{\phantom{x}} \qquad \breve{\phantom{x}} \; \breve{\phantom{x}} \; \underline{\phantom{x}} \breve{\phantom{x}} \underline{\phantom{x}} \qquad \breve{\phantom{x}} \; \underline{\phantom{x}} \; \breve{\phantom{x}}$$

Adeste, hendecasyllabī, quot estis

(Catullus 42.1)

3. When a word ending in a vowel followed by **m** is followed by a word which begins with a vowel or a vowel preceded by **h**:

$$\underline{\phantom{x}} \; \breve{\phantom{x}} \; \breve{\phantom{x}} \; \underline{\phantom{x}} \; \underline{\phantom{x}} \; \breve{\phantom{x}} \; \breve{\phantom{x}} \; \underline{\phantom{x}} \qquad \underline{\phantom{x}} \; \underline{\phantom{x}} \; \breve{\phantom{x}} \; \breve{\phantom{x}} \; \underline{\phantom{x}} \; \breve{\phantom{x}}$$

Nūlla fidēs ūllō fuit unquam in foedere tanta

(Catullus 87.3; p. 174)

There is some dispute as to whether elision means the total omission in pronunciation of the first of the two syllables or a more rapid combination of the two sounds in order to fit them into the reduced temporal allotment. In order to acquaint himself or herself with the rules for elision and also to acquire some sense of Latin rhythm, the beginner would do well to omit the first of the two syllables when reading the line aloud. Once some degree of security has been acquired, the reader may, if desired, experiment with the rapid combination of the sounds.

In addition to scanning the lines as we have done, it is possible to divide them into smaller measures of time called "feet". A "foot" is a measure composed of a sequence of long and short syllables. The type or types of feet employed in a given line of verse determine the rhythm of that verse. The following feet are basic and appear in some of the selections in this book:

| | |
|---|---|
| $\underline{\phantom{x}}\,\breve{\phantom{x}}\,\breve{\phantom{x}}$ | dactyl |
| $\underline{\phantom{x}}\;\underline{\phantom{x}}$ | spondee |
| $\breve{\phantom{x}}\,\breve{\phantom{x}}\,\underline{\phantom{x}}$ | anapest |
| $\breve{\phantom{x}}\;\underline{\phantom{x}}$ | iamb |
| $\underline{\phantom{x}}\;\breve{\phantom{x}}$ | trochee |
| $\underline{\phantom{x}}\,\breve{\phantom{x}}\,\breve{\phantom{x}}\,\underline{\phantom{x}}$ | choriamb |

The scansion of the following lines of verse shows the quantities of the various syllables as well as the division into feet (indicated by |):

$$\underline{\phantom{x}} \quad \underline{\phantom{x}}|\breve{\phantom{x}}\underline{\phantom{x}}|\underline{\phantom{x}} \quad \underline{\phantom{x}}|\breve{\phantom{x}}\;\underline{\phantom{x}}|\breve{\phantom{x}} \quad \underline{\phantom{x}}|\underline{\phantom{x}}\breve{\phantom{x}}$$

Quem bāsiābis? Cui labella mordēbis?

$$\underline{\phantom{x}} \quad \underline{\phantom{x}}|\underline{\phantom{x}} \quad \breve{\phantom{x}}\;\breve{\phantom{x}}|\underline{\phantom{x}}\breve{\phantom{x}} \quad \breve{\phantom{x}}|\underline{\phantom{x}} \quad \breve{\phantom{x}}\;\breve{\phantom{x}}| \underline{\phantom{x}} \quad \breve{\phantom{x}} \quad \breve{\phantom{x}}|\underline{\phantom{x}}\breve{\phantom{x}}$$

Ō passī graviōra, dabit deus hīs quoque fīnem.

The rhythmic analysis of Latin poetry is both intricate and fascinating. Although the observations offered above have been necessarily simplified, they should help to give at least an initial impression of the rhythm and the music of the selections of poetry encountered at this early stage in one's study of the Latin language and literature. By applying these rules, it will be possible to read the selections in this book with some attention to their rhythm and so with greater appreciation.

# NUMERALS

| | CARDINALS | ORDINALS | DISTRIBUTIVES | ADVERBS |
|---|---|---|---|---|
| I | ūnus, -a, -um<br>'one' | prīmus, -a, -um<br>'first' | singulī, -ae, -a<br>'one by one, one each' | semel<br>'once' |
| II | duo, duae, duo<br>'two' | secundus, -a, -um<br>(alter, altera, alterum)<br>'second' | bīnī, -ae, -a<br>'two by two, two each' | bis<br>'twice' |
| III | trēs, tria<br>'three' | tertius, -a, -um<br>'third' | ternī, -ae, -a<br>(trīnī, -ae, -a)<br>'three by three, three each' | ter<br>'three times' |
| IV (IIII) | quattuor[1]<br>'four' | quārtus, -a, -um<br>'fourth' | quaternī, -ae, -a<br>'four by four, four each' | quater<br>'four times' |
| V | quīnque | quīntus, -a, -um | quīnī, -ae, -a | quīnquiē(n)s |
| VI | sex | sextus, -a, -um | sēnī, -ae, -a | sexiē(n)s |
| VII | septem | septimus, -a, -um | septēnī, -ae, -a | septiē(n)s |
| VIII | octo | octāvus, -a, -um | octōnī, -ae, -a | octiē(n)s |
| IX (VIIII) | novem | nōnus, -a, -um | novēnī, -ae, -a | noviē(n)s |
| X | decem | decimus, -a, -um | dēnī, -ae, -a | deciē(n)s |

[1] Unless otherwise specified, the numbers are indeclinable.

## NUMERALS—*cont.*

| | CARDINALS | ORDINALS | DISTRIBUTIVES | ADVERBS |
|---|---|---|---|---|
| XI | ūndecim | ūndecimus, -a, -um | ūndēnī, -ae, -a | ūndeciē(n)s |
| XII | duodecim | duodecimus, -a, -um | duodēnī, -ae, -a | duodeciē(n)s |
| XIII | tredecim (decem [et] trēs) | tertius, -a, -um decimus, -a, -um (decimus, -a, -um [et] tertius, -a, -um) | ternī, -ae, -a dēnī, -ae, -a | ter deciē(n)s |
| XIV (XIIII) | quattuordecim | quārtus, -a, -um decimus, -a, -um | quaternī, -ae, -a dēnī, -ae, -a | quater deciē(n)s |
| XV | quīndecim | quīntus, -a, -um decimus, -a, -um | quīnī, -ae, -a dēnī, -ae, -a | quīnquiē(n)s deciē(n)s (quīndeciē[n]s) |
| XVI | sēdecim | sextus, -a, -um decimus, -a, -um | sēnī, -ae, -a dēnī, -ae, -a | sexiē(n)s deciē(n)s (sēdeciē[n]s) |
| XVII | septendecim | septimus, -a, -um decimus, -a, -um | septēnī, -ae, -a dēnī, -ae, -a | septiē(n)s deciē(n)s |
| XVIII | duodēvīgintī (octōdecim) | duodēvīcē(n)simus, -a, -um (octāvus, -a, -um decimus, -a, -um) | octōnī, -ae, -a dēnī, -ae, -a (duodēvīcēnī, -ae, -a) | duodēviciē(n)s (octiē[n]s deciē[n]s) |

| | | | | |
|---|---|---|---|---|
| XIX (XVIIII) | ūndēvīgintī (novendecim) | ūndēvīcē(n)simus, -a, -um (nōnus, -a, -um decimus, -a, -um) | novēnī, -ae, -a dēnī, -ae, -a (ūndēvīcēnī, -ae, -a) | ūndēvīciē(n)s (noviē[n]s deciē[n]s) |
| XX | vīgintī | vīcē(n)simus, -a, -um (vīgēnsimus, -a, -um) | vīcēnī, -ae, -a | vīciē(n)s |
| XXI | vīgintī ūnus, -a, -um (ūnus, -a, -um et vīgintī) | vīcē(n)simus, -a, -um prīmus, -a, -um (ūnus, -a, -um et vīcē[n]simus, -a, -um) | vīcēnī, -ae, -a singulī, -ae, -a | semel et vīciē(n)s (vīciē[n]s semel) |
| XXX | trīgintā | trīcē(n)simus, -a, -um | trīcēnī, -ae, -a | trīciē(n)s |
| XL (XXXX) | quadrāgintā | quadrāgē(n)simus, -a, -um | quadrāgēnī, -ae, -a | quadrāgiē(n)s |
| L | quīnquāgintā | quīnquāgē(n)simus, -a, -um | quīnquāgēnī, -ae, -a | quīnquāgiē(n)s |
| LX | sexāgintā | sexāgē(n)simus, -a, -um | sexāgēnī, -ae, -a | sexāgiē(n)s |
| LXX | septuāgintā | septuāgē(n)simus, -a, -um | septuāgēnī, -ae, -a | septuāgiē(n)s |
| LXXX | octōgintā | octōgē(n)simus, -a, -um | octōgēnī, -ae, -a | octōgiē(n)s |
| XC (LXXXX) | nōnāgintā | nōnāgē(n)simus, -a, -um | nōnāgēnī, -ae, -a | nōnāgiē(n)s |
| C | centum | centē(n)simus, -a, -um | centēnī, -ae, -a | centiē(n)s |

## NUMERALS—*cont.*

| | CARDINALS | ORDINALS | DISTRIBUTIVES | ADVERBS |
|---|---|---|---|---|
| CC | ducentī, -ae, -a | ducentē(n)simus, -a, -um | ducēnī, -ae, -a | ducentiē(n)s |
| CCC | trecentī, -ae, -a | trecentē(n)simus, -a, -um | trecēnī, -ae, -a | trecentiē(n)s |
| CCCC | quadringentī, -ae, -a | quadringentē(n)simus, -a, -um | quadringēnī, -ae, -a | quadringentiē(n)s |
| D | quīngentī, -ae, -a | quīngentē(n)simus, -a, -um | quīngēnī, -ae, -a | quīngentiē(n)s |
| DC | sēscentī, -ae, -a | sēscentē(n)simus, -a, -um | sēscēnī, -ae, -a | sēscentiē(n)s |
| DCC | septingentī, -ae, -a | septingentē(n)simus, -a, -um | septingēnī, -ae, -a | septingentiē(n)s |
| DCCC | octingentī, -ae, -a | octingentē(n)simus, -a, -um | octingēnī, -ae, -a | octingentiē(n)s |
| DCCCC | nōngentī, -ae, -a | nōngentē(n)simus, -a, -um | nōngēnī, -ae, -a | nōningentiē(n)s (nōngentiē[n]s) |
| M | mille[2] | mīllē(n)simus, -a, -um | mīllēnī, -ae, -a (singula mīl[l]ia)[3] | mīliē(n)s (mīlliē[n]s) |

[2] The singular is indeclinable; the plural is **mīlia, -ium** (third declension i-stem).
[3] Both parts decline.

# VOCABULARIES

These lists (Latin-English and English-Latin)
contain all the words necessary to do
the exercises in this book. Words that
are glossed in the main body of the text
and that do not appear in the
formal Unit Vocabularies are not included.

# LATIN–ENGLISH VOCABULARY

The entry (1) after a verb form indicates that the verb belongs to the first conjugation and has the regular principal parts in **-āre, -āvī, -ātus**. The numbers in the left-hand column refer to the Unit in which the word or phrase first appears.

UNIT

## A

| | |
|---|---|
| 2 | **ā, ab** (*prep. + abl.*), (away) from; by (*only with living beings*) |
| 16 | **abeō, abīre, abiī (abīvī), abitus,** go away, depart |
| 15 | **absēns, absentis,** absent |
| 15 | **absum, abesse, āfuī, āfutūrus,** be away, be absent |
| 6 | **ac** *or* **atque** (*conj.*), and |
| 5 | **accēdō, accēdere, accessī, accessus,** go to, approach |
| 14 | **accidō, accidere, accidī, – –,** fall upon; happen, occur |
| 12 | **accipiō, accipere, accēpī, acceptus,** receive, accept; hear |
| 8 | **ācer, ācris, ācre,** sharp, keen, fierce |
| 3 | **acerbus, acerba, acerbum,** bitter, harsh |
| 2 | **ad** (*prep. + acc.*), to, toward |
| 14 | **adeō** (*adv.*), so, so much, so far |
| 13 | **admīrātiō, admīrātiōnis,** *F.*, admiration |
| 15 | **adsum, adesse, adfuī, – –,** be present |
| 13 | **adulēscēns, adulēscentis,** young, youthful |
| 14 | **adveniō, advenīre, advēnī, adventus,** come to, arrive |
| 16 | **adversus, adversa, adversum,** opposite, hostile, adverse |
| 18 | **aestimō** (1), estimate, reckon |
| 17 | **aetās, aetātis,** *F.*, time of life, age, life |
| 4 | **aeternus, aeterna, aeternum,** eternal; **in aeternum,** forever |
| 10 | **afferō, afferre, attulī, allātus,** bring to, present |
| 3 | **ager, agrī,** *M.*, field |
| 11 | **aggredior, aggredī, aggressus sum,** go to, approach |

UNIT

15   **agitō** (1), disturb, stir up

4   **agō, agere, ēgī, āctus,** do, drive, discuss, spend (*time*), conduct

9   **aiō** (*defective verb*), say, affirm (*present* **aiō, ais, ait, – –, – –, aiunt;** *imperfect* **aiēbam,** etc., *complete; present subjunctive* – –, **aiās, aiat,** – –, – –, **aiant**)

16   **aliēnus, aliēna, aliēnum,** belonging to another, strange, out of place

13   **aliquī, aliqua, aliquod** (*adj.*), some, any

13   **aliquis, aliquid** (*pron.*), someone, something; anyone, anything

10   **alius, alia, aliud,** other, another; **alius...alius,** one...another; **aliī... aliī,** some...others

10   **alter, altera, alterum,** the other (*of two*)

4   **altus, alta, altum,** high, tall, deep

1   **ambulō** (1), walk

9   **amīcitia, amīcitiae,** *F.*, friendship

4   **amīcus, amīca, amīcum,** friendly (+ *dat.*)

16   **āmittō, āmittere, āmīsī, āmissus,** let go, lose

7   **amō** (1), love

7   **amor, amōris,** *M.*, love

12   **an** (*conj.*), or (*introducing the second part of a double question*); whether (*introducing a single indirect question*); – –...**an,** whether...or; – –...**an nōn,** whether...or not (*in direct double questions*)

2   **anima, animae,** *F.*, soul, spirit, life force

17   **animadvertō, animadvertere, animadvertī, animadversus,** turn one's attention to, notice

6   **animal, animālis, animālium,** *N.*, animal

14   **animus, animī,** *M.*, mind, rational spirit, soul

7   **annus, annī,** *M.*, year

5   **ante** (*prep.* + *acc.; adv.*), before, in front of; *as adverb* before, previously

15   **antequam** (*conj.*), before

5   **antīquus, antīqua, antīquum,** ancient

16   **aperiō, aperīre, aperuī, apertus,** open

15   **appāreō, appārēre, appāruī, appāritus,** appear, come in sight, be apparent

10   **apud** (*prep.* + *acc.*), at, near, among; at the house of

1   **aqua, aquae,** *F.*, water

2   **āra, ārae,** *F.*, altar

11   **arbitror, arbitrārī, arbitrātus sum,** think, believe, judge

5   **ardeō, ardēre, arsī, arsus,** burn, be on fire; desire

5   **arma, armōrum,** *N. pl.*, arms, weapons

10   **ars, artis, artium,** *F.*, skill, art

UNIT

| | |
|---|---|
| 18 | **as, assis, assium,** *M.*, as (*a small denomination of money*) |
| 7 | **Asia, Asiae,** *F.*, Asia |
| 6 | **Athēnae, Athēnārum,** *F. pl.*, Athens |
| 6 | **atque** *or* **ac** (*conj.*), and |
| 7 | **auctor, auctōris,** *M.*, producer, founder, author |
| 14 | **auctōritās, auctōritātis,** *F.*, authority |
| 10 | **audācia, audāciae,** *F.*, boldness, courage |
| 10 | **audāx, audācis,** bold, courageous |
| 11 | **audeō, audēre, ausus sum,** dare |
| 3 | **audiō, audīre, audīvī, audītus,** hear, listen (to) |
| 10 | **auferō, auferre, abstulī, ablātus,** carry away |
| 12 | **aura, aurae,** *F.*, breeze, wind, air |
| 5 | **aureus, aurea, aureum,** golden, of gold |
| 6 | **aurōra, aurōrae,** *F.*, dawn |
| 5 | **aurum, aurī,** *N.*, gold |
| 14 | **aut** (*conj.*), or; **aut...aut,** either...or |
| 5 | **autem** (*postpositive conj.*), however, moreover |
| 10 | **auxilium, auxiliī,** *N.*, aid |

## B

| | |
|---|---|
| 3 | **bellum, bellī,** *N.*, war |
| 5 | **bene** (*adv.*), well |
| 3 | **bonus, bona, bonum,** good |

## C

| | |
|---|---|
| 9 | **cadō, cadere, cecidī, cāsus,** fall |
| 3 | **caecus, caeca, caecum,** blind, hidden, secret |
| 4 | **caelum, caelī,** *N.*, heaven, sky |
| 15 | **calamitās, calamitātis,** *F.*, disaster, calamity |
| 3 | **campus, campī,** *M.*, plain, level surface |
| 5 | **canō, canere, cecinī, cantus,** sing (of) |
| 2 | **capiō, capere, cēpī, captus,** take, capture |
| 6 | **careō, carēre, caruī, caritus,** lack, be without (+ *abl.*) |
| 8 | **carmen, carminis,** *N.*, song, poem, incantation |
| 14 | **Carthāgō, Carthāginis,** *F.*, Carthage (*a city on the coast of North Africa*) |
| 4 | **cārus, cāra, cārum,** dear (+ *dat.*) |
| 9 | **cāsus, cāsūs,** *M.*, fall, accident, occurrence, chance |
| 16 | **causa, causae,** *F.*, cause, reason; **causā** (*preceded by gen.*), for the sake of |

UNIT

| | |
|---|---|
| 5 | **cēdō, cēdere, cessī, cessus,** go, move, yield |
| 13 | **celer, celeris, celere,** swift |
| 17 | **celeritās, celeritātis,** *F.*, speed, swiftness |
| 2 | **cella, cellae,** *F.*, storeroom, (small) room |
| 2 | **cēlō** (1), hide, conceal |
| 11 | **cēna, cēnae,** *F.*, dinner |
| 10 | **certus, certa, certum,** certain, sure |
| 4 | **cibus, cibī,** *M.*, food |
| 18 | **cingō, cingere, cīnxī, cīnctus,** surround, gird |
| 4 | **circum** (*prep.* + *acc.*), around |
| 7 | **cīvis, cīvis, cīvium,** *M. or F.*, citizen |
| 8 | **cīvitās, cīvitātis,** *F.*, citizenship; state |
| 1 | **clāmō** (1), shout |
| 3 | **clārus, clāra, clārum,** bright, clear, famous |
| 10 | **coepī, coepisse, coeptus,** began (*defective verb*; *it occurs only in the perfect system*) |
| 2 | **cōgitō** (1), think, ponder, consider |
| 5 | **cognōscō, cognōscere, cognōvī, cognitus,** learn; *in perfect* know |
| 14 | **colloquor, colloquī, collocūtus sum,** speak, talk, converse with |
| 12 | **comes, comitis,** *M. or F.*, companion |
| 10 | **cōnferō, cōnferre, contulī, collātus,** bring together, collect; compare; *reflexive* **sē cōnferre,** take oneself (*i.e., to a place*), go |
| 7 | **cōnficiō, cōnficere, cōnfēcī, cōnfectus,** complete |
| 11 | **cōnfiteor, cōnfitērī, cōnfessus sum,** confess |
| 10 | **coniūnx, coniugis,** *M. or F.*, husband, wife, spouse |
| 11 | **cōnor, cōnārī, cōnātus sum,** try, attempt |
| 9 | **cōnsilium, cōnsiliī,** *N.*, counsel, plan, advice |
| 13 | **cōnstituō, cōnstituere, cōnstituī, cōnstitūtus,** set, establish, decide |
| 11 | **cōnsul, cōnsulis,** *M.*, consul |
| 15 | **contrā** (*prep.* + *acc.*; *adv.*), against, facing; opposite, in opposition, in turn |
| 12 | **cōpia, cōpiae,** *F.*, abundance, supply; *pl.* troops |
| 1 | **corōna, corōnae,** *F.*, crown, wreath |
| 1 | **corōnō** (1), crown |
| 6 | **corpus, corporis,** *N.*, body |
| 16 | **cottīdiē** *or* **cotīdiē** (*adv.*), daily |
| 11 | **crēdō, crēdere, crēdidī, crēditus,** be credulous, believe; be trusting, trust (+*dat.*) |
| 9 | **crūdēlis, crūdēle,** cruel |

UNIT

| | |
|---|---|
| 2 | **culpa, culpae,** *F.,* guilt, fault |
| 1 | **cum** (*prep.* + *abl.*), with |
| 15 | **cum** (*conj.*), when, after, since, although |
| 11 | **cupidus, cupida, cupidum,** desirous, eager, fond of (+*gen.*) |
| 12 | **cūr** (*adv.*), why, for what reason |
| 1 | **cūra, cūrae,** *F.,* care, concern, anxiety |
| 13 | **currō, currere, cucurrī, cursus,** run |
| 10 | **custōs, custōdis,** *M.,* guardian |

## D

| | |
|---|---|
| 2 | **dāmnō** (1), condemn, sentence |
| 1 | **dē** (*prep.* + *abl.*), concerning, about; (down) from |
| 4 | **dea, deae,** *F.,* goddess |
| 5 | **dēbeō, dēbēre, dēbuī, dēbitus,** owe, ought |
| 16 | **decōrus, decōra, decōrum,** fitting, suitable; handsome |
| 17 | **dēfendō, dēfendere, dēfendī, dēfēnsus,** defend |
| 10 | **dēferō, dēferre, dētulī, dēlātus,** bring away, bring down, offer; report |
| 4 | **dēleō, dēlēre, dēlēvī, dēlētus,** destroy |
| 12 | **dēligō, dēligere, dēlēgī, dēlēctus,** select, choose, gather |
| 9 | **dēmēns, dēmentis,** mad, raving |
| 17 | **dēnique** (*adv.*), finally, at last |
| 15 | **dēsinō, dēsinere, dēsiī, – –,** stop, cease (*frequently with infinitive or ablative*) |
| 17 | **dēsistō, dēsistere, dēstitī, dēstitus,** stop, desist |
| 16 | **dēsum, dēesse, dēfuī, – –,** be missing, fail (*often* + *dat.*) |
| 17 | **dēterreō, dēterrēre, dēterruī, dēterritus,** deter, prevent, hinder, keep from |
| 4 | **deus, deī,** *M.,* god, deity (*nom. pl.* **dī**; *gen. pl.* **deōrum** *or* **deum**; *dat. & abl. pl.* **dīs**) |
| 3 | **dexter, dextra, dextrum,** right (*as opposed to left*), favorable |
| 3 | **dextra, dextrae,** *F.,* right hand; **ad dextram,** to the right |
| 6 | **dīcō, dīcere, dīxī, dictus,** say, tell, speak |
| 8 | **diēs, diēī,** *M.,* day |
| 10 | **differō, differre, distulī, dīlātus,** differ |
| 9 | **difficilis, difficile,** difficult |
| 14 | **dīgnus, dīgna, dīgnum,** worthy, deserving, suitable (+*abl.*) |
| 3 | **dīligentia, dīligentiae,** *F.,* diligence |
| 5 | **discēdō, discēdere, discessī, discessus,** go from, depart, leave |
| 16 | **discō, discere, didicī, – –,** learn |
| 9 | **dissimilis, dissimile,** dissimilar, unlike (+*gen. or dat.*) |

UNIT

| | |
|---|---|
| 6 | **diū** (*adv.*), for a long time |
| | **diūtius** (*adv.*), *comparative of* **diū** |
| 11 | **dīvitiae, dīvitiārum,** *F. pl.*, riches, wealth |
| 1 | **dō, dare, dedī, datus,** give, grant |
| 10 | **doceō, docēre, docuī, doctus,** teach |
| | **doctus, -a, -um,** learned |
| 14 | **dolor, dolōris,** *M.*, pain, grief, sorrow |
| 5 | **dominus, dominī,** *M.*, master, lord |
| 6; 8 | **domus, domūs/domī,** *F.*, house, home |
| 15 | **dōnec** (*conj.*), while, until, as long as |
| 1 | **dōnō** (1), give, present, reward |
| 3 | **dōnum, dōnī,** *N.*, gift |
| 2; 18 | **dubitō** (1), hesitate (*with infinitive*); doubt (*with indirect question or* **quīn** + *subjunctive*) |
| 17 | **dubium, dubiī,** *N.*, doubt, hesitation |
| 17 | **dubius, dubia, dubium,** doubtful |
| 4 | **dūcō, dūcere, dūxī, ductus,** lead; consider |
| 8 | **dulcis, dulce,** sweet, pleasant |
| 15 | **dum** (*conj.*), while, until, as long as; if only, provided that |
| 15 | **dummodo** (*conj.*), if only, provided that |
| 13 | **duo, duae, duo,** two |
| 5 | **dūrus, dūra, dūrum,** hard, harsh |
| 11 | **dux, ducis,** *M. or F.*, leader, guide |

# E

| | |
|---|---|
| 1 | **ē, ex** (*prep.* + *abl.*), out of, from |
| 10 | **efferō, efferre, extulī, ēlātus,** carry out; bring forth |
| 14 | **efficiō, efficere, effēcī, effectus,** effect, bring about |
| 7 | **ego, meī** (*pron.*), I |
| 11 | **ēgredior, ēgredī, ēgressus sum,** go out, go away |
| 18 | **emō, emere, ēmī, ēmptus,** buy |
| 1 | **enim** (*postpositive conj.*), indeed, of course |
| 8 | **eō, īre, iī (īvī), itus,** go |
| 10 | **errō** (1), wander, err |
| 1 | **et** (*conj.*), and; *adv.* even; **et...et,** both...and |
| 14 | **etiam** (*adv.*), even |
| 15 | **etsī** (*conj.*), although, even if (+ *indicative*) |
| | **ex,** *see* **ē** |
| 6 | **exemplar, exemplāris, exemplārium,** *N.*, copy, model, example |
| 6 | **exemplum, exemplī,** *N.*, example |

UNIT

| | |
|---|---|
| 15 | **exiguus, exigua, exiguum**, small |
| 12 | **exorior, exorīrī, exortus sum**, rise, arise, appear, start |
| 2 | **expellō, expellere, expulī, expulsus**, push out, drive out |
| 11 | **experior, experīrī, expertus sum**, try, put to the test, experience |
| 12 | **expōnō, expōnere, exposuī, expositus**, set forth, expose, explain |
| 15 | **exspectō** (1), wait (for), expect |

# F

| | |
|---|---|
| 9 | **facilis, facile** (*adj.*), easy; **facile** (*adv.*), easily |
| 4; 18; 14 | **faciō, facere, fēcī, factus**, make, do; *with gen. of indefinite value* reckon, consider; **facere ut**, to see to it that (+ *subjunctive*) |
| 4 | **factum, factī**, *N.*, deed |
| 1 | **fāma, fāmae**, *F.*, talk, report, rumor, fame, reputation |
| 11 | **familia, familiae**, *F.*, household, family |
| 11 | **fateor, fatērī, fassus sum**, confess |
| 13 | **faveō, favēre, fāvī, fautus**, be favorable, favor (+ *dat.*) |
| 8 | **fēlīx, fēlīcis**, happy, fortunate |
| 1 | **fēmina, fēminae**, *F.*, woman |
| 10 | **ferō, ferre, tulī, lātus**, bring, carry, bear, endure |
| 5 | **ferrum, ferrī**, *N.*, iron, sword |
| 8 | **fidēs, fideī**, *F.*, faith, trust, trustworthiness |
| 10 | **figūra, figūrae**, *F.*, figure, form, shape |
| 4 | **fīlia, fīliae**, *F.*, daughter |
| 4 | **fīlius, fīliī**, *M.*, son |
| 7 | **fīnis, fīnis, fīnium**, *M.*, end, boundary, limit |
| 13 | **fīō, fierī, factus sum**, be made, be done, happen, become (*passive for* **faciō, -ere**) |
| 5 | **flamma, flammae**, *F.*, flame, fire |
| 11 | **flūmen, flūminis**, *N.*, river, running water |
| 10 | **foedus, foederis**, *N.*, pact, treaty, agreement |
| 15 | **fore** = **futūrus (-a, -um) esse** (*future infinitive of* **sum**) |
| 1 | **fōrma, fōrmae**, *F.*, form, shape, figure, beauty |
| 15 | **fors, fortis, fortium**, *F.*, chance |
| 8 | **fortis, forte**, strong, brave |
| 11 | **forum, forī**, *N.*, open space, market place, public square |
| 6 | **frāter, frātris**, *M.*, brother |
| 8 | **frīgidus, frīgida, frīgidum**, cold |
| 8 | **frūctus, frūctūs**, *M.*, enjoyment; fruit; profit; **frūctuī esse** to be (for [the purpose of]) a profit, be an asset to (+ *dat.*) |
| 16 | **frūstrā** (*adv.*), in vain |

UNIT

10    **fuga, fugae,** *F.,* flight
10    **fugiō, fugere, fūgī, fugitus,** flee
8    **fulgeō, fulgēre, fulsī, – –,** flash, shine
15    **fulgor, fulgōris,** *M.,* lightning, flash, brightness

## G

**Gallus, Gallī,** *M.,* a Gaul
10    **gaudium, gaudiī,** *N.,* joy
10    **gēns, gentis, gentium,** *F.,* race, people
7    **genus, generis,** *N.,* descent, origin, race, sort
3    **gerō, gerere, gessī, gestus,** conduct, manage, wage
3    **gladius, gladiī,** *M.,* sword
2    **glōria, glōriae,** *F.,* glory, renown
9    **gracilis, gracile,** slender, unadorned, simple
11    **gradior, gradī, gressus sum,** step, walk
**Graecus, -a, -um,** Greek
15    **grātus, grāta, grātum,** pleasing (*+dat.*)
8    **gravis, grave,** heavy, severe, important

## H

1    **habeō, habēre, habuī, habitus,** have, hold, possess, consider
13    **herī** (*adv.*), yesterday
13    **hīc** (*adv.*), here
7    **hic, haec, hoc,** this, the latter
6    **homō, hominis,** *M.,* human being, man
4    **honestus, honesta, honestum,** respected, honorable, distinguished
18    **honor, honōris,** *M.,* honor, distinction, office
7    **hōra, hōrae,** *F.,* hour, season
12    **horridus, horrida, horridum,** horrible, rough
11    **hortor, hortārī, hortātus sum,** urge, encourage (*+ut or nē and subjunctive*)
9    **hospes, hospitis,** *M.,* guest, host
12    **hostīlis, hostīle,** of an enemy, hostile
7    **hostis, hostis, hostium,** *M.,* enemy, public enemy (the plural is frequently translated collectively as 'enemy')
14    **hūc** (*adv.*), to this place
9    **humilis, humile,** humble, lowly

UNIT

# I

| | |
|---|---|
| 8 | **iaciō, iacere, iēcī, iactus,** throw |
| 8 | **iactō** (1), throw, scatter, shake; boast |
| 10 | **iam** (*adv.*), now, by this time, already |
| 12 | **ibi** (*adv.*), there; then |
| 12 | **īdem, eadem, idem,** same |
| 15 | **igitur** (*postpositive conj.*), therefore |
| 6 | **ignis, ignis, ignium,** *M.,* fire (*abl. sing.* **igne** *or* **ignī**) |
| 13 | **īgnōscō, īgnōscere, īgnōvī, īgnōtus,** be forgiving, forgive, pardon (+ *dat.*) |
| 7 | **ille, illa, illud,** that, the former |
| 13 | **illīc** (*adv.*), there |
| 14 | **illūc** (*adv.*), to that place, up to that time |
| 12 | **immortālis, immortāle,** immortal, everlasting |
| 17 | **impediō, impedīre, impedīvī (impediī), impedītus,** deter, impede, prevent |
| 11 | **imperātor, imperātōris,** *M.,* commander, general |
| 5 | **imperium, imperiī,** *N.,* authority, power, empire |
| 5 | **imperō** (1), give (an) order(s), give (a) command(s). (*The person ordered is in the dative case; the thing ordered is expressed by* **ut** *or* **nē** *with the subjunctive.*) |
| 5 | **impius, impia, impium,** irreverent, wicked, impious |
| 1 | **impleō, implēre, implēvī, implētus,** fill, fill up |
| 1 | **in** (*prep.* + *acc. or abl.*), into, onto (*motion toward—requires accusative*); in, on (*place where—requires ablative*) |
| 10 | **incertus, incerta, incertum,** uncertain, unsure |
| 2 | **incipiō, incipere, incēpī, inceptus,** begin |
| 2 | **incola, incolae,** *M.* (*occasionally F.*), inhabitant |
| 2 | **incolō, incolere, incoluī, – –,** inhabit |
| 14 | **indīgnus, indīgna, indīgnum,** unworthy, unsuitable (+ *abl.*) |
| 8 | **īnfēlīx, īnfēlīcis,** unhappy, unfortunate |
| 10 | **īnferō, īnferre, intulī, illātus,** carry into; inflict |
| 16 | **īnfirmus, īnfirma, īnfirmum,** weak, unhealthy |
| 15 | **ingenium, ingeniī,** *N.,* nature, talent, disposition, natural quality |
| 8 | **ingēns, ingentis,** huge |
| 11 | **ingredior, ingredī, ingressus sum,** go into, enter, advance, begin |
| 15 | **inimīcitia, inimīcitiae,** *F.,* hostility |
| 4 | **inimīcus, inimīca, inimīcum,** unfriendly, hostile (+ *dat.*) |
| 2 | **īnsidiae, īnsidiārum,** *F.* (*used only in pl.*), ambush, plot, treachery |
| 16 | **īnstituō, īnstituere, īnstituī, īnstitūtus,** set (up), establish, arrange |
| 1 | **īnsula, īnsulae,** *F.,* island |

UNIT

| | |
|---|---|
| 4 | **intellegō, intellegere, intellēxī, intellēctus**, understand |
| 14 | **intendō, intendere, intendī, intentus**, stretch out, extend, aim, exert |
| 14 | **inter** (*prep.* + *acc.*), between, among |
| 15 | **interdum** (*adv.*), sometimes |
| 16 | **interest, interesse, interfuit, – –**, it is of importance, it concerns, it is of interest |
| 5 | **interficiō, interficere, interfēcī, interfectus**, kill |
| 5 | **invādō, invādere, invāsī, invāsus**, go into, invade, attack |
| 7 | **inveniō, invenīre, invēnī, inventus**, come upon, discover, find |
| 2 | **invidia, invidiae**, *F.*, envy, jealousy |
| 12 | **ipse, ipsa, ipsum**, self, very |
| 8 | **īra, īrae**, *F.*, wrath, anger |
| 13 | **īrātus, īrāta, īrātum**, angry |
| 7 | **is, ea, id**, this, that; he, she, it |
| 12 | **iste, ista, istud**, that (of yours), that (*with pejorative sense*) |
| 14 | **ita** (*adv.*), so, in this way |
| 6 | **Italia, Italiae**, *F.*, Italy |
| 10 | **iter, itineris**, *N.*, journey, route |
| 8 | **iubeō, iubēre, iussī, iussus**, order, command (+*infinitive, not with an* **ut** |
| • | *clause of indirect command*) |
| 15 | **iūdex, iūdicis**, *M.*, judge, jury |
| 15 | **iūdicium, iūdiciī**, *N.*, trial, judgment, decision |
| 10 | **iungō, iungere, iūnxī, iūnctus**, join |
| 6 | **Iūnō, Iūnōnis**, *F.*, Juno (*sister and wife of Jupiter*) |
| 6 | **Iuppiter, Iovis**, *M.*, Jupiter (*god of the sky*) |
| 13 | **iūs, iūris**, *N.*, right, law |
| 12 | **iussum, iussī**, *N.*, command, order (*the abl. sing. is* **iussū**, by order) |
| 11 | **iuvenis, iuvenis**, *M. or F.* (*not i-stem*), youth, young person |

# L

| | |
|---|---|
| 16 | **lābor, lābī, lāpsus sum**, slip, glide, fall |
| 2 | **labōrō** (1), work |
| 2 | **lacrima, lacrimae**, *F.*, tear |
| 3 | **laetus, laeta, laetum**, happy |
| 9 | **laudō** (1), praise |
| 9 | **laus, laudis**, *F.*, praise |
| 13 | **lēgātus, lēgātī**, *M.*, legate, envoy |
| 4 | **legō, legere, lēgī, lēctus**, choose, select; read |
| 16 | **lēx, lēgis**, *F.*, law |

UNIT

| | |
|---|---|
| 16 | **libenter** (*adv.*), freely, willingly, gladly |
| 3 | **līber, lībera, līberum**, free |
| 4 | **liber, librī**, *M.*, book |
| 6 | **līberō** (1), free |
| 8 | **lībertās, lībertātis**, *F.*, freedom |
| 16 | **licet, licēre, licuit (licitum est)**, it is permitted |
| 4 | **littera, litterae**, *F.*, letter (*of the alphabet*); *pl.* letter (*epistle*) |
| 8 | **lītus, lītoris**, *N.*, shore, beach |
| 7 | **locus, locī**, *M.*, place, spot |
| 8 | **longus, longa, longum**, long; **longē** (*adv.*), far off, at a distance, far and wide |
| 11 | **loquor, loquī, locūtus sum**, speak, talk |
| 6 | **lūmen, lūminis**, *N.*, light |
| 2 | **lūna, lūnae**, *F.*, moon, moonlight |
| 8 | **lūx, lūcis**, *F.*, light; **prīmā lūce**, at the first light, at daybreak |

# M

| | |
|---|---|
| | **magis**, *comparative of* **magnopere** |
| 5 | **magister, magistrī**, *M.*, superior, director, master, teacher |
| 9 | **magnopere** (*adv.*), greatly |
| 3 | **magnus, magna, magnum**, large, big, great |
| 9 | **maior, maius**, *comparative of* **magnus, magna, magnum**; **maiōrēs, maiōrum**, *M. pl.*, ancestors |
| 9 | **male** (*adv.*), badly |
| 11 | **mālō, mālle, māluī, – –**, prefer, choose rather |
| 3 | **malus, mala, malum**, evil, bad, wicked |
| 12 | **maneō, manēre, mānsī, mānsus**, remain |
| 8 | **manus, manūs**, *F.*, hand; band, troop |
| 3 | **Marcus, Marcī**, *M.*, Marcus (*proper name*) |
| 6 | **mare, maris, marium**, *N.*, sea |
| 9 | **Mārs, Mārtis**, *M.*, Mars (*god of war*) |
| 6 | **māter, mātris**, *F.*, mother |
| | **maximus, maxima, maximum**, *superlative of* **magnus, magna, magnum** |
| 5 | **medius, media, medium**, middle of, middle |
| | **melior, melius**, *comparative of* **bonus, bona, bonum** |
| 18 | **meminī, meminisse** (*defective verb*), remember |
| 8 | **memor, memoris**, mindful, remembering (+*gen.*) |
| 15 | **memoria, memoriae**, *F.*, memory |
| 6 | **mēns, mentis, mentium**, *F.*, mind, disposition, intellect |

## UNIT

| | |
|---|---|
| 4 | **mēnsa, mēnsae,** *F.*, table |
| 17 | **metuō, metuere, metuī, – –,** fear |
| 8 | **metus, metūs,** *M.*, fear, dread |
| 7 | **meus, mea, meum,** my, mine, my own |
| 6 | **mīles, mīlitis,** *M.*, soldier |
| | **minimus, minima, minimum,** *superlative of* **parvus, parva, parvum** |
| 11 | **minor, minārī, minātus sum,** jut forth, threaten |
| | **minor, minus,** *comparative of* **parvus, parva, parvum** |
| 13 | **mīror, mīrārī, mīrātus sum,** wonder (at), be amazed (at), admire |
| 15 | **misceō, miscēre, miscuī, mixtus,** mix, intermingle, blend |
| 3 | **miser, misera, miserum,** miserable, unhappy, wretched |
| 12 | **misereor, miserērī, miseritus sum,** pity (+*gen.*) |
| 16 | **miseret, miserēre, miseruit (miseritum est),** it pities, it moves to pity |
| 4 | **mittō, mittere, mīsī, missus,** send |
| 12 | **modus, modī,** *M.*, way, manner, limit; kind; **quō modō,** in what way, how |
| 14; 15 | **modo** (*adv.*; *conj.*), only; if only, provided that |
| 6 | **moenia, moenium,** *N. pl.*, (city) walls |
| 2 | **moneō, monēre, monuī, monitus,** warn, remind |
| 6 | **mōns, montis, montium,** *M.*, mountain |
| 4 | **mōnstrō** (1), show, point out, demonstrate |
| 2 | **mora, morae,** *F.*, delay |
| 11 | **morior, morī, mortuus sum,** die |
| 13 | **moror, morārī, morātus sum,** delay, stay, hinder |
| 7 | **mors, mortis, mortium,** *F.*, death |
| 10 | **mōs, mōris,** *M.*, custom; *pl.* character |
| 8 | **mōtus, mōtūs,** *M.*, motion, movement |
| 5 | **moveō, movēre, mōvī, mōtus,** move |
| 5 | **mox** (*adv.*), soon |
| 9 | **multum** (*adv.*), much, very |
| 3 | **multus, multa, multum,** much, many |
| 9 | **mūniō, mūnīre, mūnīvī, mūnītus,** fortify |
| 2 | **mūtō** (1), change, exchange |

## N

| | |
|---|---|
| 9 | **nam** (*conj.*), for |
| 11 | **nāscor, nāscī, nātus sum,** be born, descend from |
| 2 | **nātūra, nātūrae,** *F.*, nature |

UNIT

3    **nātus, nātī,** *M.,* son, child

1    **nauta, nautae,** *M.,* sailor

11    **nāvis, nāvis, nāvium,** *F.,* ship

3; 18    **nē** (*conj.*), in order that…not; that (*after expressions of fearing*)

12; 15    **nē** (*adv.*), not; **nē…quidem,** not even (*enclosing the word or words they emphasize*)

1    **-ne** (*enclitic*), *added to the first word of an interrogative sentence or clause*; *it indicates a question*

12    **-ne…an,** whether…or

12    **-ne…an nōn,** whether…or not (*in direct double questions*)

12    **-ne…necne,** whether…or not (*in indirect double questions*)

16    **necesse** (*indeclinable adj.*), necessary

12    **necne** (*conj.*), or not (*generally used as the second part of a double indirect question, representing* **an nōn** *in the direct question*); --…**necne,** whether…or not (*in indirect double questions*)

11    **neglegō, neglegere, neglēxī, neglēctus,** disregard, neglect

10    **negō** (1), deny, say no

13    **nēmō, nēminis,** *M. or F.,* no one

17    **nemus, nemoris,** *N.,* grove, wood

2    **neque** *or* **nec** (*conj.*), and not, nor; **neque (nec)…neque (nec),** neither… nor

12    **nesciō, nescīre, nescīvī (nesciī), nescītus,** not know, be ignorant

10    **neuter, neutra, neutrum,** neither

2    **nihil** *or* **nīl** (*indeclinable noun*), nothing

18    **nihilum, nihilī,** *N.,* nothing

2    **nisī** (*conj.*), unless, if…not; except

13    **noceō, nocēre, nocuī, nocitus,** be harmful, harm (+*dat.*)

11    **nōlō, nōlle, nōluī,** --, be unwilling, wish…not

8    **nōmen, nōminis,** *N.,* name

1; 6    **nōn** (*adv.*), not; **nōn sōlum…sed etiam,** not only…but also

12    **nōnne** (*adv.*), *in a direct question, anticipates the answer* "*yes*"; *if not, whether not* (*in an indirect question*)

5    **nōscō, nōscere, nōvī, nōtus,** learn; *in perfect* know

7    **noster, nostra, nostrum,** our, ours, our own

14    **nōtus, nōta, nōtum,** known, well-known, customary

5    **novus, nova, novum,** new, strange

6    **nox, noctis, noctium,** *F.,* night

2    **noxa, noxae,** *F.,* harm, injury

10    **nūllus, nūlla, nūllum,** no, none

UNIT

| | |
|---|---|
| 12 | **num** (*adv.*), *in a direct question, anticipates the answer "no"*; whether (*in an indirect question*) |
| 8 | **nūmen, nūminis**, *N.*, divinity, divine spirit |
| 18 | **numerus, numerī**, *M.*, number |
| 5 | **numquam** *or* **nunquam** (*adv.*), never |
| 2 | **nunc** (*adv.*), now |
| 14 | **nūntiō** (1), report, announce |
| 14 | **nūntius, nūntiī**, *M.*, messenger, message |
| 14 | **nūper** (*adv.*), recently |
| 15 | **nusquam** (*adv.*), nowhere |
| 15 | **nūtrīx, nūtrīcis**, *F.*, nurse |

# O

| | |
|---|---|
| 8 | **ob** (*prep.* + *acc.*), on account of |
| 17 | **obitus, obitūs**, *M.*, a going down, setting; downfall, ruin |
| 18 | **oblīvīscor, oblīvīscī, oblītus sum**, forget |
| 17 | **obstō, obstāre, obstitī, obstātus**, stand in the way of, hinder (+*dat.*) |
| 15 | **occidō, occidere, occidī, occāsus**, fall, set, die |
| 12 | **occultē** (*adv.*), secretly |
| 3 | **oculus, oculī**, *M.*, eye |
| 7 | **ōdī, ōdisse** (*defective verb lacking in the present system; perfect forms have present meanings*), hate |
| 9 | **odium, odiī**, *N.*, hatred |
| 10 | **offerō, offerre, obtulī, oblātus**, bring before; offer; expose |
| 15 | **omnīnō** (*adv.*), all in all, as a whole, entirely |
| 8 | **omnis, omne**, every, all |
| 8 | **opīniō, opīniōnis**, *F.*, opinion |
| 16 | **oportet, oportēre, oportuit, – –**, it is necessary, it is proper |
| 4 | **oppidum, oppidī**, *N.*, town |
| 7 | **opprimō, opprimere, oppressī, oppressus**, press upon, overwhelm, suppress, oppress |
| 6 | **oppūgnō** (1), attack, fight against |
| 12 | **ops, opis**, *F.*, power, strength; *pl.* resources, wealth |
| | **optimus, optima, optimum**, *superlative of* **bonus, bona, bonum** |
| 1 | **optō** (1), desire, wish (for), choose |
| 7 | **opus, operis**, *N.*, work; **opus est**, there is need of (+*nom. or abl.* [*instrumental*] *of thing needed; less frequently gen.*) |
| 13 | **ōrātiō, ōrātiōnis**, *F.*, oration, speech |
| 11 | **ōrātor, ōrātōris**, *M.*, speaker |

UNIT

10 **orbis, orbis, orbium,** *M.*, ring, orb, circle; **orbis terrārum**, circle of lands; the world
17 **orior, orīrī, ortus sum**, rise, arise, begin
3 **ōrō** (1), beg (for)
17 **ortus, ortūs,** *M.*, rising, source
14 **ōs, ōris,** *N.*, mouth, expression
14 **ostendō, ostendere, ostendī, ostentus**, show, expose, make plain

# P

13 **paene** (*adv.*), almost
16 **paenitet, paenitēre, paenituit, – –**, it repents
13 **parcō, parcere, pepercī, parsus**, be sparing, spare (+*dat.*)
11 **parēns, parentis,** *M. or F.*, parent
13 **pāreō, pārēre, pāruī, pāritus**, be obedient, obey (+*dat.*)
14 **parō** (1), prepare, make ready, provide, get
10 **pars, partis, partium,** *F.*, part
9 **parum** (*adv. and indeclinable adj.*) too little, not enough
9 **parvus, parva, parvum**, little, small
6 **pater, patris,** *M.*, father
11 **patior, patī, passus sum**, suffer, endure, allow
1 **patria, patriae,** *F.*, native land, country
12 **paucī, paucae, pauca**, few
14 **paulus, paula, paulum**, little, small (compares irregularly: **minor, minus; minimus, -a, -um**)
11 **pauper, pauperis**, poor
14 **pāx, pācis,** *F.*, peace
8 **pectus, pectoris,** *N.*, heart, breast
1 **pecūnia, pecūniae,** *F.*, money
   **peior, peius,** *comparative of* **malus, mala, malum**
2 **pellō, pellere, pepulī, pulsus**, push, drive (off)
2 **per** (*prep. + acc.*), through
4 **perdō, perdere, perdidī, perditus**, destroy, lose, waste
15 **pereō, perīre, periī (perīvī), peritus**, die, perish
7 **perficiō, perficere, perfēcī, perfectus**, accomplish, complete, finish
4 **perīculum, perīculī,** *N.*, danger
13 **persuādeō, persuādēre, persuāsī, persuāsus**, be persuasive, persuade (+*dat.*)
17 **perveniō, pervenīre, pervēnī, perventus**, arrive (at) (+**ad**)

UNIT

| | |
|---|---|
| 7 | **pēs, pedis,** *M.*, foot |
| | **pessimus, pessima, pessimum,** *superlative of* **malus, mala, malum,** worst |
| 3 | **petō, petere, petīvī, petītus,** seek (*with* ā + *abl.*), ask (for) |
| 15 | **piger, pigra, pigrum,** lazy, slow |
| 16 | **piget, pigēre, piguit (pigitum est),** it disgusts |
| 5 | **pius, pia, pium,** loyal, dutiful, pious |
| 7 | **placeō, placēre, placuī, placitus,** be pleasing to, please (+*dat.*) |
| 13 | **plēbs, plēbis,** *F.*, common people |
| | **plūrimus, plūrima, plūrimum,** *superlative of* **multus, multa, multum** |
| | **plūs,** *neuter comparative of* **multum;** *pl.* **plūres, plūra** |
| 1 | **poena, poenae,** *F.*, penalty, punishment; **poenās dare,** to pay a penalty |
| 1 | **poēta, poētae,** *M.*, poet |
| 14 | **polliceor, pollicērī, pollicitus sum,** promise |
| 4 | **pōnō, pōnere, posuī, positus,** put, place, set aside |
| 5 | **populus, populī,** *M.*, people (*use only in singular*) |
| 1 | **porta, portae,** *F.*, gate |
| 3 | **portō (1),** carry |
| 12 | **poscō, poscere, poposcī, – –,** beg, demand |
| 5 | **possum, posse, potuī, – –,** be able, can |
| 5 | **post** (*prep.* + *acc.*; *adv.*), after, behind (*prep.*); afterwards, after, behind (*adv.*) |
| 5 | **postquam** (*conj.*), after (+*indicative*) |
| 13 | **praeferō, praeferre, praetulī, praelātus,** bring (place) before, prefer |
| 13 | **praeficiō, praeficere, praefēcī, praefectus,** make before (at the head of), put in command of |
| 11 | **praemium, praemiī,** *N.*, reward |
| 13 | **praesum, praeesse, praefuī, – –,** be before (at the head of), be in command of |
| 11 | **precor, precārī, precātus sum,** beg, request |
| 7 | **premō, premere, pressī, pressus,** press, press upon, press hard |
| 18 | **pretium, pretiī,** *N.*, price; value |
| 9 | **prīmus, prīma, prīmum,** first; **quam prīmum,** as soon as possible |
| 9 | **prius** (*adv.*), before, previously |
| 15 | **priusquam** (*conj.*), before |
| 8 | **prō** (*prep.* + *abl.*), in front of, for, on behalf of, instead of, in return for |
| 11 | **proficīscor, proficīscī, profectus sum,** set forth, set out, start |
| 8 | **profugus, profuga, profugum,** fugitive, banished, exiled |
| 11 | **prōgredior, prōgredī, prōgressus sum,** go forth, advance, proceed |
| 17 | **prohibeō, prohibēre, prohibuī, prohibitus,** keep from, prohibit, prevent |

UNIT

| | |
|---|---|
| 9 | **prope** (*adv.*), near |
| 14 | **properō** (1), hasten |
| | **propius** (*adv.*), *comparative of* **prope** |
| 10 | **propter** (*prep.* + *acc.*), on account of, because of |
| 15 | **prōsum, prōdesse, prōfuī, – –,** be useful, do good, benefit, profit (+*dat.*) |
| 2 | **prōvincia, prōvinciae,** *F.*, province |
| 9 | **proximus, proxima, proximum,** nearest, next |
| 8 | **pūblicus, pūblica, pūblicum,** public |
| 16 | **pudet, pudēre, puduit (puditum est),** it shames |
| 2 | **puella, puellae,** *F.*, girl |
| 3 | **puer, puerī,** *M.*, boy; child |
| 18 | **pūgna, pūgnae,** *F.*, battle, fight |
| 3 | **pūgnō** (1), fight; (*with* **cum** + *abl.*), fight with (*i.e., against*) |
| 3 | **pulcher, pulchra, pulchrum,** beautiful |
| 15 | **putō** (1), think |

## Q

| | |
|---|---|
| 8 | **quaerō, quaerere, quaesīvī, quaesītus,** look for, search for, seek, ask |
| 14 | **quālis, quāle,** (of) what kind (of) |
| 9 | **quam** (*conj.*), than (*used in comparisons*) |
| 8 | **quam ob rem,** on account of which thing, for what reason, why |
| 9 | **quam prīmum,** as soon as possible |
| 12 | **quamdiū** (*adv.*), how long |
| 5 | **quamquam** (*conj.*), although (+*indicative*) |
| 15 | **quamvīs** (*conj.*), although (+*subjunctive*) |
| 12 | **quandō** (*adv.*), when; since |
| 10 | **quantus, quanta, quantum,** how much, how great |
| 12 | **quārē** (*adv.*), by what means, why; and therefore |
| 15 | **quasi** (*adv.*), as if, as it were |
| 1 | **-que** (*enclitic*), and |
| 13 | **quī, qua, quod** (*adj.*), some, any |
| 7 | **quī, quae, quod** (*relative pron. and interrogative adj.*) who, which, that (*relative*); which, what (*interrogative*) |
| 12 | **quia** (*conj.*), because |
| 12 | **quīdam, quaedam, quiddam** (*pron.*), a certain one *or* thing |
| 12 | **quīdam, quaedam, quoddam** (*adj.*), certain |
| 15 | **quidem** (*adv.*), indeed; **nē...quidem,** not even (*enclosing the word or words they emphasize*) |

UNIT

17     **quīn** (*conj.*), but that, that not (*used after expressions of prevention, negative doubting, etc.*)

7     **quīnque** (*indeclinable adj.*), five

13     **quīque, quaeque, quodque** (*adj.*), each, every

7; 13     **quis, quid** (*interrogative and indefinite pron.*), who, what; someone, something; anyone, anything

13     **quisquam, quidquam** *or* **quicquam** (*pron.*), someone, anyone, something, anything (*used with a negative or a virtual negative*)

13     **quisque, quidque** *or* **quicque** (*pron.*), each one, everyone, each thing, everything

13     **quō** (*adv.*), (to) where

15     **quōad** (*conj.*), as long as, as far as, until (*takes same construction as* **dum** *and* **dōnec**)

4; 18     **quod** (*conj.*), because; the fact that; **quod sī**, but if

17     **quōminus** (*conj.*), by which the less, that not, from (*used in positive or negative clauses of prevention*)

15     **quoniam** (*conj.*), since (*+ indicative*)

10     **quot** (*indeclinable adj.*), how many

# R

17     **radius, radiī,** *M.*, rod, ray

12     **recipiō, recipere, recēpī, receptus,** take back, regain, recover; **sē recipere,** withdraw, take oneself

15     **redeō, redīre, rediī, reditus,** return, go back

10     **referō, referre, rettulī, relātus,** bring back, report

16     **rēfert, rēferre, rētulit, – –,** it is of importance

1     **rēgīna, rēgīnae,** *F.*, queen

4     **rēgnum, rēgnī,** *N.*, realm, kingdom

6     **regō, regere, rēxī, rēctus,** rule

17     **religiō, religiōnis,** *F.*, religious awe, reverence, integrity, sanctity

17     **relinquō, relinquere, relīquī, relictus,** leave behind, abandon

17     **reliquus, reliqua, reliquum,** remaining, rest of

12     **remaneō, remanēre, remānsī, remānsus,** remain

5     **removeō, removēre, remōvī, remōtus,** remove, take away, set aside

8     **rēs, reī,** *F.*, thing, matter, affair, situation; **rēs pūblica,** state, republic

4     **respondeō, respondēre, respondī, respōnsus,** answer

17     **retegō, retegere, retēxī, retēctus,** uncover, reveal

6     **rēx, rēgis,** *M.*, king

14     **rīdeō, rīdēre, rīsī, rīsus,** laugh (at)

UNIT

| | |
|---|---|
| 12 | **rogō** (1), ask (for) |
| 6 | **Rōma, Rōmae,** *F.,* Rome |
| 3 | **Rōmānus, Rōmāna, Rōmānum,** Roman |
| 5 | **ruīna, ruīnae,** *F.,* fall, downfall, ruin, destruction |
| 6 | **rūmor, rūmōris,** *M.,* rumor, gossip |
| 5 | **ruō, ruere, ruī, rutus,** fall, go to ruin, rush |
| 6 | **rūs, rūris,** *N.,* country (*as opposed to city*) |

## S

| | |
|---|---|
| 9 | **saepe** (*adv.*), often |
| 8 | **saevus, saeva, saevum,** cruel |
| 7 | **salūs, salūtis,** *F.,* health, safety; **salūtem dīcere,** say hello, greet |
| 6 | **sānus, sāna, sānum,** sound, healthy, sane |
| 9 | **sapiēns, sapientis,** wise |
| 9 | **sapientia, sapientiae,** *F.,* wisdom |
| 9 | **satis** (*adv. and indeclinable adj.*), enough |
| 3 | **saxum, saxī,** *N.,* rock, stone |
| 11 | **scelus, sceleris,** *N.,* wicked deed, crime |
| 6 | **sciō, scīre, scīvī, scītus,** know |
| 3 | **scrībō, scrībere, scrīpsī, scrīptus,** write |
| 16 | **scrīptor, scrīptōris,** *M.,* writer |
| 1 | **sed** (*conj.*), but |
| 2 | **semper** (*adv.*), always |
| 14 | **senex, senis,** old |
| 8 | **sēnsus, sēnsūs,** *M.,* sensation, feeling |
| 2 | **sententia, sententiae,** *F.,* feeling, thought, opinion |
| 2 | **sentiō, sentīre, sēnsī, sēnsus,** feel, perceive |
| 11 | **sequor, sequī, secūtus sum,** follow |
| 9 | **serēnus, serēna, serēnum,** serene, calm |
| 6 | **servitūs, servitūtis,** *F.,* slavery |
| 11 | **servō** (1), save, preserve, rescue, keep |
| 3 | **servus, servī,** *M.,* slave |
| 2 | **sī** (*conj.*), if |
| 14 | **sīc** (*adv.*), so, in this way |
| 6 | **sīdus, sīderis,** *N.,* constellation, star; heaven |
| 10 | **signum, signī,** *N.,* signal, sign |
| 9 | **similis, simile,** like, similar (to) (+*gen. or dat.*) |
| 15 | **simul ac** (*or* **atque**) (*conj.*), as soon as (+*indicative*) |
| 5 | **sine** (*prep.* + *abl.*), without |

## UNIT

| | |
|---|---|
| 5 | **socius, socia, socium,** allied; **socius, sociī,** *M.,* ally |
| 10 | **sōl, sōlis,** *M.,* sun |
| 11 | **soleō, solēre, solitus sum,** be accustomed; be customary |
| 13 | **sollers, sollertis,** skilled, expert |
| 10 | **sōlus, sōla, sōlum,** alone, only |
| 9 | **solvō, solvere, solvī, solūtus,** loosen, free, untie |
| 15 | **somnus, somnī,** *M.,* sleep, dream |
| 6 | **soror, sorōris,** *F.,* sister |
| 12 | **sors, sortis, sortium,** *F.,* lot, destiny |
| 6 | **spargō, spargere, sparsī, sparsus,** scatter, sprinkle, distribute |
| 8 | **speciēs, speciēī,** *F.,* appearance |
| 3 | **spectō** (1), look at |
| 7 | **spērō** (1), hope (for) |
| 8 | **spēs, speī,** *F.,* hope |
| 11 | **statua, statuae,** *F.,* statue |
| 16 | **stō, stāre, stetī, stātus,** stand |
| 13 | **studeō, studēre, studuī, – –,** be zealous, study, pay attention to (+*dat.*) |
| 16 | **studiōsus, studiōsa, studiōsum,** fond of, partial to, studious (+*gen.*) |
| 4 | **studium, studiī,** *N.,* enthusiasm, zeal |
| 2 | **sub** (*prep.* + *acc.*), under (i.e., going to a place under); (*prep.* + *abl.*), under (i.e., at *or* in a place under) |
| 10 | **sufferō, sufferre, sustulī, sublātus,** undergo, endure |
| 7 | **– –, suī** (*reflexive pron.*), himself, herself, itself, themselves |
| 1 | **sum, esse, fuī, futūrus,** be, exist |
| 9 | **summus, summa, summum,** highest, top (of) |
| 2 | **superō** (1), overcome, conquer |
| 15 | **supersum, superesse, superfuī, – –,** be left over, survive |
| 8 | **superus, supera, superum,** above, upper; **superī, superōrum,** *M. pl.,* the gods above |
| 9 | **supplex, supplicis,** suppliant, humble |
| 16 | **sustineō, sustinēre, sustinuī, sustentus,** support, maintain |
| 7 | **suus, sua, suum,** his own, her own, its own, their own |

## T

| | |
|---|---|
| 2 | **taceō, tacēre, tacuī, tacitus,** be (*or* keep) silent |
| 1 | **taeda, taedae,** *F.,* torch |
| 16 | **taedet, taedēre, taeduit (taesum est),** it bores; it disgusts |
| 14 | **tālis, tāle,** such, of such a sort; **tālis...quālis,** such...as |
| 9 | **tam** (*adv.*), so; **tam ... quam,** so ... as, as ... as |

UNIT

5  **tamen** (*adv.*), nevertheless

12  **tamquam** (*adv.*), as if, as, as it were

12  **tandem** (*adv.*), at last, at length

10  **tantus, tanta, tantum,** so much, so great; **tantus...quantus** *or* **quantus...
tantus,** as (so) much...as; as (so) great...as

4  **tēctum, tēctī,** *N.*, roof, house

4  **tegō, tegere, tēxī, tēctus,** cover, conceal

14  **tempestās, tempestātis,** *F.*, weather, storm, season

9  **templum, templī,** *N.*, temple

10  **temptō** (1), try, attempt

7  **tempus, temporis,** *N.*, time, period, season

2  **teneō, tenēre, tenuī, tentus,** hold, keep, possess

17  **tergum, tergī,** *N.*, back

2  **terra, terrae,** *F.*, earth, land

1  **terreō, terrēre, terruī, territus,** frighten, alarm, terrify

1  **timeō, timēre, timuī, – –,** fear, be afraid (of)

6  **timor, timōris,** *M.*, fear, dread

10  **tot** (*indeclinable adj.*), so many; **tot...quot** *or* **quot...tot,** as many...as

10  **tōtus, tōta, tōtum,** all, whole

4  **trādō, trādere, trādidī, trāditus,** hand over, betray

14  **trāns** (*prep.* + *acc.*), across, on the other side of

7  **tū, tuī** (*pron.*), you

14  **tum** (*adv.*), then, at that time

14  **tunc** (*adv.*), then, at that time

1  **turba, turbae,** *F.*, crowd, uproar

17  **turpis, turpe,** foul, ugly

9  **tūtus, tūta, tūtum,** safe

7  **tuus, tua, tuum,** your, yours, your own (*sing.*)

# U

12; 15  **ubi** (*adv.*; *conj.*), where, when

14  **ubīque** (*adv.*), everywhere, anywhere, wherever

10  **ūllus, ūlla, ūllum,** any

4  **umbra, umbrae,** *F.*, shadow

5  **umquam** *or* **unquam** (*adv.*), ever

17  **ūnā** (*adv.*), together, at the same time

2  **unda, undae,** *F.*, wave

12  **unde** (*adv.*), from where

10  **ūnus, ūna, ūnum,** one, alone

UNIT

6    **urbs, urbis, urbium,** *F.*, city
4    **urna, urnae,** *F.*, urn
13   **ūsus, ūsūs,** *M.*, use, advantage, enjoyment
3; 11  **ut** (*adv.*; *conj.*), as, when (+*indicative*); in order that (+*subjunctive in purpose clauses*); that...not (+*subjunctive after expressions of fearing*); that (+*subjunctive in result clauses*)
10   **uter, utra, utrum,** which (of two)
16   **ūtilis, ūtile,** useful, beneficial
12   **utinam** (*adv.*), I wish! Would that! If only!
11   **ūtor, ūtī, ūsus sum,** use, enjoy, experience (+*abl.*)
12   **utrum** (*conj.*), whether
12   **utrum...an,** whether...or
12   **utrum...an nōn,** whether...or not (*in direct double questions*)
12   **utrum...necne,** whether...or not (*in indirect double questions*)

# V

3    **validus, valida, validum,** strong, healthy
16   **vel** (*conj.*), or; **vel...vel,** either...or
3    **vēlum, vēlī,** *N.*, cloth, covering, sail; **vēla dare,** to set sail
18   **vendō, vendere, vendidī, venditus,** sell
3    **venia, veniae,** *F.*, indulgence, favor, kindness, (obliging) disposition
2    **veniō, venīre, vēnī, ventus,** come
17   **vēnor, vēnārī, vēnātus sum,** hunt, go hunting
3    **ventus, ventī,** *M.*, wind
3    **verbum, verbī,** *N.*, word
11   **vereor, verērī, veritus sum,** reverence, fear, dread
14   **vēritās, vēritātis,** *F.*, truth
8    **vertex, verticis,** *M.*, head, top, summit; whirlpool, whirlwind
17   **vertō, vertere, vertī, versus,** turn
4    **vērus, vēra, vērum,** true, real; **vērē** *or* **vērō** (*adv.*), truly, indeed
7    **vester, vestra, vestrum,** your, yours, your own (*pl.*)
17   **vetō, vetāre, vetuī, vetitus,** forbid
16   **vetus, veteris,** old; **veterēs, veterum,** *M. pl.*, the ancients; **vetera, veterum,** *N. pl.*, antiquity
1    **via, viae,** *F.*, way, road, path, street
1; 4  **videō, vidēre, vīdī, vīsus,** see; *in passive* seem *as well as* be seen
6    **vigor, vigōris,** *M.*, liveliness, activity, vigor
4    **vīlla, vīllae,** *F.*, country house, farmhouse
14   **vincō, vincere, vīcī, victus,** conquer, beat, overcome

UNIT

| | |
|---|---|
| 16 | **violō** (1), do violence to, break (an agreement, the law) |
| 3 | **vir, virī,** *M.,* man |
| 10 | **virtūs, virtūtis,** *F.,* manliness, courage, excellence, virtue |
| 6 | **vīs;** *pl.* **vīrēs, vīrium,** *F.,* force, power; *pl.* strength |
| 2 | **vīta, vītae,** *F.,* life |
| 5 | **vīvō, vīvere, vīxī, vīctus,** be alive, live |
| 13 | **vix** (*adv.*), hardly, scarcely |
| 5 | **vocō** (1), call |
| 11 | **volō, velle, voluī, ––,** wish, want, be willing |
| 7 | **vōx, vōcis,** *F.,* voice |
| 18 | **vulnerō** (1), wound |

# ENGLISH–LATIN VOCABULARY

## A

**able: be able,** possum, posse, potuī, – –

**about,** dē (*prep.* + *abl.*)

**account: on account of,** propter (*prep.* + *acc.*); ob (*prep.* + *acc.*)

**across,** trāns (*prep.* + *acc.*)

**after,** post (*prep.* + *acc.*; *adv.*); postquam (*conj.*); cum (*conj.*); *or use ablative absolute*

**aid,** auxilium, -ī, *N.*

**all,** omnis, -e; tōtus, -a, -um

**ally,** socius, -ī, *M.*

**alone,** sōlus, -a, -um

**already,** iam (*adv.*)

**altar,** āra, -ae, *F.*

**although,** quamquam (*conj.*); etsī (*conj.*); cum (*conj.*); *or use ablative absolute*

**always,** semper (*adv.*)

**ancient,** antīquus, -a, -um

**and,** et (*conj.*)

**animal,** animal, -ālis, -ium, *N.*

**any,** ūllus, -a, -um

**anyone,** aliquis, aliquid; quis, quid

**appearance,** speciēs, -ēī, *F.*

**approach,** aggredior, -ī, aggressus sum; accēdō, -ere, -cessī, -cessus

**arms,** arma, -ōrum, *N. pl.*

**around,** circum (*prep.* + *acc.*)

**arrive (at),** adveniō, -īre, -vēnī, -ventus (+ad); perveniō, -īre, -vēnī, -ventus (+ad)

**art,** ars, artis, -ium, *F.*

**as...as possible,** quam + *superlative*; **as soon as possible,** quam prīmum

**ask (for),** petō, -ere, petīvī, petītus; quaerō, -ere, quaesīvī, quaesītus

**ashamed,** *use impersonal verb* pudet, **it shames**

**attack,** oppūgnō (1)

**attempt,** temptō (1); cōnor, cōnārī, cōnātus sum

**author,** auctor, -ōris, *M.*

434

# B

**be,** sum, esse, fuī, futūrus
**be in charge of,** praesum, praeesse, -fuī, – – (+*dat.*)
**bear,** ferō, ferre, tulī, lātus
**beautiful,** pulcher, pulchra, pulchrum
**because,** quod (*conj.*); quia (*conj.*)
**because of,** propter (*prep.* + *acc.*)
**beg,** ōrō (1)
**begin,** incipiō, -ere, incēpī, inceptus
**believe,** crēdō, -ere, crēdidī, crēditus (+*dat.*)
**betray,** trādō, -ere, trādidī, trāditus
**big,** magnus, -a, -um
**body,** corpus, corporis, *N.*
**bold,** audāx, -ācis
**boldness,** audācia, -ae, *F.*
**book,** liber, librī, *M.*
**bore,** *use impersonal verb* taedet, **it bores**
**both...and,** et...et
**boy,** puer, -ī, *M.*
**brave,** fortis, forte
**breast,** pectus, pectoris, *N.*
**bright,** clārus, -a, -um
**bring (it) about,** efficiō, -ere, -fēcī, -fectus + ut (+*subjunctive*)
**brother,** frāter, frātris, *M.*
**burn,** ardeō, -ēre, arsī, arsus
**but,** sed (*conj.*)
**buy,** emō, -ere, ēmī, ēmptus
**by,** ā, ab (*prep.* + *abl.*)

# C

**can,** possum, posse, potuī, – –
**capture,** capiō, -ere, cēpī, captus
**care,** cūra, -ae, *F.*
**carry,** portō (1); ferō, ferre, tulī, lātus
**change,** mūtō (1)
**character,** mōs, mōris, *M.* (*in pl.*)
**charge: be in charge of,** praesum, praeesse, -fuī, – – (+*dat.*)
**child,** nātus, -ī, *M.*; puer, puerī, *M.*
**choose,** optō (1); legō, -ere, lēgī, lēctus
**citizen,** cīvis, cīvis, -ium, *M. or F.*
**city,** urbs, urbis, -ium, *F.*
**city walls,** moenia, -ium, *N. pl.*

come, veniō, -īre, vēnī, ventus
command: put (place) in command of, praeficiō, -ere, -fēcī, -fectus
commander, imperātor, -ōris, M.
commit, faciō, -ere, fēcī, factus
complete, cōnficiō, -ere, -fēcī, -fectus; perficiō, -ere, -fēcī, -fectus
condemn, dāmnō (1)
confess, fateor, fatērī, fassus sum; cōnfiteor, cōnfitērī, cōnfessus sum
conquer, superō (1); vincō, -ere, vīcī, victus
consider, habeō, -ēre, -uī, -itus; dūcō, -ere, dūxī, ductus
constellation, sīdus, sīderis, N.
consul, cōnsul, cōnsulis, M.
country, patria, -ae, F.
courage, virtūs, virtūtis, F.
cover, tegō, -ere, tēxī, tēctus
crime, scelus, sceleris, N.
crowd, turba, -ae, F.
crown, corōnō (1)
cruel, saevus, -a, -um; crūdēlis, -e

# D

danger, perīculum, -ī, N.
dare, audeō, -ēre, ausus sum
daughter, fīlia, -ae, F.
day, diēs, -ēī, M.; (at) daybreak, prīmā lūce
delay, moror, -ārī, -ātus sum
demonstrate, mōnstrō (1)
desire, optō (1)
desirous, cupidus, -a, -um (+gen.)
destroy, dēleō, -ēre, -ēvī, -ētus
destruction, ruīna, -ae, F.
die, morior, morī, mortuus sum; pereō, -īre, -iī (-īvī), -itus
difficult, difficilis, -e
diligence, dīligentia, -ae, F.
disgust, use impersonal verb piget, it disgusts
distinguished, honestus, -a, -um
do, faciō, -ere, fēcī, factus; agō, -ere, ēgī, āctus
doubt, dubitō (1)
drive, pellō, -ere, pepulī, pulsus
drive back, repellō, -ere, -pulī, -pulsus
drive out, expellō, -ere, -pulī, -pulsus
dutiful, pius, -a, -um

# E

**each,** quisque, quidque (*pron.*); quīque, quaeque, quodque (*adj.*)
**easy,** facilis, -e
**empire,** imperium, -ī, *N.*
**enemy,** inimīcus, -ī, *M.*; hostis, hostis, -ium, *M.*
**enter,** ingredior, -ī, ingressus sum
**even,** etiam (*adv.*); et (*adv.*); **not even,** nē...quidem
**everyone,** quisque
**evil** (*adj.*), malus, -a, -um; (*noun*) malum, -ī, *N.*
**explain,** expōnō, -ere, -posuī, -positus
**eye,** oculus, -ī, *M.*

# F

**fact: the fact that,** quod
**faith,** fidēs, -eī, *F.*
**fall,** cadō, -ere, cecidī, cāsus
**fame,** fāma, -ae, *F.*
**famous,** clārus, -a, -um
**far and wide,** longē (*adv.*)
**fast,** celeriter (*adv.*)
**father,** pater, patris, *M.*
**fear,** (*verb*) timeō, -ēre, -uī, – –; vereor, -ērī, -itus sum; metuō, -ere, metuī, – –;
    (*noun*) timor, timōris, *M.*; metus, -ūs, *M.*
**feel,** sentiō, -īre, sēnsī, sēnsus
**few,** paucī, -ae, -a
**field,** ager, agrī, *M.*
**fight,** pūgnō (1); **fight with** (*i.e., against*), pūgnō cum (+*abl.*)
**fill,** impleō, -ēre, implēvī, implētus
**find,** inveniō, -īre, -vēnī, -ventus
**fire,** ignis, ignis, -ium, *M.* (*abl. sing.* igne *or* ignī)
**five,** quīnque (*indeclinable adj.*)
**flee,** fugiō, -ere, fūgī, fugitus
**food,** cibus, -ī, *M.*
**foot,** pēs, pedis, *M.*
**for,** (*on behalf of*) prō (*prep.* + *abl.*)
**forbid,** vetō, -āre, -uī, -itus
**force,** vīs, *F.*
**forget,** oblīvīscor, oblīvīscī, oblītus sum (+*gen.*)
**fortify,** mūniō, -īre, -īvī, -ītus
**forum,** forum, -ī, *N.*
**free,** līber, lībera, līberum

**freedom**, lībertās, -tātis, *F.*
**friend**, amīcus, -ī, *M.*
**frighten**, terreō, -ēre, -uī, -itus
**from**, (*out of*) ē, ex (*prep.* + *abl.*); (*away*) ā, ab (*prep.* + *abl.*)
**fugitive**, profugus, -ī, *M.*

# G

**gate** (*of a city*), porta, -ae, *F.*
**general**, imperātor, -ōris, *M.*
**get**, parō (1)
**gift**, dōnum, -ī, *N.*
**gird**, cingō, -ere, cīnxī, cīnctus
**girl**, puella, -ae, *F.*
**give**, dō, dare, dedī, datus; dōnō (1)
**glory**, glōria, -ae, *F.*
**go**, eō, īre, iī (īvī), itus
**god**, deus, -ī, *M.*
**golden**, aureus, -a, -um
**good**, bonus, -a, -um
**gossip**, rūmor, rūmōris, *M.*
**great**, magnus, -a, -um; **so great**, tantus, -a, -um
**grievous**, gravis, -e
**guardian**, custōs, custōdis, *M.*
**guest**, hospes, hospitis, *M.*

# H

**hand**, manus, -ūs, *F.*
**handsome**, decōrus, -a, -um
**happen**, fīō, fierī, factus sum
**happy**, laetus, -a, -um
**harm**, noceō, -ēre, -uī, -itus (+*dat.*)
**hate**, ōdī, ōdisse (*defective verb lacking in the present system; perfect forms have present meanings*)
**have**, habeō, -ēre, -uī, -itus; *or dative of the possessor with* sum
**he**, *supplied by* is
**healthy**, validus, -a, -um; sānus, -a, -um
**hear**, audiō, -īre, -īvī, -ītus
**heavy**, gravis, -e
**help**, auxilium, -ī, *N.*
**her** (**own**), suus, -a, -um
**here**, hīc (*adv.*); **be here, be present**, adsum, adesse, adfuī, – –

**hide,** cēlō (1)
**his (own),** suus, -a, -um
**home,** domus, -ūs (-ī), *F.*
**honorable,** honestus, -a, -um
**hope,** (*verb*) spērō (1); (*noun*) spēs, speī, *F.*
**hostile,** inimīcus, -a, -um
**house,** tēctum, -ī, *N.*; domus, -ūs (-ī), *F.*; **country house,** vīlla, -ae, *F.*
**how,** quō modō
**how many,** quot
**humble,** humilis, -e
**hunt,** vēnor, -ārī, -ātus sum
**husband,** coniūnx, coniugis, *M.*

# I

**I,** ego; *pl.* nōs
**if,** sī (*conj.*)
**if...not,** nisī (*conj.*)
**if only,** utinam (*adv.*)
**impious,** impius, -a, -um
**in,** in (*prep.* + *abl.*)
**indeed,** enim (*postpositive conj.*)
**inhabitant,** incola, -ae, *M.*
**in order (that, to),** ut (+*subjunctive*)
**in order not to,** nē (+*subjunctive*)
**into,** in (*prep.* + *acc.*)
**invade,** invādō, -ere, -vāsī, -vāsus
**island,** īnsula, -ae, *F.*
**it,** *supplied by* id

# J

**join,** iungō, -ere, iūnxī, iūnctus
**Juno,** Iūnō, Iūnōnis, *F.*
**Jupiter,** Iuppiter, Iovis, *M.*

# K

**keep from, prevent,** prohibeō, -ēre, -uī, -itus (+*infinitive*); dēterreō, -ēre, -uī, -itus
   (+*subjunctive clause of prevention*)
**kill,** interficiō, -ere, -fēcī, -fectus
**kindness,** venia, -ae, *F.*

**king**, rēx, rēgis, *M.*
**know**, sciō, -īre, -īvī, -ītus; **not know**, nesciō, -īre, -īvī (-iī), -ītus

# L

**land**, terra, -ae, *F.*
**large**, magnus, -a, -um
**law**, lēx, lēgis, *F.*
**lead**, dūcō, -ere, dūxī, ductus
**leader**, dux, ducis, *M.*
**learn**, cognōscō, -ere, -nōvī, -nitus; nōscō, -ere, nōvī, nōtus; discō, -ere, didicī, – –
**legate**, lēgātus, -ī, *M.*
**liberty**, lībertās, -tātis, *F.*
**life**, vīta, -ae, *F.*
**lifetime**, aetās, -tātis, *F.*
**light**, lūmen, lūminis, *N.*; lūx, lūcis, *F.*
**listen (to)**, audiō, -īre, -īvī, -ītus
**live**, vīvō, -ere, vīxī, vīctus
**lofty**, altus, -a, -um
**long**, longus, -a, -um; **for a long time**, diū (*adv.*)
**look (at)**, spectō (1)
**love**, (*verb*) amō (1); (*noun*) amor, amōris, *M.*

# M

**make**, faciō, -ere, fēcī, factus
**man**, vir, virī, *M.*; homō, hominis, *M.*; **old man**, senex, senis, *M.*; **young man**, iuvenis, -is, *M.* (*not i-stem*)
**many**, multus, -a, -um
**Marcus**, Marcus, -ī, *M.*
**master**, dominus, -ī, *M.*; magister, magistrī, *M.*
**middle (of)**, medius, -a, -um
**mindful**, memor, memoris
**model**, exemplar, -āris, -ium, *N.*
**money**, pecūnia, -ae, *F.*
**moon**, lūna, -ae, *F.*
**more**, plūs
**mother**, māter, mātris, *F.*
**mountain**, mōns, montis, -ium, *M.*
**move**, moveō, -ēre, mōvī, mōtus
**much**, multus, -a, -um
**must**, dēbeō, -ēre, -uī, -itus; *or use passive periphrastic conjugation expressing obligation*
**my**, meus, -a, -um

# N

**name**, nōmen, nōminis, *N.*
**native land**, patria, -ae, *F.*
**nature**, nātūra, -ae, *F.*
**neglect**, neglegō, -ere, neglēxī, neglēctus
**neither...nor**, neque...neque *or* nec...nec
**never**, numquam (*adv.*)
**no**, nūllus, -a, -um
**no one**, nēmō, nēminis, *M. or F.*
**nor**, nec; neque
**not**, nōn; nē
**not even**, nē...quidem
**not only...but also**, nōn sōlum...sed etiam
**now**, nunc (*adv.*)
**nurse**, nūtrīx, -īcis, *F.*

# O

**obey**, pāreō, -ēre, -uī, -itus (+ *dat.*)
**offer**, offerō, offerre, obtulī, oblātus
**old**, senex, senis
**old man**, senex, senis, *M.*
**on**, in (*prep.* + *abl.*)
**only**, sōlus, -a, -um
**opinion**, sententia, -ae, *F.*; opīniō, -ōnis, *F.*
**oppress**, opprimō, -ere, -pressī, -pressus
**order**, iubeō, -ēre, iussī, iussus (+ *infinitive*); imperō (1) (+ ut *or* nē *and the*
    *subjunctive*); **in order to**, ut (*conj.*)
**other**, alius, -a, -ud; **other people's**, aliēnus, -a, -um
**our**, noster, nostra, nostrum
**out (of)**, ē, ex (*prep.* + *abl.*)
**overcome**, superō (1)

# P

**pain**, dolor, dolōris, *M.*
**pardon**, īgnōscō, -ere, -nōvī, -nōtus (+ *dat.*)
**part**, pars, partis, -ium, *F.*
**peace**, pāx, pācis, *F.*
**people**, populus, -ī, *M.* (*use in singular*)
**place**, pōnō, -ere, posuī, positus
**please**, placeō, -ēre, -uī, -itus (+ *dat.*)
**poem**, carmen, carminis, *N.*

**poet,** poēta, -ae, *M.*
**possible: it is possible,** fierī potest ut (+*noun clause of result*)
**praise,** laudō (1)
**prefer,** praeferō, -ferre, -tulī, -lātus
**previously,** ante (*adv.*)
**price,** pretium, -ī, *N.*
**profit,** prōsum, prōdesse, prōfuī, – –
**prohibit,** prohibeō, -ēre, -uī, -itus
**provided that,** dum (*conj.*); dummodo (*conj.*); modo (*conj.*)
**province,** prōvincia, -ae, *F.*
**punishment,** poena, -ae, *F.*
**put (place) in command (of),** praeficiō, -ere, -fēcī, -fectus

## Q

**queen,** rēgīna, -ae, *F.*
**quick,** celer, celeris, celere

## R

**raving,** dēmēns, dēmentis
**read,** legō, -ere, lēgī, lēctus
**realm,** rēgnum, -ī, *N.*
**remain,** maneō, -ēre, mānsī, mānsus; remaneō, -ēre, -mānsī, -mānsus
**republic,** rēs pūblica, reī pūblicae, *F.*
**reputation,** fāma, -ae, *F.*
**reveal,** retegō, -ere, -tēxī, -tēctus
**right: to the right,** ad dextram
**rock,** saxum, -ī, *N.*
**Roman,** Rōmānus, -a, -um
**Rome,** Rōma, -ae, *F.*
**ruler,** regēns, regentis, *M.* (*present participle of* regō, -ere)
**rumor,** fāma, -ae, *F.*; rūmor, rūmōris, *M.*
**run,** currō, -ere, cucurrī, cursus
**rush,** ruō, -ere, ruī, rutus

## S

**safe,** tūtus, -a, -um
**safety,** salūs, salūtis, *F.*
**sail,** vēlum, -ī, *N.*; **set sail,** vēla dare
**sailor,** nauta, -ae, *M.*

**sanctity,** religiō, -ōnis, *F.*
**save,** servō (1)
**say,** dīcō, -ere, dīxī, dictus
**sea,** mare, maris, -ium, *N.*
**see,** videō, -ēre, vīdī, vīsus
**seek,** petō, -ere, petīvī, petītus; quaerō, -ere, quaesīvī, quaesītus
**sell,** vendō, -ere, vendidī, venditus
**send,** mittō, -ere, mīsī, missus
**serve (as),** *use dative of service (purpose) in double dative construction*
**set out,** proficīscor, proficīscī, profectus sum
**set sail,** vēla dare
**severe,** gravis, grave
**she,** *supplied by* ea
**shine,** fulgeō, -ēre, fulsī, – –
**ship,** nāvis, -is, -ium, *F.*
**shore,** lītus, lītoris, *N.*
**should,** dēbeō, -ēre, -uī, -itus; *or use passive periphrastic conjugation expressing obligation*
**shout,** clāmō (1)
**show,** mōnstrō (1)
**silent: be** *or* **keep silent,** taceō, -ēre, tacuī, tacitus
**since,** quoniam (*conj.*); cum (*conj.*); *or use ablative absolute*
**sing (of),** canō, -ere, cecinī, cantus
**sister,** soror, sorōris, *F.*
**skill,** ars, artis, -ium, *F.*
**slave,** servus, -ī, *M.*
**so,** tam (*adv.*); ita (*adv.*); adeō (*adv.*); sīc (*adv.*)
**so great,** tantus, -a, -um
**so that,** ut
**soldier,** mīles, mīlitis, *M.*
**someone,** aliquis
**soon,** mox (*adv.*); **as soon as possible,** quam prīmum
**son,** fīlius, -ī, *M.*; nātus, -ī, *M.*
**sorrow,** dolor, dolōris, *M.*
**sort, kind,** genus, -eris, *N.*
**soul,** anima, -ae, *F.*
**spend (a lifetime),** agō, -ere, ēgī, āctus
**state,** cīvitās, -tātis, *F.*; rēs pūblica, reī pūblicae, *F.*
**statue,** statua, -ae, *F.*
**stop,** dēsinō, -ere, dēsiī, – –
**storm,** tempestās, -tātis, *F.*

**street**, via, -ae, *F.*
**strength**, vīrēs, vīrium, *F. pl.*
**strong**, validus, -a, -um; fortis, -e
**such**, tālis, -e
**such (so) great**, tantus, -a, -um
**such great...as**, tantus...quantus
**suffer**, patior, patī, passus sum; sufferō, sufferre, sustulī, sublātus
**summit**, vertex, verticis, *M.*
**sword**, gladius, -ī, *M.*

# T

**tall**, altus, -a, -um
**tear**, lacrima, -ae, *F.*
**tell**, dīcō, -ere, dīxī, dictus
**temple**, templum, -ī, *N.*
**terrify**, terreō, -ēre, -uī, -itus
**than**, quam (*conj.*)
**that**, ille, illa, illud (*adj.*); is, ea, id (*adj.*); ut (*conj.*; *introducing a clause of result*)
**their (own)**, suus, -a, -um
**think**, cōgitō (1)
**this**, hic, haec, hoc; is, ea, id
**threaten**, minor, -ārī, -ātus sum
**through**, per (*prep.* + *acc.*)
**throw**, iaciō, -ere, iēcī, iactus
**time**, tempus, temporis, *N.*; **for a long time**, diū (*adv.*)
**to, toward**, ad (*prep.* + *acc.*)
**torch**, taeda, -ae, *F.*
**town**, oppidum, -ī, *N.*
**treachery**, īnsidiae, -ārum, *F. pl.*
**treaty**, foedus, foederis, *N.*
**troops**, cōpiae, -ārum, *F. pl.*
**try**, temptō (1)

# U

**understand**, intellegō, -ere, intellēxī, intellēctus
**unfortunate**, īnfēlīx, īnfēlīcis
**unlike**, dissimilis, -e
**urn**, urna, -ae, *F.*
**use**, ūtor, ūtī, ūsus sum (+ *abl.*)

# V

**value highly,** maximī faciō (-ere, fēcī, factus)

# W

**wage,** gerō, -ere, gessī, gestus
**wait (for),** exspectō (1)
**walk,** ambulō (1)
**walls** (*of a city*), moenia, -ium, *N. pl.*
**want,** volō, velle, voluī, − −
**war,** bellum, -ī, *N.*
**warn,** moneō, -ēre, monuī, monitus
**wealth,** dīvitiae, -ārum, *F. pl.*
**weapons,** arma, -ōrum, *N. pl.*
**well,** bene (*adv.*)
**what,** quid (*pron.*); quod (*adj.*)
**when,** ubi (*conj.*); cum (*conj.*); *or use ablative absolute*
**where,** ubi (*adv.*); **(to) where,** quō (*adv.*)
**whether,** num (*adv.*); utrum (*adv.*); *both can be used as adverbial conjunctions*
**which,** quī, quae, quod (*relative pron.*)
**who,** quī, quae, quod (*relative pron.*)
**whole,** tōtus, -a, -um
**why,** cūr (*adv.*)
**wicked,** malus, -a, -um
**willing,** volēns, volentis (*present participle of* volō, velle, voluī, − −)
**wind,** ventus, -ī, *M.*
**wish,** optō (1)
**with,** cum (*prep.* + *abl.*)
**withdraw,** sē recipere (recipiō, -ere, -cēpī, -ceptus)
**without,** sine (*prep.* + *abl.*)
**woman,** fēmina, -ae, *F.*
**wonder,** mīror, -ārī, -ātus sum
**word,** verbum, -ī, *N.*
**work,** (*verb*) labōrō (1); (*noun*) opus, operis, *N.*
**world,** orbis terrārum (orbis, orbis, -ium, *M.*)
**wound,** vulnerō (1)
**wretched,** miser, misera, miserum
**write,** scrībō, -ere, scrīpsī, scrīptus

# Y

**year,** annus, -ī, *M.*
**yesterday,** heri (*adv.*)

**you,** tū (*sing.*); vōs (*pl.*)
**young man,** iuvenis, iuvenis, *M.* (*not i-stem*)
**your,** tuus, -a, -um (*sing.*); vester, vestra, vestrum (*pl.*)

# Z

**zeal,** studium, -ī, *N.*

**INDEX**

# INDEX